Oxford Socio-Legal Studies

World Jury Systems

OXFORD SOCIO-LEGAL STUDIES

Oxford Socio-Legal Studies is a series of books exploring the role of law in society for both an academic and a wider readership. The series publishes theoretical and empirically-informed work, from the United Kingdom and elsewhere, by social scientists and lawyers which advances understanding of the social reality of law and legal processes.

WORLD JURY SYSTEMS

Edited by
NEIL VIDMAR

OXFORD
UNIVERSITY PRESS

Great Clarendon Street, Oxford OX2 6DP

Oxford University Press is a department of the University of Oxford.
It furthers the University's objective of excellence in research, scholarship,
and education by publishing worldwide in

Oxford New York

Athens Auckland Bangkok Bogotá Buenos Aires Cape Town
Chennai Dar es Salaam Delhi Florence Hong Kong Istanbul Karachi
Kolkata Kuala Lumpur Madrid Melbourne Mexico City Mumbai Nairobi
Paris São Paulo Shanghai Singapore Taipei Tokyo Toronto Warsaw

with associated companies in Berlin Ibadan

Oxford is a registered trade mark of Oxford University Press
in the UK and in certain other countries

Published in the United States
by Oxford University Press Inc., New York

First published 2000

British Library Cataloguing in Publication Data
Data available

Library of Congress Cataloging in Publication Data
World jury system / edited by Neil Vidmar.
p. cm. (Oxford socio-legal studies)
Includes bibliographical references and index.
1. Jury. I. Vidmar, Neil. II. Series.
K2292. W67 2000
347'.0752 dc21

ISBN 0-19-829856-0

3 5 7 9 10 8 6 4 2

Printed in Great Britain
on acid-free paper by
Bookcraft Ltd., Midsomer Norton, Somerset

General Editor's Introduction

The jury is at once one of the great sacred objects of the legal system and one of its most controversial and least understood institutions. The idea of trial by jury prompts contrasting responses from lawyers, policy-makers, politicians, and members of the public. It is regarded by many as a powerful democratic element in the process of delivering justice, a means by which ordinary people can pronounce on the merits of the case before them. It is viewed by others, however, as an irrational, costly, and cumbersome institution which demands that ordinary people, with all their frailties of inattentiveness, ignorance, and prejudice pronounce upon sometimes extraordinarily complex and consequential matters.

Reliance on the jury has declined in a number of countries, a decline that with few exceptions has almost reached the point of extinction in civil cases. In England, the jury's place in criminal justice has also been steadily eroded. Meanwhile, proposals that the use of the jury should be further restricted in English criminal cases in the interests of greater rationality, efficiency, or economy have provoked vigorous opposition. Debates about the merits or disadvantages of jury trial, however, take place with little understanding of how juries work, and little knowledge of the character of jury trial in other countries. This collection of comprehensive essays by specialist authors on the role of the jury in a wide variety of different jurisdictions is most welcome and should go far not only to inform but also at the same time to dispel misunderstanding of the institution. This book should raise debate about the jury to a new level.

Preface

The idea for a book about contemporary world jury systems began to form in my mind as early as the beginning of the 1980s, while I was still a faculty member at the University of Western Ontario. In my research and consulting I was constantly impressed by the very substantial differences between the jury systems of Canada and the United States. I was also struck by the often incorrect stereotypes that Canadian judges, lawyers, and academics had about the US jury system and the almost total ignorance that American judges, lawyers, and academics had about the Canadian jury. In doing background research for the book that I wrote with Valerie Hans, *Judging the Jury* (1986), I became superficially acquainted with differences between the jury systems of these two countries and that of England. I began to collect a few historical references to jury systems in other countries, and the file thickened when I moved to Duke Law School in 1987. In 1988 I began an outline for a book on comparative jury systems after I learned about juries in the Caribbean, but the project was put on a back burner, in fact, consigned to a folder along with other 'potential' projects in my files.

In 1994 I became more acquainted with the English jury system when I served as a consultant on the pretrial publicity aspects of the *Maxwell* fraud trial, that is discussed in one Lloyd-Bostock and Thomas chapter on the English jury in this volume. The *Maxwell* case gave me an additional insight, namely that, more than just satisfying scholarly curiosity, a comparative study of jury systems could shed practical insights on policy issues concerning juries. Despite differences in the emphasis on fair trial versus free press issues in England, Canada, and the United States all three countries had to face the consequences of pretrial publicity generated in an age of global television and newspapers, fax machines, and the internet. Shortly following the *Maxwell* case, I became acquainted with the jury system in New Zealand when I was asked to consult about media effects in one case involving a motion for a change of venue and another on a contempt of court charge against a television station. The New Zealand experiences further increased my interest in a comparative volume. The final incident overcoming my inertia on developing a book was when Michael Chesterman presented a comparative analysis of how Australia and the United States dealt with pretrial publicity in a paper entitled 'O.J. and the Dingo' that he presented at the 1996 meetings of the Law and Society Association in Glasgow, Scotland.

Upon returning to Duke I discussed an issue on comparative jury systems with the editorial board of *Law & Contemporary Problems* and began contacting highly qualified scholars to write articles about the jury in Australia, England and Wales, New Zealand, Northern Ireland, The Republic of Ireland, Scotland, and the United States. I decided to write the article about the Canadian criminal jury system and persuaded my colleague, William Bogart, to write about the Canadian civil jury. I became aware of Steve Thaman's work on the new Russian and Spanish juries, and he agreed to write an article. At about the same time a Duke law student, Lester Kiss, dropped by my office and informed me that he wanted to write a paper about Japanese interest in reviving the jury system in that country.

Somewhere in the process of developing the law review issue three additional insights emerged. The first was that I should expand my scope and attempt to survey other contemporary jury systems that I knew existed. The second insight was that many factors in addition to prevention of and remedies for pretrial prejudice distinguished jury systems: the jury needs to be viewed in its broader legal, procedural, and political context. The third insight was that an expanded project had appeal beyond the scholarly readership of *Law & Contemporary Problems* and should appear in book form. The end result is that this book has a first chapter that reviews the history of the development of the jury in England and sets forth a framework for comparative analysis of the jury systems discussed in the chapters that follow. Authors of other chapters have updated their chapters. In addition, a final chapter surveys most of the more than three dozen other contemporary jury systems that, directly or indirectly, are offshoots of the English jury and remain important parts of that country or dependency's legal system.

I believe that I, and the contributors to this volume, have met the original goal of providing a comparative perspective on jury systems that will be of use to students and scholars. Hopefully, it will also have a broader readership among professionals who make legal policy.

Neil Vidmar

Duke Law School
Durham, NC, U.S.A.
July 2000

Acknowledgements

My first debt is to all of my colleagues who wrote chapters for this book: Sally Lloyd-Bostock, Cheryl Thomas, Nancy King, Michael Chesterman, Neil Cameron, Susan Potter, Warren Young, Peter Duff, John Jackson, Katie Quinn, Tom O'Malley, Stephen Thaman, Lester Kiss, Stephan Landsman, and William Bogart. Never could it be more truly said that the project could not have been completed without them. A second debt is to the student editorial staff of *Law & Contemporary Problems,* led by B. J. Priester, Paul Rozelle, and Matt Witsil, and their faculty advisor, Theresa Newman, who spent so many hours editing what are now chapters 2 through 12. I also am grateful to Mr Richard C. Nzerem of the Legal and Constitutional Affairs Department of the Commonwealth Secretariat in London, England, who wrote to all of the members of the Commonwealth inquiring about their jury systems and Margaret A. Brare who collated the responses. The resulting Commonwealth Survey forms the backbone of Chapter 13. Duke Law School has provided exceptional support, as it has with all of my projects. JE also deserves thanks for many things.

Contents

1 A Historical and Comparative Perspective On the Common Law Jury

Neil Vidmar*

I. Introduction

As many scholars and practitioners have commented over the centuries, the common law jury that evolved in England and was transplanted in other parts of the world is a unique institution.[1] It brings together a small group of lay persons who are assembled on a temporary basis for the purpose of deciding whether an accused person is guilty of a criminal act or which of two sides should prevail in a civil dispute. The jurors are conscripted and often initially reluctant to serve. They are untutored in the formal discipline of law and its logic. They hear and see confusing and contested evidence and are provided with instructions, most often only in oral form, about arcane legal concepts and sent into a room alone to decide a verdict without further help from the professional persons who developed the evidence and explained their duties. In criminal cases the jury's decision determines if an accused person may be subject to prison or, in some instances, execution, or may instead be set free or confined to a mental institution. In civil cases juries decide complex matters involving causation and liability and determine compensatory and exemplary damages, sometimes involving very large sums.

Early on in the history of the jury these oddities were also recognized as its strengths. Juries inject community values into the formal legal process, and thus they can bring a sense of equity and fairness against the cold and mechanistic application of legal rules. In both state trials and in common criminal or civil disputes juries served as sometimes the only guard against the power of the state and the social class or other biases of appointed judges or corrupt officials. Although for

* Russell M. Robinson II Professor of Law and Professor of Psychology, Duke University.

[1] See , e.g. William Blackstone, Commentaries on the Laws of England (1769/1966, Clarendon edition); William Forsyth, History of Trial by Jury (1875/1994, The Lawbook Exchange); Alexis de Tocqueville, *Trial by Jury in the United States Considered as a Political Institution*, in Alexis De Tocqueville, Democracy in America 318 (1835/Phillips Bradley Trans., 1960); Patrick Devlin, Trial by Jury 164 (1956); Ramesh Deosaran, Trial By Jury: Social and Psychological Dynamics (1985).

centuries jury service was restricted to wealthy or otherwise privileged male members of society, the jurors were from the community in which the events transpired, and they added insights about facts and community values that the judges, riding the circuit, would not have. For these and other reasons the jury came to personify fairness and justice, and trial by jury came to be regarded as the 'right of Englishmen'. Never mind that the jury was not, nor could it be realistically expected to be, a perfect institution. It was viewed as better than the alternatives. When England began its expansion into empire, the jury was imported to the colonies in America, Africa, and Asia. Admiration for the institution of the jury in the nineteenth century led to its adoption in various forms in France, parts of Germany, Russia, Spain, and other European countries and in parts of South and Central America.

Modern commentary on the jury system by scholars and legal practitioners continues to extol its virtues as a vehicle for injecting democratic values into the legal process, as a vesicle of common wisdom, as a guard against judicial power, as an institution for educating people about the law and as an institution that brings legitimacy to the law.[2]

Nevertheless, it needs to be observed that enthusiasm for the jury has waxed and waned over the centuries, but even when enthusiasm was at its zenith, it has had harsh critics who doubted the competence, rationality, and motives of juries. That is true today. Some contemporary critics of the jury system charge that it is an absurd and ill-conceived institution whose only claim to legitimacy is its archaic roots.[3] They assert that it has no place in a modern system of rational law that is increasingly complex and ill-suited to decisions made by lay persons.[4] They also

[2] See, e.g., VALERIE HANS AND NEIL VIDMAR, JUDGING THE JURY (1986); JEFFREY ABRAMSON, WE, THE JURY (1994) for a review of this commentary.

[3] For discussion see, e.g., MARK FINDLAY AND PETER DUFF, THE JURY UNDER ATTACK (1998); JAMES GOBERT, JUSTICE, DEMOCRACY AND THE JURY (1997); JEROME FRANK, COURTS ON TRIAL (1945); FRANKLIN STRIER, RECONSTRUCTING JUSTICE, ch. 4 (1966); C. Howard, *Weak Link in Justice Chain*, ADELAIDE ADVERTISER, Aug. 2, 1985, in Richard W. Harding, *Jury Performance in Complex Cases* 74, in MARK FINDLAY & PETER DUFF, THE JURY UNDER ATTACK, 74, 75 (1988); Doug Small, *Judging Juries*, NATIONAL 16 (Aug.–Sept., 1999).

[4] It should be noted that many criticisms of the jury are made by appeals to 'logic', 'experience', and by anecdotes purporting to show jury incompetence or malfeasance. The critics tend to ignore a substantial body of empirical research that has developed over the last half century indicating that these claims often have little or no support, see, e.g., Neil Vidmar, *The Performance of the American Civil Jury: An Empirical Perspective*, 40 ARIZONA LAW REVIEW 849 (1998); T. M. Honess, M. Levi, and E. A. Charman, *Juror Competence in Processing Complex Information: Implications from a Simulation of the Maxwell Trial*, CRIMINAL LAW REVIEW 763 (1998). As the chapter on England explains, major changes to the English jury, including the abolition of peremptory challenges, were initiated by largely unsub-

point out that, with the exception of the United States and parts of Canada, the jury has been largely abandoned for civil cases, that its use in criminal cases has declined, and that many countries that experimented with criminal juries long ago abandoned them.

Nevertheless, as we begin the twenty-first century, the criminal jury appears alive and mostly well[5] in Australia, Canada, England and Wales, Northern Ireland, the Republic of Ireland, New Zealand, Scotland, the United States, and at least 46 other countries and dependencies around the globe. For example, juries are an inherent part of legal systems in Africa (e.g. Ghana; Malawi), Asia (e.g. Sri Lanka; Hong Kong), the Mediterranean (e.g. Gibraltar; Malta), the South Pacific (e.g. Tonga; The Marshall Islands), South America (e.g. Guyana; Brazil) and the Caribbean (e.g. Montserrat; Barbados; Jamaica).[6] Both Spain and Russia have recently re-introduced trial by jury, and in Japan, which had a jury system from 1929 through 1943, there has been discussion of the possibility of reviving it.[7] Denmark, Austria, Belgium, and Norway have variations on the jury that are still actively used.[8]

This volume presents in-depth coverage of the common law jury systems of Australia (by Michael Chesterman), Canada (Vidmar on the criminal jury and William Bogart on the civil jury), England and Wales (by Sally Lloyd-Bostock and Cheryl Thomas), Northern Ireland and the Republic of Ireland (by John Jackson, Katie Quinn, and Tom O'Mally), New Zealand (by Neil Cameron, Susan Potter, and Warren Young), Scotland (by Peter Duff), and the United States (by Nancy King on criminal juries and Steve Landsman on civil juries) plus the new systems in Spain and Russia (by Steve Thaman) and discussion of the potential

stantiated claims. Undocumented charges about the competence of juries in complex fraud cases have been made in England, Australia, and New Zealand. Charges of jury bias and incompetence have been made against both civil and criminal juries in the United States. That is for another day and another book. Instead, the goal of this volume is to provide descriptive and interpretive accounts, written by experts on each country, of the background, characteristics and values associated with each jury system, including the ways that each system addresses problems that are often shared in other countries.

[5] There are qualifications about the health of some jury systems, including England and Ireland, that are discussed in ch. in this book.

[6] These systems are discussed in Ch. 13.

[7] In addition to Kiss' ch. on Japan in this volume see also Takashi Maruta, The Jury Experiment in Imperial Japan and Prospects for Its Reintroduction. Paper presented at the International Conference on Lay Participation in the Criminal Trial in the 21st Century. Siracusa, Sicily, Italy, 26–9 May, 1999; Richard Lempert, *A Jury for Japan* 40 American Journal of Comparative Law 37 (1992).

[8] These systems are discussed in Ch. 13.

for a jury system in Japan (by Lester Kiss). Although only two separate chapters are devoted to civil juries, they are discussed in other chapters. Chapter 13 (by Vidmar) provides an overview of the spread of the jury as England built its empire and surveys 46 other contemporary jury systems around the world.

Although a few comparative studies of juries have been made, they have been limited in scope.[9] A comparative perspective within a single volume is overdue. Legal scholars, social[10] scientists, and jurists are frequently very parochial in their knowledge about the jury and tend to make unwarranted, simplistic comparisons with other countries. For instance, Australian, Canadian, English, and Scots commentators tend to have the view that every American trial involves extensive questioning of jurors by the opposing lawyers assisted by jury experts.[10] While this may be true in high profile trials that come to public attention through the news media, in ordinary trials in most federal courts the questioning is conducted by the judge in a truncated hearing.[11] In many state courts the questioning process is also short and dignified and the judge maintains tight control over the proceedings. Foreign observers do not seem to consider that the need for a more extensive process in the exceptional trials results in large part from pretrial publicity generated by the almost unfettered freedom that the media enjoy under the Constitution's First Amendment, a freedom that is restricted in their own country by *sub judice* or statutory contempt of court laws.

To take another example, in the United States there has been concern about the use of peremptory challenges to thwart a goal of ensuring fair representation of members of minority groups and women on the jury. This is a serious matter deserving the attention it receives, but it has also prompted some American judges and legal commentators to make naïve

[9] See, for example, Forsyth *supra* note 1: A.V. Sheehan, Criminal Procedure in Scotland and France (1975); Weems, *A Comparison of jury selection procedures for criminal trials in New South Wales and California*, 10 Sydney Law Review 330 (1984); Michael Chesterman, *O.J. and the Dingo: How Media Publicity Relating to Criminal Cases Tried by Jury is Dealt with in Australia and America*, 45 American Journal of Comparative Law 109 (1997); Mark Findlay and Peter Duff, The Jury Under Attack (1998); A. Schioppa, The Trial Jury in England, France and Germany: 1700–1900 (1987).

[10] See, e.g., in R.v. Kray *et al.* (1969) 53 Cr. App. R. 412 (England); *R.* v. *Hubbert* (1975) 29 C.C.C. (2d) 279; *R.*v. *Williams* (1994) 30 C.R. (4th) 277 (Canada); McCadden v. H.M. Advocate [1985] J.C. 98 (Scotland).

[11] There are many exceptions to this general statement. In some courts questioning is often extensive. I have also learned that in Connecticut and Philadelphia (though not necessarily in other courts in Pennsylvania) the judge is absent and lawyers conduct the questioning and choose the jurors. The judge plays a role in cases of conflict.

generalizations from the fact that England has abolished peremptory challenges.[12] In effect these commentators suggest, 'England abolished peremptory challenges so the consequences would be minimal if we did so'. The chapter on England makes clear that these commentators have failed to take cognizance of a number of other differences that characterize the English jury.[13] Foremost among them is the fact that England has also abolished almost all challenges for cause, though in some cases the Crown prosecutor has a limited right to vet jurors through exercising a 'stand aside', which is effectively a peremptory challenge, and a privilege not shared by the defendant. Because of the contempt of court laws pretrial publicity from mass media is usually prevented and, on rare occasions when it has occurred, the court has sometimes permanently stayed criminal proceedings. Even in serious criminal cases the English jury may return a verdict of guilty by a majority verdict of ten of the twelve jurors. Scotland and the Republic of Ireland have also abolished peremptory challenges, but Australia, New Zealand, Northern Ireland, and Canada all retain peremptory challenges, as do many of the jury systems in countries discussed in Chapter 13.

Reading the chapters as a group makes abundantly clear the fact that, despite their English heritage and similar overall structure, the jury systems in each country have evolved in different, sometimes subtle, ways. Juries occupy different roles in the political ethos of the country. The legal systems that surround them place different emphases on which cases juries are permitted to decide. The substantive laws and procedural systems differ as well. The potential influence of mass media on the jury, the degree of jury autonomy relative to the judge, the forms and types of evidence jurors are permitted to hear, the culture of courtrooms, and a variety of other characteristics also differ. In short, selecting one characteristic from one country fails to consider the issues in their broader cultural, systemic, and legal context.

The success or failure of a jury system depends upon many exogenous factors, including philosophies and bureaucratic structures associated with modes of procedure. These include the above mentioned symbolic

[12] See e.g. Eugene Sullivan and Akhil Reed Amar, *Great Debate on Jury Reform: England* v. *United States*, 33 AMERICAN CRIMINAL LAW REVIEW 1141 (1996); Morris B. Hoffman, *Peremptory Challenges Should Be Abolished: A Trial Judge's Perspective*, 64 UNIVERSITY OF CHICAGO LAW REVIEW 809, 815–22 (1997); HAROLD J. ROTHWAX, GUILTY: THE COLLAPSE OF CRIMINAL JUSTICE (1996); WILLIAM T. PIZZI, TRIALS WITHOUT TRUTH (1999).

[13] See the Lloyd-Bostock and Thomas ch. on England in this volume and JAMES GOBERT, JUSTICE, DEMOCRACY AND THE JURY (1997).

role that layperson decision making plays in the society and the relative homogeneity of its population, or at least the ability of the legal system to reduce racial and other political cleavages that would otherwise raise questions about fairness and impartiality. Similarly, changes within one part of the jury system may have impacts on other parts of the system.

On another front, all of the countries that continue to use the jury system have raised questions about its adaption to modern social, political, and legal conditions. Can it be made more democratic without interfering with the fairness of the trial? Can concerns of minority groups about the legitimacy and fairness of legal decisions be addressed by changes in the jury system? In an age of mass media—newspapers, television, the internet, fax machines—how can tainting of jurors be prevented or remediated? What substantive and procedural changes are necessary to address problems posed by expert evidence such as that involving DNA analysis, international money transfers in complex fraud cases, or psychological profiles like rape trauma and battered spouse and child syndromes.[14] A wide range of jury trial innovations have been taking place in the United States over the last decade or so.[15] These include attempts to improve instructions, encouraging jurors to take notes, to ask questions of witnesses, and in one jurisdiction to discuss evidence during the trial. New Zealand has recently conducted a study of its jury system with the goal of discovering problems and suggesting reforms.[16] Can the insights gained from this experience benefit other countries or are the jury systems too different to allow generalizations? Considerable insight can be gained from comparative analysis.

The remainder of this chapter is devoted to outlining some of the central characteristics that differentiate jury systems. The outline is not intended to be comprehensive of all of the potential differences but it addresses the major ones. The focus of the book is on contemporary jury systems, but the subheadings frequently contain summary forays into historical developments in English common law. These forays help to define the common ground from which the various systems developed and to highlight divergences over time and between countries.

[14] For discussion about the factors affecting the production and diffusion of expert evidence see Sophia Gatowski, *et al.*, *The Globalization of behavioral science evidence about battered women: A theory of production and diffusion*, 15 BEHAVIORAL SCIENCES AND THE LAW 285 (1997).

[15] G. THOMAS MUNSTERMAN, PAULA I. HANNAFORD, AND G. MARC WHITEHEAD, JURY TRIAL INNOVATIONS (1997); B. Michael Dann and George Logan III, *Jury Reform: The Arizona Experience*, 79 JUDICATURE 280 (1996).

[16] See Ch. 5.

An editorial note is appropriate here. I have intentionally been sparse in footnotes involving material and discussion that is contained in the chapters that follow. This decision was intended to avoid cluttering this chapter with more footnotes than necessary. I have, however, footnoted sources not contained in the chapters.

II. The Jury's Role in Democratic Theory and Practice

This volume's chapters on the American criminal and civil juries by Landsman show that the jury system not only reached its apotheosis in America, it remains a strong and vibrant institution even as it suffers criticism and calls for reforms. In contrast, the chapter on the English jury, the mother of the other jury systems, indicates that, relatively speaking, it appears to be an institution on the decline.[17] The civil jury has all but disappeared in England and Wales and a number of other developments have reduced the right to jury trial in criminal cases. Critics in England have even asserted that the right to jury trial should be abolished for serious fraud cases.

Some of these differences are due to the role which the jury occupies in the political consciousness and historical traditions of the United States and England. From its beginning the right to jury trial in England was reserved for serious crimes, with less serious charges being decided by magistrates.[18] In contrast, colonial Americans' experience with the British government and its judiciary led them to enshrine the right to jury trial for a much wider range of criminal and civil cases in the Constitution and in its Bill of Rights.[19] With minor exceptions this broad right to jury trial was echoed in each of the constitutions of the fifty states. Added trust in the jury, as opposed to professional judges, accrued from the fact that in the post-colonial period a paucity of trained legal professionals led Americans to lack confidence in the legal abilities of their judges, many of whom had no formal law education.[20] Even today, the fact that many American judges are either elected or subject to electoral recall arguably makes them more susceptible to influence from

[17] In addition see MARK FINDLAY AND PETER DUFF, THE JURY UNDER ATTACK (1988); and GOBERT *supra* note 13.

[18] See Blackstone *supra* note 1 and Thayer *supra* note 1; also see Penny Darbyshire, *The Lamp that Shows that Freedom Lives—Is it Worth it?* [1991] CRIM. L. REV. 740, 744.

[19] In addition to the chapters in this volume, see Albert Alschuler and Andrew G. Deis, *A Brief History of the Criminal Jury in the United States*, 61 U. CHIC. L. REV. 867, 871 (1994).

[20] Stephen Landsman, *The Civil Jury in America: Scenes from an Unappreciated History*, 44 HASTINGS L. J. 579, 598–601 (1993); HANS AND VIDMAR, *supra* note 2.

outside sources. All of these factors help to foster a preference for the combined wisdom of twelve citizens.

Alexis de Tocqueville's observations in the mid 1800s about the educational and politicizing role of the jury in the democratic ethos of American society are well known. Many readers will recall that Tocqueville argued that the jury is 'pre-eminently a political institution'.[21] He added that:

> The jury . . . serves to communicate the spirit of the judges to the minds of all the citizens; and this spirit, with the habits which attend it, is the soundest preparation for free institutions.[22]

Tocqueville's statements on the functions of the jury were quoted by Forsyth in his important 1875 treatise on the English jury.[23] And they are often set side-by-side with Lord Devlin's lecture in the 1950s in which he borrowed from Tocqueville and Blackstone to argue that:

> Each jury is a little parliament. The jury sense is the parliamentary sense. I cannot see the one dying and the and the other surviving. The first object of any tyrant in Whitehall would be to make Parliament utterly subservient to his will; and the next to overthrow or diminish trial by jury, for no tyrant could afford to leave a subject's freedom in the hands of twelve of his countrymen. So that trial by jury is more than an instrument of justice and more than one wheel of the Constitution: it is the lamp that shows that freedom lives.[24]

Often overlooked in Tocqueville's encomium, however, is the fact that he actually contrasted the American jury with the English jury. While acknowledging the English attachment to the jury and its exportation to English colonies around the world, Tocqueville noted important differences regarding the jury's role in American political life:

> In England the jury is selected from the aristocratic portion of the nation; the aristocracy makes the laws, applies the laws, and punishes infractions of the laws; everything is established upon a consistent footing, and England may with truth be said to constitute an aristocratic republic. In the United States the same system is applied to the whole people. Every American citizen is both an eligible and legally qualified voter. The jury system as it is understood in America appears to me to be as direct and extreme a consequence of the sovereignty of the people as universal suffrage.[25]

[21] Tocqueville *supra*, note 1.
[22] Ibid., at 317, 319.
[23] Forsyth, *supra* note 1 at 354–5, 357.
[24] Devlin, *supra* note 1, 164.
[25] Tocqueville, *supra* note 1, 318.

To be sure, in 1974 following a number of prior developments Parliament moved the English jury toward a representative institution with the Juries Act, requiring juries to be selected randomly from the population.[26] However, this step must be viewed against the Criminal Justice Act of 1967 that, in effect, allows an accused person to be convicted by a majority vote of ten of the twelve jurors, even for the most serious crimes, and the gradual reclassification of crimes by Parliament that in practice make them ineligible for jury trial.[27] England also abolished peremptory challenges for reasons more related to prosecution interests than to concerns about whether the jury is representative of the population.[28] At the same time the more representative jury pool has also opened the Englist jury system to charges that juries are incompetent. For example, Sir Robert Mark asserted that:

> if the one person in the criminal justice process most fitted by education, training and experience to decide the issue, namely the judge, is to be denied that right (to determine alone whether the accused is guilty) how much more illogical is it to confer upon any one of 12 randomly selected jurymen, least fitted by deafness, stupidity, prejudice, or one of a hundred other reasons.[29]

In 1985 the Roskill Committee, dealing with the issue of serious fraud, asserted that complex fraud cases 'cannot reasonably be expected to be understood by a jury selected at random'[30] and that 'many jurors are out of their depth'.[31]

Additionally, claims that jurors are sometimes bribed or intimidated in cases involving organized crime have figured in the English debate,[32] and assertions have been made that juries are inclined to wrongly convict out of prejudice or ignorance.[33]

[26] *See* Nicholas Blake, *The Case for the Jury*, in Mark Findlay and Peter Duff, *supra* note 17, 142 *Cf.* Darbyshire, *supra* note 18, 744.

[27] In addition to the Lloyd-Bostock and Thomas ch. in this volume see GOBERT, *supra* note 13.

[28] James J. Gobert, *The Peremptory Challenge—An Obituary*, [1989] CRIM. L. REV. 528.

[29] Sir Robert Mark, IN THE OFFICE OF CONSTABLE (1978); Peter Duff and Mark Findlay, *The Politics of Jury Reform*, in THE JURY UNDER ATTACK, 213–14 (1988).

[30] ROSKILL COMMITTEE REPORT 1985 ¶ 1.6, *in* Richard W. Harding, *Jury Performance in Complex Cases*, *in* THE JURY UNDER ATTACK, 74–5 (Mark Findlay & Peter Duff eds.1988).

[31] Ibid., § 8.35, at p. 76.

[32] Peter Duff and Mark Findlay, *The Politics of Jury Reform*, *in* THE JURY UNDER ATTACK, 213–14 (Mark Findlay & Peter Duff eds. 1988).

[33] Ibid., at 221–4; Michael Levi, *The Role of the Jury in Complex Cases*, *in* THE JURY UNDER ATTACK 97 (Mark Findlay & Peter Duff eds. 1988); Sarah McCabe, *Is the Jury Research Dead*, *in* THE JURY UNDER ATTACK 35 (Mark Findlay & Peter Duff eds. 1988).

A further factor in England's disenchantment with juries involves the perceived financial and administrative pressure that jury trials have on the administration of justice, thereby causing some critics to urge that many 'minor' crimes be made ineligible for jury trial.[34] We can also perhaps detect the impact of trends toward professional aggrandizement that roughly parallel responses of continental European countries to the jury system in the 1800s. Mark, for example, argued for the greater competence of the professional judge and the same argument was reflected in the report of the Roskill Commission. It is also important to consider that the English judicial system merges the judiciary and the legislature in the House of Lords, an idea rejected in American Constitutional and political culture. English academics and defense lawyers have expressed dismay at these developments in English law. Perhaps it is even fair to say that the elitist strains in English law that Tocqueville identified 150 years ago continue to affect jury theory and practice.

It needs to be said that severe criticisms directed at the jury system exist in other countries besides England. With respect to Australia, Howard wrote:

> It is often suggested that the jury is a corrective to the individual attitudes of particular judges. This may or may not be the case. It is also not the point. . . . There is no reason to suppose that a more or less random selection of ordinary people is going to have any less impressive an array of prejudices than a judge.[35]

In the United States both civil and criminal juries have had their share of criticism. In the 1970s American critics argued that a complexity exception should be made for the right to jury trial in civil cases.[36] Continuing right up into the 1990s the jury system is blamed for a 'tort crisis' and variously alleged to be incompetent, irresponsible, and prejudiced.[37] Following some highly publicized trials in the mid-1990s the criminal jury has been claimed to be acquittal prone, to be seduced by defendants who offer an 'abuse excuse', to be driven by racial tensions, and to be

[34] *See* Peter Duff and Mark Findlay, *The Politics of Jury Reform*, *in* The Jury Under Attack, 211–12 (Mark Findlay & Peter Duff eds. 1988).

[35] C. Howard, *Weak Link in Justice Chain*, Adelaide Advertiser, Aug. 2, 1985, as discussed *in* Richard W. Harding, *Jury Performance in Complex Cases* 74, *in* The Jury Under Attack, 74, 75 (Mark Findlay & Peter Duff eds. 1988).

[36] For a review see Peter Sperlich, *The Case for Preserving Trial by Jury*, 65 Judicature 394 (1982).

[37] See Marc Galanter, *An Oil Strike in Hell: Contemporary Legends About the Civil Justice System*, 40 Arizona Law Review 717 (1998); Stephen Daniels and Joanne Martin, Civil Juries and the Politics of Reform (1995).

prone to nullify laws.[38] This criticism has resulted in a spate of proposals for reforms, including caps on punitive damages in personal injury cases and urging of adoption of a majority verdict rule rather than a unanimity rule in criminal cases. However, few American critics would seriously suggest that the basic right to jury trial be abolished or curtailed in criminal cases. Even severe criticism of the civil jury is usually directed toward reforms and constraints rather than abolition.

Much of the robustness of the institution of jury trial in the United States is due to the fact that it is a guaranteed right in the federal and state constitutions. Additionally, American schoolchildren are heavily socialized about the importance of the jury. But this does not explain the whole story. Another part derives from the fact of elected rather than appointed judges in many states. Making a comparison between England and the United States, Mirjan Damaska has drawn attention to the fact that English judges are more 'technically oriented' whereas '[t]he American professional judiciary is notoriously politicized and expected to consider 'the equities' of cases so that the door remains open to the consideration of various extralegal factors'.[39] The American jury assists in this equitable functioning and helps to buffer judges against criticism.  Additionally, the relatively high frequency of jury trial with the conscription of large numbers of citizens to serve on these juries may have the socializing and legitimizing functions that Tocqueville identified in American culture almost 150 years ago. Lastly, television coverage of infamous trials and even a special television channel, Court TV, devoted to trials has now created a mass audience and further pushes the jury into the awareness of American life.[40] Thus, the American jury is arguably more deeply implicated in the actual and the symbolic administration of justice than the English jury and this helps account for its robustness as an institution.

The English and American contrast helps us view other jury systems as well. The chapter on Scotland points out that while an accused has a right to jury trial for a limited number of very serious crimes, there is neither a written nor a common law right to jury trial for most crimes. Rather, only the prosecutor has the right to decide whether the trial shall

[38] See Neil Vidmar *et al.*, *Should We Rush to Reform the Criminal Jury? Consider Conviction Rate Data*, 80 Judicature 286 (1997) for references to criminal jury critics, and to data that are contrary to the claims of these critics.

[39] Mirjan Damaska, The Faces of Justice and State Authority (1986).

[40] See Paul Thaler, The Watchful Eye: American Justice in the Age of Television (1994).

be by jury or by judge. The facts that the Scottish prosecution service is independent, and that it is not accountable to the police, the courts, victims of crime, or the accused probably account for the lack of serious political controversy over the jury in that country.

The separation of Australia, New Zealand, and Canada from England was by devolvement rather than revolution and their legal systems have remained closer to the English model. Australia has a written constitutional guarantee of the right to jury trial for Commonwealth crimes that has been interpreted as existing for the benefit of society, rather than the accused, and therefore cannot be waived. Nevertheless jury trial is limited by other considerations. These include the fact that the individual Australian states and territories retained power to legislate their own criminal offenses and determine whether the offenses are subject to jury trial. Additionally, in creating new Commonwealth offences, the Commonwealth Parliament can avoid jury trial by stipulating that the offence must not or need not be tried on indictment. The jury in New Zealand is maintained by common law custom and the 1990 Bill of Rights Act rather than a written constitutional guarantee. As is the case in England the right to jury trial is subject to legislative definition of crimes as indictable or subject to summary conviction. For crimes involving a potential sentence of fourteen years or more jury trial is mandatory. For other crimes, the accused has a right to elect for jury trial if the sentence could result in more than three months' imprisonment, but the Bill of Rights Act makes an exception that excludes jury trial for certain types of assault, such as an assault on a police officer. There has also been debate in New Zealand regarding whether jury trial should be retained in complex fraud cases.

Although Canada separated peacefully from England and looked toward England for most of its legal history, the criminal jury has gained elevated status in the political life of that country. With the adoption of a written constitution in 1982, the Charter of Rights and Freedoms, Canadian law has moved closer to American law in many subtle ways, including jury law. Canada retains a distinctions between non-indictable crimes and indictable crimes, but Section 11(f) of the Charter guarantees the right to jury trial for serious crimes. A number of subsequent Canadian Supreme Court decisions have taken cognizance of the jury's political importance or approved procedures that, in limited ways, show similarities to the American system. At the same time, however, a number of so-called hybrid offenses allow the Crown Prosecutor to lay charges that avoid jury trial, and the number of such hybrid crimes has increased in recent years without major protests from the public.

The Republic of Ireland is a special case. The right to jury trial for criminal cases was enshrined in the Irish Constitution of 1937. However, for reasons related to Ireland's unhappy historical experience with England and to the demographic nature of portions of the country, jury trial has not been as central a part of Irish political consciousness.

Chapter 13 provides discussion on a number of other countries that were influenced by English law at one point in their history. Some retained the jury system and others abandoned it. The reasons for success or failure of the jury in these countries involve many complicated factors, including competition from indigenous legal systems, but these histories also are tied to political context and socialization.

The main point of this overview is to suggest that political culture and tradition are important influences on the jury. None of the above is to suggest that the jury could be readily abolished in any of the above countries or that the jury is not an important part of the political and legal culture, but it does suggest strongly that countries vary along a continuum in the extent to which they are wedded to the jury system. These political and legal traditions should also be considered in thinking about the longer term success of the new jury systems in Russia and Spain and in thinking about proposals for a jury system in Japan.

III. Adversary Procedure and the Jury

It is also important to consider the modern jury within the context of adversarial and inquisitorial modes of legal procedure. Some recent changes in jury law and practice, particularly in the United States, have begun to modify some rules arising out of adversary system assumptions that have constrained the jury for more than a century. Additionally, consideration of procedural assumptions is, as the chapters on the Russian and Spanish jury systems and on Japan remind us, essential to the understanding of success of jury systems. A procedural perspective also provides insight when thoughts are given to the legitimacy accorded to the jury system by persons working on different cultural assumptions as is the case among the Maori of New Zealand, Inuit and Indian groups within Canada and the United States, and aboriginal people in Australia.

Although Mirjan Damaska's incisive treatise, *The Faces of Justice*,[41] cautions against making oversimplifying distinctions, the essence of the adversary system, as developed in England and spread to her colonies, involves a number of characteristics that can be stated in simplified and summary fashion for present purposes as it pertains to jury trial. In adversarial procedure each party to the dispute has responsibility for the development and presentation of the trial evidence. The evidence is presented in a single hearing before the judge and jury, neither of whom has foreknowledge of the evidence. There is a prescribed order of presentation in which the prosecutor or plaintiff presents first, with each witness being subject to cross-examination by the other side. Then the defense presents its witnesses, who are also subject to cross-examination by the opposing side. At the end of the defense case, each side presents its arguments to the jury and the judge instructs the jury on the law before sending it out to deliberate and return a verdict. Throughout this process both judge and jury remain passive listeners. Neither the judge nor the jury is allowed to consider *ex parte* evidence. The judge's role is confined to that of referee for the 'contest' according to certain rules of evidence and other procedure. Because the contending parties develop the evidence there is a strong emphasis on oral presentation at trial so that the judge and jury can judge the merits of the evidence first hand in order to detect any biases or inconsistencies. Additionally, since the jury is composed of conscripted lay persons it is essential that the proceedings be completed in a compressed period of time—a single hearing of evidence, or 'trial'—so that the jurors may return to their occupations and personal lives. Also, because lay persons have no legal training, certain rules of evidence have been developed to filter what jurors may hear in order that they not be influenced by illogical or extra-legal considerations.

In contrast, inquisitorial modes of legal procedure used on the European continent and in most other parts of the world are structured around a model of bureaucratic investigation.[42] Once a crime has been discovered the court or some court-affiliated authority takes over the

[41] Damaska, *supra* note 39.

[42] See Damaska, *supra* note 39; Bron McKillop, *Anatomy of a French Murder Case*, 45 American Journal of Comparative Law 527 (1997); John Langbein, *The German Advantage in Civil Procedure*, 52 U. Chi. L. Rev. 823 (1985). Note, however, that in civil cases the process is more adversarial than commonly portrayed, see Herbert Bernstein, *Whose Advantage After All? A Comment on the Comparison of Civil Justice Systems*, 21 U. Cal., Davis L. Rev. 587 (1988).

process. Officials interview the witnesses, undertake the discovery of other evidence, and write reports about the investigations. A series of court hearings may be held as the case develops; and in the light of new information the reports are revised. The court places heavy emphasis on these written reports. For example, in contrast to adversary procedure a written deposition taken by an official during a hearing may be used at the formal trial to challenge live testimony. At the formal trial primary questioning of the witnesses is conducted by the judge or judges—often there is more than one judge as well as lay person members of the tribunal[43]—and the lawyers for the parties play a relatively passive role. In contrast to the formalized rules of direct and cross-examination in the adversary system, testimony is taken in narrative form. The court determines the order of evidence presentation. Rules of evidence involving what may or may not be admitted at trial are largely absent since it is assumed that the professional judges can make the appropriate weighting of evidence and explain it to the lay persons on the judicial tribunal. There are other differences. In inquisitorial systems the judges are trained from the beginning to be judges and they operate in a hierarchical system. The trial judges have less individual autonomy than adversary judges, and upon appeal their total decision-making processes are reviewed by officials at a next level of the bureaucratic hierarchy.

One important implication of inquisitorial procedure is that it contains elements that conflict with elements important to trial by jury. The public part of trial, which is so important in the adversary system, is less important in inquisitorial systems. The emphasis on reports and multiple hearings to develop a picture of causation and guilt is less amenable to allowing jurors to develop their verdict on the facts independently of the judge and court investigators. Moreover, in a system in which court officials have used their professional efforts and expertise in developing the case, it is not surprising that they are reluctant to have their work potentially overturned by an informal group of amateurs called a jury. These themes are discussed in more detail in Thaman's chapter on Spain and Russia, but even this simplified discussion helps to explain part of the reason why jury systems thrived or failed to thrive in different legal cultures.

[43] See, e.g., McKillop, *supra* note 42: Sanja Ivkovic, Lay Participation in Criminal Trials: The Case of Croatia (1999); Stefan Machura, Interaction Between Lay Assessors and Professional Judge in German Mixed Courts. Paper presented at International Conference on Lay Participation in the Criminal Trial in the 21st Century, Siracusa, Sicily, Italy, 26–9 May 1999.

However, there are additional insights that can be gleaned from consideration of assumptions about adversary procedures. Scholarly studies have fairly convincingly demonstrated that the adversary system only developed at the end of the eighteenth century, primarily as a result of developments in legal thinking that allowed accused persons to have legal representation. That development allowed lawyers to challenge evidence set forth by private prosecutors and professional thief catchers.[44]

Well into the eighteenth century the ordinary English criminal jury trial bore greater resemblance to an inquisitorial than to an adversary system.[45] The primary evidence was produced by the prosecutor. The accused was not allowed to testify under oath in his or her own behalf nor allowed legal counsel. Though he or she could question witnesses the primary questioning was conducted by the judge and jurors. Jurors were selected for the sitting of an assize, perhaps several weeks, and often the same names appeared on the jury in later assizes. Juries routinely heard multiple cases in a single day, sometimes in succession, before they retired to deliberate and announce verdicts for the cases. Often the cases had the same legal elements in the charges so that at least after a few days the jurors would be reasonably versed in the law and have fact comparisons derived from similar cases, making them somewhat educated on the law. *Bushell's case* in 1670, freeing the jury from the threat of attaint for a false verdict, is frequently cited as the landmark case in which the jury was recognized as an independent fact finder. However, a study of historical records in decades after *Bushell's case* was decided indicates that judges still took a very active, indeed dominating, role in instructing the jury not only on the law but on what the verdict should be. Apparently the juries usually followed instructions. There is additional evidence that judges directed verdicts of guilty as well as not guilty despite the presence of a jury.[46]

Much more needs to be learned about the development of the adversary system as it relates to the jury, but it is clear that in the late eighteenth and then nineteenth centuries, the role of the judge gradually became more passive and similar to the form we know today. The vestiges of judge control over the jury, however, remain in all countries, although much less so in the United States. That is to say that, the US excepted, the trial judge in the other countries that are reviewed in this

[44] Stephan Landsman, *The Rise of the Contentious Spirit: Adversary Procedure in Eighteenth Century England*, 75 Cornell L. Rev. 497 (1990); John Langbein, *The Criminal Trial Before Lawyers*, 45 U. Chi. L. Rev. 263 (1978)

[45] Langbein, *supra* note 44. [46] Ibid.

book has the positive duty of not only instructing the jury on the law but also of reviewing the theories of the prosecution and defense and even commenting on the credibility of evidence.

Over time the role of the jury became even more passive in the sense that legal theory and actual legal practice developed around the notion that the jury should be seen and not heard. By the middle of the twentieth century juries were not ordinarily instructed of their right to ask questions and in fact usually discouraged from asking them.[47] They were also instructed that they should not discuss any of the evidence among themselves until after the closing arguments and instructions from the judge.[48]

Strikingly, a number of developments in parts of the United States and in other countries near the end of the twentieth century have shifted adversary procedure slightly more toward the inquisitorial end of the continuum. In the most far reaching changes, the State of Arizona has instituted new rules that require the judges to instruct the jurors that they may ask questions of witnesses (through written notes vetted by the judge and opposing counsel). Arizona juries are also instructed that they may discuss the evidence during the trial whenever all jurors are together in the jury room during recesses and before the court opens for the day.[49] Other reforms attempted in various US jurisdictions include juror tutorials on evidence in complex cases, preinstruction for juries, improved instructions and even dialogues with jurors when they reach an impasse on the verdict.[50] It is noteworthy that in New Zealand recommendations encouraging question asking have also been put forward and will most likely be passed into law. All of these types of changes are moves from passive to more active evidence integration on the part of the jury.

Another development in the United States involves a series of cases decided by the Supreme Court that vest in the judge the responsibility

[47] Michael Wolfe, *Juror questions: a survey of theory and use*, 55 MISSOURI L. REV. 817 (1990) reviews case law on this issue. It is important to observe that no court had forbidden question asking and that, acting on their own subjudice authority, individual trial judges made exceptions to the general practice.

[48] Following the American Revolution the jury had a much more active role in the trial process but this faded to a great extent after the taming of the frontier and the fading of Jacksonian democracy ideals, see HANS & VIDMAR, *supra* note 2; Alschuler & Dies, *supra* note 19.

[49] B. Michael Dann and George Logan III, *Jury Reform: The Arizona Experience* 79 JUDICATURE 280 (1996).

[50] See MUNSTERMAN *et al.*, *supra* note 15.

to screen the expert evidence for reliability and accuracy before it can be presented as trial evidence.[51] This development arose out of concerns about unreliable evidence, sometimes labeled 'junk science', but the consequences of these decisions may ultimately have a major impact on other forms of traditional expert evidence such as medical and psychiatric testimony, handwriting analysis, ballistics tests, and arson causation as well as bodies of expertise in the social sciences. This development, too, is a shift away from adversarial thinking since it transfers some of the evidence control from the parties to the judge. Of course, it also removes some of the traditional assumptions that the jury is to determine the weight of the evidence. Some of these developments are undoubtedly the result of liberal rules of evidence and a free wheeling adversary culture in the United States.[52] These issues have not as yet become as controversial outside the US, but new developments in highly technical forensic evidence may eventually see judges in other countries struggling with the same problems of admissibility when questions arise about reliability of forensic evidence.

Mention has already been made to the fact that in Scotland prosecutions are brought by a highly independent office, and the accused has no say in the mode of trial. In England and Wales, Canada, Australia, and New Zealand there are a substantial number of crimes for which the accused has the discretion to opt for trial by judge or by jury. In some Australian states the accused may opt for trial by judge alone even in cases where the law prescribes trial by jury. In Australia it is still theoretically possible for victims or their surrogates to press private prosecutions. The same holds true in Canada, although in practice the Crown has final say on whether charges will go forward.[53] In Spain the victim or the victim's family may be represented by a private prosecutor independently of the public prosecutor.

In short, where countries fall with respect to a continuum of adversary versus inquisitorial procedure must be considered in jury comparisons.

[51] Daubert v. Merrell Dow Pharmaceuticals, 113 S.Ct. 2786 (1993); Kumho Tire Co v. Carmichael, 119 S.Ct. 1167 (1998); see Steven Coronado, *The Question Is, Was, and Should Always Remain: Is it Reliable?* FOR THE DEFENSE (November supplement) 1 (1999).

[52] Sophia Gatowski *et al.*, *The Diffusion of Scientific Evidence: A Comparative Perspective of Admissibility Standards in Australia, Canada, England and the United States and Their Impact on Social and Behavioural Sciences*, 4 EXPERT EVIDENCE 86 (1996).

[53] Personal communication from Professor David Paciocco to the author regarding Sections 505 and 507 of the Canadian Criminal Code.

IV. Composition, Challenges, and Contempt: An Historical Perspective

The basic assumption behind allowing lay persons rather than professionals to decide important legal matters is that jurors provide useful insights regarding contested facts and inject community values of equity and fairness into their decisions. Juries also create a sense of legitimacy about the legal process. Consequently, the matter of who sits on the jury, that is the composition of the jury, is a matter of considerable importance. At the same time, from the early origins of the jury to today there has been concern that those jury members must be impartial, or at least must be perceived to be impartial. The jury of peers is limited to impartial peers. A number of characteristics separate contemporary jury systems with respect to how the goal of a broadly representative jury is reconciled with the need to have its members be and be seen to be impartial. The way that these conflicts are addressed is related to the cognizable grounds upon which potential jurors may be excluded from serving on any particular jury, the laws that control selection of the jury, and the laws intended to prevent tainting of the jury pool.

The universal trend toward democratizing jury pools combined with the alleged complexity of the evidence or the number of litigants involved in some modern trials has led to arguments in some countries in favor of specially selected criminal juries. Jury composition issues are also relevant to concerns about legitimacy and fundamental fairness with respect to visible minorities who are often disproportionately represented on criminal dockets. An additional area involves the question of how to deal with the potential impact of mass media on the jury pool. These are all separate topics, but they overlap with regard to the substantive and procedural laws bearing on how the petit jury is selected. Although the individual jury systems have evolved in different ways, they all have roots in the past. A brief and selective foray into the history of the English jury helps with comparative analysis.

A. Competence and Bias Issues

Despite the fact that Blackstone, echoing commentators before him, described trial by jury as 'the glory of English law',[54] the jury was not infrequently seen to be composed of persons who were ignorant or

[54] Blackstone, *supra* note 1.

biased or both. James Oldham has referred to a 1607 Proclamation for Jurors by James I that asserted that jury service:

> oftentimes resteth upon such as are either simple and ignorant, and almost at a gaze in any cause of difficultie, or else upon those that are so accustomed and inured to passe and serve upon Juries, and they have almost lost that tendernesse of Conscience, which in such cases is to bee wished, and make the service, as it were an occupation and practice.[55]

The problems alleged in this charge and in subsequent claims in later centuries arose out of complex causes. One factor was corrupt sheriffs who were responsible for assembling the jury list and summoning the jurors.[56] Sheriffs might be bribed into choosing jurors who were favorable to one side or, on the other hand, allowing wealthy, educated jurors to pay to be relieved from the hardships of jury service, leaving the jury roles to be filled by persons who were available. In other instances property requirements to serve on juries were sometimes so high that in certain localities even an honest sheriff might have difficulties finding qualified veniremen. In any event, in both criminal and civil cases challenges to the adequacy of the jury list were not unusual events. There were also problems with jurors being bribed. Additionally, in important state trials involving treason or other serious matters it was assumed that the matters should be tried by men of high social standing, that is, 'men of quality'.

B. Challenges

By the middle of the 1700s English law allowed challenges to the jurors that were called for jury duty on the grounds that they were not eligible to serve or not impartial with regard to a 'manifest presumption of partiality "or" to the favour.'[57] Ineligibility would include persons who were not landholders or persons convicted of a crime. 'Manifest partiality' involved such matters as a juror having a consanguinity relationship to one of the parties in the litigation; having accepted money or gifts; having owed money to one of the parties; or having expressed an opinion about matters in dispute at the trial. In short, there was a *prima facie*

[55] James C. Oldham, *The Origins of the Special Jury*, 50 U. Chi. L. Rev. 137, 142 (1983).

[56] Ibid. at 141–59 for all statements contained in this paragraph.

[57] See James Kennedy, Law and Practice of Juries, 90 (1826); Blackstone, *supra* note 1 at 359–65 and Forsyth, *supra* note 1 for sources of statements contained in the rest of this paragraph.

assumption that the juror was not impartial. In contrast, challenges 'to the favour' involved what we would today call attitudinal biases and prejudices. Challenges could be made to the whole panel, or array, on the grounds that the selection of the array was procedurally incorrect or to the polls, that is, to the individual jurors.

Challenges on the grounds of 'manifest partiality' were usually decided by the court, but the decision could be placed in the hands of two *triers*.[58] However, all challenges 'to the favour' were required to be decided by triers. The triers were two members from the jury pool who were sworn as arbiters to determine the truth of the challenge. They listened to the evidence, including the sworn testimony of the juror who was challenged, and rendered a verdict as to the validity of the challenge. The use of triers is interesting for a number of reasons. First, the matter of non-manifest biases was recognized early in the development of the jury. Secondly, the decision about prejudice was placed in the hands of some of the members of the jury panel rather than the court. Thirdly, the trier system existed (and still exists) in other countries:

Nancy King's research, which may surprise many readers, indicates that the trier procedure persisted into the late nineteenth century in some federal and state courts in the United States.[59] However, today the trier procedure remains as a common procedural practice only in the Canadian jury system, although it is available, but rarely used, in Australia. Its disappearance in other countries probably is involved with such factors as the development of restricted views about bias 'on the favour' and legislation that places any judgments about juror fitness to serve in the hands of the trial judge. It is reasonable to hypothesize that the disappearance of the trier procedure in the United States was due primarily to the fact that litigants were given relatively extensive powers to question jurors and reject them through the use of peremptory challenges or challenges for cause made through motions to the judge.[60] Confirmation of the hypothesis awaits further historical research.

Although in the earliest development of the jury system the Crown had an unlimited number of peremptory challenges, by the fourteenth century only the defendant could exercise them.[61] In capital cases the

[58] KENNEDY, *supra* note 57 at 102 and BLACKSTONE, *supra* note 1.

[59] Nancy J. King, *Silencing Nullification Advocacy Inside the Jury Room and Outside the Courtroom*, 65 U. CHI. L. REV. 433, 467 (1998).

[60] In some states it apparently existed simultaneously with the expanded rights of litigants to challenge jurors, see ibid. for references.

[61] See Hoffman, *supra* note 12, 819–21.

number of peremptory challenges was set at thirty-five. The accused did not need to give reasons for exercising them, and most commentators believe that peremptories provided the accused with a safeguard against biases favoring the Crown and also provided the symbolism of fairness. However, while the Crown's peremptories were taken away, it had an unlimited number of *stand asides*. The stand aside was a procedure whereby the Crown could require that any juror that it viewed unfavorably for any reason could cause that juror to be passed over in favor of the next juror. Only if the jury pool was exhausted through peremptories or challenges for cause was that juror called back to sit on the jury. In practice the stand aside provision gave the Crown the equivalent of peremptory challenges without offering any reasons and without numerical limitations. As noted above, the stand aside provision still exists in England, even though the defendant's peremptory challenges have been abolished. This Crown privilege is supposed to be used sparingly, but no statistics appear to exist as to its frequency of use. Stand asides still exist in Australia. In Canada the stand aside procedure lasted until 1992 when it was abolished by the Supreme Court on the ground that it appeared to give the Crown prosecutor an unfair advantage over the defense. Subsequently, the number of Crown peremptories was increased to bring parity with the accused.

C. *Change of Venue*

The presumption of English law was that the trial should take place in the locality of the offence.[62] Nevertheless, when 'the great ends of justice warrant' there was no impropriety in moving the trial to another venue. Changes of venue were probably often to the advantage of the Crown because of local hostility to the prosecution, but they might also have helped a defendant who was out of favor with the community.

D. *Special Juries*

Another mechanism to avoid some of the problems seen in the jury system was the *special jury*. James Oldham's research[63] indicates that, historically, there were three types of special juries: a jury composed of

[62] BLACKSTONE, *supra* note 1 at 384.

[63] Oldham, *supra* note 55; and James Oldham, *Special Juries in England: Nineteenth Century Usage and Reform*, 8 JOURNAL OF LEGAL HISTORY 148 (1987) for all references in this paragraph.

persons from a higher class; a jury of experts; and a 'struck jury'. A fourth type that did not have the technical designation of 'special' was the jury *de medietate linguae*. All of these jury types were used both before and after the middle of the seventeenth century when the jury system was exported to England's colonies. The special jury of 'quality' jurors, that is, those of higher political standing was used in cases involving national importance, such as state trials for high treason or seditious libel. The expert jury involved persons who had special knowledge bearing on a dispute in a particular area. Expert juries were formed from panels composed of, for example, cooks or fishmongers. Although women were not permitted to serve on ordinary juries, all-female juries were empaneled to determine if a condemned woman was pregnant, thereby delaying execution until after she gave birth.

The struck jury had its roots in the early development of the jury system wherein each litigant could strike twelve jurymen from a panel of forty-eight names.[64] Usually the litigant personally paid for the jurors, and the purpose was to hopefully avoid incompetent, biased, or corrupt persons that might be called by the sheriff.

Parliament recognized special juries in 1730,[65] apparently as a form of expert jury, but their actual use evolved differently, often to obtain a 'higher class' of juror, particularly one that might be favorable toward the party requesting it. Lord Mansfield made use of special juries to a great extent between 1770 and 1790 during his tenure on the Court of King's Bench. These special jury panels were composed of merchants, bankers, and tradesmen and, in one instance, a 'slop seller'. The important point, as Oldham's research shows, is that only about 27 percent of the trials were involved with purely commercial subjects while another 34 percent involved general business disputes like debt and bankruptcy. However, the remaining 31 percent involved noncommercial litigation on such matters as negligence, trespass, trover, assault, criminal conversation, nuisance, libel, and perjury. The special jury was used less frequently after Lord Mansfield's time. Nevertheless the special jury lingered on the statute books until 1949, and an exception remained for the City of London until 1971.[66] In 1982 an English

[64] Oldham I, *supra* note 55, 176; Oldham, *supra* note 63, 153.

[65] Oldham, *supra* note 55, 139–40; Oldham, *supra* note 63, 153 for all statements in this paragraph.

[66] The last case, involving a commercial matter, tried to a special jury in London occurred in 1950, see Report of the Departmental Committee on Jury Service, April 1965.

law reform body, the Fraud Trials Committee, considered revival of special juries involving experts for major fraud trials but ultimately rejected the concept. Oldham's research has also found that special juries were used in the United States in criminal cases as late as the 1950s and were provided for civil jury trials in the statutes of at least twenty states.

The possibility of prejudice against a party in a civil or criminal suit was also recognized in the concept of the *jury de medietate linguae*.[67] These special juries arose as early as the thirteenth century to deal with disputes involving Englishmen (or the Crown) and Jews and foreigners.[68] The origins of such juries involved state interests in protecting international commerce[69] and part of the rationale behind them was based on recognition of conflict of laws.[70] Another rationale, largely implicit, was the assumption that a jury of Englishmen might be prejudiced in rendering a verdict against an outsider.[71] The jury *de medietate linguae* was typically composed of half Englishmen and half members of the Jews' or foreigners' community.[72] Except for a 1554 statute that excluded mixed juries in treason cases, the jury *de medietate linguae* existed until 1870, during the reign of Queen Victoria.[73]

Deborah Ramirez suggests that the jury *de medietate linguae* presented many practical difficulties, including finding enough qualified jurors.[74] Moreover, these special juries could be seen as stigmatizing Englishmen—and their legal system—as prejudiced.[75] It is noteworthy that at the same time that special juries were abolished in the Naturalization Act of 1870, aliens were granted the right to serve on juries in cases that did not necessarily involve aliens.[76] Although the historical record is sketchy, the inclusion of aliens on jury lists may be seen as a switch of one procedural remedy for prejudice for another. Rather than setting up

[67] Oldham I, *supra* note 55, 167.

[68] Deborah A. Ramirez, *The Mixed Jury and the Ancient Custom of Trial by* Jury De Medietate Linguae: *A History and a Proposal for Change*, 74 B.U. L. Rev. 777, 783–6 (1994); Oldham I, *supra* note 55, 168.

[69] Ramirez, *supra* note 68, 785–6.

[70] Marianne Constable, The Law of the Other 7–12 (1994).

[71] Oldham I, *supra* note 55, 167; J. Thayer, A Preliminary Treatise on Evidence at the Common Law 94–7, 419 n.1 (1898 & photo. Reprint 1969).

[72] Ramirez, *supra* note 68, 785; Constable, *supra* note 67, 16–22.

[73] Ramirez, *supra* note 68, 786.

[74] Ramirez, *supra* note 68, 787, *quoting* 199 Hansard Parliamentary Debates 3d, col. 1129 (Mar. 3, 1870 statement of the Earl of Derby).

[75] Ibid. [76] Ibid.

special juries, inclusive eligibility was seen as a remedy that, at least in theory, allowed a chance of minority representation on the jury. That chance helped to justify claims of legal fairness.[77]

It is worthwhile noting here that it is easy to see the parallel of this reasoning with the steps that have been made in contemporary common law countries to increase jury representativeness with particular concerns about including minority populations. Indeed, this rationale arguably offers one explanation for the elimination of peremptory challenges and challenges for cause in the modern English jury, namely that universal opportunity for jury service randomizes prejudices and causes them to be canceled out, thereby eliminating the need for juror vetting. These notions also play an important part in the contemporary jury systems of Australia, Canada, and New Zealand.

Juries *de medietate linguae* were used in New Zealand for cases involving Maori accused of crimes and were not officially abolished until 1961. However, because of continuing concern with Maori under-representation on jury panels the idea of all-Maori juries or juries de *medietate linguae* has been revived, though not acted upon.

Juries *de medietate linguae* were also imported to the American colonies and used for criminal matters involving colonists and Native Americans.[78] After the United States became an independent nation, they continued to be accepted as part of the common law tradition and were provided for in the states of Kentucky, Maryland, Massachusetts, Pennsylvania, New York, Virginia, and South Carolina. In 1823 Supreme Court Chief Justice John Marshall permitted a mixed jury in a case involving an alien accused of piracy and murder.[79] However, in a 1936 case, *U.S. v Wood*,[80] the U.S. Supreme Court declared that the right to a mixed jury was not guaranteed in the Sixth Amendment to the Constitution.

As described in Chapter13, the notions of mixed juries were also imported into African and Asian colonies with provisions for cross-race crimes. A Commonwealth survey published in 1943 indicated that provisions for mixed juries remained in the British colonies in Aden, Barbados, Brunei, the Federated Malay States, Gold Coast, Johore, Kelantan, Kenya, Nigeria, North Borneo, and Nyasaland.[81]

[77] Ibid., 783–6. [78] Ibid., 789–90.

[79] Ibid., 792; see also United States v. Cartacho, 25 F. Cas. 312 (C.C.D. Va. 1823) (No. 14738). See also Alschuler & Deiss, *supra* note 19, 880 for additional discussion.

[80] Ramirez, *supra* note 68, 793.

[81] Alex Brown, The Juryman's Handbook (1951).

It needs to be noted that despite a legal rationale that would seem to be against special juries in contemporary English law, there is revived talk about ensuring selection of a certain percentage of minority persons on the jury in cases where racial issues are central to the case. In the United States roughly similar concerns about racial diversity have led to discussions about forms of stratified selection of the jury pool in order to ensure adequate representation of minorities on the jury panel.[82]

E. Jury Size and Verdict Rule

Historically, the size of the English petit jury was set at twelve and the verdict had to be unanimous.[83] These attributes of the jury may also be considered to be related to the issue of jury composition.

These historic characteristics of the English jury still exist for criminal trials in Australia, Canada,[84] New Zealand,[85] and federal and most state court trials in the United States. However, England and Wales, the Republic of Ireland, and two state courts in the United States have reduced the unanimity requirement in favor of super majority rules. These changes are mid-twentieth century developments for criminal trials in those countries. Scotland is the exception that, as far as can be known, always used a simple majority rule with its jury composed of fifteen members and the option of a 'not proven' verdict. However, as Chapter 13 indicates, when the jury was transported to England's colonies in Africa and Asia in the late eighteenth and early nineteenth centuries, neither the jury size nor unanimity requirements were considered essential, and they varied from colony to colony.

The size of the civil jury was often altered downward from twelve in all countries. This includes the United States and Canada. Similarly, in many countries the unanimity requirements were not considered essential for civil cases when juries were used.

[82] Nancy King and Thomas Munsterman, *Stratified Juror Selection: Cross-section by Design*, 79 JUDICATURE 273 (1996).

[83] BLACKSTONE *supra* note 1; Kennedy *supra* 57, 40.

[84] Canada had an exception in the Northwest Territories for juries composed of 7 members but today all juries are composed of 12 persons.

[85] However, at one time juries of six were allowed for some lesser crimes in New Zealand.

F. The Law of Contempt by Publication

The legal conception of contempt of court was referenced as far back as 1250 in the *Rolls and Year Books*.[86] The records indicate that mere words that 'scandalised' the court or its officers were sufficient to bring charges and conviction of contempt, even if the scandalising words occurred outside of the courtroom. Nevertheless, the law of contempt for publishing words calculated to interfere with the administration of justice or to prejudice the fair trial of a pending case became most fully developed in the eighteenth century with the flourishing of the press and pamphleteers in England. A leading case involved the printers of *The Champion* and *The St James Evening Post* in 1742 for printing matters that were considered libelous against the widow of a deceased man and the testators of his will, and therefore alleged to prejudice the fair trial of pending court proceedings.[87] In his opinion in the case the presiding judge, Lord Hardwicke, stated:

> Nothing is more incumbent upon courts of justice, than to preserve their proceedings from being misrepresented; nor is there any thing of more pernicious consequence, than to prejudice the minds of the publik against persons concerned as parties in causes, before the cause is heard.[88]

Lord Harwicke went on to rule that it was no defense for a publisher to claim no knowledge of the contents of a publication, thus setting a standard of strict liability.[89] The ruling on *The St James Evening Post* reached far into the twentieth century in England, subjecting the mass media to substantial judicial control, but by standards that were frequently unclear. Finally, in 1981 the the laws of contempt were revised by statute to provide clearer standards for journalists and publishers.[90]

[86] David Eady and A. T. H. Smith, Arlige, Eady and Smith on Contempt (1999). Statements in this paragraph are derived from this source.

[87] See also Blackstone, *supra* note 1 at Vol 4, 283–5.

[88] Quoted in Eady and Smith, *supra* note 86, 19.

[89] Ibid. at 21. Those authors assume that Lord Hardwicke based his reasoning on the law of criminal libel, in which lack of intent was no defense.

[90] Ibid. at 21; see also S.H. Bailey, *The Contempt of Court Act* (1982) 45 Modern Law Review 301; Clive Walker, Ian Cram, and Debra Brogarth, *The Reporting of Crown Court Proceedings and the Contempt of Court Act 1981* (1992) 55 Modern Law Review 647.

V. Contemporary Juries: Comparative Issues Concerning Composition, Competence, and Impartiality

With this historical sketch serving as context, we can turn to contemporary jury systems. Arising from this common background, the jury has developed differently in each of the countries in response to unique characteristics associated with the broader legal, political, and social systems in which it is enmeshed. In this section juries are compared with respect to a number of important dimensions.

A. *Representativeness*

In the latter half of the twentieth century most of the property, gender, and ethnic/racial qualifications for jury eligibility that characterized the historical jury have been eliminated.[91] Trends toward universal jury eligibility appear to be the norm. Nevertheless, in most of the countries covered in this volume's chapters, concerns have been expressed about the *de jure* or *de facto* exclusion of persons who rank among the better educated members of society. The strongest movement in the direction of universal eligibility for jury service has occurred in the United States where a series of legislative actions and Supreme Court decisions have established doctrine shifting the rationale for representativeness from the rights of accused to the rights of the citizenry to serve on the jury.[92] Many state jurisdictions in the US have eliminated traditional statutory exemptions so that even lawyers and judges are called for jury service. In most other countries the trends have not reached this far and exemptions for lawyers, police officers, and citizens considered necessary to provide essential services, such as physicians and veterinarians, remain. In South Australia a trial court has the authority to order a jury composed of men only or women only in special circumstances, but the chances of such juries being formed is remote.

In England, the United States, Canada, New Zealand, and Australia there is continuing concern about the under-representation of members of racial and ethnic groups in the jury pool despite the fact that minorities frequently are over-represented as accused persons in numbers greater than their proportions in the population. In England the elimi-

[91] However, Ch. 13 reports instances in which such qualifications still exist.

[92] In addition to Nancy King's chapter in this volume see also Andrew Leipold, *Constitutionalizing Jury Selection in Criminal Cases: A Critical Evaluation*, 86 Georgetown Law Journal 945 (1998).

nation of peremptory challenges and challenges for cause has not solved the problem of under-representation. As mentioned earlier, there has been discussion of something very roughly akin to juries *de medietate linguae* in order to include minority input into verdicts, but the idea has not been acted upon. In New Zealand some jurisdictions have made overt attempts to construct the racial composition of the jury to match the ethnic background of the accused. In the United States concern with under-representation of minorities has resulted in discussion of schemes, also not acted upon, involving stratified sampling or other measures to increase minority representation in the jury pool.[93] Canada's law makes provision for trial in one of the two official languages, and a small body of case law is concerned with the improper construction of jury lists involving aboriginal communities. The issue of aboriginal and minority group representation has caused comment in Australia and New Zealand. In Australia a judge discharged a jury when the prosecution challenged all Aboriginal members of a jury panel.

The widespread concern with minority representation raises an important policy and doctrinal issue that was articulated in an insightful essay by Jeffrey Abramson.[94] Abramson suggested that there are two rationales for a jury that is representative of the community. In Abramson's formulation the 'democratic ideal' rationale is concerned with obtaining minority views on the issues and evidence that will provide an opportunity to promote the most robust discussion and examination of the facts in the trial. The 'representative ideal' rationale is concerned with having minority group members present on the jury to represent the values and interests of those groups. Both views strive for increasing the legitimacy of the legal process, but Abramson argued that the 'representative ideal' is ultimately divisive because it perpetuates or aggravates differences between minority and majority groups. In contrast, a jury system emphasizing the democratic ideal allows an opportunity for all members of the community to be represented on the jury but promotes fair evaluation of the evidence through robust discussions arising from diverse perspectives that are independent of group loyalties. With regard to the United States, Abramson expressed concern that the representative ideal has often come to predominate over the democratic ideal.

[93] King and Munsterman, *supra* note 82. The schemes face a number of constitutional problems.

[94] Jeffrey Abramson, *supra* note 2 at ch. 3.

Abramson's distinctions are worth pondering in comparisons between countries. The degree to which these differing rationales regarding representativeness or democratic deliberation are made in the statutes and case law of different countries is not clear, nor is it necessarily the case that judges and legislators have even thought about the implications of Abramson's analysis. However, to the extent that provisions for mixed juries or for empaneling certain proportions of minorities are considered as part of possible jury reforms, as has been suggested in England and New Zealand, the representative ideal is arguably predominating over the democratic ideal. These are value choices, and ones that reflect on the role of the jury in legitimating law.

B. Jury Size

The traditional size of the criminal jury has remained at twelve in England, Canada, Northern Ireland, the Republic of Ireland, New Zealand, and the federal courts in the United States. In Australia, the jury size remains at twelve for Commonwealth crimes, but may be smaller for some crimes involving state jurisdiction. In some state jurisdictions in the United States smaller juries are also permitted for some crimes. However, in the United States, and occasionally in Australia, a number of alternate, or 'reserve', jurors are chosen in the event that one or more jurors are discharged before the trial is completed. Other countries make no provision for alternate jurors but instead provide for a valid verdict based on a jury of at least ten if jurors have to be discharged for some reason. In New Zealand the number can be smaller still if both prosecution and defense consent. The Scots jury of fifteen persons must be treated as a separate case, particularly in light of its simple majority verdict rule and 'not proven' verdict alternative. In contrast, the civil juries of the United States and Canada and the rare civil juries in other countries show considerable deviation from the number twelve, though not ordinarily dropping below six persons, except in New Zealand where four person juries were authorized for civil and minor criminal cases in the recent past.

The Russian jury consists of twelve members and two alternates. In Spain the jury is composed of nine members and two alternates. In many of the other countries that have a jury system, as described in more detail in Chapter 13, jury sizes range between seven and nine members, though for the most serious crimes a twelve-person jury may be required.

C. Decision Rule

The historical juror unanimity rule has shown considerable erosion in England and the Republic of Ireland. In those countries the jury is told to deliberate under a unanimity rule, but after a period of time, typically around two hours, it is informed that a majority of ten is sufficient. In Canada, New Zealand,[95] and federal and most state courts in the United States unanimity is required. However, in Oregon and Louisiana majority verdicts are allowed for criminal trials. Majority verdicts are also allowed in civil trials in many U.S. states.

In Australia the verdict must be unanimous for Commonwealth crimes but majority verdicts are authorized by statute in some of the states when state criminal charges are involved. Many of the countries discussed in Chapter 13 also allow super-majority verdicts. Scotland's jury is unique with its rule allowing a bare majority of eight of the fifteen members for a valid verdict. Another thing that distinguishes the Scots jury from all other juries is that if a majority of eight cannot be achieved, the accused is entitled to an acquittal. In other countries, failure to achieve unanimity or the requisite majority for conviction or acquittal permits the prosecution to retry the case to a new jury.

D. Jury Sentencing

The United States stands almost alone in allowing the jury a significant role in determining the punishment of a person found guilty of a crime. In the overwhelming majority of states where capital punishment is used, the jury determines whether the convicted person should die or be sentenced to a lesser punishment. In five states—Missouri, Arkansas, Kentucky, Virginia, and Texas—the jury may be called upon to determine the sentence of a person convicted of a non-capital crime.[96] In the remaining states punishment is determined by the judge, as is the case in all other countries. There are a few qualifications to this general rule. In Australia the jury may make a recommendation of mercy, though the judge is not bound by the recommendation. In Canada in cases involving a conviction of second degree murder the jury can

[95] However, there have been calls for majority verdicts in New Zealand.

[96] In addition to King's ch. in this book see also, Randall Jackson, *Missouri's Jury Sentencing Law: A Relic the Legislature Should Put to Rest*, 1999 JOURNAL OF THE MISSOURI BAR 14 (January–February, 1999).

make a non-binding recommendation within a selected range, regarding the appropriate sentence. Special Canadian juries may also be convened to determine if a mandatory sentence of twenty-five years to life for murder should be shortened after the convicted person has served fifteen years.

E. Challenges

As described earlier in this chapter, there were three historical forms of challenges to jurors: challenges for cause; 'stand by' privileges (functionally serving as challenges); and peremptory challenges. All contemporary jury systems allow challenges for cause, but additional factors in each country determine the extent to which they are exercised. The idea of challenge for cause is relatively simple when the matter concerns statutory qualifications for eligibility, juror competence with respect to language, or a physical handicap or illness.

The matter is more complicated when it comes to the issue of attitudinal biases, or prejudices, that might affect the juror's impartiality to decide the case at hand. Jury systems differ in the extent to which they are inclined to recognize potential biases among jurors. For comparative purposes it is useful to identify four types of prejudice by imposing an artificial typology.[97] *Interest* prejudice involves instances in which a juror may have a direct stake, or the appearance of a stake, in the outcome of the case. Blackstone referred to this type as involving a 'manifest presumption of partiality'.[98] Interest prejudice usually is recognized when the juror is related to one of the parties or witnesses in the suit, has financial or political dealings with one of the parties, or could be affected in some way by the verdict. Recall that this form of prejudice was one of the earliest forms recognized in English jury law, and it is still recognized as a ground for excusing a juror in all countries. *Specific* prejudice involves attitudes and beliefs about the particular case or the parties that could potentially cause the juror to be incapable of deciding the case with an impartial mind. These attitudes and beliefs may result from personal knowledge or biases about the case, public discussion and rumor, or from mass media coverage of the crime or the parties. *Generic*, or general, prejudice involves the transferring of bias as a result of juror stereotyp-

[97] See Vidmar's ch. on the Canadian jury in this volume for additional discussion and references.

[98] Blackstone, *supra* note 1, 363; also, Kennedy, *supra* note 57, 90.

ing of the defendant, victims, witnesses, or the nature of the crime itself. The stereotyping is accompanied by assumptions about categories of persons who fall into these categories, assumptions that the juror declares he or she cannot set aside in evaluating the evidence. Biases against members of racial or ethnic groups is one example; prejudice against homosexuals or large or foreign corporations is another example. Both specific and generic prejudice would fall under what Blackstone identified as 'bias on the favour'. Recall that juries *de medietate linguae* were established in England at least partly because of the recognition that English jurors might not be indifferent to the evidence when one of the parties was a foreigner. Arguably, some special juries evolved out of the same types of concerns. Finally, *conformity* prejudice arises when the case is of significant interest to the community such that a juror may perceive that there is a strong public consensus about the case and the proper outcome. As a consequence, some jurors may be influenced by felt pressures to reach a verdict in accord with the community consensus rather their own personal judgement regarding the weight of the evidence.

All of the jury systems discussed in this book have provisions for attempting to find and eliminate persons who may have interest prejudice. These include challenges to the jury pool based upon faults in the procedures used to draw up the jury list, initial questions directed to the assembled panel by the judge, and provisions for either of the parties to challenge a particular juror. Theoretically, in England and Wales, Scotland, both Irelands, Australia, and New Zealand specific, generic, and conformity prejudice could be grounds for a challenge. However, because in each of these countries the parties have so little opportunity to obtain knowledge about jurors before trial, because the law requires that the challenge be made *before* the juror is called, and because judges are ordinarily hostile to such attempts, challenges are extremely rare events. The case and statutory law and practice directions in these countries rely on the rationale that jurors will follow their oaths to be impartial, that the judge's instructions will have a curative effect on bias, that jury deliberation will cancel out individual biases, and, in majority verdict jurisdictions, such as England and Wales and the Republic of Ireland, that the biased or unreasonable juror can be outvoted by the majority. An additional factor, discussed separately below, is the heavy reliance on contempt of court laws to control outside influences on the jury.

The law in the United States stands almost alone in taking practical cognizance of all forms of bias through pretrial questioning of jurors by the judge or judge and opposing counsel. Although jury screening by this means is often truncated and under control of the judge, in other cases the questioning is detailed and judges grant challenges with regularity. At the same time, recent Supreme Court case law has given judges considerable authority to limit the extent of juror questioning even in state courts.[99]

Canada stands between these two extremes. In most trials jury selection proceeds without challenges for cause in a manner similar to the practices in England and Wales, Australia, and New Zealand. Jurors are seated in the jury box as randomly called unless they are excluded by a peremptory challenge from the Crown or the defense. However, provisions for challenges have been provided in the Criminal Code upon a showing of evidence by the moving party. Over the past decade and a half some trial judges have increasingly tended to allow challenges based upon some combination of each of the four types of prejudice described above. Further, settled law now gives accused persons who are members of visible racial minorities challenges on racial bias as a matter of right. The questioning of the potential juror is very circumscribed and the verdict on whether the challenge is valid is determined by two triers in a process similar to that described by Blackstone and Kennedy, as reported in Section IV B above. In Australia triers may also be used in challenges to the array or challenges to the polls, but, as noted, challenges are rare.

In Spain's new jury system lawyers for the litigants are permitted to question the jurors. However, in Russia questioning is conducted by the judge.

F. Peremptory Challenges

England and Wales, the Republic of Ireland, and Scotland have abolished peremptory challenges, but Australia, Canada, New Zealand, Northern Ireland, and the United States retain them. Typically, both sides have a certain number of peremptory challenges, though the number tends to vary depending on the seriousness of the charges and other factors. There are historical trends toward reduction of the number of allotted challenges in many of the countries. In the Australian state of Tasmania only the defense retains challenges.

[99] In addition to King's and Landsman's ch. on the US criminal and civil jury systems see Mu'Min v. Virginia 111 S.Ct. 1899 (1991) and, more generally, NANCY GERTNER AND JUDITH MIZNER, THE LAW OF JURIES (1997), ch. 10 (The Jury and the Media).

Peremptory challenges are subjects of continuing controversy for different reasons. In Australia and New Zealand the absence of a jury questioning procedure and often the opportunity to obtain the jury list until just before trial handicap the rational and informed use of the peremptory challenges, requiring defenders of this privilege to assert that their value is in imparting a perception of fairness. The fact that the prosecution has the advantage of vetting the list through police sources has raised questions about fundamental fairness.

In Canada the majority of trials are conducted under conditions similar to those in New Zealand and Australia, that is, the lawyers have little information on which to base a peremptory challenge, except that the Crown prosecutor frequently has the police review the jury list. In cases where challenges for cause are allowed, the peremptory challenge can be exercised after the juror has been questioned and the triers have found the juror impartial. Nevertheless, the very limited questioning allowed during challenges, usually consisting of one or two questions requiring the juror to answer only yes or no, provides extremely limited information about the juror beyond demeanor and appearance. Peremptory challenges have not, to date, been particularly controversial in Canada.

While peremptory challenges remain entrenched in the American jury system,[100] they are a source of controversy, and litigation, in both criminal and civil trials because of their perceived negative effect on a policy goal of obtaining juries that include a fair representation of minority members and gender. The perceived abuse of peremptory challenges to eliminate jurors based on stereotypes about group attitudes has produced calls for their abolition. Similar concerns have been voiced in New Zealand with respect to the exclusion of Maori. There have been discussions about reducing the number of peremptory challenges allowed to both prosecution and defense in order to reduce the opportunity to influence the representativeness of the jury. Jury vetting is also a source of controversy in Australia. In Canada an issue of gender bias arose in a case heard before the Supreme Court, but it involved Crown exercise of its stand aside privileges, and that was mooted when stand asides were abolished. In Spain and Russia both sides have a limited number of peremptory challenges.

[100] It should be noted, however, that the US Supreme Court has ruled that peremptory challenges are not mandated by the Constitution, see GERTNER AND MIZNER *supra* note 99 at 4-1 (peremptory challenges).

G. Stand By Privileges

Despite elimination of peremptory challenges, in England the prosecution retains 'stand by' privileges. Potential jurors can be moved to the back of the line until the jury panel is exhausted. Stand bys are supposed to be exercised sparingly under guidelines set by the Attorney General. The guidelines allow for use of the stand by not only to screen out persons who are ineligible because of a criminal record but also to eliminate persons who might be biased against the Crown's case. Stand bys are functionally a form of peremptory challenge because it would be a rare case in which the jury panel is exhausted and those stood aside are called to serve. In short, English jury practice does recognize specific and generic prejudice with respect to Crown interests. The stand by guidelines also permit vetting of the jury list by the police. There are apparently no publicly available statistics on the frequency of use of the stand by in England.

Australia also retains the stand by procedure, there called the *stand aside*, but it remains controversial among the defense bar. In jurisdictions in which the jury list is made known to the parties in advance, the prosecution may lawfully engage the police to scrutinize it. However, a difference with England is that the defense retains peremptory challenges. In New Zealand the judge may stand aside a juror upon granting a motion by either of the parties, or by the judge's own motion. Canada, as noted above, retained the stand aside as a Crown privilege until 1992 when it was ruled unconstitutional because of the potential of actual or perceived unfairness to the defense. Subsequently, the number of peremptory challenges allowed the Crown was increased to obtain balance with the defense. Ireland abolished the stand by provision in its 1976 Juries Act.

H. Contempt: The Mass Media and Jurors

The laws of contempt and its application in attempts to prevent or control trial prejudice vary substantially between common law jury systems. The impact of contempt laws involves two topics: what, when, and how the media may publish materials about court proceedings; and what jurors may disclose about the jury's deliberations.

The United States and England may be seen to occupy two ends of a continuum with respect to controls on the media, the issue commonly

characterized as 'free press versus fair trial'.[101] In the United States the First Amendment has been interpreted by the Supreme Court as allowing the media extensive access to all the major phases of the trial process.[102] The privileges include the right to engage in extensive reporting of the results of preliminary hearings, independent journalistic investigation reports before trial, and commentary on the judicial proceedings before, during, or after the trial. There are a few *sub judice* devices that a judge may use to control dissemination of prejudicial publicity, but these are weak compared to other countries and applied on a case by case basis. In short, the United States may be classified as a 'no prior restraints' country.

In contrast, statutory and common law in England place severe restraints on what the media may report, subjecting violators to sanctions involving heavy fines or even jail.[103] After charges have been laid against an accused, the media are constrained to reporting only the barest information about proceedings before trial, such as the names of persons involved and the place and date of a preliminary hearing or inquiry. Ordinarily, the public will not be barred from these proceedings, but the rules prevent wide dissemination of their contents. Once the trial begins the media are constrained to report accurately on the proceedings and in a way that will not jeopardize present or future proceedings, including a future trial of the accused on other charges or the trial of some other party. In theory a strict liability standard may be applied in adjudicating charges of violation of these rules, although in practice reporting constitutes contempt only if the reporting gives rise to a 'substantial risk' that the trial will be 'seriously impeded or prejudiced'.[104] The presence of the contempt laws typically serves their deterrent goal, but contempt charges are laid from time to time when proscriptions are seen to be violated. Scotland is similar to England in enforcing contempt rules. Ireland, too, places limits on what the media may report and on timing of what is reported.

[101] Scotland, according to Peter Duff in this volume, may occupy a position slightly beyond England on the fair trial end of the continuum.

[102] Gertner and Mizner, *supra* note 99 at ch. 10 (The Jury and the Media). A guide to judicial thinking on the problems encountered in American courts as a result of emphasis on a free press is G. Wetherington, H. Lawton, and D. Pollock, *Preparing for the High Profile Case: An Omnibus Treatment for Judges and Lawyers*, 51 Florida Law Review 425 (1999).

[103] See David Eady and A. T. H. Smith, Arlidge, Eady and Smith on Contempt (1999).

[104] Ibid.; see also David Corker and Michael Levi, *Pretrial Publicity and Its Treatment in the English Courts*, Criminal Law Review 623 (1996).

Australia tends to follow in the British tradition on the matter of contempt, although under *sub judice* rather than statutory law. However, the rules are more flexible. A defense to charges of contempt is that the impact of the prejudicial material is outweighed by free speech and media reporting on matters of public concern. Restraints on reporting of preliminary proceedings occur, but the nature of the apprehended prejudice must be very clearly spelled out. The laws in New Zealand also place constraints on the media and there is a substantial body of case law involving contempt proceedings, but the laws appear to be applied somewhat more laxly with respect to certain matters.[105] In particular, the New Zealand media rather routinely report the contents of preliminary hearings involving highly prejudicial material without charges being laid. Canada also places some constraints on the media. The Criminal Code, for example, allows the accused the right to request an order forbidding publication of the contents of a preliminary inquiry. There is recent case law involving judicial rulings placing restraints on dissemination of material that might jeopardize upcoming trials. However, in comparison to England, Australia, and New Zealand the use of prior restraint is more limited and infrequent, and judicial rulings in these matters are continually contested by the media under the Canadian constitution's guarantee of a free and unfettered press.

The matter of laws bearing on juror disclosure of information about the deliberations appears to have developed somewhat independently of media controls, but the topic also bears on mass media dissemination of trial information. In the United States the same First Amendment considerations that disallow prior restraints on the media also disallow post-trial restraints on the jurors themselves. Jurors are free to discuss their deliberations after the trial and even sell their story to a tabloid, book publisher, or television station. This right sometimes creates serious mischief for courts in high publicity trials because jurors engage in deceptive behavior out of financial motives to sell the inside story of jury deliberations. Additionally, jurors may be aggressively sought out by inquisitive journalists and jury consultants. Under special circumstances some courts have placed limitations on the press, what individual jurors may say to the press, and even limitations on what

[105] For additional discussion of New Zealand see John McGrath, *Contempt and the Media: Constitutional Safeguard or State Censorship*, New Zealand Law Review 371 (1998); B. D. Gray, *The Private Interest in Restriction of Pre-trial Publicity in Civil Cases*, New Zealand Law Review 389 (1998).

jurors are permitted to disclose,[106] but, in general, there are few restraints on jurors.

In England, Northern Ireland, and Canada the law forbids jurors from disclosing the content of jury deliberations, avoiding many of these problems. In Australia the law is more circumscribed: the press may be subject to contempt proceedings for approaching jurors after trial, but individual jurors may disclose information about the deliberations on their own initiative, though not for remuneration. New Zealand has no statutory provision for keeping jury deliberations secret. However case law has resulted in contempt prosecutions against mass media for attempts to interview jurors.

In England, Canada, Australia, and New Zealand the jury confidentiality constraints have prevented legal and social science scholars from interviewing jurors even though the information derived from the activity might shed light on contentious policy debates about the jury. However, in both Australia and New Zealand those restraints have recently been loosened to allow researchers access to jurors for purposes of studying jury policy issues.

Questions about the efficacy of contempt laws controlling pretrial publicity in a modern technological society have been raised in England, Australia, Canada, and New Zealand. The internet, fax machines, and easy public access to media and publications originating outside of the jurisdiction of a court increase the possibility that jury pools may be tainted in cases that arouse high degrees of public interest. How courts should respond to these challenges is a nascent area of jury law. The *Bernardo* case in Canada, the '*Dingo*' case in Australia, and the Kevin *Maxwell* case in England[107] provide interesting examples of the problems and court responses to meet those problems. *Maxwell* is particularly interesting because, despite the laws of contempt, a number of factors resulted in publicity throughout England and Wales that was as extensive and prejudicial as any that has occurred in the United States. Maxwell and his co-defendants were charged with fraud involving a pension plan that left many pensioners without benefits. The trial judge considered public opinion polls tendered by the defense and then deviated from the standard English practice of randomly selecting jurors without questioning them. He authorized a detailed jury

[106] See, e.g. United States v. Thomas, 116 F.3d 606 (1997) for a review of case law and Gertner and Mizner *supra* note 99, at ch. 10 (The Jury and the Media).

[107] These cases are discussed in the chs. on Canada, Australia, and England. Additional discussion of the *Maxwell* trial can be found in Corker and Levi, *supra* note 104.

questionnaire and allowed in-chambers questioning of jurors in order to select an impartial jury.

I. Change of Venue

All common law jury systems retain change of venue as a remedial measure when there is concern that the jury pool may be tainted from media publicity or from interpersonal sources of tainting when the crime is of particular concern to large segments of the community. A number of factors may influence its use. The first, of course, is the frequency with which one party or the other seeks a change of venue. A second is the extent to which judges are wedded to the legal presumption that the trial should be held in the community in which the charges are laid. A third factor is the belief that existing remedies are sufficient to cancel out bias. These include faith in the efficacy of judicial instructions, the jurors' oaths, and the time lapse between the publicity and the trial. In the United States, and to some extent Canada, the existence of mechanisms for questioning jurors (e.g. *voir dire* in the United States; challenge for cause in Canada) influence judicial attitudes about the need for a change of venue on the ground that these are alternative remedies. Another important factor involves the ability of the requesting party to produce evidence of widespread tainting of the community. In the United States and Canada courts admit expert testimony based on scientific surveys assessing the state of public attitudes in the community near the time of trial. Courts in Australia, England,[108] Ireland, Scotland, and New Zealand have generally been disinclined to accept this type of evidence, thereby placing a heavy burden on the concerned litigant to produce grounds of cause. In Australia change of venue is also complicated by low population densities in some areas and absence of a regulatory scheme to allow for transfers between states.

J. Stays of Proceedings: Temporary and Permanent

A temporary stay of proceedings (also called 'adjournments' or 'continuances') to allow memories to fade and community emotions to cool is another option to deal with a biased community, and appears to be an option in all common law countries.

[108] Corker and Levi, *supra* note 104 report that the trial judge in the *Maxwell* case acknowledged that experts are allowed to testify about survey evidence in trademark infringement cases but indicated his belief that he did not need the assistance of experts to interpret the surveys on pretrial prejudice tendered by the accused.

However, in England in recent years there have been a number of cases in which a judge ordered a permanent stay of proceedings against accused persons, in part because of the presumed extent and degree of prejudicial publicity. A permanent stay of proceedings on these grounds would be most unlikely in the United States because of the availability of remedial options that are absent in England. In Scotland there apparently has never been a permanent stay of proceedings as a result of pre-trial publicity. There has been at least one case in Australia.

K. Jury Consultants

The growth of research firms that provide lawyers with information about the probable attitudes of prospective jurors based on surveys, focus groups, and courtroom assessment of juror behavior has increased enormously in the United States over the past three decades. While their use is frequent in many important criminal and civil cases, they remain a topic of controversy within the United States because of the perception that they corrupt the ideal of an impartial jury and because of the effects on the costs of litigation.[109] Jury consultants appear to be largely confined to the United States, although they have been occasionally used in Canada and in a highly controversial case in Australia. Reasons for their failure to spread to the other countries are related to the absence of '*voir dire*' practices and to judicial hostility toward these practices.[110]

VI. Judicial Control over the Jury

A. Summing Up

An extremely important consideration in jury system comparisons involves the degree to which the judge exercises control over the jury

[109] See Franklin Strier, *Whither Trial Consulting? Issues and Projections* 23 LAW AND HUMAN BEHAVIOR 93 (1999). Claims about the efficacy of jury consultants' techniques have also been raised: see Shari Diamond, *Scientific Jury Selection: What Social Scientists Know and Do Not Know*, 73 JUDICATURE 178 (1990); Michael Saks, *The Limits of Scientific Jury Selection: Ethical and Empirical*, 17 JURIMETRICS JOURNAL 3 (1976).

[110] It needs to be noted that in addition to attempts to select jurors consultants also assist lawyers in decisions on how to organize and present a case to a jury, see Diamond, *supra* note 108. This does not require a visible presence in court, and there are no available reports about whether jury consultants have been used in this capacity outside the United States and Canada. The present author has been involved in pretrial jury research in several Canadian cases, but these efforts have not been published and there is no other published account of such activities.

through reviewing the evidence as well as the law and also the ability of the judge to direct a verdict. Following fairly closely the practices developed in the seventeenth and eighteenth centuries in England, in all countries except the United States and Scotland judges have the positive duty to not only instruct the jury on the applicable law but to also impartially review the trial evidence. This review may include commenting on the strengths and weaknesses of witnesses and discussion of how the totality of evidence fits with the theories of the opposing sides. Although such commentary would be permissible in federal courts and some state courts in the United States, in practice it appears to be obsolete. In consequence, it may be seen that in all the other countries the influence of the judge over how the jury understands and weighs the evidence is likely to be much greater than in the United States. In Scotland the judge is not required to summarize but does have the authority to do so.

B. Form of the Verdict

The general rule in most countries with respect to the criminal jury verdict is that it is a 'general verdict', that is to say, a binary decision of guilty or not guilty, and it requires no explanation from the jurors.[111] However, in Australia in special cases the judge may require a special verdict or a verdict on a special fact.

In both Spain and Russia the general verdict is not used. The jury is presented with a set of questions. In Spain the list of facts and suppositions may be very detailed. Additionally, the jury is required to give a rationale for its verdict.

In the US and Canada, and in other countries as well, the verdict rules are more complicated with respect to findings of liability and damages in civil cases. Juries may be required to give special verdicts or assess causation, negligence, compensatory damages, and exemplary damages in separate stages of the trial.

C. Directed Verdicts and Judgment Notwithstanding the Verdict

The general rule for all countries in most criminal cases is that a verdict of not guilty is final. (Nevertheless, there is one partial exception to this rule in Canada that is covered under appellate review, as discussed

[111] Peter Duff, Ch. 7 this volume, proposes that Scots jury's 'not proven' verdict may be a form allowing jury nullification.

below.) Additionally, the judge has the power to direct a not guilty verdict if he or she determines that the prosecution's evidence is not sufficient to convict. Additionally, if the jury returns a verdict of guilty, but upon consideration the judge concludes that the evidence was not sufficient, the verdict may be set aside. In Australia in an unusual and highly controversial case involving an admission of guilt by the accused led to a judge's direction to the jury that it should convict. The instruction was upheld by the High Court.

In civil cases, in all countries, the judge has substantial power to direct a verdict or alter it before judgment is rendered.

D. Rulings on Admissible Evidence and Qualification of Experts

Trial judges have a great deal of discretion to rule on whether evidence is admissible and the scope of testimony. Out of concerns of length, this topic receives scant attention in the chapters in this book, but it should not be ignored. Judicial rulings on admissibility have a major impact on what the jury is allowed to hear. Laws with respect to hearsay and illegally obtained evidence, for example, differ significantly from country to country. The chapters on the English and Scots juries provide a striking contrast with regard to corroboration requirements.

This is also the case with respect to expert evidence. Countries differ considerably with respect to admissibility and guidelines regarding the evaluation and scope allowed expert testimony.[112] In the United States the Federal Rules of Evidence, which also influence many state rules, provide that expert evidence should be admitted if it will assist the trier of fact and its impact is more probative than prejudicial. One consequence of these very open-ended rules is that US courts have allowed a great range of expert testimony.[113] Canada has been more conservative

[112] Sophia Gatowski, *et al.*, *supra* note 52; D. Carson, *Some Legal Issues Affecting Novel Forms of Expert Evidence*, 1992 EXPERT EVIDENCE 79 (1992); Peter Thornton, *A New Look at Eye Witness Testimony* (1995) 145 NEW LAW JOURNAL (Supplement, January 27, 1995) at 94; Jeffrey Bayes, *Choosing a Forensic Accountant for the Defense in a Criminal Case* (1995) 145 NEW LAW JOURNAL (Supplement, January 27, 1995) at 102; Iain Goldrein, *Court Management and Experts* (1995) 145 NEW LAW JOURNAL (Supplement, January 27, 1995) at 104; Iain Goldrein, *Court Management and Experts*, II, (1995) 145 NEW LAW JOURNAL (March 17, 1995) at 381.

[113] See e.g. DAVID FAIGMAN, DAVID KAYE, MICHAEL SAKS, & JOSEPH SANDERS, MODERN SCIENTIFIC EVIDENCE (1997); FEDERAL JUDICIAL CENTER, MANUAL ON SCIENTIFIC EVIDENCE (1994).

with regard to expert evidence, but liberal relative to Australia, England, and New Zealand.[114]

In a series of recent cases the US Supreme Court has asserted that judges have a responsibility to assess the reliability of all expert evidence before allowing it to be considered by a jury.[115] The cases also contain a non-inclusive list of general guidelines that judges should consider in making those decisions. In Canada the case law is less settled, but there are a series of cases that suggest factors that a judge should consider.[116] In contrast Australia and England utilize general tests of relevancy and helpfulness but no specific lists of criteria or guidelines have been articulated.[117]

A specific example of comparative differences involves the admission of psychological and other social science evidence. In the United States a wide range of such evidence bearing on such topics as eyewitness identification, the potential states of mind of abused spouses and rape victims, victims of sexual abuse, and a wide range of syndrome evidence.[118] Canada has been more conservative regarding admissibility on these topics, but experts have been allowed to testify on some of these matters, particularly battered woman syndrome and sex abuse syndromes. However, while these forms of evidence are not unknown in England, Australia, and New Zealand, judges have tended to take the view that these subjects are within the ken of the jury and will infringe upon the jury's fact finding functions.[119] In short, judicial culture and law regarding expert evidence vary and influence what juries see and hear.

A related point concerns the warnings and admonitions that judges give the jurors. Admonitions regarding such matters as eyewitness

[114] See Gatowski *et al.*, *supra* note 52.

[115] Daubert v. Merrell Dow Pharmaceuticals, 113 S.Ct. 2786 (1993); Kumho Tire Co. v. Carmichael, 119 S.Ct. 1167 (1998).

[116] See Gatowski *et al.*, *supra* note 52; David Paciocco, *Expert Evidence: Where Are We Now? Where Are We Going?*, Canadian Bar Association Institute of Continuing Legal Education (1988); P. Brad Limpert, *Beyond the Rule in Mohan: A New Model for Assessing the Reliability of Scientific Evidence*, 54 U. Toronto Fac. L. Rev. 65 (1996).

[117] Gatowski *et al.*, *supra* note 52.

[118] See generally, Faigman *et al.*, *supra* note 113.

[119] Gatowski *et al.* *supra* note 52; Ian Freckelton, *Child Sex Abuse Accommodation Evidence: The Travails of Counterintuitive Evidence in Australia and New Zealand*, 15 Behavioral Sciences and the Law 247 (1997); A. M. Coleman and R. D. Mackay, *Psychological Evidence in Court: Legal Developments in England and the United States.* 1 Psychology, Crime and Law 261 (1995); R. D. Mackay and A. M. Coleman, *Equivocal Rulings on Expert Psychological and Psychiatric Evidence: Turning a Muddle into Nonsense* [1996] Criminal L. Rev. 88.

identification, corroboration, character, confessions, and previous convictions, to take just a few examples, also differ from country to country. These differences are generally a result of judge-made law that develops out of different conceptions of the role and competence of the jury; and they have a direct effect on the evidence that the jury is allowed to consider.

E. *Juror Question Asking*

Whether the jury is to remain a passive body during the evidence phase of the trial or engage in more active participation bears indirectly on judicial control. There has been a trend in some jurisdictions in the United States to encourage jurors to ask questions.[120] In Arizona, a state that leads in jury reforms, jurors are specifically instructed that they may ask questions of witnesses through written submissions to the judge, and they are encouraged to do so. The judge reviews the questions to ensure they do not violate legal rules before they are allowed and ordinarily the judge will read them. Despite the fact that common law practice or statutes bearing on juries theoretically make question asking permissible in other common law countries, the practice appears to be rare, primarily because judges do not inform jurors of their right to ask questions. In New Zealand, for example, jurors are also allowed to put questions in writing for the judge but it appears that the practice is 'rare and not encouraged'.

F. *Appellate Review of Verdicts*

A given in all jury systems is that a verdict of guilty can be appealed to a higher court on the basis of legal errors, or under highly limited circumstances, even on evidential grounds. Canada, however, also allows the prosecution to appeal an acquittal on the narrow ground that the jury was erroneously instructed on the law. If a finding of legal error is made at the higher level, the case may be sent back for retrial. These cases are rare, but have occurred in recent years. Australia also allows the prosecution to appeal an acquittal for clarification of the law, but whatever decision is rendered on the legal issue cannot affect the not guilty verdict in the appealed case. The highly controversial Australian '*Dingo*' case involving murder charges against the mother of a baby that

[120] See Munsterman *et al.*, *supra* note 15; Dann and Logan, *supra* note 49.

had disappeared has caused commentators to raise questions about the narrowness of grounds of appeal, particularly when questionable expert testimony is involved.

In Russia an acquittal can be appealed by the prosecutor or by a victim or the victim's family.

VII. Other Factors Bearing on Jury System Differences

There are a number of other factors that are different between jury systems and that surely have degrees of importance in comparing the systems. These are not always explicit in the chapters in this book, but they should be kept in mind, not only for the present writings but as sources for future investigation.

A. Substantive and Procedural Laws

Laws differ in their definition of issues and in the elements that are necessary to be proved in order for a jury to reach its verdict. Laws involving homicide differ from country to country, not only in the way that the elements are specified in the definitions but in the lesser included offences that the jury may consider in reaching its verdict. Another striking example in this volume is comparison of England and Scotland with respect to corroboration. In Scotland the rules require that the prosecution's evidence must be corroborated, whereas in England an accused may be convicted on the testimony of a single eyewitness or an uncorroborated confession. Today in England the law allows the jury to be told of an accused's exercise of the right to silence at the police station or at trial and that they may draw an inference from this fact.

Similar differences exist with respect to exclusionary rules. Exclusionary rules in the United States have been eroded to some degree since the 1980s, but they still stand in contrast to other countries.[121] For example, in New Zealand, in cases where there is a breach of the Bill of Rights Act, such as a forced confession or an unreasonable search, there is a

[121] See e.g. Silas Wasserstrom, *The Incredible Shrinking Fourth Amendment*, 21 AMERICAN CRIMINAL LAW REVIEW 257 (1984); Silas Wasserstrom, *The Court's Turn Toward a General Reasonableness Interpretation of the Fourth Amendment*, 27 AMERICAN CRIMINAL LAW REVIEW 119 (1989). Compare criminal procedures of Canada, England and Wales, and the United States in CRAIG M. BRADLEY, CRIMINAL PROCEDURE: A WORLDWIDE STUDY (1999); see also D. J. Gottlieb, *Rhetoric and Reality: Control of Police Interrogation in Britain and the United States*, in J. M. Reijntjes and J. F. Nijboer (eds), PROCEEDINGS OF THE FIRST WORLD CONFERENCE ON NEW TRENDS IN CRIMINAL INVESTIGATION AND EVIDENCE (1995).

presumption in favor of exclusion. However, the presumption may be rebutted where there is no causal link between the breach and the evidence (e.g. the confession would have been made in any event) or it is otherwise fair and right to admit the evidence (e.g. the breach is trivial).[122]

These substantive differences affect the evidence that juries see and hear and the instructions that they are given.

B. Procedural Differences

Although there are undoubtedly many subtle procedural differences between countries, one of the most striking involves order of presentation of arguments and evidence at trial.[123] Again England and the United States provide useful contrasts. In England, the defence does not get an opportunity to address the jury until the prosecution has finished its case. The order of trial is as follows: prosecution opens; prosecution presents evidence (with defence having the opportunity to cross-examine each prosecution witness as called); defence opens (although there is an option not to open); defence witnesses are called with the defendant going first if he or she is giving evidence; prosecution closing arguments; defence closing arguments; judge summation and instructions on the law.

In the United States the prosecution has the opening argument but the defence has a right to address the jury immediately following the prosecution's address. The defence may defer its opening until it begins evidence, but in most cases does not. The typical order of presentation at trial, therefore, is as follows: prosecution address; defence address; prosecution evidence; defence evidence; prosecution closing summation; defence closing summation; prosecution rebuttal summation; and judge instructions only on the law. There are variations on this scheme. In some states, for example, if the defence chooses not to present evidence, then the prosecution must summarize first and the defence gets the last word. Nevertheless, the general reasoning, at least as articulated by some courts, is that in both criminal and civil cases the party bearing the burden of proof should get the last word. It should be added that in recent years in some jurisdictions judges have given the jury preliminary instructions on the law at the beginning of trial.

[122] Personal communication to the author from Professor Warren Young.

[123] I have constructed this section primarily through communications with lawyers who are familiar with the procedures in their respective countries.

In Scotland neither side presents opening arguments: the jury relies on the written indictment, which is a narrative of the charges against the accused. In New South Wales, Australia, the prosecutor opens and the defence may make an opening statement, but need not do so. However, even if it makes an opening statement the defence may again address the jury before it calls its evidence. The defence also has the right of final address before the judge begins summing up. In Canada the prosecution opens and calls its evidence, and the defence does not get to address the jury until its case is opened. At the end of the defence case the prosecutor makes a final argument and this is followed by the defence argument before the judge sums up and instructs the jury on the law. In New Zealand the prosecution traditionally made an opening address covering the broad outlines of the case, often accompanied by admonitions to be fair and impartial, but the defence did not address the jury until it opened its case. However, in recent years some judges have allowed the defence an opening statement following the prosecution, and there is serious discussion about expanding this privilege to all trials. In Spain the lawyer for the victim or victim's family is allowed to make opening and closing statements in addition to those of the public prosecutor.

One can easily develop competing hypotheses about the relative efficacy and fairness of these different trial organization procedures. Such a task is beyond the goals of this book, but their potential differential impact on the jury deserves serious consideration.

C. Case Selection: Crimes, Prosecutorial Discretion, and Guilty Pleas

What percentage of cases is selected for the jury to hear? In every country except the United States a common estimate is that the rate of criminal jury trial is around 1 percent or less, whereas in the US the rate is often given as about 8 percent. How one determines these rates depends on which denominator is used, however.[124] Is it of all crimes or just crimes eligible for jury trial? Do the statistics involve only felony cases or do they include misdemeanors? In fact other statistical estimates of criminal jury trial rates range from 15 percent of all felony cases to as low as 2.1 percent in some state jurisdictions.[125]

[124] This issue is discussed in more detail in Neil Vidmar, *Pap and Circumstance: What Jury Verdict Statistics Can Tell Us About Jury Behavior and the Tort System*, 28 Suffolk L. Rev. 1205 (1994).

[125] See Abramson, *supra* note 2 at 251–2 and accompanying footnotes for citations to these studies.

There are some clear statutory, common law, and constitutional constraints on the right to jury trial in each country, as discussed previously. However, focusing solely on which cases are eligible for jury trial obscures a number of other differences that undoubtedly vary from country to country.[126] The first is the actual crime rate. In all countries charges of murder are eligible for jury trial. However, the rate of homicide differs from country to country, and thus *caeteris paribus*, we should still expect rates of jury trial to differ between countries. When other crimes are considered, the constitutional, statutory, or common law factors affect eligibility for jury trial, but this is far from the end of the story. With 'either way' offenses that are characteristics of the criminal laws of common law countries, excepting the United States, the rates that prosecutors charge accused persons with summary or indictable crimes and the rates by which accused persons then opt for judge or jury also affects trial rates. Even when jury trial is a right or has been chosen after a prosecutorial decision to proceed by way of indictment, the rates at which trials occur are affected by decisions on the part of the accused to enter a plea of guilty instead of going to trial. Duff's chapter on Scotland points out, for example, that incidence of jury trial is less than 1 percent if calculated one way and over 7 percent if a different, but equally appropriate denominator is chosen. Differences in rates of guilty pleas among those charged likely vary between countries, and this too affects rates of trial.

A similar problem of case selection differences affects comparisons of civil jury verdicts as well. For example, in the United States the number of lawsuits that reach trial in motor vehicle accidents is between 1 and 2 percent, whereas in medical malpractice cases the percentages of trial cases are around 8 percent. In addition to types of cases, trial selection rates confound comparisons over time and between cases tried by juries versus judges for both civil and criminal cases.[127] In short, comparison of trial rates involves some very complicated chains of events and comparisons between countries must be made with extreme caution.

D. *Sidebar Conferences*

The so-called 'sidebar conference' wherein lawyers for the two sides approach the bench and huddle with the judge out of earshot of the jury

[126] Indeed, this admonition applies to jurisdictions within a single country, as the US statistics cited in the preceding paragraph indicate.

[127] See Vidmar, *supra* note 124; Brian Ostrom, David Rothman, and John Goerdt, *A Step Above Anecdote: A Profile of the Civil Jury in the 1990s*, 79 JUDICATURE 233 (1996).

and courtroom spectators to discuss points of law is a procedure that is unique to the United States. On occasions where the jury is out of the courtroom and discussions take place between judge and lawyers in open court, it is not unusual for any media representatives present to report the proceedings if they are deemed of interest. In all other countries the jury is sent to the jury room while points of law are argued in open court. For the media to report anything that is said outside the presence of the jury while the trial is in progress opens the door to possible contempt charges.

E. Radio and Television Coverage

Radio or television coverage of trials is permitted in many US state courts and in some courts has become routine, except in special cases when a judge excludes cameras and microphones under *sub judice* authority. However, in federal courts television cameras and other electronic recording devices are not allowed. In other countries covered in this book, cameras and electronic recordings by the media are not allowed.

As a side note, the media freedom in the United States allows the general public a first hand view of legal proceedings in high visibility cases, factors that may affect perceptions of the legitimacy of the jury trial, for better or for worse, depending on the circumstances.

F. Courtroom Culture

One of the most striking features a juror will be faced with is the culture of the courtroom, and this differs substantially from country to country. It is unclear what the impact may be, but these cultural differences need to be acknowledged.

Consider, for example, a typical Canadian court. The judge's bench is raised above the rest of the courtroom by as much as three or four feet. Legal counsel are seated at tables and address the court from lecterns that are either on the table or beside the table. The accused sits in the prisoner's box for the entire proceeding regardless of whether in custody or free on bail or self recognizance.[128] In most courts witnesses

[128] There have been some recent recommendations changes in Ontario as a result of a high profile case that resulted in a wrongful conviction. Ontario prosecutors have been told to address the defendants by their proper name rather than referring to them as the 'accused', and defendants not being held in custody should be allowed to sit beside their lawyers at courtroom counsel tables, see Steven Skurka, *The Morin Inquiry: A Personal Account*, 22 The Champion 9 (1998).

testify standing in the witness box, although this practice is declining and witnesses may be offered chairs. The opening of court is announced by the bailiff in a formal and loud address to the courtroom. The judge presides in a black robe with a striking scarlet sash around the waist and crossing over one shoulder. Legal counsel also wear black robes and vests, white, broad bow ties, and striped pants. The psychological distance of the judge is maintained by his being led into the court by a formally dressed bailiff and by the fact that legal counsel never approach the judge's bench. Witnesses in the box are approached with the judge's permission. Bailiffs vigilantly remind visitors in the public gallery to maintain silence and decorum. Upon entering the court and upon the entrance of the judge the lawyer effects a slight bow with his or her head in formal deference to the court. In oral submissions to the judge or to the jury counsel refer to opposing counsel formally as ' My Friend'. Until very recently the Canadian judge was always addressed as 'Your Lordship'or 'Ladyship', although in recent years it is deemed appropriate to address the judge as 'Your Honor'.

The atmosphere of formality that characterizes Canadian courts is probably even greater in courts in England, Australia, Northern Ireland, the Republic of Ireland, and Scotland. In those countries the judge and the barristers (called 'advocates' in Scotland) also wear wigs and engage in other formalities. In New Zealand barristers also wear gowns while in High Court, but wigs for judges and lawyers were abandoned some years ago.

Contrast this formality with the typical American court in which the judge's bench, though raised, is relatively on a closer horizontal plane with the other legal actors. The lawyers are dressed in business suits and frequently confer with the judge at the bench. The judge, while robed in black, is, relatively speaking, more informal in relation to lawyers, witnesses, and jurors. It is difficult to assess how these differences in courtroom culture may affect jurors, but combined with other differences between countries, they arguably could have substantial effects on jurors' willingness to attend to the judge's directions or to bend facts to fit their own notions of the equities in a particular case.

G. Lawyer Culture

Lawyer culture is closely related to courtroom culture. In the chapter on the American jury Nancy King correctly points out that in the United States the average trial takes place without lawyers giving press briefings on courthouse steps and that in many states the rules of professional conduct restrict what a lawyer may say publicly about his or her case.[129] Nevertheless, in contentious criminal and civil trials American lawyers often do make their cases public in attempts to influence the outcome of the trial. Often this is justified by the lawyers on the ground that in a society with nearly complete freedom of the press and publicly elected prosecutors making statements about the defendant, going public is the only way to counter adverse publicity for their clients. In some cases, however, the actions are more accurately viewed as unconstrained advocacy. Similar attempts to influence public opinion and the jury occur in civil cases as well.

Thus, the United States stands in stark contrast to all other countries in this regard. *Sub judice* case law and socialized rules of professional conduct proscribe such activity in the other countries. The effect of these culture of the lawyers combined with the culture of the courtroom must be considered in making cross-national comparisons of jury systems.

VIII. A Partial Picture but an Important Start

The discussion and outline presented in this introductory chapter necessarily form an incomplete picture. They do not do justice to the subtleties and complexities contained in the individual chapters bearing on the jury systems of the countries. They undoubtedly neglect some other differences. Nevertheless, the historical sketches provide some useful background on common roots and the divergences from those roots as the countries evolved separately and responded to their own cultural environments. The purpose of the discussion of main dimensions along which contemporary jury systems differ has already been stated. It is to draw attention to the fact that the systems must be viewed as self-contained systems. Recognition of this fact does not preclude borrowing insights or experience from one country and applying them to another, but it does counsel caution. These caveats, however, should not detract from the insights that can be gained. An examination of other systems and common historical roots can help to illuminate each system, cause us to reflect on how it deals with problems, and hopefully generate ideas about how it can be made better.

[129] See e.g. Gentile v. State Bar of Nevada, 501 U.S. 1030 (1991), a decision permitting bar associations to place restrictions on what lawyers may say to the press. See also Gertner and Mizner, *supra* note 99 at ch. 10 (The Jury and the Media).

2 The Continuing Decline of the English Jury

Sally Lloyd-Bostock* and Cheryl Thomas**

I. Introduction

The English[1] jury evokes passionate and often extreme views. On the one hand trial by jury is vigorously defended as an ancient right,[2] a guardian of liberty and democracy,[3] and a means whereby ordinary people's common-sense views can inform decisions and contain the powers of government.[4] On the other, the jury is increasingly regarded much more cynically as a costly, sometimes incompetent anachronism that merely creates opportunities for exploitation by 'professional' criminals at great public expense. During the twentieth century in England the second of these views appears to have gained ground. The scope and powers of the English jury have markedly declined, and jury trial is increasingly seen as excessively expensive and time-consuming. Juries have all but disappeared in civil cases, and sustained growth in the number of criminal trials, together with growing government interest in efficiency and crime control, has produced a continuing threat to the jury in criminal cases.

The English jury may be long established, but its constitutional position leaves it vulnerable. This chapter begins with an historical

* Reader in Socio-Legal Studies, Faculty of Law, University of Birmingham.

** Research Associate, Centre for Socio-Legal Studies, University of Oxford.

[1] The United Kingdom embraces three separate legal systems (for England and Wales, Scotland, and Northern Ireland), each with a different jury system. This ch. is concerned with England and Wales, but for simplicity and following custom, will refer to 'England' to include both England and Wales.

[2] The right of a freeman to the 'legal judgement of his peers' is mentioned in Clause 39 of Magna Carta (1215).

[3] Devlin writes:

> 'Each jury is a little parliament. . . . No tyrant could afford to leave a subject's freedom in the hands of twelve of his countrymen. So that trial by jury is more than an instrument of justice and more than one wheel of the constitution: it is the lamp that shows that freedom lives.'

Sir Patrick Devlin, *Trial by Jury* (1956) 164.

[4] Freeman writes: 'Juries infuse "non-legal values" into the trial process. They are the conscience of the community: they represent current ethical conventions. They are a constraint on legalism, arbitrariness and bureaucracy'. M. D. A. Freeman, 'The Jury on Trial' (1981) 34 *Current Legal Probs.* 65, at 90.

look at the English jury, and then briefly places the jury and jury reform in the context of the English legal and political system. After outlining the limited role remaining for juries in civil cases, the remainder of the chapter focuses on the shrinking right to jury trial in criminal trials, and the rules governing such matters as the selection of jurors, the conduct of the trial, and verdicts. In all these areas there have been recent changes or proposals for change. However, the impetus for reform has come from immediate political concerns, high-profile cases, and anecdote as much as from systematic information or reliable research.

II. Evolution of the English Jury

The idea of an ancient right to jury trial makes an attractive argument, and the present-day English jury does indeed have roots that can be traced back 800 years or more.[5] But the jury has continuously adapted and evolved, and its functions have changed fundamentally over the years. As well as changes to the jury itself, other changes to the criminal justice system have transformed the nature of the right to a jury trial. In particular, the growth of legal aid in criminal cases during the twentieth century[6] means that virtually all criminal defendants can be represented by a trained lawyer, strengthening the position of the defendant whilst placing an increasing burden on the public purse.

The original concept of the jury was probably imported into England after the Norman Conquest in 1066. The Normans had developed the practice of putting a group of local individuals under oath (hence the term 'juror') to tell the truth. Early jurors in England acted as sources of information on local affairs—for instance, gathering information

[5] There are many accounts of the early emergence of the English jury. This summary draws in particular on overviews by S. H. Bailey and M. J. Gunn, *Smith & Bailey on the Modern English Legal System* (3rd edn., 1996), at 888–9; W. Cornish, *The Jury* (1968); Devlin, *Trial By Jury*, *supra* note 3; and G. Robertson, *Freedom, the Individual and the Law* (7th edn., 1993) 348–51. Classic accounts include W. Forsyth, *History of Trial by Jury* (1852) and F. Pollock and F. W. Maitland, *The History of English Law before the Time of Edward I* (2nd edn., 1898), i, 138–50 and ii, 618–50; A. Sanders & R. Young *Criminal Justice* (1994).

[6] The legal aid system provides government-funded legal assistance in both criminal and (decreasingly) civil cases. A number of schemes run by the bar and judiciary existed in the 19th century to provide free or cheap legal advice to some prisoners in criminal cases. However, it was the Poor Prisoners' Defence Act 1903 that first introduced substantial provision for legal aid from public funds in cases heard by a judge and jury. See T. Goriely, 'The Development of Criminal Legal Aid in England and Wales' in R. Young and D. Wall (eds.), *Access to Criminal Justice* (1996) 26.

for the Domesday Book—but they gradually came to be used as adjudicators in both civil and criminal disputes. By 1367 it had been established that a unanimous verdict was required. The jury in legal disputes started as a group of people called upon for their prior knowledge of the case or the people involved. Only later did the principle emerge that, on the contrary, they should have no previous knowledge of the case or the parties to a dispute: by the eighteenth century, a juror with personal knowledge of a case was required to excuse himself from serving on the jury. Until the mid-nineteenth century jury trial was the only form of trial in the common law courts and, until the early twentieth century, it continued to predominate for civil as well as criminal cases.

The jury in criminal cases became firmly established when Pope Innocent III withdrew the support of the Roman Catholic Church from trial by ordeal of fire and water in 1215. However, early jurors could themselves face physical ordeals in carrying out their duties. They might be bullied into submission by being locked up without food or heat until they returned a guilty verdict, and the Star Chamber was known to punish jurors who refused to convict by seizing their land and possessions. *Bushell's Case*[7] in 1670 was a significant turning point. Twelve jurymen refused to convict the Quakers William Penn and William Mead of seditious assembly, and were locked up for two nights without food, water, fire, tobacco or chamber-pot. When this failed to force them to retract their not guilty verdict, the jurors were themselves sentenced to prison until they had paid a fine. Four of the jurors, led by Bushell, refused to pay and challenged their incarceration by a writ of *habeas corpus*.[8] The Lord Chief Justice released them in a landmark decision establishing the jury as the sole judge of fact. A jury had the right to give a verdict according to conscience, and could not be penalized for taking a view of the facts which was at odds with that of the judge.[9] A plaque recounting the story of the *Bushell* jury hangs in the Old Bailey, and it is under the principles established in that case that the jury has been acclaimed as 'the lamp that shows that freedom lives'[10] and 'the bulwark of liberty'.[11] The jury has complete power over the verdict and is not

[7] 124 Eng. Rep. 1006 (C.P.1670). [8] Ibid., at 1012. [9] Ibid., at 1018.

[10] Devlin, *supra* note 3, at 164.

[11] *Ford* v. *Blurton* (1922) 38 T.L.R. 801, 805 (Lord Atkin describing jury trial as: 'the bulwark of liberty, the shield of the poor from the rich and powerful'). Blackstone described an Englishman's right to trial by jury as 'the grand bulwark of his liberties'. W. Blackstone, *Commentaries Book 4* (1769) at 342.

required to give any explanation or justification.[12] A defendant may appeal against conviction, but not simply on the ground that the jury's decision is unjustified or mistaken.

The right of a jury to exercise judgement according to conscience continued to generate controversy over the centuries following *Bushell*, as juries continued to acquit with impunity where the law and evidence clearly indicated the defendant's guilt. Juries' refusals to convict radicals charged with publishing seditious attacks on George III and his government are among the most historic exercises of these rights. In the late eighteenth and early nineteenth centuries juries persistently undervalued stolen property in theft cases, evidently because they wished the accused to escape hanging.[13] The acquittal of Clive Ponting in 1985 of offences under the Official Secrets Act 1911 stands out as a contemporary example of a jury verdict according to conscience.[14] Ponting, a senior Ministry of Defence official, was charged with violating section 2 of the Act, which prohibited any government employee from revealing information obtained in the course of his or her job without the authorization of a superior.[15] At his trial Ponting admitted that he had passed to a Member of Parliament classified documents indicating that government ministers had lied to Parliament about the sinking of the Argentine warship the *General Belgrano* during the Falklands War. He argued that he owed a greater duty to make the information public than to observe the Official Secrets Act, and it appears the jury agreed with him.[16] The right of juries to decide in defiance of the law, or 'jury nullification' is central to the jury's democratic function and is discussed further below (Part XIII).

[12] The judge may halt a case and direct the jury to acquit where it becomes apparent after the case has started that the prosecution case is inadequate. Although strictly the jury could (and very occasionally does) object, judge-directed acquittals are not generally considered to be jury verdicts. See e.g., J. Baldwin, 'Understanding Judge Ordered and Judge Directed Acquittals in the Crown Court' [1997] *Crim. L. Rev.* 536.

[13] J. M. Beattie. *Crime and the Courts in England 1660–1800* (1986) 424–45. For a history of the role of juries deciding according to conscience see T. A. Green, *Verdict According to Conscience: Perspectives on the English Criminal Trial 1200–1800* (1985).

[14] J. C. Smith and D. J. Birch, 'Case and Comment—*R.* v. *Ponting*' [1985] *Crim. L. Rev.* 318.

[15] A new Official Secrets Act was passed in 1989. S.2 was abolished, but the new restrictions relating to disclosure of government information are considerable. See Robertson, *supra* note 5, at 167–73.

[16] Smith & Birch, *supra* note 14, at 320.

III. Legal and Political Context of the English Jury

Roy Amlot[17] writes that the spirit of trial by jury 'is burnt into the consciousness of every Englishman—to such an extent that the jury's detractors might as well attempt to do away with Parliamentary democracy as trial by jury'.[18] While it is certainly true that any perceived attack on the jury can expect to meet with vociferous resistance, the English jury is much more vulnerable to attack than the jury in the United States where the right to jury trial is enshrined in an entrenched, written constitution. In England, the nature and extent of the right to trial by jury are governed by ordinary parliamentary statute, which in turn can be altered by a simple Act of Parliament. To the extent that the government of the day controls Parliament, it can in principle radically change or even abolish the jury. However, while changes to the jury system are legally comparatively simple, the political barriers are considerable, and governments generally tread cautiously. Changes have tended to be piecemeal and incremental rather than sweeping.

The government departments most likely to be concerned with jury reform are the Lord Chancellor's Department and the Home Office.[19] Over the past thirty-five years a series of *ad hoc* Departmental Committees of Inquiry and Royal Commissions have examined aspects of the jury and made recommendations for reform, some of them implemented and others still discussed. They include those of the Royal Commission on Criminal Justice chaired by Viscount Runciman (1993),[20] the Fraud Trials Committee chaired by Lord Roskill (1986),[21] the Royal Commission on Criminal Procedure (1981),[22] the James Committee on the Distribution of Criminal Business between the Crown Court and the Magistrates Court, which addressed the defendant's right to elect trial by jury (1975),[23] and the Morris Departmental Committee on Jury

[17] Then Chairman of the Criminal Bar Association.

[18] R. Amlot, 'Leave the Jury Alone' in *The Effectiveness of Juries and the Use of the Civil Courts in the Control of Crime*, papers presented at a seminar on 10 Dec. 1997, British Academy of Forensic Sciences (1997) at 42.

[19] The Lord Chancellor broadly has responsibility for the administration of justice, although responsibility for the penal system lies with the Home Secretary.

[20] *Royal Comm'n on Crim. Just., Report*, 1993, Cm 2263 (herinafter Runciman Commission).

[21] *Fraud Trials Comm., Report*, 1986 (hereinafter Roskill Committee).

[22] *Royal Comm'n on Crim. Proc., Report*, 1981, Cmnd. 8092.

[23] *Interdepartmental Comm. on the Distribution of Crim. Bus. Between the Crown Court and Magistrates' Courts, Report*, 1975, Cmnd. 6323 (hereinafter James Committee).

Service (1965).[24] The main statute governing the present day jury is the Juries Act 1974. Important provisions relating to the jury are also contained in the Criminal Justice and Public Order Act 1994[25] and the Contempt of Court Act 1981.[26]

One of the most controversial statutory provisions regarding juries has been section 8 of the Contempt of Court Act 1981, which prohibits any enquiry into jury deliberations. The section was inserted after the former Liberal Party leader Jeremy Thorpe was acquitted of conspiracy to murder in a highly publicized jury trial.[27] One of the jurors gave an interview to the *New Statesman* magazine explaining how the jury had reached its decision. The magazine was prosecuted, but the High Court refused to find that it had committed a contempt of court in publishing the story.[28] The government moved immediately to insert a new clause into the Contempt of Court Act making it a criminal offence to 'obtain, disclose or solicit any particulars of statements made, opinions expressed, arguments advanced, or votes cast by members of a jury in the course of their deliberations'.[29]

There have been increasing calls for a relaxation of this ban for the purposes of academic research. Not all research on juries requires the questioning of actual jurors, but the Contempt of Court Act has been a major inhibition to jury research in England.[30] In 1986, the Roskill Committee expressed frustration at being unable to question jurors for its examination of the future of fraud trials.[31] Lack of research on juries meant that the Runciman Commission felt unable to make recommendations on whether there is a case for raising the age limit for jury service, or whether there should be literacy or comprehension requirements for jurors. The Commission recommended that the Contempt of Court Act be amended 'so that informed debate can take place rather than argument based only on surmise and anecdote'.[32] Following the *Maxwell* fraud case, discussed below, support for lifting the prohibition on questioning jurors came from the Bar, the Law Society, senior members of the

[24] *Departmental Comm. on Jury Service, Report*, 1965 Cmnd. 2627 (hereinafter Morris Committee).

[25] S. 31. [26] S. 8.

[27] *Attorney General* v. *New Statesman & Nation Publ'g Co. Ltd.* [1981] Q.B. 1.

[28] Ibid., at 6. [29] Contempt of Court Act 1981, s. 8.

[30] Sarah McCabe, for example, laments the paucity of research on the English jury. S. McCabe 'Is jury research dead?' in M. Findlay and P. Duff (eds.), *The Jury Under Attack* (1988) 27.

[31] Roskill Committee, *supra* note 21, paras. 8.10–8.11, app. A para. 7.

[32] Runciman Commission, *supra* note 20, at 2.

judiciary, and the Serious Fraud Office.[33] Some have suggested that the jury would not survive close scrutiny—that secrecy must surround the jury room if the jury is to be workable.[34] But the jury has survived extensive research in the United States. As Robertson argues, '[the ban] has not worked as its advocates predicted to protect the jury system from attack: on the contrary it has imposed yet another layer of secrecy which handicaps those who would wish to defend the system with more than anecdotal evidence'.[35]

IV. The Scope of Jury Trial

The role of the English jury today is almost entirely confined to the more serious criminal cases. Juries also occasionally sit in civil trials and, even less frequently, in the Coroner's Court.[36]

A. The Jury in Civil Cases

The frequency of civil jury trials in England and Wales steadily declined from the middle of the nineteenth century, when judges were given the right to refuse trial by jury. Today, less than one per cent of civil trials are jury trials.[37] The Supreme Court Act 1981[38] gives a qualified right to trial by jury in only four types of civil case: libel and slander, fraud, malicious prosecution, and false imprisonment. Even in those cases, the right can be denied where the court is of the opinion that the trial requires 'prolonged examination of documents or accounts or any scientific or local investigation which cannot be conveniently made with a jury'.[39] A large proportion of civil actions in England and Wales are personal injury cases, where jury trial is no longer a right, though it may still be granted at the discretion of the court. *Ward* v. *James*, decided in 1965, is often considered to have been the death blow to civil juries in such cases: the Court of Appeal held that personal injury litigation should be heard by a single judge unless there were special

[33] See F. Gibb, 'The Result of the Maxwell Brothers' Case Has Put the System Under the Spotlight', *The Times*, 30 Jan. 1996, at 31.

[34] e.g. E. Devons, 'Serving as a Juryman in Britain' (1965) 28 *Mod.L.Rev.* 561.

[35] Robertson, *supra* note 5, at 361.

[36] The Coroners Amendment Act 1926 enabled the coroner to sit without a jury in almost all cases. Coroner's juries are still usually required where the death occurred in custody or involves the conduct of the police.

[37] See C. Elliott and F. Quinn, *English Legal System* (2nd edn., 1998) at 138.

[38] S. 69. [39] Ibid.

considerations.[40] However, by then it was already rare for the parties to ask for a jury in personal injury cases.[41]

Today, civil juries are used most often in defamation cases. The excessively large awards juries sometimes make in such cases have caused concern. In 1975 the Faulks Committee on Defamation recommended that the function of the jury in defamation cases should be limited to deciding issues of liability and that the assessment of damages should be left to the judge.[42] The recommendation was not implemented, however, and in 1995 the Court of Appeal in *John* v. *MGN Ltd*[43] took action to curb excessive awards through the instructions given to juries. The singer Elton John had successfully sued the *Sunday Mirror* newspaper for libel, and the jury had awarded him £350,000 (£75,000 compensatory damages and £275,000 exemplary damages). The Court of Appeal reduced the jury's award to a total of £75,000 (£25,000 compensatory and £50,000 exemplary damages). At the same time the court held that, in future, both the judge and counsel could give libel juries guidance on the size of damages awards. The guidance could refer to appropriate awards and award brackets, and to conventional personal injury awards to check the reasonableness of awards that juries were proposing to make.[44] The Defamation Act 1996 further curtailed the role of juries in libel cases, establishing a summary procedure whereby judges, not juries, can dispose of libel actions up to £10,000.[45]

Following its action in defamation cases, the Court of Appeal has also laid down guidelines on the directions to be given to juries assessing damages in cases of false imprisonment and malicious prosecution brought against the police.[46] The guidelines relate in particular to exemplary damages, and evidently came in response to a request from Sir Paul Condon, then Metropolitan Police Commissioner, who claimed that jurors were being influenced by previous cases in which large sums had

[40] *Ward* v. *James* [1966] 1 Q.B. 273.

[41] In 1990, a personal injury claim related to the underground fire at Kings Cross was refused a jury trial because, in the court's view, the case involved technical and far-reaching issues which were not suitable for a jury. See Elliott and Quinn, *supra* note 37, at 138 (citing *Singh* v. *London Underground*, *The Independent*, 25 April 1990).

[42] *Committee on Defamation, Report*, 1975, Cmnd. 5909 at 141–3, 180 (The Faulks Committee).

[43] [1996] 2 All E.R. 35.

[44] Ibid., at 52–5.

[45] Defamation Act 1996, ch.31 s. 8.

[46] *Thompson* v. *Commissioner of Police of the Metropolis* [1997] 2 All E.R. 762 (consolidated with *Hsu* v. *Commissioner of Police of the Metropolis*). Thompson sued the police for false imprisonment, and the case included a claim for damages for personal injury. Hsu sued for malicious prosecution.

been awarded.[47] £50,000 was held to be the maximum appropriate award for exemplary damages in such cases, and then only when very senior officers had been involved. The jury could also be told that exemplary damages represent a windfall to the plaintiff who will have already been awarded compensatory damages, and (in the case of the Metropolitan Police) would be payable out of police funds, thereby reducing money available for other purposes.[48]

B. The Jury in Criminal Cases

Even in criminal cases, jury trials represent only approximately one or two per cent of trials.[49] More than 200 years ago Blackstone warned that an Englishman's right to trial by jury, although not openly attacked, might gradually be 'sapped and undermined' by the introduction of other, 'convenient' methods of trial, including trial by justices of the peace.[50] The vast majority of criminal cases are now tried in the magistrates' courts, usually by a bench of three lay magistrates.[51] A small number are tried by legally trained, stipendiary magistrates, but most magistrates have no legal qualifications and receive no remuneration. The English criminal justice system is highly unusual in the extent to which it relies on the services of lay judges (i.e. lay magistrates or justices of the peace).[52] Only where a case goes to the Crown Court[53] and the defendant pleads not guilty will there be a jury trial.

The possibility of a Crown Court trial is determined by the category of offence. Criminal offences are grouped into three categories.[54] 'Summary offences' are the least serious and are triable only in the magistrates' courts. They include, for example, minor traffic offences,

[47] See S. Tendler, 'Yard Wants Court to Set Limits on Damages Payouts', *The Times*, 7 May 1996 at 3.

[48] *Thompson* [1997] 2 All E.R. at 776.

[49] Estimates vary around 1 to 2%, depending on exactly how 'cases' are counted and the year taken.

[50] W. Blackstone, *Commentaries on the Laws of England*, Book IV, 343–34 (1769/1996) Clarendon Editions.

[51] On 1 Jan. 1999 there were 30,260 justices of the peace, 93 full-time stipendiaries and 104 acting stipendiaries. *Lord Chancellor's Department Judicial Statistics Annual Report*, 1998, Cm 4371 at 90–1.

[52] For comparison with a number of continental European countries, see Cheryl Thomas, *Judicial Appointments in Continental Europe* (Lord Chancellor's Department Research Series No. 6/7, Dec. 1997).

[53] The lowest tier of the Supreme Court of England and Wales exercising criminal jurisdiction.

[54] Criminal Law Act 1977, pt. II.

avoiding payment of a train fare, and soliciting. The most serious criminal offences are classified as 'indictable only', and are triable only in the Crown Court. Intermediate between these two are indictable offences classified as 'triable either way'. 'Either way' offences may be tried either in the Crown Court or (if the magistrates are willing to assume jurisdiction and the defendant consents) in the magistrates' court.[55] If they are tried in the Crown Court, and the accused pleads not guilty,[56] he or she will be tried before a jury.

Government statistics give an indication of the division of criminal business between the magistrates' courts and the Crown Court. In 1997 approximately 1,860,000 defendants were proceeded against in the magistrates' courts, while the total for trial in the Crown Court was 91,300, 67 per cent of whom entered pleas of guilty.[57] Of contested trials before a jury, 40 per cent resulted in acquittal. Only 19 per cent of cases tried in the Crown Court were indictable only and could therefore be tried only in the Crown Court.[58]

Adjustments to the borderlines between the different categories of criminal offence have produced progressive erosion of the right to jury trial over the past twenty-three years, and the trend seems likely to continue. The Criminal Law Act 1977 made criminal damage below £200 a summary offence, with no right to jury trial.[59] The Criminal Justice Act 1988 further extended the powers of the magistrates' court by expanding summary offences to include, for example, taking and driving away a car without the owner's consent, and common assault and battery, as well as raising the limit for criminal damage cases.[60] In July 1998 the government published proposals to make a number of further offences into summary offences, including some categories of theft.[61]

At present, in either way cases the defendant can insist on jury trial even though the magistrates are willing to try the case summarily. However, the government announced in 1998 that it was considering

[55] Magistrates Court Act 1980, s. 17. As discussed later in the ch., at the time of writing the government is pressing ahead with measures to remove the defendant's right to refuse consent and elect jury trial in either-way cases.

[56] The case may be discharged or otherwise disposed of before a jury is sworn in. A trial may also be halted by the judge and the jury directed to acquit.

[57] *Criminal Statistics for England and Wales*, 1997, Cm 4162, at 136. Amongst defendants in the magistrates' court, 486,000 were proceeded against for either-way offences that could have gone to the Crown Court, 531,600 for summary non-motoring offences; and 838,000 for summary motoring offences. Ibid., at 124.

[58] Ibid., at 136. [59] S. 22 (sched.4). [60] SS. 37–8.

[61] Home Office, *Determining Mode of Trial in Either Way Cases* (1998).

removing the defendant's right to elect Crown Court trial for either-way offences,[62] and at the time of writing is pressing ahead with legislation to implement the proposal.[63] The move is highly controversial as it strikes very directly at the right to jury trial. The James Committee discussed but rejected the idea in 1975.[64] In 1993 the Runciman Commission recommended that the defendant should no longer be able to insist that his or her case should be heard in the Crown Court,[65] but the proposal was not implemented. A 1997 Home Office report by Narey recommended, as had the Runciman Commission, that defendants should no longer be able to refuse to consent to summary trial in either-way cases,[66] and the present government based its proposal to legislate on similar arguments to those in the Narey report.

The main reason for removing the defendant's right to elect jury trial appears to be that Crown Court trial is very much more expensive than trial in the magistrates' court.[67] Refusal to consent to summary trial is viewed as vetoing the decision of magistrates to retain jurisdiction over cases and incurring expense that could legitimately be saved. According to Home Office figures, 22,000 defendants charged with either-way offences elected to be tried in the Crown Court in 1997 even though the magistrates were willing to try them.[68] The likely saving from removing their right to do so is difficult to estimate with any precision. The Home Secretary proposed a figure of over £120 million a year when he presented the Mode of Trial Bill to the House of Commons,[69] but the estimate, which included savings arising from lighter sentencing by

[62] Ibid.

[63] The Criminal Justice (Mode of Trial) (No. 2) Bill was introduced into the House of Commons on 22 Feb. 2000.

[64] James Committee, *supra* note 24.

[65] Runciman Commission, *supra* note 20. This is already the position in Scotland, although differences between the two systems make comparisons with the Scottish system of deciding venue of limited value—see P. Duff, 'The Scottish Jury: A Very Peculiar Institution' (1999) 62 *Law & Contemp. Probs.* 173, 177–8.

[66] *Review of Delay in the Criminal Justice System, A Report*, 1997 (hereinafter Narey report) (Home Office).

[67] The Home Office estimates that the average cost of a magistrates' court proceeding for indictable offences is £750, whilst the average cost of a Crown Court proceeding is £8,600. Richard Harries, *The Cost of Criminal Justice*, Home Office Research, Development and Statistics Directorate, Research Findings No 103 (1999), 1. The cost of a not-guilty plea at the Crown Court is estimated at an average £17,550, whilst a not guilty plea (indictable offences) in the magistrates' court is estimated at an average £1,700 (ibid., at 2).

[68] Home Office, *supra* note 61, at 2.

[69] Debate on Second Reading of Criminal Justice (Mode of Trial) (No. 2) Bill, Hansard vol. 345 No. 58, Tuesday 7 Mar. 2000, 886.

magistrates, was greeted with some scepticism. The Home Office notes that the number of defendants electing to be tried in the Crown Court is anyway falling, and suggests this may be because research has shown that they could risk a heavier sentence in the Crown Court than in a magistrates' court.[70] It reports that 72 per cent of triable-either way cases tried in the Crown Court were committed because the magistrates had declined jurisdiction, and that the proportion is rising. It indicates also that the implementation of the 'plea before venue' provision in the Criminal Procedure and Investigations Act 1996 section 49 has cut by about 15,000 the number of cases committed to the Crown Court for trial. We do not know whether the magistrates would decline to try more cases under the new regime, and the additional burden on the magistrates' courts and the likely additional costs of appeals if the defendant can no longer elect jury trial also need to be considered. Nonetheless, there is a large perceived opportunity to cut costs by removing the defendant's right of election.

A substantial proportion of potential jury trials become what are known as 'cracked trials', where preparations are made for a jury trial and court time is allocated, but the trial does not go ahead. Often the reason is that the defendant pleads guilty on the day of the trial. Judicial statistics for 1998 show that 17,393 Crown Court trials 'cracked'; 10,858 of them because the defendant pleaded guilty at a late stage.[71] Trials crack for many reasons, including poor prosecution decisions and preparation of cases. Nonetheless, the cost to the public purse that cracked trials represent has sometimes been attributed to defendants' abuse of the system, and is one of the arguments used for abolishing the ability of defendants to elect jury trial.[72]

Arguments with reference to cost are supplemented by arguments that, in a large number of cases, the expense of Crown Court trial is unjustified. Research indicates that where defendants elect to be tried in the Crown Court, it is often because they and their solicitors believe that they will have a fuller and fairer hearing and that the chances of acquittal are higher.[73] There is some evidence that black defendants in par-

[70] Home Office, *supra* note 61, at 2.

[71] Lord Chancellor's Department, *supra* note 51.

[72] See, e.g. Narey report, *supra* note 66; M. Zander and P. Henderson, *Crown Court Study, Research Study No. 19 for the Royal Commission on Criminal Justice* (1993) (hereinafter Crown Court Study).

[73] C. Hedderman and D. Moxon, *Magistrates Court or Crown Court? Mode of Trial Decisions and Sentencing* (HMSO, London, 1992), at 20.

ticular lack confidence in magistrates' courts, seeing them as 'police courts'; that black defendants choose jury trial more frequently than white or Asian defendants; and that jury trial may enhance the confidence that minority communities have in the criminal justice system.[74] There is also some evidence to support the belief that the chances of acquittal are higher in the Crown Court. Julie Vennard, for example, concluded that, in her sample of offences triable either-way, the rate of acquittal was about twice as high in the Crown Court as in the magistrates' courts.[75] Darbyshire also found a higher acquittal rate in the Crown Court than in the magistrates' courts. However, we cannot conclude that jury trial favours the defendant. The allocation of either-way offences to the Crown Court or magistrates' court is obviously not random. It may be that cases with a good defence more often go to the Crown Court, so that comparisons in rates of acquittal in the two courts are not comparing like with like. Moreover, by no means all acquittals in the Crown Court are jury acquittals.[76]

In its 1998 consultation paper on mode of trial, the Home Office suggests that the great majority of defendants electing Crown Court trial are simply seeking delay, or hoping that difficulties with witnesses will hamper the case, or hoping to put pressure on the Crown to accept a guilty plea to a lesser offence.[77] However, these claims appear to be based on anecdote. As in other areas of discussion of the jury, the language of 'abuse' of the justice system is frequently found. For example, Narey writes:

> these recommendations would . . . stop improper manipulation of the justice system. Magistrates would be well able to distinguish those defendants who . . . were justified in seeking a Crown Court hearing. . . . One senior and distinguished magistrate succinctly summarised the current scope for abuse: . . . 'Inevitably, the ones who elect are experienced defendants, the ones who know how to play the system'.[78]

Narey recalls the 1975 James Committee's hesitation to recommend removing the right of election from the defendant, given the substantial body of opinion opposed to such a step, but points out that few

[74] F. Gibb, 'Blacks Will Be Hit Most by Jury Changes', *The Times*, 21 Nov. 1998.

[75] J. Vennard, 'The Outcome of Contested Trials' in D. Moxon (ed.), *Managing Criminal Justice* (HMSO, London, 1985), at 131.

[76] In 1998, 64% of defendants in the Crown Court who pleaded not guilty to all counts were acquitted. Of these, 35% were acquitted by a jury, and 65% discharged or acquitted by direction of the judge. Lord Chancellor's Department, *supra* note 50, at 65.

[77] Home Office, *supra* note 61, at 4.

[78] Narey report, *supra* note 66, at 35.

jurisdictions regard it as necessary or desirable to build in an element of personal choice by the defendant as to the court in which he or she will be tried. He also suggests that the right to insist on a jury trial is not as ancient as is sometimes thought, as there was no right to claim jury trial until 1855.[79] This glosses over the difference between the right to a jury trial and the right to *elect* jury trial. As Narey himself points out, until that date felonies, as distinct from misdemeanours, were always tried on indictment, as distinct from summarily in the magistrates' court. Defendant election only became relevant as it became possible for an increasing range of indictable offences to be tried summarily, *with the defendant's consent.* The proposed change in effect removes the opportunity for the defendant to refuse to consent to being tried summarily, and greatly increases the level of sentence to which a defendant is exposed without the chance to elect jury trial.

At the time the Narey report appeared the Conservative Party was still in power in Britain. In opposition the Labour Party said it would not support the proposed change. However, in government the Labour Party revived discussion of the proposal, and in November 1999 introduced the Criminal Justice (Mode of Trial) Bill[80] to put it into effect. Parliament's reaction to the Bill and the surrounding debate in the press illustrate clearly the vigorous opposition that a perceived attack on the jury can expect to encounter. In January 2000 the Bill suffered a heavy defeat in the House of Lords. On 7 March a slightly revised Bill[81] was presented to the House of Commons by the Home Secretary and provoked a backbench revolt. The Bill was attacked on many grounds, including the absence of reliable audited estimates of any likely cost savings,[82] and the absence of reliable evidence of substantial and continuing abuse of the current system.[83] It was also argued that it was wrong for the government to use its 'massive and quiescent majority' to force through such a change especially when it had not been in the election manifesto.[84] The government was not defeated, but the Home Secretary did indicate during the debate that amendments might be made before the Bill became law.[85] The eventual outcome remains uncertain. However, given the Labour Government's substantial majority in the Commons, it is likely that it will eventually succeed in carrying through the reform.

[79] Narey report, *supra* note 66, at 31–2.
[80] Criminal Justice (Mode of Trial) Bill (H.L.).
[81] Criminal Justice (Mode of Trial) (2) Bill.
[82] e.g. by Mr Garnier, Hansard, *supra* note 69, 909; Mr Marshall-Andrews, ibid., 918.
[83] e.g. by Mr Hughes, ibid., at 925, 926.
[84] Mr Marshall-Andrews, ibid., at 918.
[85] Hansard, *supra* note 69, at 892.

C. *Juries in Fraud Cases*

Juries' competence to try complex cases, especially complex fraud prosecutions, has been questioned repeatedly, and was the subject of inquiry by the Fraud Trials Committee chaired by Lord Roskill, which reported in 1986.[86] Research conducted for the Roskill Committee by psychologists at Cambridge University showed that juror comprehension of complex information could be significantly improved by providing aids such as glossaries and written summaries, and using visual aids to present the information.[87] Nonetheless, the Roskill Committee recommended that complex fraud trials should no longer be tried by juries but by a Fraud Trials Tribunal comprising one judge and two lay experts.[88] The recommendation was not implemented, but is still widely discussed.[89] Other proposals include the introduction of a new straightforward offence of fraud, which would make cases easier to present to juries; or a system of smaller fraud juries of six or seven jurors who are required to reach a certain educational standard.[90]

Debate over the role of juries in serious fraud cases intensified following the *Maxwell* case in 1996, in which a jury acquitted the Maxwell brothers of conspiracy to defraud a company pension scheme.[91] The acquittals followed an extremely expensive investigation, and a lengthy, high-profile trial, and the outcome was highly embarrassing to the Serious Fraud Office which called for the abolition of jury trial in serious fraud cases.[92] The Bar staunchly opposed such a move.[93] The

[86] Roskill Committee, *supra* note 21.

[87] Ibid., at annex (Medical Research Council Applied Psychology Unit, Cambridge University, *Improving the Presentation of Information to Juries in Fraud Trials: A Report of Four Research Studies*).

[88] Roskill Committee, *supra* note 21, at 147.

[89] *Juries in Serious Fraud Trials: A Consultation Document*, The Home Office, Feb. 1998. M. Levi, *The Investigation, Prosecution and Trial of Serious Fraud. Research Study 14 for the Royal Commission on Criminal Justice* (1993).

[90] R. Rice, 'Jury Role in Fraud Trials to Be Probed', *Financial Times*, 21 Sept. 1996, at 6.

[91] Kevin and Ian Maxwell were accused of being implicated in illegal activity, including misuse of pension funds, uncovered when the death of their father (Robert Maxwell) precipitated an investigation into his business affairs. See, e.g. Gibb, *supra* note 33, at 31.

[92] The Serious Fraud Office was set up by the Criminal Justice Act 1987 following the Roskill Committee's report in 1986. It investigates, and institutes and conducts, prosecutions in a comparatively small number of the most serious fraud cases. The prosecution of other serious fraud cases continues to be handled by the Fraud Investigation Group within the Crown Prosecution Service.

[93] F. Gibb, 'Not Guilty Verdicts Put System Back in the Dock', *The Times*, 20 Jan. 1996, at 3.

Commissioner of the City of London Police called for more research and a review of the role of juries in complex fraud cases.[94] The *Maxwell* case has not so far led to extensive reform, but the judge's management of the case was innovative in several respects, and showed the extent to which procedures already within the powers of the judge could enable juries to deal more easily with complex cases. Steps taken by Phillips J to simplify the charges and provide aids to comprehension accord with the recommendations of the Cambridge research team for the Roskill Committee.[95]

More than thirteen years after the Roskill Committee reported, debate over the use of juries in fraud trials is still very much alive. There are indications that the Labour Government is considering the case for abolishing juries in some categories of fraud trial, and the Home Office has produced a consultation document setting out various options.[96] However, at the time of writing there has been no firm statement. The Serious Fraud Office has had greater success in obtaining convictions since the *Maxwell* case, which may reduce the pressure to abolish juries in fraud cases.

V. Selection for Jury Service

The qualifications and prohibitions determining who can serve on a jury have undergone significant changes in the last few decades. The number of jurors has remained at twelve,[97] but in 1972 eligibility was extended to include anyone on the electoral register who is not excluded for some specific reason,[98] and in 1988 the lower age limit was reduced to 18 years and the upper limit raised to 70.[99] Before 1972 jurors were drawn only

[94] 'Police Urge Jury Review', *The Times*, 17 Oct. 1996, at 28.

[95] Phillips J reduced the indictment from 10 charges to 2 and introduced a court day of 9:30 am to 1:30 pm, reserving the afternoons for legal argument so that the jurors did not have to concentrate all day, or wait while counsel discussed legal points in their absence. Prosecuting counsel provided a 'map' of all documents that they would call, and specific passages to be examined were displayed on monitors around the courtroom. Before the jury retired Phillips J provided them with a written summary of his three and a half day summing up, although he refused to allow jurors to have daily transcripts. Gibb, *supra* note 86.

[96] Home Office, *supra* note 89.

[97] The historical reasons for using this number are unknown, although Devlin points out that it is the number of the Apostles of Christ, the ancient tribes of Israel, the 12 patriarchs, and the 12 officers of Solomon. *Trial by Jury*, *supra* note 3 at 14.

[98] The governing provision is now the Juries Act 1974, s. 3.

[99] Juries Act 1974, s. 1 (as amended by the Criminal Justice Act 1988, s. 119).

from those who owned property of a prescribed rateable value, which tended to ensure that juries were 'predominantly male, middle-aged, middle-minded and middle class'.[100] To qualify for jury service a person must have been ordinarily resident in the United Kingdom for at least five years since the age of 13.[101] People who have ever been sentenced in the United Kingdom to a period of imprisonment of more than five years are disqualified from serving, as are people who have served any part of certain sentences in the past ten years, been placed on probation in the last five years, or are currently on bail in criminal proceedings.[102]

Several categories of people are ineligible as distinct from disqualified. These are the judiciary, others concerned with the administration of justice (including barristers, solicitors, police officers, prison officers, and court staff), the clergy, and the mentally disordered.[103] In addition, members of several professions currently have the legal right to refuse to serve. They are Members of Parliament, peers, doctors, dentists, nurses, vets, chemists, and anyone in the armed forces. Potential jurors may also be excused because of illness, or specific commitments, such as business commitments or holidays already booked. However, the Criminal Justice Act 1988 introduced the possibility of deferral of jury service, so that those who have specific commitments can be asked to serve at a later date.[104]

Potential jurors are now randomly selected from the electoral register. Research has shown that the new criteria have resulted in profound changes in the composition of juries since 1972. They have become much younger and less middle class, but there still appears to be an under-representation of women and ethnic minorities.[105] The extension of the jury franchise in 1972 followed the recommendation of the Morris Committee in 1965.[106] In contrast to other changes in the rules relating to

[100] Devlin, *supra* note 3, at 20. Bailey and Gunn cite the instance of a case in Derby in 1932, in which Bernard Rothman and others were tried on charges relating to mass trespass on private land in the Peak District. The jury was reported to consist of two brigadiers-general, three colonels, two majors, three captains, and two aldermen. Bailey and Gunn, *supra* note 5, at 891 n.15.

[101] Juries Act 1974, s. 1.

[102] Ibid. (as amended by the Juries Disqualification Act 1984, s. 1). The last category, those on bail, was added by the Criminal Justice and Public Order Act 1994, s. 40.

[103] Ibid., sched. 1 (as amended by the Mental Health Amendment Act 1982, sched. 3 and the Mental Health Act 1983, sched. 4).

[104] Criminal Justice Act 1988, s. 20 (amending Juries Act 1974, s. 9).

[105] The research findings are summarized in Bailey and Gunn, *supra* note 5, at 891–3. Sources include J. Baldwin and M. McConville, *Jury Trials* (1979) and Zander and Henderson, *supra* note 72.

[106] *Departmental Comm. on Jury Service*, *supra* note 23.

juries over the past 25 years, this change appears to have been dictated by concerns with due process rather than crime control.[107] The 'elite' nature of the composition of the jury had come to be seen as a threat to its legitimacy in a democratic society, and to claims that it introduced common sense and protected the ordinary citizen from the state. However, Nicholas Blake suggests that the results of the changes in juror qualification were not to everyone's liking. According to Blake, there were complaints from the police, judges, and some lawyers of a deterioration in the standard of jurors, who were now too stupid, too irresponsible, too easily bribed or intimidated, or too much of a security risk.[108]

Random selection of jurors from the electoral register has been done by computer since 1981. The people selected receive a summons requiring them to attend at the Crown Court at a specified time. Those summoned constitute the panel from which the jury for an individual case will be selected if a plea of not guilty is entered. Twelve people are selected from the jury panel by ballot, which is conducted in open court. After an opportunity for challenges, as discussed below, the jury is sworn, and the trial can begin. Selection of prospective jurors by computer is the practice rather than a required procedure. This was illustrated in *R.* v. *Salt* in 1996.[109] A Crown Court usher called on his son to sit as a member of the jury at Salt's trial when the number of jurors available was insufficient: a summons was issued, a ballot card created, and the son became one of the twelve jurors. When Salt appealed against his conviction on the ground of improper empanelling of the jury, the court held that every practicable effort should be made to ensure random jury selection, but that there is no rule of law requiring it. Indeed, an officer of the court can require an eligible member of the public to come in off the street to serve on a jury if there are insufficient numbers.[110] However, in *Salt* it transpired that the son had sat on five or six Crown Court juries during the previous year. The Court of Appeal decided that the son of an usher who regularly attended as a juror fell within the spirit of the disqualification that made officers and staff of the court ineligible.[111]

[107] For discussion of this point see P. Duff and M. Findlay, 'The Politics of Jury Reform' in *The Jury Under Attack*, *supra* note 30, at 251–6.

[108] N. Blake, 'The Case for the Jury' in *The Jury Under Attack*, *supra* note 30, at 140–3.

[109] 'Son of Crown Court Usher Acted Regularly As A Juror', *The Times*, 1 Feb. 1996, at 38.

[110] Juries Act 1974, s. 6(1). See, e.g., 'PC Pounds Beat in Search of Jury', *The Times*, 2 Mar. 1999, at 38.

[111] The disqualification making officers and staff of the court ineligible is found in the Juries Act 1974, s. 1.

Jury service, especially on long trials, can present work and domestic difficulties, and the basic subsistence allowance does not compensate for most people's loss of earnings. Many of those called for jury service ask for either exemption or deferral. While in opposition, the Labour party announced that, if elected, it would act to stop people avoiding jury service by citing business commitments, holidays, or minor illness, and would revise the list of professionals who have the legal right to be excused. It was feared that exemptions and excusals were resulting in juries skewed towards the working class and unemployed, who might be unsympathetic to the police and more likely to acquit criminals.[112] However, the occupations of jurors in the Crown Court Study matched the general population quite closely.[113]

If a trial is expected to last more than ten days, prospective jurors will be asked at court if this would be difficult for them. The jury-summoning officer can use his or her discretion to excuse people or grant a deferral, usually on the basis of work or childcare commitments and booked holidays. However, a genuine reason is needed, and people will not generally be excused because they have a demanding job, even if they are self-employed.[114] They may also be screened for possible bias against the defendant. In the *Maxwell* case, for example, potential jurors were screened for their ability to stay the course of a trial lasting several months, and 550 of 700 potential jurors summoned were excused on 'personal hardship grounds' to do with business or professional commitments or family obligations.[115] They were also screened to ensure that they were not biased against the defendants as a result of the extensive pre-trial publicity (see further below, Part IX). Illiteracy is not in itself a ground for excusing a potential juror,[116] but it is evident that in the *Maxwell* case questionnaires were also used to identify and excuse jurors with serious literacy problems.[117]

[112] See Jill Sherman, 'Labour Warns Jury Dodgers', *The Times*, 7 Feb. 1996, at 1.

[113] Zander and Henderson, *supra* note 72, at 239. They note that there was 'a slight over-representation of clerical workers and under-representation of skilled manual workers'.

[114] A first-hand account of the process from the perspective of an Old Bailey juror is given by Trevor Grove. See T. Grove, *The Juryman's Tale* (1998).

[115] *Juries in Serious Fraud Trials: A Consultation Document*, *supra* note 89, at 6. Jury selection in the *Maxwell* case took two weeks and involved the use of lengthy questionnaires and oral questioning by both judge and counsel. See Gibb, *supra* note 86, at 3.

[116] The Juries Act 1974 s. 10 gives the judge the power to discharge a juror with insufficient understanding of English, leading to doubt about his or her capacity to act effectively as a juror.

[117] *Juries in Serious Fraud Trials: A Consultation Document*, *supra* note 89, at 14.

After a trial has begun, the judge has powers to discharge jurors if they become ill or for any other reason are incapable of continuing to act, and the entire jury may be discharged if the jurors speak to outsiders after the jury has retired to deliberate. Jurors may also be discharged for a range of irregularities including frivolous behaviour, drunkenness, acquisition of information that the juror should not have, or discovery of bias that becomes apparent too late to be dealt with at the time for challenge.[118] In July 1998, for example, the judge removed a juror after he asked the judge for the defendant's birth date in order to draw up a star-chart.[119] The remaining eleven jurors continued, and in due course acquitted the defendant. England has no system of alternate jurors attending the trial and ready to take the place of discharged jurors, but as long as the jury does not fall below nine in number the trial can continue.[120]

VI. Jury Challenges

There is only restricted scope for jury challenges in England. The opportunity for the defence to influence the composition of the jury was all but eliminated in 1988, when the defence's long-standing right of peremptory challenge was completely abolished.[121] In contrast, the prosecution's right to stand jurors by was unchanged. The right of either side to challenge for cause remains, but it is of limited use in practice.

Before 1988, the opportunity to challenge peremptorily occurred after the clerk had asked twelve members of the jury panel to step into the jury box. Counsel for the accused (or the accused if unrepresented) would call out 'challenge' immediately before the juror in question took the oath. No reason needed to be given for the challenge, and the juror was replaced by another. The right of the defence to challenge jurors was steadily eroded over time. In 1925 the number of peremptory challenges allowed was reduced from twenty-five to twelve; in 1949 it was further reduced to seven (seven per defendant where several were

[118] There are complex rules governing the powers of the court in respect of juries and how the judge should handle various situations that may arise. These are set out in some detail in *Archbold* (2000), paras. 4-253–4-263.

[119] P. Wilkinson, 'Juror Wanted to Find Truth in the Stars', *The Times*, 9 July 1998, at 3.

[120] Juries Act 1974, s. 16.

[121] Criminal Justice Act 1988, s. 118. The right dated back to the 15th century when it was introduced to redress the balance in favour of the defendant.

tried together); in 1977 it was reduced yet further to three; and in 1988 the Criminal Justice Act removed the right altogether.

Blake details how the reductions were precipitated by particular cases.[122] The 1977 restriction followed a case in which a number of youths, mainly black, were tried for causing criminal damage and disorder. The defence used their peremptory challenges to try to achieve a representation of ethnic minorities on the jury, and the youths were acquitted.[123] Prior to the eventual abolition of the peremptory challenge in 1988, concern had arisen about defendants pooling their challenges in multi-defendant trials. One trial in particular, the 'Cyprus Secrets' case, fuelled the campaign for the abolition of peremptory challenges.[124] When eight men in the Royal Air Force were tried for offences under the Official Secrets Act 1911 it was claimed that their counsel agreed amongst themselves to exercise their peremptory challenges to ensure a young male jury. The defendants were all acquitted, but it is questionable whether this was because of the composition of the jury, since the case was weak and there were other reasons why a jury might be sympathetic. In fact, as Blake comments, data on the peremptory challenge were available at the time, based on a study of 2,500 cases, showing that the use of peremptory challenges was not associated with an increased likelihood of acquittal.[125]

The right of the defence to a number of peremptory challenges was clearly intended to provide an opportunity for the defendant to attempt to achieve a more sympathetic jury, and predates the principle that a jury should be selected at random. However, it was discussed by its opponents as if it represented an erosion of the principle of random selection, and as if its use to attempt to achieve a more sympathetic jury amounted to abuse, or an attempt to rig the jury. The Roskill Committee, for example, stated that '[t]he existence of the peremptory right of challenge must necessarily . . . tend to erode the principle of random selection, and may even enable defendants to ensure that a sufficiently large part of a jury is rigged in their favour'.[126]

[122] Blake, *supra* note 108. [123] Ibid., at 147.

[124] The use of the peremptory challenge in the case was discussed in Parliament whilst the 1986 Criminal Justice Bill was on its way through Parliament. 113 Parl. Deb. H.C. (6th ser.) 991–2 (1987) For further details see Michael Zander, *A Matter of Justice: The Legal System in Ferment* (1988) 217–19.

[125] J. Vennard and D. Riley, 'The Use of Peremptory Challenge and Stand By of Jurors and their Relationship to Trial Outcome' [1988] *Crim. L. Rev.* 731.

[126] Roskill Committee, *supra* note 21, at 126.

One serious consequence of the abolition of the peremptory challenge is that a potential means of ensuring a racial mix on juries was lost. Even a jury representative of the adult population may contain few or no jurors of the same race as the defendant. In 1989 the Court of Appeal in *R.* v. *Ford* held that there is no principle that a jury should be racially balanced, that race should not be taken into account in selecting jurors, and that the trial judge had no power to interfere with the composition of the jury to achieve a multi-racial jury.[127] To do so, it was held, would interfere with both the random selection of jurors and the responsibility of the Lord Chancellor's Department to summon jurors; and such a power would have to be granted by statute.[128] The Runciman Commission agreed with this position in most cases, but put forward a limited proposal for ensuring that a jury includes at least three members from the same ethnic group as the defendant in exceptional cases.[129] The Commission for Racial Equality has continued to press for special procedures in cases with a racial dimension, and where the defendant from an ethnic minority believes an all-white jury is unlikely to give him or her a fair trial.[130] As Bailey and Gunn state, '[s]imply relying upon random selection, and failing to address real concerns about jury composition is not likely to satisfy the deep concerns held about the criminal justice system by many people from an ethnic minority'.[131]

Even though the right to challenge for cause remains, it is normally an empty right for the defence, since the challenging party must adduce *prima facie* evidence to support the challenge before the juror may be questioned about his or her suitability. The defence has practically no information on which to base such a challenge, and no right to ask potential members of the jury exploratory questions about their backgrounds or attitudes with a view to showing that they should not be on the jury. Not surprisingly, challenges for cause are generally believed to be rare, although statistics are not available.

The right to ask questions of prospective jurors was severely restricted after the so-called Angry Brigade Trial in 1972 which involved charges

[127] *R.* v. *Ford* [1989] 3 All E.R. 445. The defendant was charged with six offences relating to unlawful use of a motor car. His counsel applied to the judge for a multi-racial jury, but the application was refused. The defendant was convicted and appealed.

[128] Ibid., at 447.

[129] Runciman Commission, *supra* note 20, at 133–4. The Commission gives as an example of such a case one in which 'black people [are] accused of violence against a member of an extremist organisation who they said had been making racial taunts against them and their friends'.

[130] Ibid., at 133.

[131] Bailey and Gunn, *supra* note 5, at 893.

arising from, amongst other things, bombings of the houses of Members of Parliament. The trial judge agreed to ask jurors to exclude themselves on a number of grounds, including if they had relatives serving in Northern Ireland or in the police force, or if they were members of the Conservative Party. A large number of jurors were questioned and challenged, and a total of thirty-nine were removed.[132] Shortly after the case the Lord Chief Justice issued a Practice Note designed to stop questions about such matters.[133] Jurors' occupations used to be available, but that too was stopped in 1973 because the Lord Chancellor decided there was evidence of 'abuse' by the defence, who were making use of the information in deciding to exercise peremptory challenges in cases with political overtones.[134]

The Roskill Committee wrote of the peremptory challenge as an erosion of the principle of random selection, and was particularly critical of its use with reference only to superficial appearance such as dress or the carrying of a particular newspaper.[135] Yet it was not in favour of providing the defence with fuller information. The Committee conceded that if the right to peremptory challenge were abolished there would be a case for returning to the practice of including jurors' occupations; but 'beyond this we do not think that any further disclosure of information about prospective jurors need be made available to the defence as of right'.[136] The Committee referred to worries that abolition of the right of peremptory challenge might lead to increased use of the challenge for cause, which in turn might lead to 'the kind of protracted proceedings which sometimes take place in the United States—the so-called voir dire'.[137]

In some circumstances not even the names of jurors will be known. The standard procedure is that the clerk of the court invites members

[132] See Zander, *supra* note 124, at 223.

[133] Practice Note [1973] 1 All E.R. 240 (stating that it was 'contrary to established practice for jurors to be excluded on . . . general grounds such as race, religion or political beliefs or occupation'). The specific practice note has been superseded, but the practice remains not to allow such questions.

[134] Practice Direction (1973) 57 Crim. App. R. 345.

[135] Roskill Committee, *supra* note 21 at 129.

[136] Ibid., at 129.

[137] The Committee was confident that: 'no such practice would ever be entertained by the judiciary in this country . . . we would expect judges to continue to be firm and adhere to well-established principles in carrying out their statutory duty of determining the propriety of a challenge for cause and of following the well established practice of not permitting such a challenge . . . without the prima facie evidence referred to above'. Ibid., at 128–9.

of the jury in waiting to answer to their names, calls out the name of each juror selected by ballot, and then explains that any challenge is to be made after the names are called. However, the Court of Appeal has held that there is no objection to the withholding of jurors' names if it is thought desirable to do so in order to prevent a jury being 'nobbled', provided that the defendant's right of challenge is preserved.[138] In this drugs-related case, after the first jury had been discharged, a second group of jurors was called to the jury box only by numbers allocated to them by the court clerk, sworn in, and given police protection.[139]

VII. Stand-By for the Prosecution and Jury Vetting

The now defunct defence right of peremptory challenge is paralleled by the prosecution right to stand a juror by. The technique of standing by for the Crown was developed when the Crown's right to challenge peremptorily was abolished in 1305 due to concern about the prosecution stacking juries.[140] The effect of standing a juror by is to remove him or her without showing cause. There is no limit on the number who may be stood by. The juror goes back into the pool and may in theory be called again if the pool runs out. The prosecution can thus defer having to show cause until the pool is exhausted. It was widely expected that prosecution's right to stand a juror by would be removed with the peremptory challenge, but that did not happen. The government argued that the right was being used sparingly in practice, and that in the absence of evidence of improper use there was no need to abolish it.[141] The Attorney General did, however, issue a new set of guidelines on the use by the prosecution of the right of stand by following the abolition of the peremptory challenge in 1988,[142] which state that it should only be used on the basis of clearly defined and restrictive criteria, either under vetting procedures (see below) or where the juror is 'manifestly unsuitable'—for example where a juror for a complex case is illiterate.[143]

[138] *R.* v. *Comerford* [1998] 1 W.L.R. 191, 198–9. The Court of Appeal held that s. 12(3) of the Juries Act 1974 did not contain a mandatory requirement that names be called, as the purpose of that provision was to define the time at which a challenge was to be made. Ibid., at 200.

[139] Ibid., at 194.

[140] See Bailey and Gunn, *supra* note 5, at 899.

[141] Ibid.

[142] 'Attorney-General's Guidelines on the Exercise by the Crown of its Right of Stand By' (1989) 88 Cr. App. R. 123, 123–4.

[143] Ibid., para. 5b.

In addition, the prosecution may have access to information on jurors obtained by the police or security services for purposes of jury vetting.[144] It has long been known that vetting takes place at least occasionally. In 1978, in response to public pressure, the Attorney-General revealed the guidelines, which were amended in 1986 and 1989.[145] The guidelines allow that the panel of jurors may be investigated in cases involving national security where some evidence may be held *in camera*, and terrorist cases. It is up to the Director of Public Prosecutions to authorize vetting in such cases. In addition, guidelines laid down by the Association of Chief Police Officers (ACPO) permit the police to undertake jury vetting, for example where it is suspected that a juror is disqualified, or where jury nobbling is thought likely. Jurors rejected as a result of vetting are stood by, which means that no reason is given publicly. The clandestine way in which jury vetting has been conducted causes great concern. In *R.* v. *McCann* it was argued that jury vetting is unconstitutional and contrary to the principle of random selection, but the arguments were rejected.[146] Robertson suggests that vetting may be challengeable under Article 6 of the European Convention on Human Rights, which guarantees the right to a fair trial, since availability of information about jurors to the prosecution but not the defence breaches the principle of 'equality of arms' between prosecution and defence.[147]

VIII. The Experience of Being a Juror

Discussion of juries in England has tended to neglect the perspective of the juror, but it is recognized that serving on a jury can have a powerful emotional and psychological impact. The impact was explored in a BBC television documentary broadcast in 1997, in which jurors who had served on a number of murder cases spoke of long-term psychological problems resulting from the experience.[148] Stressful experiences described by them included exposure to horrific evidence and, in some cases, intimidation. Some had lingering doubts about the wisdom of the outcome.

The government has begun to acknowledge that jury service can have lasting effects. At the close of the 1995 Rosemary West murder trial, the

[144] See Archbold (2000) 4-212–4-218.

[145] The 1989 version of the Attorney-General's guidelines are found in (1989) 88 Cr. App. R. 123, at 124.

[146] (1991) 92 Cr. App. R. 239.

[147] Robertson, *supra* note 5 at 359. Since Robertson wrote, the Human Rights Act 1998 IV, E incorporates Art. 6.

[148] *Modern Times* (BBC 2, 16 Apr. 1997).

Lord Chancellor's Department offered counselling to the jurors to deal with their distress. The case had exposed jurors to particularly horrific and graphic details of the murders of a number of young women. The jurors were given the opportunity to make use of a free telephone help line, consult family doctors, or come together for a group session with the Department's own welfare officers.[149] Since the *West* case, court-appointed welfare officers have been made available to speak to jurors if they request it, or in cases deemed exceptional by judges.

It is also said that jury trials are time-consuming and in some cases boring for jurors.[150] In a generally positive account of his own experience of serving on a jury in a long running case at the Old Bailey, the journalist Trevor Grove illustrates many jurors' concerns, such as the emotional impact of distressing evidence, the strain of giving the verdict, the tedium of frequent delays and periods of inactivity, and the sense of exclusion that comes from being repeatedly sent out of the courtroom so that matters can be discussed in the jury's absence.[151]

IX. Juries and Pre-Trial Publicity

The English approach to pre-trial publicity contrasts with the approach in the United States, where a high degree of publicity is tolerated before and during jury trials in the interests of freedom of the press. In England it is increasingly likely that the press will be restrained to protect the defendant from the possible effects of publicity on jury decision-making. The press may even be prevented from reporting court proceedings after the trial is over for fear of prejudicing a future trial. Prejudicial publicity is dealt with in two main ways. Under the provisions of the Contempt of Court Act 1981, the media are quite frequently barred from, and occasionally prosecuted for, publishing prejudicial material before or during a trial; and under its abuse of process jurisdiction, the court has the power to stay criminal proceedings on the ground that a fair trial has become impossible.[152] Vidmar argues that the use of the provisions of the

[149] D. Cohn, 'Counselling for Counsel', *The Times*, 2 Jan. 1996, at 29.

[150] Hedley Goldberg comments 'It has been said that the most interesting thing that can happen to a juror during a trial is being allowed to sit in a different chair'. H. Goldberg, 'A Random Choice of Jury?' *The Times*, 13 June 1995, at 41.

[151] T. Grove, *supra* note 114.

[152] For discussion see D. Corker and M. Levi, 'Pre-trial Publicity and its Treatment in the English Courts' [1996] *Crim. L. Rev.* 622. On the Contempt of Court Act see S. Bailey, 'The Contempt of Court Act 1981' (1982) *45 Mod. L. Rev.* 301. On abuse of process jurisdiction in this situation see Archbold (2000) 4–73.

Contempt of Court Act in England (including the prohibitions on talking to jurors), together with increasing use of the power to stay proceedings, place England and the United States at opposite ends of a continuum where the protection of jury trials from the media is concerned.[153]

Regarding prosecutions under the Contempt of Court Act, Corker and Levi argue that there is a lacuna in the law which severely limits the ability of the Attorney-General to regulate and deter press coverage. For a prosecution to succeed it must be shown that a particular article or broadcast has created a substantial risk of prejudice. However, in practice the effect is often cumulative, involving a number of editors, newspaper articles, or broadcasts over a period of time. They argue that this weakness in the law forces responsibility for dealing with prejudicial publicity onto the trial judge, who can influence coverage only after the trial has started.[154]

Until the 1990s, stays of proceedings on the ground of pre-trial publicity were rare, and jurors were treated as capable of following the judge's instructions to avoid prejudice.[155] But Corker and Levi identify a marked change since then, with a growing case law recognizing that publicity can cause substantial prejudice, and a corresponding willingness on the part of the courts to intervene. In several cases in the early 1990s proceedings were halted or convictions overturned in part on the basis that pre-trial publicity made or would make a fair trial impossible.[156] In *R.* v. *McCann* the Court of Appeal overturned the conviction of alleged Irish terrorists because the trial judge did not discharge the jury following a sudden wave of publicity in the closing stages of the case.[157] The defendants had exercised their right to remain silent under police questioning, and shortly before the jury retired to consider its verdict both Tom King (then Secretary of State for Northern Ireland) and the former Master of the Rolls Lord Denning made widely-publicized statements in television interviews suggesting that people who refused to answer police questions were probably guilty.[158] The Court of Appeal stated that 'we are left with a definite impression that the impact which the statements in the television interviews may well have had on the fairness of the trial could not be overcome by any direction to the jury'.[159] Another

[153] N. Vidmar, 'The Canadian Criminal Jury: Searching for a Middle Ground', this vol.

[154] Corker and Levi, *supra* note 152, 628–30.

[155] Corker and Levi (ibid., at 625) quote, for example, Taylor CJ in *Ex parte The Telegraph Plc* [1993] 1 W.L.R. 980, 987.

[156] Corker and Levi, *supra* note 152, at 624.

[157] (1991) 92 Crim. App. R. 239.

[158] Ibid., at 249–50.

[159] Ibid., at 253.

example is the prosecution of detectives responsible for investigating the bombing of two Birmingham public houses in 1974, for which the Birmingham Six were wrongfully convicted. The trial judge controversially ruled that the effect of pre-trial publicity damaging to the detectives was irremediable.[160] In a further case in 1995, following the arrest of a soap opera star and her partner for having oral sex in their car while parked on the exit lane of a motorway, a stay of proceedings was ordered when a number of newspapers published details of the man's previous criminal convictions and incidents involving the police that would have been inadmissible at trial. In ordering the stay the trial judge stated 'I have absolutely no doubt that the massive media publicity in this case was unfair, outrageous and oppressive'.[161]

In the *Maxwell* case an application for a stay of proceedings was not granted, but, as Corker and Levi describe, the judge took a number of other steps to deal with prejudicial publicity.[162] In England it is unusual for the selection of jurors to include screening for their contact with prejudicial pre-trial publicity, but potential jurors in the *Maxwell* case were screened for what they had read or heard about the case in the media, and the judge ordered that a transcript of his warning to editors to refrain from future prejudicial publicity be widely distributed. Unlike US and Canadian courts, English courts are generally resistant to expert testimony on the effects of publicity on jury decision-making. When Maxwell applied for a stay of proceedings on the ground of prejudicial pre-trial publicity, three Gallup opinion polls were submitted as evidence to Phillips J. In rejecting the application for a stay, Phillips J. found such evidence of little use and expressed the hope that 'their use in this case will not be taken as a precedent in the future'.[163] Nonetheless, when it came to jury selection he permitted Kevin Maxwell to give opinion poll evidence on the depth of prejudice against him, and he permitted screening of jurors despite the general preference in England for retaining a randomly selected jury as far as possible.

X. Evidence and Instructions Heard by the Jury

As in other jurisdictions, there are many rules limiting the evidence that English jurors may hear, and requiring judges to give them particular instructions. The rules are often implicitly based on assumptions about

[160] Corker and Levi, *supra* note 152, at 627. [161] Ibid., at 628.
[162] See ibid., at 628–31. [163] Ibid., at 614 n.45.

the limits to jury competence and the likelihood that juries will be unduly prejudiced by certain types of evidence. The courts have established, for example, that juries should be warned that several impressive and truthful identification witnesses can be in error, a jury instruction referred to as the 'Turnbull direction'.[164] Evidence of the defendant's previous convictions is generally excluded unless there are specific reasons to allow it.[165]

On the other hand, the jury in England is charged with deciding questions that in other jurisdictions are considered matters for experts. Under the rule set out by the Court of Appeal in *R.* v. *Turner*,[166] expert evidence is not admissible if it is 'within the common knowledge and experience of jurors'.[167] As a result, the scope for expert evidence from psychologists and psychiatrists in England is very much more limited than in the United States. The reliability of witness testimony, for example, is considered a matter of common sense, and expert evidence from psychologists is not normally admitted on this question.[168] The rule has particularly restricted expert psychiatric evidence. In *Turner* Lawton LJ expressed the view that '[j]urors do not need psychiatrists to tell them how ordinary folk who are not suffering from any mental illness are likely to react to the stresses and strains of life'.[169] While specific rules and practices have become established in relation to some categories of evidence, it is for the individual judge to decide whether expert evidence will be admitted and what comment on it, if any, he or she will make. Gatowski *et al.* characterize the approach of the English courts as based on a test of 'relevancy and helpfulness'. The judge considers whether the probative value of evidence outweighs any prejudicial effects, and whether it is outside jurors' common knowledge .[170]

One type of evidence that has given rise to controversy is evidence of

[164] *R.* v. *Turnbull* [1977] Q.B. 224.

[165] For an account of the current law see Law Comm'n, *Evidence in Criminal Proceedings: Previous Misconduct of a Defendant* (Consultation Paper No. 141, 1995).

[166] [1975] Q.B. 834. [167] Ibid., at 841.

[168] G. Gudjonsson, 'Psychological Evidence in Court' (1996) 9 *Psychologist* 213.

[169] [1975] Q.B. at 841. For further discussion of expert evidence from psychology and psychiatry see R. D. Mackay and A. M. Colman, 'Equivocal Rulings on Expert Psychological and Psychiatric Evidence: Turning a Muddle into a Nonsense' [1996] *Crim. L. Rev.* 88.

[170] S. Gatowski *et al.*, 'The Diffusion of Scientific Evidence: A Comparative Analysis of Admissibility Standards in Australia, Canada, England and the United States and Their Impact on Social and Behavioural Sciences' [1996] *Expert Evidence* 86–92. See also D. Carson, 'Expert Evidence in the Courts' [1992] *Expert Evidence* 3; D. Carson 'Some Legal Issues Affecting Novel Forms of Expert Evidence', ibid., 79.

previous convictions for similar offences in cases of sexual abuse of children. There has been a growing sense that the current exclusionary rules may favour the defendant too much. However, research conducted for the Home Office indicates that caution about allowing such evidence to go to a jury is well founded.[171] In a simulation study, evidence of a previous conviction for indecently assaulting a child appeared to be particularly prejudicial. The study also showed the dangers of making assumptions about jury bias. Some of the findings were unexpected, and indicated that revealing a previous conviction for an offence dissimilar to the one currently charged may actually be favourable to the defendant. The research also confirmed earlier findings[172] that instructions from the judge to use the information to decide propensity rather than credibility are likely to be totally ineffective.

The defendant's right of silence is another area where rules favourable to the defendant have come under attack. The right clearly has considerable symbolic significance, though its actual effects are unclear. As the result of a change introduced in the Criminal Justice and Public Order Act 1994, a jury can now be told that it may draw adverse inferences from a defendant's refusal to answer questions in police custody, or from the fact that a defendant chooses not to testify in his or her own defence.[173] The change was justified on the ground that professional or hardened criminals were taking advantage of the right of silence and avoiding conviction, although the available research evidence did not support this claim.[174] The effects of the change and the new instructions on juries' decisions are as yet unknown.

Although the judge has considerable discretion, his or her directions to the jury are likely to be based very closely on specimen directions prepared by the Judicial Studies Board.[175] Using the specimen directions minimizes the likelihood of an appeal. The judge's summing up will nor-

[171] Law Comm'n., *supra* note 165, app. D: The Oxford Study. A final report from the Law Commission on the law relating to evidence of previous misconduct is imminent at the time of writing.

[172] R. Wissler and M. Saks, 'On the Inefficacy of Limiting Instructions' (1986) 9 *Law and Hum. Behav.* 37.

[173] Criminal Justice and Public Order Act 1994 ss. 34–35. These sections deal with the inferences a jury could reasonably draw from a defendant's failure to answer questions when interviewed, and failure to give evidence. Recommendations on the essential points to be included in a judge's direction were made by the Court of Appeal in *R.* v. *Cowan* [1996] Q.B. 373.

[174] See D. Dixon, *Law in Policing: Legal Regulation and Police Practices* (1997) 229–30.

[175] The specimen directions are not officially recognized, but in practice their existence and use have been openly acknowledged and indeed encouraged by senior judges. See R. Munday, 'The Bench Books: Can the Judiciary Keep a Secret?' [1996] *Crim. L. Rev.* 296.

mally include directions as to the respective tasks of judge and jury; the burden and standard of proof; and the definition of the offence or offences charged and the facts that must be proved. Directions may include, for example, the legal definition of 'intention' or 'knowing or believing', or a direction that some questions, such as whether there was indecency or dishonesty, are for the jury to answer on the basis of their ordinary common sense. The judge may also warn the jury to exercise caution in using certain types of evidence, such as evidence of confessions to the police, previous convictions, or identification.[176]

Researchers conducting the 1993 Crown Court Study had the unusual opportunity to ask jurors in a large number of criminal cases to complete questionnaires. The jurors were asked whether they had any difficulty understanding and remembering the evidence, including scientific evidence, and following the judge's instructions. Most jurors thought they had no great problems. To every question on these matters, more than 90 per cent answered that it had been 'not at all' or 'not very' difficult.[177] As the researchers rightly stress, the fact that jurors report that they think they understood evidence and instructions does not prove they actually did understand them.[178] People are not always very good at describing how well they remember facts and how they make decisions. As with the research on judges' summing up outlined below, which was conducted as part of the same study, the restrictions in section 8 of the Contempt of Court Act 1981 meant that jurors' replies could not be related to other information about the cases.

Jurors may take notes and ask questions during the trial if they wish, although they rarely do so.[179] After retiring to deliberate they may send out questions, but they cannot be provided with any new evidence at this stage. In the Crown Court Study, 32 per cent of jurors said that one or more jurors in their case had wanted to ask the judge for further directions after they had retired to consider their verdict. However, in 27 per cent of cases the question had not in fact been put, often because the jurors had not realized they could do so.[180]

[176] See e.g. Bailey and Gunn, *supra* note 5, at 881–6.

[177] Zander and Henderson, *supra* note 72, at 206, 216–17. The questioning of jurors was conducted within the constraints of the Contempt of Court Act 1981 s. 8.

[178] Ibid., at 205.

[179] The procedure for asking questions (or indeed for making any kind of request of the judge such as asking for a break) is for the juror to write it down and catch the attention of an usher who will pass the note to the judge. There may of course be reasons why the question a juror wants to ask cannot be put to a witness.

[180] Zander and Henderson, *supra* note 72, at 214. It is a little difficult to distinguish jurors from cases in these data.

XI. The Influence of the Judge

Hints from the judge are likely to be a powerful influence on jury verdicts.[181] The last stage of the trial before the jury retires is a summing up from the judge, which will include a summary of the evidence as well as directions on matters of law. The judge has considerable latitude to let the jury know his or her view of the evidence, and the summing up often lasts several hours. An extreme example of a biased summing up by the judge is that given in the case of David Bentley in 1953. In July 1998, Bingham LCJ overturned Bentley's conviction for murder after more than forty years of campaigning by Bentley's family. Lord Bingham heavily criticized the summing up at the original trial by Lord Goddard (then Lord Chief Justice), which, he said, gave the jury little choice but to convict and deprived Bentley of his birthright as a British citizen, a fair trial.[182] The wide scope for English judges to comment on evidence and witnesses during the summing up contrasts markedly with the restricted scope allowed to judges in the United States where, in most courts, interpreting the evidence is the sole responsibility of the jury. [183] The contrast was apparent in the 1997 case of the British *au pair* Louise Woodward, who was convicted in a Massachusetts court of murdering a child in her care.[184] The judge did not comment on the evidence, but gave only the customary directions on the law. The contrast with the practice in England gave rise to discussion in the British newspapers.[185]

The 1993 Crown Court Study explored jurors' views about the judges' summing up in a sample of more than 800 Crown Court cases.[186] Nearly half the jurors surveyed did not think their task would have been any more difficult if the judge had not summed up on the facts. However, 19 per cent said it would have made their task 'much harder'. Not surprisingly, the longer the case, the more likely jurors were to say the

[181] See e.g. Z. Bankowski, 'The Jury and Reality', in *The Jury Under Attack*, *supra* note 30, at 8–26.

[182] *R.* v. *Bentley* [1998] T.L.R. 492.

[183] In US federal courts and in some state courts the judge has the legal authority to comment on the evidence. But this power is rarely exercised, and then only under limited conditions.

[184] The conviction was reduced by the judge to one for manslaughter. The decision was appealed by both the prosecution and the defence; the result was affirmed. See *Commonwealth* v. *Woodward*, 694 N.E.2d 1277 (Mass.1998), aff'g *Commonwealth* v. *Woodward*, No.Crim. 97-0433, 1997 WL 694119 (Mass. Super. Ct., 10 Nov. 1997).

[185] e.g. F. Gibb, 'Trial Exposes Worst Traits of US Justice', *The Times*, 31 Oct. 1997 at 4.

[186] Zander and Henderson, *supra* note 72, 214–19, 249.

judge's summing up on the facts was useful.[187] Remarkably few jurors (just over 6 per cent) reported finding the judge's directions on the law difficult,[188] though of course we do not know whether their perceptions were accurate.

The extent to which jurors are swayed by comments or hints from the judge has proved difficult to study, but the Crown Court Study provides some intriguing findings. The samples of jurors were asked whether they thought the judge's summing up pointed towards conviction or acquittal, and to what extent they felt any 'tilt' was justified by the evidence.[189] The results were complex. Thirty-three per cent of jurors said the summing up was 'tilted' towards either conviction or acquittal—almost exactly equally often in each direction.[190] The tilt in the summing up was, as expected, very closely associated with the result of the case, but there were cases in which the jury acquitted even though the judge was perceived as summing up for conviction. Thus, 9 per cent of jurors who viewed the summing up as pro-conviction reported that the jury had nonetheless acquitted. Of those viewing the summing up as 'somewhat' for conviction, 13 per cent reported that the jury acquitted.[191] This suggests that juries are capable of resisting the influence of the judge if they disagree with his or her view. However, other results showed sometimes juries acquitted or convicted against what they saw as the weight of the evidence, because of the way the judge had summed up.[192] It is important to bear in mind that when it comes down to these subgroups the numbers of cases are quite small. In addition, the research was hampered by the provisions of the Contempt of Court Act 1981, which prevented the jurors' answers to questions from being directly related to other information the researchers had collected about the cases. Relaxation of these restrictions would allow much more informative research to be conducted.

[187] Ibid., at 214–15. [188] Ibid., at 216. [189] Ibid., at 217–18.

[190] Ibid., at 218. 16% said that it pointed slightly or strongly to acquittal, and 16% that it pointed slightly or strongly to conviction. Where they felt it had been tilted one way or the other, 88% thought the tilt was supported by the weight of the evidence. Ibid.

[191] Ibid., at 219. Note that these results are for individual jurors reporting their views of the summing up and their recall of the verdict.

[192] Using a score of average juror responses, the researchers conclude that when the judge was said to have summed up for an acquittal 'against the weight of the evidence' the judge directed an acquittal in four cases and the jury acquitted in the other nine. By the same averaging measure, they conclude that when the judge was said to have summed up for a conviction 'against the weight of the evidence', the jury acquitted in four cases, but convicted in four, and in the remaining four cases convicted on some charges.

XII. The Verdict

For centuries juries' verdicts in England had to be unanimous, and this rule was widely adopted for juries in other countries. However, in England the requirement of a unanimous verdict was dropped by the Criminal Justice Act 1967, which introduced majority verdicts of ten to two.[193] Juries are now initially instructed by the judge that they must seek a unanimous verdict, but that 'a time may come' when a majority verdict will be permissible, at which point they will receive further directions. Juries must try for at least two hours to reach a unanimous verdict. Statistics for 1998 show that 20 per cent of convictions following a plea of not guilty in the Crown Court were majority verdicts.[194] When the jury delivers its verdict the foreman will be asked in open court whether or not the verdict is unanimous, and, if not, by what majority.

Debate surrounding the change to majority verdicts has again been cast in terms of the tension between crime control and the due process rights of the defendant.[195] According to Sanders and Young, the official rationale for the change was to prevent professional criminals from escaping conviction by intimidating or bribing individual jurors. It has also been argued that majority verdicts allow the views of extremists to be discounted in jury decisions. Critics believe the change was motivated more by a desire to save the expense of retrials, and that it undermines the principle that the prosecution must prove guilt beyond a reasonable doubt.[196] Sanders and Young argue that there is a double standard at work in the argument that a majority verdict can neutralize extremists: as with jury vetting, the government accepts the defects of a random selection procedure when this serves prosecution interests, but not when it serves the interests of the defence.[197] Sanders and Young further argue that it is misleading to draw bare comparisons with the Scottish system, where it is possible to convict on a simple majority of seven out of fifteen, because Scotland has means of safeguarding the defendant that have no parallel in England. For example, in England a defendant can be convicted on the uncorroborated evidence of a single witness, whereas the rules in Scotland require the prosecution evidence to be corroborated.[198] Moreover, if a Scottish jury cannot achieve a majority for conviction the

[193] The governing provision is now the Juries Act 1974, s. 17.

[194] Lord Chancellor's Dep't, *Judicial Statistics*, *supra* note 51, at 66.

[195] Or 'crime control' and 'due process' models of criminal justice processes as developed by Herbert Packer in *The Limits of the Criminal Sanction* (1968).

[196] For discussion of the arguments see Sanders and Young, *supra* note 5, at 361–4.

[197] Ibid., at 363.

[198] See P. Duff, *supra* note 65, 190–4.

defendant is entitled to be acquitted, whereas in England a majority of less than ten out of twelve jurors for acquittal results in a 'hung' jury, and the possibility of a retrial. Sanders and Young suggest that requiring the same majority for acquittal as for conviction is not reconcilable with the presumption of innocence.[199]

XIII. 'Questionable' Verdicts and Jury Nullification

Throughout the centuries of their existence, English juries have been known to acquit in the face of both overwhelming evidence of guilt and a judicial direction indicating conviction. Such acquittals may be unpopular with those seeking a conviction, but they have long been legally justified. In the sedition trial of the Dean of St. Asaph in 1784, Lord Mansfield stated that the jury might follow 'the prejudices of their affections or passions'. The judge might direct the jury how to reach the right legal answer, but the jury had it in their power to do wrong 'which is a matter entirely between God and their own conscience'.[200]

The right of juries to decide according to conscience and refuse to apply the law is essential to the democratic role claimed for the jury. As Roy Amlot writes, 'Parliament enacts and a powerful government with a strong whip may enact harsh laws. But no jury can be forced to implement what it considers to be a harsh law. In this way a jury plays a vital part in the democratic process.'[201] Various categories of 'jury nullification' can be distinguished.[202] In some cases it appears that juries are objecting, not to the law itself, but to its application in a particular case, especially where individuals have taken a stand against government. A prime example is the jury's refusal to apply section 2 of the Official Secrets Act 1911 in the *Ponting* case, discussed above. In another well-known case, Pottle and Randle were acquitted in 1991 of their part in the escape of the traitor George Blake from Wormwood Scrubs prison in 1966, in spite of a published admission in their book subtitled *How We Freed George Blake—And Why*.[203] In another example, in August 1996,

[199] Sanders and Young, *supra* note 5, at 363.

[200] *R.* v. *Shipley*, 99 Eng. Rep. 774, 820–4 (1784). For discussion of the case see P. Devlin, 'The Judge and the Jury I: The Power without the Right', *The Judge* (1981) 118–35.

[201] Amlot, *supra* note 18, at 42.

[202] See N. S. Marder, 'The Myth of the Nullifying Jury' (June 1998), draft paper presented at the Annual Meeting of the Law and Society Association in Aspen, Colorado.

[203] For discussion of the *Pottle and Randle* case, see S. Jolly, 'Images and Ideologies of the Jury' (1995), draft paper presented at the Annual Meeting of the Law and Society Association in Toronto, Canada.

four women were acquitted of damaging a British Aerospace Hawk jet in protest against their sale to third world regimes.[204]

In other cases, juries may be refusing to apply what they see as bad law. For instance, the legal definition of murder in England does not require an intention to kill. In a case heard before Lord Goff the jury appeared to reject this definition of murder.[205] The defendant had rammed a jagged glass into his victim's face and severed the man's jugular vein. The defendant did not intend to kill him, and indeed was horrified at his victim's death. However, he clearly did intend to cause 'really serious harm' which was sufficient *mens rea* for murder.[206] The jury, despite being directed to that effect, acquitted him of murder. According to Lord Goff, the jurors could not bring themselves to call him a murderer—a position with which Lord Goff himself entirely sympathized. In other instances juries may be protesting about something other than a specific law, such as racism, poverty, or police misconduct.

Instances of deliberate jury nullification would seem to be different in kind from cases where the jury appears simply to have got it wrong. It is important to remember that the impact of a doubtful acquittal on the victim of the crime in question can be devastating. Cornish writes that 'what appears at first glance to be lay common sense may well on closer scrutiny prove to be undeserved sympathy or bigoted obtuseness'.[207] However, it is not always possible to distinguish clearly between verdicts where a jury is using its power to decide in defiance of the law or government and verdicts where the jury has been confused or incompetent or prejudiced. As Bankowski points out, the notion that a verdict can be 'wrong' or 'perverse' is premised on a particular view of the nature of truth and jury trials.[208] 'A perverse verdict' may mean little more than 'a verdict I disagree with'. Baldwin and McConville's study of the Birmingham Crown Court in the 1970s revealed a lack of consensus amongst those involved in trials as to what constitutes a questionable verdict.[209] Adopting a method similar to that used by

[204] See 'Jury Out on Trial Research: Recent Verdicts Have Sparked Concern Says Robert Rice', *Financial Times*, 6 Aug. 1996, at 22.

[205] R. Goff, 'The Mental Element in the Crime of Murder' (1988) 104 *Law Q. Rev.* 30.

[206] See the guidance given by the House of Lords in *R.* v. *Nedrick* [1986] 1 W.L.R. 1025, 1028. The direction to be given a jury on the *mens rea* required to establish murder remains unsettled despite a series of House of Lords decisions since the 1960s, and was considered again by the House of Lords in *R.* v. *Woollin* [1998] 4 All E.R. 103.

[207] Cornish, *supra* note 5, at 254.

[208] See e.g. Bankowski, *supra* note 181.

[209] Baldwin and McConville, *supra* note 105.

Kalven and Zeisel,[210] they asked judges, lawyers, and police involved in jury trials for their opinions on the juries' verdicts, both acquittals and convictions. A clear pattern emerged in acquittals. Those involved on the defence side tended to see the acquittals as justified, while those involved on the prosecution side tended to see the acquittals as questionable. Acquittals were seen as fully justified 83 per cent of the time by defence solicitors, compared with 65 per cent by prosecuting solicitors, and 48 per cent by the police. The defence solicitor only expressed 'serious doubts' about 10 per cent of acquittals, while the prosecuting solicitor expressed 'serious doubts' in 26 per cent of acquittals and the police in 44 per cent.[211]

Not surprisingly, the pattern was reversed in cases of doubtful conviction, with prosecuting solicitors doubting the convictions least often and defence solicitors doubting them most often. Surprisingly, however, the police expressed more doubts than all other respondents about convictions as well as acquittals, suggesting an overall scepticism of jury verdicts. Although questionable verdicts may be either acquittals or convictions, the consequences of doubtful convictions can clearly be much more serious and may result in a deprivation of liberty. Baldwin and McConville observed that little research had been done on the question of doubtful jury convictions,[212] and that remains true today.

XIV. Conclusion

The jury may be one of the most venerated institutions in the English legal system, but it is proving vulnerable to attack. The right to trial by jury was steadily eroded throughout the twentieth century, from the virtual abolition of jury trial in civil cases to the removal of the option of jury trial in a large number of criminal cases. Increasingly serious criminal offences are being tried before benches of lay magistrates which is, as McBarnet puts it, 'a different brand of justice altogether'.[213] Several writers cited in this chapter have expressed disquiet at the jury's relentless decline.[214] The trend looks set to continue. The Labour Government

[210] H. Kalven Jr. and H. Zeisel, *The American Jury* (1996) 10.

[211] Baldwin and McConville, *supra* note 105, at 46.

[212] Ibid., at 68–9.

[213] D. J. McBarnet, *Conviction: Law, the State and the Construction of Justice* (1979) 122.

[214] e.g. Devlin, *supra* note 3; Devlin, *supra* note 200; Freeman, *supra* note 4; Findlay and Duff, *supra* note 30. In a lecture in 1979 Sir Patrick Devlin warned that 'if we lose the jury in the twentieth century we shall not be given it back in the twenty-second'. P. Devlin, *supra* note 200, 176.

is pressing ahead with legislation to remove the defendant's right to insist on jury trial in either way cases, and is looking at proposals to limit the role of juries in fraud trials.

Jury trials are undeniably more costly and time-consuming than trials in magistrates' courts, but many of the other criticisms made of juries and arguments for limiting jury trial are much more questionable. Arguments both for and against the jury quickly become entangled in ideology and metaphor, the politics of crime control and efficiency, and the rhetoric of justice and liberty. Justifications put forward for change often include claims that jury trial tends to favour the defendant, but these claims have frequently been based on no more than anecdote and have sometimes run counter to the evidence available. There was no reliable evidence, for example, that the right of silence was being abused by professional criminals, nor that the peremptory challenge was leading to acquittals by stacked juries. It is by no means clear that juries acquit in serious fraud cases because they cannot understand complex evidence. There is no systematic evidence that most defendants who elect jury trial do so for unjustifiable reasons, and the benefits of abolishing the right to jury trial in either way cases are uncertain.

To seek sound justification for reform in terms of the jury's rationality, competence, or efficiency may be to miss the point. Many commentators have stressed the importance of understanding the jury in terms of politics and the organization of power.[215] Brown and Leal write, for example, that several centuries ago:

> jury trial became an element in the historical struggle between a judiciary claiming pre-parliamentary, constitutional authority grounded in the Magna Carta and parliament exercising its prerogative to create summary jurisdiction by statute. . . .
>
> To the present day . . . governments have not liked them. They rightly thought that juries could not be relied on to convict in certain sorts of cases.[216]

It is ironic that the English jury, having served as a model in many parts of the world, is in a state of continuing decline just as jury trial is being revived in a number of countries. Spain has reintroduced the right to trial by jury in limited cases, and in a number of former communist regimes in Eastern Europe, including Russia, the introduction of jury trials is seen as a move towards the establishment of the rule of law. It

[215] See generally *The Jury Under Attack*, *supra* note 30.

[216] D. Brown and D. Neal, 'Show Trials: The Media and the Gang of Twelve', in ibid. at 126, 129.

remains to be seen whether the decline of the English jury is terminal. In a subset of criminal trials at least, it has so far proved robust, maintaining strong support amongst the general public and many senior members of the legal profession who are well aware of its failings and drawbacks. The jury has great symbolic significance and is still highly prized, not least because it continues to exercise its long-standing right to reach a verdict based on conscience, against the letter of the law, and occasionally in defiance of government.

3 The American Criminal Jury

Nancy Jean King

I. Introduction

The criminal jury, after its importation to North America by English settlers, evolved into a unique institution in the United States. Several prominent features of American law and culture have left their mark on the criminal jury: Americans' distrust of the judiciary, their passion for open procedures and unfettered public discourse about those procedures, their struggle to overcome racial and ethnic injustice, their commitment to adversarial adjudication, and the dual state–federal justice system. This brief exposition will describe the American criminal jury generally, focusing on those aspects of that institution that distinguish it from juries in other parts of the world.

II. The Criminal Jury in the New Nation

It was a highly publicized case from the colonial era, the trial of newspaperman John Peter Zenger, that was credited with 'impress[ing] thousands of Americans with the importance of the right to a jury as a bulwark against official oppression'.[1] In 1734, Zenger was charged by the British Crown with the crime of seditious libel for mocking the Royal Governor, a widely detested man named Cosby, in the *New York Weekly Journal*.[2] Court officials took pains to ensure that the jury pool included supporters of Cosby,[3] but some of the veniremen were of Dutch ancestry and maintained anti-British sentiments.[4] The jury seated included a mariner, a brewer, a vintner, an artisan, a baker, a merchant, a blacksmith, a carpenter, a currier, a tradesman, and a clerk.[5] An aging but renowned lawyer, Andrew Hamilton of Philadelphia, defended

[1] John Guinther, The Jury in America 30 (1988).

[2] See Leonard W. Levy, Emergence of a Free Press 39–40 (1985).

[3] See ibid., at 41 (noting that the original panel, ultimately challenged by lawyers for Zenger, was made up of Cosby appointees and friends).

[4] See Livingston Rutherfurd, John Peter Zenger, His Press, His Trial and a Bibliography of Zenger Imprints 62 (1904).

[5] See James Alexander, A Brief Narrative of the Case and Trial of John Peter Zenger 210 n.56 (1963).

Zenger.[6] Barred by the judge from presenting witnesses who could testify as to the truth of what Zenger had published, Hamilton exhorted the jury, 'it is not the cause of a poor printer, nor of New York alone, which you are now trying. No! It may in its consequence affect every freeman that lives under a British government on the main of America. It is the best cause. It is the cause of liberty.'[7] The jury acquitted Zenger, he was released, and news of the trial spread throughout the colonies and to England.[8]

Thirty years later, the British prosecuted American colonists for revenue violations in admiralty courts without juries, rather than in common pleas courts where juries could have acquitted and thus freed protesters. Trials for treason were to be conducted in England, removing them entirely from the scrutiny or participation of colonists.[9] These practices helped to precipitate the American Revolution;[10] Thomas Jefferson stated in the *Declaration of Independence* that one of the reasons requiring separation from England was Britain's conduct 'depriving us, in many cases, of the benefits of Trial by Jury'.[11] Even before the *Declaration*, each of the twelve states that had adopted a written constitution had included the right of the accused to a jury trial—'the only right that these twelve constitutions declared unanimously'.[12]

Not surprisingly, Article III of the Constitution of the United States, the document establishing and limiting the power of the federal government, also guarantees the right to a jury trial. It provides that '[t]he Trial of all Crimes, except in the Cases of Impeachment, shall be by Jury; and such Trial shall be held in the State where the said Crimes shall have been committed'.[13] But this assurance was not specific enough for some who feared federal tyranny. Patrick Henry, for example, argued

[6] See Levy, *supra* note 2, at 41. [7] Ibid., at 42–3.

[8] See ibid., at 44; Albert W. Alschuler & Andrew G. Deiss, *A Brief History of the Criminal Jury in the United States*, 61 U. Chi. L. Rev. 867, 874 (1994) ('In the half-century between Zenger's trial and the ratification of the Sixth Amendment [a pamphlet account of the trial] was reprinted fourteen times. More than any formal law book, it became the American primer on the role and duties of jurors.').

[9] See Alschuler & Deiss, *supra* note 8, at 875 (citing Edmund Burke, *Letter to the Sheriffs of Brison*, in The Works of the Right Honorable Edmund Burke, ii, 189, 192 (9th ed. 1889)).

[10] See Carl Ubbelohde, The Vice-Admiralty Courts and the American Revolution 209 (1960).

[11] The Declaration of Independence para. 20.

[12] Alschuler & Deiss, *supra* note 8, at 870; see also William Edward Nelson, Americanization of the Common Law: The Impact of Legal Change on Massachusetts Society, 1760–1830, at 96 (1975).

[13] U.S. Const. art. III, § 2, cl. 3.

that by selecting jurors 'from any part of the state', the federal authorities 'can hang anyone they please, by having a jury to suit their purposes'.[14] Others argued that the Constitution should include more particular protections concerning the selection of jurors and the procedures governing their deliberations. Ultimately, however, agreement upon the 'accustomed requisites' of the jury could not be reached because the jury practices among the states were too diverse.[15] The Sixth Amendment provided simply that a person accused of violating federal criminal law receive 'a speedy and public trial by an impartial jury of the State and district wherein the crime shall have been committed, which district shall have been previously ascertained by law'.[16]

III. A Patchwork of Jury Laws: The Laws of the Federal Government, and of the Several States

For nearly two centuries, judges interpreted the jury provisions in Article III and the Sixth Amendment to govern only prosecutions in the courts of the United States for violations of federal criminal law. However, the number and breadth of state crimes dwarfed the meager collection of federal crimes, and only a tiny fraction of all criminal prosecutions took place in federal court. As a result, the United States Constitution did not protect the majority of criminal defendants—those who faced state criminal charges in the courts of the several states. In state court the right to a jury trial depended upon not federal law, but the statutes, constitutional provisions, and common law of that state. Even though every state guaranteed the right to a jury trial for at least some criminal charges, state law differed as to what that right entailed. This patchwork system of justice, with the state and federal courts following separate laws, sometimes resulted in striking differences in jury procedures. It was not until 1968 that the United States Supreme Court declared that the right to jury trial guaranteed by the Sixth Amendment was an element of the 'due process' safeguarded for all state citizens by the Fourteenth Amendment.[17] Thus, every court, state or federal, was bound to provide defendants with at least those fundamental aspects of the jury trial

[14] Francis H. Heller, The Sixth Amendment to the Constitution of the United States: A Study in Constitutional Development 25–6 (1951).

[15] Ibid., at 26–33; see also Drew L. Kershen, *Vicinage*, 29 Okla. L. Rev. 801, 817–44 (1976) (providing a historical account of the debate over vicinage and the Sixth Amendment).

[16] U.S. Const. amend. VI.

[17] See Duncan v. Louisiana, 391 U.S. 145 (1968).

embodied in the Sixth Amendment. The Court explained in *Duncan* v. *Louisiana*:

> The guarantees of jury trial in the Federal and State Constitutions reflect a profound judgment about the way in which law should be enforced and justice administered. . . . Providing an accused with the right to be tried by a jury of his peers gave him an inestimable safeguard against the corrupt or overzealous prosecutor and against the compliant, biased, or eccentric judge. If the defendant preferred the common-sense judgment of a jury to the more tutored but perhaps less sympathetic reaction of the single judge, he was to have it. . . . The deep commitment of the Nation to the right of jury trial in serious criminal cases as a defense against arbitrary law enforcement qualifies for protection under the Due Process Clause of the Fourteenth Amendment, and must therefore be respected by the States.[18]

Since *Duncan*, the Supreme Court has construed the Sixth Amendment to dictate many aspects of the jury trial, such as juror selection procedures and jury size.[19] Yet the Sixth Amendment does not regulate every detail of the criminal jury trial in the United States. Individual state courts and legislatures have considerable room to experiment with different jury procedures consistent with the minimum protections of the Sixth Amendment, and have sometimes expanded upon its guarantees, providing more protection than the United States Constitution requires. The thousands of juries convened each day (over 90 percent of them in state courts)[20] are governed by hundreds of state constitutional provisions, statutes, and court rules of varying complexity and content. Congress, too, has supplied a multitude of statutes and rules governing jury trials in the federal courts, also supplementing the constitutional commands of the Bill of Rights. The federal constitutional declarations of the US Supreme Court, in other words, are only the common core of a much larger body of jury law in the United States which varies significantly from jurisdiction to jurisdiction. A jury trial in California, for example, may be conducted quite differently than a jury trial in Colorado. This state autonomy, particularly in matters of criminal justice, continues to be fiercely defended against federal control. State autonomy has made it possible for states to try out different jury procedures over the years, supplying a rich source of empirical information about

[18] See Duncan v. Louisiana, at 155–6. [19] See *infra* Part IV.

[20] See Bureau of Justice Statistics, Sourcebook of Criminal Justice Statistics 1997, at tbl. 5.16 (1998) (noting that in 1995, there were approximately 3,150 felony jury trials in federal court); ibid., tbl. 5.47 (noting that in 1994, there were over 51,000 felony convictions after jury trials in state court).

jury reforms and techniques for other jurisdictions to adopt or decline. The discussion of the American criminal jury in this chapter is therefore necessarily imprecise, sometimes providing a rough generalization of a common practice instead of a detailed breakdown of variations in practice among the fifty states and the federal courts.[21] The following section outlines the core requirements of the Sixth Amendment and several of the most common procedural variations from the traditional common law jury.

IV. The Right to a Jury Trial Under the Sixth Amendment and Local Variations

History has served as the US Supreme Court's guide in interpreting many aspects of the jury right guaranteed by the Constitution. For example, although the Sixth Amendment promises a jury 'in all criminal prosecutions', the Supreme Court has not required courts to provide juries for 'petty' offenses. Using the legislature's chosen punishment as a proxy for seriousness, the Court has refused to recognize a right to jury trial when the charge that the defendant faces carries a penalty of six months or less, even when a defendant faces conviction on several such charges in one trial.[22] For a fine alone to trigger the right to a jury trial, the amount must be quite substantial.[23] In its decisions exempting petty offenses from the jury trial right, the Court has repeatedly relied upon the historical practice of trying petty offenses before judges without juries.[24]

Tradition, however, was abandoned in other decisions interpreting the right to a jury trial. One of the most fundamental changes in the scope of the jury guarantee was brought about by the Court's 1930 decision holding that the jury trial was optional rather than mandatory in federal felony cases. *Patton* v. *United States*[25] gave defendants the option of

[21] This article also does not address the law governing jury trials in courts of military justice, juvenile courts, or Native American tribal courts.

[22] See Lewis v. United States, 518 U.S. 332 (1996) (no right to a jury when charged with two separate counts, each carrying up to sixth months' imprisonment).

[23] Compare Muniz v. Hoffman, 422 U.S. 454 (1975) (labor union fined $10,000 for a violation of criminal contempt not entitled to jury trial), with International Union, UMW v. Bagwell, 512 U.S. 821 (1994) (fines of over $64 million imposed for contempt required jury trial).

[24] See, *e.g.*, Duncan v. Louisiana, 391 U.S. 145, 160 (1968); Cheff v. Schnackenberg, 384 U.S. 373, 379 (1966); District of Columbia v. Clawans, 300 U.S. 617, 624 (1937); Schick v. United States, 195 U.S. 65, 69–71 (1904).

[25] 281 U.S. 276 (1930).

dispensing with the jury and proceeding to trial before a judge alone.[26] As a result, bench trials in felony cases, rare at common law, are now commonplace.[27]

The challenge of reconciling the variations and innovations in state practice with the Sixth Amendment prompted the Court to authorize several other modifications of the common law jury. The Court upheld Massachusetts's two-tier trial system in which a defendant received a jury only if he was first convicted by a judge.[28] The Court also held that the Constitution does not require that a jury rather than a judge make the decision to impose the death penalty or to spare a capital defendant's life.[29] However, only a few states have chosen to exclude the jury from the capital sentencing process and turn it over to judges completely.[30] In a handful of states, defendants retain the option even in a noncapital case to have the jury pronounce the sentence, but elsewhere sentencing by the judge is the norm.[31]

To comply with the Sixth Amendment, a state felony jury may have as few as six jurors,[32] and it need not decide the issue of guilt or inno-

[26] See also Singer v. United States, 380 U.S. 24 (1965) (upholding a rule conditioning the defendant's ability to waive a jury upon the consent of prosecutor and judge).

[27] See Sean Doran *et al.*, *Rethinking Adversariness in Nonjury Criminal Trials*, 23 Am. J. Crim. L. 1, 1–10 (1995) (reporting data from 13 states on the percentage of felony trials tried to the bench: three states reported less than 10%, one reported over 77%, and nine ranged between 14% and 69%); Susan C. Towne, *The Historical Origins of Bench Trial for Serious Crime*, 26 Am. J. Legal Hist. 123, 152 (1982).

[28] See Ludwig v. Massachusetts, 427 U.S. 618 (1976). In 1978, Massachusetts changed its law so that the first trial before a judge was optional, not mandatory. This modified law was upheld against a double jeopardy challenge in Justices of Boston Municipal Court v. Lydon, 466 U.S. 294 (1984).

[29] See, *e.g.*, Spaziano v. Florida, 468 U.S. 447 (1984) (upholding judge's decision to impose death penalty after jury's recommendation of a life sentence).

[30] See Ariz. Rev. Stat. § 13–703(B) (1997); Idaho Code § 19–2515 (1997); Mont. Code. Ann. § 46–18–301 (1997); Neb. Rev. Stat. § 29–2520 (1997). Four others leave the final determination of whether to impose the death penalty to the judge rather than the jury, but require the jury to make a recommendation to the judge based upon its evaluation of aggravating and mitigating factors. See Ala. Code § 13A–5–47(c) (1997); Del. Code Ann. tit. 11, § 4209 (1997); Fla. Stat. Ann. § 921.141 (West 1997); Ind. Code Ann. § 35–50–2–9 (West 1997); see also Nev. Rev. Stat. §§ 175.554, 175.556 (1997) (three-judge panel may decide sentence if jury cannot agree).

[31] Seven states permit some jury sentencing in noncapital cases. For a collection of citations to state statutes, see Wayne LaFave *et al.*, Criminal Procedure § 26.2(b) (2d ed. forthcoming).

[32] See Ballew v. Georgia, 435 U.S. 223 (1978) (five-member panel deprived defendant of his right to trial by jury); Williams v. Florida, 399 U.S. 78 (1970) (six-member panel met due process requirements).

cence with a unanimous vote.[33] Few jurisdictions have taken advantage of these streamlined procedures, however. All but four states require that twelve jurors be seated initially in noncapital felony cases (some allow for juror attrition during the trial), and only Louisiana and Oregon allow nonunanimous verdicts in felony cases.[34] Recent proposals to allow for nonunanimous juries have surfaced again in some localities, however, prompted by concern with the frequency of hung juries.[35]

While the Court has allowed for some narrowing of the safeguards provided by the common law jury to criminal defendants, it has also erected jury trial procedures for the benefit of the accused that did not exist at common law. Like the constitutional requirements adopted in the mid-1900s for other phases of criminal investigation and prosecution, these changes began as responses to injustices suffered by African-Americans prosecuted in state courts.[36] Particularly significant are the rules governing the selection of jurors. Elsewhere in this volume, Professor Stephan Landsman examines in some detail the restrictions on the exercise of peremptory challenges under the Equal Protection Clause, restrictions that originated in *Batson* v. *Kentucky*,[37] a criminal case.[38] The Court has also held that the Constitution regulates the process by which potential jurors are selected and summoned to the courthouse, a topic addressed separately below.[39]

[33] See Burch v. Louisiana, 441 U.S. 130 (1979); Apodaca v. Oregon, 406 U.S. 404 (1972); see also Schad v. Arizona, 501 U.S. 624 (1991) (discussing when unanimity is required regarding alternative means of committing a single offense).

[34] See David B. Rottman *et al.*, State Court Organization 1993, at 274–9 (1995) (state-by-state listing of jury size and verdict rules).

[35] See, for example, the discussion of unanimity in the Report of the California Blue Ribbon Commission on Jury System Improvement 70–9 (1996) (recommending a modified unanimity procedure in which a nonunanimous verdict of 11–1 would be permitted after the jury had deliberated for at least six hours, except where the punishment may be death or life imprisonment). See also sources cited *infra* notes 145–6 (collecting hung-jury rates).

[36] See, *e.g.*, Randall Kennedy, Race, Crime, and the Law 21 (1997) ('Several of the most basic protections enjoyed by all Americans, for example, the right to an attorney when charged with a serious offense, the right to be free of torture, and the right to a trial absent mob intimidation, are protections that arose in response to the racially motivated mistreatment of black defendants.'); Carol S. Steiker, *Second Thoughts About First Principles*, 107 Harv. L. Rev. 820, 838 (1994) ('The efforts of twentieth-century judges to forge new connections in the Fourth Amendment between 'reasonableness' and warrants and to create a Fourth Amendment remedy of evidentiary exclusion have been linked, both chronologically and ideologically, to attempts to address the larger problem of racial injustice.').

[37] 476 U.S. 79 (1986).

[38] See Stephan Landsman, *The Civil Jury in America*, 62 Law & Contemp. Probs. 285, 293–5 (Spring 1999).

[39] See *infra* Part VI.

Beyond these departures from the common law jury expressly addressed by the Supreme Court, a host of other innovations have become well established. In many states, jurors receive instructions about the case before the presentation of evidence.[40] Jurors in many jurisdictions may take notes during trial and review them during deliberations, although some courts continue to prohibit note-taking.[41] Some courts will allow jurors to submit questions to the judge to be asked of witnesses, but this is not nearly as popular as the practice of juror note-taking.[42] Pattern jury instructions have for the most part replaced the idiosyncratic jury charges of yesteryear.[43] Most courts today provide the jurors with written copies of the jury instructions to take into the jury room.[44] Unlike the jurors of 1800 who were typically subject to sequestration—locked in the jury room together, even overnight, until they reached a verdict[45]—today's jurors are rarely sequestered.[46] When a juror becomes unable to continue serving due to illness or misconduct, the trial need not be aborted; many jurisdictions allow the jury to continue deliberating with depleted numbers, and several jurisdictions allow the substitution of juror alternates even during deliberations.[47]

[40] See JURY TRIAL INNOVATIONS 151–3 (G. Thomas Munsterman *et al.* eds., 1997) (discussing preinstruction).

[41] See Larry Heuer & Steven Penrod, *Increasing Juror Participation in Trials Through Note Taking and Question Asking*, 79 JUDICATURE 256 (1996); Larry Heuer & Steven Penrod, *Juror Note Taking and Question Asking During Trials*, 18 LAW & HUM. BEHAV. 121 (1994); see also JURY TRIAL INNOVATIONS, *supra* note 40, at 141–7. Louisiana still prohibits the use of juror notes in the jury room. See LA. STAT. ANN. art. 1794 (West 1997).

[42] See Larry Heuer & Steven Penrod, *Some Suggestions for the Critical Appraisal of a More Active Jury*, 85 NW. U. L. REV. 226, 229 (1990) (reporting survey of judges that revealed note-taking occurred in about one-third of trials, while permission to ask questions was reported in only one percent of trials); see also Douglas G. Smith, *Structural and Functional Aspects of the Jury: Comparative Analysis and Proposals for Reform*, 48 ALA. L. REV. 441 (1997) (discussing advantages, disadvantages, and empirical information concerning juror questioning). Juror questioning apparently has 'honorable antecedents in older English and American trials, but has fallen out of use in American jurisdictions.' Michael E. Tigar, *Foreword: The Waiver of Constitutional Rights: Disquiet in the Citadel*, 84 HARV. L. REV. 1, 27 (1970).

[43] See LAFAVE *ET AL.*, *supra* note 31, § 24.8(c) (discussing use of pattern instructions).

[44] See Howard H. Lehman, *A Critical Survey of Certain Phases of Trial Procedure in Criminal Cases*, 63 U. PA. L. REV. 754, 771 (1915); Annotation, 91 A.L.R.3d 382 (1979 & Supp. 1997).

[45] See Nancy J. King, *Juror Delinquency in Criminal Trials in America, 1796–1996*, 94 MICH. L. REV. 2673, 2679–81 (1996).

[46] See Marcy Strauss, *Sequestration*, 24 AM. J. CRIM. L. 63, 68 n.22 (1996) (noting that G. Thomas Munsterman, Director, Center for Jury Studies for the National Center for State Courts, estimates that no more than 100 juries per year are sequestered during the trial period).

[47] See, *e.g.*, Miller v. Stagner, 757 F.2d 988, 995 (9th Cir. 1985) (upholding substitution); see also King, *supra* note 45, at 2749.

Another change from the traditional common law jury trial is the rule in most states barring the trial judge from sharing his opinion of the evidence with the jurors.[48] Unlike the rule in many other countries requiring judicial comment on the evidence (known as 'summing up'), this prohibition in the United States is unique.[49] Most states outlawed such comment in the 1800s by constitutional provision, statute, or judicial decision, although it is still an option in federal courts and in the courts in a minority of states.[50] The ban is based on the principle that the jury is the sole judge of the facts, combined with the traditional American distrust of the judiciary. In essence, most state legislatures and courts have decided that the judge's opinion of the evidence is at best irrelevant and meddlesome, and at worst, partisan advocacy.[51] Even in jurisdictions where judges are permitted to comment on the evidence, they must be careful not to give a 'one-sided rendition' of the case.[52] Indeed, at least one recent study showed that American jurors may be deeply suspicious of judicial comment on the evidence.[53] In some ways, this rigid exclusion of judges from factfinding complements the equally uncompromising exclusion of juries from interpreting the law in all but a few states.[54] Nevertheless, the no-comment rule continues to be criticized by some as further 'isolating' the jury laymen from 'learned guidance', thus exacerbating the problem of juror misunderstanding.[55]

[48] See, *e.g.*, People v. Kelly, 179 N.E. 898, 905 (Ill. 1931) (DeYoung, J., dissenting) ('A jury trial in which the judge is deprived of the right to comment on the evidence and to express his opinion on the facts . . . is not the jury trial which we inherited.').

[49] *Cf.* generally Symposium, *The Common Law Jury*, 62 LAW & CONTEMP. PROBS. 1 (Spring 1999).

[50] See LAFAVE *ET AL.*, *supra* note 31, § 24.6(e) (collecting current state statutes, constitutional provisions, and decisions); Kenneth A. Krasity, *The Role of the Judge in Jury Trials: The Elimination of Judicial Evaluation of Fact in American State Courts from 1795 to 1913*, 62 U. DET. L. REV. 595, 622–7 (1985) (listing state-by-state the law first barring judicial evaluation).

[51] See *The Right of a Judge to Comment on the Evidence in His Charge to the Jury*, 6 F.R.D. 317, 330 (1947); see also Krasity, *supra* note 50, at 611–12 (hypothesizing that the shift to elected judges may have diminished the respect for judicial expertise regarding factual matters); Hon. Jack B. Weinstein, *The Power and Duty of Federal Judges to Marshall and Comment on the Evidence in Jury Trials and Some Suggestions on Charging Juries*, 118 F.R.D. 161 (1988).

[52] State v. Hernandez, 590 A.2d 112 (Conn. 1991).

[53] See Dennis Turner & Solomon Fulero, *Can Civility Return to the Courtroom? Will American Jurors Like It?*, 58 OHIO ST. L.J. 131, 153–4 (1997) (finding, in mock trial study involving variations on judicial comment, that judicial comment 'did not find favor with the American jurors', and that the jurors had a 'strong preference' that the judge not sum up the evidence).

[54] See Krasity, *supra* note 50, at 620–1. On the role of juries in deciding law as well as fact, see the discussion of nullification at *infra* Part V.

[55] John H. Langbein, *Mixed Court and Jury Court: Could the Continental Alternative Fill the American Need?*, 1981 AM. B. FOUND. RES. J. 195, 202; Smith, *supra* note 42, at 538–47.

Judicial influence over factfinding remains considerable despite no-comment rules. American jury trials involve complex and pervasive judicial control of juries through the rules of evidence.[56] A judge may not be allowed to tell jurors what to deduce from the evidence they hear, but he can prevent them from hearing it at all. Certain kinds of proof offered by the prosecution, for example, must be excluded in order to comply with constitutional commands. Hearsay is inadmissible against a criminal defendant absent adequate indicia of reliability, due to the Sixth Amendment's guarantee that the accused be allowed to 'confront the witnesses against him'.[57] Evidence seized in an unlawful search must be excluded in order to ensure that government agents live up to the Fourth Amendment's command that 'the right of the people . . . against unreasonable searches and seizures, shall not be violated'.[58] Statements of the defendant are inadmissible when obtained in violation of his Fifth Amendment right not to 'be compelled in any criminal case to be a witness against himself'.[59]

Other incriminating evidence may be barred by statute or court rule for fear that the jury would be unable to assess its proper weight and relevance, such as evidence of other bad deeds by the accused.[60] Still other exclusions are meant to encourage the litigants to engage in remedial activities or settlements, such as the rule barring the admission of statements made during plea negotiations.[61] Evidence offered by the defense, too, may also be excluded on the grounds that it is unreliable or irrelevant.[62] Juries judging guilt or innocence are not allowed to hear evidence of a rape victim's prior sexual history, for example, or to learn about the punishment a defendant faces upon conviction.[63] Intoxication, insanity, duress, and other defenses are carefully regulated by the judge and often

[56] See generally John H. Langbein, *Historical Foundations of the Law of Evidence: A View from the Ryder Sources*, 96 COLUM. L. REV. 1168 (1996).

[57] U.S. CONST. amend. VI; see, *e.g.*, Idaho v. Wright, 497 U.S. 805 (1990).

[58] U.S. CONST. amend. IV. See generally WAYNE LAFAVE, SEARCH AND SEIZURE: A TREATISE ON THE FOURTH AMENDMENT (3d ed. 1996).

[59] U.S. CONST. amend. V. See generally LAFAVE *ET AL.*, *supra* note 31, ch. 6.

[60] See, *e.g.*, FED. R. EVID. 404.

[61] See, *e.g.*, ibid., 410.

[62] See, *e.g.*, Taylor v. Illinois, 484 U.S. 400, 410 (1988) (noting that 'the accused does not have an unfettered right to offer testimony that is incompetent, privileged, or otherwise inadmissible under standard rules of evidence').

[63] See, *e.g.*, FED R. EVID. 412 (limiting evidence of victim's past sexual behavior); Rogers v. United States, 422 U.S. 35, 40 (1975) (noting that 'the jury had no sentencing function and should reach its verdict without regard to what sentence might be imposed'); United States v. Davidson, 367 F.2d 60 (6th Cir. 1966) (discussing ban on juror consideration of punishment).

by statute.[64] As in civil trials, a judge in a criminal case may in some circumstances exclude a witness's testimony or other evidence as a sanction for a party's failure to comply with rules of pretrial discovery.[65] The Supreme Court has held that even a defendant may be precluded from presenting the testimony of a witness whose name defense counsel deliberately failed to list prior to trial.[66] For example, readers who followed the trial of O. J. Simpson may recall both sides arguing over the sanction of exclusion for alleged failures to disclose witnesses and other evidence prior to trial.

In addition, the judge serves as the gatekeeper for technical, scientific, and other expert testimony, allowing the jury to hear such evidence only after determining that the testimony will assist the jury in finding the facts.[67] In *Daubert* v. *Merrell Dow Pharmaceuticals, Inc.*,[68] the Supreme Court established a framework within which federal judges must evaluate expert evidence. This formula has been adopted by several state courts as well.[69] One recent study of three cities found that about six of every ten criminal trials includes expert testimony.[70] Occasionally, a defendant will raise as a defense a claim that he was suffering from insanity or some other mental impairment, a claim that usually will necessitate testimony by mental health professionals. The insanity defense, however, is raised infrequently and is rarely successful.[71] Acquittals due to insanity probably make up no more than about 0.26 percent of terminated felony prosecutions.[72] Expert testimony may also be presented by a defendant who claims that her actions were the reasonable response of a person suffering from battered woman syndrome or any of a variety of other mental or emotional conditions. Prosecutors in sex offense cases sometimes present expert testimony concerning child sex abuse syndrome or rape trauma syndrome in order to help the jury understand the behavior of alleged victims. Experts on eyewitness identification have testified in a number of cases

[64] See generally Paul H. Robinson, Criminal Law Defenses (1984).

[65] See LaFave *et al.*, *supra* note 31, § 20.6.

[66] See *Taylor*, 484 U.S. at 415–16.

[67] See Fed. R. Evid. 702; Daubert v. Merrell Dow Pharm. Inc., 509 U.S. 579 (1993).

[68] 509 U.S. 579 (1993).

[69] See, *e.g.*, Joseph R. Meaney, Note, *From* Frye *to* Daubert: *Is a Pattern Unfolding?*, 35 Jurimetrics J. 191 (1995) (listing states following *Daubert*).

[70] See Daniel W. Shuman *et al.*, *An Empirical Examination of the Use of Expert Witnesses in the Courts—Part III: A Three City Study*, 34 Jurimetrics J. 193, 204 (1994).

[71] See Hugh McGinley & Richard A. Pasework, *National Survey of the Frequency and Success of the Insanity Plea and Alternate Pleas*, 17 J. Psychiatry & L. 205, 208–14 (1989).

[72] See Andrew Blum, *Debunking Myths of the Insanity Plea*, Nat'l L.J., Apr. 20, 1992, at 9.

as well, although many courts continue to exclude such testimony as unhelpful.[73]

V. Jury Nullification

As illustrated by the Zenger trial,[74] jurors in criminal cases do not always follow the instructions given to them by judges. When their failure to follow the law results in conviction, a defendant may appeal the conviction, and in turn may receive a new trial. However, when jurors depart from the law to acquit, the Double Jeopardy Clause of the Fifth Amendment protects the defendant from being retried for that crime.[75] This power of the jury to disregard the law and to acquit a defendant accused of a crime, even when the proof at trial demonstrates guilt beyond a reasonable doubt, is known as 'jury nullification'. As noted above, nullification provided a shield against British oppression before the Revolution. American juries have, since colonial times, exercised leniency by acquitting against the evidence and law in cases in which a conviction would be followed by a mandatory death sentence.[76] Before the Civil War, antislavery juries nullified in cases in which defendants were charged with treason for resisting the enforcement of the 1850 Fugitive Slave Law, a draconian statute enacted to assist slave owners in recovering runaway slaves.[77] Following the war, Southern juries refused to convict those accused of violence against African-Americans and, in Utah, Mormon jurors refused to convict defendants charged with bigamy or polygamy.[78] Prohibition era juries refused to convict liquor law violators, Vietnam War era draft-dodgers escaped punishment through acquittals, and jurors today may be nullifying in cases involving police oversight or abuse, lengthy mandatory sentences, charges of assisted suicide, drug possession, or the use of firearms.[79]

[73] See Steven D. Penrod *et al.*, *Expert Psychological Testimony on Eyewitness Reliability Before and After* Daubert: *The State of the Law and the Science*, 13 Behav. Sci. & L. 229 (1995).

[74] See *supra* notes 1–8 and accompanying text.

[75] See U.S. Const. amend. V ('[N]or shall any person be subject for the same offense to be twice put in jeopardy of life or limb. . . .').

[76] See Woodson v. North Carolina, 428 U.S. 280, 293 (1976).

[77] See Stanley W. Campbell, The Slave Catchers: Enforcement of the Fugitive Slave Law, 1850–1860, at 148–69 (1968); Robert M. Cover, Justice Accused: Antislavery and the Judicial Process 191 (1975); Jane H. Pease & William H. Pease, The Fugitive Slave Law and Anthony Burns (1975).

[78] See Nancy J. King, *Silencing Nullification Advocacy Inside the Jury Room and Outside the Courtroom*, 65 U. Chi. L. Rev. 433, 461–4 (1998).

[79] See ibid., at 433–4, 466; Alschuler & Deiss, *supra* note 8, at 890–2.

Ever since the ratification of the Constitution, judges and scholars have debated whether nullification is good or bad, whether it is a right or a *de facto* power, and what courts can and cannot do to control it. For some, nullification 'is what the jury system is about'.[80] For others, it is a necessary cost of allowing the jury unfettered freedom to find facts, and of protecting an acquitted defendant from the ordeal of a second trial.[81] The Supreme Court has avoided entering this controversy directly for more than a century. Its last significant discussion of nullification appeared in an 1895 decision denying a criminal defendant's claim of entitlement to an instruction about a lesser-included charge that was unsupported by the evidence, a decision in which a majority of the Court sternly disapproved of such jury lawlessness and declared that it was the role of the judge, not the jury, to determine the law.[82]

While the debate continues about how much leeway jurors should be given to reject judge-directed law, there is no question that the Constitution now prohibits some judicial efforts to restrict nullification. The Double Jeopardy Clause of the Fifth Amendment bars retrial after acquittal for the same offense,[83] and the Jury Clause of the Sixth Amendment has been interpreted to prohibit judges from entering a judgment of conviction absent a jury's verdict of guilt in cases where the defendant has not waived a jury trial.[84] A court may not bar a defendant from litigating anew a factual issue decided previously against him.[85] And most courts consider special verdicts, by which a jury is asked to find the facts so that the judge can apply the law and determine guilt or innocence, to be unconstitutional.[86]

At the same time, numerous limitations on the jury's nullification power thrive in criminal courtrooms, indicating either that the power is quite narrowly confined, or an ambivalent judicial commitment to that power, or both. Federal courts remain free to retry a defendant acquitted by a state jury, as may the court of a different state, on the theory that when a defendant violates the law of more than one 'sovereign',

[80] Jeffrey Abramson, We, the Jury: The Jury System and the Ideal of Democracy 95 (1995).

[81] See King, *supra* note 78, at 444–58 (reviewing origins and explanations of jury nullification).

[82] See Sparf v. United States, 156 U.S. 51 (1895).

[83] See, *e.g.*, United States v. Ball, 163 U.S. 662 (1896).

[84] See Connecticut v. Johnson, 460 U.S. 73, 84 (1983); *Sparf*, 156 U.S. at 105.

[85] See United States v. Pelullo, 14 F.3d 881 (3d Cir. 1994); Richard B. Kennelly, Jr., Note, *Precluding the Accused: Offensive Collateral Estoppel in Criminal Cases*, 80 Va. L. Rev. 1379 (1994).

[86] See LaFave *et al.*, *supra* note 31, § 24.9.

each sovereign may exact its own punishment regardless of what another sovereign chooses to do.[87] For example, following the state acquittals of the police officers charged with beating African-American motorist Rodney King, the federal government successfully prosecuted the same officers under federal law.[88] Also, a defendant's sentence for a crime of which he was convicted may be based on the commission of another offense of which he was acquitted.[89] A 'civil penalty' may follow a criminal acquittal as well, even when the penalty looks suspiciously like a fine for the same wrongdoing.[90]

In addition, trial judges take pains to prevent nullification from occurring. Potential jurors who reveal during jury selection that they have doubts about the law are regularly excused for cause, and jurors exposed as nullification advocates during deliberations may, in some instances, be removed from the jury.[91] Judges routinely prevent defendants from introducing evidence or argument to support defenses that are not authorized by law, although occasionally a sympathetic judge may permit defense counsel to hint at a forbidden reason for the jury to exercise leniency, such as the steep punishment a defendant would face if convicted. Defendants are almost without exception denied instructions that will inform jurors that they have the power to acquit even when they believe that a defendant may be guilty under the law.[92] Instead, judges are allowed to instruct the jury that it must convict if the government proves each element of the crime charged with proof beyond a reasonable

[87] See LaFave *et al.*, *supra* note 31, § 25.5. A state may also prosecute a defendant for the same offense after acquittal in federal court.

[88] See Koon v. United States, 518 U.S. 81 (1996).

[89] See United States v. Watts, 519 U.S. 148 (1997).

[90] See Hudson v. United States, 522 U.S. 93 (1997) (holding that double jeopardy does not bar the imposition of civil and criminal penalties for the same offense). At least one court has authorized the retrial of a defendant should the prosecutor prove that the defendant bribed his judge to acquit him. See Aleman v. The Honorable Judges of the Circuit Court of Cook County, 138 F.3d 302 (7th Cir. 1998). While it would be a simple matter to confine this exception to the finality of acquittals to bench trials without intruding on the sanctity of jury decisions, the Court has so far refused in its double jeopardy cases to extend less protection to acquittals by judges than to acquittals by juries. See United States v. Martin Linen Supply Co., 430 U.S. 564, 573–5 (1977); Kepner v. United States, 195 U.S. 100, 133–4 (1904).

[91] See King, *supra* note 78, at 484–5; see also United States v. Thomas, 116 F.3d 606 (2d Cir. 1997) (reviewing case in which judge during trial dismissed juror alleged to have been misbehaving and refusing to follow instructions, noting that trial judges have the duty to dismiss jurors who intend to nullify).

[92] In Indiana and Maryland, however, the state constitution permits juries to determine both the law and the facts. See Ind. Const. art. 1, § 19; Md. Const. Decl. of Rts. art. 23.

doubt.[93] As the Court held in 1895, defendants are not entitled to instructions informing the jury of a lesser-included offense unless the evidence supports that charge.[94] Judges may require a jury to deliberate further if it returns with an acquittal on one count that is inconsistent with its verdict on another.[95] And sometimes judges ask jurors to answer special interrogatories along with their verdict of guilt or innocence—factual questions that may focus the jury on the legal issues as presented by the judge and away from extra-legal reasons for acquitting the defendant such as conscience or prejudice.[96]

Judges and legislators refuse to give the criminal jury any more discretion than this because they are concerned that greater leeway would free jurors to misuse their power. A juror may vote to acquit a defendant because she believes that the conduct proscribed by the charge is not a crime, that the defendant does not deserve punishment, that the police acted in bad faith, that God would not punish the defendant, that the victim needs no protection from the law, that she will earn a personal benefit if she acquits, that the defendant or those who support his innocence will harm her if she votes to convict, that the Constitution requires fingerprint evidence to prove identity beyond a reasonable doubt, or for any other reason at all. It is not so long ago that jurors refused to punish those responsible for torturing and terrorizing African-Americans throughout the South.[97] Those wary of nullification recognize that criminal jury trials today may still involve victims who are unpopular yet deserve protection, or laws that, while opposed in some communities, reflect the will of the state or the nation. It is in these types of cases that the jury's decision to refuse to enforce the law can be most disturbing. In any event, as Professors Harry Kalven and Hans Zeisel's classic study of American juries demonstrated, judge/jury disagreement is the exception, not the rule.[98] Most acquittals are probably due to genuine doubts about the facts, rather than overt disregard for the law.[99]

[93] See King, *supra* note 78, at 475 n.158.

[94] See Sparf v. United States, 156 U.S. 51, 59–64 (1895).

[95] For a full discussion of inconsistent verdicts and their treatment by courts, see Eric L. Muller, *The Hobgoblin of Little Minds? Our Foolish Law of Inconsistent Verdicts*, 111 Harv. L. Rev. 771 (1998).

[96] See LaFave *et al.*, *supra* note 31, § 24.9.

[97] See *supra* note 78 and accompanying text.

[98] See Harry Kalven, Jr. & Hans Zeisel, The American Jury 56 (1966) (noting that in sample of 3,576 trials, judges agreed with jurors in over 75% of cases).

[99] See ibid., at 116.

VI. Jury Composition

Given the ability of jurors to block the enforcement of criminal law, it was inevitable that the identity of those who sit in the jury box would be a subject of intense controversy. The Sixth Amendment gave little guidance, insisting only that the jury be 'impartial' and drawn from a 'previously ascertained' 'district', leaving plenty of room for courts and legislatures to define further the qualifications for service as a juror.[100] Until the Civil War, federal courts followed the juror selection procedures of the state in which the court was located, and all but one of the states effectively limited jury service to white men who were property owners or taxpayers.[101] Often local statutes would require that jurors be of 'intelligence' or 'of fair character', requirements judged exclusively by those men charged with the job of creating jury lists. These men, called sheriffs, trustees, or selectmen, would choose the initial names to be summoned, with virtually no check on their discretion.[102] When not enough of those enlisted for jury service responded to their summonses, or showed up drunk or sick, bystanders were chosen to make up the remainder.[103] By manipulating the initial list, local officials could attempt to stack a jury with sympathizers, while a defendant could do the same by trying to control who showed up and who was standing around to take the place of no-shows.[104]

Following the Civil War, Congress prohibited states from disqualifying citizens from jury service on account of race, and for a short time during Reconstruction, African-Americans served on juries in some communities.[105] But the right of African-Americans to serve on juries in most Southern communities remained unrealized: their names were rarely on jury lists, and when they were, they were never selected.[106] The

[100] See Kershen, *supra* note 15, at 843.

[101] Although only three states explicitly limited service to whites, other limitations effectively ensured all-white juries. See Alschuler & Deiss, *supra* note 8, at 877; see also Kennedy, *supra* note 36, at 169 ('Prior to the Civil War, only one state, Massachusetts, permitted blacks to serve on juries.').

[102] See Alschuler & Deiss, *supra* note 8, at 879–80; see also Jon M. Van Dyke, Jury Selection Procedures: Our Uncertain Commitment to Representative Panels 86–8 (1977) (cataloguing continued use of 'key-man' jury selection systems in several states in the mid-1970s).

[103] See King, *supra* note 45, at 2682.

[104] See Alschuler & Deiss, *supra* note 8, at 879–80; King, *supra* note 45, at 2682–5.

[105] See Alschuler & Deiss, *supra* note 8, at 886. For further discussion, see Kermit L. Hall, *Political Power and Constitutional Legitimacy: The South Carolina Ku Klux Klan Trials, 1871–1872*, 33 Emory L.J. 921 (1984).

[106] See Alschuler & Deiss, *supra* note 8, at 877.

Court's efforts to remedy these persistent practices began in 1880. Striking down an express statutory exclusion of African-Americans from juries, the Court in *Strauder* v. *West Virginia*[107] concluded that the statute denied equal protection of the law to the African-American defendant who must submit to a trial by a jury from which all members of his race had been excluded. But the Court's decision served only to shift discrimination from the text of statutes to the actions of those who enforced them. Keeping juries all-white remained business as usual well into the twentieth century. The names of African-Americans were essentially 'nailed to the bottom' of the boxes, if they appeared there at all.[108] Courts occasionally ordered relief after finding that nothing else but race discrimination could explain the total absence of African-Americans on juries over several years, rejecting claims that no qualified African-Americans existed or that those in charge did not know any. Yet, as Professor Randall Kennedy has pointed out, bringing such a challenge was not a realistic option for most defendants: Even for those defendants able to afford an attorney, attorneys remained 'dependent on the good will of whites', and were 'unwilling to jeopardize their careers' by challenging discriminatory practices.[109] In addition, state judges rarely recognized the practices in their own courts as unlawful.[110] Eventually, after the United States Supreme Court overturned the convictions of several defendants convicted by all-white juries during the 1930s, 1940s, and 1950s due to intentional race discrimination, state courts began to attempt to include African-Americans in jury pools. Even then, officials in some communities made sure to summon only as many as were necessary to avoid a successful legal challenge.[111]

A system for selecting jurors randomly from voter lists was adopted by Congress in 1970, freeing federal courts from the more discretionary state jury selection schemes and eliminating the exemptions for certain professions which had skewed jury pools in the past.[112] But in interpreting the commands of the Constitution, which bind the states, the Court stopped short of mandating random selection. The Court refused to

[107] 100 U.S. 303 (1879); see also Neal v. Delaware, 103 U.S. 370 (1880).

[108] Alschuler & Deiss, *supra* note 8, at 895.

[109] See Kennedy, *supra* note 36, at 174.

[110] See ibid.

[111] As late as the 1970s for example, attorneys and jury commissioners in Putnam County, Georgia, had conspired to minimize the number of African-Americans and women on the county's jury lists. See ibid., at 180 (describing Amadeo v. Zant, 486 U.S. 214 (1988)).

[112] See generally Carl H. Imlay, *Federal Jury Reformation: Saving a Democratic Invention*, 6 Loy. L.A. L. Rev. 247 (1973).

hold unconstitutional the key-man jury selection system that allowed state jury commissioners to select those potential jurors they felt were most qualified. Instead, the Court held in 1975 that the Sixth Amendment guarantees only that juries be drawn from a 'cross-section' of the community.[113] If a defendant could show that a cognizable group in the population was underrepresented on the venire, he deserved a new trial unless the state could show that the underrepresentation was due to a selection procedure that advanced a significant state interest.[114] Although the cases that established this doctrine involved the exclusion of women from juries, the cross-section concept was immediately employed to combat racially discriminatory selection practices.[115] Subsequent cross-section and equal protection challenges,[116] together with the court systems' acquisition of computer technology, led states to adopt random selection procedures and remove from commissioners the discretion to pick and choose among qualified potential jurors.[117] Today, in nearly every American jurisdiction, the names of citizens who are mailed summonses for jury service are selected randomly, by computer, from lists of registered voters or licensed drivers.[118]

But random selection has not resolved the ongoing litigation over the composition of juries—far from it. First, random selection highlighted the discrimination that occurred later in the selection process during the *voir dire* stage. Getting a representative group of prospective jurors into the courtroom was a big step. Ensuring diversity in the jury box was something else. Through peremptory challenges, attorneys could use whatever criteria they wished to tailor the jury pool in their favor—race, sex, ethnicity, you name it. *Batson* and the cases extending the ban against race-based peremptory challenges followed.[119] A decade of experience

[113] See Taylor v. Louisiana, 419 U.S. 522 (1975).

[114] See Duren v. Missouri, 439 U.S. 357, 367–8 (1979).

[115] See Andrew D. Leipold, *Constitutionalizing Jury Selection in Criminal Cases: A Critical Evaluation*, 86 Geo. L.J. 945, 968 n.111 (1998).

[116] See Castaneda v. Partida, 430 U.S. 482 (1977) (finding that a statistically significant gap between the proportion of Mexican-Americans in the adult population (79.1%) and the proportion of those summoned for grand jury duty in the preceding 11 years (only 39%) was enough to establish intentional discrimination on the part of those jury commissioners responsible for summoning jurors). For more on the cross-section challenge under the Sixth Amendment, see Leipold, *supra* note 115.

[117] For a discussion of state reform efforts, see G. Thomas Munsterman, *A Brief History of State Jury Reform Efforts*, 79 Judicature 216 (1996).

[118] See ibid., at 216.

[119] See Batson v. Kentucky, 476 U.S. 79 (1986); Powers v. Ohio, 499 U.S. 400 (1991); Edmonson v. Leesville Concrete Co., 500 U.S. 614 (1991); Georgia v. McCollum, 505 U.S. 42 (1992); J.E.B. v. Alabama, 511 U.S. 127 (1994).

with the *Batson* rule has demonstrated its futility, however,[120] causing some scholars and judges to suggest the elimination of the peremptory challenge altogether.[121] Unlike the challenge for cause, which is necessary to ensure the defendant the 'impartial' jury guaranteed by the Constitution, the peremptory challenge is not protected by the Constitution and is not an essential element of the defendant's right to an impartial jury.[122] The peremptory challenge is thus subject to elimination by legislatures. Already, efforts have been made in some states to reduce the number of peremptory challenges provided to each party. Presently, eight states allow four challenges or fewer per side, five states allow twelve or more challenges, and the rest fall somewhere in between.[123]

Critics of the peremptory challenge argue that not only does the challenge permit, and perhaps even encourage, invidious discrimination against potential jurors, it causes jurors to become 'frustrated and cynical about the justice system'.[124] The challenge, claim some critics, also wastes time and promotes reliance on 'jury experts', which, in turn, exacerbates the imbalance between parties who possess unequal resources to pay for such services. Actually, trial consultants offer such a wide variety of help with trial presentation and strategy that the elimination of the peremptory challenge may not have much of an effect on the market for their services. Expert assistance on how to present evidence, clients, and witnesses to a particular jury during jury selection and the remainder of trial will continue to be useful to attorneys, even if peremptory challenges were unavailable.

Jury reformers sometimes point to the successful eclipse of the peremptory challenge in other countries as evidence that the same could be accomplished here.[125] But the ability of other nations to shed the

[120] See Kenneth J. Melilli, Batson *in Practice: What We Have Learned About* Batson *and Peremptory Challenges*, 71 NOTRE DAME L. REV. 447 (1996).

[121] See, *e.g.*, ibid.; Albert W. Alschuler, *The Supreme Court and the Jury: Voir Dire, Peremptory Challenges, and the Review of Jury Verdicts*, 56 U. CHI. L. REV. 153 (1989); Raymond J. Broderick, *Why the Peremptory Challenge Should Be Abolished*, 65 TEMP. L. REV. 369 (1992); Morris B. Hoffman, *Peremptory Challenges Should Be Abolished: A Trial Judge's Perspective*, 64 U. CHI. L. REV. 809 (1997).

[122] See Ross v. Oklahoma, 487 U.S. 81, 88 (1988); Stilson v. United States, 250 U.S. 583, 586 (1919).

[123] See COUNCIL FOR COURT EXCELLENCE DISTRICT OF COLUMBIA JURY PROJECT, JURIES FOR THE YEAR 2000 AND BEYOND (1998) (hereinafter YEAR 2000).

[124] Ibid., at 29 (quoting Hoffman, *supra* note 121, at 862, 'Is it any wonder that these people leave our courtrooms thinking that the whole trial process is just as trivial and flawed as jury selection?').

[125] See Alschuler, *supra* note 121, at 166–7.

challenge does not necessarily portend an easy transition in the United States. Other countries may enjoy conditions more favorable to this change, including a history of less litigant autonomy during *voir dire*, more effective regulation of trial publicity, more homogenous jury pools, and widespread acceptance of nonunanimous verdicts. Should the peremptory challenge erode in America, it is likely that litigants would attempt to make greater use of challenges for cause. Presently, challenges for cause are employed in most trials; an estimated 15 to 25 percent of potential jurors brought to court for each criminal case are excused for cause.[126] If the challenge for cause were expanded to allow for disqualification of jurors for bias that was less obvious or clear,[127] the frequency of challenges for cause would undoubtedly increase.

Two additional constitutional regulations of the *voir dire* process deserve mention. First, the Court has held that there is a right to ask potential jurors about racial bias in a very narrow class of criminal cases raising racially sensitive issues.[128] Secondly, in capital cases, the Court has held that the defendant's right to an impartial jury is violated when the prosecutor excludes for cause jurors who are opposed to the death penalty but nevertheless are able to impose it.[129] As a result, questioning of potential jurors in capital cases typically is quite detailed.[130] The Court has imposed very few other constitutional constraints on the *voir dire* process. It has refused to recognize a constitutional right to question potential jurors about the extent of their exposure to pretrial publicity, for example, insisting only that the judge assure himself that the jurors

[126] Usage will vary with the individual case and the jurisdiction. See telephone interview with Paula L. Hannaford, Senior Research Analyst, National Center for State Courts, Williamsburg, Va. (Oct. 23, 1998).

[127] See, for example, Year 2000, *supra* note 123, at 35, proposing that peremptory challenges be abolished, but that cause challenges be

> 'expanded to mandate the exclusion of any juror as to whom any reasonable doubt exists about the juror's impartiality, based on either the juror's demeanor or substantive answers to questions during *voir dire*; and where a trial judge is uncertain regarding the existence of such a reasonable doubt, the judge's uncertainty should be resolved in favor of striking the challenged juror.'

[128] See Morgan v. Illinois, 504 U.S. 719 (1992) (requiring an inquiry of potential jurors in capital cases as to whether they would automatically impose a death sentence after a guilty verdict); Turner v. Murray, 476 U.S. 28 (1986) (requiring an inquiry about racial bias in prosecution of African-American defendant charged with murder of a white victim); Ham v. South Carolina, 409 U.S. 524 (1973) (requiring an inquiry about racial bias in prosecution of black civil rights activist).

[129] See Wainwright v. Witt, 469 U.S. 412 (1985); Witherspoon v. Illinois, 391 U.S. 510 (1968); see also *infra* notes 183–4.

[130] See *infra* Part IX.

could 'put aside what they had read or heard and render a fair verdict based on the evidence'.[131] Thus, the trial judge still has almost complete control over the amount of information litigants will learn about jurors during *voir dire*. Some judges allow attorneys great leeway to question (and begin indoctrinating) jurors; others do not allow the attorneys to question the prospective jurors, preferring instead to pose a minimum number of quite general questions from the bench. In complex or high-profile cases, courts may allow the use of detailed written juror questionnaires as a supplement to in-court questioning. This permits the jurors somewhat more privacy, facilitates the disclosure of more information about jurors, and conserves judicial resources. Some commentators have recommended that questionnaires be used routinely due to these advantages.[132]

With the widespread adoption of random selection systems, concern about discrimination shifted not only to later phases of jury selection, but also to an earlier stage of the selection processes: the creation of the juror lists themselves. In some courts, critics have claimed, the geographic boundaries of the community from which jurors are drawn create racially skewed jury lists due to the persistence of residential segregation. An example is the controversy recently resolved in the federal court for the Eastern District of New York, a district divided into two predominately white counties on Long Island and the three more racially diverse boroughs of Queens, Bronx, and Brooklyn. Out of concern for the difficulties faced by lower-income residents living in the city who had to find transportation to courthouses on Long Island, the five-county district had for years drawn jurors for its two Long Island courthouses exclusively from the two Long Island counties, while jurors for other courthouses were drawn from all five counties.[133] Recently, this system came under attack. Defendants tried in Queens, Bronx, or Brooklyn courthouses alleged that their juries were diluted with whites from Long Island, while defendants tried on Long Island alleged that they were deprived of minority jurors from the rest of the District.[134] After considering several alternative proposals to alleviate racial imbalances, the court eventually abandoned trying to carve up its racially polarized

[131] Mu'Min v. Virginia, 500 U.S. 415, 432 (1991) (O'Connor, J., concurring).

[132] See YEAR 2000, *supra* note 123, at 34; Nancy J. King, *Nameless Justice: The Case for the Routine Use of Anonymous Juries in Criminal Trials*, 49 VAND. L. REV. 123 (1996).

[133] See *In re* Jury Plan of the Eastern District of New York, 27 F.3d 9 (2d Cir. 1994).

[134] See, *e.g.*, United States v. Miller, 116 F.3d 641 (2d Cir. 1997); United States v. Bhana, 68 F.3d 19 (2d Cir. 1995).

vicinage and adopted a plan which drew jurors for all courthouses from the entire District.[135]

Concerns about racial representation in jury pools have also caused some litigants, judges, and lawmakers to question whether otherwise random and race-neutral procedures for summoning and qualification actually exclude a disproportionate number of minority citizens. Studies have shown that in some communities, minority citizens are statistically less likely to appear on lists of voters or licensed drivers, to remain at one address long enough to receive a jury summons, or to be able to obtain transportation to the courthouse or time off from work to serve as jurors.[136] To compensate, many jurisdictions are considering adding to their juror source list the names of those who may not be licensed to drive but who pay income tax, receive public assistance, or have recently become American citizens.[137] A few courts have experimented with 'oversampling' minority neighborhoods or other efforts to achieve racial balance in the jury pool.[138] The federal court in Detroit, Michigan, for example, replicated on the list of qualified jurors the racial demographics of the population from which the list was drawn by striking the appropriate number of non-African-Americans. However, the Court of Appeals recently found that such racial 'balancing' was unconstitutional,[139] and the District has discarded the system.[140]

VII. The Criminal Jury Trial: An Empirical Snapshot

No discussion of the American criminal jury would be complete without some mention of how seldom those charged with crime in the United States actually face a jury, yet how influential the jury remains. For most defendants, the jury, if not irrelevant, is at least inaccessible. A remark-

[135] See *In re* Jury Plan of the Eastern District of New York, 61 F.3d 119 (2d Cir. 1995); Nancy J. King, *Jurymandering Is Asking for Trouble*, NEWSDAY, Sept. 22, 1994, at 36; Susanne H. Vikoren, *Justice or Jurymander? Confronting the Under Representation of Racial Groups in the Jury Pool of New York's Eastern District*, 27 COLUM. HUM. RTS. L. REV. 605 (1996); see also United States v. King, 134 F.3d 1173 (2d Cir. 1998).

[136] See Nancy J. King, *Racial Jurymandering: Cancer or Cure? A Contemporary Review of Affirmative Action in Jury Selection*, 68 N.Y.U. L. REV. 707, 712–14 (1993).

[137] See, *e.g.*, YEAR 2000, *supra* note 123, at 8.

[138] See King, *supra* note 136, at 723–4.

[139] See United States v. Ovalle, 136 F.3d 1092 (6th Cir. 1998).

[140] See Tim Doran, *Ruling Puts a Roadblock into Federal Jury Selection*, DETROIT FREE PRESS, Mar. 17, 1998, at 3B (reporting that '[t]he U.S. District Court in eastern Michigan agreed to stop removing non-blacks from jury pools').

ably small percentage of felony cases go to trial, only 3 to 10 percent.[141] Plea bargaining or 'settlement' is the norm, due to powerful incentives to avoid the risk and expense of trial, incentives that influence both prosecution and defense. In more than a third of the small percentage of felony cases that are tried, the defendant opts for trial by a judge without a jury.[142] As Professor Albert Alschuler states, 'American criminal procedure has become an administrative process rather than the adjudicative process it once was'.[143]

But even though only a tiny proportion of defendants are willing or able to submit their fate to juries, the jury retains importance in other ways. Attorneys settling cases often try to predict whether a jury would convict or acquit, bargaining in the shadow of the jury. While juries actually convict in two-thirds to three-quarters of all felony cases submitted to them, the conviction rate varies considerably depending on the type of crime.[144] Only about 3 percent of federal criminal cases tried to a jury end in hung juries;[145] in some localities, that percentage is higher.[146]

The justice system continues to devote a hefty portion of its resources to maintaining the criminal jury. Trial judges spend a significant amount of time trying criminal cases, and appellate judges expend considerable time reviewing them. In the federal courts, for example, although criminal case filings represented only 13 percent of all cases filed in 1994, 42 percent of all trials were criminal trials, and most of those were jury trials.[147] Jury administration costs to each court system include the expense of preparing and updating juror lists and pattern jury instructions, juror fees (up to fifty dollars per day in some jurisdictions, but in many states, much less),[148] jury administrators' salaries, jury summoning

[141] See BRIAN J. OSTROM & NEAL B. KAUDER, EXAMINING THE WORK OF STATE COURTS, 1993: A NATIONAL PERSPECTIVE FROM THE COURT STATISTICS PROJECT 48 (1995).

[142] See ibid. (noting figures for state courts).

[143] Alschuler & Deiss, *supra* note 8, at 925.

[144] See BUREAU OF JUSTICE STATISTICS, *supra* note 20, tbl. 5.28 (1997); OSTROM & KAUDER, *supra* note 141, at 50. For a thorough statistical profile of trials, and other steps in the criminal justice process, see LAFAVE *ET AL.*, *supra* note 31, § 1.3.

[145] See Michael J. Saks, *What Do Jury Experiments Tell Us About Jury Decisions?*, 6 S.C. INTERDISC. L.J. 1, 40 (1997) (collecting hung jury statistics in federal criminal jury trials from 1980 to 1993).

[146] See Roger Parloff, *Race and Juries: If It Ain't Broke . . .*, AMERICAN LAWYER, June 1997, at 5 (collecting statistics on acquittal rates and hung jury rates, finding that acquittal rates vary greatly, and that hung jury rates in Los Angeles have remained between 12% and 16% for over a decade).

[147] See David L. Cook *et al.*, *Criminal Caseload in U.S. District Courts: More Than Meets the Eye*, 44 AM. U. L. REV. 1578, 1591 (1995).

[148] See Munsterman, *supra* note 117, at 217.

and qualification mailings, proceedings to enforce jury summonses, jury education programs,[149] juror meals, and, for some cases, the cost of sequestering the jury during deliberations.[150]

Although criminal trials are much longer and more complex than the several-a-day trials of centuries past, they are still quite short. Nationwide, each felony jury trial takes about two to four days to complete, not weeks or even months as recent (and unusually lengthy) murder trials such as that of O. J. Simpson or Louise Woodward might suggest.[151] Complex, multi-defendant, or capital cases take longer to try than most felonies. The jury selection phase of a felony case can last less than an hour or can drag on for several days, but on average seems to take up about 20 to 35 percent of total trial time.[152] Often parties will not use all of their allotted peremptory challenges. *Batson* objections to these challenges are quite common in some courtrooms, rare in many others. During the government's case-in-chief, the prosecution typically presents several witnesses, often including a police officer or the crime victim, and in many cases will call an expert to the stand to assist the jury in evaluating evidence concerning illegal substances, firearms, wounds, injuries, physical conditions, or fingerprint, DNA, or other forensic analysis. The defendant may choose not to present any witnesses at all, opting instead to impeach the credibility of the government's witnesses. When the defense does present testimony, it usually takes up less time than the prosecution's case.[153]

[149] See, *e.g.*, Year 2000, *supra* note 123, at 5–6 (describing use of juror orientation video and recommending program to improve public attitudes toward jury service).

[150] Until it abandoned mandatory felony jury sequestration in 1996, the State of New York was spending more than $4 million annually just to house and supervise sequestered jurors in criminal cases. See The Jury Project, Report to the Chief Judge of the State of New York 13 (1994).

[151] See Commonwealth v. Woodward, 694 N.E.2d 1277 (Mass. 1998) (noting trial lasted three weeks).

[152] See Dale Anne Sipes *et al.*, On Trial: The Length of Civil and Criminal Trials 40 tbl. 18 (1988).

[153] For information on the length of trials, see ibid. Criminal jury trials in federal court average in length about four and one half days. See Cook *et al.*, *supra* note 147, at 1592–3. On the types of evidence submitted in felony trials in several urban courts, see Sipes *et al.*, *supra* note 152; Dale Ann Sipes & Barry Mahoney, *Toward Better Management of Criminal Litigation*, 72 Judicature 29, 34 (1988) (reporting that while a typical prosecution in Oakland and Marin Counties in California involved at least one expert witness and three officials (police officers, etc.), prosecutors in other urban areas studied used only two officials and rarely used experts); see also Ostrom & Kauder, *supra* note 141, at 50 (reporting that actual trial time for a typical felony jury trial in the cities they studied averaged 11 hours and that the prosecution consumed about twice as much time as the defense).

The criminal jury trial plays a prominent role in the nation's psyche as well as its budget. Many believe, or at least believed at one time, that one of the jury's primary functions is to educate citizens in democracy through their participation as jurors.[154] Yet most Americans will never have the experience of deliberating as a juror. Each year, about one-quarter to one-half of the estimated twenty million individuals who receive jury qualification questionnaires in the mail will be exempted, disqualified, or excused from serving.[155] Others will be summoned but will not show up.[156] Less than half of those who do appear for jury service will become sworn jurors in any case, criminal or civil.[157] Some citizens experience juries as defendants, witnesses, attorneys, or court officers. A far greater number of Americans learn about criminal juries second-hand, schooled about the criminal jury through media accounts of jury trials.[158] Criminal jury trials continue to be front-page, box-office, best-seller material year after year, and now are even available on their own cable channel, Court TV.[159] This endless supply of dramatic highlights of real and imaginary prosecutions is, for much of America, the only source of information about the criminal jury.[160]

[154] See, *e.g.*, Vikram Amar, *Jury Service as Political Participation Akin to Voting*, 80 CORNELL L. REV. 239 (1995).

[155] See G. THOMAS MUNSTERMAN, JURY SYSTEM MANAGEMENT 47 (National Center for State Courts 1996).

[156] See ibid.

[157] These figures vary greatly from jurisdiction to jurisdiction. For example, in Washington, D.C., of those summoned for jury service, 19% purposely ignored their summonses, and 43% never received it through the mail. See YEAR 2000, *supra* note 123, at 1. Other jurisdictions report near-perfect compliance. See King, *supra* note 45, at 2697 n.89 (collecting response rates ranging from over 93% to less than half of those summoned). The National Center for State Courts recommends that courts design their jury systems so that no more than half of the jurors reporting go home without being sworn in as jurors. See Munsterman, *supra* note 155, at 86 tbl. 7-1.

[158] See SUSANNA BARBER, NEWS CAMERAS IN THE COURTROOM: A FREE PRESS-FAIR TRIAL DEBATE xiv (1987):

> 'Though television is only one source of citizens' knowledge about courts and law, it may well be the single most common and pervasive source of *shared* information and imagery. . . . [T]ypical viewers of prime time dramatic network programs will see 43 law enforcers, 6 lawyers, and 3 judges every week—all fictional but realistically portrayed. They nearly all work on criminal cases. . . . The legal process is practically invisible . . . Viewers rarely see arraignments, indictments, pre-trial hearings, plea-bargaining, jury selection, or jury deliberations.'

[159] See PAUL THALER, THE WATCHFUL EYE: AMERICAN JUSTICE IN THE AGE OF THE TELEVISION TRIAL 3–6 (1994).

[160] See ibid., at 6–10.

VIII. Publicity and the Jury

The American public has always been fascinated by crime and criminals, eagerly consuming news of crime before, during, and even after a prosecution. In the United States, as in other countries where the jury is employed, the jurors' views of a case may be influenced by media accounts of the crime, the victims, or the alleged perpetrator, including information that would not be admissible at trial. As elsewhere, this kind of influence can threaten the impartiality of the jury and the legitimacy of its decision. But in America, the fear of the influence of publicity on verdicts is more pronounced than in other countries. For example, whatever prejudices English jurors may bring with them to the jury room are assumed in that country to cancel each other out in the decision making process.[161] Not so in the United States.

Jurors' exposure to publicity can be fatal to a verdict. Judges and attorneys often take great care to empanel jurors who have not heard much about the case and to protect those jurors from publicity during the course of the trial.[162] The intensified concern about media taint in the United States may be due to the greater potential for such influence. Unlike the law of other countries, American law does not control the effects of publicity on jurors by barring the press from disseminating information about a criminal case before and during a trial.[163] Such restrictions, even if they could be effective in the age of the Internet, are contrary to the First Amendment protection of freedom of speech.[164] A defendant's inadmissible confession or prior record, the details of the victim's loss, legal pundits' speculation about the trial and sentence, reports of rulings made outside the hearing of the jury, and other inadmissible information may be freely broadcast into the homes and delivered to the doorstep of every juror and potential juror prior to and during the trial. The Constitution guarantees the press access to trials as well as the freedom to report whatever it learns, forbidding exclusion of the press except when 'necessitated by a com-

[161] See Sally Lloyd-Bostock & Cheryl Thomas, *Decline of the 'Little Parliament': Juries and Jury Reform in England and Wales*, 62 Law & Contemp. Probs. 7, 25 (Spring 1999) (noting that '[t]he defence has practically no information on which to base . . . a challenge and no right to ask potential members of the jury exploratory questions').

[162] See King, *supra* note 45, at 2729; Strauss, *supra* note 46, at 83–8.

[163] See Lloyd-Bostock & Thomas, *supra* note 161, at 28–31.

[164] See Nebraska Press Ass'n v. Stuart, 427 U.S. 539 (1976).

pelling governmental interest', and by means 'narrowly tailored to serve that interest'.[165]

Instead of the media, then, it is the jurors, together with the judge, who carry the burden of keeping the trial process free from information untested in the crucible of trial procedure. Jury selection is expected to screen adequately those potential jurors whose exposure to publicity has left them irreparably influenced,[166] even though the result may be a jury stripped of people who stay informed about the greater world around them.[167] At times, an entire community may be saturated with outrage, suspicion, or rumor, so that jurors who lack strong views about a case are hard to find. In such cases, a judge may order a change of venue to a different location.[168] Jurors who are chosen are expected to follow the court's instructions not to pay attention to media accounts or other discussions of the case during the trial, subject to dismissal from the jury should they disobey. In some cases, a court may keep the names and addresses of jurors from the press and even from the parties, to relieve juror anxiety about being approached by parties, witnesses, sympathizers for one side or the other, or by reporters.[169]

After the trial, free speech principles continue to influence a judge's ability to regulate jurors. For example, judges cannot issue gag orders preventing jurors from seeking out members of the press and telling all about their deliberations.[170] At most, a court might be able to prohibit the press and others from approaching hesitant jurors and pressing them for information about their secret deliberations after the trial.[171]

Despite all of these protections for the press, and the impression one might get by watching the television news, the vast majority of criminal

[165] Press Enterprise Co. v. Superior Court, 478 U.S. 1, 13–14 (1986); Globe Newspaper v. Superior Court, 457 U.S. 596, 606–7 (1982); Richmond Newspapers, Inc. v. Virginia, 448 U.S. 55 (1980).

[166] See *Press Enterprise Co.*, 478 U.S. at 14.

[167] Barring news consumers from juries is, in Jeffrey Abramson's view, 'rabidly antidemocratic'. Abramson, *supra* note 80, at 248.

[168] For an in-depth look at a change of venue controversy, see Laurie L. Levenson, *Change of Venue and the Role of the Criminal Jury*, 66 S. Cal. L. Rev. 1533 (1993) (discussing the state prosecution of the officers charged with beating motorist Rodney King).

[169] See King, *supra* note 132, at 130–2.

[170] See Marcy Strauss, *Juror Journalism*, 12 Yale L. & Pol'y Rev. 389 (1994).

[171] See United States v. Cleveland, 128 F.3d 267 (5th Cir. 1997) (upholding, against First Amendment challenge by press, trial judge's mandate that, 'absent a special order by' the judge, 'no juror may be interviewed by anyone concerning the deliberations of the jury').

trials in the United States go forward quietly, without attorneys giving press conferences on the courthouse steps, without debriefings on nightly television talk shows, and without cameras broadcasting live courtroom events. Most criminal trials are covered only by local press, if at all. Many courtrooms in the United States still lack video recording equipment. Although several states have installed such equipment and also allow for television coverage, other courts continue to ban cameras or audio recording equipment in the courtroom, allowing access only to representatives of the print media.[172] Attorneys, too, are barred in many states by rules of professional conduct from commenting in any detail about their trials, a restriction that has been upheld by the Supreme Court as consistent with the First Amendment.[173]

IX. The Capital Jury: The American Death Penalty

One of the most unique tasks of the criminal jury in the United States is deciding whether a convicted criminal will be put to death for his crime.[174] Presently, the federal government and about three-quarters of the states have authorized the death penalty, and in most of these states the jury, not the judge, decides whether the defendant should be sentenced to death.[175] The Court has interpreted the prohibition against 'cruel and unusual punishment' in the Eighth Amendment to bar the imposition of the death penalty except for the most serious crimes, so that today essentially only murderers are sentenced to death. Hence, capital jury trials are relatively uncommon. Of the 2,000 to 4,000 defendants a year charged with a crime that makes them eligible for the death penalty, only about 6 to 15 percent receive a death sentence, an average of about 250 death sentences per year.[176]

For much of American history, jurors were given little, if any, guidance on how they should decide who would live or die, and judges had little power to review a jury's sentencing decision. As Professor Randall Kennedy has vividly portrayed in his book *Race, Crime, and the Law*, capital trials in the United States have been plagued by racial

[172] See, *e.g.*, United States v. Edwards, 785 F.2d 1293 (5th Cir. 1986); Westmoreland v. CBS, Inc., 752 F.2d 16 (2d Cir. 1984).

[173] See Gentile v. State Bar, 501 U.S. 1030 (1991).

[174] For a complete listing of which nations authorize the sentence of death, see THE DEATH PENALTY IN AMERICA: CURRENT CONTROVERSIES 78–83 (Hugo A. Bedau ed., 1997).

[175] See LAFAVE *ET AL.*, *supra* note 31, §§ 26.1(b), 26.3(b).

[176] See ABRAMSON, *supra* note 80, at 213–14; THE DEATH PENALTY IN AMERICA, *supra* note 174, at 31–2.

injustice.[177] The death penalty was employed frequently in cases in which African-American men were convicted of raping white women, for example.[178] In 1972, in *Furman* v. *Georgia*,[179] the Supreme Court attempted to put a stop to arbitrary death sentencing. The decision struck down dozens of state sentencing schemes as violative of the Eighth Amendment's prohibition of cruel and unusual punishment.[180] Within five years, however, the Court upheld revised state sentencing statutes that were designed by state legislatures to ensure that the death penalty would be imposed in a more consistent, yet more individualized, manner.[181] In dozens of subsequent decisions, the Court has continued to map out the complex procedures required by the Constitution in order to impose the penalty of death.[182] A brief summary of those procedures follows.

The trial of a person charged with a capital crime has two separate stages: the determination of guilt or innocence, and the selection of a sentence. Only after the guilt-or-innocence phase ends with a verdict of guilt does the jury hear evidence concerning the appropriate sentence. Yet because the same jurors who decide the sentence also decide guilt, the questions during *voir dire* often focus on the sentencing decision. Potential jurors are carefully interrogated about their attitudes about the death penalty. While many of these potential jurors will have never thought seriously about capital punishment before, others will voice strong, sometimes religiously based views for or against capital punishment. For nearly two centuries, those potential jurors who revealed conscientious scruples about sentencing someone to death, or who were otherwise opposed to capital punishment, were struck from the juries in capital cases 'for cause'. In 1968, the Court found that this practice violated the defendant's rights to due process and to an impartial jury under the Sixth Amendment.[183] Today, potential jurors who cannot impose a sentence of death and thus lack the capacity to apply the law are subject to disqualification for cause, but those who might be able to sentence someone to death (and are simply

[177] See Kennedy, *supra* note 36.

[178] Eventually, the Supreme Court in 1977 held that the death penalty was an unconstitutionally severe punishment for the crime of rape. See Coker v. Georgia, 433 U.S. 584 (1977).

[179] 408 U.S. 238 (1972).

[180] See ibid., at 239.

[181] See Jurek v. Texas, 428 U.S. 262 (1976); Gregg v. Georgia, 428 U.S. 153 (1976).

[182] For useful discussions of the death penalty and the jury, see Abramson, *supra* note 80, at 207–39, and Jordan Steiker, *The Limits of Legal Language: Decisionmaking in Capital Cases*, 94 Mich L. Rev. 2590 (1996).

[183] See Witherspoon v. Illinois, 391 U.S. 510 (1968).

reluctant to do so) are qualified to serve.[184] Government attorneys nevertheless strike such moderate opponents of the death penalty from capital juries when they can with peremptory challenges. Indeed, both parties in capital cases are usually allotted more peremptory challenges than in noncapital cases, ostensibly to provide greater assurance that the jurors who remain on the panel are fair.

The sentencing phase of a capital case is a trial-like, adversarial hearing during which the parties present evidence of certain aggravating or mitigating factors. The government and the defense may present information about the character of the convicted defendant and, in many states, the jurors are exposed to victim-impact evidence. Jurors are instructed that they must unanimously agree that specified aggravating factors have been established beyond a reasonable doubt before they can impose a death sentence. For these jurors, the process of deciding whether to sentence a defendant to death is always a trying, and often a confusing, ordeal. A mammoth study involving lengthy interviews with hundreds of people who have served as jurors in death penalty proceedings[185] has revealed that jurors often misunderstand what will happen to the defendant if they decide not to impose the death penalty, believe that their decision is merely advisory, or misunderstand which factors can and cannot be considered, what level of proof is required, and what degree of concurrence is required for aggravating and mitigating factors.[186]

The dozens of decisions fine-tuning the death sentencing process have failed to dispel the belief, still held by a significant percentage of Americans, that the death penalty is imposed in a racially discriminatory manner.[187] In 1987, lawyers seeking to overturn the death sentence of Warren McCleskey, an African-American man convicted of murdering Frank Schlatt, a white police officer, presented studies that many believed demonstrated that the race of the victim consistently influenced capital sentencing decisions in Georgia.[188] In particular, defendants convicted of killing whites were much more likely to receive the death

[184] See Witherspoon v. Illinois, 391 U.S. 510 (1968).

[185] See William J. Bowers, *The Capital Jury Project: Rationale, Design, and Preview of Early Findings*, 70 Ind. L.J. 1043, 1077–85 (1995) (describing study).

[186] See William J. Bowers, *The Capital Jury: Is It Tilted Toward Death?*, 79 Judicature 220 (1996).

[187] See, *e.g.*, Dan Smith, *Death Penalty Supported in State*, Sacramento Bee, Mar. 14, 1997, at A3 (stating that 40% of respondents polled in California believe racial discrimination is a 'big factor in the application of the death penalty').

[188] See McCleskey v. Kemp, 481 U.S. 279, 286 (1987).

penalty than those who murdered African-Americans. The Court assumed the studies were valid, but refused to overturn McCleskey's sentence absent proof that the decision maker in McCleskey's case discriminated on the basis of race.[189] The Court's decision in *McCleskey* prompted the House of Representatives to endorse a federal statutory remedy for capital defendants whose statistical evidence of discrimination could not be rebutted by the state, but the bill failed to pass the Senate.[190] Studies continue to suggest that prosecutors are more likely to seek, and jurors more likely to impose, the sentence of death if the victim of the crime was white.[191] The problem of how to remedy discrimination in capital cases continues to confound courts and critics, dividing them into those who favor removing discretion entirely through either mandatory death sentences or the abolition of the death penalty, and those who seek to maintain, but somehow limit, sentencing discretion.[192]

X. Conclusion

The jury system in America took root in the midst of political conflict between those who served as jurors and those who served as judges. Today, judges in the United States are either elected by the people or appointed by elected officials; they are no longer agents of a foreign nation. Still, jurors and judges continue to disagree, coming from different backgrounds, with different attitudes about crime, about police, and about those who file in and out of witness boxes. Juries regularly surprise the system's insiders, sometimes through dramatic verdicts, sometimes in other, less momentous ways, such as the juror who one day, presumably out of frustration with the repetitive nature of the evidence, brought a sign with him to court that read, '[w]e got it the first time',[193] the juror who holds out for acquittal against the rest, or the juror who wants a question asked of the witness. Clearly, an independent spirit lives within some American jurors.

[189] See ibid., at 312–13.

[190] See Kennedy, *supra* note 36, at 345–8.

[191] See David C. Baldus & George Woodworth, *Race Discrimination and the Death Penalty: An Empirical and Legal Overview, in* America's Experiment with Capital Punishment: Reflections on the Past, Present and Future of the Ultimate Penal Sanction 385, 397–403 (James R. Acker *et al.*, eds., 1998).

[192] See ibid.

[193] See *Malpractice Suit Jury Impatient*, Detroit Free Press, Nov. 21, 1997, at 4B (reporting that a juror brought two signs into court, one said, 'We got it the first time' and the other said, 'Stop the Insanity').

As juries become both less common and more expensive, some have questioned the wisdom of preserving the criminal jury in its present form.[194] The benefits of the jury are difficult to quantify, but jury verdicts continue to earn widespread acceptance by the public and trial by jury remains a cherished right of most Americans. In any event, many basic features of the criminal jury in the United States cannot be modified without either constitutional amendment or radical reinterpretations of the Bill of Rights. Judges and legislators continue to tinker within constitutional confines, some hoping to improve the jury trial by helping jurors deliberate more carefully, others hoping to improve the speed and flexibility of jury trials, still others hoping to promote greater juror participation. Ultimately, the success or failure of any jury reform will depend on its ability to accommodate those values unique to American criminal justice: a fierce attachment to adversarial advocacy, respect for state autonomy, an improving sensitivity to racial equality, the expectation of jury independence from judicial control, and a deep commitment to freedom of speech.

[194] See, *e.g.*, Parloff, *supra* note 146 (noting efforts to scrap unanimity requirement).

4 Criminal Trial Juries in Australia: From Penal Colonies to a Federal Democracy

Michael Chesterman*

I. Introduction: History of Criminal Juries

As recently as forty years ago, Australians within certain social classes and age-groups regularly described a journey to England as 'going home', even if they had in fact been born in Australia to Australian parents. It is therefore no surprise that, along with numerous other English social, cultural, and legal practices, the English model of trial by jury was adopted in each of the Australian colonies at a relatively early stage of its development and remains an enduring feature of the Australian legal system. Interesting adaptations of this model are to be found in Australia, as this chapter will demonstrate, but the core concept remains essentially unchanged.

A. Juries in the Australian Colonies of the Nineteenth Century

The introduction of juries[1] during the nineteenth century into Britain's colonies in Australia played an integral role in moving the country toward democratic government and the establishment of the rule of law.[2]

* Professor of Law, University of New South Wales; Acting Judge, District Court of New South Wales. I am very grateful to Pamela Verrall for carrying out valuable research, to the Australian Research Council for funding this research, and to Professor David Brown of the University of New South Wales Law Faculty for critical commentary on a draft version.

[1] This account of juries in Australia addresses only the trial of criminal offences by petit jury. Grand juries, although briefly used in some of the Australian colonies during the 19th century, and still available in Victoria in theory, have never been of practical significance in Australia. Civil juries are still used, but in a decreasing minority of cases. Apart from the fact that in some jurisdictions they have only four members, they present no features of special interest. This ch. lays out the history of the establishment of juries in Australia, and discusses how juries have been utilized and limited. It also examines some of the difficult issues facing juries and analyzes the protections established to protect jury impartiality.

[2] The ensuing historical summary draws heavily on the work of DAVID NEAL, THE RULE OF LAW IN A PENAL COLONY ch.7 (1991); see also LAW REFORM COMM'N OF VICTORIA, BACKGROUND PAPER NO. 1, THE ROLE OF THE JURY IN CRIMINAL TRIALS app. 9 (1985); NEW SOUTH WALES LAW REFORM COMM'N, DISCUSSION PAPER NO. 12, THE JURY IN A CRIMINAL TRIAL ch. 1 (1985); J. M. Bennett, *The Establishment of Jury Trial in New South Wales*, 3 SYDNEY

It gave ordinary citizens a significant role to play in the administration of justice, making inroads into the potentially oppressive authority of judges, colonial governors, and, at a more remote level, the British Colonial Office.

In the first-established colony, New South Wales, this familiar political dimension of a community's adoption of jury trial had an unusual twist to it. In this instance, the struggles over jury trial formed part—an important part—of a wider battle over full citizenship rights for ex-convicts. Four of the six Australian States (New South Wales, Queensland, Tasmania, and Victoria, but not South Australia or Western Australia) began life as penal colonies, to which numerous convicted criminals were transported from Britain as punishment. By modern standards, the convicts' crimes were often trivial: for example, a theft of property worth less than two pounds. Thefts to the value of two pounds or more were punishable by hanging.

In the first thirty-odd years after the arrival of the First Fleet in Sydney,[3] New South Wales, in January 1788, the only 'juries' used comprised of six military officers, chosen by the Governor, sitting with a military judicial officer, the Judge-Advocate. During this period, many convicts served their sentences, elected to stay in the colony, and acquired sufficient land to qualify them for jury service. Yet they were still subject to a form of trial in which any resentment or prejudice against them on the part of the Governor or his military associates could weigh heavily against them.

During this time, free settlers ('Exclusives') who migrated from Britain did not leave their prejudices behind along with their homes. But freed convicts ('Emancipists') greatly outnumbered them, so much so that trial by jury of civilians would not be feasible unless Emancipists could be empanelled as jurors. Predictably, the Exclusives strongly resisted this measure. They argued that Emancipists would be far too willing to acquit and, moreover, that they themselves should not suffer the indignity of trial before jurors who were still tainted by their criminal records, even though they might now be law-abiding people who were able to satisfy a property qualification.

L. Rev. 463 (1959–60); A. C. Castles, *The Judiciary and Political Questions: The First Australian Experience, 1824–1825*, 5 Adel. L. Rev. 294 (1975); H. V. Evatt, *The Jury System in Australia*, 10 Austl. L. J. 46 (1936).

[3] White settlement commenced in Australia when the first group of convict ships to be sent out from England, known as the 'First Fleet', reached what is now Sydney Harbour on Jan. 26, 1788. Its commander, Arthur Phillip, became the first Governor of New South Wales.

These arguments were put forward in the context of fierce political resistance by Exclusives to the broader notion that Emancipists should be recognized as full citizens, with the capacity, among other things, to be appointed to public office or to practise as lawyers. The Emancipists, for their part, freely engaged in political rhetoric about juries found in other British colonial settlements at a similar stage of development; for example, that trial by one's peers was the 'birthright' of every Englishman. But this was more a power-struggle over equality of status between these two clearly defined groups within the colony than a legal debate about the merits and demerits of juries within a small community.

The efforts of Emancipists to secure jury trial for the colony, beginning in 1819 with a petition to the Colonial Office, produced only partial success during the ensuing twenty years. Between 1824 and 1828, juries of twelve, from which Emancipists were excluded, were used in Quarter Sessions trials, but not in the Supreme Court. Under British legislation passed in 1828, a Supreme Court judge could grant trial by jury in civil cases on the application of either party, but amending legislation was needed in 1829 to permit Emancipists to sit as jurors. At last, in 1833, criminal trial juries with twelve members were introduced in the Supreme Court, yet the accused could choose instead to be tried by a military panel of seven members. Not until 1839 was this option abolished.

Significantly, transportation of convicts from Britain had ceased by this time. The first important steps toward representative government in the colony were taken only three years later. The Emancipists, while winning the battle over juries, had also won the war over equal citizenship at a sufficiently early stage to participate in the first democratic institutions of government in Australia.

In the other Australian colonies, the process of establishing jury trial was not so long or painful. In Victoria, for instance, which was first settled in 1836, the first jury trial took place in 1839 and the jury system was permanently introduced in 1847. Each of the other four colonies (Queensland, South Australia, Tasmania, and Western Australia) found their way to jury trial well before the end of the nineteenth century.

B. Federation, with a Constitutional Provision for Jury Trial

At the beginning of the new century, in 1901, the six colonies federated to become the Commonwealth of Australia. Under the Commonwealth

Constitution, which entered into force on January 1, 1901, the former colonies, transformed into States, retained their former general legislative powers over matters of criminal law and procedure, including the process of jury trial. The new central Commonwealth Government obtained no general power to legislate on these matters, except in relation to the territories, over which it acquired plenary power. Within the last twenty years, however, it has granted limited self-government to the two principal Territories—that is, the Australian Capital Territory and the Northern Territory—which now control their general criminal law. For practical purposes, the legislative powers of the Commonwealth Government are confined to a number of specific subject-matters—for example, external affairs, interstate trade and commerce, taxation, and communications—and to matters relating to Commonwealth Government institutions.

Although the Commonwealth Constitution limits the federated government's powers, the Commonwealth can create criminal offences as part of such legislation, and has done so frequently. For example, corporate fraud offences and offences relating to the importation of prohibited drugs from overseas are Commonwealth offences, enacted under the Commonwealth's powers to regulate corporations and to control imports, respectively. Nonetheless, all Commonwealth offences are tried in State or Territory courts. Federal courts have been created by the Constitution itself—namely, the High Court, which functions both as the court of constitutional interpretation and the highest general court of appeal—and by Commonwealth legislation (the Federal Court and the Family Court). None of these courts, however, possesses any original criminal jurisdiction.

Accordingly, while federation set in motion the creation of an important body of Commonwealth criminal law, it did not give rise to new trial procedures at the Commonwealth level. But one provision of the Constitution, governing the trial of these offences in State courts, has a direct impact on criminal procedure. Section 80 of the Constitution begins with the words '[t]he trial on indictment of any offence against any law of the Commonwealth shall be by jury . . .'.[4]

This provision is remarkable because the Australian Constitution, unlike that of the United States, from which it borrows many significant elements, contains no general Bill of Rights and very few guarantees of

[4] CONST. s. 80 (Austl.).

citizens' rights.[5] The inclusion of this clause requiring jury trial for Commonwealth offences—though not, it should be emphasised, for the much larger range of State offences, which include the 'classic' common law crimes—is a striking testament to the importance attributed to criminal jury trial by Australian politicians and lawyers 100 years ago. Jury trial was said in the debates leading up to the preparation of the Constitution to be 'a necessary safeguard to the individual liberty of the subject in every state'.[6]

The impact of section 80 has been distinctly weaker than might have been expected or hoped for.[7] Although the fight to incorporate juries into the Australian legal system was won during the nineteenth century, the interpretation of this constitutional guarantee of jury trial has served to limit its effect throughout the present century.

II. Use of Juries in Criminal Cases

A. *Offences Arising Under the Common Law or Under a Statute of a State or a Territory*

The bulk of criminal offences in Australia arise under the common law or under State or Territory statutes. The availability of juries when these offences are tried in the appropriate State or Territory court is thus an issue of primary importance. The most important classification of criminal offences in Australian law is between 'indictable' and 'nonindictable' (more normally called 'summary') offences. The distinction between these two classes of offence determines substantially, but by no means wholly, whether an offence will be tried before a jury.

An indictable offence under State or Territory law is one which *may* be tried on indictment. If it is so tried, three things follow. First, the offence will be tried in a superior court—that is, the Supreme Court of a State or Territory—or an intermediate court, such as a District or County Court. Secondly, it will be prosecuted in the name of the Crown

[5] The Australian Constitution provides only limited protection of citizen's rights against Commonwealth laws. For example, the Constitution establishes limited guarantees of freedom of religion (s. 116) and freedom from discrimination on grounds of place of residence (s. 117), and requires the Commonwealth to compensate citizens whose property is compulsorily acquired (s. 51(xxxi)).

[6] Official Record of the Debates of the Australian Federal Convention 350 (3d Sess. 1898), vol.1.

[7] See *infra* text accompanying notes 14–23.

through a formal document under the hand of an Attorney-General, a Director of Public Prosecutions, or some other state-authorized officer. Thirdly, a twelve-member jury will normally be empanelled. Investigation into whether sufficient evidence is available to warrant the case going to trial is generally entrusted to committing magistrates, though Attorneys General and Directors of Public Prosecutions can bypass committal proceedings by filing an *ex officio* indictment. The characterization of an offence as indictable is frequently stipulated expressly in the legislation creating it. Alternatively, it may be determined by a general provision to the effect that any offence carrying a maximum sentence above a specified limit—typically, one year's imprisonment—is to be deemed to be indictable unless the contrary intention appears in the provision.

The classification of an offence as indictable does not necessarily mean, however, that any charge laid for the offence *must* be tried on indictment. Although this is the rule for the most serious indictable offences, such as murder or rape, in a wide range of other such offences, the option exists between trying them on indictment or as summary offences in a magistrates' court. In some instances, these 'hybrid' offences carry a substantial maximum penalty, such as imprisonment for ten years. The question whether such an offence will in a given case be tried on indictment or summarily is governed by one or more of a wide range of factors, generally spelled out in relevant legislation. These include, in particular, the seriousness of the criminal conduct alleged against the accused, the opinion or wishes of the accused, and the views of the prosecutor and of the court which would hear the case if it proceeded summarily. When a hybrid offence is tried summarily, a significantly lower maximum sentence is available to the court than if it were tried on indictment.

By contrast, a proceeding for a nonindictable or summary offence is not, in formal terms, a 'plea of the Crown'. It may be prosecuted by a police officer or a private citizen and it is tried by a magistrate or bench of magistrates, sitting without a jury. Another form of summary trial exists for cases of contempt (which in strict terms is not a criminal offence even though it attracts criminal penalties). These are tried by a single judge or magistrate or by a full bench of a superior court, again without a jury.

A further complication is that in four Australian jurisdictions (the States of New South Wales, South Australia, and Western Australia, and the Australian Capital Territory), a person who has been prosecuted on indictment in a superior or intermediate court may elect to be tried by a judge sitting alone. To prevent 'judge-shopping', the accused is required to make the election before the identity of the trial judge is known to him or her. Except in Western Australia, the judge must be satisfied that the accused has been advised on this issue by a legal practitioner. In New South Wales and Western Australia, the legislation requires the consent of the prosecutor as well, but prosecutorial vetoes rarely occur in practice.[8] On occasions, trial judges—who do not possess any veto power—have expressed concern about the idea that the trial of a major indictable offence may take place without a jury.[9]

In South Australia, where this form of trial by judge alone was first introduced, thirty-eight of them were held in the Supreme Court between 1989 and 1993 (the annual proportion of all criminal trials in the Court ranged between 3.9 percent and 8.9 percent).[10] In New South Wales, less than 5 percent of criminal trials in the District Court during a nine-month period in 1991–92 were conducted without a jury.[11]

The overall trend in recent decades clearly has been toward enhancement of the range of offences that will in practice be tried summarily (regardless of whether they fall within the category of 'indictable'). To illustrate this, in New South Wales in 1994, juries were used in no more than 1 percent of all criminal cases (including those with pleas of guilty) and 4 percent of those where a plea of not guilty was entered.[12] Yet changes introduced in that State in the following year reduced jury use even further. They replaced a system of requiring an accused person's consent to summary trial within a range of offences with a system that requires the accused to elect positively for trial on indictment. A wide range of thefts and other offences involving dishonesty, plus offences involving corruption of witnesses or jurors or escape from lawful custody, are now normally tried summarily by a magistrate, whereas before 1995

[8] Consent was recently refused by the prosecution in New South Wales when Ivan Milat, the accused in a very high-profile case called the 'backpacker murders', elected trial by judge alone, claiming that a jury would be prejudiced against him because of media publicity. Judicial review of this refusal by the Director of Public Prosecutions was then refused by the Supreme Court. See M. v. DPP (June 3, 1996) (unreported) (Dunford, J).

[9] In *R.* v. *Marshall* (1986) 43 S.A.S.R. 448 (Sup. Ct. S. Austl.), the first murder trial to be conducted alone by a judge in Australia, the trial judge expressed misgivings about shifting many important value judgements from jury to judge. See ibid., at 496–9; see also Justice D. C. Heenan, *Trial by Judge Alone*, 4 J. Jud. Admin. 240 (1995); Justice P. Hidden, *Trial by Judge Alone in New South Wales*, 9 Jud. Officers Bull. 41 (1997); John Willis, *Trial by Judge Alone*, 7 J. Jud. Admin. 144 (1998).

[10] See Heenan, *supra* note 9, at 243.

[11] See ibid.

[12] See generally David Brown *et al.*, Criminal Laws 253–4 (2d ed. 1996), vol. 1.

they were invariably tried on indictment before a jury in the District Court.[13]

B. Commonwealth Offences

As already indicated, offences under Commonwealth laws relate only to specific subject matters that fall within Commonwealth legislative power. Comparatively speaking, they are not numerous, though they cover some areas of considerable significance in modern times, notably the importation of prohibited drugs. They are classified in the same way as State and Territory offences and are tried in State or Territory courts.

When tried in a state court, commonwealth offences[14] are subject to the requirement in section 80 of the Commonwealth Constitution that '[t]he trial on indictment of any offence against any law of the Commonwealth shall be by jury . . . .'[15] But the foregoing outline of classifications of offences should be enough to show that this phraseology is, on a straightforward interpretation, distinctly circular. Literally interpreted, it means merely that when a Commonwealth offence is tried under the procedure, involving trial by jury, which is generally stipulated for offences prosecuted on indictment, there shall indeed be trial by jury. This is not to require that all *indictable* offences—which would at least bring in the hybrid category described above—must be brought before a jury, but only that those which *are in fact prosecuted on indictment* must be tried in this way.

Despite some powerful dissenting judgments,[16] this literal interpretation has in fact been adopted by the High Court of Australia.[17] A Chief Justice of the Court has quite openly acknowledged that in consequence '[w]hat might have been thought to be a great constitutional guarantee has been discovered to be a mere procedural provision'.[18] Section 80, so

[13] See Trevor Nyman, *New Procedures Under Criminal Procedure Act*, 33(8) L. Soc'y J. 15 (1995).

[14] These do not include offences created by the Commonwealth Parliament in the exercise of its power to legislate for a territory. See *R.* v. *Bernasconi* (1915) 19 C.L.R. 629 (Austl. H. Ct.); see also *supra* text accompanying notes 4–6.

[15] Const. s. 80 (Austl.).

[16] See *Kingswell* v. *R.* (1985) 159 C.L.R. 264, 296 (Austl. H. Ct.) (Deane J); *Li Chia Hsing* v. *Rankin* (1978) 141 C.L.R. 182, 196–203 (Austl. H. Ct.) (Murphy J); *R.* v. *Federal Court of Bankruptcy ex parte Lowenstein* (1938) 59 C.L.R. 556, 581–5 (Austl. H. Ct.) (Dixon & Evatt JJ).

[17] See *Li Chia Hsing* (1978) 141 C.L.R. at 182; *Zarb* v. *Kennedy* (1968) 121 C.L.R. 283 (Austl. H. Ct.); *R.* v. *Archdall & Roskruge ex parte Corrigan & Brown* (1928) 41 C.L.R. 128 (Austl. H. Ct.).

[18] *Spratt* v. *Hermes* (1965) 114 C.L.R. 226, 244 (Austl. H. Ct.) (Barwick CJ).

interpreted, gives full leeway to the Commonwealth Parliament to choose summary trial rather than trial on indictment for any Commonwealth offence, no matter how serious, or to characterize the offence as hybrid, leaving the mode of trial to be determined by the prosecutor, the court, and the accused in each individual case. The sole outcome of the section, to quote another High Court judge, is that 'if there be an indictment, there must be a jury; but there is nothing to compel procedure by indictment'.[19]

The reason for the choice of wording of section 80 seems to have been that the drafters of the Constitution believed that it might avert the problems that the courts of the United States had encountered in interpreting the phrase 'all Crimes' in the guarantee of trial by jury contained in Article III, Section 2 of the United States Constitution. Yet they were warned of the inherent circularity of the wording they adopted.[20] In an eloquent dissenting judgment opposing the accepted literal interpretation of section 80, Deane J in *Kingswell* v. *R.* argued that the section 'reflected a deep-seated conviction of free men and women about the way in which justice should be administered in criminal cases'[21] and that it should in fact be interpreted along lines similar to those adopted in the United States for the phrase 'all Crimes'—namely, that it should apply to any 'serious' offence against a Commonwealth law. He tentatively suggested that an offence should be deemed 'serious' if it was punishable by a maximum prison sentence of more than one year.[22] Only a wholly new interpretation such as this would, in his view, eliminate the 'potentially mischievous mockery' of the Constitution inherent in the accepted literal interpretation.[23]

This literal interpretation does not, however, leave section 80 wholly devoid of content. One form of trial currently open for some State and Territory offences which are actually prosecuted on indictment is a trial by judge alone,[24] when the accused so elects and (in most versions) the prosecutor consents. In *Brown* v. *R.*,[25] the High Court held by majority that section 80 invalidated this mode of trial for Commonwealth

[19] *Archdall & Roskruge* (1928) 41 C.L.R. at 139–40 (Higgins J).

[20] See, *e.g.*, Graham Fricke, Trial by Jury 3–4 (1997); Sam Ricketson, Trial by Jury (1983).

[21] (1985) 159 C.L.R. 264, 268 (Austl. H. Ct.).

[22] See ibid., at 319.

[23] Ibid., at 307. The notion that a literal interpretation of s. 80 makes a 'mockery' of the Constitution is drawn from *R.* v. *Federal Court of Bankruptcy ex parte Lowenstein* (1938) 59 C.L.R. 556, 580–2 (Austl. H. Ct.) (Dixon & Evatt JJ dissenting).

[24] See *supra* text accompanying notes 8–11.

[25] (1986) 160 C.L.R. 171 (Austl. H. Ct.) (3–2 majority decision).

offences. The majority took the view that, unlike Article III, Section 2 of the United States Constitution (when read in conjunction with the Sixth Amendment), section 80 does not simply confer a private right of a jury trial on the accused, which he or she can waive at will. The right, the High Court held, exists for the benefit of society generally, and fosters 'the ideal of equality in a democratic community'.[26] It also promotes public acceptance of decisions in criminal trials since they are not made either by 'a judge or magistrate who might be, or be portrayed as being, over-responsive to authority or remote from the affairs and concerns of ordinary people' or 'by reference to sensational or self-righteous publicity or the passions of the mob'.[27]

The existence of section 80 poses a broad question of policy for the trial of Commonwealth offences when an indictment is filed. These offences are uniform in substantive terms throughout the Commonwealth and have been tried, since 1995, according to a uniform law of evidence. But the versions of trial by jury adopted within the States differ from each other. There are different rules, for instance, in relation to exemptions from jury service, grounds to be excused, and challenges of individual jurors. The underlying policy question is whether the variations between the States should be permitted to remain, so that each State has a uniform jury process for all its jury trials on indictment, or whether the Commonwealth should legislate to require that where section 80 is applicable, the jury process is uniform irrespective of where in Australia the trial takes place.[28] To date, the former approach prevails.

Section 80 regularly calls for the resolution of significant procedural questions. The ensuing pages of this chapter contain discussion of its impact on State law procedures permitting verdicts by juries of fewer than twelve people, reserve jurors, 'jury vetting',[29] majority verdicts,[30] and directed verdicts of guilty.[31] A further example may be mentioned here. Some Commonwealth offences tried by a jury on indictment carry more than one maximum sentence, with the choice between them to be made by the judge in the course of sentencing, by reference

[26] (1986) 160 C.L.R., at 202 (Deane J).

[27] Ibid., at 216 (Dawson J), (citing the dissenting judgment of Deane J in *Kingswell* (1985) 159 C.L.R. at 301–2).

[28] See generally Arie Freiberg, *Jury Selection in Trials of Commonwealth Offences*, *in* THE JURY UNDER ATTACK 112 (Mark Findlay & Peter Duff eds., 1988).

[29] See *infra* Part III.A.3. [30] See *infra* Part IV.

[31] See *infra* text accompanying notes 159–67.

to stipulated factual criteria (such as whether the quantity of heroin an offender conspired to import was 'commercial' or 'trafficable').[32] In 1985, the High Court held by majority that this relegation of specific factfinding to the judge does not contravene section 80, provided that the alternative penalties all operate within the boundaries of a single offence.[33]

III. Determining Who Should Sit on a Jury

In all Australian jurisdictions, the standard number of jurors in a criminal trial is twelve. In Victoria, up to fifteen can be sworn in for a long trial on the basis that a ballot must be held to reduce the number to twelve before the jury retires to consider its verdict.[34] If after a trial begins the judge discharges one or more jurors for reasons such as ill health, a verdict may still be rendered by those remaining, provided (generally speaking) that the number does not fall below ten.[35] Reserve jurors, of which the maximum number permitted ranges between two and six, may be used in four jurisdictions.[36]

It has been held recently in State courts that both the delivery of a unanimous verdict by a jury of fewer than twelve[37] and the use of reserve jurors,[38] if in conformity with these provisions, can take place in the trial of a Commonwealth offence without any contravention of section 80 of the Constitution.

The primary aspiration of the processes for selection of the twelve jurors is to obtain a jury which is both 'representative of the community'[39] and impartial. But it is recognised that neither of these characteristics can be achieved in absolute terms. It is also recognised that '[t]here has always been some tension between the objective of obtaining a jury which is randomly selected and representative of the community, on the one hand, and the desire to ensure that such a jury is impartial and indifferent to the cause on the other.'[40]

32 See, *e.g.*, Customs Act 1901, ss. 233 B(1), 235(2) (Austl.).

33 See *Kingswell* v. *R.* (1985) 159 C.L.R. 264 (Austl. H. Ct.) (4–2 majority decision).

34 See Juries Act 1967, ss. 14A, 48A (Vict.).

35 Under the Jury Act 1977, s. 22 (N.S.W.), the number can drop below ten if both sides agree, or can drop to no lower than eight if the trial has been in progress for at least two months.

36 Queensland, Tasmania, Western Australia, and the Northern Territory.

37 See *R.* v. *Brownlee* (1997) 41 N.S.W.L.R. 139 (N.S.W. Ct. Crim. App.).

38 See *Ah Poh Wai* v. *R.* (1995) 132 W.A.R. 708 (W. Austl. Ct. Crim. App.).

39 See, *e.g.*, *R.* v. *Su* (1997) 1 V.R. 18 (Vict. Ct. App.).

40 Ibid.

A. *The Jury Should Be 'Representative of the Community'*

The generally accepted method of ensuring representativeness is random selection—for example, by a computer—from the electoral roll.[41] This method of selection fails to achieve full representativeness in so far as migrants who do not have Australian citizenship cannot be on the electoral roll and many rural Aborigines do not take the necessary steps to ensure that they are enrolled.[42]

There is little jurisprudence on what should be deemed to constitute the relevant 'community': that is, whether it is Australia as a whole, or the State or Territory where the trial takes place (being generally also the State or Territory where the alleged offence was committed), or some smaller region. In practice, the subdivision of the States into 'jury districts' (which may or may not coincide with electoral districts) for the purpose of summoning jury panels produces the result that the relevant community will be a district in which the court conducting the trial is located or has regular sittings. This will often, but by no means invariably,[43] be the district where the alleged offence was committed.[44]

This loose concept of selecting a jury which 'represents' a geographically defined 'community' does not imply that the jury must be deliberately constructed so as to represent a cross-section of all different types of people within that community (defined, for instance, in terms of race, gender, social status, and so on). Reliance on random selection indicates as much. By the same token, Australian courts do not apply the concept that accused persons are entitled to a jury of their 'peers', for example, of members of some 'community', defined other than geographically, to which they belong.[45] In 1988, the Supreme Court of

[41] In New South Wales, random selection is required by statute. See Jury Act 1977, s. 12 (N.S.W.). See generally LAW REFORM COMM. OF THE PARLIAMENT OF VICTORIA, JURY SERVICE IN VICTORIA vol. 1, paras. 2.20–2.34 (1996), and for critical commentary on this report, see Brendan Cassidy, *12 Angry Persons Still Needed*, 23 ALTERNATIVE L. J. 9 (1998).

[42] This problem is discussed in relation to Aboriginal people in Queensland in *Binge* v. *Bennett* (1989) 42 A. Crim. R. 93, 106–7 (N.S.W. Sup. Ct.).

[43] Two exceptions are where an offence committed outside a city or town where the State Supreme Court sits is serious enough to warrant Supreme Court trial, and where the venue is shifted to another location because of concerns about local prejudice against the accused.

[44] See *Duvoric* v. *R.* (1994) 4 Tas. R. 113 (Tas. Ct. Crim. App.) (upholding trial court's decision to refuse a change of venue although pretrial publicity of the case was significant).

[45] For critical comment, see Meredith Wilkie, *Composition of Juries*, in THE CRIMINAL INJUSTICE SYSTEM, vol. 2, 111, 114–18 (George Zdenkowski *et al.*, eds., 1987).

Queensland specifically held in *R.* v. *Walker*[46] that even if this notion, as expressed in clause 39 of Magna Carta,[47] was received into Queensland colonial law as part of English common law, it was subsequently overruled by legislation, and accordingly that Queensland law 'does not recognise the possibility of a jury drawn exclusively from a particular ethnic or other distinctive group in the community'.[48] A statutory exception to this general principle exists in South Australia: the trial court may order, on application by a party or on its own motion, that the jury be composed of men only or of women only if the nature of the case so requires.[49]

A consequence of the general principle of random selection is that any exclusion of a major grouping—for example, of women—through the deliberate act of the sheriff or through challenges by one of the parties may give grounds for applying to have the selection set aside. For example, in 1981, the judge in a District Court trial of an Aboriginal defendant in a New South Wales country town discharged a jury which comprised only white people because the Crown had challenged all Aboriginal members of the panel.[50] He did so in the exercise of a generally recognized judicial power to stand aside a whole jury, or one or more individual jurors, where unfairness, on account of bias or for some other reason, would otherwise result.[51] Similarly, in 1990, the Full Court of the Supreme Court of Queensland held null and void a trial in which the male accused had been permitted to challenge for cause all women on the jury panel on the ground that it was against his religious beliefs (and 'an abomination of God') to be tried by women.[52] It may, however, be necessary in such a case to show affirmatively that the actual motive for the challenges was an improper one—for example, that it was based simply in racial or gender considerations.[53]

[46] [1989] 2 Qd.R. 79 (Queensl. Sup. Ct.); see also *R.* v. *Grant & Lovett* [1972] 1 V.R. 423 (Vict. Sup. Ct.) (refusing application to discharge jury when defence took part in empanelling the jurors).

[47] MAGNA CARTA cl. 39 (Eng. 1215) (proclaiming that '[n]o freeman shall be taken, or imprisoned, or disseized, or outlawed, or exiled, or in any way harmed—nor will we go upon or send upon him—save by the lawful judgment of his peers or by the law of the land').

[48] *Walker* [1989] 2 Qd.R. 86 (McPherson J).

[49] See Juries Act 1927, s. 60A (S. Austl.).

[50] See *R.* v. *Smith* (1981) (unreported), *discussed in* AUSTRALIAN LAW REFORM COMM'N, THE RECOGNITION OF ABORIGINAL CUSTOMARY LAWS, vol. 1, paras. 593–4 (1986).

[51] See, *e.g.*, *R.* v. *McDonald* (1979) 21 S.A.S.R. 198, 210 (S. Austl. Sup. Ct.); *R.* v. *Searle* [1993] 2 V.R. 367, 370–6 (Vict. Ct. Crim. App.) (Marks & McDonald JJ).

[52] See *R.* v. *A Judge of District Courts & Shelley ex parte Attorney General* [1991] 1 Qd.R. 170 (Queensl. Sup. Ct.).

[53] See *Binge* v. *Bennett* (1988) 13 N.S.W.L.R. 578, 598 (N.S.W. Ct. App.) (Mahoney, J. A.); (1989) 42 A. Crim. R. 93, 106 (N.S.W. Sup. Ct.) (Smart J).

A number of further factors undermine the representativeness of Australian juries. Three of them will be discussed here: (1) the existence of categories of ineligible persons, grounds of exemption, and grounds to be excused from jury service; (2) the exercise of rights of challenge or 'standing aside'; and (3) 'jury vetting'.

1. Exclusions from Jury Service

The various grounds on which persons may escape jury service through being deemed ineligible, exempted, or excused are less broad-ranging than they once were. As the High Court of Australia pointed out in *R.* v. *Cheatle*, at the time of Australian federation (1901), only men who satisfied a property qualification were permitted to serve on juries because at the time they were perceived to be 'the only true representatives of the wider community'.[54] The Court added that it would be 'absurd'[55] to perpetuate this notion nowadays. Yet the equal status of women with men in regard to jury service dates back only to the mid-1970s. Other exclusions removed only around this time included people of 'bad fame or of immoral character and repute'.[56]

At the present day, a wide range of potential jurors still do not in fact serve as jurors. This is for reasons as diverse as old age, pregnancy, child-care responsibilities, medical condition, place of residence, prior criminal convictions which jury legislation classifies as 'disqualifying', insufficient ability to understand English, conscientious objection, professional involvement with the legal system, occupational status, and individual hardship.

In recent years, concern from rather different points of view has been expressed about the degree of unrepresentativeness caused by two particular forms of exclusion. First, the fact that people falling within a number of skilled occupational groups—for example, doctors, schoolteachers, ministers of religion, and senior bureaucrats—can claim exemption as of right without needing to show specific hardship in the circumstances in which they are summoned deprives the jury pool of a significant stratum of educated members.[57] A recent survey of juries in New South Wales revealed that about one half of those selected for a draft jury roll were covered by some form of exclusion which prevented

[54] *R.* v. *Cheatle* (1993) 177 C.L.R. 541, 560 (Austl. H. Ct.).
[55] Ibid.
[56] See generally Mark Findlay, Jury Management in New South Wales 232–5 (1994).
[57] See, *e.g.*, Law Reform Comm. of the Parliament of Victoria, *supra* note 41, vol. 1 at ch. 3.

them being summoned.[58] Secondly, the low incidence of Aboriginal persons on jury panels (already mentioned in connection with the requirement of electoral registration) is enhanced because of broad rules of disqualification on account of prior custodial sentences for criminal offences and exemption as of right for people living at a prescribed distance (in Victoria, for example, thirty-two kilometres) from the courthouse.[59]

2. Challenging or 'Standing Aside' Jurors

Australian jury law retains traditional common procedures whereby the prosecution or defence may prevent jurors presented by the sheriff from being sworn in.[60] Their practical utility differs amongst Australian jurisdictions according to whether and, if so, when the composition of the jury panel may be ascertained by the parties. Provisions on this issue vary widely. For example, in New South Wales, the names of the panel may not be revealed; in Victoria, the identity of those with prior criminal convictions (or, it seems, with other 'unsuitable' characteristics) may be made known to the prosecution; in South Australia, both sides must have access to the list at least seven days before the trial.

It has been held in the High Court of Australia that where a right of objection has been improperly denied, the trial is a nullity.[61]

Four types of objection may be distinguished. First, on specified grounds[62] involving default or bias on the sheriff's part in constructing the panel, a 'challenge to the array', that is, to the composition of the whole panel, may be made. However, this scarcely ever occurs.[63]

[58] See FINDLAY, *supra* note 56, at 173.

[59] See Owen Trembath, *Judgment by Peers: Aborigines and the Jury System*, 123 LAW INST. J. 44 (1993); see also Wayne T. Westling & Vicki Waye, *Promoting Fairness and Efficiency in Jury Trials*, 20 CRIM. L. J. 127, 129 (1996) (pointing out that 'the arrest and imprisonment rates of Aboriginal persons for minor offences is [*sic*] almost 15 times higher than those of the white majority').

[60] See generally LAW REFORM COMM. OF THE PARLIAMENT OF VICTORIA, *supra* note 41, vol. 1, paras. 6.32–6.45; NEW SOUTH WALES LAW REFORM COMM'N, REPORT NO. 48, THE JURY IN A CRIMINAL TRIAL paras. 4.49–4.75 (1986); FINDLAY, *supra* note 56, at 45–57, 235–6; KERRY D. STEPHENS, VOIR DIRE LAW ch. 3 (1997); Freiberg, *supra* note 28.

[61] See *Johns* v. *R.* (1979) 141 C.L.R. 409 (Austl. H. Ct.); *Corbett* v. *R.* (1932) 47 C.L.R. 317 (Austl. H. Ct.).

[62] For recent emphasis of this point, see *Greer* v. *R.* (1996) 84 A. Crim. R. 482, 485 (W. Austl. Ct. Crim. App.).

[63] See, *e.g.*, Freiberg, *supra* note 28, at 120.

Secondly, individual jurors may be challenged 'for cause'. The permitted grounds are as follows:[64] lack of any necessary qualification; personal defects creating an incapacity to serve as a juror; partiality; having served on another jury in the same matter; and past conviction for an 'infamous', but not necessarily disqualifying, crime.[65] In any case where a challenge is sought to be made, the grounds must be specified and must normally be supported by an affidavit.[66] Challenges for cause are rare, for three reasons: as just pointed out, the parties' advance knowledge about the panel is often limited, the procedural requirements rule out 'fishing expeditions', and it is in any event easier for a party to make objections without having to assign reasons, in the ways now to be mentioned.

Thirdly, either side (except for the prosecution in Tasmania) may make 'peremptory' challenges to a specified number of individual jurors,[67] and fourthly, in four Australian jurisdictions,[68] the prosecution may in addition (or instead) 'stand aside' jurors until the panel is exhausted, either as of right or with the court's leave. The important feature of these two procedures is that no ground of objection need be put forward. In practice, these are the two important forms of objection that may be raised at the stage of swearing in the jury. They are regularly used by both sides.

These two forms of objection in which no cause need be shown clearly impair the random element in jury selection. It has been cogently asked[69] whether any of the presumed countervailing benefits—notably that of eliminating jurors who might be unduly biased in one direction or another—are present. Where, as in New South Wales, the challenges are 'blind' because no prior access to the jury list has been granted, the lawyers on either side are driven to rely virtually entirely on crude assess-

[64] For High Court endorsement of these features of challenges for cause, see *Murphy* v. *R.* (1989) 167 C.L.R. 94, 102 (Austl. H. Ct.) (Mason CJ & Toohey J); see also *Bush* v. *R.* (1993) 43 F.C.R. 549 (Fed. Ct.).

[65] As to this last ground, see *R.* v. *Robinson* [1989] 1 V.R. 289 (Vict. Sup. Ct.).

[66] See *Murphy* (1989) 167 C.L.R. at 104.

[67] Currently, the generally permitted maximum number of peremptory challenges for both sides in the trial of a single accused person ranges between three (New South Wales) and eight (Queensland). More challenges may be permissible if the offence is treason or murder, if there are more than one accused, or by agreement. Usually each side is entitled to the same number of peremptory challenges. There is no rule that the prosecution is subject to a specific duty (not owed by defence counsel) to challenge only when there is a sound reason for doing so: see *Katsuno* v. *R.* (1999) 73 A.L.J.R. 1458, 1464–5 (Aust. H. Ct.) (Gaudron, Gummow, and Callinan JJ).

[68] Tasmania, Western Australia (by leave, up to four), the Australian Capital Territory, and the Northern Territory (up to six).

[69] See Findlay, *supra* note 56, at 45–57 (reporting on the results of observing the selection of juries in 10 trials).

ments of appearances (for example, apparel, demeanour, apparent social status) or on preconceived notions of whether jurors of a particular race or gender would or would not be sympathetic to their cause. The process may have some symbolic value, notably in permitting the accused to have some say in the process of jury selection,[70] but it is anything but scientific.[71]

In addition, where access to the jury list, or some aspects of it, has been granted to either side a significant period before the trial, the opposite danger arises. There may be scope for undesirable manipulation of the process of selection, through 'jury vetting'.

3. Jury Vetting

The practice of jury vetting in its most familiar form involves engaging the police to scrutinize draft jury panels to identify those who have disqualifying criminal convictions and also those who might, in the police's view, be 'unsuitable' as jurors because (for instance) of nondisqualifying convictions or perceived antagonism to the police. Typically, the disqualified people are identified to the sheriff in accordance with a statutory procedure so that they may be struck off the panel, and the 'unsuitable' people are identified for the prosecutor, who may then exercise rights of challenge or standing by (if he or she so wishes) in order that they do not in fact serve on the jury. This practice is feasible only where the prosecution is permitted access to the list of jurors to be empanelled.[72]

In addition, where, as used to be the case in Queensland,[73] the defence as well as the prosecution may gain access to jury panels some significant time before the trial, jury vetting may be carried out by the defence. The most notorious Australian instance occurred in 1991 in the course of the trial, on charges of corruption, of a former National Party Premier of Queensland, Sir Joh Bjelke-Petersen.[74] The publication of

[70] But see ibid., at 50, where it is pointed out that generally defence counsel did not consult the accused during the challenge process.

[71] For suggestions about how lawyers on both sides could receive carefully limited briefing about each potential juror just before the challenge process, see Westling & Waye, *supra* note 59.

[72] This is the case in Tasmania, Victoria, Queensland, Western Australia, and the Australian Capital Territory, but not in New South Wales or South Australia.

[73] Under the Jury Act 1981, s. 23(2) (Queensl.) (now repealed).

[74] The ensuing summary is drawn from the CRIMINAL JUSTICE COMM'N OF QUEENSLAND, REPORT BY THE HONOURABLE W. J. CARTER QC ON HIS INQUIRY INTO THE SELECTION OF THE JURY FOR THE TRIAL OF SIR JOHANNES BJELKE-PETERSEN (1993). The trial, including events within the jury-room, became the subject of an Australian Broadcasting Corporation docu-drama, *Joh's Jury*.

the members of a number of jury panels twelve days before the trial provided an opportunity for jury consultants employed by the defence to (1) procure the discharge of all of the panel likely to be employed in the trial by representing falsely to the defence lawyers (and through them, to the court) that they had all been contacted and polled as to their political opinions, and (2) ensure that the first juror in the substituted panel who was *not* challenged by the defence lawyers was (unknown to them) a member of the National Party with strong sympathies for the ex-Premier. The outcome of the trial was a hung jury, in which (as later emerged) this juror was an unyielding minority supporter of a verdict of not guilty. Under legislation subsequently passed in Queensland, the list of those summoned for jury service must be made available to either party, but only on the afternoon before the trial, and any information acquired by a party showing that a potential juror is unsuitable must be given to the other parties.[75]

The practice of jury vetting has been criticized by academic commentators[76] and in law reform reports.[77] The principal grounds of criticism have been that it undermines representativeness, that when carried out by the prosecution it frequently operates to the disadvantage of the defence (who may not get to see the information provided to the prosecution), that it may be used to exclude minority viewpoints or (at worst) to manipulate jury selection so as to provoke a hung jury, and that it may deter people from jury service because they may fear that their past indiscretions will be brought up against them.

Despite these arguments, the Victorian Court of Appeal held in *R.* v. *Su*[78] that, at least in relation to people on the panel with non-disqualifying convictions, jury-vetting by the prosecution did not contravene any principle of common law or express or imply prohibition in Victoria's jury legislation (the Juries Act 1977). In so far as it contravened the principle of random selection, it was justifiable because it served the accompanying aim of impartiality. It permitted the prosecution to eliminate those potential jurors who might, in its view, be so antagonistic to

[75] See Jury Act 1995, ss. 30, 35 (Queensl.).

[76] See, *e.g.*, MARK FINDLAY *ET AL.*, CRIMINAL JUSTICE IN AUSTRALIA 141 (1994); Freiberg, *supra* note 28; Meredith Wilkie, *Composition of Juries*, in THE CRIMINAL INJUSTICE SYSTEM, vol. 2, *supra* note 45, at 111, 122–4.

[77] See, *e.g.*, LITIGATION REFORM COMM'N, REFORM OF THE JURY SYSTEM IN QUEENSLAND: REPORT OF THE CRIMINAL PROCEDURE DIVISION 27 (1993); NEW SOUTH WALES LAW REFORM COMM'N, *supra* note 60, paras. 4.43–4.45.

[78] [1997] 1 V.R. 1 (Vict. Ct. App.).

the police or to the lawful authority of the state that they would be likely to harbour undue bias against the prosecution.[79]

The Victorian Court of Appeal in *R.* v. *Su* dismissed two other objections to jury-vetting raised by defence counsel. One was that the failure to make the list of people with nondisqualifying convictions available to the defence infringed an implied principle of equality between prosecution and defence in the matter of jury selection, deriving from recent Victorian jury legislation giving them equal rights of peremptory challenge. The other was that because the drug offences in the case were created by Commonwealth law, section 80 of the Constitution was applicable, and this section imposed an 'essential requirement' of representativeness through random selection which was contravened by this form of jury-vetting. It had been held to do this by the High Court in *R.* v. *Cheatle*,[80] in a unanimous judgment in which the long history of jury trial was carefully considered. The Court of Appeal's response to this argument was that jury-vetting was just a process of supplying relevant information to the prosecution so that it could more effectively exercise its rights of challenge or 'standing by', which had always been part and parcel of the process of jury selection despite its potential to impair full 'representativeness'.[81]

In the later case of *Katsuno* v. *R.*,[82] however, the High Court of Australia held that the Victorian practice did after all contravene two provisions of the Juries Act (sections 21(3) and 67(b)), which taken together prohibited the Cheif Commissioner of Police from disclosing to anyone other than the Sheriff the identity or criminal history of members of jury panels who had prior convictions. But the Court, by majority, ruled that this breach of the Juries Act did not constitute a failure to observe the requirements of the criminal process in a fundamental respect. Nor, in relation to trials of Commonwealth offences, did it contravene any implicit requirement of representativeness deriving from section 80 of the Constitution. Even though the Director of Public Prosecutions made use of this information to challenge peremptorily a member of the jury panel who had prior convictions, this did not render the jury 'unrepresentative'. This was because the requirement of representativeness applied only to the jury panel, which must be 'randomly and impartially selected rather than chosen by the

[79] See ibid., at 12–15.

[80] (1993) 177 C.L.R. 541 at 560. This case is discussed *infra* in the text accompanying notes 136–41.

[81] *Su* [1997] 1 V.R. at 18–21.

[82] (1999) 73 A.L.J.R. 1458.

prosecution or the State'.[83] It did not apply to the jury ultimately selected, in which the random element could quite legitimately be diminished on account of challenges, whether or not based on sound information, made by both prosecution and defence. The two dissenting judges, McHugh and Kirby JJ, disagreed with these conclusions, with the former specifically endorsing the view (rejected in *R.* v. *Su*) that the prosecution's use of the relevant information was wrongful because it thereby gained an unfair advantage over the defence.[84]

The Victorian Court of Appeal's endorsement of prosecution jury-vetting in *R.* v. *Su* was subject to one significant limitation (on which the High Court in *Katsuno* made no specific comment). This is that it covered only the vetting of people with nondisqualifying convictions, not those listed as 'unsuitable' (albeit formally qualified) for other reasons. It may therefore be open in a subsequent case to argue that in this latter situation the influence exerted on jury selection by the police, applying highly subjective criteria, does in fact contravene the requirement of representativeness. In a recent law reform report in Victoria,[85] it has recommended that jury vetting continue to be permissible, but that it be made subject to two significant limitations: It should be carried out by the sheriff instead of the police, and at the swearing-in stage, with the leave of the trial judge, the defence should have access to the information acquired through vetting.

B. *The Jury Should Be 'Impartial'*

In a number of the foregoing situations where the selection of a jury in Australia is not wholly random because of a process such as challenge, the ground on which the general aim of 'representativeness' is departed from is frequently that the concomitant aim of impartiality must also be pursued. Australian courts have acknowledged that a right of 'fair trial', derived from both the common law and the Constitution, includes a requirement that any jury employed should be reasonably impartial.[86]

[83] See (1999) 73 A.L.J.R. at 1468 (Gaudron, Gummow, and Callinan JJ), repeating a phrase used in *Cheatle* (1993) 177 C.L.R. 541 at 560–1.

[84] (1999) 73 A.L.J.R. 1458 at 1469–71.

[85] See Law Reform Comm. of the Parliament of Victoria, *supra* note 41, vol. 1, paras. 2.20–2.34.

[86] The leading High Court case is *Dietrich* v. *R.* (1992) 177 C.L.R. 292; see also Justice K. P. Duggan, *Reform of the Criminal Law with Fair Trial as the Guiding Star* (1995) 19 Crim. L. J. 258; Sir Anthony Mason, *Fair Trial* (1995) 19 Crim. L. J. 7.

They have, however, given little precise content to the notion of impartiality.

Potentially, a conflict arises between representativeness and impartiality when defence counsel in a trial makes a peremptory challenge in the belief (correct or otherwise) that the challenged juror is likely to harbour a prejudice against persons of the same lifestyle or social class or race as the accused. In addition, circumstances may arise where the jury as a whole, even though randomly selected, may be claimed to lack impartiality because some or all of its members are likely to be unduly prejudiced for or against the accused. An example is where a case of alleged child sexual abuse is tried at a time of exceptionally strong public anger and anxiety about this type of offence. But for practical purposes, there is only one situation in which an alleged risk of general jury prejudice of this nature receives direct and sustained attention from Australian law. This is where prejudice has allegedly been created by media publicity dealing specifically with the case or with particular issues directly raised in it.

A basic principle of Australian criminal procedure is that the jury's primary duty is to reach an impartial verdict on the basis only of the admissible and admitted evidence and the argument put before it in the courtroom.[87] It is bound also to give full weight to the law's presumption of innocence and the principle that guilt be proved beyond reasonable doubt.[88] There is accordingly a particular concern that the rules designating certain categories of evidence to be inadmissible on the ground that they are more prejudicial than probative will be ineffective if media publicity is left wholly unregulated and nothing is done to prevent such evidence from reaching the jury or to counter any effects that it has on the jury.[89] Media allegations that the accused has prior criminal convictions,[90] or has confessed (unless the confession has been held by the trial court to be genuinely voluntary),[91] are deemed particularly harmful in this sense.

[87] For High Court affirmation, with particular reference to the problems created by media publicity, see *Murphy* v. *R.* (1989) 167 C.L.R. 94, 98–99 (Austl. H. Ct.) (Mason CJ & Toohey J).

[88] See, *e.g., Woolmington* v. *Director of Public Prosecutions* [1935] App. Cas. 462, 481 (Eng. H.L.).

[89] See Australian Law Reform Comm'n, Report No. 35, Contempt, paras. 282–3 (1987).

[90] See *Hinch* v. *Attorney-General* (1987) 164 C.L.R. 15, 19–20 (Austl. H. Ct.).

[91] See *Attorney-General for N.S.W.* v. *TCN Channel Nine Pty. Ltd.* (1990) 20 N.S.W.L.R. 368 (N.S.W. Ct. App.).

At the same time, the Australian legal system attaches significant weight to considerations of freedom of speech, particularly in relation to what the High Court has called 'government or political matters',[92] and to the allied principle that, *prima facie* at least, legal proceedings should be conducted in open court and be freely reportable.

In seeking to reconcile these competing considerations of fair trial, free speech, and open justice, the overall response of Australian law can be outlined as follows.[93] It gives primacy to the fairness of trials as against claims of the media (and others) for freedom of speech. But the principle of open justice, being viewed as a safeguard for the fairness of trials generally, is frequently, though not invariably, treated as superior to concerns that openness of proceedings and freedom of reporting might jeopardise the fairness of any specific trial (including the trial being reported). Several legal strategies are invoked in order to implement this general approach.

The primary strategy is deterrence of the media through penal sanctions. Under the so-called *sub judice* principle,[94] a branch of the law of contempt of court, the media (and others) may be subject to penal sanctions (usually fines) for publishing material which is found, through proof beyond reasonable doubt, to have had a 'real and definite tendency, as a matter of practical reality' to prejudice the fairness of a current or forthcoming criminal trial by virtue of influence on the jury.[95]

In determining whether this tendency exists, it is assumed, however, that jurors will 'exercise a critical judgment of what they see, read or hear in the media',[96] and will do their best to focus only on the evidence and argument put to them in the courtroom.[97] In addition, there are two important grounds of exoneration a media defendant may raise. One, reflecting the principle of 'open justice', is that the prejudicial material

[92] Speech on these topics is protected by an implied constitutional principle of freedom of political communication. But it is primarily defined in terms of speech which might bear upon decisions on how to vote in elections, and in any event the constitutional principle is subject to common law principles (such as those of contempt law) which are held to be reasonably adapted and appropriate to a countervailing legitimate purpose (such as protecting juries from media prejudice). See *Lange* v. *Australian Broad. Corp.* (1997) 189 C.L.R. 520 (Austl. H. Ct.).

[93] This outline is adapted from Michael Chesterman, *OJ and the Dingo: How Media Publicity Relating to Criminal Cases Tried by Jury Is Dealt with in Australia and America*, 45 AM. J. COMP. L. 109, 114–24 (1997); see also AUSTRALIAN LAW REFORM COMM'N, *supra* note 89, paras. 246–7, 271–9.

[94] See Chesterman, *supra* note 93, at 116–17.

[95] *John Fairfax & Sons Pty. Ltd.* v. *McRae* (1955) 93 C.L.R. 351 (Austl. H. Ct.).

[96] *Duff* v. *R.* (1979) 39 F.L.R. 315, 333 (Fed. Ct.).

[97] See, *e.g.*, *Attorney-General* v. *TCN Channel Nine Pty. Ltd.* (1990) 20 N.S.W.L.R. 368, 383 (N.S.W. Ct. App.).

formed part of a fair and accurate report of legal proceedings held in open court and not subject to any rule of law or court order restricting reporting.[98] The other, reflecting free speech values up to a point, is that the prejudice occasioned by this material is outweighed by the countervailing public interest in the freedom of discussion of, and the dissemination of information about, matters of public concern. But the High Court has warned that it will be difficult, if not impossible, to invoke this ground of exoneration if the prejudice to the criminal trial was intentional, or if the central issue in the trial (that is, the guilt or innocence of the accused) was canvassed in the published material, or if information recognized to be highly prejudicial, such as the accused person's criminal record, was disclosed.[99]

As an ancillary strategy, the law provides in limited circumstances for specific prevention. When presented with clearly established grounds, a court may grant an injunction forbidding the publication of specified prejudicial material which, if published, would be in contempt.[100] A court or an investigatory body, if appropriately empowered, may make an order that the reporting of prejudicial material disclosed in proceedings which it is conducting should be prohibited or postponed.[101] In this situation, contrary to the normal outcome, the principle of open justice gives way to concerns that a jury might be prejudiced.

The strategies outlined so far do not affect the composition of the jury in the relevant criminal trial. They seek instead to ensure, by deterrence or by direct prevention, that no media publication creating a significant risk of jury prejudice occurs. If despite these legal constraints prejudicial publicity does occur, either before or during the trial, the presiding judge may decide that it is sufficient to warn the jury to ignore the publicity and focus only on the evidence and argument.[102] This may be

[98] See *Hinch* v. *Attorney-General* (1987) 164 C.L.R. 15, 25–6, 43, 83 (Austl. H. Ct.); *R.* v. *Pearce* (1992) 7 W.A.R. 395, 426–7 (W. Austl. Sup. Ct.) (Malcolm CJ). But when open court proceedings in a criminal trial are conducted in the absence of the jury—for example, to determine the admissibility of specific evidence—reports of them are not protected by this principle. See *R.* v. *Day* [1985] V.R. 261 (Vict. Sup. Ct.).

[99] See *Hinch* (1987) 164 C.L.R. at 43.

[100] See, *e.g.*, *John Fairfax Publications Pty. Ltd.* v. *Doe* (1995) 37 N.S.W.L.R. 81, 84 (N.S.W. Ct. App.).

[101] But the evidence of prejudice must be strong. See, *e.g.*, *Friedrich v. Herald & Wkly. Times Ltd.* [1990] V.R. 995 (Vict. Sup. Ct.).

[102] For discussion at the High Court level, see *R.* v. *Glennon* (1992) 173 C.L.R. 592, 601, 603–4. For examples of judicial warnings in leading cases, see J. L. Glissan & S. Tilmouth, Australian Criminal Trial Directions 3–600–10; see also *Connell* v. *R. (No. 6)* (1994) 12 W.A.R. 133, 154–8 (W. Austl. Sup. Ct.).

termed a 'remedial' strategy of a low-key variety. It is frequently employed irrespective of whether the publicity in question would attract contempt sanctions.

However, there are other, more substantial remedial measures available, which will or may (according to the circumstances) affect the composition of the jury to which the trial is ultimately committed. These are as follows:[103]

(1) the start of the trial, and with it the selection of the jury, may be delayed until it is considered that any influence exerted on the potential jury by the offending publicity has sufficiently died down;[104]
(2) the presiding judge may briefly question the jury panel to ascertain whether any of them have encountered the publicity and, if so, invite or require the relevant jurors to stand down if it seems that they are likely to be influenced by it in arriving at a verdict;[105]
(3) questioning of potential jurors by counsel on a 'challenge for cause' may also be permitted, though only (as mentioned above) when before the questioning begins there is sufficient evidence to raise a *prima facie* case of the probability that the individual juror being questioned is biased as a result of the publicity;[106]
(4) the court may order the severance of the trials of two or more co-accused;[107]

[103] See generally *Glennon* (1992) 173 C.L.R. at 601, 611–15; *Dietrich* v. *R.* (1992) 177 C.L.R. 292, 363 (Austl. H. Ct.); *Jago* v. *District Court of New South Wales* (1989) 168 C.L.R. 23, 46–7, 49 (Austl. H. Ct.); *Murphy* v. *R.* (1989) 167 C.L.R. 94, 99 (Austl. H. Ct.).

[104] For example, the start of the trial in *Murphy* v. *R.* (1989) 167 C.L.R. 94 (Austl. H. Ct.), was delayed for one week. The trial judge's rejection of a defence application for a delay of six months was endorsed by the High Court. See also *R.* v. *Keogh* (Dec. 22, 1995) (unreported) (S. Austl. Ct. Crim. App.); *R.* v. *Plunkett* (July 1, 1997) (unreported) (S. Austl. Ct. Crim. App.) (refusing to overturn a trial judge's decision not to delay the start of a trial even though it was held in a country town and the offending publicity appeared in a local newspaper on the morning when the trial began).

[105] For a description of the procedure, see, *e.g.*, *Glennon* (1992) 173 C.L.R. at 601; *Bush* v. *R.* (1993) 43 F.C.R. 549, 558 (Fed. Ct.). Under s. 47 of the Jury Act 1995 (Queensl.), the trial judge, on prior application with supporting grounds, can authorize questioning of a potential juror by a party, having first put his or her own questions. This is the only Australian jury legislation to permit questioning by a party.

[106] See *Murphy* v. *R.* (1989) 167 C.L.R. 94, 95 (Austl. H. Ct.); *R.* v. *Stuart and Finch* [1974] Q.R. 277 (Queensl. Sup. Ct.); *Bush* (1993) 43 F.C.R. at 549; *Connell* v. *R. (No. 6)* (1994) 12 W.A.R. 133, 162–8 (W. Austl. Sup. Ct.).

[107] See *Murphy* (1989) 167 C.L.R. at 99.

(5) where the publicity occurred during the trial, the jury may be discharged before a verdict is reached, and a new trial ordered;[108]

(6) the venue for the trial may be moved to an area where the offending material was not published or had only limited circulation;[109]

(7) in four Australian jurisdictions,[110] where the offence is created by Commonwealth law, the accused must be tried by a jury. In all other jurisdictions,[111] the accused may elect to be tried by a judge sitting alone; and

(8) in exceptional circumstances, a guilty verdict may be set aside on the ground that prejudicial publicity rendered the trial unfair, even though one or more of the foregoing remedial techniques was employed, or a permanent stay of proceedings against the accused may be granted, on the ground that there is nothing that a trial judge could do to repair the consequences of such publicity so as to make a subsequent trial fair.[112]

It should be noted that these 'remedial' techniques of jury trial management operate independently of the rules determining whether or not a publisher is liable to sanctions for contempt under the *sub judice* doctrine. A jury may be discharged on account of publicity in respect of which the publisher is held not liable in contempt proceedings,[113] or

[108] See, *e.g., Registrar, Court of Appeal* v. *Willesee* (1985) 3 N.S.W.L.R. 650, 664–73 (N.S.W. Ct. App.). In New South Wales, under s. 55D of the Jury Act 1977, jurors may be questioned under oath by the trial judge to determine whether they have encountered the publicity and, if so, whether it has influenced them.

[109] In addition to the trial court, the Attorney General, who has primary responsibility for determining the venue, may direct a change of venue. See *R.* v. *Cattell* [1968] 1 N.S.W.L.R. 156 (N.S.W. Ct. App.). The applicant for a change of venue must furnish significant evidence of the likelihood of prejudice. See *R.* v. *Pepperill* (1981) 54 F.L.R. 327 (N. Terr. Sup. Ct.); *R.* v. *Webb* (1992) 64 A. Crim. R. 38 (S. Austl. Sup. Ct.); *Durovic* v. *R.* (1994) 4 Tas.R. 113 (Tas. Ct. Crim. App.).

[110] New South Wales, South Australia, Western Australia, and Australian Capital Territory.

[111] See *Brown* v. *R.* (1986) 160 C.L.R. 171, 176 (Austl. H. Ct.).

[112] It appears that the only case where a permanent stay has been granted is *Tuckiar* v. *R.* (1934) 52 C.L.R. 335, 344, 347 (Austl. H. Ct.) (conviction set aside on other grounds, but post-conviction publicity held to rule out any possibility of a fair trial in the future). The leading authority is *R.* v. *Glennon* (1992) 173 C.L.R. 592, 598–9 (Austl. H. Ct.), where a conviction set aside by the Victorian Supreme Court because of prejudicial publicity was restored by a majority of the High Court. The High Court minority considered the Victorian Court's order to be within the limits of its discretion on the facts. See also *Duff* v. *R.* (1979) 39 F.L.R. 315 (Fed. Ct. Austl.); *R.* v. *Donald* (1983) 34 S.A.S.R. 10 (S. Austl. Ct. Crim. App.); Lewis (1992) 63 A. Crim. R. 18 (Queensl. Ct. App.); *R.* v. *Von Einem* (1991) 55 S.A.S.R. 199, 218–19 (S. Austl. Sup. Ct.) (Duggan J pointing out that the existence of a right for the accused to elect to be tried by a judge alone was a factor in favour of not granting a permanent stay).

[113] See, *e.g., Willesee* [1985] 3 N.S.W.L.R. at 654 (Kirby P).

indeed is not even prosecuted for contempt.[114] Conversely, a publisher may be convicted of *sub judice* contempt for material published even though the trial judge refused to discharge the jury on the ground of prejudice to the fairness of the trial.[115] The High Court has explained this apparent discrepancy on the ground, *inter alia*, that the issue of contempt liability is determined with regard to the situation as at the time of the publication, which is generally a different time than when a remedial measure is considered.[116] A further reason for the discrepancy is that some aspects of the rules governing contempt liability—for example, exoneration on the ground of 'public interest'—have no relevance to the trial court's decision whether or not to employ such a measure.[117]

Because Australian law, like English law, relies principally on the deterrent effect of contempt law to curb media publicity that may prejudice a trial, the use of these techniques for finding a jury that, despite such publicity, can be expected to reach an impartial verdict is relatively uncommon.[118] Trial judges frequently express concern about the likely impact of publicity on the jury, but then declare themselves satisfied, in the light of their own experience as trial judges, that the integrity and good sense of the jury, reinforced by judicial warnings to ignore the publicity, will result in an impartial verdict.[119] Appeal courts frequently defer to the decisions of trial judges, to whom a broad discretion is permitted,[120] that major remedial measures, such as aborting

[114] This occurred in New South Wales in Sept. 1997. Observations by the New South Wales Police Minister to the effect that people convicted of paedophilia offences had generally committed such offences many times before they were arrested and charged induced two trial judges—almost certainly unnecessarily—to discharge juries currently engaged on paedophilia trials. There was never any likelihood that the media organizations reporting the Minister's observations would be charged with contempt, let alone held liable.

[115] See, *e.g., Nationwide News Pty. Ltd. ex parte Director of Public Prosecutions (Commonwealth)* (1997) 94 A. Crim. R. 57 (W. Austl. Sup. Ct.).

[116] See *R.* v. *Glennon* (1992) 173 C.L.R. 592, 605–6 (Austl. H. Ct.) (Mason CJ & Toohey J); ibid., at 612–15 (Brennan J).

[117] This explains why a criminal jury was discharged on the ground of prejudice caused by a television broadcast the night before it was due to consider its verdict, but in subsequent proceedings for contempt the broadcasters were held not liable. See *Willesee* [1985] 3 N.S.W.L.R. at 650. For further discussion see M. Chesterman, *Media Prejudice During a Criminal Jury Trial: Stop the Trial, Fine the Media, or Why Not Both?* (1999) 1 UNIV. TECHNOLOGY SYDNEY L. REV. 71.

[118] See Chesterman, *supra* note 93, at 133–7.

[119] See *R.* v. *Connell (No. 3)* (1993) 8 W.A.R. 542, 559–60 (Sup. Ct. W. Austl.) (Seaman J).

[120] This was made clear by the High Court in *R.* v. *Glennon* (1992) 173 C.L.R. 592 (Austl. H. Ct.). This was a significant element in the majority's ruling that the Victorian Court of Criminal Appeal should not have reversed the 'discretionary judgment' of the trial judge. See ibid., at 598.

or delaying a trial, are not after all necessary.[121] There appears generally to be significant judicial resistance to adopting these measures in a whole-hearted fashion.

These points are probably best illustrated in relation to the questioning of jurors before they are sworn in. Generally, the judge simply tells the panel that any among them who feel that they might have been unduly influenced by publicity, or might have a good reason to stand down from the jury, should identify themselves. Further questioning of individual jurors by the judge is rare. Questioning by counsel is even more rare, because the threshold requirements for challenges for cause are not easily complied with. Doubts have indeed been expressed in the High Court about the efficacy of challenges for cause in detecting bias.[122] The contrast between the Australian approach and the lengthy *voir dire* interrogations typical of high-profile American trials is very striking.[123]

Attempts by defence lawyers to introduce expert evidence to show that media publicity is likely to predispose the jury against their clients have had a frosty reception. In two recent cases,[124] defence lawyers, seeking leave to challenge individual jurors for cause or to obtain a temporary or permanent stay of proceedings, tendered the results of telephone surveys within the relevant region and called an expert witness to interpret and comment on them. In both cases, this evidence was rejected on methodological grounds by the trial judge, whose decision on this point was upheld on appeal. In the earlier case, one of the appellate judges remarked that 'it would be an exceptional case' to have survey evidence that went as far as to provide grounds for a challenge for cause to every member of the panel.[125] Although doubted in the later of the two

[121] See, *e.g.*, *R.* v. *George, Harris & Hilton* (1987) 9 N.S.W.L.R. 527, 534 (N.S.W. Ct. Crim. App.) (Street CJ).

[122] See *Murphy* v. *R.* (1989) 167 C.L.R. 94, 103–4 (Austl. H. Ct.) (Mason CJ & Toohey J); ibid., at 123–4 (Brennan J).

[123] See, *e.g.*, Philip R. Weems, *A Comparison of Jury Selection Procedures for Criminal Trials in New South Wales and California* (1984) 10 Sydney L. Rev. 330, 340–7 (estimating that the average time spent selecting a jury in New South Wales was 30 minutes, whereas in California it could take up to six weeks).

[124] See *Bush* v. *R.* (1993) 43 F.C.R. 549 (Fed. Ct.); *Connell* v. *R. (No. 6)* (1994) 12 W.A.R. 133, 167 (W. Austl. Sup. Ct.) (affirming the ruling of Judge Seaman in *R.* v. *Connell (No. 3)* (1993) 8 W.A.R. 542, 550–7 (W. Austl. Sup. Ct.)); see also Hugh Selby, *The Pre Trial Use of Survey Evidence by Trial Judges, in Another Dimension* (Proceedings of the 28th Australian Legal Convention, Hobart, Sept. 1993, 125).

[125] *Bush* (1993) 43 F.C.R. at 555 (Drummond J). For a recent *sub judice* case, illustrating this judicial attitude yet again, see *Attorney-General for N.S.W.* v. *John Fairfax Publications Pty. Ltd.* [1999] N.S.W.S.C. 318.

cases,[126] this remark is symptomatic of Australian judicial reluctance to explore fully the possible remedial approaches to the problem of pretrial prejudicial publicity.

In addition, judges regularly draw attention to the expense, delay, inconvenience, and (in some circumstances) hardship occasioned by the more drastic of these techniques, such as aborting a part-heard trial or reversing a conviction.[127] Australian courts are a good deal less willing than their American counterparts to subject the state, the accused, and the witnesses to these detriments.

Similarly, even though it was recently said by an appellate court that 'where a trial judge is faced with a situation in which pre-trial adverse publicity has a potential to prevent the fair trial of the accused the first step to take is to consider a change of venue',[128] the actual use of this expedient is uncommon. The States and Territories have not yet agreed on a general scheme of cross-border changes of venue, which means that the technique will not produce much benefit in any of the smaller ones, such as Tasmania or the Australian Capital Territory.[129]

Commentators have labelled the Anglo-Australian reliance on restricting media publication, instead of developing and applying sophisticated remedial techniques, as unduly hostile to freedom of speech and unduly narrow in focus.[130] They have also criticized it for failing to account for the inevitable incidence of cases—likely to increase in frequency as electronic technologies of communication become more sophisticated and more global—where despite legal restraints potential jurors come into contact with prejudicial material.[131] In response, the Australian legal community has at least begun to accept that remedial strategies involving departures from the normal processes for finding a jury should be thought about seriously. They are distinctly more on the agenda nowadays than, say, ten years ago. But as has been made clear, they are a long way from supplanting prosecutions for *sub judice* contempt as the primary strategy to deal with publicity that might jeopardize a jury's impartiality.

[126] See *Connell* (1994) 12 W.A.R. at 166.

[127] See, *e.g.*, Gallagher (1987) 29 A. Crim. R. 33, 41 (Vict. Ct. Crim. App.).

[128] *Connell* (1994) 12 W.A.R. at 167.

[129] See *Bush* (1993) 43 F.C.R. at 553.

[130] See, *e.g.*, Matthew Lippman & Thomas Webber, *The Law of Constructive Contempt: A Comparative Perspective*, 8 Anglo-Am. L. Rev. 210, 225, 237–8 (1979).

[131] See Clive Walker, *Fundamental Rights, Fair Trials and the New Audio-Visual Sector* (1996) 59 Mod. L. Rev. 517, 519–25, 533–5, 538–9.

IV. The Question of Unanimity of Verdict

The common law rule, dating back in England to the fourteenth century, that a criminal jury verdict must be unanimous is maintained and reinforced by statute in three Australian jurisdictions, namely New South Wales, Queensland, and the Australian Capital Territory.[132] Strangely, however, there is no hard-and-fast rule that a jury must be expressly directed to this effect, though if anything said by the judge (for example, in answer to a juror's question) conveys the impression that a non-unanimous verdict will suffice, this will give grounds for quashing a conviction on appeal.[133]

In the other five major Australian jurisdictions, majority verdicts are authorized by statute, though subject to significant limitations.[134] The minority may never be more than two in number and under some provisions—namely when the number of jurors has fallen below twelve and in all cases in Victoria—may constitute only one juror. In South Australia, Tasmania, and Western Australia, there may be no majority verdict in cases of murder.[135] The jury may not deliver a majority verdict until they have tried for a stipulated time (ranging between three and six hours under the different provisions) to reach a unanimous verdict.

A further important limitation on these majority verdict provisions is that they do not apply to trials of offences against the laws of the Commonwealth, by virtue of section 80 of the Constitution. The High Court made a unanimous ruling to this effect in 1993, in the case of *Cheatle* v. *R.*[136] Its principal reasons were that when the Australian colonies agreed in 1900 to form a federation, jury unanimity was 'a basic principle of the administration of criminal justice'[137] in each of them, that unanimity ensured a genuine consensus of all the jurors, thereby reducing the danger of unduly hasty verdicts and reflecting the fundamental rule that guilt must be proved beyond reasonable doubt,

[132] See Jury Act 1997, s. 56 (N.S.W.); Jury Act 1995, s. 59 (Queensl.); Juries Act 1967, s. 38 (A.C.T.). For authoritative discussion of the common law rule requiring unanimity, see the joint judgment of all seven Justices of the High Court of Australia in *Cheatle* v. *R.* (1993) 177 C.L.R. 541, 550–9.

[133] See *Milgate* v. *R.* (1964) 38 A.L.J.R. 162 (Austl. H. Ct.), *approved by Lalchan Nanan* v. *State* [1986] 1 App. Cas. 860, 873–4 (P.C.).

[134] See Juries Act 1927, s. 57 (S. Austl.); Jury Act 1899, s. 48(2) (Tas.); Juries Act 1967, s. 47 (Vic.); Juries Act 1957, s. 41 (W. Austl.); Criminal Code, s. 368 (N.T.).

[135] The same applies to treason in South Australia and Tasmania, and to any other offence punishable by life imprisonment in Western Australia.

[136] (1993) 177 C.L.R. 541 (Austl. H. Ct.).

[137] Ibid., at 551.

and that it was supported by case law authority in Australia, England, and America.

From time to time, the incidence of hung juries in trials where no majority verdict is allowed prompts calls for the introduction of majority verdicts in those jurisdictions which do not permit them.[138] A familiar reason advanced is the waste of criminal court time caused by the need to retry cases that would have been resolved the first time around if majority verdicts were permitted. But some degree of inhibition on this change is imposed by the *Cheatle* decision. In addition, a survey of members of thirty-three hung juries by the New South Wales Bureau of Crime Statistics and Research[139] showed that, contrary to popular and (generally speaking) professional expectation, the proportion of these juries in which there were only one or two jurors in the minority was less than half (about 42 percent). There was no generally recurring pattern of one or two minority jurors holding out against the rest. The survey report pointed out that the proportion of these juries from which a verdict could actually have emerged if majority verdicts had been permitted along the lines just set out would in fact be less than 42 percent because six of the trials surveyed (18.2 percent) involved Commonwealth offences, for which a unanimous verdict was mandatory. It concluded that because hung juries were relatively rare (less than 10 percent of jury trials) and because a high proportion of cases with hung juries (in recent years in New South Wales, about 43 percent) were not in fact re-tried, the actual saving of criminal court time which might be achieved from introducing majority verdicts in New South Wales might be as little as 1.7 percent.

It is worth adding here that if a trial judge encountering the prospect of a hung jury exerts undue pressure on the jury to reach agreement, a verdict of guilty may be set aside on appeal. The High Court, in so ruling in 1993,[140] specifically held that it would be improper for the judge to draw attention to the inconvenience and expense occasioned by the failure to agree, or to suggest that jurors should compromise with each other to reach a verdict. Referring to the Court's decision in *Cheatle*, Deane J said: '[a]ny suggestion that a minority juror should democrati-

[138] In Sept. 1995, for instance, the Attorney-General of New South Wales announced that he was considering this measure.

[139] See Pia Salmelainen *et al.*, *Hung Juries and Majority Verdicts*, CRIME & JUST. BULL., July 1997, at 1.

[140] *R.* v. *Black* (1993) 179 C.L.R. 44 (Austl. H. Ct.), discussed in Paul A. Fairall, *Resolving Jury Deadlock in Criminal Cases*, 24 W. AUSTL. L. REV. 112 (1994).

cally submit to the view of the majority is antithetical to the jury process under the common law of this country'.[141]

V. Division of Functions Between Judge and Jury

In Australian criminal jury trials, the tasks of judge and jury are demarcated along traditional lines. In the words of a former Chief Justice of South Australia, '[i]t is fundamental to trial by jury that the law is for the judge and the facts are for the jury'.[142]

The jury's task is to resolve the relevant questions of fact and apply the law, as outlined by the judge, so as to arrive at a verdict. This will normally be a general one: that is, guilty or not guilty as charged. A possible alternative is a partial verdict—guilty on some counts charged but not others. On rare occasions, the court may seek a special verdict[143] or a verdict on a special fact. Here the jury makes the relevant finding or findings of fact but the court determines the legal implications.

Australian juries play no role in the sentencing of those whom they have found guilty, except that they may make a recommendation for mercy. The trial judge is not bound, however, to accept this recommendation.[144]

This demarcation of functions does not mean that the judge plays no role at all in the factfinding process. So much is clear from the following typical passage in a judge's summing-up to a jury:

> It is the function of the judge to control the trial, to rule on questions of the admissibility of evidence and to define the issues that are to be decided. It is also the duty of the judge to instruct the jury as to the law which applies in the case and the practice by which evidence is to be evaluated or weighed and you are required, by your oath, to follow the directions on the law as I give them to you.[145]

This duty of the judge to instruct the jury about the evaluation of the evidence as well as about the application of substantive criminal

[141] (1993) 179 C.L.R. at 56.

[142] *R.* v. *Prasad* (1979) 23 S.A.S.R. 161, 162–3 (S. Austl. Sup. Ct.) (King CJ).

[143] In Queensland, Tasmania, Victoria, Western Australia, and the Northern Territory, there is statutory provision for special verdicts. See Criminal Code, s. 624 (Queensl.); Criminal Code, s. 383(3) (Tas.); Crimes Act 1958, s. 569(3) (Vict.); Criminal Code, s. 642 (W. Austl.); Criminal Code, s. 369 (N.T.).

[144] See *Whittaker* v. *R.* (1928) 41 C.L.R. 230 (Austl. H. Ct.).

[145] *R.* v. *Manunta* (Dec. 20, 1988) (unreported) (O'Loughlin J) (quoted in GLISSAN & TILMOUTH, *supra* note 102, para. 1–600–30).

law principles is implemented in procedural terms through a requirement that the judge should sum up on the evidence as well as the law before the jury retires to consider its verdict.[146] In the course of doing this, the judge must put the issues fairly and in a balanced way. This does not mean that the relative strengths and weaknesses of each side in the case must be glossed over,[147] though by virtue of the presumption of innocence, the judge should ensure that any ground of defence that might be supported by the evidence should be considered by the jury, even if defence counsel has deliberately or inadvertently failed to raise it.[148]

The judge may also convey his or her own views on aspects of the evidence, though not too freely and forcefully.[149] But this is subject to the important proviso that the jury must be clearly directed to ignore these views if its own conclusions are different. The judicial summing-up just quoted continues as follows:

> But having said that, let me with equal emphasis state that the facts of the case are the exclusive province of the jury; you are the sole judges of the facts. You exclusively decide what are the facts of this case. You ignore any view of the trial judge, you ignore any of the views of counsel if it should come to pass that the views expressed by the judge or by counsel do not accord with your own views.[150]

An issue of the judge/jury demarcation that for a time provoked significant debate in Australia is whether and, if so, in what circumstances the judge may direct a verdict. Most of the debate has focussed on directed acquittals.[151] An investigation of these in New South Wales[152] suggested that they occurred in about 2 percent of jury trials. They are uncontroversial when they happen because the prosecution has, in effect, discontinued the case by offering no evidence. This may be because plea-bargaining has taken place at the last minute or

[146] See J. L. Glissan & S. Tilmouth, The Right Direction: A Casebook of General Jury Directions in Criminal Trials s. 5 (1990).

[147] See *Ali Ali* (1982) 6 A. Crim. R. 161, 165 (N.S.W. Ct. Crim. App.) (Street CJ).

[148] See *Van Den Hoek* v. *R.* (1986) 161 C.L.R. 158, 161–2 (Austl. H. Ct.).

[149] See *Cunningham* v. *Ryan* (1919) 27 C.L.R. 294, 298–9 (Austl. H. Ct.).

[150] *Manunta* (quoted in Glissan & Tilmouth, *supra* note 102, para. 1–600–30).

[151] For a summary of the course of the case law, see Glissan & Tilmouth, *supra* note 146, paras. 7–2000–1ff.

[152] See New South Wales Law Reform Comm'n, Discussion Paper No. 37, Directed Verdicts of Acquittal (1995).

because some unexpected difficulties have arisen in relation to essential evidence. The controversial issue is instead the criterion to be applied when the prosecution has presented what it believes to be a fully substantiated case, but the judge is nonetheless minded to direct an acquittal.

The broader of two competing criteria, adopted in cases during the 1970s, is that the judge should direct an acquittal when he or she believes that a verdict of guilty would be 'unsafe or unsatisfactory'.[153] But a narrower test, set out in a 1979 case in South Australia,[154] became accepted in State courts of criminal appeal during the 1980s.[155] A High Court decision in 1990 confirmed the narrower test, with some modifications, declaring that an acquittal should not be directed unless 'there is a defect in the evidence such that, taken at its highest, it will not sustain a verdict of guilty'.[156] This comes close to saying that, in effect, there must be an absence of evidence. The important element differentiating this criterion from the earlier, broader one is that it leaves to the jury the assessment of the weight of any evidence that has actually been admitted (albeit with a warning from the judge) on the basis that it may have probative value. Accordingly, in the High Court's words, 'if there is evidence (even if tenuous or inherently weak or vague) which can be taken into account by the jury in its deliberations and that evidence is capable of supporting a verdict of guilty, the matter must be left to the jury for its decision'.[157]

This narrower principle, despite its affirmation of the traditional scope of the jury's function, has encountered some criticism.[158] It has, for instance, been argued that since the broader test of a guilty verdict being 'unsafe or unsatisfactory' is the same as an appeal court invokes in deciding whether a conviction should be set aside on appeal, it would be better put into operation during the trial.[159] The trial judge is generally accepted to be better placed than an appeal court to assess the quality of the prosecution's case.

[153] See, *e.g.*, *R.* v. *Falconer-Attlee* (1973) 58 Crim. App. 348 (Ct. Crim. App.) (Eng.).

[154] See *R.* v. *Prasad* (1979) 23 S.A.S.R. 161 (S. Austl. Ct. Crim. App.).

[155] See, *e.g.*, *Attorney-General's Reference (No. 1)* [1983] 2 V.R. 410 (Vict. Sup. Ct.).

[156] *Doney* v. *R.* (1990) 171 C.L.R. 207, 214 (Austl. H. Ct.).

[157] Ibid., at 214–15.

[158] See, *e.g.*, James Glissan, *Unsafe and Unsatisfactory: The Law as to Directed Verdicts*, 63 Austl. L. J. 283 (1989); Donald Just, *Judicially-Directed Acquittals*, 65 Law Inst. J. 933 (1991).

[159] This point was made implicitly by Dawson J in the High Court in *Whitehorn* v. *R.* (1983) 152 C.L.R. 657, 689.

The converse issue of a judge's instruction to a jury that it should bring in a verdict of guilty has also provoked some disagreement. In the leading High Court case, *Yager* v. *R.*,[160] four out of the five members of the court agreed that, in view of a number of admissions of the accused relating to the importation of a prohibited drug, which in effect left no relevant issue of fact to be determined by the jury, it was appropriate for the judge to make it clear to the jury that the appropriate verdict was guilty. Three members of this majority[161] indicated that this could, in effect, be put in the form of a direction to convict. The fourth, Gibbs J, considered the judge's formulation to be acceptable, but only because it did not amount to a formal direction.[162] The judge, in his view, could tell the jury that 'if they do their duty they will return a verdict of guilty', but 'he cannot dictate the verdict they are to return'.[163] This followed from 'the fundamental principle of our constitutional law that a juror may not be punished for returning a verdict against the direction of the court, and hence may not be intimidated into returning a particular verdict'.[164]

Murphy J, the lone dissenter, held that the judge's statement, being tantamount to a direction, had deprived the accused of her right under section 80 of the Constitution to trial by jury for an offence against a Commonwealth law which had been prosecuted on indictment.[165] In an earlier case,[166] he had explicitly linked this view on directed verdicts of guilty to the principle that juries had traditionally 'refused to convict when there was oppression in the law or its administration, despite overwhelming evidence of guilt'.[167]

The position adopted by Gibbs J seems as far as a judge should be permitted to go in instructing a jury to declare that the accused is guilty. The principle that a jury cannot be ordered to render its verdict one way or the other or be punished for bringing in a perverse verdict is well-established. It was, for instance, affirmed by the High Court in 1969 in the context of a jury's acknowledged power, under both common law and statutory principles, to bring in a verdict of manslaughter in any trial of an accused for murder.[168]

[160] (1977) 139 C.L.R. 28 (Austl. H. Ct.).
[161] Barwick CJ and Mason and Stephen JJ.
[162] See (1977) 139 C.L.R. at 38–9. [163] Ibid., at 38.
[164] Ibid., at 38–9. [165] See ibid., at 51.
[166] See *Jackson* v. *R.* (1976) 134 C.L.R. 42, 54 (Austl. H. Ct.). [167] Ibid.
[168] See *Gammage* v. *R.* (1969) 122 C.L.R. 444, 451 (Austl. H. Ct.) (Barwick CJ); ibid., at 463 (Windeyer J).

VI. Appellate Review of Jury Verdicts

A. Acquittals

The rule called *autrefois acquit* and the rule against double jeopardy preclude any appeal against a jury verdict of not guilty.[169] These rules are indeed broad enough to rule out any appeals against decisions by judges that an accused person is not liable to penal sanctions: for example, on grounds of criminal contempt.[170] In 1995, the New South Wales Law Reform Commission was asked to consider whether the law should be changed to permit prosecution appeals against directed acquittals in jury trials. Its recommendation was that since such acquittals occurred only rarely, the incidence of errors of law would be very low indeed, and it would not be appropriate to introduce this limited exception to the long-established rule against double jeopardy.[171]

In consequence, when the prosecution believes an acquittal to have been incorrect on legal grounds, it is restricted to submitting the relevant issue of law to an appeal court. This must be done on the basis that the decision on the appeal will not affect the verdict of not guilty.[172]

It is noteworthy that this approach leaves full scope for 'jury equity'. It may on occasion seem highly likely that the reason underlying a jury verdict of not guilty is not that the necessary evidence to establish guilt was lacking but that the jury believed the relevant principles of criminal law to be unjust and oppressive. In conformity with traditional views about this prerogative of a jury,[173] there will be no redress for the prosecution because an appeal against the verdict itself is simply not allowed, nor can any punitive action be taken against the jury.

In 1855, a series of highly politicized trials of thirteen gold prospectors for treason took place in Melbourne following one of the most famous events in nineteenth century Australian history—the 'Eureka stockade'. Together with a number of fellow prospectors, the accused had established the stockade in an attempt to escape the highly

[169] See, *e.g.*, Brown *et al.*, *supra* note 12, vol. 1, at 155–6.

[170] See *Director of Public Prosecutions* v. *Chidiac* (1991) 25 N.S.W.L.R. 372, 375–7 (N.S.W. Ct. App.). The prohibition does not, however, apply to liability for civil contempt. See *Microsoft Corp.* v. *Marks (No. 1)* (1996) 69 F.C.R. 117, 137 (Fed. Ct.).

[171] See New South Wales Law Reform Comm'n, *supra* note 152, at 30.

[172] See, *e.g.*, Criminal Appeal Act 1912, s. 5A(2) (N.S.W.).

[173] See, *e.g.*, Lord Devlin, *The Conscience of the Jury* (1991) 107 Law Q. Rev. 402.

oppressive enforcement of a regime of licensing of gold exploration. The acquittal of all of them after very short periods of deliberation by the juries represents an outstanding instance of 'jury equity' in Australia. In the first of the trials, the presiding judge, being unable to vent his anger about the acquittals upon the jury, had to be content with sentencing two spectators in the courtroom, randomly chosen, to a week in prison for contempt of court for participating in the spontaneous applause which followed the jury's delivery of its verdict.[174]

B. Convictions

Appeals against convictions in jury trials may be on matters of fact or law or mixed law and fact. Generally they allege errors of law by the trial judge: for example, that the substantive law has been misstated, or evidence has been wrongly admitted or excluded. In so far as they are based on the issues of fact which have been entrusted to the jury, the general principle on which Australian courts of criminal appeal operate is that a verdict of guilty which is found to be unreasonable or which cannot be supported having regard to the evidence may be set aside, but not unless it has resulted in a 'miscarriage of justice'.[175] In a number of leading cases,[176] the High Court has established that this requires a finding that the jury's verdict of guilty was 'unsafe or unsatisfactory', which in turn means that a jury, acting reasonably, *must* have entertained a reasonable doubt about the guilt of the accused. This is not the same as saying that the appeal court itself entertained such a doubt,[177] because this would be to substitute the appeal court's own assessment of the evidence for that of the jury.

[174] For an attractive account of these events, see Graham L. Fricke, *The Eureka Trials* (1997) 71 AUSTL. L. J. 59.

[175] This is the net effect of a statutory provision operating throughout Australia. Appeals against a jury's conclusion that an accused is guilty may be allowed if this conclusion is found by the appeal court to be unreasonable or insupportable on the evidence, or on any ground where there has been a miscarriage of justice, provided however that the appeal court may dismiss the appeal if it considers that in all the circumstances 'no substantial miscarriage of justice has actually occurred'. See Criminal Appeal Act 1912, s. 6 (N.S.W.); Criminal Code, s. 668E (Queensl.); Criminal Law Consolidation Act 1935, s. 353 (S. Austl.); Criminal Code, s. 402 (Tas.); Crimes Act 1958, s. 568 (Vic.); Criminal Code, s. 689 (W. Austl.).

[176] See *Chidiac* v. *R.* (1990) 171 C.L.R. 432 (Austl. H. Ct.); *Morris* v. *R.* (1987) 163 C.L.R. 454 (Austl. H. Ct.); *Chamberlain* v. *R. (No. 2)* (1984) 153 C.L.R. 521 (Austl. H. Ct.); *Whitehorn* v. *R.* (1983) 152 C.L.R. 657 (Austl. H. Ct.).

[177] This was the formulation advocated in *Chamberlain* v. *R. (No. 2)* (1984) 153 C.L.R. 521, 617–22 (Austl. H. Ct.) (Deane J dissenting).

Even this relatively remote consideration of the jury's verdict requires that the appeal court must conduct its own independent review of the evidence. In so doing, it must remember that certain issues, notably the credibility and reliability of oral testimony, are pre-eminently issues for the jury. But occasions may still arise where the court concludes that 'the Crown case rests upon oral testimony which is so unreliable or wanting in credibility that no jury, acting reasonably, could be satisfied of the accused's guilt to the requisite degree'.[178] In addition, the appeal court may decide that the jury has attached undue weight to testimony within a category which the law has traditionally treated with great caution. The examples given by the High Court in a leading case in 1990 are unsatisfactory identification evidence and the uncorroborated evidence of accomplices and of complainants in sexual offence cases.[179]

One of the High Court cases establishing these general principles was an appellate proceeding in Australia's most celebrated criminal trial in the last two decades, the Chamberlain case.[180] In August 1980, Azaria Chamberlain, a ten-week-old baby, disappeared from her family's tent in a camping ground near Uluru (Ayers Rock) in the central Australian desert. Her mother, Lindy, claimed that Azaria had been carried off by a dingo,[181] but after two coronial inquiries Lindy was herself tried and convicted in the Northern Territory Supreme Court of the murder of her daughter, whose body was never found. She appealed unsuccessfully to the Federal Court[182] and thence to the High Court, where her appeal again failed, though only by a three to two majority.[183] The majority judges expounded and applied the criteria of 'unsafe or unsatisfactory' verdict that have just been outlined, while the minority were more inclined to believe that if the court itself had a reasonable doubt in relation to the prosecution case, which was based entirely on circumstantial evidence, the conviction should not be allowed to stand.

This 'dingo baby' case had attracted enormous publicity, and the Australian community was sharply divided on whether Lindy Chamberlain had killed her daughter. The level of popular controversy is graphically shown in a film made about the case, called *Evil Angels* (entitled in the United States, *A Cry in the Dark*), which starred Meryl Streep as Lindy

[178] *Chidiac* v. *R.* (1990) 171 C.L.R. 432, 444 (Mason, CJ).

[179] See ibid., at 444–5 (Mason CJ).

[180] See *Chamberlain* (1984) 153 C.L.R. at 521.

[181] A dingo is a variety of indigenous wild animal resembling a hunting-dog.

[182] See *Chamberlain* v. *R.* (1983) 72 F.L.R. 1 (Fed. Ct.).

[183] See *Chamberlain* v. *R. (No. 1)* (1983) 153 C.L.R. 514 (Austl. H. Ct.).

Chamberlain and Sam Neill as her husband Michael. Eventually, after Lindy Chamberlain had spent about four years in jail, she was released on account of continued campaigning by her supporters and the appearance of significant new evidence which cast further doubt on the reliability of the jury's verdict. The conviction was in fact formally quashed a further two years later, following a Royal Commission in which important defects were revealed in the scientific evidence that had been put to the jury.[184]

The Chamberlain case is one of a number which have given cause for concern[185] that the criteria for allowing appeals against jury convictions may be drawn too narrowly. It is recognized, however, that to give appeal courts too much discretion in this context may jeopardize the essential independence of the jury. The final defence against unjust convictions may therefore have to be special investigatory review procedures, such as the Royal Commission in the Chamberlain case. Yet the danger here is that generally a government is unwilling to establish such an inquiry unless it is compelled to do so by public pressure. Very few criminal convictions have anything like the high public profile of the Chamberlain case, which developed essentially because the claim of Lindy Chamberlain that her baby had been taken from a tent by a dingo so fiercely gripped the public imagination.

VII. Protection from Interference

In general, Australian jurors are reasonably well shielded from forms of interference which might either prevent them from carrying out their duties impartially and to the best of their capacities or deter them or their fellow citizens from being willing in the future to serve on a jury. The shield provided by the law is not, however, impenetrable. These general statements may be briefly illustrated by reference to three matters: anonymity, protection from improper contacts during the trial, and confidentiality of deliberations.

As the above discussion of jury vetting shows,[186] ascertainment of the identity of jurors is generally feasible for the parties and their advisers.

[184] For non-legal accounts of the case, see, *e.g.*, JOHN BRYSON, EVIL ANGELS (1985) (on which the film was based); NORMAN H. YOUNG, INNOCENCE REGAINED (1989).

[185] See, *e.g.*, ACADEMICS FOR JUSTICE, LAW SCHOOL, MACQUARIE UNIVERSITY, NEW SOUTH WALES, TRAVESTY! MISCARRIAGES OF JUSTICE (Kerry Carrington *et al.*, eds., 1991); BROWN *ET AL.*, *supra* note 12, vol. 1, at 307–9.

[186] See *supra* Part III.A.3.

But the trend in recent times has been toward restricting access to their names. This is particularly observable in Queensland, where in the wake of the *Bjelke-Petersen* trial, this information, instead of being easily accessible at least five days before the trial, is now made available to parties only after 4:00 p.m. on the previous day. In New South Wales, amendments to section 38 of the Jury Act 1977, enacted in 1997, prevent the open disclosure of jurors' names even when they are called to be sworn. They are instead to be called up by numbers, though their names will be made known to the parties in order to help them decide whether to challenge them. This is reinforced by section 68 of the Act, which makes it an offence to publish, broadcast, or otherwise disclose any matter likely to lead to the identification of a juror or former juror, unless the juror consents.

These provisions in New South Wales go further than their equivalents in other jurisdictions in seeking to keep jurors anonymous. Yet they do not prevent a juror's identity becoming known to any person who attends the court and is acquainted with the juror. In a small country town, and even in larger communities, absolute or even relative anonymity will be impossible so long as the court is open to the public and the jury sits in full view of the court.

The possibility of interference with jurors—for example, their being approached by 'outsiders' wishing to influence them—is in general terms viewed seriously. However, the issue of isolating them during their deliberations has shown a change of approach. While the days of jurors being sequestered throughout a trial are gone, it was until recently the invariable practice not to allow them to separate once they had retired to consider their verdict.[187] Accordingly, in a case in 1986,[188] for instance, a conviction was overturned because three of the jurors travelled in a taxi without a 'keeper' on their way to their overnight accommodation during the period of deliberation. Yet perhaps surprisingly, the modern trend, at least in New South Wales, is toward allowing them to go home for the night even during this period, having been duly warned by the judge not to discuss the case with anyone or let themselves come into contact with media stories about it.[189] This faith in the power of judicial admonitions seems surprising, though it seems in line with apparent

[187] See, *e.g.*, *Ah Poh Wai* v. *R.* (1995) 132 A.L.R. 708, 720–30 (W. Austl. Ct. Crim. App.).

[188] See *R.* v. *Chaouk* [1986] V.R. 707 (Vict. Ct. Crim. App.).

[189] See *Brownlee* v. *R.* (1997) 41 N.S.W.L.R. 139 (N.S.W. Ct. Crim. App.); ibid., at 145–6 (Grove J). In New South Wales, a judicial discretion to permit this is conferred by statute. See Jury Act 1977, s. 54 (N.S.W.).

judicial confidence in the effectiveness of warnings about prejudicial publicity.

With confidentiality of deliberations, as with anonymity, the trend is toward tightening up the law. In Tasmania, each juror swears an oath not to reveal deliberations. During the last thirty years and in each case following some highly publicized revelations from the jury-room, four Australian jurisdictions (Victoria in 1986, New South Wales in 1987, Queensland in 1995, and the Australian Capital Territory in 1997) have introduced specific provisions in their jury legislation prohibiting media reporters or other people from soliciting former jurors to obtain their accounts of jury room deliberations, particularly when there is any prospect of these accounts being published generally.[190] In New South Wales, but not Queensland, Victoria, or the Australian Capital Territory, it remains permissible, under these provisions, for former jurors to offer this information of their own accord, though not in return for payment. The statutory restrictions in New South Wales, Queensland, and the Australian Capital Territory leave scope for officially authorized research into jury decision making.[191] In jurisdictions other than these four, the issue is controlled generally by a loose principle of contempt law that the disclosure or publication of jury deliberations may constitute contempt if in the circumstances it constitutes an interference with the administration of justice.[192]

This concern for confidentiality is reinforced by a common law rule that evidence relating to jury deliberations may not be tendered in any appeal against the jury's verdict.[193] Even when this evidence might raise serious doubts about the propriety of the verdict, it cannot be received.[194] Juror misconduct occurring after the jury has retired, but not while

[190] See Jury Act 1977, ss. 68A, 68B (N.S.W.); Jury Act 1995, s. 70 (Queensl.); Juries Act 1967, s. 69A (Vic.); Juries Act 1967, s. 42C (A.C.T.).

[191] The importance of leaving scope for research into jury deliberation is emphasised in Mark Findlay, *Politics of Secrecy and Denial*, CRIM. JUST., Mar. 1996, at 368.

[192] See *Attorney-General* v. *New Statesman & Nation Publ'g Co. Ltd.* [1981] Q.B. 1 (Div. Ct.) (Eng.).

[193] For an overview of these issues, see the article of the Honorable Chief Justice of New South Wales (as he then was), A. M. Gleeson, *The Secrecy of Jury Deliberations*, 1(2) NEWCASTLE L. REV. 1 (1996).

[194] See, *e.g.*, Medici (1995) 79 A. Crim. R. 582 (Vict. Ct. Crim. App.). For an extreme instance in the Privy Council, see *Lalchan Nanan* v. *The State* [1986] 1 AC 860 (P.C.), where it was alleged that the jury, having not been specifically instructed to reach a unanimous verdict, had found the accused guilty of murder by a majority of eight to four. Although the accused had been sentenced to death, this evidence was still not admissible to challenge the conviction.

strictly speaking they are deliberating, is not however caught by this rule.[195] It has been held in Victoria[196] that a statutory exception to the confidentiality restrictions, permitting evidence of misconduct during deliberations to be revealed to a court, the Attorney General, or an investigating or prosecuting authority, does not detract from this rule relating to criminal appeals.

VIII. Conclusion

The recent history of juries in Australia reveals an interesting clash between the endeavours of State and Territory governments to reduce the costs associated with jury trial by various means—for example, relegating more and more cases to summary trial by magistrates, allowing for trial on indictment by judges sitting alone, and introducing majority verdicts—and the determination of the High Court of Australia, in its decisions on section 80 of the Constitution, to reassert the traditional values and features of jury trial. While the scope of the High Court's efforts is circumscribed—it can only affect the trial of Commonwealth offences and it appears committed to retaining its long-standing literal interpretation of the section, robbing it of much of its potential force—the court's judgments do operate as strong reminders of the reasons why jury trial travelled from England to Australia in the first place.

One suspects that the community generally is scarcely aware of this conflict. Although sometimes the media and other contributors to public debate ask whether juries are really worthwhile, sustained bursts of criticism are not common and defenders of the jury system are generally quick to make the arguments in favour of it.[197]

Australian life and culture have diversified enormously in the last twenty to thirty years, due chiefly to the arrival of large numbers of migrants from many countries with very different legal traditions. The inflow from South East Asian countries has been especially prominent. Nevertheless, the 'little bit of England' that is trial by jury remains more or less intact. Although its range of operation may continue to shrink, it is reasonably well assured of a continuing role in the Australian criminal justice system.

195 See, *e.g.*, Gleeson, *supra* note 193, at 13.

196 See *Medici* (1995) 79 A. Crim. R. at 582; *Portillo* (1996) 88 A. Crim. R. 283 (Vict. Ct. App).

197 The last significant wave of public criticism of juries was in the mid-1980s, provoking a series of eloquent replies in The Jury Under Attack, *supra* note 28.

5 The New Zealand Jury: Towards Reform

Neil Cameron,* Susan Potter,** and Warren Young***

I. Introduction

The colonial history of the courts in New Zealand is one of confusion and often makeshift adaptation. Legislative and ideological structures, including those surrounding the venerable institution of the common law jury, often meshed poorly with the realities of colonial society and everyday legal practice. Initial attempts to accommodate or incorporate the interests and customs of the majority indigenous population further clouded the picture. These attempts were largely nullified by settler antagonism and the cultural destruction wrought by the colonization process.

Jury trial in New Zealand dates back to the earliest years of colonization and initially represented an uninterrupted transmission of the English legal heritage.[1] Both the Supreme Court and the lesser courts were established in 1841, the year following the formal annexation of the colony and its separation from the Australian colony of New South Wales. The new courts had their jurisdiction defined in terms of the existing jurisdiction of the English courts, drew their personnel from English-born and -qualified practitioners, and operated according to English procedure. Grand, common, special juries and even the ancient aliens jury, *de medietate linguae*, were all pressed into service.

Not surprisingly, the colonists soon adapted the English traditions and structures to the realities of their colonial setting. In this chapter, we briefly sketch the subsequent evolution of both the civil and criminal jury and of the attempts to incorporate the indigenous Maori people within a set of notionally separate arrangements which were nonetheless exclusively derived from European notions of criminal justice. We

* Senior Lecturer in Law, Victoria University of Wellington.

** Senior Legal Researcher, New Zealand Law Commission. The views expressed here are her own and do not necessarily represent those of the Commission.

*** Professor of Law, Victoria University of Wellington.

[1] Surprisingly, there is very little information available on the history of jury trial in New Zealand. For a brief but useful introductory discussion, see REPORT OF THE ROYAL COMM'N ON THE COURTS pt. 1 (AJHR Paper H2, 1978).

then outline the current structures and the issues and concerns that have emerged with some force over the last few years. As with many common law jurisdictions that still retain trial by jury, the civil jury in New Zealand is seldom used. However, the criminal jury has undergone something of a revival over the last decade and a half. This, in turn, has generated concerns at the political, judicial, administrative, and public levels that are currently being addressed by the New Zealand Law Commission and through a major research project that has been undertaken on behalf of the Commission. In particular, over the last few years, attention has focused on issues including the so-called 'hung jury crisis' and the desirability of majority verdicts,[2] the availability of jury trial generally, the selection of jurors (especially the issue of Maori representation on juries), the use of juries in complex cases, the provision of proper assistance to jurors both at trial and during the decision making process, and the problems of pretrial publicity and juror prejudice.

II. The History of Jury Trial in New Zealand

A. *The Development of the Criminal Jury*

The Supreme Court Ordinance of 1841 provided for a criminal jury of twelve men for all cases tried on indictment.[3] Sensibly, it also provided for any criminal case to be tried by judge alone should the need arise.[4] In the absence of a grand jury in the infant colony, cases were to be commenced by the presentation of an indictment under the signature of the Attorney General or a Crown Prosecutor 'as if the same had been presented by a grand jury'.[5] At the same time, the Sessions Courts Ordinance of 1841 constituted an intermediate tier of courts of general and quarter sessions, presided over by justices, which also had the jurisdiction to try indictable matters before a jury.[6] Summary matters were heard by justices sitting alone,[7] or, from 1846, by a resident magistrate.[8]

In 1858, the sessions courts were replaced by a system of district courts presided over by judges drawn from the practising legal profession.[9] The

[2] See, *e.g.*, John Goulter, No Verdict: New Zealand's Hung Jury Crisis (1997).
[3] See Supreme Court Ordinance 1841, § 19 (N.Z.).
[4] See ibid., § 22. [5] Ibid., § 20.
[6] See Sessions Courts Ordinance 1841, § 6 (N.Z.).
[7] See Summary Proceedings Ordinance 1842, § 1 (N.Z.).
[8] See Resident Magistrates Courts Ordinance 1846, § 1 (N.Z.).
[9] See District Courts Act 1858, § 4 (N.Z.).

district court handled the less serious jury trials on indictment, while the Supreme Court dealt with the most serious cases.[10] The first major consolidating Act, the Juries Act 1868, finally introduced the grand jury as an intermediate step in Supreme Court cases, although district courts were left to proceed simply on the basis of an indictment signed by the Attorney General or a Crown prosecutor.[11]

In practice, district courts were only ever declared in five districts of the colony.[12] Hence, although in theory there were three distinct levels of criminal trial—one summary and two by jury—in most parts of the colony, the choice was between summary trial in the resident magistrates' court and jury trial in the Supreme Court. By the end of the century, most district courts had ceased to function, their jurisdiction cannibalized by the Supreme Court and the emergent magistrates' courts.[13] District courts were effectively abolished in 1909 with the abolition of the court districts, although the 1858 Act itself was not finally repealed until 1925.[14]

Initially, eligibility for jury service in the Supreme Court, with the exception of those working in certain occupations, was restricted to male residents between 21 and 60 years of age who held an estate in fee simple in land or tenements.[15] The chaotic state of land titles in the early years of the colony, however, rendered the property qualification impractical, and as a temporary expedient the Supreme Court initially adopted the solution arrived at in the Sessions Courts Ordinance in 1841, whereby eligibility was based simply on British citizenship and residence in the colony for six months or more.[16] In any event, the property qualification was never in fact implemented.

From the first Juries Ordinance in 1841, a wide range of political, legal, civil service, and essential industries personnel were either disqualified or excused from jury service. These categories gradually expanded until most state employees could claim exemption. Women

[10] See ibid., § 29. [11] See ibid., § 145.

[12] These districts were Hawke's Bay, Otago Goldfields, Taranaki, Timaru, and Westland. See Report of the Royal Comm'n on the Courts, *supra* note 1, at 9.

[13] See Magistrates' Courts Act 1893, §§ 28–40 (N.Z.) (replacing the Resident Magistrates' Courts with Magistrates' Courts).

[14] See District Courts Abolition Act 1925, § 2 (N.Z.).

[15] See Juries Ordinance 1841, § 1 (N.Z.). The professions that were exempt from jury duty were legislators, appointed officials, judges, ministerial officers, coroners, constables, full-pay military men, clergymen, barristers, physicians, revenue officers, licensed pilots, and seamen. See ibid.

[16] See Supreme Court Ordinance 1841, § 6 (N.Z.).

were excluded until 1942, and even then were not admitted on the same terms as men.[17] Characteristically, settler law also excluded Maori from the common jury,[18] although 'half-castes' not living as part of a tribal group or community were classified as non-Maori for this purpose.[19] It was not until 1962, with the abolition of the last of the mixed race jury provisions, that Maori became eligible for service on common juries,[20] and it was not until 1976 that women became eligible on the same terms as men.[21]

In the Supreme Court, the cumbersome grand jury process—which required a preliminary hearing before a magistrate or justice to determine if there was a *prima facie* case, followed by the laying of an indictment before the grand jury,[22] and then the empanelling of a common, special, or Maori jury to hear the actual case—was abolished in 1961.[23] Indeed, although we have no information on the frequency of grand jury hearings prior to 1961, it seems likely that, because the preliminary hearing before the justices effectively performed the same task as the grand jury hearing, many cases in the Supreme Court already largely bypassed the process. At the same time, the criminal jurisdiction of the magistrates' court was progressively expanded—most radically in 1952.[24] As a result, by the early 1970s, although criminal jury trials continued

[17] Women had to be at least 25 years old and under 60, and to serve had to notify the Sheriff in writing of their desire to do so. See Women Jurors Act 1942, § 2 (N.Z.). In comparison, men 21 to 65 years of age who were non-Maori were automatically eligible to serve. See Juries Act 1908, § 3 (N.Z.).

[18] See Jury Amendment Ordinance 1844, § 1 (N.Z.).

[19] More fully, 'Maori' was defined as including all persons of the 'Aboriginal New Zealand race, all Aboriginal Polynesian Melanesian and Australasian Natives, and all persons one of whose parents was a Native of such race and which persons are herein designated "half-caste". Provided that no half-caste shall be deemed to be a Maori for the purposes of this Act unless he shall be living as a member of some Native tribe or community.' Jury Law Amendment Act 1862, § 2 (N.Z.).

[20] See Juries Amendment Act 1962, § 2 (N.Z.).

[21] See Juries Amendment Act 1976, § 2 (N.Z.).

[22] For the procedure to select a grand jury, see Juries Act 1908, §§ 51–60 (N.Z.).

[23] See Crimes Act 1908, § 407 (N.Z.). These provisions were repealed by the Crimes Act 1961 (N.Z.). For a succinct description of the relevant legislative provisions and the process in practice, see J. M. E. Garrow, The Crimes Act 1908 (Annotated) 185–6 (2d ed. 1927).

[24] The Summary Jurisdiction Act 1952 (N.Z.), empowered magistrates, with the consent of the defendant, to try almost all indictable offences against property and all but the most serious sexual and violent offences. On summary conviction in such cases, the magistrates' court was, however, limited to the imposition of a maximum sentence of three years' imprisonment, whatever the nominal maximum sentence for the offence. See also Report of the Royal Comm'n on the Courts, *supra* note 2, at 12.

to increase in absolute terms,[25] the proportion of defendants eligible for jury trial who actually elected it was in fact dropping rapidly. By 1976, for example, only 0.24 percent of those charged with criminal offences and 2.6 percent of those with the right to elect trial by jury were actually being tried by jury.[26]

Nevertheless, the overall growth in the volume of criminal trials began to produce problems for the Supreme Court. In 1978, the Royal Commission on the Courts recommended the creation of a new district court structure to reinstate elements of the old nineteenth century three-tier trial system and provide for two distinct levels of jury trial.[27] In the Commission's view, a structural change of this sort was clearly preferable to trying to cope with the problem simply by appointing more judges and would enable a 'reallocation of the workload of the High Court and the District Courts so that judicial attributes match case importance'.[28] As a result, a series of statutory amendments in 1979 and 1980 renamed the magistrate's court and the Supreme Court, which became the district court and the High Court respectively, and provided for designated district court judges to conduct jury trials in all but the most serious offences.[29] In 1991, the process of removing criminal jury trials from the High Court was accelerated by dividing those remaining offences exclusively within the High Court jurisdiction into two groups: a small group reserved only for High Court trial and a rather larger group of so-called 'middle band' offences which, if the interests of justice or the demands of administrative convenience required it, could be transferred to the district court for trial.[30]

The end product of this process has been the increasing simplification of the criminal jury and its transfer from the High Court to the district court. At the same time, although the overall use of criminal juries seems to have initially increased with the introduction of jury trial in the district court, the downward trend in the proportion of cases going to jury trial has probably resumed over the last couple of years. Unfortunately, it is virtually impossible to confirm these impressions on the basis of the available data on jury trial in New Zealand. While a crude ratio

[25] The increase in criminal jury trials sparked concerns that the seriousness of offending and the greater availability of criminal legal aid had resulted in more defendants opting for jury trial.

[26] See Report of the Royal Comm'n on the Courts, *supra* note 1, at 366.

[27] See ibid., at 113.

[28] Ibid., at 98.

[29] For a review of this legislation, see R. A. McGechan, *Trial by Triad—District Courts, Summary Proceedings and Crimes Amendment (No. 2) Acts 1980* (1982) 10 N.Z. U. L. Rev. 17.

[30] See District Courts Act 1947, § 28A(1)(e) (N.Z.).

of jury trials to summary trials can be obtained, more sophisticated data, such as the proportion of offenders eligible to elect jury trial who actually elect it, are unobtainable at present. It seems that jury trials make up considerably less than 1 percent of total nontraffic criminal trials, and we know that whereas in 1990 only 57 percent of the committals were to the district court, by 1997 this had risen to 78 percent; beyond that the data are either unavailable or ambiguous.[31]

B. *The Civil Jury*

1. Supreme/High Court Trial

In addition to criminal cases tried on indictment, the Supreme Court Ordinance of 1841 provided for a jury of twelve men in all civil trials.[32] As in the criminal jurisdiction, however, special provisions were made for cases involving the indigenous inhabitants. The Jurors Ordinance of 1842 provided for the enrolment of Maori jurors to serve on mixed race juries in actions in which one party was Maori.[33] Not surprisingly, this provision and similar attempts to accommodate the interests of the majority population attracted considerable settler hostility and, as a result, seems to have remained largely, if not entirely, a dead letter.[34]

The first general step away from jury trial at this level came in 1860 with the provision that, with the consent of the parties, issues of fact could in the future be tried by judge alone.[35] In 1862, a system of 'minor juries' was instituted to deal with cases under £100 in value. Minor juries consisted of six members balloted from a panel of twelve and were used at the discretion of the trial judge.[36] By 1882, this had been reduced to a jury of four, available at the request of either party, in cases involving sums of more than £50 and less than £500.[37] The 'minor jury' was finally abolished in 1977.[38]

Prior to 1880, civil juries essentially had to reach a unanimous verdict, as they were discharged only if they failed to reach agreement after

[31] See unpublished statistics for June 1990 to June 1997, Dep't for Courts, Wellington (on file with authors).

[32] See Supreme Court Ordinance 1841, § 19 (N.Z.).

[33] See Jury Law Amendment Act 1862, § 9 (N.Z.).

[34] See Report of the Royal Comm'n on the Courts, *supra* note 1, at 14.

[35] See Supreme Court Amendment Act 1860, § 22 (N.Z.).

[36] See Supreme Court Amendment Act 1862, § 7 (N.Z.).

[37] See Supreme Court Act 1882, sched. 2, cl. 251 (N.Z.).

[38] See Judicature Amendment Act 1977, § 9(i) (N.Z.).

twelve hours' deliberation.[39] In 1898, this statute was amended to allow hung juries to be discharged after a 'reasonable' period of deliberation, provided that it was not less than four hours.[40] In the meantime, the Juries Act of 1880 had provided for all civil juries to render a three-quarters majority verdict after a minimum of three hours' deliberation if unanimity could not be achieved.[41] In 1980, the minimum deliberation time was increased to four hours.[42]

At the same time as the power to conduct judge-alone trials was extended and alternatives to the cumbersome jury of twelve were devised, the provision of special juries was restricted and finally abolished. Although special juries seem to have been available since the inception of the Supreme Court in 1841, formal recognition of their availability did not occur until 1844,[43] and it was not until 1868 that it was made clear that the parties could demand one as of right in all civil cases.[44] Nevertheless, by the Juries Act of 1908, a special jury could be empanelled only by leave of the court when a party petitioned, or alternatively a judge could order it on a requirement of loosely defined 'expert knowledge'.[45] In 1937, this requirement was tightened by limiting special juries to cases in which the judge was satisfied that 'difficult questions in relation to scientific, technical, business or professional matters are likely to arise'.[46] Special juries could consist of either twelve or four jurors in the usual way.[47] They were abolished by the Juries Act of 1981.

In 1980, the Supreme Court became the High Court.[48] The availability of civil juries in the High Court is now governed by sections 19A and B of the Judicature Act of 1908. In theory, jury trial is available in

[39] See Juries Act 1868, § 53 (N.Z.).

[40] See Juries Amendment Act 1898, § 13 (N.Z.).

[41] See Juries Act 1880, § 156 (N.Z.).

[42] See Judicature Amendment Act 1980, § 5 (N.Z.) (inserting a new § 54A that increased the deliberation time to four hours).

[43] Prior to 1844, no specific rules relating to special juries existed in New Zealand. In the absence of such rules, the Supreme Court followed the 'practice of Her Majesty's Superior Courts at Westminster', which included special juries at the request of the parties. See Juries Amendment Ordinance 1844, § 6 (N.Z.). The Supreme Court Rules Ordinance of the same year formally recognized such juries by providing for a Special Jury List to be compiled for use '[w]henever a special jury shall be allowed by a Judge of the Supreme Court.' Supreme Court Ordinance 1844 §§ 74–5 (N.Z.).

[44] See Juries Act 1868, § 20 (N.Z.).

[45] Juries Act 1908, § 71 (N.Z.).

[46] Statutes Amendment Act 1937, § 37 (N.Z.).

[47] See Juries Act 1889, § 71 (N.Z.).

[48] See Judicature Amendment Act 1979, § 2 (N.Z.). This legislation came into force on Apr. 1, 1980.

most civil trials at the request of either party.[49] In practice, it is so rare that the Department for Courts no longer even keeps statistics on it.

2. The District Court

In 1858, a number of civil courts, presided over by justices of the peace and Commissioners, were abolished and a simplified three-tier trial court system was established. Minor civil suits were to be heard by justices at petty sessions and by resident magistrates without benefit of jury.[50] Suits involving sums of not less than £20 and not more than £100 were to be heard in the district court; more serious matters went to the Supreme Court.[51] At the district court level, either party could require a jury trial. From the start, district court juries consisted of only four members,[52] selected by the parties from a panel of twelve by a series of alternating challenges.[53] By 1893, the jurisdiction of the district court had been extended to £500 but, as previously noted, district courts had never been proclaimed in all districts of the colony, and their civil business seems to have been gradually usurped by the consent jurisdiction of the resident magistrates' court. By the time the Magistrates Courts Act of 1893 was enacted,[54] district courts had largely ceased to function and were effectively abolished in 1909.[55]

When, in 1980, the magistrates' court was redesigned and became the new district court with the ability to conduct jury trials in some criminal cases, the civil side of its jurisdiction was left largely untouched.[56] Hence, while criminal trials may take place before a jury in either the district or the High Court, civil jury trial is confined to the High Court.

C. *The Trial of Maori Cases*

In 1841, the embryonic colonial administration had little claim or desire to deal with the affairs of the indigenous population.[57] Settler justices

[49] See Judicature Act 1908, §§ 19A–19B (N.Z.).

[50] See Petty Sessions of the Peace Act 1858 (N.Z.); Resident Magistrates' Courts Acts 1858 (N.Z.).

[51] See District Courts Act 1858, § 15 (N.Z.).

[52] See ibid., § 62.

[53] See ibid., § 66.

[54] The Magistrates Courts Act of 1893 replaced the resident magistrate's court with a court of record presided over by a stipendiary magistrate.

[55] In 1909, all the remaining court districts were abolished by proclamation. The District Courts Act 1858, itself was not, however, formally repealed until 1925. See REPORT OF THE ROYAL COMM'N ON THE COURTS, *supra* note 1, at 9.

[56] See generally McGechan, *supra* note 29.

[57] See generally REPORT OF THE ROYAL COMM'N ON THE COURTS, *supra* note 1; ALAN WARD, A SHOW OF JUSTICE: RACIAL 'AMALGAMATION' IN NINETEENTH CENTURY NEW ZEALAND (1983).

were initially instructed simply to 'compromise or adjust' minor disputes involving natives in accordance with native custom.[58] In theory at least, more serious matters were, from the start, subject to settler law and procedure, but the practical realities of life in the emergent colony meant that few such cases came to notice. Furthermore, from 1844 onward, minor civil disputes in which one or both parties were Maori and criminal cases in which both parties were Maori were subject to special procedures that made use of tribal authority structures and native assessors.[59] In addition, the Juries Amendment Ordinance of 1844 provided for mixed race juries in both civil and criminal cases in all courts where jury trial was available where 'the property or person of any Aboriginal Native of New Zealand may be affected'.[60]

Parallel to the development of the district court in the 'European' arena, the Native Circuit Courts' Act of 1858 provided for a system of native circuit courts to deal with disputes involving Maori in those districts in which native land title had not yet been extinguished. These courts were staffed by resident magistrates—whose jurisdiction in the 'European' domain was exclusively judge alone—who sat with Maori assessors and, if the parties requested it, with all-Maori juries in both civil and criminal cases.[61] However, the potential impact of these provisions was limited because they applied only in those outlying districts for which they had been proclaimed by the Governor in Council. Indeed, even where they were in force, they are likely to have been a relatively cost-free gesture toward indigenous justice, since it was clear that the government-appointed resident magistrate was to largely control the process.[62] Furthermore, it seems likely that in some districts, at least, Maori juries were seldom, if ever, used. In any event, although the use of Maori assessors in civil cases was retained in the Circuit Court until 1893, the provision for Maori juries in civil cases was abolished in 1867.[63] In criminal cases

[58] See Report of the Royal Comm'n on the Courts, *supra* note 2, at 14. Maori methods of conflict resolution and the behavioural standards that informed them were almost always referred to in colonial literature and legislation as 'native custom', thus clearly distinguishing it from the 'legal' codes and procedures of the European colonists.

[59] See Native Exemption Ordinance 1844 (N.Z.); see also Resident Magistrates' Court Ordinance 1846 (N.Z.).

[60] Juries Amendment Ordinance 1844, § 1 (N.Z.).

[61] See Native Circuit Courts' Act 1858, §§ 2, 6–10 (N.Z.).

[62] For example, although the jury list was compiled by the native assessors, the initial panel of 12 was selected by the resident magistrate. See ibid., § 6 (N.Z.). Furthermore, on conviction by the jury, the court was free to disregard the verdict if it thought fit, and, in the event of jury disagreement, the court could simply decide the case itself. See ibid., § 10.

[63] See Resident Magistrates' Act 1867 (N.Z.). This Act consolidated the powers of resident magistrates but did not reenact the provisions of the Native District Courts Act 1858, for Maori juries in civil cases between Maori.

the jurisdiction of the native circuit court seems to have remained, at least in theory, until 1891, when it was abolished as obsolete, like the district court, its function usurped by the magistrates' court.[64]

In theory, all-Maori juries were available in both civil and criminal cases in the Supreme Court. In civil cases, Maori juries were available if both parties were Maori and if both concurred. In criminal cases, they were available if both parties were Maori and the accused requested it. In addition, in civil cases where one party was Maori and requested an all-Maori jury, or both parties were Maori and one wanted a Maori jury but the other did not, the court could order trial by a mixed jury composed of six jurors drawn from the Maori roll and six from the common roll.[65] We have little information on the extent to which Maori and mixed juries were ever used. However, a Maori or mixed jury would be available to the parties only if Maori jurors were available on that day. As there was never any requirement that the authorities compile or maintain a Maori jury roll, and the legislation was always quite clear that if Maori jurors were not available the jury could be drawn from the available common jurors,[66] the use of such juries probably was rare. By the time of their abolition in 1962, Maori juries were already described as obsolete—in spite of the fact that an all-Maori jury had been used in a criminal trial the year before.[67] The abolition of Maori and mixed juries in 1962 accompanied the belated extension to Maori of the right to sit on ordinary juries.[68]

In describing these structures, it may be correct to conclude, as the Report of the Royal Commission on the Courts does, that:

> a principal thread of development during the nineteenth century involved a difficult question of whether special tribunals, judicial officers, and rules should govern disputes involving the Maori people; particularly in districts where the Maori formed a majority population. By the end of the century this issue had been settled, if not resolved. Except in respect of Maori land and certain related matters, the Maori people were to be governed almost completely by the English derived law.[69]

[64] A process that culminated in the Magistrates' Courts Act 1893 (N.Z.), which repealed the special provisions of the 1867 Act relating to Maori.

[65] The provisions dealing with Maori and mixed juries in both the civil and the criminal jurisdiction were consolidated by the Juries Act 1868, §§ 45–52 (N.Z.), and retained that form largely unchanged until their abolition in 1962.

[66] See Juries Act 1868, § 50 (N.Z.).

[67] See PETER WILLIAMS, A PASSION FOR JUSTICE 89–91 (1997).

[68] See Juries Amendment Act 1962, § 2 (N.Z.).

[69] REPORT OF THE ROYAL COMM'N ON THE COURTS, *supra* note 1, at 2.

However, in so far as trial by jury was concerned, the issue was effectively settled in the first few years of colonization. In practice, the provision of mixed and Maori juries seems to have been little more than a perfunctory gesture intended, at the most, to justify a system that progressively destroyed the indigenous legal structures while denying Maori the right to participate as full citizens in the administration of the new system of justice to which they were to be subjected. Furthermore, as noted above, the extension of 'special' procedures to Maori always took place in the context of a system that was founded exclusively on values derived from the English common law. Indeed, the very concept of the jury, generously extended to the Maori people by the colonial authority, was a concept alien to the legal and social culture of the indigenous race.

D. The Juries Act of 1981

The Juries Act of 1981 marks something of a watershed in the history of the jury in New Zealand. In particular, the Act significantly extended the democratic reach of the jury by sweeping away many of the old occupational exemptions and limiting the grounds on which citizens could apply to be excused from jury service. Jury procedure was simplified and largely removed from the statute into a comprehensive set of Jury Rules, thus reducing the length of the statute from 184 sections to thirty-seven. Special juries were finally abolished, and the jury of twelve was declared as the only form of jury available.

III. The Availability of Jury Trial

A. Civil Trials

In any civil case heard in the High Court, section 19A of the Judicature Act provides that either party may request a jury trial where the only relief claimed is payment of a debt, pecuniary damages, or recovery of a chattel to the value of more than $3,000.[70] Where the case does not fall within section 19A, trial is to be by judge alone unless the court

[70] See Judicature Act 1908, § 19A(1)–(2) (N.Z.), amended by Judicature Act 1977, § 6 (N.Z.). The $3,000 lower limit means that in practice all damages claims that are likely to reach the court will be eligible for jury trial—what research we have indicates that the minimum level at which litigation through the courts becomes economic is $15,000. This is undoubtedly an understatement. See REPORT OF THE NEW ZEALAND JUDICIARY 16 (1997).

orders otherwise on the ground that any proceedings or issue 'can be tried more conveniently' before a jury.[71] The right to jury trial under section 19A is, however, not absolute. The judge may still, on the application of either party, direct trial of the whole case or of any particular issue before a judge alone if one of two conditions is satisfied: The case or issue involves the consideration of difficult questions of law, or the case involves the prolonged examination of documents or accounts or difficult questions of a scientific, technical, business, or professional nature which 'cannot conveniently be made with a jury'.[72]

For most of its history, the use of the civil jury in New Zealand, while not rare, has been limited to a number of specific types of case. Since the turn of the century, its use has largely been confined to defamation and personal injury cases, and the occasional action against governmental bodies, such as the police. The effective abolition of the vast majority of personal injury actions in 1972 (and their replacement with a comprehensive 'no-fault' state-administered compensation scheme) has now relegated the civil jury to only one or two cases per year.[73] While recent changes to the accident compensation scheme may have begun to open the door to a revival of some forms of personal injury action, the High Court seems likely to adopt a cautious approach to the application of jury trial under such instances.[74]

The future of the civil jury is unclear. On the one hand, if personal injury claims and, in particular, exemplary damages and Bill of Rights Act claims are permitted to develop,[75] plaintiffs may well continue to press

[71] Judicature Act 1908, § 19B(2) (N.Z.).

[72] Ibid., § 19A(5). However, the High Court has recently confirmed that § 19A does not confer a 'general discretion' on the court in this area. Even though a trial would 'be much more sensibly, economically and conveniently managed and conducted before a judge alone', a jury trial cannot be refused unless the factors specifically identified in § (5)(a)–(b) are made out by the party resisting trial by jury. M & Ors v. L & Ors (Mar. 3, 1998) High Court, Auckland Registry, CP. 226–9/96, CP. 279–80/96, at 23 (unreported).

[73] In 1960, civil jury trials accounted for 35.75% of the total civil actions heard in the Supreme Court. By 1976, after three years of operation of the accident compensation scheme, *see* Accident Compensation Act 1972, §§ 4–5 (N.Z.), the number had fallen to 12.65%. See REPORT OF THE ROYAL COMM'N ON THE COURTS, *supra* note 1, at 125–6.

[74] See, e.g., the comments of Elias J in *Innes* v. *Attorney-General* (1997) 4 H.R.N.Z. 251, 256.

[75] Currently, the view of the Court of Appeal is that public law compensation under the Bill of Rights Act is not 'pecuniary damages' and is accordingly not covered by the 'right' conferred by § 19A of the Judicature Act of 1908. In addition, the consideration of compensatory damages is not appropriate for jury determination and accordingly should not be ordered under § 19B. See Simpson v. A-G (Baigent's Case) [1994] 3 N.Z.L.R. 667, 677.

for jury trial. On the other hand, neither defendants nor the judiciary are likely to evince much enthusiasm for the process. However, given the iconic status of jury trial in general, there is unlikely to be much enthusiasm for outright abolition, either. The likelihood seems to be that New Zealand will continue to retain a theoretical right to jury trial in civil cases, which will continue to be rarely, if ever, exercised effectively.

B. Criminal Trials

Criminal offences in New Zealand can be divided into two basic categories: the more serious indictable offences, which can be tried on indictment before a judge and jury, and the lesser summary offences, which can be tried summarily before a district court judge or before justices. The picture is, however, complicated by the fact that many indictable offences also can be tried summarily and that some summary offences may, if the accused so elects, be tried on indictment. In broad terms, therefore, a case may proceed to jury trial for one of three reasons: it involves an offence which by statute is laid on indictment; it involves an offence which may be laid either summarily or on indictment but which the prosecution has chosen to lay indictably; or the charge has been laid summarily but the accused has exercised a right to elect jury trial.

Jury trial may take place either before a district court presided over by a trial judge[76] or before the High Court. The district court has jurisdiction to conduct jury trials in the following situations:

(1) where the accused elects trial by jury, having been charged either with a summary offence carrying a maximum penalty in excess of three months' imprisonment,[77] or with an indictable offence in which the prosecution has chosen to proceed in summary form;[78]

[76] That is, a district court judge appointed by the Governor-General under § 28B of the District Courts Act of 1947 to exercise the jurisdiction of the district court in respect to trials on indictment.

[77] See Summary Proceedings Act 1957, § 66(1) (N.Z.); see also New Zealand Bill of Rights Act 1990, § 24(e) (N.Z.). There are a few notable exceptions to this right. The offences of common assault and assault on a law enforcement officer under ss. 9 and 10 of the Summary Offences Act 1981, which both carry a maximum penalty of six months' imprisonment, can only be tried summarily.

[78] Those indictable offences in respect of which the prosecution may choose to proceed either on indictment or summarily are listed in s. 6(2) of and in the First Schedule to the Summary Proceedings Act 1957.

(2) where the accused has been charged with an indictable offence which may be laid summarily but the prosecution elects to proceed by way of indictment;
(3) where the accused has been charged with one of the twenty-seven offences listed in Part I of Schedule 1A of the District Courts Act of 1947.[79] These offences comprise a band of the less serious offences under the Crimes Act of 1961 and are triable only on indictment;
(4) where the accused has been charged with one of the seventeen so-called 'middle band' offences listed in Part II of Schedule 1A of the District Courts Act of 1947, such as rape, kidnapping, and wounding with intent, and the proceedings have been transferred from the High Court to the district court following a determination by a High Court judge on the papers that in the interests of justice or administrative convenience it is more appropriate for the trial to be held in the district court.[80]

The High Court has jurisdiction to try all indictable offences and all offences where the accused is proceeded against summarily and elects jury trial. However, in practice most of these cases now proceed to the district court and the High Court will hear cases only in the following situations:[81]

(1) where the offence falls in the 'middle band' and a High Court judge has determined that trial in the district court is not appropriate;
(2) where the offence is indictable and is neither triable summarily nor listed as a 'middle band' offence in Part II of Schedule 1A to the District Courts Act 1947. This small group of offences, all carrying maximum penalties of fourteen years' imprisonment or more, essentially comprise the most serious offences in the Crimes Act 1961 and must be tried in the High Court;
(3) where, on the application of either party, a High Court judge orders the transfer of the case from the District Court.

Although trials on indictment at both levels still generally involve jury trial, in all but a relatively small number of offences, the accused may now apply for trial by judge alone.[82] There is a statutory presumption in

[79] District Courts Act 1947, § 28A(1)(d) (N.Z.).
[80] See ibid., § 28A(1)(e); Summary Proceedings Act 1957, § 168A(a)(1) (N.Z.).
[81] See District Courts Act 1947, § 28J(1)–(2) (N.Z.).
[82] See Crimes Act 1961, § 361B (N.Z.). An application for trial by judge alone may not be made where the accused is charged with an offence punishable by imprisonment

favour of granting the application,[83] and the courts have taken the view that, in general, the accused is to be seen as the best judge of the situation.[84] Unlike a number of other jurisdictions, there is no requirement that the prosecution consent to the application, nor is there any requirement that the accused obtain legal advice prior to the application.

In practice, whether an accused is tried by jury, and, to a lesser extent, where the trial takes place, depend on a number of factors and distinctions which frequently seem arbitrary. These factors range from the maximum penalty for the offence charged, whether the offence is classified as summary or indictable (which may well be largely a matter of historical accident), the form (summary or indictable) in which the prosecution has chosen to commence the proceedings, and whether the accused elects to be tried by jury or seeks trial by judge alone. The result is that offenders who have committed similar offences can have very different levels of control over the form and venue of their trial, as well as the potential penalties to which they will be exposed.

Leaving aside the question of the availability of trial by jury in complex or otherwise exceptional cases,[85] the current rules on the availability of jury trial raise a number of distinct issues. First, as noted above, the present law provides for mandatory jury trial in all cases where the maximum penalty is fourteen years' imprisonment or more.[86] While there are certainly good arguments for a presumption of jury trial in such cases,[87] it is difficult to see a justification for a blanket rule that applies whether or not the case raises issues which are particularly appropriate to jury resolution. We accordingly agree with the New Zealand Law Commission in its 1998 discussion paper on criminal jury trials when it suggests that in all such cases it should in the future be left to the accused to assess whether jury trial is the appropriate forum for the case.[88]

for life or a term of 14 years or more, such as homicide or sexual violation. See ibid., § 361B(5).

[83] See ibid., § 361B(4).

[84] See R. v. Narain [1988] 1 N.Z.L.R. 580, 589.

[85] See *infra* Part III.C.

[86] See *supra* text in note 82.

[87] See, e.g., the comments of Williams J in *R.* v. *Maguire* (Dec. 8, 1992) High Court, Auckland Registry, T. 267/90, at 3 (unreported), the VICTORIAN LAW REFORM COMMITTEE, JURY SERVICE IN VICTORIA ¶ 2.27 (Issues Paper No. 2, 1995), and, in relation to murder, the comments of White J in *R.* v. *Marshall* (1986) 43 S.A. St. R. 448, 449.

[88] See NEW ZEALAND LAW COMM'N, JURIES IN CRIMINAL TRIALS PART ONE, at 22–30 (1998) (hereinafter Jury Trials Part One). This paper was the Commission's first substantive discussion of the role of the jury in criminal trials in New Zealand. It was followed in November 1999 by two further papers: *Juries in Criminal Trials Part Two: A Discussion Paper* (1999) (hereinafter Jury Trials Part Two) and *Juries in Criminal Trials Part Two: A Summary of the Research Findings* (1999) (hereinafter Summary of Research).

Secondly, as noted above,[89] although the Summary Proceedings Act provides for an accused to have the right to elect jury trial if charged with an offence punishable by more than three months' imprisonment, and although this right is confirmed by the New Zealand Bill of Rights Act of 1990,[90] persons charged with either assault or assault on a law enforcement officer face a maximum penalty of six months' imprisonment and yet may not elect trial by jury.[91] While the precise rationale for this exclusion is unclear, the High Court has recently linked it to 'the view that the [c]ourt system could not accommodate the luxury of jury trials for the very common type of prosecution for assault suitably brought under the Summary Offences Act'.[92] The logic of the exclusion of these two offences from the right recognized in the Bill of Rights is not compelling. If the offence is properly considered to be a minor one for which summary trial is appropriate, then it should be visited only with the generally accepted 'minor' penalty of three months' imprisonment or less. If it is a serious offence which merits a potential penalty of six months' imprisonment, then, like similar offences in that penalty range, it should attract the right to jury trial. In its 1998 discussion paper, the New Zealand Law Commission proposes the repeal of section 43 of the Summary Offences Act of 1981 to remedy this anomaly.[93] Although we agree with the Commission's criticism of the provision, and although we recognize the political difficulties involved, it would be preferable in our view to deal with the anomaly by reducing the maximum penalty for the offences in question to three months' imprisonment, thus rendering section 43 redundant.

Thirdly, the current system, whereby a large number of offences are *prima facie* indictable but may, at the discretion of the police, be charged either indictably or summarily, enables the police to dictate jury trial in circumstances where the accused might well prefer the case to be tried by judge alone. At present there are no guidelines, legislative or otherwise, for the exercise of this discretion, and little or no input into police decision making by the Crown Prosecutor, who, if the case does eventually go to trial before a jury, will be responsible for drawing up the indictment and presenting the case in court. As a result, practice seems

[89] See *supra* text accompanying note 77.

[90] New Zealand Bill of Rights Act 1990, § 24(c) (N.Z.). This section also provides, however, that there is no right to a jury trial where the offence is under military law and tried before a military tribunal. See ibid.

[91] See Summary Offences Act 1981, § 43 (N.Z.).

[92] Reille v. Police [1993] 1 N.Z.L.R. 587, 591.

[93] See New Zealand Law Comm'n, Jury Trials Part One, *supra* note 88, ¶ 128.

to vary considerably between police districts and even police investigators within the same district,[94] with the decision being made primarily on the basis of the individual officer's perception of the seriousness of the accused's conduct.

While the prosecution will always have a choice over the precise charge to lay, and this may sometimes dictate the mode of trial and limit the choices available to the accused, permitting the prosecution to determine directly the mode of trial by choosing the *form* in which the charge is laid is anomalous. This is a view which has been consistently taken by the New Zealand Law Commission and is repeated in its 1998 discussion paper on criminal jury trials.[95] In our view, this power should be removed and the offences currently subject to it treated simply as summary offences. Hence, the accused would retain the right to elect jury trial and, where the accused declines this right, the court would retain the residual power to decline summary jurisdiction where appropriate.[96]

If it is accepted that a blanket provision for mandatory jury trial is inappropriate, not least because crude statutory criteria based on maximum sentence length or general offence categories are essentially arbitrary in their operation, and that the prosecution generally should not have the power to dictate the mode of trial, the historical distinction between indictable and summary offences becomes largely irrelevant. Consistent with the provisions of the New Zealand Bill of Rights Act, offences carrying three months' imprisonment or less should continue to be triable summarily. All other offences should also be triable by a judge alone unless the defence elects trial by jury. As in the civil jurisdiction, it may, however, be desirable to give the court power to decline jury trial in cases of particular complexity.[97]

C. *Jury Trial in Complex Cases*

The principal debate in relation to criminal cases is whether the right to jury trial should be removed in some or all complex cases. At present,

[94] See WARREN YOUNG *ET AL.*, NEW ZEALAND DEP'T OF JUSTICE, THE PROSECUTION AND TRIAL OF ADULT OFFENDERS IN NEW ZEALAND 23–6 (1989); see also NEW ZEALAND LAW COMM'N, CRIMINAL PROSECUTION 40–1 (1997).

[95] See NEW ZEALAND LAW COMM'N, THE STRUCTURE OF THE COURTS (1989) and Jury Trials Part One, *supra* note 88, para. 147.

[96] See Summary Proceedings Act 1957, § 44 (N.Z.). This enables the court, for example, to deal with the situation where defendants in multiple defendant trials choose different modes of trial.

[97] See *infra* Part III.C.

there is no provision in New Zealand law for complex trials, such as fraud cases, to be tried automatically by judge alone, or indeed by any other form of special tribunal. It is the defendant's decision whether to make an application for a judge-alone trial.[98]

This procedure was inserted into the Crimes Act in 1979 in response to concern expressed by the Court of Appeal that in complex fraud cases some mechanism was needed to permit trial by judge alone.[99] More recently, the difficulties experienced by the judge and parties in *R.* v. *Adams*,[100] otherwise known as 'the Equiticorp case', led the trial judge to observe that such cases should never be tried by jury.[101] In this case, seven company directors were accused on an indictment containing thirteen counts of fraud. All the defendants applied for, and were granted, trial by judge alone. The trial lasted six months, and the Crown called 105 witnesses who testified. An additional ninety witnesses presented written briefs to the court. The evidence raised complex factual issues and difficult points of civil and criminal law.

The problems produced by complex and often lengthy cases have been considered by both the New Zealand Law Commission[102] and reform bodies in a number of other commonwealth jurisdictions. The most comprehensive recent discussion is to be found in the consultation paper published by the English government in 1998, which outlines and discusses most of the reform options available for such cases.[103]

Proponents of judge-alone trials in these cases argue that such a procedure is desirable because juries are not competent to cope with complex and extensive evidence, often from expert witnesses, especially where the case extends over a lengthy period of time. However, professional opinion on this is divided, in terms of both the nature of the problem and its significance. Furthermore, what research we have is equivocal.[104] While some 'complex' cases undoubtedly produce perverse jury verdicts through the failure of juries to understand the evidence,

[98] See *supra* text accompanying notes 82–4.

[99] See R. v. Jeffs & Others (Apr. 28, 1978) (Court of Appeal), quoted in REPORT OF THE ROYAL COMM'N ON THE COURTS, *supra* note 2, ¶ 399. The legislation enacted did not follow the Royal Commission's recommendation in para. 400 that the defendant be able to *elect* trial by judge alone and that the Crown be able to object to that election.

[100] (Dec. 18, 1992) High Court, Auckland Registry, T 240/91 (unreported).

[101] See NEW ZEALAND LAW COMM'N, Jury Trials Part One, *supra* note 88, at 40.

[102] Jury Trials Part Two, *supra* note 88, 53–4.

[103] See HOME OFFICE, JURIES IN SERIOUS FRAUD TRIALS: A CONSULTATION DOCUMENT (1998).

[104] Jury Trials Part Two, *supra* note 88, 54; Summary of Research, *supra* note 88, 25–6.

this is likely to be true for some noncomplex cases as well. On the other hand, the provision of special judge-alone or specialist tribunal regimes for a limited range of predominantly white-collar offences runs the risk of giving the appearance of the establishment 'looking after its own' or conversely, of an establishment exercise in scapegoating. In other words, such cases, however defined, may well be precisely the ones in which the political or symbolic value of the jury as an avenue for community input is most significant. Moreover, the New Zealand research strongly suggests that at least some of the difficulties juries confront in such cases result from aspects of trial procedure, such as the way in which evidence is presented, the lack of explanation of legal terms, unhelpful or untimely judicial instructions, and reliance on oral proceedings.[105]

Notwithstanding these considerations, there is a strong argument that some cases are simply unsuited to the jury process. The problem lies in defining which cases fall into this category. Fraud trials are not the only kind of complex trial, and, as a blanket category, not all fraud trials are automatically complex. Scientific evidence may make a murder trial complex and the evidence difficult to understand, or myths regarding female sexuality in a rape trial may cloud issues of consent and sexual behaviour. It would be neither possible nor desirable, therefore, to eliminate the problem of complex trials solely by reference to the offence category or the length of trial. It would be possible to do so only by giving judges the discretion to order a judge-alone trial where they believe that, because of the complexity of the case, a jury trial would be contrary to the interests of justice. Although, if implemented, the exercise of such discretion would likely become a fruitful area for pretrial litigation or appeals, it would go a long way toward eliminating the problems that stem from trial by jury in complex cases.

IV. The Selection of Jurors in Criminal Trials

A. Eligibility for Jury Service

Prior to the selection of the jury at court, a number of legal rules determine who is able to serve on a jury. The Juries Act of 1981 states positively that registered electors between 20 and 65 years of age are

[105] Summary of Research, *supra* note 88, Part 3. How procedures in these respects might be modified to enhance jury decision making is discussed *infra*, text following note 173.

qualified to serve on juries within the jury district in which they reside.[106] This includes noncitizens who are permanent residents and are registered on the electoral rolls.[107]

As in other jurisdictions, those individuals with a close connection to either the administration of the law or the criminal justice system cannot serve.[108] Such individuals excluded from service include members of the Executive Council of New Zealand, Members of Parliament, judges, certain justices of the peace, barristers and solicitors, police officers,[109] and certain employees in the justice system. Persons who have been convicted of a criminal offence and imprisoned[110] for life or a term of three years or more, or sentenced to preventive detention, are also disqualified from serving on a jury, as are those who, within the last five years, have been either imprisoned for three months or more or sentenced to corrective training.[111]

B. The Out-of-court Selection Process

The first step in the selection process is the compilation, by random selection, of jury lists from the General and Maori electoral rolls for each jury district.[112] From the jury lists, a number of potential jurors are randomly selected by the court registrars of individual courts (the jury panel) and sent a summons to appear in court for jury service. Jurors are summoned to appear at the beginning of the working week (usually Monday morning) and must remain available to be selected for any jury commencing during that week. The registrar may ask potential jurors not selected on the first day, or persons who serve on a jury for one or two days, to return later in the week for another jury empanelment. Sum-

[106] See Juries Act 1981, § 6 (N.Z.).

[107] See Electoral Act 1993, § 74 (N.Z.).

[108] See Juries Act 1981, § 8 (N.Z.).

[109] There is no statutory prohibition on former police officers serving on juries, but in practice counsel apply for the discharge of the juror or the jury if such information comes to hand. See, *e.g.*, R. v. Ryder (No. 3) (Sept. 28, 1994) High Court, Christchurch, T 68/94 (unreported); R. v. Turner (July 25, 1996) Court of Appeal, CA 439/95 (unreported).

[110] Prior to 1981, s. 5 of the Juries Act 1908 (N.Z.) disqualified people who had been *convicted* of any offence *punishable* by death or imprisonment for a term of three years or more.

[111] See Juries Act 1981, § 7 (N.Z.).

[112] The Juries Act 1981 (N.Z.) and the Jury Rules, S.R. 1990, No. 226 (N.Z.) set out the system for selecting persons for jury service. The Electoral Enrolment Centre compiles the jury lists and the Department for Courts screens the lists for potential jurors who may be disqualified. A jury district is defined arbitrarily as those places within 30 kilometres by the most practicable route from a courthouse in the town or city in which jury trials may be held. See Juries Act 1981, § 5(3) (N.Z.).

moned potential jurors may apply to the registrar to be excused from jury service. The registrar may grant that application if:

(1) the potential juror, another person, or the general public may suffer a serious inconvenience or hardship because of the nature of the person's occupation or business or any commitment arising from it, or because of the person's health, family commitments, or other personal circumstances;
(2) the potential juror has either served as a juror or attended for jury service within the last two years;
(3) the potential juror has been excused from jury service for a period that has not yet expired; or
(4) the potential juror is a member of a religious sect or order that holds jury service to be incompatible with its beliefs.[113]

Potential jurors are excused fairly readily on these grounds. A survey conducted by the then Department of Justice in 1993[114] found that only 26 percent of persons summoned appeared in court for jury service;[115] 56 percent were excused by the registrar before or on the day of court;[116] and the remaining 18 percent did not turn up, either because they ignored the summons or because residential or postal addresses were out of date.[117]

Excusing more than half of the summoned potential jurors from jury service has a significant impact on the representation of particular community groups. Anecdotal evidence suggests that professional groups, teachers, the self-employed, and women at home with children are particularly likely to be excused. Similarly, the significant numbers who fail to turn up without contacting the court are no doubt drawn disproportionately from some groups—probably the unskilled and the highly mobile.

Consequently, of the quarter of summoned jurors who turn up for jury service, some demographic groups are seriously under-represented compared to the jury district population. In particular, in the *Trial by Peers*

[113] See ibid., § 15.

[114] See New Zealand Dep't of Justice, Trial by Peers?: The Composition of the New Zealand Jury 45–54 (1995) (hereinafter Trial by Peers). The period surveyed was Sept. 13 to Oct. 8, 1993.

[115] Even this figure may still be too high. Other data collected by the Department for Courts indicate that the figure is more likely to be around 20%–22%. See ibid., at 42.

[116] This group included anyone who was disqualified or ineligible to serve and who informed the registrar of this fact.

[117] See Trial by Peers, *supra* note 112, at 42.

study, Maori, Maori women, women in general, and younger age groups were under-represented. Five out of the ten occupational groups had lower than expected proportions in the jury panel ('legislators, administrators and managers', 'professionals', 'agriculture and fishery workers', 'trades', and 'elementary occupations'). The difference between the expected and actual proportion was most striking for the elementary occupations.[118]

Under-enrolment of eligible voters, a significant proportion of whom are Maori and Pacific Islanders compared with the general electorate, is being addressed by the Electoral Enrolment Centre by the use of special enrolment campaigns.

Based on the assumption that jury representativeness is a desirable goal, it appears that the proportions either being excused or failing to turn up pose a significant problem. It may not be worth tackling the problem of 'no-shows'; many fail to turn up because their addresses on the electoral roll are out of date, and it would be time-consuming, difficult, and resource-intensive to bring successful prosecutions against those who deliberately ignore the summons. The existing liberal policy in relation to excuses, however, is another matter; for citizens to take jury service seriously as a duty for which they should make themselves available, it is untenable to operate a system which excuses more than half of those called upon. Mindful of this problem, the Department for Courts is at present conducting research on excusing jurors, and will be investigating the usefulness of providing guidelines to court registrars. It remains to be seen whether this will prove to be enough to remedy the problem.

C. Selection at Court

Upon arrival at court, summoned jurors normally have their attendance noted by a court official and are then shown an introductory video.[119] They are also told, in a number of languages, that they must be able to speak and understand English and, if they do not, they are excused by the registrar.[120]

[118] This classification included labourers, cleaners, building caretakers, messengers, door-keepers, and refuse collectors. See Trial by Peers, *supra* note 112, at 42.

[119] See *infra* text accompanying notes 167–9.

[120] Although registrars have no specific powers to excuse on this ground, it is likely that they can do so within the general terms of the statutory provision giving them the power to excuse jurors. See Juries Act 1981, § 15(1)(b) (N.Z.).

There is an initial ballot for each jury trial commencing on that day which selects about thirty potential jurors for the case. Those thirty or so jurors are then taken to the courtroom. Before final balloting, counsel read the full names of the defendant(s) and all witnesses to be called by the prosecution and the defence, and the potential jurors are asked to disclose whether they know any of the people whose names have been read out and, if so, the nature of that knowledge. The judge then decides whether to excuse any potential juror on the basis of such personal knowledge.[121] Following that, there is a final ballot to select the twelve jurors who will serve on the case.

As jurors are called, they may be challenged by prosecution or defence[122] before they sit down in the jury box, or they may be directed by the judge to 'stand by'.[123] There are three different types of challenges: challenge for want of qualification, challenge for cause, and peremptory challenge. Before we consider each of these, however, it should be noted that information upon which challenges can be based is very limited.

Any party to the proceedings can request that the registrar make available a copy of the jury panel for inspection or copying up to five working days before the jurors are due to be summoned for the week in which the proceedings are scheduled to start.[124] Any other person may inspect and copy the jury panel during the same period with the court's permission.[125] However, the panel list is drawn from the electoral roll entry and lists only names, addresses, and occupations. In addition, in most centres, the police provide the prosecution with information on each potential juror's previous criminal convictions. In a few cases, the police officer in charge of the case will also go through the prosecution's jury list to see if there is anybody he or she does not want on the jury. The police may also annotate the jury list to indicate that a potential juror is an associate of repeat offenders.

The defence has more limited resources with which to check out the jury. Counsel may review the jury list with their client to see if any person should be excluded. At times, information from the jury list is also discussed. In smaller centres, counsel may make use of personal contacts,

[121] See ibid., § 16(b). [122] See ibid., § 19.

[123] See ibid., § 27. Jurors who are stood by (either by consensus between the parties or on the judge's own motion if he or she believes that there is a difficulty with that juror) may be recalled if the number of potential jurors is exhausted before a panel of 12 has been selected.

[124] See ibid., § 14(1). [125] See ibid., § 14(2).

or may try to discover information on potential jurors by circulating the jury list around the office.

Hence, although jury vetting is not prohibited, the reality is that the scope for it is very limited. Furthermore, only in exceptional circumstances may a judge allow counsel to cross-examine jurors before they take their seats.[126] Indeed, there is no reported New Zealand case in which such questioning has been permitted, and in practice it does not occur. The effective absence of a *voir dire* procedure at this stage, coupled with the very restricted nature of any vetting that might take place, means that in the vast majority of cases there is little or no opportunity to assess the knowledge, attitudes, and prejudices of potential jurors prior to challenge.

1. Challenge for Want of Qualification

While all jury lists are screened by the Department for Courts with regard to disqualifications and exclusions, counsel for both prosecution and defence are entitled to challenge any balloted potential juror 'for want of qualification', that is, on the basis that sections 6–8 of the Juries Act 1981 prevent the person from serving. This kind of challenge occurs very rarely[127]—presumably because either the pretrial screening process is generally effective or nobody at court is aware of the features that may disqualify a juror under these sections.

2. Challenge for Cause

The prosecution and defence may challenge potential jurors for cause on the ground that they are not 'indifferent between the parties'. By virtue of section 25 of the Juries Act 1981, such challenges are to be determined by the judge in private and in such manner and on such evidence as he or she thinks fit. Because of the absence of information upon which to determine whether such bias exists, challenges for cause are also very rare. The *Trial by Peers* study recorded none, and as far back as 1957 the Court of Appeal described them as obsolete.[128] Where possible prejudice may exist—for example, because the potential juror is known to be an associate of repeat offenders—he or she is instead subject to a peremptory challenge.

Rather oddly, other grounds available at common law on which a juror could be challenged for cause, such as intoxication, the imper-

[126] See R. v. Sanders [1995] 3 N.Z.L.R. 545, 549.
[127] None was recorded in the *Trial by Peers* study. See Trial by Peers, *supra* note 112.
[128] See R. v. Greening [1957] N.Z.L.R. 906, 914.

sonation of a juror, or an inability to understand the language in which the trial is being conducted, are not available under the Juries Act 1981. If such cases occur, counsel must rely on using a peremptory challenge or the stand-by procedure.[129] The latter option is not entirely satisfactory, however, since the person stood by may still be called for jury service if there are no prospective jurors left and the jury does not yet number twelve. If such a situation arose, the juror could only be discharged if the court were prepared to exercise its inherent jurisdiction.[130]

3. Peremptory Challenge

The prosecution or defence may also challenge a limited number of potential jurors without the need to give any reason for doing so. Generally, the prosecution and defence may each challenge six potential jurors in this way. In trials involving more than one defendant, the Crown has a maximum of twelve challenges, while defence counsel may challenge six potential jurors for each defendant. It appears that defence counsel challenge twice as often as prosecutors.[131] There is no law prescribing the proper and nondiscriminatory exercise of peremptory challenges; they may be exercised on any basis and are not open to scrutiny or objection.

Peremptory challenges are sometimes exercised by prosecution counsel on the basis of information about criminal convictions or criminal associations provided to them by the police. Because of the absence of other information about the background and attitudes of potential jurors, such challenges are usually based on perceived age, address, occupation, gender, ethnicity, general appearance, and demeanour. The stereotypes derived from these characteristics—for example, that manual or trade workers are more likely to be pro-defence than professional or service occupations, and that schoolteachers cause hung juries[132]—have little or no empirical foundation. It must therefore be concluded that, for

[129] See J. N. Finn, *Aspects of the Law Relating to Jury Trials* (1984) 2 CANTERBURY L. REV. 206–7.

[130] See ibid. at 207. Although there is no authority on the matter, it may also be open to the judge to discharge such a juror under the Crimes Act 1961, s. 374(3) (N.Z.). However, that section seems intended primarily to deal with jurors who become incapacitated during the trial, rather than those who are incapacitated when initially called.

[131] See TRIAL BY PEERS, *supra* note 114, at 56.

[132] These and other stereotypes were highlighted in the *Trial by Peers* study, which was based on both the observation of actual trials and interviews with prosecution and defence counsel. See ibid.

the most part, the peremptory challenge in New Zealand is in essence exercised arbitrarily.

Once the jury pool has been assembled at court, the peremptory challenge is the most significant courtroom procedure affecting the composition, and hence the representativeness, of juries. The *Trial by Peers* study in 1993 found that, compared to the jury pool:

(1) fewer Maori men served on District Court juries, while the expected proportion served on High Court juries;
(2) men, and particularly Maori men, were under-represented;
(3) younger age groups were more likely to serve, while those aged 50 and over were under-represented; and
(4) there were fewer than expected unemployed jurors.[133]

Concern about the results of this study led the Solicitor General to issue an instruction to Crown Counsel to take whatever steps were necessary to ensure that Maori men were not challenged disproportionately by the prosecution. There is no information on the extent to which this instruction has modified prosecution practice—and it is, of course, unknown how far the under-representation of this group is actually due to prosecution practice. However, regardless of whether the situation has changed, it is likely that there is still a strong perception amongst Maori,[134] and perhaps other groups, that peremptory challenges have a discriminatory effect and exacerbate the unrepresentativeness of juries already produced by the system of disqualifications and excuses.

The rationale for peremptory challenges, especially in the absence of a *voir dire* procedure, is questionable. To the extent that they are used to alter the socio-demographic composition of the jury so as to produce an outcome favourable to one party or the other, they are surely unjustified. Similarly, the argument[135] that peremptory challenges give defendants confidence in the system by allowing them to eliminate those whom they do not wish to try the case is a spurious one: If they cannot object to a judge in a summary trial, why should they be able to object to a juror without good grounds for doing so?

[133] See Trial by Peers, *supra* note 114, at 67.

[134] See generally Moana Jackson, New Zealand Dep't of Justice, The Maori and the Criminal Justice System: He Whaipaanga Hou—A New Perspective Part 2, at 138–41 (1988).

[135] See Law Reform Comm'n of Canada, Working Paper 27, The Jury in Criminal Trials, 1980, at 54.

The New Zealand Law Commission in its 1998 discussion paper has suggested reducing the number of peremptory challenges to four. This, it is argued, would still allow biased jurors to be removed, but would make it more difficult for either side to influence the representative nature of the jury and select the jury of their choice. However, this suggestion appears to be a compromise solution with little merit. As we have said, the peremptory challenge is at best a weak and haphazard procedure for removing biased jurors, and it is difficult to see why a party who has evidence of possible bias should not be required to challenge for cause and satisfy the court of the grounds for their objection. Thus, leaving in place a right to exercise four peremptory challenges does not effectively address the bias issue, and, since it is axiomatic that most minorities are easier to remove from the jury through a challenging process, it will continue to undermine jury representativeness.

D. Maori Representation

The issue of Maori representation on juries in New Zealand is a pressing one for at least two reasons. In the first place, while we do not know what proportion of defendants in jury trials are Maori, we do know that Maori are significantly over-represented in the convicted population.[136] Secondly, in political terms, the lack of Maori representation on central legal institutions like the jury forms part of the debate about the need to recognize indigenous forms of justice and, perhaps, separate legal institutions for Maori.[137]

Clearly there are a number of levels at which the issue of Maori under-representation can be tackled. To date, mainstream concern has focused on administrative measures designed to ensure that a higher proportion of Maori are entered on the electoral roll, and hence are available for jury service, and that the prosecution does not challenge Maori

[136] Although rather more concentrated in the younger age groups, persons identifying themselves as Maori make up approximately 13% of the New Zealand population. See STATISTICS NEW ZEALAND, NEW ZEALAND NOW CRIME TABLES (1996). However, persons described as Maori account for roughly 37% of the offenders apprehended by the police, 40% of the total number of nontraffic criminal cases which are prosecuted, 42% of convicted nontraffic cases, 50% of the male prison population, and 56% of the female prison population. See PAULINE SIDDLE, RESPONDING TO OFFENDING BY MAORI: SOME CRIMINAL JUSTICE STATISTICS 20 (1996); Juan Tauri & Allison Morris, *Re-forming Justice: The Potential of Maori Processes* (1997) 30 AUSTL. & N.Z. J. CRIMINOLOGY 149.

[137] See, *e.g.*, COURTS CONSULTATIVE COMMITTEE, REPORT OF THE COURTS CONSULTATIVE COMMITTEE ON HE WHAIPAANGA HOU (1991); JACKSON, *supra* note 134; Tauri & Morris, *supra* note 134.

jurors disproportionately.[138] Although measures of this sort may have considerable potential to deal with the extremes of under-representation, so long as the Maori population is characterized by high rates of unemployment, low educational and skill levels, and high geographical mobility, they are unlikely to provide the whole answer. Furthermore, attempts to assert control over the process of challenge, whether through simply exhorting prosecutors to challenge even-handedly or through banning challenges based on ethnic, gender, or status grounds,[139] are not likely to be successful either. Faced with the ability of lawyers to find alternative rationalizations for their challenges, and being in no position to assess them, judges are unlikely to be either willing or able to police such requirements effectively. In our view, the only effective way of controlling peremptory challenges is to abolish them.

In addition to efforts to improve the selection process, some jurisdictions have also seen overt judicial attempts to 'engineer' the racial composition of juries so as to match the ethnic background of the accused.[140] Even though, in its usual form, this manipulation tends to consist of relatively minor interference designed simply to get some representation on the jury of the group in question, if it were to be done in New Zealand, it would probably require a specific legislative amendment.[141]

In 1993, the UK Royal Commission on Criminal Justice recommended such an amendment. On the application of the defence or

[138] See Advisory Committee on Legal Services, New Zealand Dep't of Justice, Te Whainga i Te Tika: In Search of Justice 42 (1986). See generally Courts Consultative Committee, *supra* note 137.

[139] See, *e.g.*, *Batson* v. *Kentucky*, 476 U.S. 79 (1986), which is the leading U.S. case holding race-based challenges to be unconstitutional under the Equal Protection Clause of the 14th Amendment. The Supreme Court held that a defendant could overcome the presumption that peremptory challenges were used legitimately by making a *prima facie* case that the challenges in the particular case were race-motivated, after which the burden shifts to the prosecutor to articulate a neutral reason for the challenge. The rule applies regardless of the race of the potential juror or the defendant, *Powers* v. *Ohio*, 499 U.S. 400 (1991), to defence as well as to prosecution challenges, *Georgia* v. *McCollum*, 505 U.S. 42 (1992), to gender-based challenges, *J.E.B.* v. *Alabama*, 511 U.S. 127 (1994), and in civil cases, *Edmonson* v. *Leesville Concrete Co.*, 500 U.S. 614 (1991).

[140] The developments in England and Wales in the 1980s reflected a similar problem in the United Kingdom. See, *e.g.*, R. v. Broderick [1970] Crim. L. Rev. 155; R. v. Binns, [1982] Crim. L. Rev. 522; R. v. Bansal [1985] Crim. L. Rev. 151; R. v. Fraser, [1987] Crim. L. Rev. 418; Simon Thomas & Others (1989) 88 Cr. App. R. 370.

[141] The English developments were brought to an end by the Court of Appeal in *R.* v. *Ford* [1989] 3 All E.R. 445 (Eng. C.A.), which held that a judge has no common law power deliberately to alter either the composition of the jury pool or the jury, or to authorize the empanelling of a multi-racial jury. New Zealand courts would be likely to adopt a similar view.

prosecution, and in exceptional circumstances, a judge would be able to order that a jury include up to three representatives of racial minority communities. In addition, counsel should be able to ask the court to designate that one of the three be of the same racial background as the accused or the victim.[142] As the New Zealand Law Commission has pointed out in its 1998 discussion paper, this recommendation fails to address either the issue of representativeness or the lack of jurors of the same ethnic background as the accused.[143] Three jurors randomly selected from three different minority racial groups will not necessarily render the jury 'more representative', nor will one juror of the same racial background as either the accused or the complainant satisfy the demands of the accused for a more appropriate tribunal of fact. Furthermore, the need to show 'exceptional' circumstances, which the Royal Commission defines as existing only where the accused can persuade the court that the 'unusual and special' features of the case are such that it is reasonable to believe that the defendant will not get a fair trial from an all-white jury, suggests that there will be very few cases indeed in which the procedure would even be arguable, let alone available.[144]

In any case, judicial tinkering of this sort is both undesirable and unnecessary. For one thing, it is likely to compromise the integrity of both the judiciary and the jury system in the eyes of jurors and of the general public. For another, if the concern is with the representativeness of the jury or with whether the jury adequately reflects the ethnic and cultural background of the accused, then, in principle, juries should be selected so as to achieve this in all cases—not just where the accused is Maori. Any such system would be impracticable and would, in any event, be unlikely to be much of an improvement on the present system—for either Maori or other minority groups. Numbers would inevitably be small, and ethnic 'representatives' would be unlikely to be either representative or a significant force in the dynamics of the jury.

More significantly, perhaps, we doubt that the current concern with Maori under-representation would be met by simply ensuring that the jury contains some Maori jurors or even that it reflects the proportion of Maori in the (local) community. Rather, the underlying criticism of the present system is based on the assertion that Maori defendants can be appropriately judged only by a body that reflects Maori cultural values

[142] See Report of the Royal Comm'n on Criminal Justice, 1993, Cm 2263, at 207–8.
[143] See New Zealand Law Comm'n, Jury Trials Part One, *supra* note 88, at 73–4.
[144] Report of the Royal Comm'n on Criminal Justice, *supra* note 142, at 133.

and attitudes. Achieving this result would require more than one or two Maori jurors on each jury where the defendant is Maori and, unless it is to be extended to all cultural minorities, would need to be based on some principled argument derived from the status of Maori as the indigenous race of New Zealand. In other words, it is a demand for the revival of the all-Maori jury, or at least a strong version of the old mixed jury.

The abolition of the right to an all-Maori jury in 1962 was justified on the basis that New Zealand was governed by 'one law for all' and the belief that under that law no section of the population should receive any 'special privileges'. It was also argued that the right was essentially arbitrary in that it discriminated between defendants whose victims were Maori and those whose victims were not.[145] Maori Members of Parliament and some influential Maori figures outside Parliament opposed the reform, arguing that the right at least ensured that Maori values would be taken into account in some cases. Recent proponents of reviving the right to an all-Maori jury in all cases where the defendant identifies as Maori base their arguments on a rejection of the 'one law for all' ideology, and of the view that the right constitutes a 'privilege' for Maori. Hence, in *He Whaipaanga Hou*, Moana Jackson attempts to develop an argument for a return to the all-Maori jury based on the right to trial by a jury of 'one's peers' flowing from Magna Carta and, more significantly, on the guarantee of Maori *rangatiratanga* (self-government, self-determination, or sovereignty) in Article Two of the Treaty of Waitangi.[146]

However one views the arguments made by Jackson in principle, there are clearly a number of significant practical difficulties that any such system would face. The small and often densely interrelated nature of Maori communities in many areas, the loss of contact between many Maori and their cultural roots, and the need to counter majority suspicions of partial juries all present real problems for any such development. Furthermore, if one accepts that the 'right' to an all-Maori jury is part of a more general claim to Maori sovereignty over things Maori, it is difficult to see how one can justify leaving Maori defendants with a choice about jury composition. More significantly, however, the notion of an all-Maori jury operating within a court and prosecution structure that is still almost entirely based upon European values is something of

[145] See 332 N.Z. Parl. Deb., H.R. 2750–1 (1962); 328 N.Z. Parl. Deb., H.R. 2840 (1961).
[146] See JACKSON, *supra* note 134, at 259–79.

a contradiction in terms and is not in fact the sort of development that Jackson is advocating. The institution of the jury is itself alien to Maori culture and Maori law.[147] In its modern form, at least, it is a product of centralized, professional, and primarily retributive justice systems. If the demand by Maori for all-Maori juries is to make any sense, it can only do so within the context of a discrete Maori justice system—shaped and informed by Maori values and, perhaps, those European institutions that Maori regard as appropriate or useful. It remains unclear whether the jury is likely to be one of those. What does appear clear is that if proposals for an alternative Maori criminal justice system were ever to be taken seriously, changes to the jury structure would be one of the more minor concerns it would generate.

E. Discharging Jurors

Once a jury is constituted, counsel no longer have the opportunity to challenge persons off the jury. However, counsel may apply to the judge to discharge a juror under section 22 of the Juries Act 1981, or section 374 of the Crimes Act 1961.

A judge may discharge a juror who is disqualified from serving as a juror under the Juries Act 1981, or who is or gives the appearance of being biased,[148] or who is unable to continue to serve by reason of the illness or death of a member of the juror's family. There is also a broad discretionary power to discharge a juror who is 'incapable' of continuing to serve, for example, because of some language difficulty or mental or physical incapacity, or because the juror refuses to perform his or her duty. The Court of Appeal has stated that an 'incapable' juror includes one whose continued presence on the jury would jeopardize the fairness of the trial to either side, or make the verdict abortive or seriously vulnerable.[149]

In determining whether the entire jury should be discharged on any of the grounds already mentioned, the judge will primarily consider whether the bias of one juror has tainted the other jurors, or whether a juror who gives the impression of bias will cause the jury's verdict to be perceived as unfair. Determining whether the jury has been contaminated by an individual juror is a matter of inference; jurors may

[147] See *supra* text accompanying notes 67–9.

[148] That is, the juror is personally concerned with the facts of the case or is closely connected with one of the parties or with one of the witnesses or prospective witnesses. See Crimes Act 1961, § 374(3)(d)–(e) (N.Z.); Juries Act 1981, § 22 (N.Z.).

[149] See R. v. M. (1991) 7 C.R.N.Z. 439, 441–2.

not be questioned about discussions between them, whether in retirement or during the course of the trial.[150]

No alternate or reserve jurors are selected at the commencement of the trial. If a juror is discharged, the court may proceed with eleven jurors, or fewer than that number if the prosecution and accused consent. Moreover, under the recently inserted section 374(4A) of the Crimes Act 1961, the court may proceed with as few as ten jurors if there are exceptional circumstances relating to the trial, including, without limitation, the length or expected length of the trial, and it is in the interests of justice to do so. The amendment was made as a direct result of expressions of concern about the possibility that some jurors would fail to cope with and have to be excused from a forthcoming trial, scheduled to last five months and involving a large number of serious criminal offences including sexual violation and murder.

At least one commentator has expressed concern publicly about the amendment and suggested that legislators ought to have considered reserve juror systems more carefully.[151] However, reserve jurors would involve additional administrative and financial costs and, more importantly, would impose the burden of jury duty upon a significant number of citizens without generally permitting them to participate in the decision making process. When that is set against the fact that fewer than twelve jurors has been accepted historically within New Zealand, and that there is no evidence that smaller numbers (especially ten or eleven instead of twelve) detract from the quality of decision making, the case for introducing reserve jurors is a decidedly weak one.

V. Jury Secrecy and the Inscrutability of Jury Verdicts

New Zealand has a tradition of jury secrecy which has been designed to protect the deliberations of juries in individual cases from outside scrutiny.[152] However, there is no statutory equivalent of the provisions of the English Contempt of Court Act 1981 to enforce this tradition.[153] Unless the court gives leave, section 370(2) of the Crimes Act 1961 merely prohibits any communication with the jury by any person other than the officer of the court who has charge of them after they have

[150] See R. v. Coombs [1985] 1 N.Z.L.R. 319, 324; R. v. Papadopoulos [1979] 1 N.Z.L.R. 621, 626.

[151] See Trevor Morley, *What About Jury Alternatives?*, Council Brief, Mar. 1998, at 6.

[152] See Jury Trials Part Two, *supra* note 88, 58ff.

[153] Contempt of Court Act 1981, § 8 (Eng.).

retired to consider their verdict. A breach of this prohibition where the communication goes to the merits of the case or might appear to an onlooker to do so may result in the jury's discharge and the declaration of a mistrial or the overturning of the verdict on appeal.[154] Beyond this, the convention is created by case law and broadly enforced in a number of ways.

In the first place, the courts have firmly established that evidence of jury discussions, both during the trial and after the jury has retired to consider its verdict, is inadmissible whether for the purposes of an appeal or otherwise. Similarly, juries cannot be required to give reasons for their decision, or to indicate or agree on any particular view of the facts. In other words, although the jurors can reach a unanimous verdict for radically different reasons and on quite different interpretations of the facts, they cannot be asked to explain what those reasons or interpretations are.

Just as importantly, an approach to one or more jurors during or after a trial may amount to a contempt of court and result in prosecution.[155] The issue of contempt was considered quite recently[156] in the 1993 prosecution of Radio New Zealand, which had sought to interview jurors about their reaction to the discovery of new evidence after the trial and whether, if this new evidence had been available, it would have affected their verdict. Holding Radio New Zealand in contempt, the High Court noted that such behaviour was likely to injure the administration of justice both by removing the protection of confidentiality from jury deliberations and by weakening community confidence in jury verdicts. The Court also stated that publicity about jury deliberations would impede frank discussions amongst jurors through fear of subsequent exposure to public criticism or ridicule, and might discourage juries from bringing in unpopular verdicts.

The New Zealand Law Commission has suggested that the law regarding jury secrecy should be clarified through codification. It has argued in its draft Evidence Code[157] that the rigorous enforcement of

[154] See R. v. Parkinson (1915) 34 N.Z.L.R. 636, 639; cf. R. v. Davis [1960] Cr. App. R. 235, 240.

[155] Contempt proceedings are in fact quite rare. The Solicitor General attempts to work cooperatively with the media to establish the parameters of appropriate publication, and prosecutes only when the case is a serious one and the breach is considered to be a blatant and gross one.

[156] See Solicitor-Gen. v. Radio N.Z. (1993) 10 C.R.N.Z. 641.

[157] New Zealand Law Commission, *Evidence* (1999). vol. 2, section 77. See also discussion in Jury Trials Part Two, *supra* note 88, 64–6.

jury secrecy may sometimes conceal a miscarriage of justice, and that, while evidence of jury deliberations concerning the substance of the case should generally remain inadmissible, evidence disclosing irregularities in the conduct of the deliberations—for example, intimidation of a juror during deliberations—should be admissible when it may disclose such a miscarriage.

Beyond this codification, however, the New Zealand Law Commission has not suggested any real liberalization of the law on jury secrecy.[158] For example, it has rejected submissions from journalists, who have contended that the media should be able to interview jurors following a trial about the experience of being a juror, as distinct from interviewing jurors about their deliberations. In fact, there is no reason to believe that the former constitutes a threat to the functioning of the jury system, and it is unclear whether it even constitutes contempt of court under the existing law.[159] This confusion demonstrates that the law in this area is decidedly vague. That, at least, has been recognized by the Commission, which has suggested that it might be desirable to[160] clarify the circumstances under which media contact with consenting jurors after trial is permissible.

Compelling though the reasons for jury secrecy are in individual cases, in many jurisdictions the conventions that have grown up to preserve it have formed a significant obstacle to jury reform. As a result of the shroud of secrecy surrounding jury deliberations and the vagueness of the legal position of journalists and potential researchers, such public debate as there is on the jury system is often ill-informed and based largely on anecdote. Policy makers and law reform bodies, too, deliberate in the absence of systematic information on how real juries actually operate in practice.

With these concerns in mind, and with the full support of the judiciary and the relevant government agencies, two of the current authors have just completed a collaborative study with the New Zealand Law Commission aimed at presenting a more accurate picture. This research involved extensive interviews with jurors in a sample of 49 trials from throughout the country designed to explore not only how jurors

[158] Jury Trials Part Two, *supra* note 88, 77.

[159] For an example of a journalistic account of the experience of being a juror, see Llewelyn Richards, *Two Trials in One*, NORTH AND SOUTH, Nov. 1997, at 28. There seems to have been no suggestion that this article, which provides details of the jury discussion in a rape case, might amount to contempt.

[160] Ibid.

approached and understood the issues in the case, but also how deliberations were conducted and decisions reached.

The results of this research have now been published by the New Zealand Law Commission in summary form[161] and the Commission's 1999 discussion paper draws heavily on them for its recommendations. Not surprisingly, in its discussion of the codification of the rules governing jury secrecy the Commission recommends specific provisions to protect the conduct of academic research in this area.[162]

VI. The Jury Trial Process

A. Hung Juries and Majority Verdicts

Jury verdicts in favour of conviction or acquittal must be unanimous. Provided that the jury has been deliberating for at least four hours,[163] it may be discharged if the court believes that it is unlikely to reach agreement. In that event, a new trial will generally be ordered, subject to the Solicitor General's power to stay proceedings. However, if the jury reports that it is having difficulty in agreeing, it will usually be given a direction to try again. That direction (known as a *Papadopoulos* direction) incorporates words to the following effect:

> One of the strengths of the jury system is that each member takes into the jury room his or her individual experience and wisdom and is expected to judge the evidence fairly and impartially in that light. You are expected to pool your views of the evidence and you have a duty to listen carefully to one another. Remember that a view honestly held can equally honestly be changed. So, within the oath, there is scope for discussion, argument and give and take. That is often the way in which in the end unanimous agreement is reached.
>
> But, of course, no-one should be false to his or her oath. No-one should give in merely for the sake of agreement or to avoid inconvenience. If in the end you honestly cannot agree, after trying to look at the case calmly and objectively and weighing carefully the opinions of others, you must say so. If regrettably that is the final position, you will be discharged and in all probability there will have to be a new trial before another jury.
>
> Therefore I am asking you, as is usual in such cases, to be good enough to retire again and see whether you can reach a unanimous verdict in the light of what I have said.[164]

161 Summary of Research, *supra* note 88.
162 Jury Trials Part Two, *supra* note 88, 65.
163 See Crimes Act 1961, § 374(2) (N.Z.).
164 R. v. Accused [1988] 2 N.Z.L.R. 46, 59.

Anecdotal evidence suggests that the length of jury deliberations has increased significantly in recent years.[165] However, there is no reliable evidence on deliberation time and whether it has in fact increased. What is more certain is that trials involving jury disagreements ('hung juries') have increased in recent years, both numerically and in proportionate terms.[166] Some of the recent hung juries, too, have occurred in particularly high-profile and lengthy trials, and have attracted considerable media comment. In particular, the prosecution of a Wellington businessman, John Barlow, on two charges of murder, resulted in two hung juries and a conviction at his third trial; each trial lasted for approximately four weeks.[167]

Not surprisingly, this trend has prompted calls for majority verdicts, similar to those permitted in England and Wales and a number of Australian states.[168] In fact, as far back as 1984, the then Minister of Justice, in response to a perceived increase in the number of jury disagreements, suggested that the idea of majority verdicts deserved serious consideration. Now the New Zealand Law Commission has stated its provisional view that, if current rates of hung juries are either substantially maintained or increased during the period prior to publication of its final report, it will recommend introducing majority verdicts.[169]

The problem in assessing the merits of majority verdicts is that we have little reliable or unambiguous evidence on the nature of hung juries or the reasons why they may be increasing. Majority verdicts are often mooted on the assumption that hung juries result from the obstinacy of one or two irrational 'rogue' jurors who hold out against the reasoned views of the majority. That assumption, however, is unproven. If it is instead the case that minority jurors rarely stick to their view without some initial support and that hung juries usually occur when there is a

[165] See, *e.g.*, the comments of the Court of Appeal in *R.* v. *Hapeta* [1995] 1 N.Z.L.R. 6, 10.

[166] In 1997, there was considerable public and political concern, inspired in part by the release of John Goulter's book *No Verdict: New Zealand's Hung Jury Crisis*, *supra* note 2, over reports that the rate of hung juries had increased rapidly from 4% or so in 1991 to 10% in 1997. This 10% figure subsequently proved to be somewhat misleading. While the rate of hung juries has certainly increased in the last decade or so, we still have no accurate official data on the rate of fully hung juries. In its 1999 paper the Law Commission suggests a figure of around 10% but this includes juries that were hung on only some of the charges, see Jury Trials Part Two, *supra* note 88, 41–3.

[167] R. v. Barlow [1998] 2 N.Z.L.R. 477.

[168] See, *e.g.*, Michael Chesterman, *Criminal Trial Juries in Australia: From Penal Colonies to a Federal Democracy*, Ch. 4, this volume.

[169] See Jury Trials Part Two, *supra* note 88, 50.

substantial division of initial opinion amongst jurors,[170] the case for majority verdicts becomes considerably weaker. Our own research suggested that in at least three of the five cases in which the jury was hung on all charges, the disagreement was genuine and rational. The other two cases both involved 'rogue' jurors, but even in these cases other jurors had misgivings that might have affected the outcome if the jury had been able to deliberate properly.[171]

B. Assisting Jury Deliberations

The limited amount of research undertaken in New Zealand so far confirms that juries sometimes misunderstand or misapply the law, become confused about the facts, draw unwarranted inferences or conclusions from them, or take irrelevancies into account. These problems are not confined to lengthy or complex trials and are said to arise not only from the varying educational and intellectual levels of jurors, but also from deficiencies in the way in which they are prepared for their role and in which the facts and the law are presented to them.[172]

To the extent that there are problems attributable to court procedure, it might be expected that improvement in the quality of the information presented to juries and the aids provided to them during the trial would go some way toward mitigating those problems. In recent years, therefore, this area has received considerable attention. The process of reform began in 1992, when the Courts Consultative Committee[173] published a report entitled *Jurors' Concerns and the Jury System*, which reviewed the facilities, information, and services provided to jurors and made recommendations for change. Since then, a number of improvements to the facilities, information, and services provided to jurors have been gradually introduced. For example, every jury summons sent to potential jurors now includes standard information dealing with such subjects as the functions of juries, the selection process, and the duties of jurors.[174] In

[170] Overseas research evidence provides some support for this proposition. See, *e.g.*, VALERIE HANS & NEIL VIDMAR, JUDGING THE JURY 168 (1986).

[171] Summary of Research, *supra* note 88, Part 9.

[172] Summary of Research, *supra* note 88, Parts 3 and 7.

[173] The Courts Consultative Committee is a committee of judges, lawyers, and officials established in 1986 to advise the Minister of Justice on the operation of all aspects of the court system.

[174] The information in the summons form is set out under various question headings such as 'What is a jury?,' 'How was I chosen for jury service?', and 'What happens if I do not report to court?'.

addition, the Department for Courts has prepared a booklet, entitled *Information for Jurors*, which is available to jurors when they first arrive at court and in the jury room. It deals with the subject matters covered in the summons form in more detail, as well as some additional matters jurors need to consider, such as choosing a jury representative[175] and the need for confidentiality. The booklet includes a glossary of terms commonly used in criminal proceedings. The Department has also prepared a short introductory video for jurors covering similar matters. Although the video is not always used, both the booklet and video are distributed throughout New Zealand jury courts.

At the start of a trial, judges may make introductory remarks to the jury. It is not uncommon at this preliminary stage for judges to instruct the jury on, for example, the prosecution's burden of proof and the need for the jurors to set aside any feelings of sympathy or prejudice. However, there is some variation in the extent to which this instruction occurs. The prosecution's opening address covers the charges against the defendant and a summary of the facts that the prosecution intends to prove. Section 367 of the Crimes Act 1961 envisages that the defence will not open its case until the prosecution has presented its evidence and prosecution witnesses have been cross-examined. There is case law suggesting that section 367 precludes the defence from making an opening statement following the prosecution's.[176] Despite this, some judges do allow defence counsel the opportunity to make an opening statement, which the defence is free to decline. The defence's opening statement may define the issues without analyzing the evidence.[177]

Once both sides have presented their evidence, cross-examined witnesses, and given closing addresses, the judge will not only give directions to the jury about the relevant law, but also sum up and make limited comment on the factual evidence presented by both sides. Judicial directions are given at this stage on such matters as the prosecution's burden and standard of proof, the relevance of circumstantial evidence, the defendant's right of silence, and the jury's use of exhibits. Judges have access to what is known as a bench-book, containing guidelines on some

[175] The jury representative is otherwise known as the 'foreman'. The term 'jury representative' is used in the booklet *Information for Jurors*.

[176] See R. v. Joseph [1994] 2 N.Z.L.R. 702, 703–4. Hammond J further noted that he doubted that Parliament intended to give the defence both the advantage of blunting the prosecution's opening statement and the last word in the closing addresses. See ibid.

[177] The Ministry of Justice has foreshadowed an amendment to s. 367(1) allowing the defence to make an opening statement as of right. See Jury Trials Part Two, *supra* note 88, 10–11.

of the more commonly used instructions as well as other trial matters. However, they make varying use of it.[178] Some prefer to formulate their own instructions, others use the bench-book as a guide on substance but not on style, and yet others follow the model directions more closely. The foreword indicates that it is entirely a matter for individual judges to determine the extent to which they make use of the bench-book. In general, the New Zealand Court of Appeal's approach to jury directions has been to encourage brevity.

Jurors are able to ask questions of the witnesses during the trial by forwarding the questions in writing to the judge, who determines whether the questions will be put. However, this practice is rare and is not encouraged in the information supplied to potential and selected jurors; in fact, the *Information for Jurors* booklet describes this practice as 'most unusual'.[179] The jury may also ask the judge questions during deliberations.

While hearing the evidence, individual jurors can take notes and refer to them in the course of deliberations. The jury is given a copy of the indictment and exhibits, and sometimes of the relevant statutory offence provisions that can be taken to the jury room. Transcripts of videotaped police interviews with defendants are technically exhibits and often are provided to the jury as the videotape is being shown. However, they are normally recovered before deliberation commences. The trial transcript—the record of all the evidence—is never given to the jury. Instead, the jury may ask to have passages of the transcript read out in open court during the course of deliberations. Juries are never given written copies of either the judge's directions or counsel's closing addresses, although during deliberations the jury may ask for the judge's directions on a particular topic to be given again orally, and enlarged upon or clarified. Where the complexity of the case warrants it, the Court of Appeal has approved the use (including during deliberations) of charts and summaries supplementing oral presentation.[180]

[178] The current bench-book for New Zealand judges was produced in early 2000 by judges of the High Court and district court. The bench-book contains guidance on pre-trial applications and other procedural matters as well as practice notes, advice on summing up, and model directions.

[179] The New Zealand Law Commission has recommended an express provision in its proposed Evidence Code codifying the right of jurors to ask questions through the judge, but it may be doubted whether this in itself will make the practice more common. See New Zealand Commission, *Evidence* (1999), vol. 1, paras. 443–4.

[180] See, *e.g.*, R. v. Egden (Feb. 17, 1995) Court of Appeal, CA 211/94, at 5–6 (unreported).

Despite these strategies for enhancing jury decision making, the research shows that many jurors still find particular aspects of trial procedure difficult or confusing, and that much more could still be done to improve the quality of the decision making process.[181] For example, greater use of visual aids or written material could significantly improve the comprehensibility of the evidence; despite some use of such devices in complex cases, evidence and instructions are still presented largely in oral form and require concentration for lengthy periods of time by jurors who may be quite unused to assimilating information imparted in this form. Jurors could also be given more advice about how to undertake their functions—for example, how to select a foreman and how to structure their decision making—since they are largely left to their own devices at present. Similarly, the judge could encourage them to depart from their role as passive participants in the process by specifically telling them that they can and should ask questions, both during the trial and at the conclusion of the summing up, in order to clarify points of fact or law about which they are uncertain.

VII. Pretrial Publicity and Prejudice

In the absence of a *voir dire* procedure for jury selection in New Zealand, it is virtually impossible to eliminate from the jury those who might be prejudiced as a result of prior knowledge of the case.[182] Given this problem, it might be expected that the courts would have imposed stringent controls on the nature and extent of pretrial publicity, so as to minimize the likelihood that bias will arise on that account. In fact, however, this is not the case. Although the rules relating to pretrial and trial publicity are more restrictive than those in the United States, the media are nevertheless generally free to report on pretrial court proceedings. Such reporting includes, in the case of charges laid on indictment and proceeding to a jury trial, the preliminary hearing at which the prosecution's evidence is presented in order to determine whether there is a *prima facie* case. Name suppression also is granted only infrequently (although more often prior to trial than subsequent to it), and rarely on the ground that it will prejudice the subsequent trial.

[181] See Summary of Research, *supra* note 88, Part 3.
[182] See *supra* text accompanying note 127.

Improper or inaccurate reporting of court proceedings, or the publication of material reflecting on the character and credibility of the accused, may amount to contempt of court. So too may any other publicity about any aspect of the investigation, the arrest and charging of the suspect, or the evidence in the case, which may suggest that the accused committed the offence or which otherwise may prejudice the chances of a fair trial. The test, however, is a vague and arguably an unduly liberal one: in striving for a balance between the freedom of the press and the accused's right to a fair trial, the courts have in fact created a presumption in favour of the former, which can be rebutted in contempt proceedings only by proof to the criminal standard that there is a 'real risk'[183] or a 'substantial risk',[184] as distinct from a remote possibility, of interference with a fair trial. Thus, they have not found contempt or unfairness in circumstances where there has been a significant lapse of time between the publication and the trial or where the circulation of the publication has been in an area 200 kilometres from the area in which the trial is to take place.[185]

Not surprisingly, contempt proceedings in such circumstances are rare. The vagueness of the test and the difficulty in identifying when publication might amount to contempt encourage media reporting in borderline cases. It is not uncommon, for example, for the media to report that a defendant arrested for a particular offence was already on bail on other charges. Furthermore, the development in recent years of a more competitive news market has likely contributed to this process, with television in particular being more prepared to push the limits than previously.[186]

Apart from preventing inappropriate pretrial publicity through the law of contempt, the effects of such publicity also may be mitigated by

[183] Solicitor-Gen. v. Wellington Newspapers Ltd. [1995] 1 N.Z.L.R. 45, 47.

[184] R. v. Coghill [1995] 3 N.Z.L.R. 651, 662.

[185] See Gisborne Herald Ltd. v. Solicitor-Gen. [1995] 3 N.Z.L.R. 563, 568.

[186] For example, in a recent paper, the Solicitor-General, John McGrath QC, has commented that:

> over the last fifteen years the conventional acceptance of the media that it needs to function in a way that protects the needs of the criminal justice system has come under pressure. Some would argue it is no longer workable. This attitudinal change appears, to this observer, to be due to the emergence of real competition in the news market, in itself linked to the corporatisation of State television and the arrival of TV3 as a competing private broadcaster.

LEGAL RESEARCH FOUNDATION SEMINAR, CONTEMPT AND THE MEDIA: CONSTITUTIONAL SAFEGUARD OR STATE CENSORSHIP? 23 (1998).

changing the venue of the trial to an area where potential jurors are less likely to have been exposed to it.[187] However, applications for change of venue are granted only sparingly, and even where the possibility of prejudice seems fairly clear, the courts are notably reluctant to accede to such requests. For example, in *R. v. Parsons*,[188] the Court of Appeal upheld a decision to refuse a change of venue where a son was charged with killing his father, a prominent local businessman, despite significant local media coverage of the charge and of the fact that bail had been denied, at least partly on the basis of affidavits from the police and from the family detailing concerns that the accused would abscond or would attempt to intimidate witnesses if bailed. The court professed itself satisfied that there was no 'real risk' that this publicity would preclude a fair and impartial trial, and noted that the refusal of bail and publication of the reasons for it occurred some fifteen months before the trial was scheduled to commence. Given that counsel cannot question potential jurors in order to explore the possibility that some prejudice may still linger, and bearing in mind the likely lack of impact of warnings to the jury not to let such publicity intrude on their decision making,[189] the court's reluctance to order a change of venue in such cases seems unduly risky. Coupled with vague, uncertain contempt laws, and increasingly rampant market-driven media, defendants in New Zealand do appear likely to be at an increasing risk of prejudice with little or no opportunity to detect its existence, let alone combat it.

The New Zealand Law Commission has tentatively suggested the enactment of a statutory offence of contempt, applying to publicity that occurs where the commencement of proceedings is highly likely and that results in a substantial risk of prejudice to a fair trial.[190]

Arguably, however, the proposed statutory offence would do little to promote greater certainty in the law or to curb unwarranted publicity. Part of the difficulty arises from the fact that the nature of the 'public interest' in potentially prejudicial pretrial publicity has not been clearly

[187] See Crimes Act 1961, § 322 (N.Z.). On adverse publicity as a ground, see *R.* v. *Brown* [1987] 3 C.R.N.Z. 132 (C.A.), and *R.* v. *Holdem* [1987] 3 C.R.N.Z. 103 (H.C.).

[188] (July 19, 1995) Court of Appeal, CA 127/95 (unreported).

[189] Most of the empirical research on the impact of judicial instructions to ignore prejudicial material suggests that they are largely ineffective in achieving their objectives. Indeed, in many cases, judicial commentary may well exacerbate the problem by focusing jurors' attention on the prejudicial material. For an overview, see Hans & Vidmar, *supra* note 162; J. Alexander Tanford, *The Law and Psychology of Jury Instructions*, 69 Neb. L. Rev. 71 (1990).

[190] Jury Trials Part Two, *supra* note 88, 73.

articulated either in court decisions or in the Law Commission's discussion of the issue. While publicity about some matters relating to the charge or the defendant may occasionally be desirable—for example, to obtain evidence or to prevent suspicion falling on others—it is difficult to see why the public generally has an 'interest' in the publication of material which has the potential, however slight, to prejudice a fair trial.

VIII. Conclusion

It is certainly the case that in New Zealand, as in many other common law jurisdictions, the recent history of the jury has been one of fairly steady decline. This is particularly so of the civil jury which, for all practical purposes, now has become virtually extinct with little realistic prospect of revival. In the criminal area, the extension of jury trial to the district court produced a brief resurgence, but the previous trends seem now to have largely reasserted themselves. Again, as with other jurisdictions, the pressures have been largely fiscal but, given the opportunity, defendants have shown no great enthusiasm for jury trial either.

Nevertheless the jury has retained a large part of its historic role as an ideological centrepiece of New Zealand criminal justice. In spite of the perception in some quarters of a 'hung jury crisis' and a corresponding interest in moving toward majority verdicts, there is no constituency at all for radical change or even for any significant restriction on the right to jury trial. At the most, there are occasional calls for a reconsideration of the availability of jury trial in complex or very lengthy cases, which can be accommodated with only relatively minor adjustments.[191] In addition, it is important to note that emerging concerns in New Zealand about wrongful or dubious convictions in a number of recent cases focus largely on failings in the investigatory and prosecution processes rather than on any failings in the jury or trial system.

On the other hand, New Zealand is currently in the throes of a series of developments designed to improve jury selection processes (particularly in relation to Maori jurors), upgrade jury facilities, enhance juror education, and provide appropriate assistance, both during the hearing and in the decision making phase. The New Zealand Law Commission

[191] See *supra* text following note 103; *supra* text following note 173.

has produced two discussion papers covering all aspects of jury trials in criminal cases, and the publication of the results of the recently completed research has provided a focus for debate—at least within the legal profession and in government circles. The concern of all this effort is primarily to ensure that, whether the actual use of the criminal jury continues to decline, it will remain as a central plank in the ideology of criminal justice in New Zealand, effectively symbolizing a number of traditional values. How far these efforts will succeed and how significant the values traditionally associated with the jury will turn out to be in the future is another question.

6 The Canadian Criminal Jury: Searching for a Middle Ground

Neil Vidmar*

I. Introduction

In many important respects, the contemporary Canadian criminal jury system may be viewed as a hybrid of the English and American jury systems. This statement does not imply a direct American influence on the conception of the jury because, as will be discussed below, Canadian judges have often expressly rejected American practices and, in the very recent past, tended to defer primarily to England when seeking guidance from case law. Nevertheless, on a number of dimensions, Canadian jury law and practice occupy a middle ground between those of these other two countries.

I can begin to make the point clear by describing a Canadian trial, *R.* v. *Bernardo*,[1] that overlapped the O. J. Simpson murder trial in the United States. Recall that Simpson, a former American football star and television celebrity, was charged with the vicious knife-slaying of his former wife and a young man just outside his ex-wife's residence. Aside from the fact that the Simpson trial involved a famous football player and television celebrity charged with gruesome knife-slayings, there were important trial characteristics that could occur only in some American jurisdictions. The preliminary hearing and the entire trial were televised. The prospective jurors were given a lengthy questionnaire that asked

* Russell M. Robinson II Professor of Law and Professor of Psychology, Duke University. I am indebted to Professor David Paciocco for comments on this article and to the Honorable Madam Justice Louise Charron, Alan D. Gold, and the Honorable Justice Henry Vogelsong for comments on an earlier article that is incorporated in this article.

[1] The case of *R.* v. *Bernardo* is unreported. For related litigation, see *Thompson Newspapers Ltd.* v. *The Queen* (1994) 121 D.L.R.4th 42 (Ont. C.A.). My account of the *Homolka* and *Bernardo* trials is developed from personal sources as well as media accounts. A reasonable summary of the *Bernardo* case can be found in the weekly issues of Maclean's magazine from May 15, 1995 through Oct. 16, 1995. More detailed accounts of the trial can be found in the *Toronto Globe and Mail* or *Toronto Star* newspapers covering that same period. See, *e.g.*, Nick Pron & John Duncanson, *Bernardo Trial Has Jury Pool of 1,500*, TORONTO STAR, Apr. 11, 1995, at A1. Other discussions of the background of the case and the trial can be found in FRANK DAVEY, KARLA'S WEB: A CULTURAL INVESTIGATION OF THE MAHAFFY-FRENCH MURDERS (1994); STEPHEN WILLIAMS, INVISIBLE DARKNESS: THE STRANGE CASE OF PAUL BERNARDO AND KARLA HOMOLKA (1996).

about their personal attitudes, beliefs, and lifestyles, and then they were questioned at length in court on their views in a process that took weeks of court time before the jury was chosen. In addition, alternate jurors were selected to sit with the other jurors in the event that one or more of the jurors were excused for illness or other reasons. The jurors were sequestered for the entire time of the months-long trial. In mid-trial, several jurors were removed and replaced by alternates, on the suspicion that they were planning to sell the story of the jury deliberations to tabloid newspapers or book publishers at the trial's conclusion. Lawyers for the prosecution and defense engaged in media interviews while the trial was in progress.

Simpson's trial captured world-wide attention when it was broadcast over the CNN television network. While in many respects Simpson's trial was an anomaly within the United States,[2] contrasting it with *Bernardo* is useful because, like the Simpson case, the crimes of which Bernardo was accused were heinous, the case captured the attention of the Canadian public, and it raised serious threats to the integrity of the Canadian legal process. However, the *Bernardo* case shows some restrictions on media coverage that evoke comparison with England, Australia, and New Zealand. Its jury selection process and trial controls contrast markedly with those of the United States. The case also raises the specter of attempts to control pretrial publicity in any country in an age of international mass media and the internet.

Against a backdrop of a series of rapes by the 'Scarborough rapist' that terrorized a number of Toronto suburbs beginning in mid-1990, two teenage girls, Linda Mahaffy and Kristen French, went missing in 1991 and 1992. Their sexually abused bodies were subsequently found. Mahaffy's body had been dismembered by a power saw, encased in cement, and dumped in a lake. Police were stymied until January 1993, when Karla Homolka, an attractive 23-year-old woman residing in St Catherines, Ontario, was severely beaten by her 29-year-old husband, Paul Bernardo. In the police investigation that followed, Homolka confessed that she had participated with Bernardo in the kidnapping, sexual enslavement, and degradation of the two teenagers. Homolka nevertheless insisted that Bernardo alone murdered the girls. She also eventually implicated Bernardo (and herself) in numerous other sexual crimes, including the drugging and rape of

[2] See Nancy Jean King, *The American Criminal Jury*, 62 Law & Contemp. Probs. 41, 60–1 (Spring 1999).

her younger sister, Tammy, that resulted in the girl's death. The incident had to that point been treated as a natural but unexplained death. Finally, she informed the authorities that the rape and torture of Mahaffy and French, each occurring over several days, had been videotaped by Bernardo.

Bernardo was arrested and charged as the Scarborough rapist in February 1993 and later charged with kidnapping, rape, and murder. Canadian and US media covered the story extensively and engaged in much speculation about the crimes, but police and prosecutors remained tight-lipped. After many searches of the couple's home over a period of seventy days, police failed to find the videotapes. Thus, Homolka became the Crown's crucial witness against her husband, and a highly controversial plea bargain was struck in May 1993. For her full cooperation and testimony, Homolka would receive two twelve-year sentences for manslaughter to be served concurrently. At her June 1993 plea and sentencing trial, the judge allowed Canadian media representatives to be present, but in an attempt to preserve the integrity of the *Bernardo* trial, he drew upon common law precedent to forbid them from publishing any details until the latter trial was completed.

Despite the reporting ban, public rumors about the Homolka and Bernardo crimes were intense. Radio and print media in nearby Buffalo, New York, as well as other American mass media, reported some of the forbidden information. A public opinion survey in December 1993 found that many persons in the trial venue (moved to Toronto from St Catherines) reported that they had learned details of the case from other persons, from reading US newspapers, or from facsimile or internet communications.[3] Bernardo's public trial did not commence until May 1995, but in the interim, the case had been kept before the public by litigation over the publication ban, the resignation of Bernardo's first lawyer and the appointment of a new defense team, publicity from various victims' rights groups, widespread dissemination of anonymous flyers reporting erroneous and gruesome details about the Mahaffy and French deaths, media editorials about the Homolka plea bargain, and allegations of police incompetence.[4] Moreover, rumors surfaced that the missing

[3] See Angus Reid Group, Inc., Public Opinion on Publication Bans and the Homolka Trial (Dec. 29, 1993).

[4] The editorials involved general discussion of the issues and the need for investigation and thorough public airing of the matter after the Bernardo trial was completed, when the media would be free from the judicial restraint.

videotapes had been found and would be used as evidence. These last rumors turned out to be true.[5]

When the trial began in May 1995, 980 prospective jurors were summoned to appear at the ballroom of the downtown Royal York Hotel, which had been turned into a large courtroom. The charges against the accused were read—two counts each of first-degree murder, kidnapping, unlawful confinement, and aggravated sexual assault, and one count of causing an indignity to a corpse. Bernardo pleaded not guilty to each count. Jury selection began. In order to eliminate persons who believed they could not serve under the trial conditions, Associate Chief Justice Patrick LeSage, the trial judge, explained to the assembled panel that the trial would last for an estimated four months and that the jurors would be required to view very explicit photographs and videos of sexual acts. Over the next three days, the remaining members of the panel were randomly called one-by-one to a nearby courtroom, placed under oath, and asked up to eight questions in a procedure that Canadian law calls a 'challenge for cause'.[6]

The questions asked of the jurors were as follows:[7] (1) have you read, heard, or seen anything about this case in the media (newspapers, radio, or television)?; (2) have you obtained information about it from anywhere else?; (3) have you read, heard, or seen anything about the accused's, Paul Bernardo's, background, character, or lifestyle?; (4) have you read, heard, or seen anything about Karla Homolka or about her trial?; (5) as a result of this case, some groups and organizations have circulated petitions or have sought support concerning issues which relate to this case, the victims, or their families. Have you supported any of these groups or associations, for example, by signing a petition, writing a letter of support, or by making a donation?; (6) as a result of any knowledge, discussion, and/or contact with any group or organization, have you formed an opinion about the guilt or innocence of the accused, Paul Bernardo?; (7) if you have formed an opinion about the guilt or innocence of the accused, are you able to set aside that opinion and decide this case only on the evidence you hear in the courtroom and the judge's

[5] Bernardo's first lawyer obtained possession of the videotapes from information provided by his client, following the 70-day police search of Bernardo's home. Eventually the tapes were turned over to the prosecution. The investigation into possible obstruction of justice is described in BERNARDO INVESTIGATION REVIEW, INVESTIGATION REVIEW: REPORT OF MR. JUSTICE ARCHIE CAMPBELL (1996).

[6] For more discussion of the challenge for cause, see *infra* Part III.B.3.

[7] See *Excerpts from* R. v. Bernardo, *in* JURY TRIALS (National Judicial Institute, Nov. 27–29, 1995).

directions on the law?; (8) answer the following question with a yes or no: is there anything we have not asked you about why you could not judge this case fairly and impartially according to the evidence heard at trial and the judge's directions on the law? Beyond their responses to these questions, no other information about the jurors, other than physical appearance and demeanor in the courtroom, was available to the Crown prosecutor or the defense lawyer.

In contrast to US practice,[8] the trial judge does not have authority to determine which jurors are impartial and which are not.[9] Rather, that decision is placed in the hands of two layperson 'triers'. For the selection of the first juror, two persons are randomly chosen from the venire panel and sworn to serve as triers.[10] They listen to the prospective jurors' answers to the questions and, under instructions from the judge, render a verdict on whether he or she is 'impartial between the Queen and the accused'. If a prospective juror is found to be not impartial, another is called, and the process continues until an unbiased juror is found. After the first juror is chosen, he or she replaces one of the triers to choose the second impartial juror. The first two jurors then serve as triers for juror number three; jurors two and three are the triers for juror four; the rotating 'trier' schedule continues until twelve jurors are seated.[11] However, even if the triers decide that a person is impartial, either

[8] See NANCY GERTNER & JUDITH H. MIZNER, THE LAW OF JURIES 2–3 (1997).

[9] Throughout the rest of this ch., I will sometimes be sparse with citations to specific authority and procedures. The interested reader should consult the following sources for details: E. G. EWASCHUK, CRIMINAL PLEADINGS & PRACTICE IN CANADA (2d ed. 1998); CHRISTOPHER GRANGER, THE CRIMINAL JURY TRIAL IN CANADA (2d ed. 1996); THE MEDIA, THE COURTS AND THE CHARTER (Philip Anisman & Allen M. Linden, eds., 1986); ALAN W. MEWETT, AN INTRODUCTION TO THE CRIMINAL PROCESS IN CANADA (2d ed. 1992); R. E. SALHANY, CANADIAN CRIMINAL PROCEDURE (6th ed. 1998); DAVID M. TANOVICH *ET AL.*, JURY SELECTION IN CRIMINAL TRIALS (1997).

[10] For a description of challenge for cause in another case and an assessment of its effectiveness, see Neil Vidmar & Julius Melnitzer, *Juror Prejudice: An Empirical Study of a Challenge for Cause*, 22 OSGOODE HALL L.J. 487 (1984). The history of this procedure in Canada has not been explored, but it undoubtedly comes directly from English law. See 3 WILLIAM BLACKSTONE, COMMENTARIES 363; JAMES KENNEDY, LAW AND PRACTICE OF JURIES 90 (1826); see also Nancy J. King, *Silencing Nullification Advocacy Inside the Jury Room and Outside the Courtroom*, 65 U. CHI. L. REV. 433 (1998) (documenting the existence of triers in colonial and post-colonial America).

[11] One consequence of this unique procedure, of course, is that to a considerable degree the members of the jury are responsible for its make-up. I do not propose to explore the implications of this self-selection process for group cohesion in this chapter, but draw the matter to the reader's attention. Another consequence is that through taking part in, as well as observing, the challenge process, the jurors are further educated about the importance of being impartial.

the Crown or the defendant can exercise a peremptory challenge—twenty are provided for each side in a murder case—necessitating other jurors to be called and tried until that juror slot is filled. If a juror is acceptable to both sides, he or she is seated in the jury box for the remainder of the proceeding. When the twelfth juror is chosen, the jury is sworn.

With some persons excused for hardship, others excused for bias, and others rejected through peremptory challenges exercised by the prosecution and the defense, 225 veniremen were called in the *Bernardo* case before a jury was seated. There were no alternate jurors. The total jury selection process took five days, an extraordinarily lengthy proceeding for a Canadian trial. When all twelve were selected, the judge admonished the jurors not to discuss the case with anyone, told them that a number of legal matters still had to be resolved, and ordered them to return in two and a half weeks for the commencement of the trial.

At the end of May, the trial began with television and print coverage that was unprecedented in Canadian history. Although radio and television were not allowed in the courtroom, the streets outside were jammed with communications equipment. Long queues of spectators waited for the limited public seating. The trial involved some of the most disturbing evidence ever heard and seen in a Canadian courtroom. Graphic videotapes of the rapes and torture of the two girls were played over and over and over for the jury. The press and public were allowed to hear the audio portion of the days and hours of the victims' torture and humiliation by Bernardo and Homolka, but only the jury and court officials saw, as well as heard, the evidence. Nevertheless, the audio portion, as well as Karla Homolka's testimony, left little for the imagination, and the print media reported it extensively. Throughout the trial, the jurors went, unescorted, back to their homes each evening. They were not sequestered until they began their deliberations some four months after the trial began. Paul Bernardo was found guilty of the murders and other charges and sentenced to life in prison.[12] We will likely never learn how the jurors reached their verdict because Canadian law forbids jurors to ever disclose anything about their deliberations.

[12] Canada permanently abolished capital punishment in 1976 after a 14-year moratorium on hanging. See GRANGER, *supra* note 9, at 331. Under the life sentence, Bernardo would be eligible to apply for parole after 25 years. However, in a subsequent proceeding initiated by the Crown, he was found to be a dangerous offender and is now serving an indefinite life sentence, although that indefinite sentence is subject to periodic review.

Before elaborating on the law and rationale behind the procedures involved in the *Bernardo* trial, let us consider the history of the Canadian jury and develop a profile of the Canadian jury today.[13]

II. Profile of the Canadian Criminal Jury

A. *The History of the Right to Jury Trial in Canada and the Scope of That Right*

English common law, including the right to trial by jury, was followed almost from the beginning of the development of the separate English colonies that eventually became the nation of Canada. For example, Nova Scotia recognized the right to jury trial in 1758 and, following the defeat of the French army on the Plains of Abraham outside Quebec City, the law of England was established in the colony of Quebec in 1763. Although French civil law was restored in Quebec in 1774, English criminal law remained in force. Under the British North America Act, which established the Dominion of Canada in 1867, the federal Parliament was granted jurisdiction over criminal law, but the provinces maintained certain rights over the administration of that law. In 1892, Parliament passed the Criminal Code that recognized the right to jury trial for serious offenses. When the Constitution Act, known as the Canadian Charter of Rights and Freedoms ('Charter'), was passed in 1982, it specifically recognized the right to jury trial: '[a]ny person charged with an offense has the right . . . except in the case of an offense under military law tried before a military tribunal, to the benefit of trial by jury where the maximum penalty for the offense is imprisonment for five years or a more severe punishment. . . .'[14]

Although the right to jury trial is enshrined in the Charter, it needs to be understood in the context of the Criminal Code.[15] When it passed the uniform Criminal Code of 1892, Parliament followed Sir James Fitzjames Stevens's draft English code of 1879,[16] and its basic structure is retained in the modern Criminal Code.[17] The Code divides offenses into

[13] For general discussion on the origins of trial by jury in criminal cases in England and Canada, see GRANGER, *supra* note 9, at 11, 26. See also generally DESMOND H. BROWN, THE GENESIS OF THE CANADIAN CRIMINAL CODE OF 1892 (1989).

[14] CAN. CONST. (Constitution Act, 1982) pt. I (Canadian Charter of Rights and Freedoms), § 11(f) (hereinafter Charter).

[15] Criminal Code, R.S.C., ch. C-46 (1985) (Can.).

[16] See generally BROWN, *supra* note 13.

[17] See GRANGER, *supra* note 9, at 36.

three types.[18] *Indictable* offenses include the most serious crimes, such as murder and treason. Murder and treason must be tried in a superior court before a judge and jury. *Summary conviction* offenses are less serious offenses, such as driving while disqualified, keeping a common bawdy house, and theft or fraud under $5,000. These offenses involve maximum punishments of no more than two years in jail (the typical maximum for a summary offense is six months in jail) and a fine of less than $5,000. Summary offenses are tried by judge alone in a lower court, and there is no right to jury trial. The third category involves *hybrid* offenses that can be tried either as an indictable crime or as a summary conviction offense. Offenses falling under this category include assaults of all kinds, serious fraud, conspiracy, being an accessory to a crime, and drug offenses. The decision to proceed by indictment is solely determined by the Crown Attorney, that is, the public prosecutor, and, with a few exceptions, is not subject to judicial review. However, once the Crown has elected to proceed by indictment, the accused person has the right to decide whether to be tried by judge and jury or by judge alone for most offenses.[19]

Canada has two official languages, English and French. Section 530 of the Code provides that an accused has the right to be tried by a judge and jury who speak the language of the accused, or, if special circumstances warrant it, a judge and jury composed of persons who speak both languages.[20] Section 531 provides that a change of venue to a different territory within a province may be made in order to obtain a jury with the required language skills.[21]

It is difficult to obtain nationwide statistics on the absolute number of criminal jury trials or what percentage of accused persons elect for jury trial when they have that option. However, in 1993 in Ontario, the largest province, with a population of eleven million persons (approximately one-third of Canada's entire population), there were 1,018 criminal jury trials in the General Division Court, a superior court.[22] In contrast, there were 1,368 nonjury trials. Some of the jury trials involved murder or other offenses that are required to be tried by judge and jury. Even discounting these cases involving no option regarding the

[18] See Granger, *supra* note 9, at 37–54.

[19] However, a few offenses are not eligible for jury trial. See Criminal Code, *supra* note 15, §§ 469, 553.

[20] See ibid., § 530.

[21] See ibid., § 531.

[22] See Ontario Law Reform Comm'n, Consultation Paper on the Use of Jury Trials in Civil Cases 6–7 (1994).

choice of factfinder, more accused persons who pleaded not guilty elected for trial by judge alone than trial by jury. When summary conviction offenses are taken into account, the vast bulk of criminal cases, at least 90 percent, are tried by judge alone.[23] Nevertheless, the institution of the criminal jury continues to occupy an important place in Canadian law.

B. The Structure and Composition of the Jury and its Verdict

The Canadian jury is always composed of twelve persons.[24] No provision is made for alternate jurors and removal of a juror is considered to be a very serious matter. However, a juror can be discharged if he or she becomes ill at any time during the course of the trial, or there is some other 'reasonable cause' to discharge a juror. The judge is also vested with the power to declare a mistrial. The judge may continue the trial as long as ten jurors remain.[25] Conviction of an accused by a jury of ten or eleven members has been held to be constitutional under the Charter.[26]

Verdicts must always be unanimous.[27] There is no provision, as in England and Wales and some American states, for a majority verdict.[28] The judge has the discretion to poll the jury if there is any doubt that the verdict is not unanimous. If the jury has difficulty in reaching unanimity, the judge may provide some guidance on reasonable doubt, but a strong charge to reach unanimity would be considered improper. If the judge concludes that further deliberation would be hopeless, the jury may be discharged and a new trial ordered.[29]

The form of the verdict is ordinarily a general verdict of guilty or not guilty. The Criminal Code provides two exceptions.[30] The first involves cases of defamatory libel where the judge may provide the jury a special verdict. The second involves instances of what used to be called the

[23] This statement is based on personal communications with Professor David Paciocco.

[24] See Criminal Code, R.S.C., ch. C-46, § 631(5) (1985) (Can.).

[25] See ibid., § 644; see also Granger, *supra* note 9, at 190–8 (discussing the discharge of jurors).

[26] See Granger, *supra* note 9, at 197–8.

[27] See ibid., at 281.

[28] See Sally Lloyd-Bostock & Cheryl Thomas, *Decline of the 'Little Parliament': Juries and Jury Reform in England and Wales*, 62 Law & Contemp. Probs. 7, 36–7 (Spring 1999); King, *supra* note 2, at 46.

[29] See Granger, *supra* note 9, at 331.

[30] See Criminal Code, R.S.C., ch. C-46, §§ 16, 317 (1985) (Can.). There appears to be no rule against special verdicts, but they are used only in cases that fall within these two exceptions.

insanity defense but is now called a 'defense of mental disorder'.[31] If a jury decides that the accused committed the act but was suffering from a mental disorder that exempts her from criminal responsibility, it may render such a verdict. In many cases, the jury also has the option of returning a verdict finding the accused guilty of a lesser-included offense.[32]

Sentencing the accused is the responsibility of the judge, not the jury.[33] In 1976, Canada abolished the death penalty and substituted a mandatory life sentence with no eligibility for parole for twenty-five years upon conviction of first-degree murder, so jury recommendations are moot on this matter.[34] However, in instances where an accused who is under the age of 18 has been found guilty of first- or second-degree murder, or an accused who is over the age of 18 at the time of the offense is found guilty of second-degree murder, the judge must then tell the jury about the possible statutory range of the sentence and ask if it wishes to make a recommendation.[35] In the instance of an adult found guilty of second-degree murder, for example, the judge must tell the jury that the accused would ordinarily be eligible for parole after a mandatory ten-year imprisonment and ask the jury if it wants to make a recommendation as to the number of years between ten and twenty-five that the accused should serve before being eligible for parole. The jury does not have to make a recommendation, and any such recommendation is not binding on the judge. The Criminal Code is silent on whether the jury can be informed of the possible sentence before the jury has reached a verdict in the case, but case law has established that it is legal error to inform the jury about possible punishment prior to its verdict on guilt for any charge, including second-degree murder.[36] Several provincial courts have ruled that the recommendation does not have to be unanimous.[37] Finally, the jury's power to decide guilt can be removed if, at the end of the prosecution's

[31] See Criminal Code, R.S.C., § 16(1).

[32] See ibid., § 317.

[33] See Granger, *supra* note 9, at 331.

[34] However, after 15 years of a life sentence have been served, a convicted person may apply for judicial review of the sentence. If the Chief Justice of the province in which the conviction took place decides a review is merited, a jury may be empanelled to hear the application and consider a reduction in the sentence. Two-thirds of the jury must agree for the sentence to be reduced. See Criminal Code, R.S.C., ch. C–46, §§ 745.6–745.64 (1985) (Can.); see also David Watt & Michelle K. Fuerst, Tremeear's Criminal Code 1195–1201 (commenting on these code sections).

[35] See Criminal Code, R.S.C., ch. C–46, § 745 (1985) (Can.); see also Granger, *supra* note 9, at 331–2 (commenting on this section); Watt & Fuerst, *supra* note 34, at 1189–95.

[36] See Watt & Fuerst, *supra* note 34, at 1189–95.

[37] See Granger, *supra* note 9, at 332.

case, the judge decides that the Crown has not produced a *prima facie* case for guilt. In such an instance, the judge will enter a directed verdict of not guilty.[38]

Although not too many years ago the typical Canadian jury consisted primarily of white males selected by the local sheriff, the jury has become much more representative of the population. The selection of the jury list is controlled by provincial statute, and the general rule in the provinces is that the list is compiled by random selection from the electoral rolls in the province or local community.[39] Litigation based on an unrepresentative jury pool is sparse. While the prosecution or defense may challenge the whole jury array at the start of the trial on the grounds of fraud, partiality, or misconduct, such challenges have been infrequent.[40] In *R.* v. *Catizone*[41] and *R.* v. *Nepoose*,[42] new arrays were ordered when too few women appeared on the original arrays. In *R.* v. *Nahdee*,[43] the accused successfully challenged the array because of irregularities in the selection of aboriginal persons, and in *R.* v. *Born With A Tooth*,[44] the Crown prevailed on a challenge to irregularities in the selection of aboriginal citizens. However, challenges to arrays on the ground that they did not contain a sufficient proportion of persons of a racial or ethnic group have tended to fail if there were no irregularities in the selection process itself. If the challenge to the array is not made at the start of trial, section 670 of the Criminal Code states that any irregularity in the summoning or empanelling of the jury shall not be grounds for reversing a verdict.[45] It is not clear how successful an appeal would be if strong evidence showing deliberate racial or gender biases in selection were produced after a conviction.

Statutory exemptions from jury service do restrict representativeness to some degree. Each province is responsible for the law on this matter and the statutes differ somewhat across the provinces. The most common exemptions are for legislators, judges and other court employees, lawyers, and police officers, but some provinces also exempt doctors, veterinarians, firefighters, ministers, and law students.[46]

[38] See ibid., at 332–40.

[39] See ibid., at 81–142; see also Tanovich *et al.*, *supra* note 9, at 39–57 (discussing the selection of jury lists from the Canadian provinces).

[40] See Granger, *supra* note 9, at 149–51.

[41] (1972) 23 C.R.N.S. 44 (Ont. County Ct.).

[42] (1988) 46 C.C.C.3d 421 (Alta. C.A.).

[43] (1993) 26 C.R.4th 109 (Ont. Gen. Div.).

[44] (1993) 81 C.C.C.3d 393 (Alta. Queen's Bench).

[45] See Criminal Code, R.S.C., ch. C-46, § 670 (1985) (Can.).

[46] See Granger, *supra* note 9, at 83–142.

C. *Jury Selection*

The jury selection process in the *Bernardo* trial is not typical of Canadian jury practice and procedure. In common practice, challenges for cause occur in only a small percentage of criminal trials. Most often, jurors are selected without any questioning at all. The trial judge may ask the assembled panel of prospective jurors if any of them has health or other problems that would pose a hardship and if anyone has a relationship with the parties or witnesses in the case. The judge may excuse such jurors. The remaining jurors are then randomly selected, and called one by one to face the accused. At this point, the Crown prosecutor and defense lawyer may exercise one of the peremptory challenges that each side is allotted. However, since no other information is available, except in some provinces the juror's occupation, the decision on a peremptory challenge is made solely on the basis of observable physical characteristics and demeanor of the juror.[47]

The legal presumption behind this practice, as enunciated in a leading case on jury law, *R.* v. *Hubbert*, is that a juror will 'perform his duties in accordance with his oath' and render a verdict with an impartial mind.[48] *Hubbert* discussed additional factors that bolster this presumption. The jury is composed of twelve persons who will deliberate and cancel any individual biases that exist. Additionally, the judge's instructions to the jury will have a salutary effect by reminding the jurors that they have a solemn duty to be fair and impartial.[49]

Hubbert recognized the utility of the challenge for cause process in some cases, but specifically expressed the view that Canadian jury selection procedures should not develop along American lines.[50] *Hubbert* was decided in 1975, but the concern about 'Americanizing' the Canadian jury continues to be expressed by members of the judiciary today[51] as a consequence of a number of decisions that have liberalized the standards under which challenges for cause should be allowed and the types of prejudices that have been legally recognized.[52] This chapter

[47] It is known, from the author's professional knowledge from interviews with judges, defense lawyers, and Crown attorneys, that the Crown frequently does search the list to determine if any jurors have a criminal record.

[48] (1975) 29 C.C.C.2d 279 (Ont. C.A.).

[49] See ibid., at 296.

[50] See ibid., at 291.

[51] See Dagenais v. Canadian Broad. Corp. [1994] 3 S.C.R. 835, 839 (Can.); R. v. Williams (1994) 30 C.R.4th 277, 283–85 (B.C.S.C.).

[52] See R. v. Sherratt [1991] 1 S.C.R. 509 (Can.); R. v. Parks (1993) 24 C.R.4th 81 (Ont. C.A.).

addresses this issue in some detail, but first it is important to discuss how Canadian law attempts to prevent certain types of prejudices from arising in the first place.

D. Balancing Free Press and Fair Trial

The *Bernardo* case introduced the delicate balancing act that the Canadian legal system attempts to maintain between the values of a free press and a fair trial.

This balancing involves the controls that the judiciary may place on the mass media to prevent pretrial publicity. England, with its severe contempt of court laws for those reporting court proceedings, emphasizes the value of fair trial over free press;[53] the United States, with *Nebraska Press Association* v. *Stuart*[54] and related cases, emphasizes the value of free press over fair trial. In contrast, Canada attempts to balance the two competing values. Section 11(d) of the Charter guarantees an accused the right 'to be presumed innocent until proven guilty according to law in a fair and public hearing by an independent and impartial tribunal', and section 2(b) provides for 'freedom of the press and other media of communication'.[55] The Criminal Code also declares the right to a proceeding in open court.[56] However, two sections of the Code place limits on these rights. Section 537 provides the judge with the power to exclude everyone but the prosecutor, the accused, and his counsel from the preliminary inquiry, ordinarily held for indictable offenses.[57] Section 486 of the Code confers the judge with authority to ban the public and press from all or part of criminal trial proceedings if it is in the interest of public morals, the maintenance of order, or the proper administration of justice.[58] The apparent contradiction between these sections of the Code and the Charter guarantees are reconciled by section 1 of the Charter, which declares that the rights and freedoms are not absolute: 'reasonable limits' may be 'prescribed by law as can be demonstrably justified in a free and democratic society'.[59]

In addition, section 539(1) of the Criminal Code provides that the accused person has the right to ask for an order banning publication of

[53] See JAMES GOBERT, JUSTICE, DEMOCRACY, AND THE JURY (1997); S. H. Bailey, *The Contempt of Court Act 1981* (1982) 45 MOD. L. REV. 301; Clive Walker *et al.*, *The Reporting of Crown Court Proceedings and the Contempt of Court Act 1981* (1992) 55 MOD. L. REV. 647.

[54] 427 U.S. 539 (1976).

[55] Charter, *supra* note 14, §§ 2(b), 11(d).

[56] See Criminal Code, R.S.C., ch. C–46, § 486 (1985) (Can.).

[57] See ibid., § 537.

[58] See ibid., § 486.

[59] Charter, *supra* note 14, § 1.

the content of the proceedings until the charges are dropped or the trial is ended.[60] The motion must be granted; the judge has no discretion. (The fact that the preliminary inquiry has been held may be reported.) Defendants frequently invoke this right, particularly in cases likely to draw public interest. Consequently, the preliminary inquiry is seldom a source of prejudicial pretrial publicity.

Although the trial judge drew upon common law precedent to ban publication of the content of the *Homolka* trial proceedings until the termination of the *Bernardo* trial, his order should be viewed in the context of the general philosophy of the Criminal Code and the Charter, that is, to balance free expression with the right of the accused to a fair trial. The philosophy was also reflected in the *Bernardo* trial with respect to the judge's decision to prohibit both the public and the press from viewing the videotapes that were shown to the jury. Canadian trial practice does not allow sidebar conferences; the jury is removed from the courtroom for all legal arguments.[61] The Code proscribes publication of anything said in the absence of the jury until the jury retires to consider its verdict, at which time sequestration is mandatory.[62] The ban does not apply if the jury is sequestered during the whole trial, but sequestration is extremely rare.[63]

Two other matters bear on the control of pretrial prejudice. The first is that cameras are not permitted in Canadian courtrooms.[64] This inhibits inflammatory publicity in sensational cases like *Bernardo*. The second is that section 649 of the Criminal Code prohibits jurors from ever disclosing anything about their deliberations under threat of a summary conviction that could result in a maximum sentence of six months' imprisonment and a fine of up to $5,000.[65] This law, passed in 1972, has the effect of curtailing improper juror motivation. Thus, the jurors in the *Bernardo* case were not tempted to lie about their lack of impartiality in anticipation of a lucrative contract with a tabloid newspaper or a book publisher at the trial's end. Fame and financial gain are not motives for Canadian jurors.

The attempt to balance competing values of fair trial and free press

60 See Criminal Code, R.S.C., ch. C–46, § 539(1) (1985) (Can.).

61 See Granger, *supra* note 9, at 213.

62 See Criminal Code, R.S.C., ch. C–46, § 539(1) (1985) (Can.); see also Watt & Fuerst, *supra* note 34, at 854–5 (commenting on this section).

63 See Granger, *supra* note 9, at 305–7.

64 See Daniel J. Henry, *Electronic Public Access to Court: A Proposal for Its Implementation Today*, in The Media, the Courts and the Charter, *supra* note 9, at 441.

65 See Criminal Code, R.S.C., ch. C–46, § 649 (1985) (Can.).

has met some difficult challenges in the face of Royal commissions of inquiry and mass media saturation, and several of these cases merit further comment. Canadian political culture often encourages the use of formal public inquiries in important matters that affect the public interest. In 1995, the government of Nova Scotia ordered an inquiry into a fatal underground explosion in the Westray Coal Mine and granted its commissioner the power to compel testimony of witnesses, including persons who might face criminal charges. The affected witnesses applied for a temporary stay of the public hearings on the ground that the publicity would jeopardize their right to a fair trial. Although the appeal was argued on the ground that the accused would elect a trial by jury, they subsequently elected trial by judge alone, thereby rendering the issue moot. Nevertheless, in *Phillips* v. *Nova Scotia*,[66] the Supreme Court addressed the problem of pretrial publicity generated by public inquiries. The court conceded that publicizing evidence might 'irreparably' prejudice jurors, but it emphasized the importance of public interest in the inquiry and placed the burden of proof on the accused to demonstrate the link between publicity and harm. In the decision, the Court stated:

> The objective of finding 12 jurors who know nothing of the facts of a highly-publicized case, is today, patently unrealistic. . . . [I]mpartiality cannot be equated with ignorance of all facts of the case. . . . [I]n order to hold a fair trial it must be possible to find jurors who, although familiar with the case, are able to discard any previously formed opinions and to embark upon their duties armed with both an assumption that the accused is innocent until proven otherwise, and a willingness to determine liability based solely on the evidence presented at trial.[67]

Phillips asserted that any remedy must be weighed against existing procedural safeguards relating to jury prejudice (such as judicial instructions and challenges for cause).[68] Moreover, *Phillips* sanctioned temporary publication bans of harmful testimony or the conclusions of the inquiry until completion of the criminal proceedings.[69]

R. v. *Kenny*[70] and *R.* v. *Burke*[71] also involved a 1989 public inquiry involving charges of obstruction of justice in the investigation of rampant sexual assaults on boys in the Mt. Cashel Orphanage in Newfoundland by numerous members of the Christian Brothers, a Catholic religious

[66] [1995] 2 S.C.R. 97 (Can.). [67] Ibid., at 168.
[68] See ibid., at 169. [69] See ibid.
[70] (1996) 108 C.C.C.3d 349 (Nfld. C.A.). [71] [1994] 8 C.C.C.3d 257 (Nfld. C.A.).

order, who were in charge of the institution. Despite defense motions to delay the inquiry until after the trials of the accused or at least to place a ban on publication, the hearing took place and was covered live on television. The testimony was very graphic about what occurred and who was involved.[72] The problem was exacerbated by statements prejudicial to the accused by public officials. Additionally, the convictions of the first members to stand trial received extensive media coverage in Newfoundland and across Canada. Kenny, one of the accused, moved for a permanent stay of proceedings on the ground of prejudicial pretrial publicity. The trial judge, while conceding that the publicity had prejudiced the community, nevertheless concluded that the risk of bias could be neutralized by jury selection procedures and judicial instructions, and denied the motion. Kenny then elected trial by judge alone and was convicted.[73] His appeal of the denial of the motion to stay was decided by the Supreme Court after *Phillips* and after *Burke*.

Another case involving the balance of a fair trial and a free press was *Dagenais* v. *Canadian Broadcasting Corp.*[74] Former and present members of a Catholic religious order who ran an Ontario training school were charged with multiple counts of sexual and physical abuse of young boys who were in their care. As their trial date approached, their defense lawyers applied for an injunction preventing the Canadian Broadcasting Company from airing a television mini-series program, *The Boys of St Vincent*, a fictional account based upon Newfoundland's Mt. Cashel Orphanage cases. Relying on common law authority, the trial judge granted a nationwide injunction on the airing of the CBC series until after the Ontario trials were finished. The Ontario Court of Appeal upheld the injunction but limited its scope to Ontario and the city of Montreal.[75] Upon further appeal, the Supreme Court applied a balancing test under section 1 of the Charter and quashed the injunction.[76] The *Dagenais* decision did not absolutely curb common law judicial authority on publication bans, but it enunciated guidelines limiting the scope of such bans and requiring the weighing of potential harms to free expression against some combination of alternative remedial measures, such as adjourning trials, changing venues, sequestering

[72] See James R. P. Ogloff & Neil Vidmar, *The Impact of Pretrial Publicity on Jurors: A Study to Compare the Relative Effects of Television and Print Media in a Child Sex Abuse Case*, 18 LAW & HUM. BEHAV. 507 (1994) (describing the testimony that appeared on television as well as a summary of other background material about the case).

[73] See *Kenny* [1996] 108 C.C.C.3d at 349.

[74] [1994] 3 S.C.R. 835 (Can.).

[75] See ibid., at 836.

[76] See ibid.

jurors, allowing challenges for cause, and providing strong judicial direction to the jury. The decision was based on a balancing of the salutary effects of a publication ban on the fairness of the trial against the deleterious effects delaying free expression guaranteed by section 2 of the Charter. In fact, *Dagenais* asserted that, unlike the American model of a clash between free press and fair trial, section 1 of the Charter requires a balancing of values. It also noted that freedom of expression and the accused's right to a fair trial are not always in conflict, such as when public scrutiny of the court process may protect the fairness of trials. Finally, it noted that publication bans can also protect the privacy of members affected by the trial and other interests.

Note that in *Bernardo*, *Phillips*, and *Dagenais*, the injunctions involved delay, not permanent bans, on media publication or airing of stories. Moreover, Canadian law provides no proscription of news stories developed from sources independent of court hearings. The *Homolka* hearing's status as a 'trial' was also ambiguous, and the ban on publication to protect the *Bernardo* trial might not have prevailed if Homolka's guilty plea and sentencing had occurred before the jury trial. As it was, the media engaged in much commentary regarding the 'leniency' of her sentence before and during Bernardo's trial, even though such commentary could taint public opinion. Finally, it appears that in recent years, the Supreme Court of Canada has increasingly relied on confidence in 'existing procedural safeguards' against jury prejudice in the face of media reporting.[77] This possibly results from the greater use of such procedural devices as the challenge for cause, and the need to allow free expression under the Charter.[78] Those matters are discussed in the next part of this chapter, but the important point is that the Canadian Supreme Court appears to be engaging in a pragmatic search for a middle ground between the English and American systems regarding the free press/fair trial issue.

III. Pretrial Prejudice and Procedural Remedies

Despite the presumption that jurors will follow their oath, and despite measures intended to prevent or minimize tainting of jurors by the mass

[77] See Phillips v. Nova Scotia [1995] 2 S.C.R. 97, 169 (Can.).

[78] In 1998, new controversy developed over the frequency and extent to which judges are prone to grant bans on publicity as a result of some controversial cases, but the matter has not been resolved at the level of appeal courts. See Brian Bergman, *To Gag or Not to Gag*, MACLEAN'S, Oct. 19, 1998, at 81.

media, Canadian law and practice recognize that some of the laypersons called to serve as jurors may not have impartial minds regarding the guilt or innocence of the accused. Sometimes this is because the measures have proven ineffective and sometimes this is because, as described below, the sources of potential prejudice arise from cases other than mass media. A number of remedies intended to constrain and guide the laypersons who form the jury are provided. During the 1990s, the courts have shifted the emphasis placed on these remedies, but not without strong controversy amongst the judiciary, the Crown, and the defense bar. Before turning to these issues, a brief discussion of legal prejudice, or partiality, is useful because it sheds light on the recent developments in case law.

A. Forms of Prejudice

For purposes of conceptual analysis, potential juror prejudice may be divided into four types.[79] Interest prejudice, sometimes also called manifest or 'obvious' prejudice,[80] involves jurors who may have a direct stake in the trial outcome or at least whose presence would appear to be unfair to one of the parties. Thus, persons who have a direct familial, social, or economic relationship with the accused, the victim, or witnesses, or who might be positively or adversely affected by the outcome of the trial would be classified as having an interest prejudice. Interest prejudice may be inferred on the basis of the juror's connection to the trial without a specific assessment of his or her attitudes.

Specific prejudice exists when the juror holds attitudes or beliefs about the specific case at trial that would prevent that person from deciding guilt or innocence with an impartial mind. These attitudes and beliefs could arise from personal knowledge about the case, publicity from the mass media, or informal discussion and rumor about the case among members of the community.

Generic, or general, prejudice involves the transferring of attitudes or beliefs about the case or its participants as a result of the juror's preexisting beliefs, or stereotyping, of the defendant, the victim/complainant, or the crime itself, such that the case is not decided impartially.[81] As contrasted to specific prejudice, knowledge about the

[79] See Neil Vidmar, *Pretrial Prejudice in Canada: A Comparative Perspective on the Criminal Jury*, 79 JUDICATURE 249, 252 (1996).

[80] R. v. Sherratt [1991] 1 S.C.R. 509, 534 (Can.).

[81] For additional elaboration of generic prejudice, see Neil Vidmar, *Generic Prejudice and the Presumption of Guilt in Sex Abuse Trials*, 21 LAW & HUM. BEHAV. 5 (1997).

case or the particular identities of the trial participants is immaterial. Rather, it is the perceived characteristics of the parties or the crime itself that cause the juror to code the case as falling within a class or category of cases in which the juror is inclined to lower the burden of proof regarding guilt or to evaluate the evidence in a biased manner. Racial or ethnic prejudice is one of the oldest recognized forms of generic prejudice. The person is judged on the basis of his or her identity as a member of a group, rather than on the specific facts brought out in the trial evidence. There are research findings indicating that the mere existence of charges of child sex abuse causes some persons to infer that the accused is likely guilty. Generic prejudice is not mere abhorrence of the crime itself, but rather the inability to decide guilt fairly on the basis of the trial evidence.

Finally, conformity prejudice exists when the juror perceives that there is such strong community interest in a particular outcome of a trial that he or she is influenced in reaching a verdict by the community's feelings rather than an impartial personal evaluation of the trial evidence.

While most psychologists would recognize all four of the above categories as sources of *potential* prejudice, the central issues in jury law are if, when, and under which circumstances a court will recognize them as legally cognizable sources of partiality and which remedies to apply if the prejudice is acknowledged. Although not under the specific terminology applied here, all common law jury systems appear to recognize interest, specific, and conformity prejudice.[82] However, only a small number of common law jury systems appear to recognize forms of generic prejudice *per se*. At the end of the middle ages, England appears to have recognized forms of generic prejudice with its provisions for a jury *de medietate linguae*, where foreigners involved in civil or criminal litigation were entitled to a jury composed of six of their countrymen and six Englishmen.[83] United States case law and practice recognize racial and other generic prejudices.

Canadian case law provides numerous attempts at definitions of juror partiality, the most general of which is not being 'indifferent between the Queen and the accused'.[84] However, in the leading case, *R.* v. *Parks*,[85]

[82] See Gertner & Mizner, *supra* note 8, at 3–9 to 3–17; Gary Knapp, Annotation, *Scope of Voir Dire Examination*, 114 L.Ed.2d 763 (1995).

[83] See, *e.g.*, Marianne Constable, The Law of the Other: The Mixed Jury and Changing Conceptions of Citizenship, Law, and Knowledge (1994) (discussing early English practice).

[84] R. v. Hubbert (1995) 29 C.C.C.2d 279, 286 (Ont. C.A.).

[85] (1993) 24 C.R.4th 81 (Ont. C.A.).

decided by the Ontario Court of Appeal (and subsequently refused leave to appeal by the Supreme Court[86]) the definition was articulated in precise form:

Partiality has both an attitudinal and behavioural component. It refers to one who has certain preconceived biases, and who will allow those biases to affect his or her verdict despite the trial safeguards designed to prevent reliance on those biases. A partial juror is one who is biased and will discriminate against one of the parties to the litigation based on that bias.[87]

This definition is broad enough to encompass all four types of prejudice described above. And, indeed, the very recent Supreme Court case of *R.* v. *Williams*[88] recognized all four types of prejudice, though without coming to grips with limits to the scope of generic prejudice. However, as will be described below, the issue of generic prejudice has been a significant source of controversy within the Canadian legal system.

B. Remedies for Prejudice

The Criminal Code and Canadian case law provide a number of remedies for juror prejudices or partiality. In addition to adjournments of proceedings, these are judicial instructions, peremptory challenges, challenges for cause, changes of venue, and trial by judge alone.[89]

1. Judicial Instructions

As already discussed, Canadian courts have expressed a strong belief in the power of judicial instructions to guide jurors to be fair and impartial. This presumption was stated in *Hubbert*, but enunciated even more strongly in *R.* v. *Corbett*,[90] a case involving the issue of whether prior convictions of the accused could be introduced in evidence bearing on character if the accused chose to testify. Rejecting social science research

[86] [1994] 1 S.C.R. x (Can.).

[87] *Parks* (1993) 24 C.R.4th at 93.

[88] (1998) 159 D.L.R.4th 493 (Can.).

[89] See Dagenais v. Canadian Broad. Corp. [1994] 3 S.C.R.835 (Can.). *Dagenais* makes reference to the remedy of adjournment of the trial until the effects of publicity have abated. Adjournments are authorized under § 645 of the Criminal Code and are under the discretion of the trial judge. However, the case law on adjournments for pretrial publicity is sparse and largely noncontroversial. I will not discuss it further here.

[90] [1988] 1 S.C.R. 670, 695 (Can.).

that indicated that jurors were influenced by knowledge of criminal records, *Corbett* asserted confidence in the experience of trial judges that firm instructions from the judge caused juries to perform their duties according to the law.[91] The reasoning of *Corbett* was specifically applied to pretrial publicity in *Dagenais*, with the caveat that judicial instructions were not invariably efficacious in eliminating the effects of pretrial publicity.[92]

2. Peremptory Challenges and Stand Asides

Following the traditions of common law and the underlying rationale, the peremptory challenge remains a part of Canadian law.[93] In cases involving treason or murder, both the prosecutor and the accused are entitled to twenty peremptories. For offenses in which the accused may be sentenced to more than five years in prison, both sides have twelve peremptory challenges, and for other offenses each side has four. In joint trials, each co-accused has the same number of peremptory challenges as if he or she were tried alone. The purposes of the peremptory challenge are recognized as the same as those articulated by Blackstone, who has been favorably quoted on the issue.[94] It provides a perception of trial fairness to the accused to be able to eliminate persons for whom the accused has an uncomfortable feeling. Additionally, in instances in which there is suspicion about the venireman's professed indifference to the matters at the bar, but there are not sufficient grounds to eliminate the person for cause, the peremptory challenge provides a mechanism for doing so.

Prior to 1992, the Crown also had the right to 'stand aside' (also called 'stand by') up to forty-eight jurors with no reasons given. The stand-aside procedure was adopted from English practice in the Criminal Code of 1892. Originally the number of stand-asides was unlimited, but in 1917 the number was reduced to forty-eight.[95] The rationale for the stand-aside was the same as in English law, namely to allow the Crown to eliminate jurors deemed unfit or hostile to the Crown. However, in 1992 in *R.* v. *Bain*, the Supreme Court concluded that stand-asides violated the Charter because a reasonable person would conclude that it provided the Crown with an unfair advantage over the accused.[96] Subsequently,

[91] See ibid. [92] See *Dagenais* [1994] 3 S.C.R. at 885.

[93] See Criminal Code, R.S.C., ch. C–46, § 634 (1985) (Can.).

[94] See R. v. Bain [1992] 1 S.C.R. 91, 152 (Can.) (quoting 4 William Blackstone, Commentaries 353).

[95] See ibid., at 109. [96] See ibid., at 105.

Parliament amended the Criminal Code and abolished stand-asides, but it simultaneously gave the Crown the same number of peremptory challenges as the accused.[97]

With the exception of the stand-aside, peremptory challenges have not been controversial as they have been in England or the United States.[98] There are probably a number of reasons, including such factors as tighter controls in Canada on the trial process, lack of extensive pre-trial questioning of jurors, rarity bordering on a near absence of in-court jury selection experts, and the fact that legal issues of jury representativeness *per se* are minimized by case law and the Criminal Code. However, *R.* v. *Biddle*[99] deserves brief comment because it can be compared with the US case of *J.E.B.* v. *Alabama*,[100] which forbids the use of gender-based peremptory challenges. Biddle was convicted by an all-female jury of two 1986 rapes, largely on the basis of contested eyewitness identification evidence. The Crown had exercised its stand-by privileges to eliminate male jurors. Biddle's conviction was overturned on other grounds and since *Bain* had subsequently ruled the stand-by unconstitutional, the question of the all-female jury was only academic. However, in a concurring opinion, one justice commented that '[w]hile representativeness is not an essential quality on the jury', it is a 'characteristic which furthers the perception of impartiality'.[101] Consequently, the prosecution's 'apparent attempt' to modify the jury's composition undermined jury impartiality.[102] However, in opinions that concurred with overturning the conviction, two justices disagreed with this assessment, with one stating:

> I agree that a jury must be impartial and competent. But, with respect, the law has never suggested that a jury must be representative. For hundreds of years, juries in this country were composed entirely of men. Are we to say that all these juries were for that reason partial and incompetent?[103]

In short, it is not clear how the Supreme Court would rule in a case in which one side exercised its peremptory challenges to systematically eliminate jurors on the basis of gender or race.

[97] See GRANGER, *supra* note 9, at 144–5. When multiple defendants are involved in a trial, each has the allotted number of peremptory challenges, but the Crown's number of peremptory challenges is not increased. See Criminal Code, R.S.C., ch. C–46, § 634 (1985) (Can.).

[98] See Lloyd-Bostock & Thomas, *supra* note 28, at 23–7.

[99] [1995] 1 S.C.R. 761 (Can.).

[100] J.E.B. v. Alabama *ex rel.* T.B., 511 U.S. 127 (1994).

[101] *Biddle* [1995] 1 S.C.R. at 788.

[102] Ibid.

[103] Ibid.

3. Challenges for Cause

In contrast to peremptory challenges, challenges for cause have evoked considerable legal controversy within the past decade.[104] They have occurred with greater frequency than in the past, and both trial and appellate judges have disagreed on the scope of permissible grounds of these challenges, as well as on the scope of the permissible questions.[105] Courts in Ontario have allowed challenges for cause with greater frequency than those of other provinces. Judges in other provinces have either actively resisted challenges for cause, or the matter has seldom arisen, at least in reported case law.[106]

As a first matter, attention needs to be drawn to the fact, alluded to earlier, that the Canadian judge does not have the power to dismiss individual jurors from the array on the grounds of prejudice.[107] The judge is allowed to dismiss some persons if he or she determines in open court that the juror has a personal interest in the matter to be tried, has a relationship with the judge or any of the parties or witnesses to the suit, or would suffer personal hardship or suffers from a disability.[108] However, the Code states that two lay triers shall decide the issue of impartiality of a challenged juror.[109] The challenge process proceeds in the manner described in the *Bernardo* trial.[110] Two laypersons are randomly chosen to serve as a mini-jury to render a verdict on the impartiality of the challenged juror. After the first impartial juror is chosen, he or she becomes a trier for the next juror, and the process of selection and trier replacement with a newly selected juror continues until a jury of twelve is selected. Ordinarily, the jury panel is removed from the courtroom for the challenging process on the theory that observing the process may affect their answers.[111]

The trial judge, however, plays a crucial role in determining whether a challenge shall be allowed and the form of the questions that may be

[104] See Austin M. Cooper, *The ABCs of Challenge for Cause in Jury Trials: To Challenge or Not to Challenge and What to Ask If You Get It*, 37 Crim. L. Q. 62 (1994); David M. Tanovich, *Rethinking Jury Selection: Challenges for Cause and Peremptory Challenges* (1994) 30 C.R.4th 310; David Paciocco, Challenges for Cause: *Cameron* and Sexual Offence Cases (Apr. 1995, unpublished manuscript on file with author); Steven Skurka, Challenge for Cause: Questions Allowed Since *R.* v. *Parks* (Nov. 11, 1994, unpublished manuscript on file with author).

[105] See Granger, *supra* note 9, at 158–88.

[106] See ibid.

[107] See ibid., at 187–8; Tanovich *et al.*, *supra* note 9, at 81–3, 161.

[108] See Tanovich *et al.*, *supra* note 9, at 77–83.

[109] See Criminal Code, R.S.C., ch. C–46, § 640 (1985) (Can.).

[110] See Tanovich *et al.*, *supra* note 9, at 151–64.

[111] See ibid., at 165.

put to the jurors.[112] Since there is a legal presumption that a juror is impartial, the burden of proof for overcoming this presumption lies with the party requesting the challenge. In practice, this is almost always the accused. The standard of proof is low, namely proof of an 'air of reality' or a 'realistic potential'.[113] The evidence introduced in support of a challenge has involved newspaper articles, testimony by persons who have knowledge of the community, and expert opinion by social scientists, sometimes buttressed with a public opinion survey designed specifically for the case.[114] In recent years, a number of judges have taken judicial notice of the existence of forms of prejudice in permitting challenges for cause. As will be described below, for certain cases where the race of the parties might be an issue, recent case law has asserted that the accused need present only a *prima facie* case to challenge on grounds of potential racial bias. However, even though the standard of proof is low, the costs of producing evidence serve to inhibit requests for challenges for cause in many cases.

The judge is charged with keeping a tight rein on the forms of questions that may be asked of jurors. In response to concerns about 'American-style' *voir dire*, *Hubbert* asserted that '[c]hallenge for cause is not for the purpose of finding out what kind of juror the person called is likely to be—his personality, beliefs, prejudices, likes or dislikes'.[115] Typically, the questions put to jurors are limited in number, often only one or two, and require only yes or no answers. Usually the questions are written out in advance and approved by the judge. The questions must directly address the juror's state of mind. The lawyer for the side that requests the challenge asks the questions.

In *R.* v. *Parks*, the jurors were asked:

> As the judge will tell you, in deciding whether or not the prosecution has proven the charge against an accused a juror must judge the evidence of the witnesses without bias, prejudice or partiality:
>
> (1) In spite of the judge's direction would your ability to judge witnesses without bias, prejudice or partiality be affected by the fact that there are people involved in cocaine and other drugs?[116]

[112] See TANOVICH *ET AL.*, *supra* note 9, at 84–106. [113] See ibid., at 95–100.

[114] See ibid., at 137–47; Vidmar & Melnitzer, *supra* note 10, at 491–3.

[115] R. v. Hubbert (1975) 29 C.C.C.2d 279, 289 (Ont. C.A.).

[116] The judge was ruled in error for having permitted this question. See (1993) 24 C.R.4th 81, 88 (Ont. C.A.).

(2) Would your ability to judge the evidence in the case without bias, prejudice or partiality be affected by the fact that the person charged is a black Jamaican immigrant and the deceased is a white man?[117]

In *R.* v. *Cameron*, the judge allowed the following question:

As His Honor will instruct you, in deciding whether or not the prosecution has proven the charge against an accused, a juror must judge the evidence of all the witnesses, both for the Crown and for the defence, without bias, prejudice, or partiality.

In spite of His Honour's direction, would your ability to judge the accused without bias, prejudice or partiality be affected by the fact that he was selling cocaine on the day in question?[118]

Most often, the judge does not allow further exploration of the juror's reasoning behind the answer. The triers make their decision based on the juror's yes or no answer about whether he or she can be fair and impartial. In practice, this process of jury selection typically consumes less than two hours of trial time.

In cases involving pretrial publicity, the judge may permit additional questions. In *R.* v. *Lesso*,[119] the judge allowed the following questions: have you discussed the case with anyone?; if yes, have you expressed an opinion about the guilt or innocence of the accused?; if no, do you have an opinion as to the guilt or innocence of the accused?; if yes, what is that opinion? In a Prince Edward Island case, *R.* v. *Cameron*,[120] involving a doctor in a small community accused of sexually assaulting his patients, the jurors were asked up to five questions: whether they had been patients or had some other relationship with the accused; whether they knew and had attitudes or beliefs about trial witnesses that would cause them to give the testimony of those witnesses more or less credibility than that of other witnesses; whether they had discussed and formed an opinion about the case; whether they had strong beliefs about sexual assault that would prevent them from being impartial; and whether they had any other beliefs about the case or about sexual assault in general that would prevent them from being impartial.

In most cases, judges have held that it is inappropriate to ask jurors whether they are members of a particular race or class of society, about

[117] Ibid. [118] (1995) 96 C.C.C.3d 346, 348 (Ont. C.A.).

[119] (1973) 23 C.R.N.S. 179, 187–91 (Ont. H.C.J.).

[120] No. GSC–13385 P.E.I.S.C. (Trial Div.) Apr. 15, 1994.

their personal experiences such as whether the juror or a member of the juror's family has been the victim of an offense, and what the prospective juror's beliefs are, including whether they belong to any groups, such as a victim support group, or fraternize with particular ethnic or racial groups.[121]

The limited questioning allowed in challenges for cause renders it an imperfect device for ferreting out prejudice since the juror might not understand the question and typically is required to answer only yes or no. However, in actual experience with challenges for cause, a number of jurors do affirm that they are not impartial and are rejected by the triers.[122] Additionally, the process of asking the juror if he or she can be impartial is believed to reinforce the judge's admonition at trial of the need to be fair and impartial.[123] Thus, Canadian jury law may again be seen as seeking a middle ground between the extensive, intrusive, and occasionally time-consuming American *voir dire* and the near refusal of English law to recognize that some jurors may not be 'impartial between the Queen and the accused'.

The primary controversy regarding challenges for cause has involved forms of generic prejudice. Since the mid-1970s, a number of trial judges in Toronto, Ontario, have taken cognizance of the existence of racial prejudice in that city and allowed challenges regarding whether jurors held racial prejudice.[124] In *R.* v. *Parks*, the Ontario Court of Appeal took judicial notice of the fact that '[a] significant segment of our community holds overtly racist views' and indicated that the black person accused of second-degree murder involving a drug transaction should have had the right to challenge jurors on their impartiality without the need to demonstrate actual prejudice.[125] The reasoning of the *Parks* decision was subsequently extended to cases outside of Toronto and to cases involving important witnesses who were members of that minority group.[126]

[121] See Granger, *supra* note 9, at 181–6; Tanovich *et al.*, *supra* note 9, at 147–50.

[122] See Vidmar & Melnitzer, *supra* note 10, at 50; Vidmar, *supra* note 81, tbl.1; Neil Vidmar, *Social Science and Jury Selection, in* Law Society of Upper Canada, Psychology and the Litigation Process 100, 125 (1976) (discussing the unreported case of *R.* v. *Doxtator*).

[123] See R. v. Koh (1998), Nos. C25944, C27462, 1998 Ont. C.A. LEXIS 859, 29 (Ont. C.A. Dec. 30, 1998).

[124] See Vidmar Melnitzer, *supra* note 10, at 488.

[125] (1993) 24 C.R.4th 81, 99 (Ont. C.A.).

[126] See R. v. Willis (1994) 90 C.C.C.3d 350 (Ont. C.A.); R. v. Morgan (1995) 42 C.R.4th 126 (Ont. Gen. Div.); see also Tanovich *et al.*, *supra* note 9, at 110–11 (discussing challenges for cause based on racial bias).

Subsequently, in British Columbia an aboriginal (Canadian Indian) defendant facing charges of robbery, requested a challenge for cause involving racial bias. In the resulting case of *R.* v. *Williams*, both the trial judge[127] and the British Columbia Court of Appeal[128] denied the motion. The judges acknowledged that there was widespread prejudice against aboriginal people in the community, but asserted there was no evidence that there was a nexus between the prejudice and the ability of jurors to decide the case impartially if properly instructed by the trial judge. The British Columbia courts also attempted to distinguish the case from *Parks*. The case was appealed, and in *R.* v. *Williams*,[129] the Supreme Court in a unanimous nine–zero decision ruled that the challenge should have been allowed and directed a new trial. The Court recognized generic prejudices beyond just racial prejudice and their potential influences on jurors, while still asserting the trial judge's discretion to decide the merits of challenges for cause on a case-by-case basis.

Both before and after *Parks*, individual trial judges have allowed challenges for cause bearing on other types of generic prejudice.[130] These have included prejudices involving other racial groups, homosexuality, HIV status, offenses involving domestic violence, violence against women, elderly persons, and the police, and drug offenses, particularly when the drug charges were intertwined with racial issues. In addition, in a substantial number of Ontario cases, trial judges have allowed challenges in cases involving sexual offenses against children.[131] Despite a substantial number of documented cases in which jurors admitted to not being impartial when an accused was charged with sexual abuse,[132] in *R.* v. *Betker*,[133] the Ontario Court of Appeal ruled that challenges based on this type of offense were inappropriate. The reasoning of the Court involved complicated issues that are beyond the scope of this overview of Canadian law. However, following the Supreme Court decision in *R.* v. *Williams*, the issue of offense-based challenges has been re-opened and a number of such challenges have been allowed by Ontario trial judges.[134]

[127] (1994) 30 C.R.4th 277 (B.C. Sup. Ct.).
[128] (1996) 106 C.C.C.3d 215 (B.C.C.A.).
[129] (1998) 159 D.L.R.4th 493 (Can.).
[130] See Granger, *supra* note 9, at 178–81; Tanovich *et al.*, *supra* note 9, at 115–37.
[131] See Tanovich *et al.*, *supra* note 9, at 119–24; Vidmar, *supra* note 81, tbl.1.
[132] See Tanovich *et al.*, *supra* note 9, at 119–94; Vidmar, *supra* note 81, tbl.1.
[133] (1997) 115 C.C.C.3d 421 (Ont. C.A.).
[134] This conclusion is based on personal conversations with Professor David Paciocco.

It is reasonable to conclude that the challenge for cause is a procedural remedy that is in a state of change and development. Although the various appeal court decisions have stated that the law as defined in *Hubbert* has not changed, the empirical result in Ontario has been a substantial expansion of the right to challenge for cause, accompanied with a partial retrenchment regarding sexual offense-based challenges. The *Parks* case and its progeny and the *Williams* decision are at once a recognition of changing social conditions in Canada and an attempt to provide a remedy to foster the legal goal of a fair trial and public perceptions of fairness. Lawyers and judges in other provinces have been more conservative regarding the use of the challenge for cause, continuing to rely more heavily on the presumption that a juror will be impartial. The *Williams* decision, however, will surely result in more frequent challenges when the accused is a member of a minority group.[135] Whether there will be spill-over effects regarding other forms of pretrial prejudice or other developments cannot be foretold at the present time.

4. Changes of Venue

The basic rule at common law was that the trial should be heard in the community in which the crime occurred, and that is still the presumption in Canada. However, the Code provides that either the accused or the prosecutor may apply for a change of venue if 'it appears expedient to the ends of justice'.[136] This could mean convenience to the parties or other matters, but is also interpreted to include situations where substantial segments of the community are believed to be so tainted by pretrial prejudice that a fair trial cannot be held. The standard for moving a trial has been a showing that there is a 'fair and reasonable probability of partiality or prejudice'.[137] Most authority seems to indicate that change of venue is a more extreme remedy than a challenge for cause.[138]

The nature of proof tendered by the applicant is similar to that in a challenge for cause application. It may be documentary evidence, *viva voce* evidence, or expert testimony. In a number of cases, a basis of the

[135] In *R.* v. *Koh* (1998) Nos. C25944, C27462, 1998 Ont. C.A. LEXIS 859 (Ont. C.A. Dec. 30, 1998), a case involving charges of narcotics trafficking, the Ontario Court of Appeal stated that racism was not unique or indigenous against blacks and extended to persons of Asian/Chinese origin. *Koh* expanded the right to challenge elaborated in *Parks* to accused who are 'minorities of colour'.

[136] Criminal Code, R.S.C., ch. C–46, § 599 (1985) (Can.).

[137] GRANGER, *supra* note 9, at 61.

[138] See ibid., at 57–78.

expert's testimony has been a public opinion poll carried out in the relevant community and sometimes in comparison communities.[139]

5. Trial by Judge Alone

Recall that there are some crimes, including murder, in which the Code specifies that the accused must be tried by judge and jury.[140] The Code indicates that this may be changed to judge alone only with the consent of both the accused and the Crown.[141] In *R.* v. *McGregor*,[142] the accused was charged with killing his estranged wife with a cross-bow on the street near the Parliament buildings in Ottawa. The killing occurred on the first anniversary of the mass killings of a number of female engineering students in the City of Montreal. There was a great deal of publicity about the killing and its relation to the 'Montreal Massacre'. The accused chose to plead not guilty by reason of insanity and wished to be tried by judge alone. The Crown would not consent, arguing that a change of venue was the appropriate remedy. Counsel for McGregor introduced survey data through two experts who indicated that there was not only extremely high prejudice in the community but that there was also substantial generic and specific evidence of lack of impartiality toward the insanity defense. However, the survey data also indicated that generic prejudice against the insanity defense would likely be substantial in the county to which the Crown proposed moving the trial, thereby raising the possibility that a challenge for cause would be required even if the trial was moved. In addition, defense counsel made other arguments, such as the need for access to Ottawa-based psychiatric consultants during the trial. Relying on section 24(1) of the Charter, which provides for a court to provide a remedy if any accused rights are in jeopardy of being infringed, the court granted trial by judge alone.

IV. Controls on the Rest of the Trial Process

The Canadian presumption about jurors following their oath and the tightly restricted questioning process when challenges for cause are

[139] See R. v. Theberge (1995) No. 2666–90, 1995 Ont. C.A. LEXIS 1206 (Ont. Gen. Div., Mar. 16, 1995); Neil Vidmar & John W. T. Judson, *The Use of Social Science Data in a Change of Venue Application: A Case Study*, 59 Canadian B. Rev. 76 (1981).

[140] See Criminal Code, R.S.C., ch. C–46, § 471 (1985) (Can.).

[141] See ibid., § 473.

[142] (1992) 14 C.R.R.2d 155 (Ont. Gen. Div.); see also Tanovich *et al.*, *supra* note 9, at 29–32 (discussing the judge versus jury issue).

allowed needs to be viewed in the context of the whole jury system. Not only does Canadian law attempt to control factors that might engender pretrial prejudice, it also provides for greater control over the jury than does the American system. In fact, in this regard, it bears greater similarity to the jury systems of England, Australia, and New Zealand.

A. Duties of the Trial Judge

The Canadian trial judge has limited discretion to summon witnesses who are not called by either the prosecutor or the defense if he or she determines that it is necessary to the 'ends of justice'.[143] The exercise of this power does not require the consent of the parties. The power must be used sparingly and is regularly exercised. The judge also has a positive duty to put questions to a witness in order to clarify an obscure answer, a misunderstanding of a question put to the witness, or an omission by legal counsel of a question that the judge believes is relevant to the issues in the case.[144] It is improper for either the Crown prosecutor or defense counsel to offer any personal opinions about the evidence or for the defense lawyer to invite the jury to ignore the law.[145]

Equally important, after the evidence and final arguments have been given, the trial judge has the positive duty of reviewing the case for the jury.[146] The judge must impartially, but substantially, review the theories of the prosecution and the defense and the evidence presented by both sides. Moreover, the judge is entitled to express an opinion to the jury about the importance of various pieces of evidence and may even offer an opinion regarding the credibility of a witness. In undertaking this commentary, the judge must make it clear that the jury is not bound to accept her opinion regarding the facts. The judge also has the obligation of raising any questions arising from the evidence that favor the accused even if they were not raised by the accused's legal counsel. The jury also must be instructed on reasonable doubt and the unanimity requirement. The judge may provide the jury with a written description of the different verdicts open to it but may not ask the jury to particularize the basis of its verdict; only a general verdict is considered to be proper.

Canadian legal thinking regards this judicial guidance to the jury as significant in the mitigation of any prejudices held by members of the

[143] See GRANGER, *supra* note 9, at 216–19. [144] See ibid.
[145] See ibid., at 221–41. [146] See ibid., at 243–304.

jury. This is a large, though implicit, factor in the presumption that jurors will follow their oath to be impartial. It is also important in the belief that even when challenges for cause are allowed, the limitations of the highly circumscribed questioning process are capable of being offset by the intervention and guidance of the judge.

B. Expert Evidence

The issue of the reliability and utility of expert evidence has engendered concern in Canada[147] as it has in the United States and other countries.[148] The concerns have focused around forensic evidence from the natural sciences such as DNA tests, fiber samples, and explosive residue. However, Canada has also seen an increase in testimony involving the behavioral sciences. In *R.* v. *Lavalee,*[149] involving a woman accused of killing her partner, the Supreme Court approved the admissibility of testimony about 'Battered Woman Syndrome'. In other cases, evidence has been tendered about the 'Child Sexual Abuse Accommodation Syndrome', reliability of eyewitness identification, and other social science evidence.[150] Issues have been raised about the validity and reliability of some of the expert evidence and upon its impact on the jury.[151]

Roughly similar to the US cases of *Daubert* v. *Merrell Dow Pharmaceuticals, Inc.*[152] and *General Electric Co.* v. *Joiner,*[153] in *R.* v. *Mohan*[154] the Supreme Court of Canada enunciated a number of criteria for determining the admissibility of expert evidence. *Mohan* stated that not only must such evidence be logically related to a fact in issue, it must also meet a threshold of reliability beyond the qualification of the expert. Additionally, when the testimony engages a novel scientific theory or technique, it should be subject to special scrutiny. *Mohan* was intended to draw the judge's attention to his or her responsibility to screen expert evidence allowed in court. An important goal of the *Mohan* decision was to prevent

[147] See P. Brad Limpert, *Beyond the Rule in* Mohan: *A New Model for Assessing the Reliability of Scientific Evidence,* 54 U. Toronto Fac. L. Rev. 65 (1996); David M. Paciocco, Expert Evidence: Where Are We Now? Where Are We Going? (Jan. 31, 1998) (unpublished manuscript presented at Canadian Bar Association 1998 Institute of Continuing Legal Education, on file with author).

[148] See David Faigman *et al.*, Modern Scientific Evidence: The Law and Science of Expert Testimony (1997); Sophia I. Gatowski *et al., The Diffusion of Scientific Evidence: A Comparative Analysis of Admissibility Standards in Australia, Canada, England, and the United States, and Their Impact on the Social and Behavioural Sciences* Expert Evidence 86 (1996).

[149] [1990] 1 S.C.R. 852 (Can.).

[150] See Paciocco, *supra* note 147, at 14.

[151] See ibid., at 33.

[152] 509 U.S. 579 (1993).

[153] 118 S. Ct. 512 (1997).

[154] [1994] 2 S.C.R. 9 (Can.).

juries from being influenced by unreliable expert evidence while still permitting new and novel evidence if it was relevant.[155] Subsequently, in *R.* v. *Olscamp*,[156] testimony about Child Sexual Abuse Accommodation Syndrome was ruled inadmissible and in another case, *R.* v. *McIntosh*,[157] expert evidence bearing on eyewitness reliability was excluded. Questions are also being raised about evidence derived from the natural sciences. However, as commentators have pointed out, Canadian courts have been inconsistent in applying the *Mohan* criteria from case to case.[158] Thus, *Mohan* set the stage for a control on what juries see and hear, but systematic application of these controls is in a developmental stage.

C. Crown Appeal of an Acquittal

It would be remiss to fail to mention a striking feature of Canadian law. While the Charter gives great weight to the presumption of innocence, the Crown does have a limited right to appeal a jury acquittal. The Code provides that the Attorney General has the right to appeal a verdict of acquittal or a verdict of not criminally responsible on account of mental disorder.[159] The grounds for an appeal must involve an issue of law, such as a claim that the jury was not properly instructed on the law. This limitation on double jeopardy requires a thorough review by appeal courts, but on occasion the Crown has been successful in obtaining a new trial. In 1986, in a highly publicized case, Guy Paul Morin was found not guilty of the murder of 9-year-old Christine Jessup.[160] His primary defense was an alibi defense but this was complicated by psychiatric testimony that Morin was suffering from severe schizophrenia such that if he did commit the crime, he would not have appreciated the nature and quality of the act. The Ontario Attorney General filed an appeal on the grounds that the judge misdirected the jury on reasonable doubt and that it had been improperly instructed about Morin's psychiatric condition. The Ontario Court of Appeal reversed the verdict and ordered a new trial.[161] The Supreme Court of Canada upheld the reversal with respect to the reasonable doubt instruction.[162] In his second trial, the issue of schizophrenia was abandoned but the alibi defense was

[155] See Paciocco, *supra* note 147, at 8–15.

[156] (1994) 35 C.R.4th 37 (Ont. Gen. Div.).

[157] (1997) 35 O.R.3d 97 (Ont. C.A.).

[158] See Limpert, *supra* note 147, at 83.

[159] See Criminal Code, R.S.C., ch. C–46, § 676 (1985) (Can.).

[160] See R. v. Morin (1987) 36 C.C.C.3d 50 (Ont. C.A.). For a synopsis of the *Morin* case from beginning to end, see Jack King, *The Ordeal of Guy Paul Morin: Canada Copes with Systemic Injustice*, CHAMPION, Aug. 1998, at 8.

[161] See R. v. Morin (1988) 2 S.C.R. 345, 351 (Can.).

[162] See ibid., at 361.

expanded. Despite new evidence of serious police misbehavior, unreliable witnesses, and demonstration of unreliable forensic conclusions regarding hair and fiber samples, after nine months of trial testimony, the jury found Morin guilty of first-degree murder following a week of deliberations. Morin appealed, but while the appeal was pending DNA evidence that had not been available during the first two trials eliminated Morin as the killer and his conviction was set aside. A subsequent public inquiry into justice system failures resulted in the lengthy 1998 Kaufman Report that made many recommendations regarding criminal procedure and the jury system.[163] The impact of the Kaufman Report cannot yet be assessed.

The *Morin* case follows by more than two decades a change in Canadian law, known as the Morgentaler Amendment,[164] that had allowed an appeals court to actually substitute a verdict of guilty despite a jury finding of not guilty. The Code now only allows ordering a new trial based on matters of law.[165] The jury is the sole interpreter of the facts. Nevertheless, even with these restrictions, section 676, as *Morin* demonstrates, is another judicial constraint on the jury.

D. Some Other Constraints

There are a few other factors bearing on the jury system that deserve brief mention. The rules of lawyer behavior outside the courtroom before, during, and after the trial are in marked contrast to those in the United States and more in line with the practice in other common law countries. A lawyer holding press conferences to discuss the evidence, the judge, or anything that could affect the trial or by innuendo bring the administration of justice into disrepute would likely face serious contempt of court charges, censure from colleagues, or, more likely, both. Indeed, the legal culture is such that even a lawyer having no

[163] Fred Kaufman, The Commission on Proceedings Involving Guy Paul Morin: Report (1998).

[164] Morgentaler, a doctor crusading for abortion rights, was found not guilty of performing an abortion after admitting to all of the elements of the charge but arguing an affirmative defense of necessity. The Quebec Court of Appeal overturned the jury acquittal and substituted a conviction, based on the trial evidence. However, the public outcry caused Parliament to amend the Criminal Code in 1975 so that while an acquittal can still be appealed, the court can only order a new trial. The details of the trial, appeal, and change in law are described in F. L. Morton, *Morgantaler* v. *Borowski*: Abortion, the Charter, and the Courts (1995).

[165] See Criminal Code, R.S.C., ch. C–46, § 676 (1985) (Can.).

connection to a case would be unlikely to offer highly evaluative commentary to the media about the conduct of the case or the witnesses, as frequently occurs in the United States. Partly because of this legal culture and partly because of the severe limitations on the jury selection process, in-court jury trial consultants have rarely been employed.[166] Under procedural rules, the Crown is required to disclose its witnesses and evidence in advance of trial, but the defense is not under a similar obligation.[167] This may help to foster a more constrained atmosphere, especially on the part of defense lawyers. Inside the superior courts, lawyers wear black vests and gowns inherited from English tradition (the wigs are, mercifully, absent) and follow formal rules of decorum. Opposing lawyers sit at a counsel table or stand at a lectern during the trial. They can approach a witness only with permission of the judge. Addresses to the jury at the beginning and end of the trial are made from the lectern.[168] Special deference is given to the judge, who until recent years was always addressed as Your Lordship or Ladyship, but the prescriptive norms also extend to the forms of address between the lawyers. For instance, even when hotly disputing a legal point, the adversaries frequently refer to their opponents as 'my friend'. It is not an easily measurable phenomenon, but the atmosphere of the Canadian courtroom surely must have an impact on the jurors.

V. Aboriginal Peoples and the Jury System

The Inuit, or Eskimo people as they were then known, were first introduced to the Canadian jury system in 1916 in what Edwin Keedy, who was present at the proceedings, aptly labeled a 'remarkable murder trial'.[169] Two priests working among the Inuit people, who were still largely isolated from Western culture, went missing. After a long hunt, a party of the Northwest Mounted Police (later the Royal Canadian

[166] There have been some instances, including several cases in which the present author participated in a low-key manner.

[167] See Criminal Code, R.S.C., ch. C–46, § 603 (1985) (Can.); see also Watt & Fuerst, *supra* note 34, at 920–6 (discussing disclosure requirements under § 603).

[168] Also noteworthy is the fact that the accused does not sit with his defense counsel. Rather, he must sit in the 'prisoner's box' throughout the trial. This rule applies even to the accused who are free on their own recognizance. However, in the light of the Kaufman Report, this practice has been changed in Ontario. See King, *supra* note 160.

[169] Edwin R. Keedy, *A Remarkable Murder Trial:* Rex v. Sinnisiak, 100 U. Pa. L. Rev. 48 (1951). For additional discussion of the incident upon which the charges were brought, see Roger Buliard, Inuk (1951); Richard Finnie, The Lure of the North (1940).

Mounted Police) uncovered the fact that two Inuit men, Sinisiak and Uluksak, had killed the priests near the Coppermine River. The two Inuit admitted the acts, and they were transported 2,000 miles south to Edmonton, Alberta, along with two interpreters and an elderly Inuit who was to be a witness. Sinisiak was appointed legal counsel and the Chief Justice of the Supreme Court of Alberta conducted his trial for murder of one of the priests. Although the trial took place in summer, in the first stage the two accused were dressed in their native dress, with a tub full of water and ice provided to soak their feet and help them stay cool. Through translators, the Inuit admitted the act of which they were accused, but testified that the priests had abused them and, moreover, created in their minds the belief that the priests were going to kill them. In fact, the Inuit subsequently ate pieces of the priests' liver as a protection against their evil spirits. At the close of the trial, the prosecution contended that the accused killed the priests for their rifles. Defense counsel argued that the Inuit should be judged by the standards of their own culture. The judge instructed the jury that the cultural defense must be rejected. He also told the jury that if Sinisiak was found guilty of murder, he would have no choice, under Canadian law, but to sentence him to death. However, the judge also stated that he would recommend clemency, which he was confident would be granted. After an hour of deliberation, the jury returned a verdict of not guilty.

The story did not end in Edmonton. Within six days, the accused were moved 200 miles south to Calgary, and both Inuit were tried for the death of the second priest. After forty-five minutes of deliberation, the jury returned a verdict of guilty but with the strongest recommendation of mercy. Both men were sentenced to death by hanging, as required by law, but the Inuit were told that the sentence was deferred until the 'Big Chief far away' could review it. On August 19, 1916, the death sentence was commuted to life in prison, and they were returned to the Arctic under custody of the Mounted Police and held first at Herschel Island and then at Great Slave Lake. In 1919, the two were released from custody and returned to their people. However, the order of release contained the requirement that they make known to others that:

> Eskimos live and are governed under a system of law . . . with equality as against both white man, Indian and Eskimo. . . . [W]hile . . . these prisoners have been visited by a dispensation of mercy whereby their lives have been spared . . . these reasons are not likely to prevail on another occasion, either for them or for any other Eskimo, seeing that the proceedings in the present case have served to inform them of their responsibilities, and that they are solemnly

charged with their duty to serve God and honour the King and carefully to observe his laws.[170]

Rex v. *Sinisiak* serves as a seminal event in attempts to establish the rule of law for aboriginal peoples living in Canada's Northern Territories, and some of its themes exist in modern attempts to provide and legitimate law among the Inuit and Indian tribal peoples living in these isolated areas. The jury system is one part of the story.[171] These territories cover almost three and a half million square kilometers, covering four time zones, with a total population of under 60,000 persons. The sixty-five communities in this area range from a population of eleven to about 14,000 persons, with an average population of approximately 500 residents; in the smaller communities, the majority are aboriginals. There are four major ethnic groups: Inuit (37 percent of the population), Dene (16 percent), Metis (7 percent), and 'nonnatives' (39 percent). Nine different languages are spoken, and some dialects are so distinct that peoples speaking the same language cannot easily understand one another. Reflecting social problems that are similar to those experienced by aboriginal peoples all over the world who come in contact with modern culture, the majority of charged crimes involve native accused.

In the first half of this century, the problems of isolation and sparse populations resulted in few jury trials. Rather, cases tended to be tried by a judge or magistrate. However, with the establishment of the Territorial Court of the Northwest Territories in 1955, accused persons have increasingly exercised the right to jury trial. In the first fourteen years, there was an average of five trials per year.[172] The Criminal Code provided for six-person juries in the Northwest Territories because of the sparseness of population, and until 1965, women were prohibited from serving. Additionally, an eligibility requirement for service was an ability to speak English. In consequence, between 1955 and 1968, despite the fact that aboriginal peoples were the accused in 55 percent of the cases, aboriginals served on only twenty-seven of the sixty-six jury trials and typically as only one of the six members.[173]

[170] Keedy, *supra* note 169, at 67.

[171] Except where otherwise noted, this discussion about the jury system is based upon Christopher Gora, *Jury Trials in the Small Communities of the Northwest Territories*, 13 Windsor Y. B. Access Just. 156 (1993).

[172] See W. G. Morrow, *A Survey of Jury Verdicts in the Northwest Territories*, 8 Alta L. Rev. 50, 54–8 (1970); see also Jack Sissons, Judge of the Far North 181–6 (1968) (discussing the legal system in the Northwest Territories).

[173] There were two all-native juries. See Morrow, *supra* note 172, at 56–7.

In 1965, women were declared eligible to serve on juries, and in 1985 the six-person jury was declared unconstitutional.[174] In 1988, an amendment to the Jury Act permitted unilingual jurors.[175] Between 1987 and 1991, the latest date for which figures are available, an average of forty-seven jury trials took place per year.[176]

Christopher Gora conducted formal interviews with judges, lawyers, and other persons connected to the court process that revealed a number of problems with the implementation of jury trials.[177] While every effort is made to keep the trial in the community in which the offense occurred, major problems have arisen in this regard. Sometimes the community is too small to obtain a jury, particularly when many of its members are related to the victim or the accused. Linguistic problems continue to be a source of difficulty because of the lack of trained interpreters. In addition, local political struggles between families and ruling cliques can prevent the formation of a jury in that location. Thus, a change of venue is required, bringing additional problems regarding preparation of the case and accessibility of witnesses. Many of Gora's respondents also noted a substantial trend toward acquittals, especially in comparison to trials before a judge alone.[178] Additionally, there appears to be a greater reluctance to serve on juries than elsewhere in Canada. Both the acquittal rates and the reluctance to serve may reflect unwillingness to pass judgement on one's neighbor. However, it also appears to reflect a preference for community values and traditional cultural ways of handling deviance that are in conflict with the legal values and processes of the broader Canadian society.

Gora discussed a number of potential reforms that might ease the difficulties of jury trial in the Canadian North.[179] These include simplifying the charge to make the language more accessible to the jurors and altering the configuration of the court[180] to make it more similar to traditional community forums, allowing the community to select the jury

[174] See R. v. Punch (1985) 22 C.C.C.3d 289 (N.W.T.S.C.).

[175] See Gora, *supra* note 171, at 162. Unilingual jurors are provided with translators. Gora noted that the issue of translators attending the actual jury deliberations had not yet arisen. See ibid., at 167.

[176] See ibid., at 170.

[177] See ibid., at 170–4.

[178] This problem was also raised during informal interviews that I undertook in Baker Lake, an Inuit community of about 1,400 persons, in the summer of 1997.

[179] See Gora, *supra* note 171, at 174–80.

[180] Having no formal courthouse, trials in smaller communities take place in hotels, community centers, or schools. The temporary spatial designs, however, are made similar to more traditional court settings.

pool, and allowing community input into sentencing. Nevertheless, in some respects the essential problems of compatibility of jury trial with the culture and values of aboriginal peoples reflected in *R.* v. *Sinisiak* remain, even as these peoples obtain greater exposure to the rest of Canada.[181]

VI. Conclusion

The Canadian jury system is at once conservative and progressive. It exhibits conservative elements of an earlier age regarding judicial control over the trial process. On the other hand, there are trends in its continuing evolution that attempt to take into account the influence of modern mass media on the fairness of trial, and potential racism resulting from changes in Canada's demographic profile. The recognition that the presumption of impartiality may not always hold even when reinforced with strong judicial instructions involves an implicit recognition of twentieth century psychological understanding of human behavior. Concern about the legitimacy of the jury system in the eyes of minority groups and the small steps that have been taken to increase the actual and perceived fairness are another indication of these progressive trends. This is not to say that the system is ideal. The balancing between competing values and policies has required compromises of substance and process. The developments in Canadian case law also help to illustrate the need to view the jury system in the context of the broader legal and social systems in which it is embedded. The effectiveness of the jury system for the demographic, social, and cultural conditions of Canada's arctic and subarctic regions can be debated. Nevertheless, as a whole, the criminal jury remains a robust institution in the scheme of Canadian life and law.

[181] On Apr. 1, 1999, the Northwest Territories were divided into two regions with an evolving mandate for self-governance in many areas of community life. The effects of these changes on the jury system cannot be foretold at this time.

7 The Scottish Criminal Jury: A Very Peculiar Institution

Peter Duff*

I. Introduction

One of the benefits of the comparative study of legal institutions is that it exposes the extent to which they are shaped by contingency as well as by logic or principle. What is regarded in one jurisdiction as the only possible or acceptable way of doing something is often revealed to be pure preconception. In other words, the comparative study of law can act as a balance to the unconscious ethnocentrism often displayed in legal and political ideology. For this reason, the Scottish criminal jury is of particular interest because it embodies several unique characteristics which may seem very peculiar to those familiar with other versions of the institution. In particular, it comprises fifteen persons; its verdicts may be reached on the basis of a bare eight–seven majority; and it has a choice between three different verdicts—guilty, not guilty, and not proven—which even many Scots regard as illogical and unprincipled. The main purpose of this chapter is to describe and discuss the Scottish criminal jury. I shall also use the above peculiarities and other aspects of the institution to question various assumptions commonly held elsewhere about trial by jury.

II. Origins and Background

While the exact origins of the Scottish criminal jury are obscure, it is clear that it developed roughly in tandem with, although in a different fashion from, its English counterpart.[1] It is thought to have derived from the Norman style of government which began to permeate Scotland in the eleventh and twelfth centuries,[2] although it is likely that there was already some form of community participation in different forums for resolving disputes.[3] In succeeding centuries, other possible methods of settling

* Professor of Criminal Justice, Law Department, Aberdeen University.

[1] See Ian Douglas Willock, The Origins and Development of the Jury in Scotland 20–30 (1966). This also summarizes the English literature on the subject.

[2] See ibid., at 20–1. [3] See ibid., at 5.

conflicts, such as trial by ordeal, trial by combat, and trial by compurgation, died out and trial by jury became more common.[4] Initially, jurors were selected for their knowledge of the circumstances of the case, but by the fifteenth and sixteenth centuries a distinction began to emerge between jurors and witnesses. By the beginning of the nineteenth century, Baron Hume, regarded as the founder of modern Scottish criminal law, was able to state that jurors had long sat solely in a judicial capacity.[5]

The Scottish civil jury has a less interesting history.[6] Unlike the criminal jury, it did not emerge spontaneously. While it may have existed in embryonic form in Scottish civil procedure, the modern version was adopted from England in 1815 and consequently possesses none of the peculiarities of its criminal counterpart.[7] Instead, it is comprised of twelve persons, whose decision originally had to be unanimous but may now be reached by majority,[8] with the normal choice of two verdicts. As elsewhere, the use of the civil jury has declined rapidly in recent years, and it was recently observed that many legal practitioners now regard it as a 'somewhat exotic creature'.[9] Its use in the Sheriff Court, the lower of the civil courts, was abolished in 1980.[10] In the higher civil court, the Court of Session, some cases are in theory still tried by jury, most notably actions for damages for personal injuries and for defamation.[11] In practice, however, there is trial by judge if the parties consent or if 'special cause' is shown.[12] If an action involves complicated questions of law or difficult calculations of damages, this will usually be considered to be sufficiently 'special' to justify dispensing with the jury.[13] As a consequence of these two exceptions, the number of civil cases heard before a jury each year does not reach double figures.[14] Thus, the rest of this chapter is concerned with the jury in criminal cases.

[4] See IAN DOUGLAS WILLOCK, at 21–30. [5] See ibid., at 197.

[6] See ibid., at 247–57 (discussing the development of the Scottish civil jury).

[7] See ibid., at 256.

[8] See Administration of Justice (Scotland) Act 1933 s. 11(1). The majority verdict was not introduced to civil procedure until 1933. See ibid.

[9] Mark Lazarowicz, *Excessive Damages and Civil Jury Trial*, 1996 SCOTS LAW TIMES (NEWS), at 251–6.

[10] See Law Reform (Miscellaneous Provisions) (Scotland) Act 1980, s. 11.

[11] See Court of Session Act 1988 s. 11. S. 11 replaced its outdated counterpart in the Court of Session Act 1825 s. 11, and removed from the ambit of jury trial a large number of types of action which never in practice went to a jury.

[12] See ibid., s. 9.

[13] See, *e.g.*, Stark v. Ford (1995) S.L.T. 69, 70 (Outer House).

[14] See *Civil Juries: Abolition?*, 1988 SCOTS LAW TIMES (NEWS), at 212; see also ALAN PETERSON & T. ST. JOHN BATES, THE LEGAL SYSTEM OF SCOTLAND 33, 43 (3d ed. 1993); Lazarowicz, *supra* note 9.

III. The Incidence of Jury Trial

At the outset, it is necessary to explain the hierarchy formed by the Scottish criminal courts of first instance: the High Court of Justiciary; the Sheriff Court sitting under 'solemn' procedure (that is, with a jury); the sheriff court sitting under 'summary' procedure (that is, without a jury); and the district court.[15] The High Court comprises around twenty-five judges who act as the ultimate tribunal for criminal appeals and also form the highest civil court of first instance (the Court of Session). Criminal trials in the High Court are always heard under solemn procedure by one judge sitting with a jury. The court sits in Edinburgh but goes on circuit as required to the other main towns in Scotland. Its powers of sentencing are unlimited.

At the next level, Scotland is divided into forty-nine sheriffdoms, each of which has a sheriff court with one or more sheriffs attached to it depending upon the volume of business.[16] For example, the Glasgow Sheriff Court has more than twenty sheriffs, whereas the sheriff courts in Orkney and Shetland share one sheriff. Sheriffs, who have both civil and criminal jurisdiction, are appointed from the ranks of long-standing legal practitioners. In criminal matters, sheriffs have a dual jurisdiction. Under solemn procedure, the sheriff sits with a jury and the maximum sentence he may impose is three years' imprisonment; under summary procedure, the sheriff sits alone, and the maximum sentences available are three months, or six months in the case of a second or subsequent offence of theft or violence, or a fine of £5,000.[17] Finally, there are district courts throughout Scotland where minor criminal cases are heard under summary procedure before one or often more lay justices of the peace. The maximum penalties available to the district court are sixty days' imprisonment or a fine of £2,500.

As in most other jurisdictions, the vast bulk of cases are processed through the lower criminal courts. Of all the criminal cases dealt with by the Scottish courts in the year up to March 31, 1995, only 2.2 percent

[15] See generally Robert Wemyss Renton & Henry Hilton Brown, Criminal Procedure ¶¶ 1–08 to 1–10, 1–17 (6th ed. 1996), for a full account of the jurisdiction and powers of the Scottish criminal courts. This is the 'bible' for Scots criminal lawyers and will frequently be referred to throughout this ch.

[16] See generally ibid.

[17] See Crime and Punishment (Scotland) Act 1997 s. 13. Though not yet implemented, the Act increases these maxima to five years' imprisonment under solemn procedure and six months (or 12 months in the case of a subsequent offence of theft or violence) under summary procedure.

were heard under solemn procedure and thus offered even the possibility of trial by jury.[18] Again, as elsewhere, most accused tend to plead guilty, and only one-third of those solemn cases result in a trial.[19] Thus, of all those persons prosecuted in the Scottish criminal courts in 1994–95, fewer than 1 percent put their case to a jury.[20] In fairness, it should be noted that because of the greater propensity of those prosecuted under summary procedure to plead guilty, jury trials comprised 7.7 percent of all trials in Scotland during that period.[21] Nevertheless, this still means that 92.3 percent of contested cases were heard either by a sheriff sitting alone or by lay magistrates.[22] Further, one cannot escape the fact that fewer than one in 100 of all persons accused of crime in Scotland have their fate determined by a jury,[23] an astonishingly low proportion given the significance invested in trial by jury and the confidence in the criminal justice system which the institution generates.

A. *Jurisdiction*

There are very few crimes which may not be prosecuted under summary procedure. The High Court, where procedure is solemn, has exclusive jurisdiction over the common law crimes of murder and rape (as well as over treason and some other extremely rare offences); thus, those accused of such crimes are always entitled to trial by jury.[24] All other common law crimes, including assault, robbery, burglary, theft, and fraud, may be tried under either solemn or summary procedure and thus need not necessarily be heard before a jury.[25] For statutory crimes, the relevant legislation sometimes specifies the mode of trial, but very few offences demand solemn procedure. Examples of statutory offences requiring solemn procedure are breaches of the Official Secrets Acts, some terrorist offences and, most commonly, the crime of causing death by dangerous driving.[26] However, the great majority of statutory crimes may be prosecuted only under summary procedure, and thus a jury can never

[18] See 1994–95 Her Majesty's Scottish Office, Crown Office and Procurator Fiscal Serv. Ann. Rep. (1995) 46; see also 1996–97 Her Majesty's Scottish Office, Crown Office and Procurator Fiscal Serv. Ann. Rep. (1997) 41 (hereinafter collectively Crown Office Reports).

[19] See Crown Office Reports, *supra* note 18. [20] See ibid.

[21] See ibid. [22] See ibid. [23] See ibid.

[24] See Renton & Brown, *supra* note 15, ¶¶ 1–08 to 1–10, 1–17.

[25] See ibid.

[26] See Official Secrets Acts 1911 and 1989, s. 10; Prevention of Terrorism (Temporary Provisions) Act 1989 s. 13; Road Traffic Act 1988 s. 1; Road Traffic Offenders Act 1988 s. 9, and sched. 2 (Scot.).

be involved in such cases.[27] Finally, some statutory offences—like most common law offences—may be heard under either summary or solemn procedure.[28]

Where a crime may be tried under either solemn or summary procedure, it is the public prosecutor who decides upon the mode of trial.[29] At this stage, it should be noted that Scotland has a long-standing tradition of the public prosecution of crime.[30] Great importance has always been attached to the independence of the Scottish prosecution service and the fact that it is unaccountable to the police, the courts, the victims of crime, or the accused.[31] In each and every case, the public prosecutor is 'master of the instance',[32] which means that it is entirely up to the prosecution whether to prosecute at all, what charges to bring, where to proceed, what procedure to use, and whether to accept a plea bargain.[33] In determining the appropriate venue and whether to prosecute under solemn or summary procedure, the main factor taken into account by the prosecutor is the adequacy of the sentencing power of the court in light of the seriousness of the crime.[34] For example, a minor assault, resulting in a black eye for the victim, will almost certainly be prosecuted either in the district court, where the maximum penalty is sixty days' imprisonment, or in the sheriff court under summary procedure, where the maximum penalty is three months. Thus, such cases will not be heard before a jury. On the other hand, a serious assault with a weapon, resulting in severe injuries, will probably be prosecuted before a jury either in the sheriff court under solemn procedure, where the maximum penalty is three years, or the High Court, with its unlimited sentencing power. In this context, it should be noted that recent legislation, not yet activated, enables the sheriff's current sentencing powers under summary procedure to be doubled.[35] The effect of this is likely to be a further decrease in the number of jury trials.

[27] See Renton & Brown, *supra* note 15, ¶¶ 1–08 to 1–10, 1–17.

[28] See ibid. [29] See ibid.

[30] See Susan R. Moody & Jacqueline Tombs, Prosecution in the Public Interest 18–22 (1982); see also Julia Fionda, Public Prosecutors and Discretion: A Comparative Survey 65–95 (1995).

[31] See Moody & Tombs, *supra* note 30, at 18–22; Renton & Brown, *supra* note 15, ¶ 3.06.

[32] Moody & Tombs, *supra* note 30, at 18–22; Renton & Brown, *supra* note 15, ¶ 3.06.

[33] See Moody & Tombs, *supra* note 30, at 18–22; Renton & Brown, *supra* note 15, ¶ 3.06.

[34] See Moody & Tombs, *supra* note 30, at 18–22; Renton & Brown, *supra* note 15, ¶ 3.06.

[35] The Crime and Punishment (Scotland) Act 1997 s. 13, increases the previous maxima of three and six months to six and 12 months.

In Scotland, if a case may be heard under either solemn or summary procedure, the accused has no say in the matter.[36] This is unlike England and Wales, where, at least with respect to the large number of 'either-way' crimes, it is the defendant, and not the prosecutor, who decides whether the case will be tried in the Crown Court before a jury or in the magistrates court without a jury.[37] In the interests of efficiency and the reduction of costs, there have been several attempts in England and Wales to limit the defendant's 'right' to opt for jury trial by making various 'either-way' offences, primarily petty dishonesty and minor violence, triable only under summary procedure. However, these proposals have been criticized as an attack on citizens' civil liberties and contrary to due process.[38] In Scotland, on the other hand, the accused has never had any such 'right', and, perhaps more significantly, there has never been any pressure to grant the accused such an option.[39] Thus, what in England is often perceived to be a fundamental principle of trial by jury is revealed simply to be the product of the way in which the institution happened to develop in that jurisdiction.

Unlike in some jurisdictions, there has been very little pressure in Scotland to curtail the role of the jury in cases involving complex commercial crime.[40] The prosecutor can always avoid jury trial, of course, by choosing to proceed under summary procedure in the Sheriff Court, but in that case the maximum penalty which can be imposed is only three months' imprisonment (or six months for a second offence) and a fine of £5,000. Various suggestions to modify or remove the jury from complicated fraud trials were considered by the Thomson Committee in the 1970s, largely because there was concern in England over the issue.[41] Nonetheless, these proposals were rejected by the majority of respondents to the enquiry and found little favour with the Committee itself.[42]

[36] See Andrew Ashworth, The Criminal Process: An Evaluative Study 247–8 (1994).

[37] See Nicholas Blake, *The Case for the Jury*, *in* The Jury Under Attack 141 (Mark Findlay & Peter Duff eds., 1988).

[38] See ibid., at 145–6; see also John Jackson, *Trial by Jury and Alternative Modes of Trial*, *in* Criminal Justice in Crisis 255–63 (Mike McConville & Lee Bridges eds., 1994); Gerry Maher, *Reforming the Criminal Process: A Scottish Perspective*, *in* Criminal Justice in Crisis, *supra*, at 62–5. For analysis of this issue, see Ashworth, *supra* note 36, at 242–52.

[39] See Thomson Committee, Criminal Procedure in Scotland, Second Report, Cmnd. 6218, ¶¶ 51.46–.47 (1975).

[40] For example, in England and Hong Kong. See generally Fraud Trials Committee, Report; see also Peter Duff *et al.*, Juries: A Hong Kong Perspective 43–51 (1992); Michael Levi, *The Role of the Jury in Complex Cases*, *in* The Jury Under Attack, *supra* note 37, at 95–111.

[41] See Thomson Committee, *supra* note 39, ¶¶ 51.34–.41.

[42] See ibid.

In a recent review of trial by jury conducted by the Scottish Office, the question of juror comprehension was briefly touched upon,[43] but there was little concern that this posed a particular problem and there were no proposals for change as regards this issue.[44] This review did not even mention the trial of complex commercial crime, largely because such cases have simply not proved to be a problem in Scotland. It should be noted, however, that Scotland has not yet had any long and complex prosecutions of large-scale commercial frauds of the sort that have caused difficulties in other jurisdictions.

B. Citing and Empanelling the Jury

In Scotland, every person aged between 18 and 65 is eligible for jury service, subject to various provisos which will be dealt with shortly.[45] Until relatively recently, there was a property qualification,[46] but this was increasingly ignored in practice and finally abolished in 1980.[47] Thus, the clerk of the sheriff court now obtains a list of names randomly drawn from the electoral roll and writes to those so chosen, requesting the details necessary to establish whether they are eligible for jury service.[48] This same procedure is also applicable to any High Court trials which take place in the sheriffdom.[49]

As in other jurisdictions, various categories of persons are ineligible because of their involvement in the criminal justice system, including members of the judiciary and court staff, legal practitioners, police and prison officers, procurators fiscal and their staff, and various types of social workers involved with the juvenile justice system and probation schemes.[50] A more recent category of persons disqualified are those who have at any time been sentenced to five years' imprisonment or more, or who have received a sentence of three months and have not yet been

[43] See Scottish Office, Juries and Verdicts, 1994, ¶¶ 4.1–.4 (hereinafter Juries and Verdicts).

[44] See Scottish Office, Firm and Fair, 1994, Cmnd. 2600 (hereinafter Firm and Fair). The jury proposals are in ch. 3.

[45] See Law Reform (Miscellaneous Provisions) (Scotland) Act 1980 s. 1, sched. 1 as amended for jury ineligibility and disqualification rules.

[46] See Jurors (Scotland) Act 1825, s. 1.

[47] See Law Reform (Miscellaneous Provisions) (Scotland) Act 1980, sched. 3. A similar reform had taken place in England and Wales some 10 years earlier under the Criminal Justice Act 1972 s. 25.

[48] See Renton & Brown, *supra* note 15, ¶ 15–07.

[49] See ibid.

[50] See Law Reform (Miscellaneous Provisions) (Scotland) Act 1980, sched. 1, pt. 1.

rehabilitated under the Rehabilitation of Offenders Act of 1974.[51] An even more recently added disqualification was for anyone on bail for any offence.[52] Further, persons suffering from serious mental disorders are disqualified from jury service.[53] Finally, in order to ensure that potential jurors have a sufficient grasp of the English language, the statute stipulates that they must have been resident in the United Kingdom for any period of at least five years since attaining the age of 13.[54]

Certain other groups of persons are entitled to be excused from jury service as of right, due to the social value of their occupations. These include doctors, dentists, nurses, pharmacists, and veterinarians,members of the armed forces, ministers of religion and those in holy orders, and members of the United Kingdom and European parliaments.[55] Those who have attended for jury service within the last five years are also entitled to be excused as of right.[56] Finally, any potential jurors may seek to be excused for good reason, for example, if they are suffering from a serious long-term illness making their attendance at court impossible.[57]

As a result of the various disqualifications and exemptions, there has been recent concern that juries are not as representative of the community as they might be. These concerns led to consideration of the problem of 'juror attrition' in a general consultation paper on the jury issued by the Scottish Office.[58] The suggestion was that the procedures for selecting and contacting jurors from the electoral roll were not working as well as they might, and, more significantly, that larger proportions of potential jurors from the middle and upper socio-economic groups were disqualified or being excused from jury service.[59] A study carried out for the consultation paper demonstrated that of 11,806 members of the public in Edinburgh eligible to serve on the jury, contact was made with only 7,500 (68 percent) by the sheriff clerk.[60] Of these, 2,520 were statutorily excluded, 1,560 were excused, and, ultimately, only 3,283 (30 percent) were present in court as potential jurors.[61]

[51] See Law Reform (Miscellaneous Provisions) (Scotland) Act 1980, pt. 2.

[52] See Criminal Justice Act 1995 s. 7 (Scot.).

[53] See Law Reform (Miscellaneous Provisions) (Scotland) Act 1980, sched. 1, pt. 1.

[54] See Renton & Brown, *supra* note 15, ¶ 15–01.

[55] See Law Reform (Miscellaneous Provisions) (Scotland) Act 1980, sched. 1, pt. 3. More cynical readers might question the inclusion of the last listed group as socially useful.

[56] See ibid.

[57] See Law Reform (Miscellaneous Provisions) (Scotland) Act 1980 s. 1(5).

[58] See Juries and Verdicts, *supra* note 43, ¶ 3.35.

[59] See ibid., app. 1, at 48.

[60] See ibid., app. 1, at 49.

[61] See ibid., ¶¶ 3.27–.28.

Further, 38 percent of potential jurors from the upper socio-economic group were excused compared with 18 percent and 23 percent from the bottom two groups.[62] This paper led to proposals for reform in a government White Paper on criminal justice,[63] and legislation was then enacted to try to reduce the level of 'attrition' and make it more difficult to secure an excusal on the ground of inconvenience.[64]

Once eligibility has been established, a list of potential jurors is drawn up and the sheriff clerk summons sufficient persons when a trial is about to take place.[65] The resulting 'list of assize' is kept in the clerk's office and, upon application, a copy is available without charge to the defence.[66] Until very recently, the list of assize had to state the occupation of the prospective jurors, but following a recommendation which resulted from the recent review of the jury,[67] this requirement was removed and the list now records only jurors' names and addresses.[68] The reason for this was that while jurors' occupations were thought to form the basis for many peremptory challenges, occupation alone was not thought sufficient to justify any challenge for cause upon the abolition of peremptory challenges.[69] Therefore, there was no 'substantive reason' for jurors' occupations to be revealed.[70] The jurors are selected by ballot in open court from those potential jurors who have appeared at court in response to being cited.[71]

C. Questioning of Jurors and Challenge for Cause

There is no equivalent to the *voir dire* procedure in Scotland, a fact which might surprise some American readers. The strong opposition of the Scottish criminal justice system to any procedure of this type is well illustrated by the observations of the Appeal Court in *McCadden* v. *H. M. Advocate*:[72]

[62] See ibid., app. 1, at 51. [63] See FIRM AND FAIR, *supra* note 44, ch. 3.

[64] See Criminal Justice (Scotland) Act 1995 ss. 6, 7.

[65] See RENTON & BROWN, *supra* note 15, ¶ 15–10. [66] See ibid. ¶ 15–08.

[67] See JURIES AND VERDICTS, *supra* note 43, ¶ 3.35; see also FIRM AND FAIR, *supra* note 44, ¶ 3.11.

[68] See Criminal Justice (Scotland) Act 1995 s. 6.

[69] For a discussion of challenges, see *infra* Parts III.C–D.

[70] FIRM AND FAIR, *supra* note 44, ¶ 3.11.

[71] See RENTON & BROWN, *supra* note 15, ¶ 18.34.

[72] 1985 J.C. 98. The opinion was given on behalf of the court by the Lord Justice Clerk, Scotland's second most senior judge.

There may never be a process which eliminates the possibility of personal prejudices existing among jurors, the nearest practical one (and it is not foolproof) being possibly the 'vetting' of jurors, a system against which the law of Scotland has steadfastly closed the doors. Evidence of how it is used and abused in countries in which it is operated only tends to confirm the wisdom of that decision.[73]

The court went on to observe that it should not be 'lightly assumed' that jurors will pursue their prejudices in defiance of their oath and the directions of the judge.[74] On a more practical note, the court pointed out that the broad base from which jurors are drawn means that any prejudices and biases tend to cancel each other out and, further, that the majority verdict, which means a bare eight-to-seven vote either way suffices, ensures that it is unlikely that one prejudiced juror can affect the outcome of the case.[75]

As a consequence, there may be no general questioning of potential jurors by the judge or by any of the parties to the case. The total antipathy of the Scottish legal system to any form of *voir dire* is also illustrated in *M.* v. *H. M. Advocate.*[76] This case involved terrorist offences which had spilled over from Northern Ireland to Scotland.[77] At the request of one of the defence counsel, potential jurors were asked by the judge whether they had lost any near relatives in the religious and political disturbances in Northern Ireland which might affect their ability to give unbiased consideration to the issues involved.[78] As it happens, no jurors declared themselves to be in this position.[79] During the course of an appeal based on other grounds, however, the Appeal Court stated that it did not approve of this procedure:

[T]here should be no general questioning . . . of persons cited for possible jury service to ascertain whether any of them could or should be excused from jury service in a particular trial. . . . The essence of the system of trial by jury is that it consists of fifteen individuals chosen at random from amongst those who are cited for possible service.[80]

Further, most views presented to the Thomson Committee on Criminal Procedure, which reported shortly after the above case, were also opposed to any kind of investigation of jurors' attitudes.[81]

[73] 1985 J.C. 98, at 102. [74] Ibid. [75] See *infra* text accompanying note 131.

[76] 1974 S.L.T. (Notes) 25 (H.C.J.). These observations were made by the Lord Justice General, Scotland's most senior judge, in the course of giving the court's opinion.

[77] See ibid. [78] See ibid. [79] See ibid. [80] Ibid.

[81] See Thomson Committee, *supra* note 39, ¶ 51.27.

Challenges for cause are permissible, but because such challenges are very rare, no clear procedure has evolved for dealing with them.[82] It has always been regarded as sufficient cause for challenge if a potential juror is clearly disabled in some way, for example, if he is insane, deaf, dumb, or blind,[83] but further development of this area of law has obviously been severely limited by the attitude to questioning jurors. It is difficult to challenge a juror for cause if one has no information about that juror beyond a name and address or, formerly, an occupation. Further, it has been held that:

> [i]t is not a sufficient cause for a juror to be excused that he is of a particular race, religion, or political belief or occupation, or indeed that the juror might or might not feel prejudice one way or the other towards the crime itself or to the background against which the crime has been committed.[84]

On the other hand, it is regarded as sufficient cause if a potential juror has a personal connection with one of the parties to the case or has personal knowledge of the facts.[85] In order to ensure that such jurors are identified, before the case is called, the clerk tells potential jurors the names of the accused, the complainant, and anyone else named in the indictment and indicates that if they know any of these persons, they should make this known.[86] Once the jury has been empanelled, the judge may remind the jurors that if they know any of the parties involved or feel that there is any reason why they should not serve on the jury, they should make this known to the court immediately.[87]

In essence, however, it can be seen that the philosophy underlying jury selection in Scotland, as well as in England and Wales, is very different from that governing the process in the United States. In Scotland, there is a very strong view that the accused, and the prosecutor, must simply accept the jurors who emerge randomly from the selection process. The feeling is that the prejudices and biases of the various individuals comprising the jury will assume little significance in the dynamic of group decision making, particularly when a bare majority suffices. There is a lot to be said for this point of view. The complete lack of information about prospective jurors means that no attempt can be made by either side to 'stack' the jury in its favour. Further, the simplicity of the selection procedure helps to ensure that the jury really does represent the

[82] See ibid., ¶ 51.23. [83] See Renton & Brown, *supra* note 15, ¶ 18.36.
[84] See M. v. H. M. Advocate (1974) S.L.T. (Notes) 25 (H.C.J.).
[85] See Pullar v. H. M. Advocate (1993) J.C. 126, 134–5 (1993).
[86] See ibid., at 134. [87] See ibid., at 135.

community, although this of course means that any prejudices generally held in the community are likely to be replicated in the jury room. In practical terms, the absence of any kind of *voir dire* procedure also renders trial by jury quicker and cheaper than on the other side of the Atlantic.

In conclusion, it is once again significant that what is perceived to be an integral part of the institution of trial by jury in one group of related jurisdictions is regarded with abhorrence in a different group of jurisdictions. It is clear that these views are shaped by specific histories and cultures rather than deriving logically and necessarily from the principles which support trial by jury.

D. Peremptory Challenge

In Scotland, the right of peremptory challenge has gradually disappeared. The position was formalized in the early nineteenth century when the accused was granted five peremptory challenges,[88] but the number was reduced to three in 1980,[89] and abolished altogether in 1995.[90] Three reasons have been cited to justify this whittling away of the peremptory challenge. First, it was sometimes argued that such challenges increased the overall inconvenience to the public of jury service because additional jurors had to be cited to cater for the possibility of such challenges, particularly in cases involving several accused.[91] Secondly, it was frequently alleged that good citizens, who were willingly attempting to fulfil their civic duty, were puzzled, embarrassed, or even angered by being challenged in open court for reasons they simply did not understand.[92] Both these arguments have some validity. The third and most influential argument, which clinched the abolition of the peremptory challenge, was the allegation that this opportunity was frequently 'abused' by the defence in an attempt to secure a jury which was less likely to convict.[93] It was suggested that prospective jurors were challenged on the basis of sex, occupation, or even dress, the wearing of a suit and tie being regarded as fatal to one's chances of making the jury

[88] See Jurors (Scotland) Act 1825 s. 16; Willock, *supra* note 1, at 193. However, Albert V. Sheehan, Criminal Procedure ¶ 1.42 (1990), states that the right of peremptory challenge was formalized in the Jurors in Criminal Trials (Scotland) Act 1822 s. 1. The last manifestation of this right was in the Criminal Procedure (Scotland) Act 1975 s. 130.

[89] See Criminal Justice (Scotland) Act 1980 s. 23.

[90] See Criminal Justice (Scotland) Act 1995 s. 8.

[91] See Juries and Verdicts, *supra* note 43, ¶¶ 3.28–.34.

[92] See ibid. [93] See ibid.

panel.[94] It was also claimed that in cases of fraud or financial crime, prospective jurors who seemed likely to be able to understand the facts in the case—for example, accountants or bankers—were routinely challenged.[95] This argument is based upon two assumptions, and it is worth examining each of these in turn.

First, there is the claim that defence solicitors and advocates regularly 'abused' their peremptory challenges in an attempt to secure the type of jury they wanted.[96] Assuming that this does amount to 'abuse', which of course might well be contested, it is fair to say that there is much anecdotal evidence to support this charge,[97] although there is virtually nothing in the way of any firm data about the extent and nature of the phenomenon. The government's recent consultation paper admitted as much, stating that 'there is no direct evidence of whether and on what scale such abuse occurs', but added that 'the procedure clearly has the potential for abuse'.[98] Of the 994 jurors in the attrition study who were balloted, 6 percent were challenged, 5 percent by the defence, and 1 percent by the Crown, and while there was no evidence of any sexual bias in the use of the challenge, it did seem that potential jurors from the upper socio-economic groups were more likely to be challenged by the defence.[99] It should be noted, however, that the numbers involved were very small. Only forty-eight jurors from the upper socio-economic group were balloted, eight of whom were challenged (17 percent) as against 306 jurors from the next highest socio-economic group, of whom 8 percent were challenged.[100] This hardly seems sufficiently convincing evidence to justify the abolition of a procedure which had formed part of trial by jury for almost 200 years.

The second step in the argument is that the 'abuse' of the peremptory challenges led to an increased likelihood of acquittal.[101] There is no evidence to support this claim. Such an argument assumes that Scottish defence practitioners, with virtually no information to go on, were successful in predicting the likely reactions of potential jurors to particular cases. Evidence from other jurisdictions suggests that even where there is much more information available about prospective jurors, it is

[94] See ibid. ¶ 3.30.

[95] See ibid.; see also THOMSON COMMITTEE, *supra* note 39, ¶ 51.29.

[96] See JURIES AND VERDICTS, *supra* note 43, ¶¶ 3.28–.34.

[97] See ibid.

[98] Ibid., ¶ 3.31.

[99] See ibid., app. 1, ¶ 10.4, tbl. 10. Of course, this might simply mean that in some cases men were routinely challenged, whereas in others, it was women that were treated in this way, and that these opposing trends cancelled each other out.

[100] See ibid.

[101] See ibid., ¶ 3.30.

extremely difficult for the lawyers involved to predict their behaviour.[102] Further, the argument assumes that, even if Scottish practitioners did have some success, three challenges (or previously five) were enough to alter the dynamics of a jury of fifteen which may reach a verdict on the basis of a simple majority. Clearly, the role of any individual juror can be much more crucial where there is a requirement of unanimity or some sort of weighted majority. Significantly, some Home Office research carried out in England and Wales before the abolition of the peremptory challenge there on similar unsatisfactory grounds[103] revealed that the acquittal rate was no higher in cases where the challenge had been used than in cases where it had not.[104]

Therefore, the reasons given for the abolition of the peremptory challenge in Scotland were unsatisfactory. There was little evidence that it was being 'abused' and no evidence whatsoever that this 'abuse' had any effect on the outcome of cases. This is regrettable because, in my view, there is a perfectly respectable argument of principle which could have been used against the peremptory challenge. Quite simply, the jury in Scotland is clearly meant to be fifteen people chosen at random from the community, and there is no justification for either side to attempt to alter its composition except where there are grounds for challenge for cause. Furthermore, the existence of the bare majority verdict means that the presence of one biased juror is very unlikely to make any difference to the outcome of the case, unlike the position where there is a requirement of unanimity. Yet this type of argument was rarely advanced by those responsible for the demise of the peremptory challenge in Scotland. The right thing was done for the wrong reasons.

Finally, it is interesting to note that the disappearance of the peremptory challenge aroused little reaction in Scotland, whereas in England, its gradual demise caused an outcry and was often portrayed as a serious attack upon the civil liberties of defendants.[105] Again, what was often

[102] See VALERIE P. HANS & NEIL VIDMAR, JUDGING THE JURY 76–8 (1986); see also SEAN ENRIGHT & JAMES MORTON, TAKING LIBERTIES: THE CRIMINAL JURY IN THE 1990s, at 63–7 (1990).

[103] See Criminal Justice (Scotland) Act 1988 s. 118. See also ENRIGHT & MORTON, *supra* note 102, ch. 4, for details.

[104] See Julie Vennard & David Riley, *The Use of the Peremptory Challenge and Stand by of Jurors and Their Relationship to Trial Outcome* [1988] CRIM. L. REV. 731–8.

[105] See Sean Enright, *Reviving the Challenge for Cause* (1989) 139 NEW L.J. 9–10, 19; see also TONY GIFFORD, WHERE'S THE JUSTICE: A MANIFESTO FOR LAW REFORM 50–1 (1986); James Gobert, *The Peremptory Challenge—An Obituary* [1989] CRIM. L. REV. 528–38; E. P. Thompson, *Subduing the Jury*, LONDON REVIEW OF BOOKS, Dec. 4, 1986, at 7–9 & Dec. 18, 1986, at 12–13.

regarded as a fundamental aspect of jury trial in England appears to have been discarded quite easily in Scotland. To some extent, this might be explained by the existence of the requirement for a ten-to-two majority in England, but it probably also reflects the differing ideologies which simply happen to have grown up around the same institution, without much basis for their differences in terms of strict logic.

E. Publicity Before and During the Trial

Essentially, all that may appear in the media about a criminal prosecution is a fair and accurate report of legal proceedings, published contemporaneously and in good faith. The Scottish judiciary takes a very severe attitude toward any potentially prejudicial publicity before or during the trial.[106] While the position is now primarily governed by legislation,[107] it is useful to examine the common law position first. One recent example will suffice to demonstrate the stringent approach invariably adopted by the Scottish courts. In *Muir* v. *British Broadcasting Corporation*, the BBC was about to broadcast an update of an earlier programme about prisoners being beaten by prison officers in Glasgow's Barlinnie prison.[108] The programme reported a prison doctor's view that a particular individual's injuries were consistent with his having been assaulted by guards.[109] The report further revealed that the doctor had been dismissed from the prison service but was being backed by the British Medical Association, and that the European Committee for the Prevention of Torture also believed the prisoner's injuries were consistent with his allegations of mistreatment.[110] The prison doctor was to be a witness in a trial of three prison officers for assaulting inmates at Barlinnie which was due to start the following month. The charges did not relate to the prisoner featured in the programme, and there was no reference to the accused in the programme nor to the proceedings against them. Nevertheless, on application by the three accused, the High Court banned the programme because there was a 'distinct risk that at least one out of the fifteen jurors may get the impression from this programme that Doctor Danson was a witness of considerable credit whose views should be taken to be of great importance'.[111] The Court observed that the test to be applied in such cases is whether there is 'more than minimal

[106] For a discussion of contempt of court in Scotland, see ERIC M. CLIVE *ET AL.*, SCOTS LAW FOR JOURNALISTS 100–31 (5th ed. 1988).

[107] See Contempt of Court Act 1981 s. 4.

[108] 1997 S.L.T. 425 (H.C.J.).

[109] See ibid.

[110] See ibid.

[111] Ibid., at 427–8.

risk of prejudice'.[112] Thus, either the accused or the Crown may apply to prevent media coverage of not only their own case, but of a much broader range of subjects which might impinge incidentally upon the forthcoming trial.

In terms of statute, the Contempt of Court Act 1981 makes it an offence of strict liability to publish, including broadcast, anything which creates a 'substantial risk' that the course of justice in any 'active' proceedings will be 'seriously impeded or prejudiced'.[113] This legislation covers Scotland, England, and Wales, but, as Alistair J. Bonnington states, 'its application in Scotland is so starkly different from that in England that it is difficult to believe that the two jurisdictions are dealing with the same statutory provisions'.[114] First, the Lord Advocate, Scotland's senior law officer, is much more likely than his English counterpart, the Attorney General, to act when there has been prejudicial publicity.[115] Secondly, the Scottish courts have interpreted the provision that there must be a 'substantial risk' to mean that there must be 'some risk, greater than a minimal one', of prejudice.[116] This rather odd interpretation of the statutory formula means that it is relatively easy in Scotland to allege contempt.[117] Finally, in Scotland, the accused himself may bring proceedings under the Act, whereas in England the Attorney General must either bring or consent to any such proceedings.[118]

Bonnington demonstrates the contrasting approaches adopted in Scotland and England with reference to a recent English case, where the Attorney General refused to take action over what was undoubtedly prejudicial reporting of a trial, on the ground that he thought that contempt proceedings were unlikely to succeed.[119] Bonnington observes that in Scotland the Lord Advocate would undoubtedly have prosecuted in such a case, and further, that if he had not, the accused could have taken action.[120] Bonnington's predicted result of such proceedings in Scotland was that 'there is little doubt that all newspapers would have been convicted and would have suffered substantial fines—in the case of the *Sun*[121]

[112] 1997 S.L.T., at 427.

[113] Contempt of Court Act 1981 s. 2.

[114] Alistair J. Bonnington, *Press and Prejudice* (1995) 145 New L.J. 1623.

[115] See ibid.

[116] H. M. Advocate v. Caledonian Newspapers Ltd. (1995) S.L.T. 926, 930.

[117] See generally Clive *et al*, *supra* note 106, at 103, who thought that this was a 'new and important' test because it clarified a previously vague standard. However, as events show, this view proved to be unduly optimistic.

[118] See Contempt of Court Act 1981 s. 7. This difference reflects the common law position in each of the jurisdictions.

[119] See Bonnington, *supra* note 114, at 1623.

[120] See ibid.

[121] The most popular tabloid newspaper in the United Kingdom.

editor, a jail sentence would have been quite likely'.[122] In summary, therefore, the strict approach of the Scottish judiciary to the possibility of prejudicial reporting has meant that the media have rarely impinged upon jury trial in Scotland. It should be remembered that, unlike in the United States, in Scotland there is no constitutional right to freedom of expression or freedom of information to counter-balance the strict laws of contempt.

Despite their draconian attitude toward potentially prejudicial publicity, Scottish judges have not looked sympathetically upon claims made by the accused about the effects of adverse publicity where this has unfortunately occurred. Bonnington observes that there has never been a successful application to prevent a trial proceeding because of prejudicial pretrial publicity, nor a successful appeal against conviction based on the grounds of prejudicial publicity.[123] He cites in illustration of this claim the rather contradictory case of *Stuurman* v. *H.M. Advocate*,[124] where the court imposed large fines on the media for 'causing "the greatest risk of prejudice"',[125] and yet only a few weeks later decided that the accused could nevertheless receive a fair trial.[126] Another interesting case is *H.* v. *Sweeney*,[127] where the trial proceeded despite overwhelming publicity, including the resignation of the Solicitor General,[128] the publication of alleged confessions by the accused, and 'no fewer than 160 articles' in the media.[129] The High Court's view was that the admittedly prejudicial coverage of the case was outweighed by the public interest in the prosecution of serious crime, the gap of several months before the trial was to commence, and the beneficial effect upon the jury of a careful direction by the judge not to be swayed by the publicity.[130]

F. *The Number of Jurors*

The Scottish criminal jury comprises fifteen persons. In the early days of jury trial, the number of jurors was not fixed, although there was always a preference for an odd number because of the existence of the

[122] Bonnington, *supra* note 114, at 1623. [123] See ibid.
[124] See ibid. (relying generally on *Stuurman*, 1980 J.C. 111, 111–13, 121).
[125] Ibid. [126] See ibid.
[127] 1983 S.L.T. 48, 55–7 (H.C.J.) (the Lord Justice-General).
[128] Scotland's second most senior law officer.
[129] See *Sweeney*, 1983 S.L.T. at 56; see also ROSS HARPER & ARNOT MCWHINNIE, THE GLASGOW RAPE CASE 139–42 (1983).
[130] See *Sweeney*, 1983 S.L.T. at 56–7.

majority verdict.[131] By the end of the sixteenth century, the jury virtually always comprised fifteen persons. This practice was eventually confirmed implicitly in the Jurors (Scotland) Act 1825.[132] In the 1970s, the Thomson Committee considered the possibility of a smaller jury.[133] Its primary concern was whether it was necessary to inconvenience quite so many members of the public, observing that the Scottish civil jury, as well as criminal juries in other jurisdictions, operated with fewer jurors.[134] Although the committee was not impressed with the argument that a slightly smaller jury was less likely to provide a representative cross-section of the population, dismissing this as 'speculative',[135] it nonetheless concluded that the number of jurors should be reduced to twelve, with a simple majority of seven votes being necessary for a guilty verdict.[136] However, this recommendation was not acted upon. The more recent Scottish Office review also raised the question of unnecessary inconvenience to citizens and asked for views on the reduction of the size of the jury to eleven, twelve, or thirteen persons.[137] Most of those who responded were not in favour of any change and thus the number of jurors was left at fifteen.[138] Both the Thomson Committee and the Scottish Office review emphasized that the size of the jury could not be looked at in isolation and was bound up with the majority required for a verdict and the three verdict system.[139] Consequently, I shall return to the number of jurors when these issues are discussed below.

G. Management of the Jury

After the jury has taken the oath, there must be no communication on the subject of the trial between a juror and non-juror.[140] If this rule is broken, the trial is not necessarily abandoned, nor is any conviction

[131] See Willock, *supra* note 1, at 184–90.

[132] Ss. 7, 17 (Scot.); *see* Willock, *supra* note 1, at 189.

[133] See Thomson Committee, *supra* note 39, ¶ 51.12. The Committee stressed that this recommendation was dependent upon the retention of the three verdict system. For a discussion of this, see *infra* Part III.I.

[134] See Thomson Committee, *supra* note 39, ¶ 51.08.

[135] Ibid., ¶ 51.11.

[136] See ibid., ¶ 51.13.

[137] See Juries and Verdicts, *supra* note 43, ¶¶ 5.1.–.4.

[138] See Firm and Fair, *supra* note 44, ¶¶ 3.20, 3.21.

[139] See Juries and Verdicts, *supra* note 43, ¶¶ 5.1–.4; Thomson Committee, *supra* note 39, ¶ 51.12.

[140] The following section is based very closely on Renton & Brown, *supra* note 15, ¶¶ 18.42–.45, where all the necessary citation of the statutory provisions and cases will be found.

necessarily quashed. The consequences of the infringement depend very much on the circumstances, in particular the severity of the breach and its potential to prejudice the trial. If the infringement is minor, it may not be necessary to excuse the juror and a direction by the judge to the jury may suffice. Alternatively, the juror may be excused and the trial may continue. However, if the breach is particularly serious and there is a danger that it may prejudice the whole jury, it may well be necessary to abandon the trial. Where a trial is adjourned overnight, the jury is not secluded (that is, sequestered) except in the most exceptional of cases. Once the verdict is being considered the matter is entirely different, and the jury must be secluded.[141]

If a juror becomes ill during a trial or is excused for some other reason, the trial may continue provided that there are not fewer than twelve jurors remaining.[142] In such cases, a majority of eight jurors is still required to return a guilty verdict; otherwise the result must be acquittal.[143] There is no provision in Scotland for alternate jurors. Such a provision has not as yet proved necessary because trials rarely last for more than a couple of days and up to three jurors may be lost without the trial having to be abandoned.[144]

It is worth noting that in Scotland there are no opening statements by the lawyers. Instead, jurors are given a copy of the indictment, which comprises a narrative of the essence of the case against the accused.[145] Immediately after the prosecution has presented all its witnesses, the defence may submit that there is no case to answer. The arguments are heard outside the presence of the jury and if the submission succeeds, the judge, rather than the jury, acquits the accused. If the submission is unsuccessful, the case simply continues.[146] In making this decision, the judge should not assess the credibility or reliability of the evidence since these are jury matters; he should simply determine whether the evidence, if accepted, would be sufficient in law for conviction.[147] It is worth noting that this procedure was unknown in Scotland until it was imported from England in 1980. As well as the statutory power to withdraw the case from the jury

[141] See *infra* notes 151, 152 and accompanying text.

[142] See Renton & Brown, *supra* note 15, ¶¶ 18.42–.45.

[143] See ibid. [144] See ibid. [145] See ibid.

[146] See Criminal Procedure (Scotland) Act 1995 s. 97.

[147] The Scottish requirement that the prosecution evidence must be corroborated is of particular importance in this context. For instance, it might be that the evidence of the victim, although totally convincing, is not corroborated by any evidence from another source, in which case the judge would be bound to accede to the defence application that there is no case to answer and acquit the accused.

at the close of the prosecution case, the judge also has a common law power, which he may exercise on application or of his own volition, to hold that there is insufficient evidence to allow the case to go to the jury. However, he may do this only after all the evidence has been heard and the closing speeches made. In this eventuality, the judge cannot acquit the accused, but must direct the jury to return a verdict of not guilty.[148]

The Sutherland Committee recently raised the question whether the judge should be empowered to withdraw a case from the jury or to direct the acquittal 'if he believes [the jury] could not reasonably reach a guilty verdict'; the Committee suggested that this matter, which was peripheral to its remit, should be given further consideration.[149] It added nothing further, but the proposal seems to imply that the judge should make some assessment of the reliability and credibility of the evidence. If so, this is a rather revolutionary proposal because it seems to involve a degree of usurpation by the judge of the jury's role. For example, if, in the judge's opinion, no jury could reasonably believe the main prosecution witness, and there is insufficient other evidence to convict, then the judge should presumably withdraw the case from the jury. As yet, the government has not taken this matter up, and it seems probable that the proposal will simply be forgotten, largely because of its radical nature.

At the end of the trial, the prosecutor and defence briefly address the jury, and then the judge directs the jury as to the law. The judge is not required to summarize the evidence, as he is in some jurisdictions, but particularly in a long or complicated trial, he would normally remind the jury of the main points.[150] When the jury retires to consider its verdict, the clerk of court, acting in practice through a court officer, encloses the jurors in a room by themselves.[151] If necessary, the jury must be secluded in overnight accommodation.[152] Apart from instructions by the judge in connection with administrative matters—for example, food and accommodation or emergencies—no one may visit the jury room, nor may any juror leave it, except where further directions are sought or given or where the jury asks to examine a production.[153] The legislation

[148] See Kent v. H. M. Advocate (1950) J.C. 38, 39; see also Renton & Brown, *supra* note 15, ¶ 18–76.

[149] Sutherland Committee on Criminal Appeals and Miscarriages of Justice Procedures, 1996, Cmnd. 3245, at 19, 20 (hereinafter Criminal Appeals). Its deliberations will be further discussed below in Part III.J.

[150] See Shepherd v. H. M. Advocate (1997) S.L.T. 525, 528 (H.C.J.).

[151] See Criminal Procedure (Scotland) Act 1995 s. 99.

[152] See Thomson v. H. M. Advocate (1998) S.L.T. 364, 365–6 (H.C.J.).

[153] See Criminal Procedure (Scotland) Act 1995 s. 99.

provides that any contravention of these provisions shall lead to the acquittal of the accused.[154]

Under the Contempt of Court Act 1981, which applies both in Scotland and south of the border, it is contempt for anyone to obtain, disclose, or solicit any particulars of the deliberations in the jury room.[155] Thus, the phenomenon in the United States of jurors revealing the secrets of the jury room, sometimes for large sums of money, cannot happen in Great Britain. This rigorous approach was implemented in 1981 following revelations in a political weekly by a juror from the trial of a prominent politician for conspiracy to murder, and the subsequent failure of an attempt to prosecute the magazine for contempt.[156] The major disadvantage of the legislation is that it makes serious research into juries' reasons for their verdicts virtually impossible. For this reason, the recent English Royal Commission on Criminal Justice recommended that the Act be amended to allow research into the process by which jurors reach decisions.[157] This proposal is still under consideration by the government.[158]

H. *The Majority Verdict*

The Scottish criminal jury may return a verdict, whether for conviction or acquittal, on the basis of a bare majority of eight to seven.[159] Consequently, there is no such thing as a hung jury; every trial produces a verdict. The jury should be directed by the judge that eight votes are necessary for conviction, and it should not be told to try for unanimity before returning a majority verdict.[160] In returning the jury's verdict, the foreman must state, or be asked, whether it is unanimous or by majority, but should not be asked for the size of the majority.[161] The Thomson Committee considered the possibility that the actual numbers of those voting for each of the three verdicts should be announced in open court in order to prevent mistakes.[162] Because it infringed upon the privacy of

[154] See ibid. [155] Contempt of Court Act 1981 s. 8(c)(1).

[156] See Attorney-General v. New Statesman and Nation Publ'g Co. [1980] 1 All E.R. 644, 646–7, 650 (holding that the Attorney General's contempt of court argument was not justified in this particular instance).

[157] See English Royal Commission on Criminal Justice Report, 1993, Cmnd. 2263, at 2.

[158] See Firm and Fair, *supra* note 44, ¶ 3.14; see also Criminal Appeals, *supra* note 149, ¶ 3.7.

[159] See Renton & Brown, *supra* note 15, ¶ 18–79. [160] See ibid.

[161] See Criminal Procedure (Scotland) Act 1995 s. 100(1).

[162] See Thomson Committee, *supra* note 39, ¶¶ 51.51–.56.

the jury room, this option did not find favour with the committee. However, the Committee suggested that the judge might be encouraged to enquire into the voting in order to satisfy himself that the verdict was correct.[163] More recently, in *McCadden* v. *H.M. Advocate*, the Lord Justice Clerk suggested that the jurors ought to be asked how many of them voted guilty,[164] but this was disregarded in practice and disapproved in the subsequent case of *Pullar*.[165] Thus, the size of the majority remains a mystery in all cases.

In his history of the Scottish jury, Willock observes that the verdict of the Scottish jury seems always to have been reached by majority vote.[166] He suggests that in medieval times, verdicts were reached by taking the sense of the meeting, or the feeling of the community, and that dissent was tolerated but not thought to be of much importance.[167] Thus, by midway through the sixteenth century, the majority verdict had become formally established as an integral part of trial by jury, encouraging the use of an odd number of jurors, and it also had become established that a majority of one was sufficient to determine the verdict.[168] In contrast, a firm rule had developed in England by the middle of the fourteenth century, remaining unaltered until very recently, that the verdict must be unanimous.[169]

The adequacy of a bare majority of eight to seven is obviously open to question. This emerges very starkly when one considers that until the abolition of capital punishment in the early 1960s, it was theoretically possible for someone to be executed on the basis of this majority. In essence, is it really safe to convict someone if seven out of fifteen jurors think that the case has not been satisfactorily proven? If almost half of the jurors are not convinced of the accused's guilt, is this not evidence in itself that the case has not been proven beyond reasonable doubt? These questions have been ably analysed by Gerry Maher, who argues that the rule of unanimity is not always necessary to show that the principle of proof beyond reasonable doubt is being taken seriously.[170] In his view, one must take into account other means by which the criminal process attempts to ensure proof of guilt at a level of practical certainty. The Scottish system, for instance, demands corroboration of the Crown

[163] See THOMSON COMMITTEE, *supra* note 39. [164] 1985 J.C. 98, 103.
[165] Pullar v. H. M. Advocate (1993) J.C. 126, 136–7.
[166] See WILLOCK, *supra* note 1, at 226. [167] See ibid.
[168] See ibid. [169] See *infra* text accompanying note 173.
[170] See Gerry Maher, *The Verdict of the Jury*, *in* THE JURY UNDER ATTACK, *supra* note 37, at 45–52.

case and provides the protection of the not proven verdict.[171] Nevertheless, Maher does question whether conviction by a simple majority does in fact give sufficient weight to the principle of requiring proof beyond reasonable doubt.[172]

Clearly, a practical advantage of the Scottish position is that there is no such thing as a hung trial. However, a less obvious point is made by Maher in his critique of the English position. The law in England now requires a majority of ten to two, whether for conviction or acquittal.[173] Where the jury splits nine to three, there will be a retrial.[174] As Maher observes, this does not sit comfortably with the presumption of innocence or with the associated principle of double jeopardy.[175] The prosecution has had its chance to prove the accused's guilt and has failed; surely the presumption of innocence means that the accused is entitled to be acquitted. As Maher puts it, '[t]he presumption of innocence therefore closes the logical space between proof of guilt and proof of innocence', and thus where the verdict is not one of guilt, the result must be acquittal rather than a retrial.[176] This criticism cannot be levelled at the Scottish position.

The majority verdict has been considered on several occasions in recent years. The Thomson Committee canvassed, without much enthusiasm, the possibility that the ratio required for a guilty verdict should be two to one, that is, ten to five or, if the size of the jury were reduced, eight to four, but the overwhelming weight of submissions was in favour of retaining the bare majority.[177] Ultimately, only one member of the Committee dissented from this view, the remainder arguing that a 'weighted' majority was unnecessary in view of other safeguards for the protection of the innocent. The Committee suggested that if its recommendation to reduce the size of the jury to twelve persons were adopted, a seven-to-five majority should be required for conviction and an even split of six to six should lead to acquittal.[178] The recent Scottish Office review also sought reaction to a possible increase in the number required for conviction, particularly if the three verdict system were to be abolished.[179] It cited the arguments both for and against the simple majority, while itself expressing no opinion on the matter.[180] The government

[171] See *infra* Part III.I. [172] See Maher, *supra* note 170, at 45–52.
[173] See ibid., at 43. [174] See ibid. [175] See ibid., at 50–2.
[176] Ibid., at 50. [177] See Thomson Committee, *supra* note 39, ¶¶ 51.06–.07.
[178] See ibid., ¶ 51.12. This would not be symmetrical and consequently avoids the practical and theoretical difficulties often posed by the 'weighted' majority verdict.
[179] See Juries and Verdicts, *supra* note 43, ch. 6.
[180] See ibid.

announced that most respondents to this review favoured the straightforward majority, and given that the size of the jury was to remain at fifteen and the three verdict system was to be retained, there was no case for changing the existing position.[181]

Finally, it is worth noting that the abandonment of the unanimity rule in England and its replacement with the requirement of a ten-to-two majority[182] provoked a great deal of vehement protest. For instance, M. D. A. Freeman claimed that 'the concept of a majority verdict strikes at the root of the fundamental principle of English law that guilt must be proved beyond reasonable doubt'.[183] Yet in Scotland, which is ruled by the same government and has a very similar culture, the principle that guilt must be proved beyond reasonable doubt has happily coexisted with the majority verdict for centuries. Further, there are several other jurisdictions where the majority verdict is not thought to prejudice the presumption of innocence, a fact which appears to be ignored by the English critics of the abandonment of the unanimity rule.

I. The Three Verdict System

Undoubtedly the most peculiar aspect of the Scottish system of trial by jury is that it allows the jury in criminal trials a choice of three verdicts: guilty, not proven, and not guilty. This phenomenon was the result of an historical accident, but it has now formed part of the Scottish criminal justice system for over 250 years.[184] The verdicts of guilty and not guilty are self-explanatory, but the intermediate verdict of 'not proven' requires some elucidation. While there is no common law or statutory definition of 'not proven', the vital point is that it has exactly the same effect as a not guilty verdict; it counts as an acquittal.[185] The difference is that the

[181] See FIRM AND FAIR, *supra* note 44, ¶ 3.20.

[182] See Criminal Justice Act 1967 s. 13.

[183] M. D. A. Freeman, *The Jury on Trial* (1981) 34 CURRENT LEGAL PROBS. 65, 69; see also ENRIGHT & MORTON, *supra* note 102, at 75–6; Blake, *supra* note 37, at 143.

[184] See WILLOCK, *supra* note 1, at 217–25.

[185] As explained above, where the jury is not unanimous, there must be at least eight votes for conviction in order to convict the accused, and the judge directs the jury to this effect. Where the votes for acquittal are split, the majority of such votes dictates whether the verdict is one of not guilty or not proven, an even split resulting in the latter verdict. See RENTON & BROWN, *supra* note 15, ¶ 18–90. This seems to indicate that if the jury is unsure which verdict to deliver, the judge should enquire into the actual figures, which is difficult to reconcile with the principle that no such enquiry should be made. See also McCadden v. H. M. Advocate (1985) J.C. 98, 103; Pullar v. H. M. Advocate (1993) J.C. 126, 136–7.

verdict of 'not guilty' is thought to mean that the accused definitely did not commit the crime, that is, it is a positive declaration of innocence, whereas the verdict of 'not proven' is thought to imply solely that the accused's guilt has not been conclusively demonstrated.[186] As a result of this uncertainty, the Court of Appeal has discouraged judges from attempting to direct jurors on the difference between not proven and not guilty, although they must be informed of the three verdicts available to them.[187] It has also been held that it is not necessary to tell jurors that not proven is a verdict of acquittal,[188] presumably because they are always told that at least eight votes of guilty are required for conviction and thus can work out the consequences of a not proven verdict for themselves.

Whatever its meaning, there is no doubt that the not proven verdict is used fairly frequently by the Scottish courts. Around one-third of all jury acquittals are the product of the not proven verdict, while the equivalent in nonjury trials is around one-fifth.[189] The verdict has attracted much criticism over the years, primarily on the ground of its lack of logic. It is argued, quite simply, that if the Crown cannot prove its case beyond reasonable doubt, the only possible verdict should be not guilty. That is dictated by the presumption of innocence, and therefore there is no place for a 'second class' acquittal.[190] Debate has tended to focus around two main arguments which are usually put forth in favour of the three verdict system.[191]

First, it is claimed that the jury may well not be convinced of the accused's innocence. Of particular significance here is the Scottish rule that the prosecution case must be corroborated.[192] It is argued that there are many cases where one witness is completely believed, but there is insufficient corroborating evidence to allow the jury, or the judge in a nonjury trial, to convict, although they may be fairly certain that the accused is indeed guilty.[193] This might be particularly so with regard to the victim of a sexual assault. The Scottish Office paper supports this

[186] See Juries and Verdicts, *supra* note 43, at 29.

[187] See McDonald v. H. M. Advocate (1989) S.L.T. 289, 299 (H.C.J.).

[188] See McRae v. H. M. Advocate (1990) J.C. 28, 28–9.

[189] See Juries and Verdicts, *supra* note 43, at 27–8. Nevertheless, four-tenths of not proven verdicts are returned in nonjury trials as a result of the far greater number of such trials. See ibid., at 28, tbls. 1, 2.

[190] See Thomson Committee, *supra* note 39, ¶ 51.05.

[191] See ibid., ¶ 51.05; see also Juries and Verdicts, *supra* note 43, ch. 10.

[192] See Renton & Brown, *supra* note 15, ¶ 24–69.

[193] See Juries and Verdicts, *supra* note 43, ch. 10.

claim by demonstrating that the not proven verdict comprised 'a slightly higher proportion' of acquittals in rape and sexual assault cases over a number of years.[194] In such cases, the not proven verdict is more satisfactory for the victim because it does not necessarily cast doubt upon her honesty or reliability. In response to this argument, it might well be observed that this does not alter the fact that the presumption of innocence demands a verdict of not guilty if the Crown case cannot be proved.

Secondly, it is claimed that if jurors were faced with a straight choice between guilty and not guilty, they might opt for guilty where otherwise they would have found the case not proven.[195] In other words, there would be an increased danger of wrongful convictions. The majority of the members of the Thomson Committee were sufficiently worried by this possibility to recommend that the not proven verdict should be retained, although they accepted the argument that the three verdict system was illogical.[196] In response, it might be observed that, first, their concern is based purely on speculation, and, secondly, there is always a danger of wrongful conviction, yet no other country in the world feels that giving the jury a choice of three verdicts is a solution to this problem.

There is a third possible argument which has not been addressed in the debate over the not proven verdict. Anecdotal evidence suggests that the verdict is sometimes used if the jury knows perfectly well that the accused is guilty but thinks that the law needs to be tempered with mercy. The classic example might be the wife who has been battered by her alcoholic husband for years and eventually stabs him to death with the bread-knife as he lies in a drunken stupor on the couch. It is not unknown in such a case for a jury to return a verdict of not proven to a charge of murder,[197] even in the face of overwhelming evidence, presumably because it sees no purpose in further punishing the accused. In essence, the not proven verdict provides the jury with a rather subtle way of 'nullifying' the law instead of having to confront it directly and openly. What the jury is really saying through the medium of a not proven verdict is that while it knows perfectly well the accused is guilty, it is not prepared to convict in this particular case. Given the issues raised by jury 'nullification', it is not surprising that this argument has not been officially cited in support of the not proven verdict.

[194] See JURIES AND VERDICTS, *supra* note 43, ¶ 10.4, tbl. 3.

[195] See ibid., ¶ 10.1.

[196] See THOMSON COMMITTEE, *supra* note 39, ¶ 51.05.

[197] The doctrine of provocation would not allow the charge to be reduced to culpable homicide in such a case.

It is worth examining in more detail the most recent controversy over the not proven verdict because it has attracted a great deal of public and political interest. The debate was started by the trial of a young man for the brutal killing of a female student, which, to the astonishment of most observers, resulted in a not proven verdict by the jury.[198] The media strongly hinted that the accused had indeed committed the crime, and the police gave the impression that as far as they were concerned the matter was closed.[199] Within weeks, the victims' parents were organizing a petition which demanded the abolition of the not proven verdict, attracting much support and a great deal of media attention.[200] Implicit in much of the criticism of the not proven verdict was the belief that were it not available, the jury would have returned a guilty verdict. This, of course, although likely, is impossible to tell.[201]

Around this time, the Lord Advocate, the senior law officer in Scotland, revealed in an extensive interview with a Sunday newspaper that he felt some 'unease' over the not proven verdict.[202] Nevertheless, he confirmed that neither he nor the Scottish Office was persuaded that there was enough dissatisfaction to justify scrutiny of the verdict.[203] However, the campaign to abolish the not proven verdict continued to gather momentum and, shortly afterwards, the BBC (Scotland) devoted its flagship documentary to the issue, entitling the programme 'Not Proven: "That Bastard Verdict"' (the latter phrase being a description of the verdict by Sir Walter Scott, who hated its illogicality[204]). Supporters of the verdict were given an opportunity on the programme to explain their point of view, but the thrust of an emotive programme was essentially hostile to the retention of the three verdict system. Further, the BBC had commissioned a public opinion poll which produced the devastating finding that the majority of the Scottish public, including those who had served as jurors, simply did not understand the not proven verdict or its

[198] For a full account of the debate, see Peter Duff, *The Not Proven Verdict: Jury Mythology and 'Moral Panics'* (1996) 41 J.R 1, 1–12.

[199] See ibid.

[200] For instance, a member of Labour's shadow ministerial team announced he would introduce a Private Member's Bill to abolish the verdict. See Joy Copley, *Bill Launched to Abolish 'Not Proven'*, Scotsman, Apr. 22, 1993, at 6.

[201] See *Not Proven: 'That Bastard Verdict'* (BBC Scotland television broadcast, Focal Point Documentary, May 13, 1993) (hereinafter BBC Broadcast); see also Firm and Fair, *supra* note 44, at 32.

[202] See Kenny Farquharson, *Law Chief Uneasy over 'Not Proven'*, Scotland on Sunday, Mar. 21, 1993, at 21.

[203] See ibid.

[204] *Quoted in* Willock, *supra* note 1, at 217.

implications.[205] Many people erroneously thought that the accused could be retried if more evidence came to light.[206]

At this time, by pure coincidence, the Scottish Office was beginning a major review of various aspects of the criminal justice process, the primary motive being to cut costs and increase efficiency.[207] The government simply added to this review an examination of the not proven verdict along with various other aspects of trial by jury, a pragmatic solution to the increasing political pressure.[208] As described above, the Scottish Office consultation paper raised several other issues, including the peremptory challenge, the size of the jury, and the simple majority verdict, but the bulk of the paper was devoted to the not proven verdict.[209] The government expressed no opinion on its future, but simply canvassed the arguments for and against it and invited the submission of views.[210]

Ultimately, the decision was to retain the not proven verdict. The consultation exercise had not revealed 'a consensus for change', among either the legal profession or the public.[211] Further, the government noted that respondents were divided about the logical case for three verdicts, some asserting that 'the three verdicts were entirely logical and, indeed, more consistent with reality than a two verdict system'.[212] Thus, in the absence of 'a considerable weight of informed opinion against the three verdict system', the government thought that it should be kept.[213] Regarding jurors' possible 'misconceptions' about the verdict, it was suggested that to some extent these would have been corrected by the consultation paper,[214] although it is perhaps somewhat optimistic to think that the public makes a habit of reading such papers. There was an assurance in the White Paper that the judiciary had taken steps to

[205] See BBC Broadcast, *supra* note 201; see also JURIES AND VERDICTS, *supra* note 43, at 31; Alistair Bonnington, *Third Option for Scots Juries*, HERALD, May 13, 1993, at 15. But cf. Lord McCluskey, *Fiddling with Scottish Justice* (1994) SCOLAG 69, 70; John Robertson & Iain Duff, *Parents Vow to Continue Campaign*, SCOTSMAN, June 28, 1994, at 4 (reporting comments of the Solicitor General).

[206] See BBC Broadcast, *supra* note 201

[207] See FIRM AND FAIR, *supra* note 44, at 1.

[208] See Joy Copley, *Justice System in Scotland Comes Under Review*, SCOTSMAN, May 26, 1993, at 1.

[209] See JURIES AND VERDICTS, *supra* note 43.

[210] See ibid.

[211] See FIRM AND FAIR, *supra* note 44, ¶ 3.16. It is interesting to note that a factor which influenced the Thomson Committee, other than their fear of wrongful convictions, was that 'there is no evidence that the public regard the system as working unsatisfactorily'. THOMSON COMMITTEE, *supra* note 39, ¶ 5.12.

[212] FIRM AND FAIR, *supra* note 44, ¶ 3.17.

[213] Ibid., ¶ 3.19.

[214] See generally ibid., ¶¶ 3.15–.19.

ensure that juries understand that a verdict of not proven does not lead to a retrial.[215]

J. Appeal: Perversity of Jury's Verdict

The right to appeal against conviction under solemn procedure[216] was introduced by the 1926 Criminal Appeal Act.[217] Three grounds were stipulated. The first two were very general: 'a wrong decision of any question of law' by the court, and 'a miscarriage of justice'.[218] The third ground was more specific, 'the verdict of the jury . . . was unreasonable or cannot be supported having regard to the evidence'.[219] Despite this wording, the Appeal Court never granted an appeal based solely on the perversity of the jury's decision, allowing appeals under this heading only where the jury's verdict was self-contradictory or illogical in some way.[220] Thus, any attempt to argue that the jury could not have reasonably convicted on the basis of the evidence was invariably doomed to failure.

These three grounds of appeal were removed and replaced with a single ground—'miscarriage of justice'—by the Criminal Justice Act 1980.[221] The intention underlying the change was probably to liberalize the attitude of the court, but it did not affect the Appeal Court's approach to claims that the evidence simply did not sustain the jury's verdict.[222] In 1984, the Lord Justice General, Scotland's most senior judge, commented:

> Questions of the reliability and credibility of witnesses are essentially, in our law, questions for the jury, and we know of no case in which this court has interfered with any conviction upon the ground that, in its opinion, a jury had been perverse in treating a key witness as both reliable and credible.[223]

As the editors of Renton and Brown observe, 'the very narrow approach adopted under the old law to factual challenges to jury

[215] See ibid., ¶ 3.18.

[216] See Lord McCluskey, Criminal Appeals s. 2 (1992) (providing general information on appeals process).

[217] See Criminal Appeal (Scotland) Act 1926 s. 2.

[218] Ibid.

[219] Ibid.

[220] See Salmond v. H. M. Advocate (1992) S.L.T. 156, 157–8 (H.C.J. Sept. 9, 1990) (appeal was allowed when a jury in an attempted murder case found the accused 'guilty . . . with extreme provocation', because this verdict was indisputably incompetent since provocation is not relevant to a charge of attempted murder).

[221] Criminal Justice (Scotland) Act 1980 s. 33.

[222] See Renton & Brown, *supra* note 15, ¶ 29–07.

[223] Rubin v. H. M. Advocate (1984) S.L.T. 369, 370–1 (H.C.J.).

verdicts has persisted into the new jurisprudence of the court'.[224] It is also useful to note that in his book on appeals, Lord McCluskey, a High Court judge himself, seems doubtful that the Appeal Court will ever 'retreat from the notion . . . that the conclusions . . . of the jury . . . are sacrosanct and inviolable whatever the weight and coherence of the evidence'.[225]

Various aspects of the appeal procedure were recently examined by the Sutherland Committee, including the question of overturning the jury's verdict.[226] The Committee agreed with the general principle that the Appeal Court should be very reluctant to interfere with a jury's verdict reached on the basis of legal sufficiency of the evidence.[227] It did think, however, that there might be a few 'exceptional' cases where 'any reasonable jury ought to have entertained a reasonable doubt', and argued that the Appeal Court should overturn the jury's verdict where that verdict is 'unreasonable and has resulted in a miscarriage'.[228] Furthermore, it recommended that this power should be specifically enshrined in statute, presumably because this might help to overcome the court's notorious reluctance to interfere with the verdict of a jury.[229]

However, the Committee did not favour the English Appeal Court's approach of overturning a jury's verdict on the basis of a 'lurking doubt' or 'gut feeling', because this would debase the original verdict and might lead to the court being 'swamped' with appeals.[230] Instead, it preferred a more objective test and, ultimately, something very close to its suggested formulation was adopted in the Crime and Punishment Act 1997.[231] This formula retains the approach of creating only one ground of appeal—a 'miscarriage of justice'—but specifically includes within this heading the granting of an appeal for 'the jury's having returned a verdict which no reasonable jury, properly directed, could have returned'.[232]

In essence, as the Sutherland Committee observed, the issue of overturning an unreasonable verdict 'strikes at the heart of the role of the jury in Scottish criminal procedure'.[233] In fact, this subject raises funda-

[224] Renton & Brown, *supra* note 15, ¶ 29–07.

[225] Lord McCluskey, *supra* note 216, at 188.

[226] See Criminal Appeals, *supra* note 149, ¶¶ 2.59–.71.

[227] See ibid., ¶ 2.66. [228] Ibid., ¶ 2.67. [229] See ibid., ¶ 2.68.

[230] See ibid., ¶ 2.69.

[231] See Crime and Punishment (Scotland) Act 1997 s. 17; see also Criminal Appeals, *supra* note 149, ¶ 2.70.

[232] Crime and Punishment (Scotland) Act 1997 s. 17.

[233] Criminal Appeals, *supra* note 149, ¶ 2.66.

mental questions about jury trial in every jurisdiction where the institution exists. The main justification for the jury is that it is alleged to be better at finding the facts than the judge(s) acting alone and, consequently, it is very difficult to justify any judicial interference with the verdict of the jury. To overturn the jury's decision is to demonstrate a lack of faith in the institution, calling its very existence into doubt. That, of course, is why appeal courts in every jurisdiction are much quicker to intervene where there has been some minor procedural hitch than when there is a query over the essential merits of the conviction. Obviously, one can frame the necessary test to review the jury's decision in a variety of ways, but whether one talks of a 'lurking doubt', or a 'perverse verdict', or 'returning a verdict which no reasonable jury could have returned', one is challenging the very *raison d'être* of trial by jury. For this reason, it seems unlikely that the new provision will make much difference to the approach of the Scottish courts.

K. Appeal: Irregularity of Procedure and Prejudice

There is little purpose in listing all the possible irregularities in procedure here. In practice, the most common ground of appeal under solemn procedure is that of misdirection by the judge.[234] It is clear, however, that most such cases stem from a general dissatisfaction with the verdict and the need of the accused's adviser to find an appropriate 'peg' on which to hang an appeal.[235] Appeals on the grounds of other types of irregularity affecting the jury are few.[236] Nonetheless, it is worth discussing allegations that the jury was prejudiced in some way because there have recently been several such appeals, and by their very nature, they go to the very heart of jury trial.

The question of possible prejudice following pretrial publicity has already been considered, and as we saw, an appeal has yet to succeed. A more common allegation is that one or two jurors were biased against the accused for some other reason. In this context, the most influential modern case is probably *McCadden*, where, it will be remembered, the

[234] See Peter Duff & Frazer McCallum, Grounds of Appeal in Criminal Cases 22, tbl. 7 (1996). In a sample of 250 appeals against conviction under solemn procedure, which produced 350 grounds of appeal, 147 of the grounds related to alleged misdirection by the judge. See ibid.

[235] See ibid.

[236] In the sample of 350 appeal grounds, only four related to alleged jury irregularity. See ibid.

Appeal Court took the opportunity to disapprove of any attempt to vet jurors in any way.[237] The appeal was based on the allegation that one juror had made remarks in a social club indicating that he was prejudiced against the accused. The appeal was rejected and while the court stated that 'it cannot be held that an appeal based on alleged malpractice by a juror . . . can never be entertained', it was made very clear that it would be extremely difficult for such an appeal to succeed. An inquiry into allegations of juror malpractice would be held only where the court was satisfied that 'the evidence placed before it to substantiate the claim is *prima facie* sufficiently substantial, convincing and trustworthy to warrant an inquiry'.[238] In the court's view, there were sufficient safeguards—the judicial direction, the jury of fifteen, the majority verdict, etc.—to prevent a miscarriage of justice. Further, there were obvious 'dangers to the administration of justice which would result from a too facile resort' to such inquiry.[239]

The importance that the courts attach to the effect of the judicial direction to consider the case dispassionately, as a counterweight to possible prejudice, can hardly be overstated. In the recent case of *Gray* v. *H.M. Advocate*, the Appeal Court summed up its approach: '[T]It has repeatedly been observed that it *must* be assumed that jurors will comply with the directions given to them by the presiding judge'.[240] In that case, the judge had stressed that the jury should ignore everything but the evidence of the witnesses given in court.[241] Despite strong indications that there had been contact during the trial between two jurors and a co-accused, against whom charges were withdrawn, the individuals who were ultimately convicted had their appeal rejected.[242]

One further case is worth citing in this context. In *Pullar* v. *H.M. Advocate*,[243] one of the jurors had been an employee of one of the two main prosecution witnesses. He had informed the clerk before the ballot but, on being questioned, had stated he did not know the accused or any of the circumstances of the case.[244] The clerk took no further action, and the juror was selected.[245] After proceedings had begun, the prosecution

[237] See McCadden v. H. M. Advocate (1985) J.C. 98, 102.

[238] Ibid.

[239] Ibid. It is fair to say that in this case the two witnesses who had allegedly overheard the juror's remarks in the social club were unconvincing; they were not of good character, and they were friends of the accused's brother.

[240] 1994 S.L.T. 1237, 1243 (H.C.J.) (emphasis added).

[241] See ibid., at 1241.

[242] See ibid., at 1244.

[243] 1993 J.C. 126. Here, the court took the opportunity to establish the procedures for ensuring that jurors do not know the parties to the case.

[244] See ibid., at 130.

[245] See ibid.

witness also informed the clerk of the relationship, and the clerk assured him that the juror had disclaimed any knowledge of the case.[246] Hearing an appeal against conviction, the Appeal Court accepted that the clerk should have passed this information to the judge and that, if this had happened, the juror would have been excused, or at least could have been challenged, because of the possibility of bias.[247] It rejected the appeal however, because this irregularity did not automatically invalidate the verdict and there was no evidence that the juror was biased or that a miscarriage of justice had occurred.[248] The accused then unsuccessfully appealed to the European Court of Human Rights, under Article 6 of the Convention, on the ground that the jury was not 'independent and impartial'.[249] The European Court of Human Rights observed that there was no evidence of bias nor any likelihood in the circumstances that the juror was more likely to believe his employer than the defence witnesses.[250] Further, the integrity of the jury was protected by various safeguards, primarily the existence of fourteen other jurors, the jurors' oath to assess the witnesses dispassionately, and the judicial direction.[251]

IV. Conclusion

This account of the Scottish criminal jury has, I hope, fulfilled two purposes. First, it has furnished a full description of the institution, and in particular, emphasized its peculiarities—principally its size, the existence of the bare majority verdict, and the rather illogical three verdict system. Secondly, it has also attempted to challenge, in passing, various common preconceptions about the nature of jury trial. For instance, it should have become clear that the institution of trial by jury does not necessarily require that the accused should have any 'right' to have his case put to a jury. Nor need it involve a complex selection procedure, with both sides having plentiful opportunities to challenge potential jurors on the ground of possible bias. Nor, finally, does conviction require unanimity on the part of the jury, or a heavily weighted majority, contrary to what is often thought.

As we have seen, the Scottish jury has existed for a long time, and without serious challenge, despite the absence of such features which are

[246] See ibid. [247] See ibid., at 133. [248] See ibid., at 134.
[249] See Pullar v. United Kingdom (1996) S.C.C.R. 755.
[250] See ibid. [251] See ibid.

often regarded elsewhere as integral parts of jury trial. It is quite easy to perceive a particular aspect of jury trial in one's own jurisdiction as a matter of logical necessity or fundamental principle, rather than realizing it is the product of mere historical accident. The benefit of this type of collection is that it ought to allow the reader to avoid such ethnocentrism and to appreciate the full range of the institution of trial by jury.

8 The Jury System in Contemporary Ireland: In the Shadow of a Troubled Past

John D. Jackson,* Katie Quinn,** and Tom O'Malley***

I. Introduction

One of the aims of this book is to demonstrate how the jury system has managed to adapt and survive in a range of very different legal and political environments. In one respect, the survival of the jury in a country that has long been riddled with political upheaval, violence, and division may be viewed as a powerful symbol of the triumph of an institution that has endured throughout the years as a living testament to the adaptability of the common law tradition with which the jury system is often associated. Not only did the jury survive the political troubles in eighteenth and nineteenth century Ireland, but it also has survived the constitutional changes of the twentieth century that brought about the partition of the island into two separate legal jurisdictions, the Republic of Ireland, an independent state comprising twenty-six out of the thirty-two counties on the island, and Northern Ireland, remaining part of the United Kingdom and comprising the other six counties.[1] Although jury trial was imposed under the English common law in Ireland, this mode of trial was enshrined for criminal cases in the Irish Constitution of 1937 and remains an important constitutional right. North of the border, jury trial has survived thirty years of recent troubles, and, although it has been suspended for cases connected with the troubles, all the protagonists in the present 'peace process' expect it to be restored once the troubles have abated.

At another level, however, jury trial may be viewed as a dying remnant from the past, more deeply in decline perhaps even than in England and Wales, with only the force of tradition saving it from complete

* Professor of Law, Queen's University of Belfast.
** Lecturer in Law, Queen's University of Belfast.
*** Lecturer in Law, University College, Galway.

[1] For a modern history of Ireland, see ROBERT F. FOSTER, MODERN IRELAND 1600–1972 (1989). For a history of Northern Ireland, see JONATHAN BARDON, A HISTORY OF ULSTER (1992).

extinction. Jury trials have almost entirely disappeared in civil cases both north and south of the border.[2] In the Republic of Ireland, civil juries are retained only for libel, slander, assault, and false imprisonment cases; in Northern Ireland, civil juries are retained only for libel claims or if the judge accedes to a particular application.[3] As the jury has ceased to play any significant role in civil cases, this chapter on the contemporary jury in Ireland does not intend to say anything more about them.

The chapter will focus on the distinctive features of criminal trial by jury in Ireland, both north and south, to explain on the one hand how the jury continues to survive within modern Ireland, and on the other hand how it also has managed to decline in significance. The constitutional guarantee of jury trial in criminal cases in the Irish Republic is subject to important exceptions, with the result that most criminal accused are tried before a judge sitting alone rather than a jury. This also holds true for Northern Ireland. As Ireland is hopefully transformed in the new millennium into a more peaceful and less divisive island, it may be that political conditions will become more conducive for jury trial and its decline will be arrested. But active steps will arguably need to be taken to deal with certain problems inherent in the present system that are likely to persist beyond any abatement of the troubles before the future of the jury trial in Ireland can be fully assured.

II. Origins and Development of Jury Trial in Ireland

The origins of jury trial in Ireland share much in common with those of England and Wales. Commencing with the Anglo-Norman invasion of 1169, the English common law tradition, with its system of trial by jury, gradually supplanted the native custom-based system of Brehon law; by the end of the seventeenth century, the common law tradition was firmly established throughout the country. The inception of the jury trial as developed in England by the Normans is outlined elsewhere in this volume and will not be rehearsed here.[4] However, the development of the Anglo-Norman jury trial and the differences that emerged in

[2] See Raymond Byrne & J. Paul McCutcheon, The Irish Legal System 102 (3d ed. 1996); Brice Dickson, The Legal System of Northern Ireland 192–3 (3d ed. 1993).

[3] The most significant recent change occurred when personal injury claims were taken out of the control of juries, first in Northern Ireland in 1987 and shortly afterward in the Republic of Ireland in 1988. This issue is discussed in Bryan M. E. McMahon, Judge or Jury? The Jury Trial for Personal Injury Cases in Ireland (1985).

[4] See Sally Lloyd-Bostock & Cheryl Thomas, The continuing decline of the English Jury, Ch. 2, This volume.

Ireland as a result of the divergent culture and history will be examined. Despite the wholesale imposition of English common law in Ireland, the particular society and circumstances in Ireland ensured that jury trial never succeeded in establishing a firm grasp on the Irish legal system, at least not to the same extent as it did in England and Wales.

Jury trial in Ireland has often had to operate in a turbulent society. During the eighteenth and nineteenth centuries in particular, when violence and sectarian tensions abounded, the jury system came under considerable strain. At certain periods and in particular parts of the country, intimidation of both jurors and witnesses, antipathy toward the state, close community ties between jurors and accused, and juror sympathy with the accused combined to create serious difficulties in securing convictions. Jurors were particularly reluctant to enforce the law in agrarian and political cases, but there is also some evidence of a reluctance to convict even in cases of ordinary, everyday crime. This has been borne out by evidence that in the latter half of the nineteenth century, conviction rates were lower than in England and Wales for all categories of crime.[5] Legal folklore also has abounded with stories of perverse jury acquittals.[6] In one of these, a judge is said to have dismissed a prisoner with the words 'you have been acquitted by a Limerick jury, and you may now leave the dock without any other stain upon your character!'[7] It has been suggested that the root problem stemmed from the dual function of the system of jury trial.[8] On the one hand, it is supposed to enforce the law of the land; on the other hand, it is supposed to represent judgment by one's peers. Where, however, many of the laws are out of harmony with jurors' own convictions and where jurors have sympathy with many of their peers who are put on trial, the jury system can undermine the entire system of criminal justice.

As a result of these problems, a number of remedial tactics were employed by the Crown and the prosecuting authorities to ensure the conviction of offenders. One tactic was the trial of a large portion of offences without the use of a jury where possible by, for example, the extension of the jurisdiction of the summary courts and trials before 'resident magistrates'. Although the sentences handed down in these

[5] For the statistical evidence see D. Johnson, *Trial by Jury in Ireland 1860–1914*, 17 Legal Hist. 270, 273–7 (1996).

[6] Some of the stories are recounted in Maurice Healy, The Old Munster Circuit (1977), and in Alexander M. Sullivan, The Last Serjeant: The Memoirs of Serjeant A. M. Sullivan (1952).

[7] Healy, *supra* note 6, at 229.

[8] See Johnson, *supra* note 5, at 289.

courts of summary jurisdiction would inevitably be lighter, the hope was that this tactic would result in more convictions.[9]

Where the use of jury trial could not be avoided, a number of more subtle tactics were developed by the Crown in an effort to ensure the punishment of offenders. Such strategies included the extensive use of the Crown's right to ask potential jurors to stand by,[10] the transfer of trials to different venues to avoid local prejudices,[11] the use of 'special jurors',[12] and the reduction of charges to convince defendants to plead guilty.[13] The use of the prosecution's right to ask potential jurors to stand by was particularly controversial and frequently led to accusations of jury packing. Indeed, it was believed by some that the prosecution used this right to select a jury more sympathetic to the prosecution's case, such as a predominantly Protestant jury where the accused was a Catholic.[14] The Crown, on the other hand, contended that the right of stand-by was used merely to ensure an unbiased jury in cases where the impartiality of potential jurors was in doubt.[15] There was also some suggestion that the sub-sheriffs who empanelled the jury were also involved in jury packing, calling only on particular categories of jurors for particular cases.[16] If it was suspected that a sheriff had manipulated the jury in this way, the English procedure of 'challenge to the array' was open to the accused or the prosecution. The potential for such 'packing' by sheriffs was, however, greatly reduced in 1873 when the Juries (Ireland) Act of 1871 came into force. This Act provided for a system of jury service by alphabetical rotation and consequently significantly curtailed the discretion of the sheriff in empanelling the jury.

These attempts by the Crown to influence the composition of the jury and thereby the outcome of the case were matched on the defence side

[9] See Johnson, *supra* note 5, at 270–1.

[10] 'Stand-by' was a right enjoyed by the Crown, under the common law, whereby an unrestricted number of potential jurors could be challenged without cause and thereby excluded from jury service. Although strictly speaking the Crown prosecutors were required to show cause for such challenges when the entire jury panel had been gone through, it appears that in practice the Crown was rarely called upon to do so. See Johnson, *supra* note 5, at 271; J. F. McEldowney, *'Stand by for the Crown': An Historical Analysis* [1979] Crim. L. Rev. 272, 275.

[11] See Johnson, *supra* note 5, at 271.

[12] See ibid. 'Special jurors' were comprised of wealthy men in the county and were often used for the trial of political or agrarian offences.

[13] See ibid.

[14] See Johnson, *supra* note 5, at 285; McEldowney, *supra* note 10, at 279–80.

[15] See McEldowney, *supra* note 10, at 278–9.

[16] See Johnson, *supra* note 5, at 272.

by the frequent use of the extensive right of peremptory challenge. Each defendant was given the right to challenge twenty jurors if accused of a felony and, from 1876, six if charged with a misdemeanour,[17] with the result that, despite the strenuous efforts of the Crown, conviction rates were kept low, particularly in 'agrarian'[18] and political cases. Although many of the strategies adopted by the government and prosecuting authorities in Ireland to increase the prospect of conviction, such as the extensive use of the summary jurisdiction and the use of stand-by, were also utilized in England and Wales,[19] periods of particular political and agrarian tension in some parts of Ireland caused these tactics to place even greater strain on Irish jury trial.

Indeed, in times of particular unrest, jury trial was suspended altogether for specified periods for certain offences and in particular locations, with the substitution of a variety of special courts. In 1882, for example, in the aftermath of a number of particularly sensational murders known as the Phoenix Park murders,[20] legislation was enacted to allow for the nonjury trial of certain serious offences. The Prevention of Crimes (Ireland) Act 1882 intended to create a 'Special Commission Court' comprising three senior judges who would try such offences in the absence of a jury. Although the Special Commission Court was never used, the very enactment of this legislation illustrates that Ireland is not a stranger to the concept of nonjury trial, particularly during troubled periods, and this may go some way to explaining the ease with which jury trial, regarded by some as a fundamental right, continues to be withdrawn from certain categories of offenders well into the twentieth century.

Given the political tensions and divided nature of Irish society in the eighteenth and nineteenth centuries, the notion of trial by an impartial jury of one's peers which would result in a conviction where the evidence of guilt was clear was always going to be a difficult achievement.

[17] See Juries Procedure (Ireland) Act 1876, 39 & 40 Vict., ch. 78, s. 10.

[18] Crime committed in rural areas, often associated with the Land Question. See FOSTER, *supra* note 1, at 406. See generally VIRGINIA CROSSMAN, POLITICS, LAW AND ORDER IN NINETEENTH CENTURY IRELAND (1996).

[19] See generally J. M. BEATTIE, CRIME AND THE COURTS IN ENGLAND 1660–1800 (1986); W. R. CORNISH & G. DE N. CLARK, LAW AND SOCIETY IN ENGLAND 1750–1950, at ch. 8 (1989).

[20] The so-called Phoenix Park murders were particularly controversial as they were believed to be politically motivated and the victims, Cavendish, the Irish Chief Secretary, and Burke, the Irish Under Secretary, were killed by a secret society known as the 'Invincibles'.

There are differing views about the extent of the difficulties encountered by the jury system in Ireland and their impact on the institution. On the one hand, it has been contended that despite its problems, jury trial was never truly doubted as the most appropriate mode of trial for criminal offences in Ireland,[21] whereas on the other hand it has been argued that, given the difficult circumstances in which jury trial was forced to operate, the persistence of a jury system in Ireland at all is 'an achievement of note'.[22] Although we cannot be sure of the extent to which jury trial was truly threatened during this turbulent time, the difficulties of the past have left their mark on the modern jury system in Ireland. If the troubles have cast a shadow on the operation of the modern jury, however, the system has been bolstered in the Republic of Ireland by a constitutional guarantee that protects the right to jury trial in criminal cases. We turn now to consider the significance of this constitutional guarantee.

III. The Constitutional Dimension: Jury Trial as a Constitutional Right

The present Constitution of the Republic of Ireland, enacted by the people in 1937, provides that, subject to three exceptions, 'no person shall be tried on any criminal charge without a jury'.[23] The exceptions referred to in Article 38.5 relate to summary trial for minor offences, trial by special courts, and trial by military tribunals. Despite the unequivocal words of Article 38.5, however, the meaning of trial by jury is left undefined in the Irish Constitution, and it has been argued that this lack of definition gives rise to some confusion about exactly what type of 'jury' the constitutional guarantee seeks to protect.[24] Must the function and composition of juries remain as they were in 1937, for example, in order to enjoy the constitutional guarantee? The Constitution is silent on what features and functions are fundamental to the constitutional notion of a jury, and, as such, there remains much which is unclear regarding the implications of Article 38.5 for jury trial in the Republic of Ireland. However, a number of important decisions have

[21] See Neal Garnham, The Courts, Crime and the Criminal Law in Ireland 1692–1760, at 133 (1996).

[22] J. F. McEldowney, Irish Jury Trial: A Survey of Some Eighteenth and Nineteenth Century Statutes 1 (1979).

[23] Const. art. 38.5 (Ir.).

[24] See J. M. Kelly *et al.*, The Irish Constitution 657 (3d ed. 1994).

been handed down which go some way toward elucidating the implications of the constitutional guarantee for jury trial in Ireland.

The importance of the constitutional guarantee in light of the troubled nature of Irish history has been expressed by one senior judge:

> The bitter Irish race-memory of politically appointed and Executive-oriented judges, of the suspension of jury trial in times of popular revolt, of the substitution therefor of summary trial or detention without trial, of cat-and-mouse releases from such detention, of packed juries and sometimes corrupt judges and prosecutors, had long been implanted in the consciousness of the people, and, therefore, in the minds of their political representatives, the conviction that the best way of preventing an individual from suffering a wrong conviction for an offence was to allow him to 'put himself upon his country,' that is to say to allow him to be tried for that offence by a fair, impartial and representative jury, sitting in a court presided over by an impartial and independent judge appointed under the Constitution, who would see that all the requirements for a fair and proper jury trial would be observed, so that, amongst other things, if the jury's verdict were one of not guilty, the accused could leave court with the absolute assurance that he would never again 'be vexed' for the same charge.[25]

This statement goes some way to explaining why it was thought necessary to entrench trial by jury in the new Constitution. In the eyes of many, the criminal justice system had been corrupted by those in authority during the troubles of the eighteenth and nineteenth centuries and the constitutionally protected jury provided a safeguard against future tyranny. This continues to provide an enduring rationale for the continuation of the jury system in other countries,[26] but in Ireland, of all places, where there had been such enormous political upheaval and strife, the risk of future tyranny could not be discounted until well into the twentieth century. It seems therefore that although the troubles provide an explanation of why the jury system never established as firm a grasp on the Irish legal system as it did in England and Wales, they also provide an explanation for its continued existence under the new Constitution.

Despite this entrenchment, however, jury trial in the Republic of Ireland has been significantly eroded in recent years. First, as previously mentioned, the Constitution itself qualifies this right considerably by exempting minor offences, special courts, and military tribunals from

[25] The People (Director of Public Prosecutions) v. O'Shea [1992] 1 I.R. 384, 432–3 (Henchy J) (delivering a minority judgment on the issue of the nonappealability of jury acquittals).

[26] See, in particular, SIR PATRICK DEVLIN, TRIAL BY JURY 164 (1956), who eloquently described trial by jury as the 'lamp that shows that freedom lives'.

jury trial. Secondly, this right is further diminished by the acceptance of majority, as opposed to unanimous, jury verdicts. It will become evident when these distinctive features of trial by jury in the Republic of Ireland are examined in more detail that, despite the apparent strength of the constitutional guarantee, official policies on jury trials in criminal cases have become decidedly abolitionist in modern Ireland. But before we examine these issues, we need to examine how the constitutional guarantee has affected the composition of the modern Irish jury.

A. Jury Composition and Selection in Ireland

The eligibility and selection of jurors in the Republic of Ireland today are governed by the Juries Act 1976. The immediate motivation for the introduction of this legislation was the decision of the Supreme Court in *de Búrca & Anderson* v. *Attorney General*,[27] although work on the bill was at an advanced stage by the time this decision was handed down. In *de Búrca*, the plaintiffs argued successfully that the existing law[28] was inconsistent with the Constitution because it confined jury service to citizens with certain property qualifications and exempted all women. Women were not, strictly speaking, *excluded* from jury service; they were merely *exempt* and could apply for inclusion on jury lists. However, in the ten years preceding the hearing of this action, only two women had actually served on a jury. So far as the property qualification was concerned, the Minister for Justice had statutory power to prescribe the rateable value of land that was to be the minimum qualification for service as a juror in that district.

All five members of the Supreme Court agreed that the property qualification was unconstitutional. Two of them held that it constituted an invidious discrimination which violated the equality clause of the Constitution. Two others held that it produced a lack of representativeness which failed to comply with the notion of a jury as required in criminal cases by Article 38.5 of the Constitution. The fifth member concurred without stating a specific reason. On the issue of women on juries, four members of the Supreme Court found the effective exclusion of women to be unconstitutional, partly on the ground of inequality and partly on the ground of lack of representativeness. The Chief Justice, O'Higgins, dissented on this issue. He held that since the state, while allowing women to serve as jurors, 'permits each woman to decide for

[27] [1976] 1 I.R. 38. [28] Juries Act 1927.

herself, in accordance with her own circumstances and special responsibilities, whether service on a jury is a right she ought to exercise or a burden she ought to undertake',[29] it could not be regarded as engaging in invidious discrimination. The 1976 Act, which was implemented partly as a result of this decision, provides simply that, subject to certain exceptions, every citizen between 18 and 70 years of age entered on the register of Dáil electors in a jury district shall be eligible for jury service.[30] There is no discrimination on the basis of gender or property ownership. The exceptions consist of persons who are ineligible[31] for or disqualified[32] from jury service, and persons excusable as of right.[33]

Turning to the rules governing the selection of juries, panels of potential jurors are first of all drawn up by each county registrar from the register of Dáil electors for the county using 'a procedure of random or other non-discriminatory selection'.[34] These jurors are then summoned to attend at court on a particular date, and at the beginning of each jury trial jurors are selected from the jury panel by ballot in open court.[35]

[29] [1976] 1 I.R. at 59.

[30] See Juries Act 1976 s. 6. The Republic of Ireland legislature consists of the President, the House of Representatives (the Dáil), and the Senate. Members of the Dáil are elected directly by the People. All citizens (and certain others) who have reached the age of 18 are eligible to vote in Dáil elections.

[31] See ibid., s. 7 and sched. 1, pt. 1. The President of Ireland, persons concerned with the administration of justice (including practising lawyers, members of the police, and prison officers), members of the defence forces, and incapable persons are all ineligible for jury service. Incapable persons are those who, because of insufficient capacity to read, deafness, or other permanent infirmity are unfit for jury service, as well as those who, on account of a mental illness or disability, are resident in a hospital or similar institution, or are regularly treated by a medical practitioner.

[32] See ibid., s. 8. A criminal record is the sole ground for disqualification from jury service. Any person who has ever been sentenced to imprisonment for five years or more, or to detention under s. 103 of the Children Act 1908 (which provides for indefinite detention of persons under the age of 17 who have been convicted of murder), or who, within the last 10 years, has served any part of a term of imprisonment or detention where the sentence was for three months or longer, is disqualified.

[33] See Juries Act 1976, s. 9 and sched. 1, pt. 2. There is a long list of persons who are excusable as of right. It includes Members of Parliament, ministers of religion, and professional people, such as doctors, veterinary surgeons, and pharmacists, provided they are actually in practice. Many others, including civil servants, local authority officials, and teachers at all educational levels may be excused following certification by a senior official in the relevant workplace that the person in question 'performs essential and urgent services of public importance that cannot reasonably be performed by another or postponed.' Ibid. All full-time students in any educational institution are also excusable.

[34] Ibid., s. 11.

[35] See ibid., s. 15(1). However, when jurors are summoned to make up a deficiency and balloting has already begun, the judge may dispense with the need for a ballot in respect of these jurors. See ibid., s. 15(2).

Before jury selection is commenced, however, the judge must warn potential jurors that ineligible or disqualified persons must not serve on the jury and outline the penalty for doing so. The judge must then go on to call upon any person who knows that he or she is not qualified, or is in doubt whether he or she is qualified to serve on the jury, or any person who may 'have an interest in or connection with the case or the parties', to inform the judge of this fact, either orally or otherwise, if selected.[36] Although having an interest in the case or the parties is not itself grounds for disqualification from jury service, such an interest or connection may form the basis of a challenge.

Like in Northern Ireland, but unlike in England and Wales,[37] the right of peremptory challenge still exists in the Republic of Ireland, alongside the right to challenge for cause. Indeed, in jury trials in this jurisdiction, both the defence and the prosecution may challenge up to seven jurors without cause.[38] In a case involving many co-defendants, each defendant may challenge seven potential jurors without cause, whereas the prosecution may never challenge more than seven jurors notwithstanding the number of co-accused.[39] No explanation whatever need be given for these peremptory challenges. Any number of jurors may subsequently be challenged with cause.[40] Finally, it appears that the right to ask potential jurors to 'stand by', once enjoyed by the Crown, no longer exists in Ireland.[41]

Unlike the situation that prevails in the United States, potential jurors in the Republic of Ireland may not be questioned by the parties to the proceedings before challenges are made. Indeed, accused persons and the prosecution are armed with little or no insight into the sympathies and prejudices of potential jurors with which to make the decision to challenge or not. Although any member of the public is entitled to reasonable facilities to inspect a jury panel, and any party to a proceeding is entitled to apply to the county registrar for a copy of the jury panel list free of charge,[42] these lists generally contain only the names and addresses of potential jurors and occasionally their occupations. Conse-

[36] See Juries Act 1976, s. 15(3).

[37] The right of peremptory challenge was abolished in England and Wales under the Criminal Justice Act 1988 (Eng.). See Lloyd-Bostock & Thomas, *supra* note 4, at 23–4.

[38] See Juries Act 1976 s. 20.

[39] See ibid.

[40] See ibid., s. 21.

[41] See Juries Act 1927 s. 59, which made statutory provision for the exercise of a right to 'stand by' by the Attorney General. This was abolished when the 1927 Act was repealed by the 1976 Juries Act.

[42] Juries Act 1976 s. 16.

quently, they provide little information for either the accused or the prosecution to decide whether to exercise their rights of challenge.

The rights of challenge (both peremptory and with cause) have so far escaped critical attention in this jurisdiction, although, as we shall see, they have been the subject of some scrutiny in Northern Ireland. They can without doubt be used to exclude women (or men), or members of racial, religious, or ethnic minorities. In the absence of any empirical research on the matter, it is difficult to assess the predominant motivations underpinning the use of this statutory privilege. Each side in a case will obviously wish to have a jury most likely to be sympathetic toward it. Age and socio-economic status are therefore likely to be the more predominant criteria informing peremptory challenges. There is evidence that peremptory challenging was commonplace in nineteenth-century trials. Kenny records that in Ireland in the past the policy of some lawyers, presumably acting for the defence, was to challenge anyone who wore a necktie.[43] It is possible that the same mentality may underpin many challenges made today.

There is no statutory requirement for gender balance on Irish juries. The Law Reform Commission recently considered the matter in the context of rape law but decided against recommending a minimum number of women on juries in rape trials.[44] Statistics for the years 1979 to 1986[45] show that the changes made in the 1976 Act have increased the representation of women on juries with the percentage of women on juries varying over those years from 23 to 44 percent. The Commission did not find any direct correlation between the gender composition of juries and verdict, and verdicts of not guilty were returned in several cases in which there had been a majority of women jurors.[46] But there is much still to be investigated about the effect of jury composition on jury verdicts.

It seems that there is a more general need for empirical investigation into the practice of jury challenges, whether with or without cause, and into patterns of jury composition. As already noted, a wide variety of citizens are eligible to be excused from jury service. Furthermore, the penalty for failure to answer a summons for jury service is merely a fine of £50.[47] It has been suggested that a fairly high percentage of jurors

[43] See J. W. Cecil Turner, Kenny's Outlines of Criminal Law 610 n.4 (19th ed. 1966).

[44] See Law Reform Comm'n, Rape (Consultation Paper, 1987).

[45] See ibid. at 81, 94–7. [46] See ibid.

[47] See Juries Act 1976 s. 34.

are likely to be unemployed.[48] All of these factors point to the necessity for an investigation of prevailing patterns of jury composition. Much of the official and rhetorical support for jury trial rests on the assumption that it consists of trial by twelve of one's peers randomly chosen, which in turn implies a reasonable guarantee of representativeness. But, for the reasons just indicated, this can no longer be assumed. Also, as Irish society becomes slowly but surely more multicultural, it is all the more important that peremptory challenges are not being used in a discriminatory fashion.

B. *The Scope of the Right to Jury Trial in the Republic of Ireland*

As mentioned above, every person charged with a criminal offence in the Republic of Ireland enjoys a constitutional guarantee to jury trial unless the offence is being tried by a court of summary jurisdiction, a special court, or a military tribunal. Non-minor offences, therefore, which do not fall within one of the other two exceptions retain the constitutional right to jury trial and are tried by a judge and jury in either the Circuit Criminal Court or the Central Criminal Court. The Circuit Criminal Court sits at various locations throughout Ireland and hears non-minor criminal offences, but the most serious criminal offences, such as rape and murder, are dealt with in Dublin in the Central Criminal Court.

The first exception to the right of trial by jury in the Republic of Ireland concerns minor offences, which may be tried by a 'court of summary jurisdiction',[49] meaning in effect the District Court. One of the more innovative aspects of the judicial system established in 1924 after the achievement of political independence was the substitution of a professional judiciary for the magistracy. Therefore, unlike England and Wales, which favour a lay magistracy, legally qualified factfinders are favoured over lay factfinders in courts of summary jurisdiction in the Republic of Ireland. Furthermore, as the qualifications for appointment as a district judge are quite stringent,[50] a reasonably extensive jurisdiction in both civil and criminal matters can be granted to the District Court.

[48] See McMahon, *supra* note 3, at 22.

[49] Const. art. 38.2 (Ir.).

[50] To qualify for appointment as a District Judge, a person must have practised as a solicitor or barrister for at least 10 years. See Court (Supplemental Provisions) Act 1961 s. 29(2). In practice, however, the vast majority of appointees will have practised for considerably longer; rarely will a person with less than 20 years' experience be considered for a judicial appointment.

Like the question of what constitutes a jury for the purposes of the constitutional guarantee, the Constitution of Ireland does not provide a definition of a 'minor' offence for the purposes of summary trial. In the absence of a constitutional or statutory definition, it has been left to the courts to identify the distinguishing characteristics of a minor offence fit to be tried summarily. The main criterion developed so far is the level of punishment which the offence may attract.[51] At present, the District Court is precluded from imposing a prison sentence in excess of one year for any one offence or two years for a combination of offences. It may not impose a fine in excess of £1,000 for an indictable offence, although many summary offences now carry fines of up to £1,500. Any offence for which the appropriate punishment would appear, in the opinion of the District Court, to exceed these sentences should not be treated as minor. The defendant should therefore be sent forward to trial to a higher court or, if he or she has pleaded guilty, be sent forward for sentence on a signed plea. Another distinguishing criterion is the moral quality of the offence—it has been held that certain offences such as murder and rape should never, on account of their heinous nature, be treated as minor.[52] The jurisdiction of the District Court in criminal matters is quite extensive, with the result that, notwithstanding the constitutional guarantee to jury trial in criminal matters, most accused in the Republic of Ireland are tried before a judge sitting alone without a jury. Indeed in 1997, 99.6 percent of all criminal cases in the Republic of Ireland were dealt with in the District Court before a legally qualified factfinder sitting alone.[53]

The other two exceptions to the right of trial by jury relate to circumstances when jury trial would be inappropriate or would be ineffective to secure the conviction of offenders. Military tribunals may be established to try persons subject to military law and to try offences during war or rebellion. But Article 38.3 of the Constitution also provides for the establishment by law of special courts 'for the trial of offences in cases where it may be determined in accordance with such law that the ordinary courts are inadequate to secure the

[51] See Conroy v. Attorney General [1965] 1 I.R. 411; Melling v. Ó Mathghamna [1962] 1 I.R. 1.

[52] See *Conroy* [1965] 1 I.R. at 436.

[53] See Unpublished Statistics provided by the Courts Division, Department of Justice, Equality, and Law Reform, Dublin (on file with authors) (hereinafter, Unpublished Statistics). This figure includes all adults sent for trial (including those who ultimately pleaded guilty) before the District Court for both summary offences and indictable offences dealt with summarily.

effective administration of justice, and the preservation of public peace and order'. Advantage has been taken of this provision on three occasions since 1939 to establish Special Criminal Courts, the most recent of which was in 1972 when the Court was re-established in response to the spill-over effects of violence within Northern Ireland.[54] The Special Criminal Court is governed by the Offences Against the State Act 1939, which provides most significantly that this court sit without a jury and that it comprise an uneven number of members not below three.[55]

The jurisdiction of the Special Criminal Court is potentially quite expansive, extending both to certain 'scheduled' and 'nonscheduled' offences. Under section 36 of the 1939 Act, the government can schedule 'offences of any particular class or kind under any particular enactment' for trial by the Special Criminal Court. This has meant that a wide range of offences have been scheduled, including offences under the Malicious Damage Act of 1861, section 7 of the Conspiracy and Protection of Property Act of 1875, the Explosive Substances Act of 1883, and the Firearms Acts of 1925–71. Persons charged with such offences must be tried before the Special Criminal Court unless the Director of Public Prosecutions directs otherwise. In addition, section 46 of the 1939 Act provides that nonscheduled offences also can be tried by the Special Criminal Court where the Director of Public Prosecutions certifies that, in his opinion, the ordinary courts are inadequate in a particular case to secure the effective administration of justice and the preservation of public peace and order. Although the rationale for the establishment of the Special Criminal Court was largely anxiety about jury intimidation by terrorist organizations, the jurisdiction of this court is not restricted to such cases and can extend also to 'ordinary' criminal conduct.[56] However, despite the potential within the 1939 Act for the extensive use of the Special Criminal Court, the court has been employed very infrequently in recent years. Indeed, between 1990 and 1997 the number of accused persons indicted in the Special Criminal Court fell from forty-nine to only twenty-six, with as few as twelve and

[54] For more detailed accounts of the Special Criminal Court, see GERARD HOGAN & CLIVE WALKER, POLITICAL VIOLENCE AND THE LAW IN IRELAND 227–44 (1989); KELLY *ET AL.*, *supra* note 24, at 642–9; MARY ROBINSON, THE SPECIAL CRIMINAL COURT (1974).

[55] The members of the Special Criminal Court may be judges, solicitors, or barristers of not less than seven years' standing or Defence Forces Officers not below the rank of commandant. See Offences Against the State Act 1939 s. 35, pt. 5.

[56] See The People (Director of Public Prosecutions) v. Quilligan [1986] 1 I.R. 495.

fifteen accused persons facing trial in the Special Criminal Court in 1995 and 1996, respectively.[57]

C. *The Jury's Verdict and the Constitutional Guarantee*

Jury trial in criminal cases in the Republic of Ireland has been further eroded by the recent concession by the Supreme Court that a majority verdict will suffice in order to uphold the constitutional guarantee. It could be argued that the very essence of trial by jury as envisaged at the enactment of the Constitution in 1937 demands a unanimous verdict by twelve jurors and, indeed, that such a fundamental alteration to the system of trial by jury would require an amendment to the Constitution and, consequently, a referendum. However, this interpretation of Article 38.5 was categorically rejected by the Supreme Court in *O'Callaghan* v. *Attorney General*.[58] In that case, the appellant, convicted in the Dublin Circuit Court of larceny and robbery by a majority verdict of ten to two, sought a declaration that section 25 of the Criminal Justice Act 1984, which allows for majority verdicts, was unconstitutional. Section 25(1) of the 1984 Act provides that '[t]he verdict of a jury in criminal proceedings need not be unanimous in a case where there are not fewer than eleven jurors if ten of them agree on the verdict'.

O'Callaghan argued that the constitutional guarantee of trial by jury demanded unanimity and, as such, section 25 was unconstitutional. In arriving at its decision, the Supreme Court recalled that the requirement of unanimity had previously been relaxed by the Juries (Protection) Act 1929, and rejected O'Callaghan's submission that unanimity was embedded in the Constitution by Article 38.5. Delivering the opinion of the court, Justice O'Flaherty took the opportunity to shed some further light on the fundamental characteristics of jury trial as protected by the 1937 Constitution:

> The purpose of trial by jury is to provide that a person shall get a fair trial, in due course of law, and be tried by a reasonable cross-section of people acting under the guidance of the judge, bound by his directions on law, but free to make their findings as to the facts. The essential feature of a jury trial is to interpose, between the accused and the prosecution, people who will bring their experience and commonsense to bear on resolving the issue of the guilt or innocence of the accused. A requirement of unanimity is not essential to this purpose.[59]

[57] See Unpublished Statistics, *supra* note 53.

[58] [1993] 2 I.R. 17.

[59] Ibid., at 25.

It is arguable, however, that Justice O'Flaherty's statement of the essential features of the constitutionally protected jury represents a considerably watered down version of the 1937 notion of jury trial which required the agreement of all twelve jurors. Indeed, it is questionable whether a majority verdict, where up to two jurors are not convinced of the guilt of the accused beyond a reasonable doubt, adequately protects the rights of the accused.[60] The Supreme Court itself conceded that if the proportion of jurors required for a majority verdict was 'substantially lowered', it might be sufficient to raise a doubt about the guilt of the accused.[61] On the other hand, it has been argued that the approach of the Supreme Court may have been influenced by practical considerations such as the vexation of finding section 25 of the 1984 Act unconstitutional and consequently all of the majority verdicts delivered under it invalid.[62]

In view of the approach of the courts, the constitutional guarantee does not appear to have rendered trial by jury in the Republic of Ireland inviolable. The courts' interpretation of the qualifications to the scope of jury trial and the verdicts of the jury arguably have chipped away at this constitutional 'right'. Indeed, further erosion may lie ahead, for as Justice O'Flaherty noted in *O'Callaghan*, in spite of the constitutional protection, '[t]he operation of jury trials in criminal cases is not to be regarded as fixed and immutable; this was made clear by the amendment of the law that was brought about as a consequence of *de Búrca* v. *Attorney General*'.[63]

This statement begs the question of how far the constitutionally protected right to jury trial may be removed from the 1937 notion of the jury system without breaching the Constitution. In the light of the Supreme Court decisions to date, it may be thought that the constitutional guarantee does little more than offer rhetorical support for the jury system, rather than any substantial protection.

D. *Juries, the Media, and Fair Trial*

Although the constitutional right to jury trial may not afford as much protection to the jury system in the Irish Republic as advocates of jury

[60] For further argument, see G. Maher, *The Verdict of the Jury*, in THE JURY UNDER ATTACK 40 (Mark Findlay & Peter Duff eds., 1988).

[61] [1993] 2 I.R. at 26.

[62] See James Casey, *Interpretation of Constitutional Guarantees: An Antipodean History Lesson?*, 31 IR. JUR. 102, 109 (1996).

[63] [1993] 2 I.R. at 24 (citing de Búrca & Anderson v. Attorney General [1976] 1 I.R. 38).

trial would like, the Supreme Court has been very insistent on the need for trials to be fair. Article 38.1 of the Constitution states that 'no person shall be tried on any criminal charge save in due course of law', and, in conjunction with other constitutional provisions, this has been interpreted by the Supreme Court to mean that every trial shall apply fair procedures.[64] Fairness is therefore an overriding requirement of all trials, whether they are jury trials or not, and this raises the question whether there are circumstances in which jury trial can become unfair.

One concern that has become particularly prevalent in recent years has been the role of the media in its coverage of criminal jury trials. While there is clearly a value in informing the public about the work of our criminal courts, increased media coverage carries with it dangers for the administration of justice, the most significant being that the outcome of a case will be influenced by media coverage. It is often assumed that juries are particularly susceptible to prejudice on account of media coverage, while judges are much less impressionable as a result of their training and experience.[65] It is debatable whether juries are more susceptible than other tribunals of fact in this regard, but it cannot be doubted that the impartiality of a jury's verdict may be compromised where the jurors are exposed to prejudicial media accounts of the parties to proceedings.

There are a number of restrictions placed on reporting and commenting on court proceedings. Although the Constitution of Ireland contains provisions laying down the principle of open justice and freedom of expression, these principles have been limited in a number of ways.[66] The traditional way in which the courts have protected parties from prejudicial comment has been by means of the law of contempt of court. The *sub judice* rule in particular, restraining or restricting comment on pending proceedings, has placed considerable limitations on media reporting.[67] As well as these restrictions, the courts have in a number of cases aborted jury trials on the ground that media reporting had created a real risk of an unfair trial.

[64] See State (Healy) v. Donoghue (1976) 1 I.R. 325, 348–9 (O'Higgins CJ). The other constitutional provisions referred to are in Article 34, which recognises the concept of open justice, and Article 40.3, which guarantees the personal rights of the citizen. See KELLY *ET AL.*, *supra* note 24, at 340–59, 589–93.

[65] See Desmond v. Glackin (No. 2) (1992) 12 I.L.R.M. 490; Weeland v. RTE (1987) 2 I.R. 662; Cullen v. Toibin & Magill (1984) 4 I.L.R.M. 577.

[66] See MARIE MCGONAGLE, A TEXTBOOK ON MEDIA LAW ch. 6 (1996).

[67] See Kevin Boyle & Marie McGonagle, *Contempt of Court: The Case for Law Reform*, in LAW AND THE MEDIA: VIEWS OF JOURNALISTS AND LAWYERS 127, 146 (Marie McGonagle ed., 1997).

The balance between the interests of fair trial and freedom of the press was recently addressed by the Supreme Court in *Irish Times Ltd.* v. *Murphy*,[68] where the Court ruled on the validity of an order made by a circuit court judge prohibiting the media from reporting the evidence which would be given in a drug trial until the conclusion of the trial. The Court agreed with Justice Denham in *D.* v. *Director of Public Prosecutions*[69] that the right of an accused person to a fair trial is a superior right to a the right of free press and, consequently, a court may interfere with the freedom of the press where it is necessary to protect an accused person's right to a fair trial. But the Court went on to rule that such interference would be justified only where there was a real risk of an unfair trial if contemporaneous reporting were allowed, and if the damage which any improper reporting would cause could not be remedied by the trial judge either by giving appropriate directions by the jury or otherwise.[70] Chief Justice Hamilton accepted that an accused's right to a fair trial included the right to have the jury reach a verdict by reference only to evidence lawfully admitted at the trial and not by reference to facts, alleged or otherwise, contained in statements or opinions gathered from the media or any other outside sources. But he considered that, provided reporting was fair and accurate, it was hard to envisage any circumstances (other than where a trial within a trial is held to determine the admissibility of evidence or where persons are jointly indicted but tried separately) where fair and accurate reporting of proceedings publicly heard before a court could prejudice the right to a fair trial. The circuit judge was not entitled to assume on the evidence before him that the reporting of the proceedings would be other than fair, and even if at any stage the reporting proved to be unfair, he was not entitled to assume that the risk of unfairness could not be avoided by appropriate rulings and directions by the judge.

The Chief Justice also made some comment on the number of recent trials that had been aborted as a result of media coverage. While he defended the right of the trial judge to discharge a jury where the risk of an unfair trial could not be remedied by appropriate rulings and directions to the jury, he urged that:

> [s]ave in exceptional circumstances, a trial judge should have confidence in the ability of the jury to understand and comply with such directions, to disregard any inadmissible evidence and to give a true verdict in accordance with the

[68] [1998] 2 I.L.R.M. 161.
[69] [1994] 2 I.R. 465.
[70] See also Z. v. Director of Public Prosecutions (1994) 2 I.R. 476.

evidence. It is only when this is not possible that the extreme step shall be taken of discharging the jury.[71]

It may be necessary to curb the freedom of the media and even, in extreme cases, to abort a trial altogether when there is a real risk of jury prejudice. But there can be little doubt that when these steps are taken the effect is to undermine confidence yet again in the institution of the jury. The Chief Justice made this very point in an earlier case when he said that when juries have regard for factors other than the evidence given at trial, they are disregarding their oath to deliver a 'true verdict in accordance with the evidence'.[72] The Chief Justice observed that in his eighteen years of practice at the Bar and nineteen years of service as a judge, he shared the confidence that the system has in the ability of juries to act in accordance with their oath. The difficulty is that there is a lack of empirical evidence to substantiate this confidence. Little is known, certainly in Ireland, about what effect media coverage has on juries and whether judicial directions to disregard media coverage can be effective. There is often cynicism expressed about the effectiveness of judicial warnings.[73] At the same time, when juries are formally instructed to follow certain directions, there is no evidence that juries do not try their best to follow them. One of the values of jury trial in an adversary system is that there is a full opportunity for the parties to present their case and for the tribunal of fact to be formally instructed on how to proceed in a manner that cannot be so easily emulated when the same tribunal has to both preside over the trial and come to a decision.[74] When, on the other hand, there is evidence that juries are unable or unwilling to give defendants a fair trial in certain circumstances, then clearly jury trial is no longer such an attractive method of trial and thought has to be given to alternatives. Confidence in juries is also undermined, of course, when juries are disinclined to give the prosecution case a fair hearing. This takes us back to the social and political context in which juries have had to operate in Ireland. Mention has been made of Ireland's turbulent past, but the troubles have lingered on well into the

[71] [1998] 2 I.L.R.M. at 174.

[72] Z. v. Director of Public Prosecutions (1994) 2 I.R. 476.

[73] See, e.g., R. Munday, *Irregular Disclosure of Evidence of Bad Character*, 1990 Crim. L. Rev. 92–7 (arguing that judicial incantations to juries exhorting them to disregard potent evidence of an accused's disposition are unconvincing).

[74] See John D. Jackson, *The Value of Jury Trial*, *in* Criminal Justice: United Kingdom Association for Legal and Social Philosophy: Twentieth Annual Conference at Glasgow, 24–6 March 1994, at 79 (Elspeth Attwood & David Golberg eds., 1995).

twentieth century, especially in Northern Ireland where violence has been rife, particularly in the last third of the century, and this has posed a major challenge for the jury system.

IV. The Northern Ireland Jury and the 'Troubles'

We have seen that Ireland's turbulent history has not provided fertile ground for the growth and flourishing of jury trial. One of the commonly invoked strengths of jury trial in criminal cases is that its lay element acts as an independent buffer within the criminal justice system between the state and the individual, allowing independent external scrutiny of the prosecution's case. This lends legitimacy to the fairness and independence of the system as a whole. When the legitimacy of the state is questioned by a sizeable proportion of the community from which the lay element is drawn, however, and it proves difficult to obtain convictions, the jury system can present formidable problems of law enforcement, especially when the conditions are extreme enough to lend themselves to violence and intimidation.

During the course of this century, there have been periods when the violence has been so extreme that the state has resorted to measures such as the introduction of martial law or the detention of suspects without trial, which have resulted not only in the disbandment of the jury system but in the disbandment of the criminal process altogether.[75] At other times, the state has reacted by taking emergency measures *within* the criminal process, for instance the introduction of trial without jury. Mention has been made of intentions to set up a 'Special Commission Court' under the Prevention of Crime (Ireland) Act 1882. Likewise, the Criminal Procedure (Northern Ireland) Act 1922 made provision for the trial of certain serious offences in Northern Ireland by a special court consisting of the Lord Chief Justice and one other judge of the Court of Appeal when the accused so requested or when the Attorney General so directed such a trial. Neither of these courts was actually constituted and put into practice, however, and the concept of trying serious cases without a jury in Ireland did not take hold until 1939 when, as we have

[75] For a discussion of the use of emergency law during the worst period of violence in Ireland this century, from 1918 to 1925, see COLM CAMPBELL, EMERGENCY LAW IN IRELAND, 1918–1925 (1994). Since then, detention without trial has been deployed periodically under emergency legislation in both parts of Ireland. The power to detain without trial still exists under emergency legislation in the south, but it was recently removed in Northern Ireland under the Northern Ireland (Emergency Provisions) Act 1998.

seen, a special three-judge court was established in the Republic of Ireland under the Offences Against the State Act 1939.

It has not been until the latest period of 'troubles', however, largely located in Northern Ireland, that extensive use has been made of nonjury courts within the criminal process. As already mentioned, the Special Criminal Court was re-established in the Republic of Ireland in 1972, but more significantly within Northern Ireland itself jury trial was suspended for a range of offences known as 'scheduled offences' under the Northern Ireland (Emergency Provisions) Act 1973 following the recommendations of a commission chaired by Lord Diplock.[76] The Diplock Commission was set up shortly after the British government prorogued the local Stormont Parliament in 1972 and assumed direct control over Northern Ireland's affairs. Its purpose was to consider what measures should be taken to deal more effectively with terrorism without resorting to internment. The use of internment by the Stormont Government in 1971 under emergency legislation dating back to 1922 had merely contributed to an intensification of the 'troubles' and there was an urgent need to consider alternative measures. Although the Commission recommended a range of measures for dealing with political violence within the criminal justice system, the recommendation that certain serious criminal offences should henceforth be tried in the ordinary courts by a single judge without a jury stood out at the time as the most drastic departure from the ordinary criminal process and has proved to be one of the most enduring measures. Until recent years, when the violence has abated, 'Diplock' trials, as trials by judge alone in emergency cases have come to be called in Northern Ireland, accounted for around a third of all serious cases in the jurisdiction.[77]

A. *Suspension of the Jury*

Although the Diplock courts have proved controversial, there has been more common ground in the Diplock debate and at the same time more shades of differing opinion within a general consensus than is sometimes recognized.[78] First of all, there has been a general consensus among

[76] See REPORT OF THE COMMISSION TO CONSIDER LEGAL PROCEDURES TO DEAL WITH TERRORIST ACTIVITIES IN NORTHERN IRELAND, 1972, Cmnd. 5185 (hereinafter Diplock Commission).

[77] See A COMMENTARY ON NORTHERN IRELAND CRIME STATISTICS 1993 (1994); A COMMENTARY ON NORTHERN IRELAND CRIME STATISTICS 1996, tbls. 4.7, 4.9 (1997).

[78] For further discussion of the Diplock debate and a full analysis of Diplock trials, see JOHN D. JACKSON & SEAN DORAN, JUDGE WITHOUT JURY: DIPLOCK TRIALS IN THE ADVERSARY SYSTEM (1995).

almost all protagonists that within the adversary system, trial by jury is the ideal method of trying serious criminal cases,[79] although there has been some dispute about whether the next best alternative ought to take the form of trial by a single judge, trial by two or three judges, or trial by a judge and lay assessors.[80] The debate has focused instead very firmly on the peculiar exigencies of the Northern Ireland situation. This seems to reflect the general consensus throughout Ireland that the jury system is still the ideal form of trial but that it is not always entirely suited to Irish circumstances.

The Diplock Commission considered that, in the circumstances of Northern Ireland in 1972, jury trial was deficient for two reasons. First, violence on the part of paramilitary organizations meant there was a persistent threat of intimidation which extended to jurors as well as witnesses, and 'a frightened juror is a bad juror even though his own safety and that of his family may not actually be at risk'.[81] Secondly, the Commission pointed to the danger of perverse verdicts by partisan jurors. The property qualifications for jury service which existed at that time were more widely met by Protestants than by Catholics, and the rights of stand-by and challenge were exercised in such a way as to accentuate Protestant representation on the jury, with the result that there was a fear that Loyalist defendants in particular had been 'unjustly acquitted'.[82] These conclusions were criticized at the time and have been criticized since on the ground of lack of empirical evidence.[83] Since then, the property qualification has been abolished in Northern Ireland, as in England and Wales, and juries are empanelled on the basis of random selection from the electoral register.[84] The enduring rationale for the

[79] The consensus has not been entirely universal. See Louis Blom-Cooper, Public Confidence and the Criminal Process 16 (1991) (Northern Ireland Criminal Justice conference unpublished paper) (arguing that trial by judge alone provides a 'model system of criminal trial and a rational system of justice').

[80] The merits and defects of three-judge trials are discussed in Review of the Operation of the Northern Ireland (Emergency Provisions) Act 1978, 1984, Cmnd. 9222 (hereinafter Baker Report), and John Jackson, *Three Judge Courts in Northern Ireland*, in Twelfth Report of the Standing Advisory Commission on Human Rights: Annual Report for 1985–86, at 63 (1987). Support for the notion of involving lay assessors is to be found in Kevin Boyle *et al.*, Ten Years on in Northern Ireland: The Legal Control of Political Violence (1980).

[81] Diplock Commission, *supra* note 76, para. 36.

[82] Ibid.

[83] See Steven C. Greer & Antony White, Abolishing the Diplock Courts ch. 4 (1986); W. L. Twining, *Emergency Provisions and Criminal Process: The Diplock Report* [1973] Crim. L. Rev. 406, 413.

[84] The law was changed shortly after the Diplock Commission reported by the Juries (N.I.) Order 1974. The relevant legislation today is the Juries (N.I.) Order 1996.

Diplock courts has therefore tended to be based on the intimidation argument rather than on the problem of perverse acquittals.[85]

The argument is still controversial, particularly so within the last few years when there has been a sharp decline in the level of violence in Northern Ireland.[86] But when it has come to discussion of the policy options available over the years, few at any time have seen the choice as a stark one between wholesale adoption of the Diplock system and immediate return of jury trial in all cases. No one, for example, has argued that the jury system works so badly in the Northern Ireland context that it is necessary to extend the present Diplock system, and at the other extreme, most of those who have been in the forefront of the demand for the restoration of jury trial have recognised that it may be necessary to abandon jury trial in specific instances where it is shown that attempts have been made to interfere with a jury.[87] The issue instead has become one of determining whether the present system strikes the correct balance between protecting against the dangers of juror bias and intimidation and upholding the ideal of jury trial where possible. This is not to say that there have not been a number of other controversial issues affecting the operation of the Diplock courts. There have been concerns about judicial case-hardening, over-reliance on confession evidence, the use of so-called 'supergrass' evidence,[88] the abrogation of the right of silence, and, most recently, miscarriages of justice. However, many of these relate to other emergency measures, such as the increased powers of arrest and detention given to the security forces, and the relaxation of the rules of evidence that have accompanied the withdrawal of jury trial.[89] It has been argued that these issues have seriously discredited the courts domestically and internationally,[90] but on the

[85] See, *e.g.*, Baker Report, *supra* note 80, ¶ 107.

[86] See COMMITTEE ON THE ADMINISTRATION OF JUSTICE, NO EMERGENCY, NO EMERGENCY LAW: EMERGENCY LEGISLATION RELATED TO NORTHERN IRELAND: THE CASE FOR REPEAL (1995).

[87] See GREER & WHITE, *supra* note 83, at 66–8.

[88] The term 'supergrass' was first coined in the early 1970s to describe those 'grasses' or informers from the London underworld who testified against their former associates in a series of high-profile mass trials. See STEVEN GREER, SUPERGRASSES: INFORMERS AND ANTI-TERRORIST LAW ENFORCEMENT IN NORTHERN IRELAND 1 (1995). In one such trial, Bertie Smalls gave evidence against a large number of persons allegedly involved in a series of robberies. See R. v. Turner (1975) 61 Cr. App. 67 (Eng.).

[89] For a full analysis of all of these issues, see JACKSON & DORAN, *supra* note 78, at 29–55.

[90] See Fionnuala Ní Aolain, *The Fortification of an Emergency Regime*, 59 ALB. L. REV. 1353, 1378 (1996); see also Paul Hunt & Brice Dickson, *Northern Ireland's Emergency Laws and International Human Rights*, 11 NETHS. Q. HUM. RTS. 173 (1993).

central question of abrogation of jury trial itself, few have argued that this is itself fundamentally unfair where the conditions truly make jury trial unworkable.[91]

There has, however, been a strongly argued view that the scheduling system at the core of Diplock court procedure has operated in such a way as to draw too many 'ordinary' cases within the Diplock net.[92] The term 'scheduled offence' derives from the fact that offences deemed appropriate for trial by judge alone in Diplock courts are listed in Schedule 1 to the Northern Ireland (Emergency Provisions) Act 1996.[93] These include a wide range of serious criminal offences which are all capable of being committed in connection with the emergency situation. The list ranges from general criminal offences such as murder, manslaughter, wounding with intent, grievous bodily harm, and assault occasioning actual bodily harm to offences more specifically related to the troubles such as membership of a proscribed organization.[94] Since not all cases where these offences have occurred have been connected to the troubles, the Attorney General is given discretion in a particular case to certify that certain scheduled offences are not to be treated as scheduled offences and are therefore to be dealt with by jury trial.[95]

One criticism has been that this power does not extend to all offences listed in the schedule, with the result that certain offences are incapable of being certified for jury trial even where there is no palpable connection with the emergency. The United Kingdom government has progressively taken steps to rectify this by extending the list of scheduled offences which can be certified out, notably the offences of robbery and aggravated burglary which, until 1996, had to be treated as scheduled offences where any weapon was used to carry out the offence.[96] But

[91] It is to be noted that Art. 6 of the European Convention on Human Rights does not guarantee a right to jury trial. It has, however, been argued that a system of trial by judge alone alongside a system of jury trial could amount to a breach of Art. 26 of the Covenant on Civil and Political Rights which guarantees equal protection under the law. See Brice Dickson, *Northern Ireland's Emergency Legislation—the Wrong Medicine* [1992] PUB. LAW 592, 607.

[92] John D. Jackson & Sean Doran, *Diplock and the Presumption Against Jury Trial: A Critique* [1992] CRIM. L. REV. 755.

[93] The first Northern Ireland (Emergency Provisions) Act dates back to 1973. Since then, there have been periodic revisions and consolidating statutes. The latest Act is the Northern Ireland (Emergency Provisions) Act 1998.

[94] See Northern Ireland (Emergency Provisions) Act 1996, at sched. 1.

[95] See ibid.

[96] See ibid. S. 2 of the more recent 1998 Act increases quite substantially the number of offences which can be certified out.

another criticism is that, as the security situation has improved, there has been no attempt made to offset the present scheduling system's presumption against jury trial by establishing a broad presumption in favour of jury trial which would require the Attorney General to certify for Diplock trial any particular case with a connection to the troubles. It has been argued that while such a move would probably not of itself dramatically affect the number of cases going to trial in Diplock courts, it would have considerable symbolic force, as it would represent an official affirmation of faith in the jury system.[97]

This raises the question whether such faith is justified, which shall be addressed shortly. As the security situation hopefully improves, it may be expected that the enduring rationale for the Diplock courts—the threat of intimidation of jurors—will become less defensible and pressures will mount for a full-scale restoration of trial by jury. At the same time, while paramilitary organizations continue to operate, there are likely to continue to be certain cases which have a paramilitary connection where the risks of juror intimidation may be as great as they ever were. One recent well-publicized case, involving eight men charged with armed robbery in Belfast, was certified for jury trial despite reports that the men had IRA connections. Seven trials involving seven juries reportedly took place before the case was finally stopped, and one of the trials collapsed amid allegations of jury tampering.[98] The case has provided reasons to be cautious about an outright restoration of jury trial.

The answer to such cases, however, may be to try to take more active steps to protect the jury from intimidation. It has been suggested that the category of scheduled offences should be used as a basis not for withdrawal of the jury but for the application of certain safeguards in the selection of juries.[99] The measures suggested include withdrawing the names and addresses of jury panels,[100] balloting of jurors by number only,[101] preventing the disclosure of the names and addresses of jurors at all stages,[102] not informing jurors whether they will serve in scheduled

[97] See Jackson & Doran, *supra* note 92, at 764. Such a procedure has been endorsed by Lord Lloyd, Inquiry into Legislation Against Terrorism 30–1 (1996) (hereinafter Lloyd Report).

[98] See John Mullin, *The Trying Game*, Guardian, Jan. 20, 1998, at 17.

[99] See C. A. Gearty & J. A. Kimball, Terrorism and the Rule of Law 56–7 (1995).

[100] See ibid.; Greer & White, *supra* note 83, at 74.

[101] See Gearty & Kimball, *supra* note 99, at 56–7; Greer & White, *supra* note 83, at 75.

[102] See Gearty & Kimball, *supra* note 99, at 56–7; Greer & White, *supra* note 83, at 75.

or nonscheduled cases,[103] keeping the jury out of sight of the public gallery in scheduled cases,[104] and favouring applications for excusal in scheduled cases from people living in areas where Loyalist or Republican paramilitaries have a particularly strong influence.[105] Although such measures represent regrettable departures from the ideals of fully open and public justice, they have been considered preferable to maintaining Diplock courts.[106]

In the absence of an all-embracing threat of political violence which plagues the effective operation of the jury system, it may be argued that there is no particular reason for distinguishing between defendants charged with particular paramilitary offences and, say, defendants charged with the kind of gangland or drug-related offences that have been familiar in London. In both cases, there is a risk of juror intimidation. But there has been little demand in England and Wales for such offences to be tried without a jury and instead the effort there has gone into steps to prevent intimidation, such as the withholding of jurors' names.[107]

This brings us, however, to the point made throughout this book that each jury system is embedded in a unique political and cultural context, and that it must not be assumed that the same approach is suitable for all systems. In England and Wales, jury trial for serious criminal offences is considered not merely an ideal mode of trial but for many an essential, ancient right; hence the controversy when it is suggested that serious criminal offences such as fraud should be tried by some other mode or that the right to elect jury trial in certain categories of cases should be removed.[108] It has already been seen that jury trial is less rooted in Irish

[103] See Gearty & Kimball, *supra* note 99, at 56–7; Greer & White, *supra* note 83, at 75.

[104] See Gearty & Kimball, *supra* note 99, at 56–7; Greer & White, *supra* note 83, at 75.

[105] See Gearty & Kimball, *supra* note 99, at 56–7; Greer & White, *supra* note 83, at 76.

[106] See Gearty & Kimball, *supra* note 99, at 56–7.

[107] Other steps have included keeping jurors out of sight of the public gallery in sensitive cases (recommended by Royal Commission on Criminal Justice, 1993, Cm 2263, at ch. 8), round-the-clock police protection (recommended by ibid.), new offences of intimidating jurors and harming or threatening harm to jurors (adopted in the Criminal Justice and Public Order Act 1994, s. 51(1)–(2) (Eng.); for commentary, see Martin Wasik & Richard Taylor, Criminal Justice & Public Order Act 1994, at 131–3 (1995)), and the retrial of defendants who have been acquitted by juries which have been 'got at' (provided for in the Criminal Procedure and Investigations Act 1996, ss. 54–7 (Eng.); for commentary, see Roger Leng & Richard Taylor, Criminal Procedure and Investigations Act 1996, at 91–106 (1997)).

[108] The U.K. government has recently invited comments on both these issues. See Home Office, Determining Mode of Trial in Either-Way Cases (1998); Home Office, Juries in Serious Fraud Trials (1998).

history. Beyond that, there is the question whether a community as divided as Northern Ireland is as suited to jury trial as less polarized communities. The Diplock Commission's reference to the danger of perverse verdicts by partisan juries was made at a time when property qualifications were more widely met by Protestants and there was a risk of under-representation of Catholics. But even with more balanced juries, there is a danger of unfair discrimination on religious or political grounds. This raises the question of how the jury in Northern Ireland has operated throughout the years of the troubles and whether it is worth placing faith in a full-scale return to the system.

B. The Jury System in Ordinary Criminal Cases

Leaving aside the scheduling system under emergency legislation, the rules governing the scope of the right to jury trial in Northern Ireland are similar to England and Wales. All offences must be tried summarily or on indictment. Some offences must be tried on indictment in the Crown Court and others, known as 'hybrid offences', may be tried either in the magistrates' court or in the Crown Court.[109] There are three kinds of hybrid offences. The first of these are summary offences for which a defendant can claim trial by jury (provided they are not scheduled offences). These offences are normally tried in the magistrates' court, but if the offence is one for which the person, if convicted, is liable to be sent to prison for more than six months, the defendant must be informed of his right to be tried by jury, unless the offence is a scheduled offence. Secondly, certain indictable offences may be tried summarily if the magistrate believes the case is not a serious one and the prosecution and defence consent. Thirdly, certain offences are stated to be triable either summarily or on indictment, which means that the prosecution decides how the case will be tried.

Since the property qualification was removed in 1974, the composition of the jury in Northern Ireland has also been based on very similar lines to that of England and Wales.[110] Every person who is between 18 and 70 and is registered as an elector is qualified and liable for jury service. There is no residence requirement. The disqualification, ineligibility, and excusal criteria provisions are almost exactly the same as for England and Wales, except that full-time teachers in any school may refuse to serve in

[109] See Magistrates' Courts (N.I.) Order 1981, arts. 29, 45, 46.
[110] *Cf.* Lloyd-Bostock & Thomas, *supra* note 4, at 20–3.

addition to all the other categories of persons who are excusable. The same rules permitting majority verdicts also apply in Northern Ireland.[111]

One significant difference, however, lies in the scope for peremptory challenging in Northern Ireland. Both parties to criminal proceedings are entitled to an unlimited number of challenges to jurors for cause, but, as in England and Wales, challenges for cause are rare. As well as this, however, each defendant is allowed to challenge up to twelve jurors without cause, and evidence suggests that this is a much more frequent occurrence.[112] Figures obtained from the Court Service for a two-month period in 1988 show that in a sample of forty-one cases, there were no challenges for cause, but the average number of peremptory challenges per defendant was nine, and in over a third of the cases defendants exercised their full rights of peremptory challenge.[113] In addition, the prosecution's right to stand-by, which is unlimited, was used to remove on average between four and five jurors per defendant.

Although it has been suggested that the peremptory challenge system can undermine the jury system by permitting the packing of juries according to religious denomination,[114] the recent Juries Order preserved the defence right to challenge up to twelve jurors. In a strong defence of the right of peremptory challenge in the Northern Ireland context, the Standing Advisory Commission on Human Rights has taken the view that the peremptory challenge provides an important 'safety valve', enabling defendants to correct any perceived religious imbalance.[115] When linked with the prosecution's right to stand-by, the right of peremptory challenge enabled the defence to have confidence in the impartiality of the jury and the prosecution to seek to secure a fair trial. Although the Commission had no doubt that panels were randomly selected, panels were unlikely to be representative of the community when exemptions and excusals were taken into account, and challenging was a mechanism whereby any perceived prejudice could be removed. There is no empirical evidence available on the grounds on which parties exercise their right to challenge or stand-by, nor is there any evidence on whether juries end up being representative of the community. The challenging system is certainly a mechanism whereby both

[111] See Criminal Procedure (Majority Verdicts) Act 1971, s. 1 (N.I.).

[112] See Juries (N.I.) Order 1996, art. 15.

[113] See Sixteenth Report of the Standing Advisory Commission on Human Rights: Report for 1990–1991, at ch. 6 (1991) (hereinafter Sixteenth Report).

[114] See Gearty & Kimball, *supra* note 99, ¶ 3.85.

[115] Sixteenth Report, *supra* note 113, ¶ 6.33.

sides can achieve a reasonably balanced jury, but questions can be asked about what message this sends about the degree of confidence that can be placed in the jury system as a system of trial by one's peers.[116]

Little is known about the operation of juries in Northern Ireland. Section 8 of the Contempt of Court Act 1981 applies in Northern Ireland as in England and Wales, with the result that jurors cannot be asked about their discussions in the jury room. Some insight into the operation of the jury system was, however, obtained by one of the authors in a survey conducted into the experiences of laypersons in the criminal justice system in Northern Ireland.[117] Questionnaires covering aspects of jury service were handed to jurors over a six-month period after their month's service at Belfast Crown Court. The 237 panellists who responded were concerned about a number of matters, including the challenging system.[118] Significantly, however, there was little evidence to support the particular concerns about juries voiced by the Diplock Commission, although the cases tried were all ordinary cases unconnected directly with the Northern Ireland emergency. As in England and Wales, large numbers of jurors were able to get excused during the fieldwork period.[119] A third of all jurors in the sample considered the possibility of excusal and 10 percent actually tried to be excused (unsuccessfully) on grounds of occupation, ill health, or a specific work problem.[120] But the most common reason for wanting to be excused was the inconvenience of jury service.[121] Forty percent said they were worried about serving, but no one mentioned fear of intimidation as the reason.[122] Fear of the unknown and ignorance of procedures seemed to be the most important factors.[123] Similarly, no one made any allegations of jurors discriminating on religious or political grounds. Fifty percent of jurors thought the jury system was fair, 15 percent unfair, and 35 percent were unsure; these proportions were similar for both Catholic and Protestant jurors.[124] Overall, 91 percent of those who served on a jury agreed with the verdicts reached in their cases, and 9 percent disagreed.[125]

[116] For further discussion on the advantages and disadvantages of peremptory challenging, see S. J. ADLER, THE JURY: TRIAL AND ERROR IN THE AMERICAN COURTROOM 221–4 (1994); John D. Jackson & Sean Doran, *Juries and Judges: A View From Across the Atlantic*, CRIM. JUST., Winter 1997, at 15, 16.

[117] See JOHN D. JACKSON *ET AL.*, CALLED TO COURT: A PUBLIC REVIEW OF CRIMINAL JUSTICE IN NORTHERN IRELAND (1991).

[118] See ibid., at 89–95. [119] See ibid., at 59–60.

[120] See ibid., at 59. [121] See ibid., at 59–60.

[122] See ibid., at 59. [123] See ibid., at 60.

[124] See ibid., at 146. [125] See ibid., at 128–9.

The survey provided no basis for speculation about how the system would cope with scheduled cases. It is also dangerous to infer too much about jury performance in ordinary cases from a small survey based on jury perceptions. But it has been argued that the survey provides little ground for believing that peculiar exigencies of the Northern Ireland situation were having an adverse effect on the workings of the jury system in ordinary criminal cases and to that extent supported the position of those who have advocated a presumption in favour of jury trial.[126]

The survey was confined to Belfast juries, where it has been suggested that there is a greater likelihood of middle class, commercial, or better educated jurors serving on the juries.[127] No research has been carried out into the workings of juries in the rural areas of Northern Ireland outside Belfast. There is some evidence to suggest that the perennial Irish problem of low jury acquittal rates manifests itself in these areas. By itself, the fact that acquittal rates have been generally higher in jury trials than in Diplock trials does not provide any ground for concern about acquittal rates.[128] There is an obvious danger in measuring jury performance against professional performance, as it cannot be assumed that the professional approach is necessarily correct.[129] What gives rise to greater concern is when there are very different rates of jury acquittals throughout a particular jurisdiction. It is part of Northern Ireland legal folklore that jury acquittal rates are much higher in the west of the province than in the east of the province, and there is some evidence to support this. North Down, for example, is reputed to have the highest conviction rate of any jury in the United Kingdom, while Fermanagh and Tyrone are reputed to have the lowest.[130] The reasons for this are no doubt varied. Interviews with prosecuting counsel by one of the authors revealed that there is a reluctance to rely on police evidence in certain parts of the country, but, according to one very senior prosecuting counsel, the reasons were less political and had more to do with the nature of the offences and close rural ties:

[126] See Jackson & Doran, *supra* note 92, at 762.

[127] See Jackson & Doran, *supra* note 78, at 238.

[128] For detailed comparison of outcomes in jury and Diplock trials, see ibid., at 35.

[129] See Zenon Bankowski & Geoff Mungham, Images of Law (1976); M. D. A. Freeman, *The Jury on Trial* (1981) 34 Current Legal Probs. 65.

[130] See Jackson & Doran, *supra* note 78, at 170. There is evidence to show that in areas such as Fermanagh and Tyrone, acquittal rates can rise higher than 60%. See Northern Ireland Court Service, Northern Ireland Judicial Statistics, 1995, tbl. 4.

> [I]n the country there's still the view that the law case is to some extent a sort of game. The point about the old Irish jury trials is that they were for such things as assaults, stealing in certain forms but very little by way of murder. But the crime problem was not a very big problem and therefore the community reacted very often by thinking that the guy being tried at all represented a punishment for him and therefore they wouldn't increase that punishment by convicting.[131]

These comments suggest that when Northern Ireland enters a genuine climate of peace, there will still be questions to be asked about the effective operation of jury trial and a need to review the existing procedures. No doubt mechanisms could be found for dealing with some of the problems. It has been suggested that fears of sectarian bias might be laid to rest if terrorist-related cases were tried in Belfast by juries selected on a province-wide basis.[132] It may be that for a range of serious criminal cases greater scope could be given to the prosecution and defence to argue for a change of venue. These mechanisms, along with peremptory challenges, are examples of how the jury system may have to be prepared to adapt itself to particular conditions and concerns. But at the same time, they also raise fundamental questions about the suitability of this mode of trial. Many of the mechanisms take the jury system further away from its original rationale, which was to provide for a mode of trial whereby a group of the defendant's peers would be randomly selected from the community to try the defendant. Widespread use of peremptory challenging and changes of venue serve to underline the point that a randomly selected jury from the defendant's community cannot be trusted to deliver a fair and impartial verdict and can ultimately serve to undermine confidence in the whole system.

At this point, questions need to be asked about the viability of other modes of trial. The point has been made that discussion of modes of trial within the United Kingdom has tended to reflect a rather myopic perception that Crown Court trial and trial by magistrates are the sole methods of bringing criminal proceedings to a satisfactory resolution, and that other modes of trial such as trial by judge alone or trial by judge and lay assessors are very much a second best.[133] As in England and Wales, a greater proportion of offences in Northern Ireland are being

[131] Jackson & Doran, *supra* note 78, at 238.

[132] See Lloyd Report, *supra* note 97, ¶ 16.18.

[133] See John D. Jackson & Sean Doran, *The Relevance to Northern Ireland of the Report of the Royal Commission on Criminal Justice*, in Nineteenth Report of the Standing Advisory Commission on Human Rights, Report for 1993–94, annex C (1994).

deemed triable by summary trial and a greater proportion of ordinary cases are therefore being tried by magistrates rather than by juries in the Crown Court. The time has perhaps come to reflect on whether the Diplock mode of trial by judge alone or by judge and lay assessors may serve as a better ideal in certain circumstances. Giving the defendant the right to elect for such a mode of trial in certain serious criminal cases, as is permitted in a number of Commonwealth countries, may, for example, prove to be a better 'safety valve' than requiring defendants to undergo jury trial, albeit with the right to exercise a large number of peremptory challenges.[134]

It has been suggested that as a first step on the road from Diplock courts, the Attorney General ought to be empowered on application by either the defence or the prosecution to order that a particular case should be tried by a judge sitting without a jury where, in his or her opinion, the existence of a conspicuous terrorist element is likely to present difficulties for the conduct of the trial and be prejudicial to the interests of justice.[135] This proposal has been made very much as a transitional measure pending full return to jury trial, but it raises questions whether such a certifying-in procedure might not be suitable for a wider range of situations and on a more permanent basis.[136] This kind of mechanism effectively exists at present in the Irish Republic, where the Director of Public Prosecutions has a fairly wide power to certify-in any particular case where 'the ordinary courts are inadequate for securing the effective administration of justice and the preservation of public peace and order'.[137] This brings us finally to a consideration of the future role and scope of jury trial within modern Ireland as a whole.

V. Conclusion

This chapter has painted a picture of a jury system in decline in both parts of Ireland. Many of the measures which have reduced the right to jury trial have mirrored changes in England and Wales, and, indeed, further inroads have been made by virtue of the nonjury courts estab-

[134] See Sean Doran & John D. Jackson, *The Case for Jury Waiver* [1997] CRIM. L. REV. 155.

[135] See LLOYD REPORT, *supra* note 97, ¶ 16.16.

[136] See the proposals of John D. Jackson & Sean Doran, *Emergency Provisions in Northern Ireland*, in TWENTY FIRST REPORT OF THE STANDING ADVISORY COMMISSION ON HUMAN RIGHTS, REPORT FOR 1995–96, at 113 (1996).

[137] CONST. art. 38.3 (Ir.); see also *supra* text following note 53 (discussing the Special Criminal Court).

lished both north and south of the border. Unlike England and Wales, however, these changes have taken place against the background of very little controversy, certainly in southern Ireland. The withdrawal of the jury in Northern Ireland and its replacement by Diplock courts has been controversial, but more on account of the emergency measures which have accompanied the withdrawal of the jury than on account of the denial of jury trial *per se*. In the Republic of Ireland, the declining reach of the jury, even the wide power given to the Director of Public Prosecutions to certify cases for nonjury trial in the Special Criminal Court, has given rise to surprisingly little controversy.[138]

The explanation for this would seem to lie in the history of jury trial in Ireland. For a variety of reasons, jury trial has not proved well suited to Irish circumstances. Jury intimidation and prejudice, distrust of the state, considerable community segregation, and the small and largely rural nature of the jurisdictions have combined to ensure that jury trial is by no means as entrenched in Irish legal culture as it is in England and Wales. Although a great number of these obstacles to the growth of a robust jury system have abated in recent times, jury trial has failed to flourish on the island.

Unlike other systems, such as those in the United States and more recently Canada, where the constitutional guarantee seems to have helped to bolster the institution of the jury,[139] the constitutional guarantee in Ireland has failed to halt the decline. The Supreme Court has adopted a pragmatic approach which in effect seems to permit the scope of jury trial and the powers of the jury to be influenced by contemporary perceptions of a fair trial. If the prevailing perception is that a fair trial can be guaranteed without a jury, it would seem that the Supreme Court is not necessarily going to stand in the way. Indeed, it can be argued that the very existence of a constitution protecting basic fundamental freedoms reduces the need for jury trial.[140] The enduring rationale for a jury system in criminal cases has been that it provides a buffer between the individual and the state and thereby a guarantee against state tyranny. We have seen that jury trial was entrenched in the Irish Constitution largely because of fear of abuse of power on the part of the state. As the Supreme Court has proved more

[138] There is also surprisingly little legal and academic literature on the contemporary Irish jury.

[139] See Neil Vidmar, *The Canadian Criminal Jury: Searching for a Middle Ground*, Ch. 6, This volume.

[140] See R. J. O'Hanlon, *The Sacred Cow of Trial by Jury* (1990) 27 Ir. Jur. 57, 65.

active in preventing encroachment on constitutional rights by the state, however, this particular justification for the jury becomes more superfluous.[141]

Other justifications, of course, remain. A further attraction of jury trial is that it acts as link between the community of professional participants who operate within the criminal justice system and the community outside, injecting, as it has been put, 'lay acid' into the system.[142] This is only an advantage, however, if it is possible to find juries who are representative of the community and who can be trusted to bring a degree of impartiality to the case. We have seen that in the past the jury system was plagued by low conviction rates. In fact, conviction rates in Ireland continue to remain quite low, at least in comparison with England and Wales. At the same time, many of the traditional reasons for very low conviction rates in Ireland seem to be diminishing. There is less suspicion of the state and less tolerance of crime (which has risen in all areas of Ireland, particularly urban property crime in the Dublin area).[143] The murder of an Irish journalist in 1996 in particular prompted concern and caused the Dáil to introduce tougher measures against criminals.[144] All this is likely to make juries more inclined to convict where there is clear evidence of guilt.

But problems of representativeness remain. The divided nature of Northern Irish society and the small and largely rural nature of both jurisdictions continue to pose problems of jury representativeness and impartiality. The use of peremptory challenges has in the past been used to mitigate some of these problems and, as we have seen, is still defended as an important 'safety valve' in the north. At the same time, this power hardly affirms confidence in the system, as it suggests that certain individuals are unable to put aside their personal prejudices when they serve on a jury. Moreover, the peremptory challenge system runs the risk of perpetuating rather than diminishing religious, political, racial, ethnic, and gender discrimination.

[141] For details of the growing activism of the Supreme Court in protecting constitutional rights, see JAMES P. CASEY, CONSTITUTIONAL LAW IN IRELAND (2d ed. 1992); KELLY *ET AL.*, *supra* note 24.

[142] Z. Bankowski, *The Jury and Reality*, in THE JURY UNDER ATTACK, *supra* note 60, at 20.

[143] See JOHN D. BREWER *ET AL.*, CRIME IN IRELAND 1945–1995: HERE BE DRAGONS 84–8 (1997).

[144] See Ian O'Donnell, *Crime Prevention More Vital Than Punishment*, IR. TIMES, July 27, 1996.

It seems that the future of the jury system in Ireland is bleak unless greater steps are taken to build confidence in its ability to render verdicts which are just and reliable and to attune it more to the needs of the modern Irish criminal justice system. It has been argued that the jury is an ideal mode of trial within an adversary system of justice, as it helps to ensure that the prosecution's case is thoroughly presented and examined.[145] Ireland inherited a strong adversary tradition from the English common law, and this tradition is maintained by a strong bar dedicated to effective advocacy.[146] Many also regard lay participation in the criminal justice system as a very valuable means of promoting confidence in the system.[147] At the same time, as these chapters illustrate, there are many different kinds of jury systems and each has to be suited to the political, cultural, and legal contexts in which it is embedded.[148] The prevalent view that juries are unsuited to the Irish context is likely to continue unless steps are taken to look more exactingly at how juries are presently selected and how they are actually working. A contrast has been drawn by one of the authors between the secretive attitude adopted toward juries in the United Kingdom and Ireland and the much more open attitude in the United States and Canada.[149] Openness carries the risk of unwelcome exposure but is arguably a healthier attitude to adopt if one is serious about the longer-term future of an institution.[150] Secrecy, on the other hand, is a sign of weakness and is likely to lead to ultimate decline. More open examination of the Irish jury might expose a number

[145] For full discussion, see JACKSON & DORAN, *supra* note 78, at 287–304; Sean Doran *et al.*, *Rethinking Adversariness in Non-Jury Criminal Trials*, 23 AM. J. CRIM. L. 1 (1995); Jackson, *supra* note 74.

[146] Some of this advocacy is well illustrated in M. MCDONNELL BODKIN, FAMOUS IRISH TRIALS (1928).

[147] The recent Belfast 'Good Friday' Agreement established a review of the criminal justice system in Northern Ireland with terms of reference which include considering 'measures to improve the responsiveness and accountability of, and lay participation in, the criminal justice system.' See REVIEW OF THE CRIMINAL JUSTICE SYSTEM IN NORTHERN IRELAND: A CONSULTATION PAPER (1998).

[148] For more general discussion of the importance of culture in shaping legal institutions, see MIRJAN R. DAMASKA, THE FACES OF JUSTICE AND STATE AUTHORITY: A COMPARATIVE APPROACH TO THE LEGAL PROCESS (1986). For the role of national culture in shaping law, see Oscar G. Chase, *Legal Processes and National Legal Culture*, 5 CARDOZO J. INT'L. & COMP. L. 1 (1997), and the comment of John D. Jackson, *Playing the Culture Card in Resisting Cross-Jurisdictional Transplants: A Comment on 'Legal Processes and National Culture,'* 5 CARDOZO J. INT'L & COMP. L. 51 (1997).

[149] See Jackson & Doran, *supra* note 116.

[150] For philosophical development of this argument, see PAUL CHEVIGNY, MORE SPEECH: DIALOGUE RIGHTS AND MODERN LIBERTY (1988).

of shortcomings with the present system, but it might also suggest particular solutions which may in the longer term help to fashion a system that is more suited to the needs of modern Ireland and is consequently more robust. Until this happens, it is likely that the jury system will sink further into the background of everyday practice in the criminal courts, still serving as a symbol of an ideal mode of justice but playing little part in the bulk of actual cases.

9 Europe's New Jury Systems: The Cases of Spain and Russia

Stephen C. Thaman*

I. Introduction

The recent reintroduction of trial by jury in both Russia (1993) and Spain (1995) is interesting for two reasons. First, it is a surprising reversal in the long-term trend toward the elimination of the classic jury in favor either of courts composed exclusively of professional judges, or of 'mixed courts' in which professional judges and lay assessors collegially decide all questions of fact, law, and sentence. Secondly, it raises the question whether the jury can act as a catalyst in the reform of Continental European criminal procedure, as it did during the nineteenth century in the wake of the French Revolution.

The modern notions of procedural fairness in criminal procedure, which have gained general international recognition in national constitutions and international human rights conventions, have their origins in the following Anglo-American concepts, which developed in the context of an adversarial trial by jury: (1) the presumption of innocence, (2) the privilege against self-incrimination, (3) the equality of arms, (4) the right to a public and oral trial, (5) the accusatory principle, and (6) the judge's independence from the executive or investigative agency. The classic separation of powers within the adversarial criminal process between a neutral judge, responsible for deciding questions of law and punishment, and a panel of lay persons responsible for questions of fact and guilt, also gave rise to common law rules of evidence. For instance, the separation of powers inspired the regulation of hearsay and relevance, the creation of exclusionary rules addressing excessively prejudicial and illegally gathered evidence,[1] and the adoption of the principle of 'free evaluation

* Associate Professor of Law, Saint Louis University. Unless otherwise noted, all translations and transliterations of foreign texts are the author's. Unpublished documents cited in the chapter are on file with the author.

[1] John H. Langbein's research has seriously called into question whether the Anglo-American rules of evidence were attributable to the division of labor between the jury and the judge or to the 'lawyerization' of criminal trials in the late 18th and early 19th centuries. See John H. Langbein, *The Criminal Trial before the Lawyers*, 45 U. Chi. L. Rev. 263, 306 (1978); cf. Mirjan R. Damaška, Evidence Law Adrift 26 (1997) ('A space

of the evidence' unfettered by formal rules of evidence.[2] Important developments affecting the presentation and evaluation of evidence in substantive criminal law, the separation of factual and legal questions,[3] and the dissection of criminal offenses into their various constitutive objective and subjective elements arguably have their roots in the need for the judge to instruct the jury on how to apply the law to the facts of the case.[4]

Although most of the principles discussed above were accepted into the formerly inquisitorial criminal procedures of civil law countries, the structural framework in which they originated—the adversarial trial by jury—has largely been rejected by the same countries as being alien to certain other principles of the inquisitorial criminal process, such as (l) the duty of the state (prosecutor, judge, and investigating judge) to ascertain the truth, (2) the necessity of reviewability of judgments, as reflected in the requirement of providing reasons for findings of guilt or innocence,[5] and (3) the principle of mandatory prosecution ('legality principle'). The legality principle is antipathetic not only to the unbridled

for technical evidence law begins to open up only when the trial court is split into two parts—one lay, the other professional.').

[2] Langbein also recognizes that the seeds of 'free evaluation of evidence' were being planted in Continental Europe before the introduction of trial by jury with the weakening of the institution of torture and the rise of 'poena extraordinaria'. See John H. Langbein, Torture and the Law of Proof 59 (1977). On the transformation of the 'romantic notion' of *intime conviction* into the 'less expansive' notion of *freie Beweiswürdigung*, which required adherence to 'extralegal canons of valid inference', see Damaška, *supra* note 1, at 21.

[3] Though Sir Edward Coke proclaimed '[*a*]*d quaestionem facti non respondent judices; ad quaestionem juris non respondent juratores*' as early as 1620, and early French and German jury legislation tried to limit juries to deciding naked 'historic facts', leaving the application of the law to the professional bench, German, and later Russian, scholars quickly understood that the jury's verdict of 'guilty' or 'not guilty' was a mixed issue of law and fact. The German response was to replace the classic jury with the mixed court, or *Schöffengericht*, in which professional judges and lay assessors decide all issues of law, fact, guilt, and sentence in joint session. See John H. Langbein, *The English Criminal Trial Jury on the Eve of the French Revolution*, in The Trial Jury in England, France, Germany 1700–1900, at 13, 34 (Antonio Padoa Schioppa ed., 1987). For a summary of the 19th century German discussion, see Peter Landau, *Schwurgerichte und Schöffengerichte in Deutschland im 19. Jahrhundert bis 1870*, in The Trial Jury in England, France, Germany 1700–1900, *supra*, at 241, 279–81, and Hugo Meyer, That- und Rechtsfrage im Geschworenengericht, insbesondere in der Fragestellung an die Geschworenen 109–280 (1860).

[4] See Ennio Amodio, *Giustizia popolare, garantismo e partecipazione*, in I giudici senza toga. Esperienze e prospettive della partecipazione popolare ai giudizi penali 1, 13 n.30 (Ennio Amodio ed., 1979). The Russian Supreme Court has made the quantum leap to treating the proof of *actus reus* as a factual question for the jury, and *mens rea* as a legal question for the professional bench. See text accompanying notes 90–2.

[5] According to Amodio, Art. III(1) of the Italian Constitution makes the reintroduction of the classic jury impossible because it requires reasons to be provided for all judicial decisions. See Amodio, *supra* note 4, at 46–8.

'discretion' of juries to acquit out of sympathy or nullify the harshness of the sentence,[6] but also to the apotheosis of party control of the criminal trial: plea-bargaining, a practice growing from the same soil as trial by jury in England and the United States.[7] Consequently, juries have largely been abolished or converted into a form of lay participation more conducive to adhering to the aforementioned principles: the 'mixed court' of professional judges and lay assessors, collectively responsible for all questions of law, fact, guilt, and sentence.

The tension between the principles and the structure of the jury system it has produced in these civil law nations raises significant questions. To what extent are the universally accepted principles derived from common law criminal procedure dependent on the classic separation of powers in an adversarial jury trial?[8] Can a judge, who has studied the investigative file and determined, before the trial, that it includes sufficient evidence for a finding of guilt, preserve the presumption of innocence and act as an impartial fact/guilt finder?[9] Is the classic jury system a useful catalyst for cementing the independence of the judge from the executive or investigative branch in order to provide a foundation for an

[6] On jury nullification in the United States, see Albert W. Alschuler & Andrew G. Deiss, *A Brief History of the Criminal Jury in the United States*, 61 U. Chi. L. Rev. 867, 871–5 (1994).

[7] On the strange symbiosis of trial by jury and plea-bargaining, see Bernd Schünemann, *Reflexionen über die Zukunft des deutschen Strafverfahrens*, in Festschrift für Gerd Pfeiffer 481 (1988).

[8] For the proposition that French and German reformers, enamored with the Anglo-American jury system, lost sight of the 'interdependencies' between that system and the procedural and evidentiary maxims of the adversary system, which were otherwise rejected, see Karl H. Kunert, *Some Observations on the Origin and Structure of Evidence Rules under the Common Law System and the Civil Law System of 'Free Proof' in the German Code of Criminal Procedure*, 16 Buff. L. Rev. 122, 147 (1967); cf. Amodio, *supra* note 4, at 13 n.30; see also K. J. Mittermaier, Das Volksgericht in Gestalt der Schwur- und Schöffengerichte 21 (1866) (hereinafter Mittermaier, Das Volksgericht); K. J. Mittermaier, Erfahrungen über die Wirksamkeit der Schwurgerichte in Europa und Amerika 667 (1865) (hereinafter Mittermaier, Erfahrungen). Mittermaier felt the principle of oral and public trials could be effectively implemented only in the form of the classic jury trial.

[9] Mittermaier doubted that judges, despite their best effort, could protect themselves from forming an unconscious 'preconceived opinion as to guilt' imbued by study of the dossier of the preliminary investigation. See Mittermaier, Das Volksgericht, *supra* note 8, at 22; Mittermaier, Erfahrungen, *supra* note 8, at 683. Modern German views range from the ultra-pessimistic contention that German criminal procedure is a Potemkin facade and the trial an orchestrated blessing of the results of the preliminary investigation, see Schünemann, *supra* note 7, at 482–3, to cautious assertions that the preliminary study of the file, while strongly influencing the presiding judge, does not make him or her incapable of objectively weighing the trial evidence: see Christoph Rennig, Die Entscheidungsfindung durch Schöffen und Berufsrichter in rechtlicher und psychologischer Sicht 177, 223, 237, tbl. 10 (1993); cf. Mirjan Damaška, *Evidentiary Barriers to Conviction and Two Models of Criminal Procedure*, 121 U. Pa. L. Rev. 506, 544 (1973).

objective 'ascertainment of the truth'?[10] If the judge has a duty to uncover the truth and the defendant invokes his or her right to remain silent, how effective is this right when the judge is also the finder of guilt?[11] What is the meaning of *intime conviction*, the French rendition of a 'verdict according to one's conscience', in a 'mixed court', where the presiding judge has unique access to the dossier and is responsible for drafting the judgment (even in the unlikely event he or she has been overruled by the lay assessors) in such a way as to withstand the formal requirements of appellate scrutiny?[12]

This comparison of the provisions of the 1993 Russian Jury Law[13]

[10] In the Netherlands, the 'pre-prepared version of the truth' is presented to the trial judge in the form of the investigative dossier. See Nico Jörg *et al.*, *Are Inquisitorial and Adversarial Systems Converging?*, in CRIMINAL JUSTICE IN EUROPE: A COMPARATIVE STUDY 41, 46–7 (Phil Fennell *et al.* eds., 1995). The '*Schulterschluß*' between the trial judge and the prosecutor, and the 'systematic distortion of the processing of information, caused by the judicial reconstruction of an historical situation' all constitute, according to its critics, 'weaknesses of truth-finding hindered by inquisitorial procedure with an accusatory facade'. See Schünemann, *supra* note 7, at 475–6, 479.

[11] This question is answered by the fact that continental defendants virtually never remain silent during the preliminary investigation or the trial itself. See MIRJAN DAMAŠKA, THE FACES OF JUSTICE AND STATE AUTHORITY 128 (1986); Damaška, *supra* note 9, at 527.

[12] As to the problems inherent in the presiding judge explaining the reasoning of the lay assessors, especially if he or she has been outvoted by them, see Damaška, *supra* note 9, at 540, 543. As to how the *freie Beweiswürdigung* of the judge, through the necessity of its having to be based in 'rules of logic, experience of the laws of nature . . . and . . . probability', has led to the re-emergence of new 'formal rules of evidence', which it was supposed to have replaced, see ibid., at 540; DAMAŠKA, *supra* note 11, at 20, 55; Kunert, *supra* note 8, at 124. On the 'guesswork' involved in the formulation of the judgment in mixed courts, see Damaška, *supra* note 1, at 42–3. In his early writings, Mittermaier warned against 'declaring legally-educated judges to be jurors' by allowing them to decide by *freie Beweiswürdigung*, because this permission would place too much power into their hands. See C. J. A. MITTERMAIER, DAS DEUTSCHE STRAFVERFAHREN 222 (2d ed. 1832).

[13] See Zakon Rossiyskoy Federatsii o vnesenii izmeneniy i dopolneniy v Zakon RSFSR O sudoustroystve RSFSR, Ugolovno-protsessual'nyy kodeks RSFSR, Ugolovnyy kodeks RSFSR i Kodeks RSFSR ob administrativnykh pravonarusheniiakh (Law of the Russian Federation on the Introduction of Changes and Amendments to the Law of the RSFSR on Court Organization of the RSFSR, the Code of Criminal Procedure of the RSFSR, the Criminal Code of the RSFSR, and the Code of the RSFSR on Administrative Infractions), VEDOMOSTI RF, Issue No. 33, Item No. 1313, at 2238–64 (1993) (hereinafter Jury Law). All citations are from Ugolovny Kodeks Rossiyskoy Federatsii, Ugolovno-protsessual'nyy Kodeks RSFSR, Ugolovno-ispolnitel'nyy Kodeks Rossiyskoy Federatsii, 185–437 (Ministry of Justice of the Russian Federation ed., INFRA/M-NORMA 1997).

The Jury Law amends several Russian codes. The amended codes in the Jury Law will be cited as Law on Court Organization (hereinafter LOC) and Code of Criminal Procedure (hereinafter UPK RSFSR).

The right to jury trial was introduced in only 9 of Russia's 89 political units: Ivanovo, Moscow, Riazan, Rostov-on-the-Don, Saratov and Ul'ianovsk Regions, Altay, Krasnodar, and Stavropol Territories.

and the 1995 Spanish Jury Law[14] will focus on the effect of their implementation and reintroduction of the classic jury system on these questions and problems.[15] The most notorious case to be prosecuted in either country, the case of Mikel Otegi, exemplifies the fragility of the new jury systems. Mikel Otegi, a young Basque nationalist, murdered two Basque policemen and was acquitted on March 7, 1997, on the grounds of diminished capacity caused by intoxication and uncontrollable rage provoked by alleged previous police harassment. The acquittal shocked the Spanish public, prompting calls to amend or repeal the jury law, or at least to suspend it in the Basque Country.

II. Brief Historical Background

While the liberal Spanish Constitutions of 1812, 1837, and 1869 provided for some kind of trial by jury, the institution found legislative form only in the Code of Criminal Procedure of 1872 and, finally, in the Law on the Jury of 1888. Only the latter law was implemented for any length of time, functioning between 1888 and 1923, when it was suspended by the Primo de Rivera dictatorship, and then again between 1931 and 1936.[16]

Trial by jury was introduced in Russia during Alexander II's judicial reforms of 1864 and survived, despite subsequent legislation removing political and press crimes from its jurisdiction, until the Bolsheviks abolished it in 1917.[17]

[14] Ley Orgánica del Tribunal del Jurado, B. O. E., 1995, 122 (amended by Ley Orgánica, B. O. E., 1995, 275) (hereinafter LOTJ); see also LEY DEL JURADO (Victor Moreno Catena ed., 2d ed. 1995).

[15] The discussion of Russia will often refer to my own investigation of the first 114 trials in 1993–4. See Stephen C. Thaman, *The Resurrection of Trial by Jury in Russia*, 31 STAN. J. INT'L L. 61 (1995) (hereinafter Thaman, *Resurrection*). For a more concise but more current treatment of the provisions of the new law and its implementation, see Stephen C. Thaman, *Das neue russische Geschworenengericht*, 108 ZEITSCHRIFT FÜR DIE GESAMTE STRAFRECHTSWISSENSCHAFT 191 (1996) (hereinafter Thaman, *Das neue russische Geschworenengericht*). For a similar in-depth analysis of the new Spanish jury system, see Stephen C. Thaman, *Spain Returns to Trial by Jury*, 21 HASTINGS INT'L & COMP. L. REV. 241 (1998) (hereinafter Thaman, *Spain Returns*). The comparison in this chap. includes new Spanish and Russian material not included in an earlier article. See Stephen C. Thaman, *Geschworenengerichte in Ost und West: Die klassische Jury und das adversarische Verfahren im Strafverfahren Rußlands und Spaniens*, 41 RECHT IN OST UND WEST 73 (1997) (hereinafter Thaman, *Geschworenengerichte*).

[16] For a history of jury trial legislation in 19th century Spain, see Thaman, *Spain Returns*, *supra* note 15, at 246–9 (citing JUAN ANTONIO ALEJANDRE, LA JUSTICIA POPULAR EN ESPAÑA: ANÁLYSIS DE UNA EXPERIENCIA HISTÓRICA: LOS TRIBUNALES DE JURADOS 79–243 (1981)).

[17] See Thaman, *Resurrection*, *supra* note 15, at 64–5.

Article 125 of the post-Franco Spanish Constitution of 1978 provided for public participation in the administration of justice through the institution of trial by jury.[18] This provision was conceived as the key to democratic reform of the criminal justice system following the Franco dictatorship.[19] However, between 1978 and 1995, the majority of Spanish jurists questioned the appropriateness of using the classic jury system as a catalyst for criminal justice reform. They stressed the perceived inadequacies of the Spanish jury experience after 1888 and maintained either that Article 125 made lay participation optional,[20] or even if Article 125 made lay participation a constitutional mandate, that the 'mixed jury' or *escabinado* would be constitutionally adequate as the equivalent of the modern form of popular participation (following the models of Germany, France, Italy, and Portugal).[21]

The movement toward recognizing adversarial trial procedure and trial by jury as constitutional foundations of the Russian administration

[18] Constitución Española (Constitution) (C.E.) art. 125 (Spain).

[19] The legislature noted that the suspension, abolition, or limitation of the jury trial in the period 1820–1939 always coincided with limitations of civil rights in periods of monarchic reaction or dictatorship. See LOTJ § I, Exposición de Motivos, *supra* note 14. Indeed, in nearly all Continental European countries, the introduction of trial by jury coincided with liberal reforms, and its abolition with the installation of dictatorial or totalitarian regimes, for example, Bolshevism in Russia (1917), Fascism in Italy (1931), the Vichy Regime in France (1941). The only exception was Germany, in which the democratic Weimar Government abolished the classic jury, albeit in an undemocratic manner, by the Emminger decree of 1924. See Ellison Kahn, *Restore the Jury? Or 'Reform? Reform? Aren't Things Bad Enough Already?*,' (1991) 108 S. Afr. L.J. 672, 678.

[20] A dubious precedent for the 'optional' nature of constitutional commands can be found in the Argentine Constitution of 1858, which called for trial by jury, but was never implemented with legislation. See Thaman, *Spain Returns*, *supra* note 15, at 251 (citing Ricardo J. Cavallero & Edmundo S. Hendler, Justicia y Participación: El Juicio por Jurados en Materia Penal 43–63 (1988)).

[21] For summaries of these discussions, and an argument for the propriety of introducing a mixed court in lieu of trial by jury, see Thaman, *Spain Returns*, *supra* note 15, at 250–6 (citing Agustín-J. Pérez-Cruz Martín, La Participación Popular en la Administración de Justicia: El Tribunal del Jurado 322 (1991); Ernesto Pedraz Penalva, *Sobre el significado y vigencia del Jurado*, in Constitución, Jurisdicción, y Proceso 60–2 (1990)). Although lay judges in the mixed courts of Germany, France, Italy, and Portugal deliberate with the professional bench, the courts in each country are still called by the old name for jury courts. On the German *Schwurgericht*, see §§ 74(2), 74(d) Gerichtsverfassungsgesetz, discussed in Theodor Kleinknecht & Karlheinz Meyer, Strafprozeßordnung 1447, 1453 (43d ed. 1997). On the French *cour d'assise*, see § 240 Code de Procédure Pénale, reprinted in Code de Procédure Pénale 363 (36th ed. 1994). On the Italian *corte di assise*, see Riodinamento dei Giudizi di Assise (L. 10 aprile 1951, n.287, Gazzelta Ufficiale 7 maggio 1951, n.102), published in Codice di Procedura Penale con Leggi Complementari (Bolzano, 1991); see also Codice di Procedura Penale § 5, reprinted in Il Nuovo Codice di Procedura Penale (La Tribuna) 93 (Piacenza, 1995). On the Portuguese *júri*, see Código de Processo Penal Anotado § 51 (Coimbra, 4th ed. 1991).

of justice[22] began during Gorbachev's *perestroika* and culminated in the Russian Jury Law. The reform was aimed at replacing the traditional Soviet 'mixed court', which had been completely ineffective as a popular corrective against judicial arbitrariness and party control of judicial decision-making.[23]

III. Jurisdiction of the Jury Court

The defendant has a right to a jury trial in Russia in any case tried in Russia's second-level courts of original jurisdiction.[24] The Spanish legislature chose to grant jurisdiction to second-level courts of original jurisdiction, the provincial courts (*audiencia provincial*), on the basis of the magnitude of threatened punishment[25] and limited trial by jury to particular types of crimes, such as crimes committed by public officials in the exercise of their duties, crimes against persons, honor, liberty, and security, and arson.[26]

[22] Art. 123 of the Constitution of the Russian Federation of 1993 guarantees an adversarial procedure and trial by jury. See Konstitutsiia Rossiyskoy Federatsii (1993) (Constitution) (hereinafter KONST. RF).

[23] See Thaman, *Resurrection*, *supra* note 15, at 66–8.

[24] See UPK RSFSR arts. 421, 36. These jury cases are mainly capital crimes of aggravated murder and rape. Before the enactment of a new Russian Penal Code in 1996, juries also heard a smattering of cases involving passing counterfeit currency and bribery. Under the new Russian Penal Code, the following crimes are also triable by the jury court: capital murder, aggravated rape, kidnapping, commerce in children, hostage-taking resulting in death, terrorism, crimes of organized criminal gangs, hijackings, mass rioting, piracy, negligent operation of public transportation resulting in death, train-wrecking resulting in death, treason, espionage, attacks against government officials and the police, various types of obstruction of justice, war crimes, genocide, ecocide, and having an accessory after the fact in the commission of a serious offense. See UPK RSFSR art. 36, referring to Ugolovnyy Kodeks Rossiyskoy Federatsii, *supra* note 13, at 3–181, arts. 105(2), 126(3), 131(3), 152(3), 205, 206(2), 206(3), 208(1), 209–11, 212(1), 227, 263(3), 267(3), 275–9, 281, 290(3), 290(4), 294–302, 303(2), 303(3), 304, 305, 316, 317, 318, 321(3), 322(2), 353–8, 359(1), 359(2), 360. The pertinent courts are called 'regional courts' or 'territorial courts', depending on the type of federal political entity involved.

[25] The Law on the Judiciary (*Ley del Poder Judicial*), before its amendment by the LOTJ, originally provided that the competence of the jury court would be determined in relation to the type of crime and the quantity of the punishment designated. See *Ley del Poder Judicial*, art. 83(2)(d) (B.O.E., 1985, 157). In the United States, the right to jury trial inures when the crime with which the defendant is charged is punishable by more than six months' deprivation of liberty. See Baldwin v. New York, 399 U.S. 66, 69 (1970).

[26] See LOTJ art. 1. The law has been criticized for including comparatively trivial crimes such as bribery of public officials, and minor threats and trespasses within the jury court's jurisdiction, and excluding serious crimes against the person such as rape. See Thaman, *Spain Returns*, *supra* note 15, at 261–2 (citing Vicente Gimeno Sendra, *La segunda reforma urgente de la Ley del Jurado*, EL TRIBUNAL DEL JURADO 27–8 (1996); JUAN-LUIS GÓMEZ

In Russia and the United States, the defendant may waive his or her procedural right to trial by jury. In Russia, a large portion of defendants waive their right to a jury trial, in favor of being tried by the traditional court of lay assessors or by a three-judge panel.[27] In Spain, on the other hand, jury courts have exclusive jurisdiction because the right to a jury trial embodies the citizens' right to participate in the administration of justice as jurors.

IV. Composition of the Jury Court

The jury court is composed of nine jurors and two alternates in Spain and twelve jurors and two alternates in Russia. One professional judge presides over the court in both countries.[28]

Voter registration lists serve as the source for prospective jurors in both Spain and Russia.[29] Although the right to vote inures at age 18 in both countries, Russia has restricted jury eligibility to registered voters who are 25 years of age or older.[30] Both countries exempt certain public officials, as well as officials in the legal and law enforcement professions, and allow discretionary excuses for age, hardship, or illness.[31]

In both countries, the jury for a particular case is selected from at least twenty prospective jurors who have been preliminarily screened and

Colomer, El proceso penal especial ante el Tribunal del Jurado 33–4 (1996)). Prosecutors and courts in Spain have assiduously avoided jury trials for such minor offenses. 57 of the first 75 trials in Spain of which the author is aware were for murder. See Thaman, *Spain Returns*, *supra* note 15, at 258–63. In Russia, only 12 of the first 109 jury trials involved noncapital offenses. See Thaman, *Resurrection*, *supra* note 15, at 135–7.

[27] It is questionable whether these 'waivers' are voluntary; many believe that they are the result of coercion or undue influence exerted by investigators, defense lawyers, or judges at the preliminary hearings. See Thaman, *Resurrection*, *supra* note 15, at 87–8; see also Thaman, *Das neue russische Geschworenengericht*, *supra* note 15, at 195. In 1994, the first full year of jury trials in the nine regions, only 20.4% of defendants chose trial by jury, but the percentage rose to 30.9% in 1995, 37.3% in 1996, and 37% in 1997. The option of being tried by a three-judge panel has not been fully implemented due to a lack of judicial resources. It was exercised only 76 times in 1994 and 61 times in 1995. See *Spravka*, Memorandum of A. P. Shurygin, President of the Cassation Panel of the SCRF (1998) (hereinafter *Spravka*); *Praktika realizatsii novykh form ugolovnogo sudoproizvodstva* (On Realization of New Forms of Criminal Procedure) 4 (1997) (memorandum of Cassational Panel of the Supreme Court of the Russian Federation, on file with author) (hereinafter *Praktika realizatsii*).

[28] See LOTJ art. 2; UPK RSFSR art. 440. Nineteenth century legislation in both countries provided for a jury of 12, presided over by a three-judge panel. See Thaman, *Spain Returns*, *supra* note 15, at 264.

[29] See LOTJ art. 8; LOC art. 80.

[30] See LOTJ art. 8; LOC art. 80.

[31] See LOTJ arts. 9–12; LOC art. 80.

summoned to the court on the day of trial.[32] After brief questioning of the juror's ability to be fair and impartial in the case,[33] the prosecution and the defense may exercise challenges for cause, or peremptorily challenge a limited number of prospective jurors (two each in Russia, four each in Spain).[34]

V. Preliminary Investigation and Preliminary Hearing in Jury Cases

The Russian jury law did not introduce changes in the procedure of the preliminary investigation, in which a legally trained official in the Ministry of the Interior or the Procurary independently and inquisitorially (that is, guided by a duty to seek the truth) collects evidence and determines whether a charge will be referred to the Procuracy for indictment.[35] The Spanish Jury Law, on the other hand, has provided for the active participation of both the defense and the prosecution following the investigative judge's determination that the crime charged is subject to the jury court's jurisdiction.[36] Once the parties are notified of the court's jurisdiction, the law provides for adversarial proceedings in which the parties may solidify their accusatory and defense pleadings and request further investigative measures.[37]

[32] See LOTJ art. 38; UPK RSFSR art. 434.

[33] The judge conducts this questioning in Russia. See UPK RSFSR art. 438. In Spain, as in many U.S. jurisdictions, the judge turns over questioning to the parties. See LOTJ art. 40. Jury selection in Spain has lasted anywhere from 30 minutes to nearly seven hours in the first trial in Bilbao. See Thaman, *Spain Returns*, *supra* note 15, at 291 (citing Interview with Jose Maria Alavrez Seijo, Presiding Judge of Oviedo Provincial Court, Oviedo (June 9, 1997); Interview with Remigio Conde Salgado, President of Lugo Provincial Court, Lugo (June 10, 1997); Javier Muñoz, *¡Una sola puñalada y la mato, caramba!*, El Correo, Apr. 8, 1997). Some Spanish lawyers have hired psychologists to aid them in *voir dire* and have often probed the biases and prejudices of the jury in a sophisticated manner. See Thaman, *Spain Returns*, *supra* note 15, at 288–91 (citing Salvador Enguix, *Juicio al Jurado*, La Vanguardia, June 2, 1996, at 4–5).

[34] See LOTJ art. 40; UPK RSFSR art. 439.

[35] At the conclusion of the preliminary investigation, the investigator, a legally-trained official in the Ministry of the Interior or the Procuracy, advises the defendant of his right to a jury trial in the mandatory presence of his counsel. See UPK RSFSR arts. 423, 424.

[36] See LOTJ arts. 25–8.

[37] See ibid. art. 29. This 'adversarialization' of the preliminary investigation, and the corresponding limitation of the powers of the investigative judge, has been criticized on grounds of equal protection (in that nonjury accuseds do not have similar rights), and as being beyond the scope of a law to introduce trial by jury. See Thaman, *Spain Returns*, *supra* note 15, at 273–4 (citing Vicente Gimeno Sendra, Ley Orgánica del Tribunal del Jurado, Comentarios práticos al nuevo proceso penal ante el Tribunal del Jurado 165–6 (1996); Victor Fairén Guillén, *Comentarios al 'Anteproyecto del Ley del Jurado'*, 2 Revista de Derecho Procesal 462 (1994)).

The preliminary hearing in Spain is conducted by the investigative judge and is considered an extension of the preliminary investigation. The hearing takes place after the performance of indispensable investigative acts and the defendant's submission of a provisional response to the accusatory pleadings.[38] At the hearing, the parties may request that the investigative judge perform further investigative acts, move to dismiss the charges or the entire accusation, or amend the charges to include a separate crime related to the 'justiciable facts'.[39] If the evidence is sufficient to charge the defendant with a crime subject to the jury court's jurisdiction, the judge issues an order setting the defendant's case for trial.[40]

The Russian preliminary hearing is conducted by the trial judge, who reviews the entire dossier of the preliminary investigation before deciding whether to set the case for trial and what evidence will be admissible at trial. Though the hearing is adversarial in nature, no new evidence is adduced and rulings suppressing evidence must be based on the contents of the investigative dossier. If the judge determines that there is insufficient evidence to proceed to trial, he or she may dismiss the case. However, the more common remedy is for the judge to return the case to the investigator for supplementary investigation.[41]

The Russian legislature has left the central role of the investigative dossier intact, but the Spanish legislature has modeled its preliminary hearing on that of the Italian Code of Criminal Procedure of 1988[42] by

[38] See LOTJ arts. 30–1. Unlike the procedure in nonjury trials, where the investigative judge must investigate the alleged crimes 'with all the circumstances which could influence its qualification and the guilt of the criminals', L.E. CRIM. art. 299, the jury procedure provides for investigation only upon motion of one of the parties, and only of subject matter relevant to probable cause to charge the crime, see LOTJ art. 27.

[39] See LOTJ art. 31.

[40] See ibid., art. 32.

[41] Supplementary investigation was performed in 18% of all cases tried from November 1, 1993, to January 1, 1995, according to the statistics of the Russian Supreme Court (hereinafter SCRF). See Thaman, *Das neue russische Geschworenengericht*, *supra* note 15, at 195. The Russian Ministry of Justice contends that 36.1% of jury cases were returned for further investigation in 1994 and 36% in 1995. See A. Gagarsky, *Miniust podvodit itogi raboty sudov*, 8 ROSSIYSKAIA YUSTITSIIA 4 (1996) (hereinafter Ross. IUST.). The percentage has fallen to 25.8% in 1996 and 22.5% in 1997. See *Spravka o praktike rassmotrenii del sudami prisiazhnykh v 1997 godu*, Memorandum prepared by G. P. Ivanov, Judge of the SCRF 3–4 (Mar. 21, 1998) (on file with author) (hereinafter *Spravka*).

[42] In Italy, however, the preliminary hearing judge (*guidice per le indagini preliminari*) is separate from the trial judge, presiding only over matters arising during investigation. This difference ensures a greater amount of structural independence. See Stephen P. Freccero, *An Introduction to the New Italian Criminal Procedure*, 21 AM. J. CRIM. L. 345, 364–5 (1994). For

largely eliminating the investigative dossier from the trial to reinforce the principle of immediacy and orality of the trial in the jury court.[43] During the preliminary hearing, the investigative judge prepares a 'trial file'. This file includes evidence that cannot be repeated at trial or that needs to be ratified at trial, or other evidence the parties intend to use at trial.[44]

The Russian constitutional prohibition against the use of evidence seized in violation of the Russian Constitution or the Code of Criminal Procedure may now be the basis for a motion to suppress evidence at the Russian preliminary hearing.[45] In particular, numerous defendants' admissions and confessions have been held inadmissible because they were elicited in violation of the defendant's right to counsel, which adheres in capital investigations from the moment of arrest,[46] or because the suspect was not informed of his or her constitutional right to remain silent.[47] Russian courts have also explicitly applied the 'fruits of the

analysis of the 'double file' innovation in the new Italian Code of Criminal Procedure, see Hans-Heinrich Jescheck, *Grundgedanken der neuen italienischen Strafprozeßordnung in rechtsvergleichender Sicht*, FESTSCHRIFT FÜR ARTHUR KAUFMANN ZUM 70. GEBURTSTAG 659 (1993); Alessandro Honert, *Der italienische Strafprozeß: die Fortentwicklung einer Reform*, 106 ZEITSCHRIFT FÜR DIE GESAMTE STRAFRECHTSWISSENSCHAFT 427, 436 (1994). (The last document was unavailable to staff editors for citation-checking because it could not be retrieved from an archive.)

[43] See LOTJ III: Exposición de Motivos. The principle of immediacy and orality ensures that the evidence will be heard first-hand through the testimony of witnesses, rather than through the reading of documents.

[44] See LOTJ art. 34. For more detail on preliminary hearings, see Thaman, *Spain Returns*, *supra* note 15, at 279–82.

[45] See KONST. RF art. 50. The constitutional right to exclude illegally gathered evidence was codified in UPK RSFSR arts. 69, 433. For a discussion of this emerging body of law, see Thaman, *Das neue russische Geschworenengericht*, *supra* note 15, at 196–7, and Thaman, *Resurrection*, *supra* note 15, at 90–4.

[46] All persons have a right to counsel upon arrest. See UPK RSFSR art. 47. Those charged with capital crimes have a right to a court-appointed lawyer from the time of the filing of an accusatory pleading. See ibid., art. 49(5). The right inures in jury cases from the time the investigation is completed. See ibid., art. 426.

[47] See KONST. RF art. 51. The SCRF has held that all suspects must be informed of their right to remain silent before being questioned during the preliminary investigation, or the statements are inadmissible in court. See Decision No. 8 of the Plenum Verkhovnogo Suda RF, O nekotorykh voprosakh primeneniia sudami Konstitutsii Rossiyskoy Federatsii pri osushchestvlenii pravosudiia, 1 BIULL. VERKH. SUDA RF 3, 6 ¶ 18 (1996). Evidence was suppressed on constitutional or lesser statutory grounds in approximately one third of all jury cases in 1994 and 1995, not including those cases returned for further investigation. See V. Voskresenskiy, *Uchastie prokurora v rassmotrenii del*, 7 ROSS. IUST. 4 (1996). The main author of the Jury Law estimates that evidence has been suppressed in 70% of all jury cases. See S. A. Pashin, *Dokazatel'stva v rossiyskom ugolovnom protsesse*, in 2 SOSTIAZATEL'NOE PRAVOSUDIE 311, 368 (S. A. Pashin *et al.* (eds.), 1996) (hereinafter SOST. PRAVO.).

poisonous tree' doctrine in suppressing certain evidence, such as semen or blood stains on clothing or objects that were not handled according to code specifications when they were gathered.[48] Motions to suppress evidence may also be made at trial, where witness testimony often reveals that evidence was illegally seized. Testimony regarding the motion is required. The illegality of investigative methods is often first revealed through witness testimony, and the parties may call additional witnesses in support of, or in opposition to, the motion.[49]

Motions to suppress evidence which allege the violation of a fundamental right during the preliminary investigation are made in Spain in preliminary proceedings in the trial court.[50] The efficacy of this remedy has been doubted because the trial judge does not possess the full investigative dossier and there are no provisions for hearing oral testimony.[51] Thus, it is generally conceded that such motions will have to be resolved at trial, though, to the author's knowledge, defendants have made no such motions during the first year of jury cases.[52]

VI. The Trial

A. *The Changing Roles of the Participants*

One of the key aims of the Russian legislature was to strip the trial judge of the inquisitorial duty of seeking the truth and to eliminate the accusatory role the Soviet-Russian procedure had imposed on the court. Therefore, the judge no longer reads the accusatory pleading nor dominates the questioning of the defendant and the witnesses in the new jury trials. The judge may no longer prevent the prosecutor's abandonment of the case, act as a prosecutor by necessity when the prosecutor

[48] See U. Liakhov and V. Zolotykh, *Sud prisiazhnykh—put' k spravedlivoy yustitsii*, 3 Ross. Iust. 10–11 (1997).

[49] The SCRF approved this practice in Decision No. 9 of the Plenum Verkhovnogo Suda RF, O nekotorykh voprosakh primeneniia sudami ugolovno-protsessual'nykh norm, reglamentiruiushchikh proizvodstvo v sude prisiazhnykh, 3 Biull. Verkh. Suda RF 2, 4, ¶ 7 (1995) (hereinafter SCRF Decision No. 9).

[50] See LOTJ art. 36(1).

[51] See Thaman, *Spain Returns*, *supra* note 15, at 283–4 (citing Gómez Colomer, *supra* note 26, at 99).

[52] According to the President of the Provincial Court of Málaga, Manuel Torres Vela, the lack of motions to suppress based on search and seizure violations has been due to the fact that no narcotics charges are heard by juries, and that the typical Spanish murder case, involving 'crimes of passion' or bar-room fights, seldom involve searches or wiretaps. See ibid., at 284.

does not appear for trial, or return the case to the investigator on his or her own motion.[53]

The Spanish criminal trial was perhaps the most adversarial on the European Continent even before the passage of the jury law.[54] Although the Spanish jury law kept the trial procedure basically unchanged, the trial judge's ability to control the collection of evidence has been drastically impeded by the lack of access to the investigative dossier. The trial begins not only with the reading of the prosecution's accusatory pleadings, but also with the pleadings of the defendant and the private prosecutor, usually representing the alleged victim, the victim's family, or its representatives.[55]

Russian and Spanish jury trials are greatly influenced by the empowerment of the victim or aggrieved party in criminal procedure.[56] In both countries, a prosecutorial motion to dismiss may be granted only if the aggrieved (the private prosecutor) agrees.[57] In the Russian trial, the aggrieved is usually uneducated, not represented by counsel, and often has no knowledge of the investigation and evidence. The aggrieved party has had a disturbing effect in many trials by displaying unpredictable outbursts of emotion, blurting out inadmissible or suppressed evidence, and necessitating laborious explanations by the judge about every aspect of the proceeding.[58] Whereas the Russian Supreme Court has winked at the victim's illegal disclosure of the defendant's prior criminal record to

[53] See Thaman, *Das neue russische Geschworenengericht*, *supra* note 15, at 199–201. I have criticized the judge's excessive discretion to remand a case for further investigation even after the jury has been sworn and has heard evidence. Such practice violates the presumption of innocence and the right to one's lawful judge, as guaranteed by Art. 47 of the KONST. RF. See Stephen Thaman, *Sud prisiazhnykh v sovremennoy Rossii glazami amerikanskogo yurista,* in 2 GOSUDARSTVO Y PRAVO 67, 70–1 (1995). Russian commentators have expressed similar criticism. See U. Liakhov, *Sudebnoe sledstvie v sude prisiazhnykh,* in SOSTIAZATEL'NOE PRAVOSUDIE 63, 80–1 (S. A. Pashin *et al.* (eds.), 1996); see also Thaman, *Resurrection*, *supra* note 15, at 100–1.

[54] The duty of the judge to ascertain the truth was phrased in terms of 'conducting the trial taking care to prevent discussions which are impertinent or do not aim at establishing the truth, without restricting the liberty necessary for the defense'. Art. 683 of the Ley de Enjuiciamiento Criminal (B.O.E. 1882, 126) (hereinafter L.E. CRIM). Very similar language has been adopted by the new Russian jury law. See UPK RSFSR art. 429.

[55] See L.E. CRIM. art. 649. The aggrieved party also has the right to court-appointed counsel in case of indigency. See ibid., art. 119.

[56] In the United States, the aggrieved is not a party in criminal proceedings, has no right to question witnesses, make a statement, or argue to the jury. The aggrieved's only input would be as a witness. For criticism of this state of affairs, see GEORGE P. FLETCHER, WITH JUSTICE FOR SOME: PROTECTING VICTIM'S RIGHTS IN CRIMINAL TRIALS 248–50 (1996).

[57] See UPK RSFSR art. § 430; LOTJ art. 51.

[58] On the role of the victim, see Thaman, *Resurrection*, *supra* note 15, at 107–8.

the jury to the point of affirming a death sentence in the face of such a procedural error,[59] it has reversed acquittals because the trial judge continued the case in the absence of the aggrieved party.[60]

In Spain, the aggrieved party is invariably represented by counsel in the trial and has had a strong impact on the jury in several of the first cases. In particular, the presence of the aggrieved in the courtroom has weakened the defendant's supposed advantages in being the sole 'common citizen' arguing to a jury of his peers against the prosecutor, the representative of the state. The presence of the victim's counsel has created a 'good cop–bad cop' situation, where the public prosecutor pursues a 'just resolution' of the case and the private prosecutor screams for blood.[61] This situation also allows the victim's counsel to push a certain theory of the case primarily aimed at a greater monetary award.[62]

B. Proceedings Preliminary to the Taking of Evidence

Russia and Spain follow the Continental European model of evidentiary proceedings. The proceedings commence with the reading of the accusatory pleading and the defendant's plea, and continue with the

[59] The RF Supreme Court affirmed the death penalty in the case of *Stepanenko* (Saratov Regional Court), although the aggrieved revealed the defendant's criminal record to the jury. The judge interrupted the aggrieved and instructed the jury to disregard the statement. Supreme Court Decision of Sept. 17, 1996 (Case of Stepanenko), Case No. 32 kp-096-7sksp.

[60] See Supreme Court Decision of Nov. 3, 1996 (Case of Karakaev), Case No. 18 kp-096–87sp (reversing the acquittal of the Krasnodar Territorial court); Supreme Court Decision of Oct. 8, 1996 (Case of Bulychev), Case No. 32 kp-096–55sp (reversing the acquittal of the Saratov Regional Court in a double-murder case).

[61] In the first case in Granada, the prosecutor and the defense asked the jury to acquit a 71-year-old woman on insanity grounds after all three psychiatric experts agreed she was not criminally responsible when she stabbed her 86-year-old neighbor to death. The private prosecutor asked for a guilty verdict based on partial lack of responsibility, and the jury returned a guilty verdict. See Thaman, *Spain Returns*, *supra* note 15, at 397–9. The private prosecutor invariably requests a higher prison sentence and damages than the public prosecutor and sometimes pleads more serious criminal charges. See ibid., at 399–400.

[62] In the second Barcelona trial, the private prosecutor was represented by a former television personality who was successful in convincing the jury that the defendant was guilty of only attempted murder of a taxi-driver, in order to support his civil suit for 50 million pesetas against the city government and the taxi company for causing the death by being dilatory in getting an ambulance to the scene. See Thaman, *Spain Returns*, *supra* note 15, at 399–400 (citing Carmen Muñoz, *La fiscal pide una pena menor por la muerte del taxista*, El periódico, Sept. 20, 1996, at 26; Blanca Cia, *El jurado dice que el acusado no quiso matar al taxista*, El País (Catalan Edition), Sept. 21, 1996, at 1,7).

interrogation of the defendant and the testimony of witnesses and experts. The trial closes with the summations and the last word of the defendant.[63] The provisions of the extant Codes of Criminal Procedure remain in force in both countries to the extent they are not in contradiction with the provisions of the new jury laws.[64]

In Spain, the parties, including the victim, are allowed to make an opening statement, following the reading of the pleadings. The statement grants the parties an opportunity to explain their pleadings, list the facts they believe will be proved, and state the verdict and sentence they believe will be just; they may even propose the hearing of new evidence.[65] The Russian legislation does not provide the parties with the same opportunity.

C. *Pleas of Guilty*

In both countries, the defendant is first asked if he or she admits the charges brought against him or her.[66] In Spain, pleas of guilty conforming to the pleadings and the longest requested sentence of either the prosecutor or the private prosecutor are permitted in jury and nonjury trials if the sentence does not exceed six years of deprivation of liberty and there is no question of the presence of a *corpus delicti* for the crime or any objection from the defense counsel. Upon reaching conformity, or *conformidad*, the trial is terminated and sentence is imposed.[67] The Spanish practice of *conformidad* is similar to one of the new Italian forms of abbreviated procedures, the *applicazione della pena su richiesta delle*

[63] For a summary of the Russian procedure, see Thaman, *Das neue russische Geschworenengericht*, *supra* note 15, at 202–4. For a summary of the Spanish procedure, see L.E. Crim. arts. 688–93.

[64] See UPK RSFSR art. 420; LOTJ art. 24.

[65] See LOTJ art. 45. Opening statements are also a part of the U.S. criminal trial.

[66] See UPK RSFSR art. 278; L.E. Crim. arts. 688–90.

[67] See L.E. Crim. arts. 694–5. The Jury Law only mentions *conformidad* after the evidence has been taken, see LOTJ art. 50, and some courts have deemed it necessary to select a jury and hear the evidence before resolving an undisputed case. This was done in the first Madrid case, the second Castellón case, and the second Bilbao case; the Bilbao judge openly condemned this perceived necessity. See Thaman, *Spain Returns*, *supra* note 15, at 314–15 (citing *Un juez de Bilbao pide que se eviten vistas con jurado 'sin contenido'*, El Correo, May 23, 1997). Most commentators have deemed that such an interpretation of the law would be uneconomical and would lead defendants to test the waters at trial before agreeing to plead guilty. See Thaman, *Spain Returns*, *supra* note 15, at 312 (citing Gimeno Sendra, *supra* note 37, at 191–2). In practice, the great majority of minor nonhomicide cases are resolved either through a *conformidad* or by manipulating the charges to avoid the jury court's jurisdiction. See Thaman, *Spain Returns*, *supra* note 15, at 311–12.

parti.[68] Coupled with the early and active adversarial participation of the defense, prosecution, and victim in both the preliminary criminal investigation and the trial, the practice is the best example of a 'reprivatization of the criminal law' on the basis of a consensual model proposed by some German commentators.[69] Although the Russian law allows a defendant to plead guilty before the jury and condones, with the consent of the judge and all the parties, an abbreviated trial or even the taking of no evidence, the jury must still deliberate and decide the defendant's fate.[70]

D. The Taking of the Evidence

Trials in both countries begin with an advisement to the defendant of his right not to testify and his privilege against self-incrimination.[71] If the defendant waives these rights, the prosecutor begins the examination of the defendant.[72] The defendant has given a statement waiving his or her right to testify and to avoid self-incrimination in nearly all of the first Spanish trials. The same was true in all but one of the first 114 Russian

[68] For discussion of the 'application of punishment upon the request of the parties', see Freccero, *supra* note 42, at 372–4, and William T. Pizzi & Luca Marafioti, *The New Italian Code of Criminal Procedure: The Difficulties of Building an Adversarial Trial System on a Civil Law Foundation*, 17 YALE J. INT'L. L. 1, 23–6 (1992).

[69] A guilty plea would follow a thorough criminal investigation in which the defendant and the victim would have full participatory rights, rights of discovery, and an opportunity to have their own evidence evaluated. A trial would be the last resort for difficult cases, but all evidence taken with the participation of both parties in the preliminary investigation would be admissible. See JÜRGEN WOLTER, ASPEKTE EINER STRAFPROZEẞREFORM BIS 2007, at 65–91 (1991); Thomas Weigend, *Die Reform des Strafverfahrens*, 104 ZEITSCHRIFT FÜR DIE GESAMTE STRAFRECHTSWISSENSCHAFT 486, 496–511 (1992). For detail, see Thaman, *Spain Returns*, *supra* note 15, at 309–16.

[70] A jury acquitted a Russian man of capital murder and rape after his guilty plea. See Thaman, *Resurrection*, *supra* note 15, at 104–5, 159–60. In the pre-revolutionary Russian jury system, Russian defendants used to plead guilty and express their remorse, winning an acquittal from the jury. For instance, one woman, charged with attempting to poison her husband, ignored her lawyer's advice to plead guilty and denied the charges in her testimony. The jury convicted her and sentenced her to hard labor in Siberia. When her lawyer asked why she did such a stupid thing, she replied that if she were acquitted, she would have to go back to living with her husband! See N.P TIMOFEEV, SUD PRISIAZHNYKH V ROSSII. SUBEBNYE OCHERKI 23–5 (1881). In up to 95% of all criminal cases in the United States, the defendant elects to waive his right to trial by jury and enters a 'plea bargain' in exchange for a sentence guaranteed to be less than if the defendant had gone to trial and was convicted. See CHARLES H. WHITEBREAD & CHRISTOPHER SLOBOGIN, CRIMINAL PROCEDURE 625 (3d. ed. 1993).

[71] See L.E. CRIM. art. 688.

[72] See ibid., arts. 699–700; UPK RSFSR arts. 278, 446.

trials, though some judges allowed the defendant to hear the prosecution's case before deciding whether to testify, as is the practice in the United States. For criminal justice systems that place emphasis on the presumption of innocence, the prosecution's burden of proof, and the defendant's right to remain silent, the interrogation of the defendant before any incriminating evidence has been presented to the factfinder is a lingering inquisitorial vestige in these two systems.[73]

In both Russian and Spanish jury trials, the questioning of the witnesses is initially left to the parties, with the opponents having a right to cross-examine. The judge intervenes only after the parties have finished their questioning.[74] Russian judges have maintained a dominant, inquisitorial role much more so than their Spanish counterparts.[75] Both jury laws allow jurors to submit written, unobjectionable questions to be asked by the presiding judge.[76]

The Russian jury law does not attempt to limit the jury court's access to the preliminary investigation file, nor to regulate the use of prior statements of witnesses or defendants included therein.[77] In Spain, however, the trial judge does not conduct the preliminary hearing and the

[73] For Russian criticism of this practice, see Liakhov, *supra* note 53, at 69; V. Zolotykh, *Sudebnoe sledstvie v sude prisiazhnykh*, in 3 VESTNIK SARATOVSKOY GOSUDARSTVENNOY AKADEMII PRAVA 189, 191 (C. V. Naumov *et al.* (eds.), 1996) (hereinafter VESTN. SAR. GOS. AKAD. PRAVA); cf. Thaman, *Spain Returns*, *supra* note 15, at 297.

[74] See UPK RSFSR art. 446; L.E. CRIM. art. 708.

[75] In the four Spanish trials I saw (the first trials in Palma de Mallorca, Valladolid, Granada, and Córdoba), the trial judges asked few if any questions, leaving the conduct of the evidentiary portion of the trial entirely in the hands of the prosecutor and lawyers. See Thaman, *Spain Returns*, *supra* note 15, at 307. Russian judges have been criticized for first asking witnesses to give a general explanation of their knowledge of the case, and then asking follow-up questions to 'clarify' matters, leaving little opportunity for the parties to dispel the opinion already created in the minds of the jury. See S. A. Nasonov, *Sudebnoe sledstvie v sude prisiazhnykh: zakonodatel'stvo, teoriia, praktika*, in 3 VESTN. SAR. GOS. AKAD. PRAVA, *supra* note 73, at 170, 174. However, some Russian judges adopted a completely passive role, as would befit a U.S. judge. See Thaman, *Resurrection*, *supra* note 15, at 102–9; Thaman, *Das neue russische Geschworenengericht*, *supra* note 15, at 202–3.

[76] See LOTJ art., 46(1). In a study of 54 cases in 1994, it was determined that jurors were much more active than lay assessors in Russian 'mixed courts' in questioning witnesses and defendants. Of the questions asked by the court, 56% were asked by the presiding judge and 43% by the jurors. See M. V. NEMYTINA, ROSSIYSKIY SUD PRISIAZHNYKH 32 (1995). One Saratov judge noted that the more he let the parties examine the witnesses, the more jurors intervened with questions in response to the lawyers' inability to cover crucial areas of testimony effectively. See Thaman, *Resurrection*, *supra* note 15, at 106. Active jury questioning happened in Spain on occasion, but was not the rule. See Thaman, *Spain Returns*, *supra* note 15, at 304–6.

[77] In cases where witnesses failed to appear in court in the first Russian trials, extensive reading from the dossier was common in order to impeach the defendant or witnesses. See Thaman, *Resurrection*, *supra* note 15, at 107.

evidentiary file is not physically present at the trial. Thus, the trial judge's knowledge, as well as that of the jurors, is restricted to the evidence introduced at trial. This difference in procedure effectively prevents a Spanish judge from assuming the inquisitorial role of his Russian counterpart.

Although the Spanish jury law allows the parties to question witnesses about prior statements that contradict their testimony at trial, these statements may not be read into evidence, nor are they admissible for the truth of the matter stated.[78] The new procedure has presented problems, however, for the lawyers. In the three murder trials I observed in Valladolid, Granada, and Córdoba, the defendants, while testifying, denied that they remembered what happened on the day of the homicide. Without being able to use the statements from the preliminary investigation, prosecutors found it very difficult to impeach the alleged lack of memory of the defendants, leading to an interrogation confusing for jurors and audience alike.[79]

The new Russian law prohibiting the introduction of illegally gathered evidence presents some complicated tactical problems for Russian defendants because jury acquittals can be appealed by the prosecutor or the aggrieved. First, many acquittals have been reversed by the Supreme Court of the Russian Federation ('SCRF') because the trial judge excluded evidence which the high court's Cassational Panel deemed admissible.[80] Thus, lawyers must carefully evaluate whether to move to

[78] See LOTJ art. 46(5). The same evidentiary procedure was introduced in the Italian Code of Criminal procedure of 1988, only to be annulled by the Constitutional Court and by subsequent legislation. See Honert, *supra* note 42, at 436. In Spanish trials before professional judges, prior statements may be read in court to impeach in-court statements. See L.E. Crim. art. 714.

[79] Even prior trial testimony is inadmissible in a retrial. Thus, in the first retrial of a Spanish jury case in Castellón, the defendant changed his testimony to improve his self-defense claim and the prosecution could not use his prior testimony because it was unsworn, as Spanish defendants are not required to testify under oath, and because the reversal of the defendant's conviction had rendered the case a 'nullity'. The defendant was acquitted the second time around. See Thaman, *Spain Returns*, *supra* note 15, at 300 (citing interview with Antonio Gastaldi Mateo, Public Prosecutor in the Castellón Provincial Court (June 20, 1997)). For detail on the banishment of the investigation dossier from the trial court and the problems it has caused, see Thaman, *Spain Returns*, *supra* note 15, at 298–301.

[80] The following acquittals have been reversed for this reason: Supreme Court Decision of Sept. 1, 1994 (Case of Bulochnikov), Case No. 51kp-094-68sp (reversing acquittal of the Altay Territorial Court for murder of two persons); Supreme Court Decision of Nov. 24, 1994 (Case of Shchepakin), Case No. 41-kp-094-112sp (reversing acquittal of Rostov-on-the-Don Regional Court for murder); Supreme Court Decision of Dec. 13, 1994 (Case of Sushko), Case No. 19-kp-094-72sp (reversing an acquittal of the Stravopol Territorial Court for the murder of two persons); Supreme Court Decision of Jan. 18, 1995, Case No. 32-kp-

exclude questionably prejudicial evidence. In addition, in some early trials, defense lawyers would sometimes wait until trial to move to exclude the evidence so the judge would not return the case for further investigation, and so the jury could hear the testimony about the unlawful tactics of criminal investigators.[81] In several cases, the Cassational Panel of the SCRF has reversed acquittals because the defense had unsuccessfully moved to exclude allegedly coerced confessions and then had, either through the testimony of the defendant, other witnesses, or through the defense lawyer's closing argument, alluded to the allegedly unlawful actions of the interrogators.[82]

Finally, the Russian legislation prohibits mention of a defendant's past criminal record before the jury.[83] To achieve parity, the SCRF ruled *en*

094-70sp (reversing acquittal of the Saratov Regional Court for an attempted murder and theft); Supreme Court Decision of Oct. 26, 1995 (Case of Volkov), Case No. 4-kp-095-94sp (reversing acquittal of the Moscow regional Court for the murder of two persons, arson, and destruction of property); Supreme Court Decision of Feb. 20, 1997 (Case of Nikitin/Savchenko/Bovisov/Grishin), Case No. 4-kp-097-13sp (reversing acquittals of the Moscow Regional Court for murder, destruction of property, and other crimes); Supreme Court Decision of Apr. 16, 1997 (Case of Vlasov/Vlasov/Kovalev), Case No. 41-kp-097-32sp (reversing convictions of Rostov-on-the-Don Regional Court for robbery-murder).

[81] See Thaman, *Resurrection*, *supra* note 15, at 92.

[82] The President of the Cassational Panel of the SCRF discusses several such cases in A. Shurygin, *Zashchita v sudoproizvodstve s uchastiem kollegii prisiazhnykh zasedateley*, 9 Ross. Iust. 6 (1997). Human rights activists, aware of the fact that criminal investigators in Russia still employ torture and other tools in their 'technology of confessions', have sharply criticized these rulings for depriving juries of evidence about the voluntariness of confessions and the credibility of the defendant. See Pashin, *supra* note 47, at 344; Stanislav Velikoredchanin, *Sud prisiazhnykh* v *Rossii*, in 25 Prava cheloveka v Rossii: informatsiannaia set, 11, 11–12 (Stanislav Velikoredchanin ed., 1997). The following acquittals were reversed for this reason: Supreme Court Decision of Nov. 24, 1995 (Case of Zhevak), Case No. 41-kp-096-24sp (reversing acquittals of the Rostov-on-the-Don Regional Court for murder); Supreme Court Decision of May 14, 1996 (Case of Kornilov/Nikilenko/Gerner), Case No. 41-kp-96-39sp (reversing the acquittal of the Rostov-on-the-Don Regional Court for the murder of several people in a bombing); Supreme Court Decision of Apr. 19, 1997 (Case of Antipov), Case No. 41-kp-097-27sp (reversing the acquital of the the Rostov-on-the-Don Regional Court for the rape of a minor); Supreme Court Decision of May 7, 1997 (Case of Grigoriev), Case No. 51-kp-097-26sp (reversing the acquittal of the Altay Regional Court for the rape of a minor); Supreme Court Decision of May 29, 1997 (Case of Popov), Case No. 32-kp-097-21sp (reversing the acquittal of the Saratov Regional Court for a robbery-murder).

[83] See Thaman, *Resurrection*, *supra* note 15, at 103. For instance, the defendant's criminal record must be omitted from the reading of the indictment. See UPK RSFSR art. 446. On the other hand, the jury has received questions related to proving prior convictions of defendants in Spanish cases when the aggravating circumstance of recidivism is pleaded. Thus in the Ugal/Martínez case in the Barcelona Provincial Court, the jury proved four prior convictions for Ugal and nine for Martínez. See Thaman, *Spain Returns*, *supra* note 15, at 347.

banc that the defendant may not introduce good character evidence before the jury.[84] This ruling hinders the defense in presenting 'sympathy' evidence to the jury inducing them to recommend leniency. Since 'sympathy' evidence can help eliminate the possibility of the death penalty, its omission has been strongly criticized.[85] For example, the SCRF has even upheld the conviction of an arguably 'battered' woman for the aggravated murder of her husband even though she was prevented from introducing evidence of his bad character. The court held that admission of such evidence would turn the case into a trial of the victim.[86]

E. The Role of Judge and Jury in Rendering Judgment

Both the Russian and Spanish legislatures have rejected the Anglo-American general verdict of 'guilty' or 'not guilty'. Instead, Russia and Spain have followed the French model, later adopted by most Continental European countries in the nineteenth century, whereby the jury is presented with a list of questions or propositions.[87]

Before arguments and the defendant's last word, the Spanish judge prepares a verdict form (*objeto del veredicto*) in the form of a list of propositions, some designated as favorable to the defendant, some as unfavorable. The jury must then decide whether they were proved or not proved during the trial. The propositions are restricted to the facts presented by the various parties during the trial and relate to the elements of the crimes charged, conditions which modify or exclude guilt, and statutory factors that aggravate or mitigate the defendant's criminal responsibility. Finally, the jury is asked to affirm or deny the proof of the defendant's

[84] See SCRF Decision No. 9, *supra* note 49, ¶ 16. In the case of Gusiev/Poliakov, an acquittal for robbery-murder was reversed because the defense read records of the defendant's illness to the jury and told the jury that an earlier conviction had been reversed by the SCRF. See Supreme Court Decision of Apr. 30, 1997 (Case of Gusiev/Poliakov), Case No. 19 kp-097-15sp (reversing decision of Stavropol Territorial Court).

[85] Defense lawyers still manage to present 'sympathy' evidence before the jury. See generally Nasonov, *supra* note 75, at 183–5; Pashin, *supra* note 47, at 385.

[86] See Supreme Court Decision of June 3, 1997 (Case of Shayko), Case No. 80 kp-097-28sp (affirming conviction handed down by Ul'ianovsk Regional Court). The woman, in an earlier trial, had been convicted of murder in the heat of passion, caused by a serious insult delivered by her husband. The SCRF reversed the conviction, finding that the 'nature' of the questions asked constituted an abuse of the judge's authority. See Supreme Court Decision of Sept. 24, 1996 (Case of Shayko), Case No. 80-kp-096-33sp (Ul'ianovsk Regional Court).

[87] See Meyer, *supra* note 3, at 48–108.

guilt of the 'criminal acts' (*hechos delictivos*) contained in the parties' pleadings. If the jury believes that guilt has been proved of one or more of the allegations, it may nevertheless recommend a suspension of sentence (*remisión condicional de la pena*) or ask that the government grant complete or partial amnesty for the offense (*recomendación del indulto*).[88] The judge's proposed verdict form must be discussed with the parties; the parties' objections to the form's contents may form the basis for an appeal.[89]

The Russian 'question list' requires the posing of three basic questions: (l) whether the *corpus delicti* of the crime has been proved; (2) whether the defendant's identity as perpetrator of the crime has been proved; and (3) whether he or she is guilty of having committed the crime.[90]

Both legislatures resorted to the 'question list' verdict form to give the professional judge a factual foundation for the imposition of a reasoned judgment. The factual foundation is a statutory or constitutional requirement in both countries.[91] Both legislatures equivocated, however, on whether they actually wished to limit the jury to deciding mere 'naked historical facts' or allowing it to make a finding of 'guilty' or 'not guilty' on each charged offense. While the Russian statute prohibits the judge from posing questions which require 'strictly juridical evaluations', it also requires the judge to instruct the jury on the substantive law as it applies to the acts imputed to the defendant, thus seeming to indicate that the jury is to apply the law to the facts. The SCRF, however, has interpreted the statutory language to reduce the jury to deciding only 'naked historical facts', depriving it even of deciding 'internal fact elements' or *mens rea*, by characterizing it as a 'question of law'.[92]

[88] See LOTJ art. 52. Unlike the Spanish 'recommendation', the Russian jury's finding of 'lenience' or 'special lenience' binds the judge in substantially lowering the sentencing parameters. See UPK RSFSR arts. 449, 460; see also Thaman, *Das neue russische Geschworenengericht*, *supra* note 16, at 206.

[89] See LOTJ art. 53.

[90] See UPK RSFSR art. 449. For a detailed discussion of the problems encountered by Russian judges in drafting the question lists in the first trials, see Thaman, *Resurrection*, *supra* note 15, at 114–23.

[91] See Constitución Española (C.E.) art. 120(3) (Spain); UPK RSFSR arts. 314, 462.

[92] In SCRF's Opinion No. 9, *supra* note 49, ¶ 18, the Court held that the jury lacked competence to decide 'juridical questions', such as whether a murder was intentional, negligent, or committed in the heat of passion or for financial gain, whether it was committed with a 'hooliganistic' motivation, extreme cruelty, or excessive force in self-defense, or whether an act amounted to robbery or rape. I have criticized the jurisprudence of the SCRF, drawing on the pre-revolutionary practice and theory discussed in Stephen Thaman, *Postanovka voprosov v sovremennom Rossiyskom sude prisiazhnykh*, 10 Ross. Iust. 8–11 (1995) (hereinafter Thaman, *Postanovka voprosov*); see also Thaman, *Das neue russische*

Spanish courts have wrestled with similar problems. Most courts have tried to phrase questions of guilt in terms of the defendant's 'having caused the death' of the victim and have eschewed using the *nomen juris* in their formulations. This has not been true in questions related to mitigating and aggravating circumstances, however, and juries have been asked directly whether a murder was committed with treachery (*alevosía*) or excessive cruelty (*ensañamiento*), often including definitions phrased in legal terminology within the question itself. Spanish courts have also not shied away from asking juries directly about the defendant's mental state, for example, whether a homicide was committed intentionally, recklessly, with gross negligence, with simple negligence, or accidentally.[93] According to some commentators, one of the main reasons for several of the more criticized verdicts in the country is jurors' hesitance to find 'intent' in the domestic and bar-room 'crimes of passion' typical of many Spanish homicides. This has led judges to instruct juries seriously on the difference between intentional and reckless murder, as well as the difference between homicide with gross or simple negligence.[94]

The Russian system separates the guilt question into three component parts, thereby permitting implicit jury nullification by allowing an acquittal even though the jury has determined that the *corpus delicti* and the defendant's perpetration of the criminal acts has been proved. In the famous *Vera Zasulich* case of 1878, the jury acquitted a young revolutionary sympathizer of shooting a Tsarist official by availing itself of this option of a 'not guilty' verdict, even though all of the elements of the crime had been proved.[95] Spanish law treats contradictions between the

Geschworenengericht, *supra* note 15, at 205–6. For similar criticism, see NEMYTINA, *supra* note 76, at 83. While *mens rea* is a 'question of fact' for the jury to decide in U.S. trials, the U.S. Supreme Court has recently decided that it does not violate due process to statutorily prevent the jury from hearing evidence relevant to the proof of the defendant's mental state, for example, evidence of intoxication. See Montana v. Egelhoff, 518 U.S. 37, 42–4 (1996).

93 See Thaman, *Spain Returns*, *supra* note 15, at 320–51, for a detailed study of the Spanish question lists. See ibid., at 335–46 on questions relating to mental states.

94 This was the opinion of the President of Sevilla Provincial Court. See Thaman, *Spain Returns*, *supra* note 15, at 340, 355 (citing Miguel Carmona Ruano & José Manuel De Paúl, Informe sobre las Causas Juzgadas por el Tribunal del Jurado 68–9 (1997) (unpublished draft commissioned by CGPJ, on file with the author)).

95 For discussions of pre-revolutionary Russian jury nullification in the context of the new statute, see Thaman, *Resurrection*, *supra* note 15, at 114–15; Thaman, *Postanovka voprosov*, *supra* note 92, at 9. In a case from the Ivanovo Region, a jury affirmatively answered the *corpus delicti* and perpetration questions. The victim had been stabbed to death, his woman friend, the defendant, had perpetrated the killing, and no legal excuses or justifications had been proved. Nevertheless, the jury found her 'not guilty' of the murder and the SCRF

questions of *corpus delicti*, the identity of the perpetrator and guilt as a defect in the verdict which the jury is instructed to correct.[96]

The Spanish system is more explicit in reducing the jury's role in determining 'guilt' by limiting the scope of the jury's involvement to finding that the defendant committed a certain criminal act rather than a finding that a 'crime' was committed in the juridical sense.[97] The stricter 'anti-nullification' approach of the Spanish legislature did not, however, prevent the stunning acquittal of Mikel Otegi of the murder of two policemen in the Basque Country. The jury was able to acquit the young man, despite clear evidence of an intentional double murder, because questions of *mens rea*, including questions of diminished capacity and insanity as a complete excuse for criminal conduct, are considered to be 'questions of fact' for the jury to decide. Spain also permits a complete excuse on grounds of temporary insanity, even when caused by voluntary intoxication or other causes.[98] In Russia, the judge must

upheld the judgment. See Thaman, *Geschworenengerichte*, *supra* note 15, at 79 n.66. In commenting on the SCRF decision affirming this case, the chief author of the jury law noted that one interpretation of the 'not guilty' verdict under the Russian law is that 'the act contains all the elements of the crime in its totality, but the jury, for reasons known to them, deprived the state of the right to achieve a conviction and apply the sanctions of the special part of the Penal Code': S. A. Pashin, *Postanovka voprosov pered kollegiey prisiazhnykh zasedateley*, in 1 Sost. Pravo., *supra* note 47, at 89, 90–1.

[96] See LOTJ art. 63(1)(d). This happened in the second Málaga trial, a prosecution for trespass and threats, in which the jury found the principal fact questions to be proved, yet returned a verdict of 'not guilty'. The judge returned the verdict for 'correction', explaining its supposed contradictoriness, and the jury blithely found the principal fact questions (as to *corpus delicti* and perpetration) to be 'not proved' and revalidated its acquittal. See Carmona Ruano & De Paúl, *supra* note 94, at 7. On the Spanish attempt to prevent jury nullification, see Thaman, *Spain Returns*, *supra* note 15, at 376–80. In its study of jury trials between April 1, 1997 and March 31, 1998, however, the CGPJ has found two cases where the jury actually engaged in jury nullification, i.e., returning a verdict based on sympathy for the defendant, and in contradiction to the facts, yet neither was appealed by the prosecution. Consejo General del Poder Judicial. *Anexo I. Aplicación de la Ley Orgánica del Tribunal del Jurado en el Período l de Abril de 1997–31 de Marzo 1998* (hereafter CGPJ *Anexo I*) (on file with author), at 56–7.

[97] LOTJ art. 60(1) originally called for a finding of guilt or lack thereof as to each 'charged crime' (*delito imputado*). In November 1995, the language was changed to 'charged criminal act' (*hecho delictivo imputado*) to effect a clean separation of questions of law from questions of fact. See Thaman, *Spain Returns*, *supra* note 15, at 336. Thus, as one critic noted, it is no longer a guilt-finding in the strict meaning of the word and is actually superfluous in the technical sense. See Thaman, *Spain Returns*, *supra* note 15, at 378 n. 609 (citing Gómez Colomer, *supra* note 26, at 122).

[98] In the Otegi Case, the bulk of the defense's 64 questions related to the defendant's drinking the evening and morning before the killings and his prior encounters with the Basque police. The jury affirmed by majority vote the following questions: (Q69): Mr. Mikel Mirena Otegi Unanue has a personality with a propensity or predisposition to experience

discharge the jury and initiate psychiatric commitment procedures if evidence of mental illness eliminating criminal responsibility arises.[99] Until the promulgation of a new penal code in 1996, the question of voluntary intoxication, a veritable national pastime in Russia, was only presented to the jury as a circumstance that aggravates the defendant's level of guilt. Despite this statutory aggravating factor, which also existed before the Russian Revolution, Russian jurors have tended to mitigate the responsibility of intoxicated defendants and have generally recommended lenience.[100]

As in the first Russian trials, some Spanish judges have limited the propositions in the verdict form to those absolutely necessary to prove the elements of the offenses and the mitigating or aggravating circumstances,[101] whereas others have had the jurors affirm or reject virtually every assertion contained in the prosecution and defense pleadings. For example, of the fifty-four propositions submitted to the first Valladolid jury, several had no relation to important elements of the offense.[102] Interviews of the jury in the notorious Otegi case in San Sebastián

feelings of harrassment and persecution on the part of the *Ertzaintza*; (Q70): In Mr. Mikel Mirena Otegi Unanue there exists a pre-existing pathological condition or an ailment or an underlying psychic disturbance in connection with the aforementioned sense of harrassment and persecution by the *Ertzaintza*, which he experienced in extreme ways intolerable for his personality; (Q76): Mikel Mirena Otegi Unanue consumed an excessive quantity of alcoholic beverages between the afternoon and evening of December 9 and 10, 1995, until he achieved a state of inebriation; (Q77): The conjunction of all of the facts laid out in numbers 69 through 76 of Part C, or, in the alternative, of those which have been declared proved, had as a result that in the moment of firing the weapon Mr. Mikel Mirena Otegi Unanue was absolutely not in control of his actions. See Verdict Form from the Otegi Case in San Sebastián Provincial Court (Mar. 7, 1997) (on file with author).

[99] See Thaman, *Resurrection*, *supra* note 15, at 127.

[100] Eighty-nine defendants in 76 of the first 109 Russian trials to reach a verdict were found to be intoxicated (an aggravating factor) at the time of commission of the crime. The jury recommended leniency to 47 of those defendants. Pre-revolutionary observers of jury trials in Russia also found that the 'views of jurors about the condition of drunkenness at the moment of the commission of a crime are diametrically opposed to those provisions of the law dealing with this object'. Timofeev, *supra* note 70, at 381; cf. Bobrishchev-Pushkin, Empiricheskie zakony deiatel'nosti Russkogo suda prisiazhnykh 355–6 (1896).

[101] For example, only nine and six propositions, respectively, were submitted to the juries in the first murder cases in Palencia and Granada.

[102] This subsequently elicited much criticism in the press, and the judge admitted the difficulty he had with the verdict in a newspaper interview. See Thaman, *Spain Returns*, *supra* note 15, at 332–3 (citing Juan Carlos León, *El jurado nos libera de una responsabilidad*, El Norte del Castillo, June 16, 1996, at 10–11).

revealed they had great trouble understanding the ninety-five questions submitted to them.[103]

Following the preparation of the verdict form, the arguments of the parties, and the defendant's last word, the presiding judge in Spain instructs the jury in a restrained manner and in a form the jury can understand as to (1) the jury's function, (2) the content of the verdict form, (3) the nature of the facts under discussion, those that determine the circumstances constituting the crime(s) charged and those that refer to allegations of exclusion and modification of guilt, (4) the rules of deliberation and voting, and (5) the form of their final verdict.[104] The judge must be sure to maintain strict impartiality during the summation and must instruct the jurors not to consider any evidence declared inadmissible at trial.[105] The judge also instructs the jurors to resolve all doubts in favor of the defendant.[106] Spanish judges have differing views on whether they should instruct juries on the legal elements of the charged crimes, inasmuch as the law expressly restricts the jury to deciding solely whether the charged acts were committed.[107] Even though the SCRF has in fact reduced Russian jurors to judges of 'naked acts', and does not even let them decide *mens rea* questions, the judge still gives a complete instruction on the substantive law during his or her summation. The judge is also required to summarize the evidence and the positions of the

[103] See Thaman, *Spain Returns*, *supra* note 15, at 333 (citing Carmen Gurrucha & Juan Carlos Escudier, *La caótica actuación del jurado del 'caso Otegi'*, El Mundo, Apr. 22, 1997, at 6–7). There have been verdict forms with over 150 questions in more than one Spanish case. CGPJ *Anexo I*, *supra* note 96, at 33. The CGPJ has urged judges to limit their questions to descriptions of only those facts necessary to constitute the elements of the charged offences, and to desist from including questions unrelated to guilt gleaned from the statement of facts in the accusatory pleading. Consejo General del Poder Judicial, *Informe del Consejo General del Poder Judicial Sobre la Experiencia de la Aplicación de la Vigente Ley Orgánica del Tribunal del Jurado*. Madrid. Jan. 14, 1998 (hereafter CGPJ *Informe*), at 49–51. In one Russian trial, 1,047 questions were submitted to the jury. See Interview with V. P. Stepalin, Judge of the Cassational Panel of the SCRF (Aug. 20, 1998) (on file with author).

[104] See LOTJ art. 54. [105] See ibid. [106] See ibid.

[107] Thus in the first Granada and Córdoba murder trials, the trial judges scarcely mentioned the elements of the charged crimes. Author's observations at trial (May 5–9, 1997). Trial judges in Lugo, Sevilla, and Girona agreed with this interpretation of the law. See Thaman, *Spain Returns*, *supra* note 15, at 354 (citing Interview with Edgar Armando Fernández Cloos, Trial Judge in Lugo Provincial Court (June 16, 1997); Interview with Antonio Gil Merino, Trial Judge in Sevilla Provincial Court (June 16, 1997); Interview with Fernando Lacaba Sánchez, Trial Judge in Girona Provincial Court (June 26, 1997)). On the other hand, the judge in the first trial in Vitoria explained in the judgment how difficult it was to explain to the jury the difference between intentional murder, reckless murder, homicide with gross and simple negligence, and accident. See ibid., at 355.

parties,[108] a practice adhered to in Spain from 1888 until 1931, when it was repealed because it was seen as tantamount to an ultimate accusation by the supposedly neutral bench at the end of the trial when no response was afforded to the defense.[109] Several convictions have been reversed by the SCRF because of the one-sidedness of the presiding judge's summation, or because he or she neglected to mention some of the evidence.[110]

F. Deliberation, Verdict, and Judgment

Jury deliberations in both Russia and Spain are entirely secret. The presiding judge is not allowed to participate and jurors may not reveal any information about the deliberations.[111] In Spain, seven of nine votes are required to prove any propositions unfavorable to the defendant, whereas only five votes are needed to prove any proposition favorable to the accused. Jurors are also allowed to alter the propositions submitted to them as long as they do not substantially alter the subject of their deliberations and the alterations do not result in an aggravation of the possible criminal responsibility of the defendant.[112] Similarly, 'guilty' verdicts require seven votes while 'not guilty' verdicts or recommendations of suspension of sentence and clemency require only five.[113] The jury can request more instructions or clarifications as to the verdict form, and if the jury has not voted after two days of deliberations, the judge can call them into court to determine whether they have had any problems understanding the verdict form.[114]

While the detailed special verdicts used in Spanish and Russian cases certainly enable the sentencing and appellate judges to divine the reasoning process of the jury, Spain has gone one step further and required

[108] See UPK RSFSR. art. 451; see also Thaman, *Das neue russische Geschworenengericht*, *supra* note 15, at 207.

[109] See Thaman, *Spain Returns*, *supra* note 15, at 356 (citing Francisco Mares Roger & José-Antonio Mora Alarcón, Comentarios a la Ley del Jurado 359 (1996)).

[110] See Shurygin, *supra* note 82, at 7. A counsel's objection to a lack of objectivity in a summation must be on the record in order to preserve the issue on appeal. See UPK RSFSR art. 451. This objection should be made in the presence of the jury so as to give the judge a chance to correct any possible errors. See ibid.

[111] See LOTJ arts. 55–6; UPK RSFSR art. 452.

[112] See LOTJ art. 59.

[113] See ibid., art. 60. A guilty verdict in Russia requires seven of the twelve jurors' votes, whereas six votes are sufficient for an acquittal or for a finding favorable to the defendant. See UPK RSFSR art. 454.

[114] See LOTJ art. 57. Russian jurors must strive for unanimity during the first three hours of deliberation, whereafter they may seek to reach a majority decision. See UPK RSFSR art. 453. Juries seldom deliberate more than the three minimum hours.

that the jury give a succinct rationale for their verdict, indicating the evidence upon which the verdict was based and the reasons for finding a particular proposition proved or not proved.[115] Other than a nonbinding statement by the jury provided for in the Austrian Code of Criminal Procedure,[116] this is the clearest attempt yet by a legislature to require that juries justify their verdicts.

While some juries gave fairly elaborate explanations of why they found a charge to be proven (for example, by explaining why they believed a witness, or did not believe the defendant, or by pointing to expert testimony), many juries just provided stock phrases like 'testimony of witnesses and experts', or 'evidence, experts, defendant's testimony'.[117] The ultimate minimalist variant was that of the jurors in the second Málaga case; that jury just wrote: 'witnesses'.[118]

Prior to the *Otegi* case, some commentators opined that requiring juries to give reasons for acquittals would violate the presumption of innocence and the principal of 'free evaluation of the evidence', since an appellate court, when reviewing a jury's verdict, need only affirm that objective elements of proof exist which could have permitted the jury to reach a certain conclusion.[119] Indeed, many of the acquittal verdicts were phrased in terms of doubt about the sufficiency of the proof.[120] On

[115] See LOTJ art. 61(1). This innovation was deemed necessary to comport with art. 120(3) of the Spanish Constitution. CONSTITUTIÓN ESPAÑOLA (C.E.) art. 120(3). It was also deemed necessary to comply with the presumption of innocence guaranteed by art. 24(2) of the Spanish Constitution and art. 6(2) of the European Convention on Human Rights. See ibid., art. 24(2); Eur. Conv. on H.R., Dec. 10, 1948, art. 6(2); Thaman, *Spain Returms*, *supra* note 15, at 364 (citing GIMENO SENDRA, *supra* note 37, at 320).

[116] See art. 331(e) StPO. It is a contested point, however, whether the reasons stated in the '*Niederschrift*' may be used as a basis for attacking the factual findings of the jury. See Einhard Steininger, *Die Anfechtung mangelhafter Tatsachenfeststellungen im Geschworenenverfahren*, 47 ÖSTERREICHISCHE JURISTENZEITUNG 686, 688–91 (1992).

[117] See Thaman, *Spain Returns*, *supra* note 15, at 365–7 (citing Carmona Ruano & De Paúl, *supra* note 94, at 54), for a list of such 'reasons', categorized as 'minimal'.

[118] See ibid., at 355. The CGPJ has studied the reasons given in 139 verdicts returned up to March 31, 1998 and has found the reasons sufficient in 70 and clearly insufficient or non-existent in 51 of the cases. CGPJ *Informe*, *supra* note 103, at 74; CGPJ *Anexo I*, *supra* note 96, at 33–4.

[119] See ibid., at 372 (citing José Antonio Díaz Cabiale, *Prueba, Veredicto, Deliberación y Sentencia*, in COMENTARIOS SISTEMÁTICOS A LA LEY DEL JURADO Y A LA REFORMA DE LA PRISIÓN PREVENTIVA 276, 290 (Agustín Pérez-Cruz Martín *et al.* (eds.), 1996); MARÉS ROGER & MORA ALARCÓN, *supra* note 109, at 398).

[120] An example would be the acquittal of the defendant in the first Ávila trial for failing to render aid after a traffic accident: 'After we heard all the testimony of witnesses and experts, the evidence was not sufficient to declare the defendant guilty'. Verdict form from the Barrero Case in Ávila Provincial Court (Oct. 7, 1996) (on file with author), reprinted in Thaman, *Spain Returns*, *supra* note 15, at 371–2.

June 27, 1997, however, the Superior Court of Justice of the Basque Country reversed the *Otegi* acquittal based on the insufficiency of the rationale given by the jury, believing that the jury had basically made just bald assertions of reasonable doubt. After lamenting that the jury did not give even a minimal explanation for its answers to the ninety-one factual questions, and provided only a 'pseudo-motivation or substitute global motivation', the Court expounded:

The invocation of doubt and the references to that which the law requires—with which the jury pretends to support its answers, which they forgot to give reasons for before—reveal that the jury, camouflaging with perplexity a psychological state which has nothing to do with serious hesitation, invents the existence of a doubt which it gratuitously prejudges, in order to use the prop of Art. 54(3) of the law. Armed with the protection of this precept, the jury proclaims that it is plagued by doubt, that it finds it impossible to dissipate it and that, because of it, it is resolving the issue in the sense most favorable to the defendant. It does not describe from where the doubt arose, nor the magnitude thereof, nor is any notion apparent of the force employed to overcome the doubt or clear up the difficulties to which it has given rise.[121]

To avoid deficiencies with the verdict, the jury may request that the secretary of the court help them in drafting the verdict.[122] Some commentators have seen this as the first step toward, or a subliminal recognition of what is in their opinion the superiority of the mixed court with lay assessors.[123] Indeed, in a few of the first trials, the legally trained secretary answered substantive legal questions posed by the jury.[124]

After receiving the verdict from the jury, the judge must review the verdict for defects and ask the jury to make any necessary corrections. In a Spanish case, if the judge returns the jury three times to correct defects in the verdict, and they fail to do so, he or she may dissolve the

[121] See Thaman, *Spain Returns*, *supra* note 15, at 373 (citing Aurora Intxausti, *Otegi volverá a ser juzgado por matar a dos 'ertzainas'*, EL PAÍS, June 28, 1997, at 13). For a general discussion on the Spanish reasoned verdicts, see Thaman, *Spain Returns*, *supra* note 15, at 364–74. The Otegi reversal was upheld by the Spanish Supreme Court. See STS, Mar. 11, 1998 (B.J.C. 4226, 6–13).

[122] See LOTJ art. 61(2).

[123] See Thaman, *Spain Returns*, *supra* note 15, at 375 (citing GIMENO SENDRA, *supra* note 26, at 34–5; GÓMEZ COLOMER, *supra* note 26, at 124).

[124] The secretary in the second Oviedo trial told me that she not only explained to the jury the effect of recommendations of clemency or a suspended sentence, but also the difference between a complete and partial excuse from criminal responsibility due to psychic disturbance. See Thaman, *Spain Returns*, *supra* note 15, at 375 (citing Interview with Evelia Alonso Crespo, Secretary in Oviedo Provincial Court (June 9, 1997)). See generally ibid., at 374–6.

jury and retry the case before a new jury. If the new jury also fails to reach a verdict due to similar problems, the judge must, on his or her own motion, enter a verdict of acquittal.[125]

The judge's ruling following a guilty verdict in both countries must be based on the facts found to be true by the jury, which the judge then juridically qualifies before imposing sentence.[126] Spanish judges have expressed frustration at having to justify jury verdicts with which they do not agree, a situation which judges could face in mixed courts, in the unlikely event they were outvoted by the lay assessors. In a twenty-six-page judgment, the judge in the thirteenth Barcelona trial expressed his disagreement with a jury's finding that the defendant did not intend to kill, when he stabbed his female companion seven times in areas of her body containing vital organs. The judge lamented, '[i]n the mind of the jurist a certain pain emerges, from the point of view of judicial technique' when one must justify a judgment when the facts 'collide with the interpretative criteria which jurisprudence utilizes to determine the intentionality of an agent'.[127] The judge in the second Córdoba trial criticized a jury's verdict which compelled him to sentence a man to thirty years in prison as 'the sentiments of the common people, struggling in the nadir of a long process of decadence', and added:

> There are times when the soul is buffeted about by anxiety when the knowledge of ancestral criteria of the technical application of the law is brought down in an instant by simple inclinations of personal sensibility, replete with honesty, but nevertheless deprived of even the simplest sense of legal culture.[128]

[125] See LOTJ art. 65. The Russian judge may also return the jury to the jury room to correct contradictions in their verdict. See UPK RSFSR art. 456.

[126] See LOTJ art. 70; UPK RSFSR art. 459. Judgments of guilt and acquittals may be appealed in both Russia and Spain. Spain provides for a first appeal, in which new evidence may be adduced, an appeal in cassation, and an appeal to the Supreme Court of Spain. See L.E. Crim. art. 846(a)–(c). Russia provides only one level of appeal in cassation, followed by a direct appeal to the SCRF. See UPK RSFSR arts. 463, 464.

[127] Thaman, *Spain Returns*, *supra* note 15, at 385–6 (citing Francesco Peirón, *Un juez critica el veredicto de un jurado que sólo consideró imprudencia matar a una mujer a puñaladas*, El País, May 31, 1997). The judgment in the case of Domingo Ortega Perez was reversed by the Superior Court of Catalonia and, upon retrial, he was convicted of murder. See *La Audiencia de Barcelona tiene que repetir un juício con jurado*, La Vanguardia Digital (visited Sept. 28, 1998) <http://www.vanguardia.es/cgi-bin/nrp_ccr_new/dia-hoy&nnk-vb2832a&sec-soc>; Francesa Peirón, *El jurado rectifica y condena por asesinato al hombre que mató a su mjuer de siete cuchilladas*, La Vanguardia Digital (visited Oct. 3, 1998) <http://www.vanguardia.es/cgi-bin/nrp_ccr_new/dia-hoy&nnk-vb032/a&sec-soc>.

[128] Thaman, *Spain Returns*, *supra* note 15, at 384 (citing *Juez firma sentencia de un jurado por imperativo legal*, Ideal, June 8, 1997, at 1). On problems related to the judge's justifying his or her sentence, see ibid., at 384–7.

VII. Conclusion

It is difficult to predict the future of trial by jury in either Russia or Spain. Despite a constitutional anchor in both countries, a decided lack of enthusiasm exists on the part of professors, judges, and lawyers as to whether it is an institution capable of helping to solve the problems plaguing the administration of justice. It also remains to be seen whether it will serve as a genuine catalyst in transforming the criminal trials in both countries into an adversarial proceeding, with increased orality and immediacy and less reliance on the investigative dossier.

Russia's new law has been in effect since late 1993, yet the institution has not spread beyond the nine original regions.[129] From December 15, 1993 to December 1, 1998, approximately 1,639 jury trials, involving 3,032 defendants, reached a verdict.[130] Defendants requesting to be tried by a jury in jurisdictions subject to the Regional or Territorial Courts have risen from 20.5 percent in 1994, to 30.9 percent in 1995, 37.3 percent in 1996, and 36.8 percent in 1997,[131] and 43.2 percent in 1998[132] indicating the increasing popularity of trial by jury at least within one part of the population. The acquittal rate, at 18.2 percent in 1994, fell to 14.3 percent in 1995, but then rose to 19.1 percent in 1996 and to 22.9 percent in 1997, falling to 20.6 percent in 1998.[133] These numbers must be compared, however, to general acquittal rates of 1.3 percent in 1994 and 1.4 percent in 1995.[134] In addition, many of the jury trials ended in convictions for lesser offenses or in verdicts of lenience or special lenience.[135] The relative lenience of Russian juries can perhaps be explained as a reaction to an excessively severe Soviet criminal justice system, coupled with profound mistrust among the population of criminal investigators and police, who are known to engage in brutal coercive tactics in interrogation and are otherwise distrusted in their testimony.[136] The parties themselves becoming more active in the presentation of evidence and examination of witnesses may also have led to a higher acquittal rate.

[129] These nine regions are named *supra* note 13.

[130] See *Praktika realizatsii*, *supra* note 27, at 4; Spravka po rezul'tatam izucheniia prichin otmeny i izmeniia prigovorov suda prisiazhnykh rassmotrennykh Verkhovny m Sudom Rossiyskoy Federatsiiv 1998 gody (1999) (on file with the author), at 3, 6–7.

[131] See *Spravka*, *supra* note 27.

[132] See Spravka (1999), *supra* note 130, at 6.

[133] See ibid.

[134] See Gagarsky, *supra* note 41, at 4.

[135] See Thaman, *Das neue russische Geschworenengericht*, *supra* note 15, at 212.

[136] See Thaman, *Resurrection*, *supra* note 15, at 66–7, 91–4, 130.

The appellate jurisprudence of the SCRF has radically restricted the jury's power to decide issues of *mens rea*, the pivotal questions in most murder trials, and aggravating circumstances, which can trigger imposition of the death penalty. These issues include statutory aggravating circumstances, the issue of intention, affirmative defenses such as necessary defense or heat of passion, and others.[137] In 1994, the SCRF reversed 42.9 percent of all judgments and 20.1 percent of all acquittals, nine total. While the SCRF reversed only 31.5 percent of the judgments in 1995 and 22.2 percent in 1996, it is still reversing a substantial number of acquittals, 17.3 percent of those appealed in 1995,[138] 30.7 percent in 1996, and 48.6 percent in 1997, and 66 percent in 1998.[139] Not only does the ability to reverse an acquittal differentiate Russian and Spanish appellate procedure from that in the United States, but in Russia, the issues subject to review by appellate courts are not limited by those framed by the appellants and respondents. This inquisitorial remnant in the new adversarial framework has enabled the SCRF to reverse many cases on issues not briefed by any of the parties.[140]

Other than in the verdict in the *Otegi* case, Spanish juries have not been excessively lenient in their first year. Of the fifty-two homicide verdicts I analyzed, the jury followed the recommendation of the public prosecutor thirty-four times, three of those prosecutorial recommendations for acquittal by reason of insanity.[141] The jury followed the more severe recommendation of the private prosecutor (victim's representative) only three times. The jury found lesser-included offenses of negligent homicide or infliction of injuries not pleaded by the public prosecutor in seven cases and acquitted ten times, seven of which were not pleaded by the public prosecutor.[142] In two cases, the jury actually returned a verdict more lenient than that requested by the defense.[143]

[137] I have argued that this could violate Art. 20 of the KONST. RF, which guarantees trial by jury in capital cases. See Thaman, *Das neue russische Geschworenengericht*, *supra* note 15, at 205; Thaman, *Postanovka voprosov*, *supra* note 92, at 10.

[138] See *Praktika realizatsii*, *supra* note 27, at 4; Gagarsky, *supra* note 41, at 4.

[139] *Spravka* (1999), *supra* note 130, at 7. See *Spravka*, *supra* note 41, at 7–8.

[140] See P. A. Lupinskaia, *Poriadok obzhalovaniia, oprotestovaniia i proverki, ne vstupivshikh v zakonnuiu silu prigovorov i postanovleniy, vynesennykh v usloviiakh al'ternativnoy formy sudoproizvodstva*, in 3 VESTN. SAR. GOS. AKAD. PRAVA, *supra* note 73, at 239, 240–1.

[141] See Thaman, *Spain Returns*, *supra* note 15, at 392–7.

[142] See ibid.

[143] See ibid. In the period up to March 31, 1997, around 30% of acquittals were registered in the 39 cases (including 50 criminal charges) that actually went to jury verdict. CGPJ *Informe*, *supra* note 103, at 24. There were 24 acquittals in the 126 cases that went to verdict in the period from April 1, 1997 through March 31, 1998 (around 19%), which is slightly lower than the acquittal average in the provincial courts in the years 1982–92, CGPJ *Anexo I*, *supra* note 96, at 29.

The CGPJ in its studies of jury cases up to March 31, 1998, has found only a handful of 'surprising' verdicts among the approximately 166 that actually went to trial (that is, verdicts different from that which a professional court would have returned).[144]

Of course, one of these 'deviant verdicts' was the acquittal of Mikel Otegi, which riveted the Spanish public's attention to the new jury courts after the institution had been neglected following the first trials in May of 1996. The *Otegi* verdict spawned calls by the ruling Popular Party to suspend jury trials in the Basque Country, because of public consensus that the verdict was not based on the evidence, but was due to either juror sympathy with the Basque Nationalists or fear of retribution if they convicted the young nationalist sympathizer.

Other reform proposals include (1) changing venue in such cases, (2) eliminating assaults on police officers and other government officials from the list of crimes subject to the jury court's jurisdiction, (3) restricting the jury's role to deciding only naked factual questions, and leaving the guilt finding and the findings of mitigating circumstances relating to mental disease or intoxication to the professional judge, (4) reforming appellate procedures to allow for broader appeal of acquittals, and (5) transforming the classic jury into a 'mixed court'.[145]

The extreme lenience of Spanish law in allowing a defense of not guilty by reason of complete or temporary insanity, whether due to mental disease or defect, alcohol or drug intoxication, or even any other circumstance of analogous significance,[146] has led to the mounting of

[144] Of the 39 verdicts returned prior to April 1, 1997, only six verdicts, including that in the *Otegi* case, were considered to have been surprising and two others 'relatively surprising'. CGPJ *Informe*, *supra* note 103, at 30–4. In the 123 cases that reached verdicts from April 1, 1997 through March 31, 1998, only nine were characterized as 'surprising'. CGPJ *Anexo I*, *supra* note 96, at 46–7. Most of such verdicts were cases in which the jury failed to find intent to kill and convicted of lesser offences despite overwhelming circumstantial evidence of such intent. Ibid., at 40–1. Nearly all of these judgments have been reversed on appeal. Ibid., at 49.

[145] See ibid., at 405–12 (citing Javier Muñoz, *El Gobierno y el PNV abrogan por reformar el jurado para que no se repitan veredictos 'absurdos'*, El Correo, Mar. 8, 1997; C. Valdecantos, *El PP quiere limitar las competencias del jurado*, El País, Mar. 8, 1997; Raimundo Castro, *El Gobierno cambiará la Ley del Jurado por el 'caso Otegi'*, El Periódico, Mar. 8, 1997; Ferran Gerhard, *Mariscal trabaja ya en la nueva Ley del Jurado*, El Periódico, Mar. 9, 1997; Salome García, *El Gobierno baraja sustraer al jurado el ataque a policías*, El Periódico, Mar. 11, 1997). On the post-*Otegi* reform proposals, see ibid., at 405–12.

[146] Arts. 20–1 of the Código Penal (B.O.E. 1995, 281). Most of the first trials were tried under similar provisions included in the Penal Code of 1973, because the 1995 Code went into effect only three days before the first trials began on May 24, 1996.

such defenses in many of the first cases.[147] While such defenses have been rejected by most juries, the *Otegi* acquittal could conceivably be an impulse for the Spanish legislature to amend its law concerning mental excuses, as was done in California following the *Dan White* verdict and in the federal system following the *John Hinckley* verdict. This would be a clear example of how the presence of a jury of lay factfinders exercises influence on the definition of crimes and their defenses in the substantive criminal law.

Despite the requirement that murder and certain other cases throughout Spain be tried by jury, there have as yet been remarkably few jury trials.[148] Prosecutors have been either charging lesser crimes or reaching agreements with defendants (*conformidad*) in the minor cases of threats, burglary, and bribery to avoid the jurisdiction of the jury court.[149]

Even though there have been relatively few jury trials held to date, the reappearance of juries on the inquisitorial soil of Continental Europe is an important phenomenon, regardless of its reception among law professors, lawyers, judges, and politicians. It breathes life into the overly written, overly bureaucratic structure of European criminal jurisprudence and makes European jurists rethink the procedural and substantive tenets upon which their criminal justice systems are based.

[147] In my study, such defenses were pleaded in 36 of the 57 homicide cases. See Thaman, *Spain Returns*, *supra* note 15, at 343 n. 444.

[148] None have yet been held in the province of Segovia and only one in Ávila, Cáceres, Ciudad Real, Cuenca, Huesca, Jaén, León, Lleida, Santander. CGPJ *Anexo I*, *supra* note 103, at 10, and Statistical Tables.

[149] See ibid., at 404.

10 Reviving the Criminal Jury in Japan

Lester W. Kiss*

I. Introduction

The last decade has spawned a reexamination of the effectiveness of the jury system in the United States.[1] Jury verdicts rendered in certain highly publicized trials have shocked the public and caused journalists and scholars alike to criticize juries as ill-equipped to handle the cases before them.[2] Some critics have even questioned the basic role of the jury as an instrument of democracy and a form of sovereignty of the people.[3] To counter this criticism, others argue that the intense attack on the jury system by scholars and journalists is a result of disgust with unexpected verdicts and is not based on empirical evidence about the system, which shows that juries reach a defensible decision most of the time.[4]

Despite the ongoing debate about the effectiveness of the American jury, several countries have recently adopted or are seriously considering

* J.D./LL.M., 1998, Duke University; Fulbright Fellow, Japan, Associate: Paul, Hastings, Janofsky, and Walker LLP, Los Angeles, CA.

[1] See, *e.g.*, Stephen J. Alder, The Jury: Trial and Error in the American Courtroom (1994) (contending that a jury system that works as badly as our system should not and will not survive); Marcus A. Brown, *Commentary: Trial by Jury—An Obsolete Concept*, 49 Consumer Fin. L.Q. Rep. 109 (Winter 1995) (arguing that jury trial should be eliminated in criminal cases and reduced in civil cases in the interests of time, cost, and justice); Tamar Jacoby & Tim Padgett, *Waking up the Jury Box*, Newsweek, Aug. 7, 1989, at 51, ('A growing number of legal scholars think the [jury] reforms will make for more reliable, accurate verdicts').

[2] See, *e.g.*, Steven I. Friedland, *The Competency and Responsibility of Jurors in Deciding Cases*, 85 Nw. U. L. Rev. 190 (1990); see also Alder, *supra* note 1; Brown, *supra* note 1.

[3] See, *e.g.*, Albert W. Alschuler & Andrew G. Deiss, *A Brief History of the Criminal Jury in the United States*, 61 U. Chi. L. Rev. 867, 927 (1994) ('Only a shadow of this communitarian institution [the jury] has survived into the urbanized America of the late twentieth century').

[4] For representative research bearing on criminal juries, see John Baldwin & Michael McConville, Jury Trials (1979); Harry Kalven, Jr. & Hans Zeisel, The American Jury (1966); Neil Vidmar *et al.*, *Should We Rush to Reform the Criminal Jury?*, 80 Judicature 286 (1997). Research on civil juries has produced some of the most solid data indicating that juries do their jobs reliably and responsibly, even in complex cases. See, *e.g.*, Neil Vidmar, Medical Malpractice and the American Jury (1995); Richard Lempert, *Civil Juries and Complex Cases: Taking Stock After Twelve Years*, in Verdict: Assessing the Civil Jury System 181 (Robert E. Litan ed., 1993).

adopting their own jury systems.[5] One of the more heated debates about adopting a jury system is occurring in Japan.[6] Because Japan actually used a jury system for criminal trials from 1928 to 1943,[7] the present-day debate focuses mainly on readopting the jury for criminal cases only.[8]

The purpose of this chapter is to analyze whether the readoption of criminal jury trials in present-day Japan would be feasible from cultural, societal, and legal viewpoints in light of Japan's prior experience with a jury system. Part II of the chapter briefly considers why reversion to trial by jury is being considered by Japanese lawyers and judges. Part III describes the jury system used in Japan from 1928 to 1943 and the problems with the system that caused its suspension. Part IV examines the two main types of layperson juries used in other countries. Part V considers the broad question of whether the adoption of one of the jury systems examined in Part IV would be feasible in Japan from cultural, societal, and legal viewpoints.

II. Why the Debate about Trial by Jury?

Just as in the United States, where certain seemingly outrageous jury verdicts have fueled the fire of criticism of the jury system, a similar phenomenon has occurred in Japan regarding its judge-based system. Exam-

[5] Spain and Russia are among the countries that recently adopted a jury system. See Stephen C. Thaman, *Europe's New Jury Systems: The Cases of Spain and Russia*, 62 LAW & CONTEMP. PROBS. 233 (Spring 1999). See also generally *Advertising Campaign Used to Introduce Jury Trials to Spain*, EUROMARKETING, Oct. 31, 1995, available in 1995 WL 11652377; Hon. Steven R. Plotkin, *The Jury Trial in Russia*, 2 TUL. J. INT'L & COMP. L. 1 (1994); Stephen C. Thaman, *The Resurrection of Trial by Jury in Russia*, 31 STAN. J. INT'L L. 61 (1995); Tunku Varadarajan, *A Jury System Under Question*, The TIMES (LONDON), Mar. 18, 1997, at 43. Japan is considering readopting its jury system for criminal trials. See Richard Lempert, *A Jury for Japan?*, 40 AM. J. COMP. L. 37, 38–9 (1992).

[6] See, *e.g.*, Kaneyoshi Hagiwara, *Sueiden keisanshin o kangaeru* (Considering the Criminal Assessor System of Sweden), 48 JIYU TO SEIGI (Liberty and Justice) 114 (1997); Takeshi Nishimura, *Keiji baishin saiban—200X nen, nihon de* (Criminal Jury Trials—in Japan in the Year 200X?), 48 JIYU TO SEIGI (Liberty and Justice) 92 (1997); Hiroshi Sato, *Naze nihon ni sanshinsei o ka* (Why Should Japan Adopt the Assessor System?), 48 JIYU TO SEIGI (Liberty and Justice) 108 (1997); Satoru Shinomiya, *Naze nihon ni baishinsei o ka* (Why Should Japan Adopt the Jury System?), 48 JIYU TO SEIGI (Liberty and Justice) 102 (1997).

[7] See Baishinho (Jury Act), Law No. 50 of 1923; Baishinho no Teishi ni Kansuru Horitsu (An Act to Suspend the Jury Act), Law No. 88 of 1943.

[8] However, some scholars have examined the possibility of adopting the jury system for civil cases. See, *e.g.*, Ichiro Kato, *The Concerns of Japanese Tort Law Today*, 1 LAW IN JAPAN: AN ANNUAL 65, 91 (1967); Lempert, *supra* note 4, at 37.

ples of such highly publicized verdicts by judges include the acquittals of four death row inmates who were imprisoned for over twenty-five years before obtaining new trials.[9]

Two of these controversial cases are *Government* v. *Akabori* (the *Shimada* case)[10] and *Government* v. *Menda* (the *Menda* case).[11] In the *Shimada* case, Masao Akabori was arrested in May 1954 for the rape and murder of a schoolgirl in Shimada City, Shizuoka Prefecture.[12] After intense questioning by the police, Akabori confessed to the rape and murder.[13] After a four-year trial, Akabori was convicted and sentenced to death in May 1958.[14] His direct appeals to the Tokyo High Court[15] and Supreme Court[16] were fruitless. Twenty-five years later, the Tokyo High Court overturned the Shizuoka District Court ruling rejecting a retrial request and remanded the case to the district court.[17] The district court granted a new trial on May 29, 1986.[18] After a trial lasting nearly two years, the Shizuoka District Court acquitted Akabori on January 31, 1989.[19] The district court acquitted on the ground that there was no evidence linking Akabori to the crime other than his own confessions, which were shown to be of little reliability.[20]

In the *Menda* case, Sakae Menda was charged with the hatchet murder of a 76-year-old prayer reader and his wife in Hitoyoshi City, Kumamoto

[9] See Daniel H. Foote, *From Japan's Death Row to Freedom*, 1 PAC. RIM L. & POL'Y J. 11–13 (1992); Toyoji Saito, *'Substitute Prison': A Hotbed of False Criminal Charges in Japan*, in COMPARATIVE LAW: LAW AND THE LEGAL PROCESS IN JAPAN 507, 508–9 (Kenneth L. Port ed., 1996).

[10] Government v. Akabori (the Shimada case), 1316 HANREI JIHO 21 (Shizuoka Dist. Ct., Jan. 31, 1989). The description of this case is based on the district court decision and Professor Foote's detailed English-language account of the court's decision. See Foote, *supra* note 9, at 50–63.

[11] Government v. Menda (the Menda Case), 1090 HANREI JIHO 21 (Kumamoto Dist. Ct., July 15, 1983). For an in-depth account of this case, see Foote, *supra* note 9, at 14–19.

[12] See 1316 HANREI JIHO at 31.

[13] See ibid.

[14] See Foote, *supra* note 9, at 55–6 (citing Government v. Akabori (the Shimada incident) (Shizuoka Dist. Ct., May 23, 1958), reprinted in Keiji saishin seido kenkyukai (Study Group on the Criminal Retrial System), Chomei saishin jiken mikokan saibanreishu daiishu (unpublished Court Decisions in Famous Retrial Cases) at 133 (hereinafter Mikokan saibanreishu)).

[15] Ibid. (citing Government v. Akabori (the Shimada incident), (Tokyo High Ct., Feb. 16, 1960), reprinted in Mikokan saibanreishu, *supra* note 14, at 144).

[16] Ibid. (citing Government v. Akabori (the Shimada incident), (Sup. Ct., Dec. 15, 1960), reprinted in Mikokan saibanreishu, *supra* note 14, at 151).

[17] 1316 HANREI JIHO at 26.

[18] Government v. Akabori (the Shimada incident), 1193 HANREI JIHO 31 (Shizuoka Dist. Ct., May 29, 1986).

[19] See 1316 HANREI JIHO 21.

[20] See ibid., at 51.

Prefecture.[21] Menda confessed to the crime a few days later after detailed questioning.[22] After a year-long trial in the Kumamoto District Court, Menda was found guilty of the murders and sentenced to death on March 23, 1950.[23] The Fukuoka High Court[24] and the Supreme Court[25] upheld the verdict on direct appeal. In 1975, after numerous failed attempts at obtaining a retrial, Menda was successful when the Fukuoka High Court granted his request.[26] The Kumamoto District Court acquitted Menda of both murders on July 15, 1983, approximately thirty-three years after he was convicted.[27] In its ruling, the court rejected Menda's confessions because it found them to be unreliable.[28]

The roots of the debate on the readoption of the jury trial, however, go far deeper than a mere reaction to erroneous verdicts by judges. Although, in theory, the Japanese criminal justice system provides criminal defendants with a wide set of legal protections,[29] in reality, these protections are diminished by the practices of judges and prosecutors. In particular, there are questions whether judges are effective finders of fact.[30] Proponents of the jury system argue that, in reality, criminal defendants are convicted before the trial even begins.[31] Prosecutors conduct the factfinding and draw legal conclusions, and judges simply 'rubber stamp' their results.[32] A jury would be a better finder of fact

[21] See Government v. Menda (the Menda case), 1090 Hanrei Jiho 21 (Kumamoto Dist. Ct., July 15, 1983).

[22] See ibid., at 85.

[23] See Foote, *supra* note 9, at 19–21 (citing Government v. Menda (the Menda incident), (Kumamoto Dist. Ct., Yatsuhiro Div., Mar. 23, 1950), reprinted in Mikokan saibanreishu, *supra* note 14, at 1).

[24] See ibid. (citing Government v. Menda (the Menda incident), (Fukuoka High Ct., Mar. 19, 1951), reprinted in Mikokan saibanreishu, *supra* note 14, at 3).

[25] See ibid. (citing Government v. Menda (the Menda incident), (Sup. Ct., Dec. 25, 1951), reprinted in Mikokan saibanreishu, *supra* note 14, at 5).

[26] See ibid., at 22.

[27] See 1090 Hanrei Jiho at 21.

[28] See ibid., at 63.

[29] See Jean Choi Desombre, *Comparing the Notions of the Japanese and the U.S. Criminal Justice System: An Examination of Pre-Trial Rights of the Criminally Accused in Japan and the United States*, 14 UCLA Pac. Basin L.J. 103, 107–8 (1995); B. J. George, Jr., *Rights of the Criminally Accused*, 53 Law & Contemp. Probs. 71 (Spring 1990).

[30] See Takeo Ishimatsu, *Can Criminal Judges Be Said to Be Judging?*, 22 Law in Japan: An Annual 143 (1989).

[31] See ibid.

[32] See Lempert, *supra* note 4, at 39. Support put forth for this theory usually begins with the statement that the conviction rate in Japan is about 99.8%. See Foote, *supra* note 9, at 81. This unusually high rate of conviction demonstrates that prosecutors must have an extremely high level of suspicion to indict, a suspicion so high that they are certain that the defendant is guilty. See ibid., at 76. Such a practice can only encourage judges to presume guilt when the case finally gets to trial, countering the presumption of innocence

because juries, unlike judges, do not hear cases on a daily basis and would not simply accept the decision of the prosecutor. Theoretically, juries would be more inclined than a judge would be to listen to the evidence and deliver a fair verdict.[33]

An area that illustrates the poor factfinding that can occur in a Japanese courtroom is the judges' ready acceptance of 'voluntary confessions'[34] of criminal defendants. It is doubtful whether such confessions, which occur with great frequency, are truly voluntary.[35] Under the Japanese system, police often have unrestricted power to interrogate a suspect, and many cases of abuse have been reported.[36] Japanese authorities often demand detailed, corroborated confessions.[37] Such confessions may then be presented at trial,[38] and although they may be attacked by the defendant and defense counsel in court, their corroboration gives judges a basis to accept them even if they are procedurally questionable.[39]

One reason for such easy acceptance of confessions by judges is a peculiarity of trial practice in Japan called 'trial by dossier'.[40] The confession is submitted to the court in the form of a confession statement

embodied in Japanese law. See ibid., at 81. Professor Foote quotes one former judge as stating:

> 'In general, there is a feeling from the outset that the defendant is guilty. On top of that, when there is a long trial focusing on whether or not the defendant is guilty, it's troublesome for judges, who face demands to dispose of cases promptly. . . . Moreover, when a judge issues an acquittal, the faces of his superiors and the displeased faces of prosecutors with whom he's become friendly will appear in his mind.'

Ibid. The term 'prosecutor justice' (*kensatsukan shiho*), which is often seen in the literature, stems from this theory. See Ryuichi Hirano, *Diagnosis of the Current Code of Criminal Procedure*, 22 Law in Japan: An Annual 129, 131 (1989).

[33] During the period when Japan had a jury system, the acquittal rate was 15.4% for defendants who chose jury trial as compared to rates between 1.3% and 3.7% for those who chose bench trials. See Foote, *supra* note 9, at 84.

[34] According to Professor Foote, '[a]n emphasis on obtaining confessions remains at the heart of Japan's criminal justice system': ibid., at 86.

[35] See Hirano, *supra* note 32, at 137.

[36] See Saito, *supra* note 9, at 508. Such abuse usually comes in the form of indirect techniques and psychological pressure rather than direct physical violence. See Hirano, *supra* note 32, at 137. For example, in the *Menda* case, prosecutors questioned Menda for almost 80 hours and did not allow him to sleep. See Foote, *supra* note 9, at 65. In the *Shimada* case, Akabori was questioned from dawn to dusk for a number of days. See ibid., at 53.

[37] See Hirano, *supra* note 32, at 135. In contrast to the Japanese case, in the United States, in most cases, simple confessions that only summarize the facts of a crime will suffice. See ibid. The problem with requiring detailed confessions is that it forces Japanese prosecutors to conduct lengthy interrogations. See ibid.

[38] See ibid. [39] See ibid. [40] See ibid., at 138.

which becomes part of a dossier. Judges then read the dossiers and often form factual conclusions in their chambers or homes rather than in open court after having heard witnesses.[41] This practice is problematic because the manner of speech and demeanor of witnesses and of the defendant can have a strong influence on the finder of fact;[42] if these elements are not fully considered, the defendant may not be receiving a fair trial. Proponents of the jury system argue that because there is little hope of judges agreeing to eliminate trial by dossier, the only solution is a switch to an American-style jury system where factual conclusions are formed only after testimony in open court.[43]

Also inhibiting effective factfinding by the Japanese judiciary is that most judges are career judges with little experience in the outside world.[44] One can become a judge after passing the extremely rigorous National Legal Examination (*shiho shiken*), followed by two years of practical training.[45] The person then has the choice of becoming either a judge, a prosecutor, or an attorney.[46] The result is a highly educated, well-trained elite group of jurists who may have attitudes and experiences quite different from those of the general public.[47] This limited range of life experience may negatively affect the factfinding abilities of these judges.

The idea of readopting the jury system has come to the forefront of possible reforms of the criminal justice system in Japan. Japanese organizations have already conducted in-depth studies of foreign jury systems. For example, a subcommittee of the Osaka Bar Association's Committee for Judicial System Reform toured the United States, Great Britain, and Germany to study citizen participation in the trial process,[48] and the Supreme Court of Japan sent several

[41] See Hirano, *supra* note 32, at 135. [42] See ibid. [43] See ibid., at 142.

[44] See Takeshi Kojima, *Japanese Civil Procedure in a Comparative Law Perspective*, 46 U. KAN. L. REV. 687 n. 12 (1998).

[45] See Edward I. Chen, *The National Law Examination of Japan*, 39 J. LEGAL EDUC. 1, 1 (1989). The practical training occurs at the Legal Training and Research Institute, which limits the number of successful applicants to approximately 500. See ibid., at 7. In recent years, less than 3% of those who took the National Legal Examination passed. See Mark A. Behrens & Daniel H. Raddock, *Japan's New Product Liability Law: The Citadel of Strict Liability Falls, but Access to Recovery Is Limited by Formidable Barriers*, 16 U. PA. J. INT'L BUS. L. 669, 677–8 (1995). Only summary court judges and five of 15 Supreme Court Justices are appointed without first being qualified for admission to the bar. See Mamoru Urabe, *Wagakuni ni okeru baishin sai ban no kenkyu* (A Study on Trial by Jury in Japan), in THE JAPANESE LEGAL SYSTEM 482 (Hideo Tanaka ed., 1976).

[46] See Chen, *supra* note 45, at 1. [47] See Lempert, *supra* note 4, at 48.

[48] See ibid., at 38.

judges to the United States, United Kingdom, Germany, and France to study juries.[49]

III. The Jury System in Japan from 1928 to 1943

Japan adopted a jury system on April 18, 1923.[50] Although enacted in 1923, the law did not take effect until 1928, and it stayed in effect for fifteen years until it was suspended on April 1, 1943.[51]

Before devising a jury system appropriate for Japan, the Japanese government investigated trial systems in France, Germany, England, and the United States.[52] The result was a uniquely Japanese jury system complementing an otherwise Continental European system of criminal procedure.[53] Therefore, although the Japanese system was influenced by the Anglo-American model of jury trial, it differed in many important respects.

First, not all defendants were entitled to a jury trial. The only cases for which a jury trial was guaranteed were those in which the maximum penalty was death or imprisonment for life[54] or where the maximum penalty was imprisonment for greater than three years and the minimum penalty was imprisonment for not less than one year.[55] In death penalty or life imprisonment cases, the law provided for trial by jury unless waived by the accused.[56] In all other eligible cases, the law provided for trial by jury only if the accused specifically requested a jury trial.[57] Furthermore, the law provided that certain crimes were not triable by jury.[58] These crimes included crimes against a member of the imperial family, riot with the purpose of overthrowing the government,

[49] See ibid., at 38–9. The Supreme Court of Japan has also published a book entitled Wagakuni de Okonowareta Baishin Seido (The Old Jury System in Japan), which is a compilation of works on the jury system used in Japan from 1928 to 1943.

[50] See Baishinho (Jury Act), Law No. 50 of 1923.

[51] See Baishinho no Teishi ni Kansuru Horitsu (An Act to Suspend the Jury Act), Law No. 88 of 1943.

[52] See Lempert, *supra* note 4, at 37 n. 1.

[53] See Urabe, *supra* note 45, at 483. More specifically, the Japanese laws in 1923 were based on the German civil law and a constitution modeled after the Prussian Constitution. See Behrens & Raddock, *supra* note 45, at 673–4.

[54] See Baishinho (Jury Act), Law No. 50 of 1923, art. 2.

[55] See ibid., art. 3. [56] See ibid.

[57] See ibid. Note that a jury trial was not available for crimes such as simple theft, embezzlement, gambling, adultery, and obscenity because the punishment for these crimes did not fall within the parameters set out in the Act. See Urabe, *supra* note 45, at 484.

[58] See Urabe, *supra* note 45, at 484.

violation of the Peace Preservation Act (*Chian Iji-ho*), espionage, and violation of laws concerning the election of public officials.[59]

Secondly, the Japanese jury did not return a general verdict of 'guilty' or 'not guilty'. Instead, it responded to questions submitted by the judge (*toshin*) and related to the existence of facts.[60] These answers were based on the views of a majority of the requisite twelve jurors.[61]

Thirdly, the jurors' responses were not binding.[62] The court, upon finding the jury's answer unwarranted, could disregard it, call another jury, and submit the case anew.[63]

Jury selection resembled the jury selection methods used in the Anglo-American system at that time. The pool of prospective jurors included 'male citizens over thirty years of age who had resided in the same city, town or village for two years or longer, who paid not less than three yen in national direct tax for the preceding two consecutive years, and who were literate'.[64]

The number of jury trials in Japan decreased drastically from 1928 to 1943.[65] The annual number of cases tried by jury was greatest in 1929, when 143 cases were put to juries.[66] The number dropped to sixty-six the next year and decreased annually until, in 1942, only two jury trials were held.[67] A total of 611 defendants chose jury trials during the fifteen years the system operated.[68] Of these, ninety-four were acquitted.[69] Why did the use of the jury system decline so precipitously during its lifetime?

One reason put forth for the decline of the jury system over this period was the political climate in the late 1920s to 1943.[70] The Jury Act was enacted in 1923 during the period known as 'Taisho Democracy'.[71] It was primarily because of this nationwide movement toward democracy

[59] See Urabe *supra* note 45, at 484 (citing Baishinho (Jury Act), Law No. 50 of 1923, art. 4).

[60] See Baishinho (Jury Act), Law No. 50 of 1923, art. 88.

[61] See ibid., art. 91.

[62] See ibid., art. 95.

[63] See ibid. In the United States, a judge in a civil trial can overrule the jury's verdict and grant a motion for a 'judgment notwithstanding the verdict' regardless of the jury's verdict; however, in a criminal trial, the judge can only enter a judgment notwithstanding the verdict in favor of acquittal, thereby reversing the jury's conviction. Compare FED. R. CIV. P. 50, with FED. R. CRIM. P. 29(c).

[64] Urabe, *supra* note 45, at 484 (citing Baishinho (Jury Act), Law No. 50 of 1923, arts. 12, 23, 27).

[65] See ibid., at 485.

[66] See ibid.

[67] See ibid.

[68] See Foote, *supra* note 9, at 84.

[69] See ibid.

[70] See Urabe, *supra* note 45, at 487 (citing Nobuyoshi Toshitani, *Minshu to Horitsuka* (The Populace and Lawyers), in 6 GENDAI NO HORISUKA (Contemporary Lawyers) 387–9 (1966)).

[71] See ibid.

that Premier Takashi Hara was able to sponsor the Act successfully and allow Japanese citizens an opportunity to participate directly in the justice system.[72] However, by the time the jury system was first used in 1928, the political climate in Japan was moving toward fascism.[73] By 1928, a great number of the members of the Communist Party were arrested, and by 1935 the basic 'organ theory of the Emperor' (*Tenno Kikan-setsu*) was suppressed.[74]

This political and cultural environment of rising militarism and fascism countered the rise of the jury system because it encouraged the *bourgeoisie* to waive the right to trial by jury[75] and prohibited access to trial by jury to those who most needed it: criminal defendants who adhered to communist and socialist ideologies.[76] Both of the main classes of society, therefore, had no concern about the fate of the jury system because they either did not care to use it or were not permitted to use it. Hence, any possible strengths of the jury system were lost under the 'fierce storm of fascism'.[77]

Another reason put forth for the decline of the jury system in Japan was the content of the Jury Act itself. Many Japanese scholars observe that it is not surprising that the jury system failed in Japan because the drafters of the Act seemed to have built in various devices to prevent the smooth working of the system.[78] The most important of these is the judge's ability to disregard the jury's answers, seat a new jury, and try the case *de novo*.[79] The drafters of the Act may have included this provision because they believed that it would be contrary to the judge's responsibility to decide each case if he or she had to give binding effect to the jury's answers.[80]

[72] See ibid., at 483. [73] See ibid., at 487 (citing Toshitani, *supra* note 70).

[74] See ibid. Urabe explains that the 'organ theory of the Emperor' was a constitutional theory under which sovereignty resided in the nation, and the Meiji Emperor was an organ of this sovereign body exercising state powers. The suppression of this theory is an example of the move toward fascism. See ibid.

[75] See ibid. The *bourgeoisie* waived trial by jury because they feared their unpopularity would work against them through the jury. See ibid.

[76] See ibid. Trial by jury was not available in these cases, known as *shiso jiken* (thought cases) because no crime of a political nature could be tried by jury. See Baishinho (Jury Act), Law No. 50 of 1923, art. 4.

[77] See Urabe, *supra* note 45, at 487–8 (citing Toshitani, *supra* note 70).

[78] See ibid. (stating that one should not feel surprised at the failure of the jury system but rather by the remarkable success of various devices which were built into the system to prevent the smooth working of trial by jury in Japan); Kitaro Saito, *Baishin* (Jury), in Keiji Hogaku Jiten (Dictionary of Criminal Law) 62 (Y. Takigawa ed., 1957) (stating that if the framer of the Jury Act had respected trial by jury, he would have provided that almost all criminal cases were to be tried by jury).

[79] See Baishinho (Jury Act), Law No. 50 of 1923, art. 91.

[80] See Urabe, *supra* note 45, at 490.

This provision effectively undermined any true power of the jury system and allowed judges to continue to make the final decisions on guilt and innocence. Criminal defendants quickly learned that acquittal by a jury had little meaning, and they would often waive their right to a jury trial from the start or simply not elect trial by jury if given the choice.[81]

Jury trials also cost criminal defendants more money and deprived them of the possibility of bringing a *koso* appeal on points of fact.[82] Because the sentence of a convicted criminal was usually mitigated upon appeal, criminal defense attorneys understandably would encourage their defendants to preserve the right to this appeal, even if it meant waiving the right to jury trial.[83]

Furthermore, public prosecutors could avoid any request by the accused for a jury trial because the law provided that jury trial was available only if the case underwent a 'preliminary investigation' (*yoshin*).[84]

Finally, the Jury Act did not allow objections to the judge's instructions to the jury.[85] Attorneys and public prosecutors often criticized the instructions given by the judge as 'soliciting answers which would lead to the guilt of the accused'.[86] Even if the jury did return its special verdicts to the effect that the defendant was not guilty, there was still a great chance that the judge would call for a new trial. Such obstacles frustrated attorneys, sometimes to the point where they would prefer to waive jury trial as a way of expressing piety to the authority of the judge in hopes of leniency in sentencing.[87]

The final factor considered to have led to the unpopularity of the Japanese jury is Japanese culture. Japanese society is often described as 'vertical' or 'hierarchical', meaning that social relationships are governed by the relative 'status' of the parties. This 'status' is often determined by, among other factors, age and occupation. The hierarchy that exists in Japanese society is evidenced by the Japanese language,[88] by the act of

[81] See Saito, *supra* note 78.

[82] See ibid. However, such a defendant was entitled to bring a *jokoku* appeal on points of law to the highest court. See Urabe, *supra* note 45, at 491.

[83] See ibid.

[84] See H. Kikuchi, *Baishin Seido ni Tsuite* (On the Jury System), 14 Nihon Horitsuka Kyokai Series 57 (1959).

[85] See Baishinho (Jury Act), Law No. 50 of 1923, art. 78.

[86] See Urabe, *supra* note 45, at 490. [87] See ibid., at 488.

[88] The Japanese language has formal and informal forms for all verbs and certain nouns. When speaking to a 'superior', a Japanese will resort to the formal form, generally called *keigo*.

bowing that occurs between persons just introduced,[89] and by the seating at formal occasions.

Many scholars are convinced that as a result of the hierarchy in Japanese society, the Japanese people prefer trial by 'those above the people' rather than by 'their fellows', and that this caused the Japanese to distrust juries from the beginning.[90] People trust judges because they have a special sense of responsibility when adjudicating cases and try to keep their moral standards high in order to ensure impartial trials.[91] Therefore, citizen participation in the judicial process is ultimately not suitable for the Japanese people because citizens would simply prefer to have a judge rather than their fellow citizens decide their case. Scholars disagree on exactly how much weight should be given to the cultural aspect of the failure of the jury system in Japan, but most agree culture played some part.

The failure of the jury system in Japan can be attributed to numerous factors. First, the fascist political climate that arose in Japan just as the jury system began to be used caused many of those charged with political crimes to desire a trial by jury, but did not allow them to have it. Secondly, inherent defects in the Jury Act prevented the jury system from gaining respect. Finally, Japanese respect for authority caused the Japanese people to prefer trial by experienced and honest judges rather than trial by their peers.

IV. Types of Jury Systems

If Japan decided to reintroduce a jury system, it would have to ensure that the new system avoided the systemic defects of the old. This would entail making jury verdicts binding, allowing defendants who elect jury trial to appeal just as if they had elected nonjury trial, ensuring that election of trial by jury would not be more expensive for the defendant, and allowing defendants to object to the trial judge's jury instructions.

Once these basic facets of any serious jury system were adopted, the Japanese would have to decide exactly what form the new jury system would take. The old system could serve as a template; juries could be

[89] The 'inferior' person should bow lower. 'Inferiority' is determined by factors such as age, rank, and occupation.

[90] Ryuichi Hirano, *Shokugyo Saibankan to Shiroto Saibankan* (Professional Judges and Lay Judges) 29 HORITSU JIHO 435, 437 (1957); see also Christopher A. Ford, *The Indigenization of Constitutionalism in the Japanese Experience*, 28 CASE W. RES. J. INT'L L. 3, 62 n. 159 (1996).

[91] See Hirano, *supra* note 90, at 437.

composed of twelve private citizens who rendered majority special verdicts. However, because of the negative aspects associated with the previous jury system, the Japanese are examining all possibilities, including the mixed court system of laypersons and professional judges.[92] This section examines the two models of jury systems that could be implemented in Japan: the Anglo-American jury composed completely of laypersons, and the Continental mixed court composed of both judges and laypersons.

A. *The Anglo-American Jury System*

A criminal jury in the Anglo-American system is composed of six to twelve jurors selected at random from the local population.[93] Such a jury can convict or acquit based on either majority or unanimous verdicts.[94] Although the goals of the jury system are numerous, one goal seems to be most important: '[t]he power to condemn citizens to criminal sanctions is potentially so dangerous that it ought not to be left entirely to the hirelings of the state'.[95] As Justice White wrote in *Duncan* v. *Louisiana*:

> [t]hose who wrote our constitutions knew from history and experience that it was necessary to protect against unfounded criminal charges brought to eliminate enemies and against judges too responsive to the voice of higher authority. The framers of the constitutions strove to create an independent judiciary, but insisted upon further protection against arbitrary action.[96]

Other purposes behind the Anglo-American jury system are to ensure fairness through group decision-making, to promote simplicity and better factfinding through lay reasoning and skills, and to allow criminal defendants to be judged by their peers.[97] Unlike judges, laymen have no

[92] See Sato, *supra* note 6.

[93] In the U.S. system, the Supreme Court in *Williams* v. *Florida*, 399 U.S. 78 (1970), held that a six-person jury in a state criminal case did not violate the Sixth Amendment right to trial by jury. Most states, however, provide 12-person juries in capital cases. See Richardson R. Lynn, Jury Trial Law and Practice 15 (1986). The sources for the jury pool include public documents such as phone books and voter registration lists. See ibid., at 41.

[94] While unanimous verdicts are still required in federal courts, states are permitted to utilize nonunanimous verdicts. See Apodaca v. Oregon, 406 U.S. 404 (1974) (holding that neither the Sixth nor the Fourteenth Amendment imposes on the states the requirement of unanimous criminal verdicts).

[95] See John H. Langbein, *Mixed Court and Jury Court: Could the Continental Alternative Fill the American Need?*, 1981 Am. B. Found. Res. J. 195, 209.

[96] 391 U.S. 145, 156 (1968).

[97] See Langbein, *supra* note 95, at 209.

connection to the criminal justice system other than the fact that they are serving as jurors and therefore lack incentive to abuse their power or misuse the system.[98]

B. The Continental Mixed Court

The second version of the jury system being considered by the Japanese is the mixed court system, in which laypersons and professional judges sit together in a single panel that deliberates and decides on all issues of verdict and sentence. This mixed court system is widespread in Europe for cases of serious crime.[99] Because the system has been most widely employed in Germany, the rest of this section will look specifically at the German system.

There are two kinds of mixed courts in modern German practice.[100] For more serious crimes, the mixed court consists of five 'judges'—two lay and three professional ('two-three court').[101] For less serious crimes, the court consists of three 'judges'—two lay and one professional ('two-one court').[102] Any decision that disadvantages the accused requires a two-thirds majority vote.[103] This means that in the two-three court, four of the five judges must agree on a verdict of conviction,[104] giving the two laymen a veto power if they act together.[105] In the two-one court, the two-thirds voting rule allows the two laymen either to convict or acquit over the opposition of the professional.[106] Thus, depending on whether the trial is for a serious or minor crime, laymen will have varying power in the decision-making process.

When the trial is over, the mixed court begins deliberations. However, unlike the Anglo-American jury, 'the presiding judge (the only professional in the two-one court and the senior professional in the two-three court) "leads" these *in camera* proceedings and "puts the questions and takes the votes"'.[107] This safeguards against the laymen making decisions based on ignorance or bias.

The mixed court system has safeguards against the inexperience of the laypersons. The selection of lay judges is much less random than the selection of jurors in the Anglo-American system. Lay judges are selected for four-year terms, and the selection process is divided into a

98 See ibid. 99 See ibid., at 195. 100 See ibid., at 198.
101 See ibid. 102 See ibid., at 198–9.
103 See ibid., at 199 (citing § 263(1) of the German Code of Criminal Procedure).
104 See ibid. 105 See ibid. 106 See ibid., at 200–1.
107 Ibid., at 200 (citing § 194(1) of the German Code of Criminal Procedure).

nomination and a selection phase.[108] German studies on the nomination practices of local authorities have revealed wide variations in practice.[109] Some authorities compile random lists of residents, others delegate the task to the political parties represented on the city council, and still others vigorously seek out volunteers.[110] Some authorities even allow the police to exercise a veto power over the provisional list.[111] In the selection phase, a 'selection commission' chooses the new lay judges from the pool of nominees.[112] The number chosen varies from year to year depending on the expected caseload. Considerable variation exists in the functioning of these commissions, and in many cases political parties have a large influence in the process.[113] While it is clear that a goal of the system is for the list of nominees to be representative of 'all groups in the population',[114] neither the statutory procedures nor the practices of the local authorities and commissions bears this out.[115] The end result is that lay judges often have educational and social backgrounds more similar to professional judges, which may diminish the effectiveness of the lay role in the mixed court system.

V. Would a Jury System Work in Japan from a Cultural, Societal, and Legal Viewpoint?

A. Japanese Culture

'Culture' is defined as 'the customary beliefs, social norms, and material traits of a racial, religious, or social group',[116] By definition, therefore, culture is a generalization of the beliefs, social norms, and traits of most members of a certain group. When discussing Japanese culture, one must remember that not every Japanese person will act in accordance with the cultural traits described.[117] A generalization of Japanese

[108] See Langbein, *supra* note 95, at 206.

[109] See ibid. (citing EKKEHARD KLAUSA, EHRENAMTLICHE RICHTER: IHRE AUSWAHL UND FUNKTION, EMPIRISCH UNTERSUCHT 23–46 (1972)).

[110] See ibid. [111] See ibid.

[112] See ibid., at 207. Langbein explains that '[t]he selection commission is chaired by a judge and contains, in addition to an administrator from the state government, ten citizens chosen by the elected local governments within the judicial district'. Ibid.

[113] See ibid.

[114] Ibid., at 208 (citing § 36(2) of the German Code of Criminal Procedure).

[115] See ibid.

[116] MERRIAM WEBSTER DICTIONARY 191 (new ed. 1994).

[117] This is especially true of younger generations of Japanese, many of whom have lived abroad and have adopted elements of foreign cultures into their own lives.

behavior patterns based on sociological evidence can nevertheless serve as a useful tool in analyzing the probable success of a jury system in Japan.

The hierarchical nature of Japanese society is difficult to miss. The language and behavior one Japanese person exhibits when meeting another for the first time is largely governed by the place each has in Japanese society.[118] This is true both in the business and personal contexts. In the business context, once business cards are exchanged and each person has determined the status of the other, each person can adapt his language and behavior to the situation. For example, if person A is a department head while person B is a new employee, person A would speak in neutral Japanese while person B would speak in extremely polite Japanese.[119] Similarly, in the personal context, a student would use honorific Japanese toward a professor, and a younger person would use similar honorific language toward an elder. In every personal interaction, therefore, the relative status of the participants influences how they behave.

Many scholars have pointed out that the Japanese have a higher level of trust for authority figures than do other societies. Such scholars often state as a basis of this trust the Confucian tradition in Japan.[120] They argue that this trust of authority is exemplified by the average Japanese citizen's lack of interest in politics and by his apathy for provoking change in a system with which he is frustrated.

The *shudan-ishiki*, or 'group consciousness', of the Japanese is also a cultural trait that could have profound effects on the actual functioning of the jury system in Japan. Chie Nakane is a leading scholar on the issue of Japanese group consciousness, and her framework for discussing this issue is useful. Nakane uses two basic criteria to define group consciousness—'frame' and 'attribute'.[121] Frame is 'a locality, an institution, or a particular relationship which binds a set of individuals into one

[118] To determine this hierarchy, the Japanese often exchange *meshi* (business cards) or explain their position when meeting each other.

[119] Almost all verbs in Japanese can be transformed into the humble form, the polite form, or the neutral form. One of the most difficult aspects of learning Japanese for Americans is that the type of Japanese used must always be adjusted according to the identity of the listener.

[120] See Dan Fenno Henderson, *Security Markets in the United States and Japan: Distinctive Aspects Molded by Cultural, Social, Economic, and Political Differences*, 14 Hastings Int'l & Comp. L. Rev. 263, 295 (1991).

[121] Chie Nakane, Japanese Society (1970), reprinted in Japanese Culture and Behavior: Selected Readings 155 (Takie Sigiyama Lebra & William P. Lebra eds., 1974).

group; in all cases it indicates a criterion which sets out a boundary and gives a common basis to a set of individuals who are located or involved in it'.[122] Attribute is a personal characteristic such as a descent group or caste that can define a group.[123] According to Nakane, Japanese group consciousness is based more on frame than attribute. For example, when a Japanese confronts another person and affixes some position to himself socially, he is inclined to give precedence to institution over kind of occupation;[124] 'rather than saying "I am a type-setter" or "I am a publisher", he is likely to say, "I am from B Publishing Group"'.[125] Nakane concludes that the criterion by which Japanese classify individuals socially tends to be that of particular institution rather than that of universal attribute.[126] The institution to which one belongs, therefore, becomes almost the sole criterion for defining one's group. This is why accounts of Japanese companies building towns for their employees, organizing group vacations for their employees and, in extreme cases, having common graves for their employees, have been prevalent in the literature.[127]

Maintenance of harmony in the group is another important aspect of Japanese culture. Scholars such as Takeyoshi Kawashima believe that Japanese society functions effectively only because of the high degree of interpersonal harmony maintained therein.[128] A natural result is that strong, contradictory personal opinions by inferiors are not voiced. Nakane describes such a phenomenon in the Japanese family 'group':

> [I]n the ideal traditional household in Japan, opinions of the members of the household should always be held unanimously regardless of the issue, and this normally meant that all members accepted the opinion of the household head, without even discussing the issue. An expression of a contradictory opinion contrary to the head was considered a sign of misbehavior, disturbing the harmony of the group order.[129]

It is difficult to say just how true Nakane's statement would be if applied outside the family context. However, a family is similar to any other type of closely knit group, and the goal of maintaining harmony in both could have the same effect.

[122] CHIE NAKANE, JAPANESE SOCIETY (1970). [123] See ibid.
[124] See ibid., at 156. [125] Ibid. [126] See ibid. [127] See ibid., at 163.
[128] See Takeyoshi Kawashima, *Nihonjin no Hoishiki* (The Legal Consciousness of the Japanese) (1967); see also Takeyoshi Kawashima, *Dispute Resolution in Contemporary Japan*, in LAW IN JAPAN 41 (A. Von Mehren ed., 1963).
[129] NAKANE, *supra* note 121, reprinted in JAPANESE CULTURE AND BEHAVIOR: SELECTED READINGS, *supra* note 121, at 165.

1. *Mixed Court Proposal.* The adoption of a mixed court in Japan is problematic. First, because of the hierarchical nature of Japanese society and the Japanese respect for authority, the danger exists that the professional judge or judges would have more than simply their intended 'guiding' influence over the laypersons. Certainly, laypersons in any country are respectful of those above them,[130] but respecting a higher authority does not mean subordinating one's views to please that authority. In Japanese culture, however, respect for higher authority combined with a desire to maintain harmony and avoid confrontation may result in listening and adopting for oneself what that authority has to say.[131] Because of this, the layperson juror in a mixed court system in Japan may have difficulty voicing any personal beliefs about the case.[132] Also because a mixed court system contains at least one professional judge, overcoming this problem requires limiting the participation of the judge, which would lead to the Anglo-American jury system.

Furthermore, even if the laypersons were told that they should speak their minds and independently determine the outcome of the case, there is no way of knowing whether a conscious decision to abandon one's cultural instincts could be effective. For example, because it is impolite in Japanese culture to blatantly disagree with a superior (on the principle of maintenance of harmony), how far would a layperson go in voicing disagreement with a professional judge's opinion even after being told he must do so? The layperson would possibly speak up once or twice, but if the judge did not somehow reinforce the viewpoint, only a courageous Japanese juror would press the issue. For these reasons, the adoption of a mixed court system in Japan seems to be undesirable compared to the adoption of a modified Anglo-American jury system.

2. *Anglo-American Proposal.* The adoption of an all-layperson jury system modeled on that in the United States would be preferable in Japan because it would create the largest chance for full participation of all jurors. Although the cultural concepts of hierarchy and respect for authority would still play a role in the jury's decision-making, there would be more leeway to work around these concepts if no legal authority figures such as professional judges were present. The hierarchical difference between, for example, a policeman and a university professor

[130] See Comment, *The Great Democratizing Principle: The Effect on South Africa of Planning a Democracy Without a Jury System*, 11 Temp. Int'l & Comp. L.J. 107, 126–7 (1997).

[131] See ibid. (citing Koshi Morita, *Lawyers Seek Return of Juries*, The Daily Yomiuri, Nov. 25, 1992, at 3).

[132] See ibid.

seems to be much less than that between a policeman and a professional judge, meaning that the policeman may be more candid in expressing his opinion to the professor than to the judge.

The all-layperson system would not be without problems, however. To examine the degree to which an all-layperson system would work in Japanese culture, it is useful to first look at the ideals of the jury system in the United States.[133] According to Samuel Kassin and Lawrence Wrightsman, there are three ideals behind the idea of jury deliberation in the United States. The first ideal is that of independence and equality.[134] 'No juror's vote should count more than any other juror's vote'.[135] and each person contributes his or her personal opinion.[136] The second ideal is an openness to be influenced by information. Jurors must debate with an open mind and withhold judgment until full deliberation by all of the jurors.[137] 'Jurors should scrutinize their own views, be receptive to others', and allow themselves to be persuaded by rational argument.'[138] The third ideal is that jurors should not be persuaded by irrational pressures. 'No juror should surrender his honest conviction as to the weight or effect of the evidence solely because of the opinion of his fellow jurors, or for the mere purpose of returning a verdict.'[139] The reasoning behind this is simple: if a juror changes his vote just to comply with the majority and not because of rational persuasion by new information, his final vote will not reflect his true beliefs.

Scholars do not agree on whether these ideals are properly achieved in juries in the United States. In one study done by social psychologist Solomon Asch, American subjects were asked to sit around a table and orally give their opinions on various subjects, one after the other.[140] Asch instructed the first five people at the table, who worked for him but acted as subjects, to give an opinion that clearly seemed wrong based on the

[133] I am assuming that in adopting an all-layperson jury system, the Japanese would want to maintain these same general ideals.

[134] See Samuel M. Kassin & Lawrence S. Wrightsman, The American Jury on Trial: Psychological Perspectives 172 (1988).

[135] Ibid.

[136] See ibid. Ideally, the jury is structured to maximize equal participation. Verdicts are to be rendered based only on the evidence before them, and jurors are discouraged from basing their arguments on private or outside sources of knowledge. To further promote equality, courts often exclude from service those who might exert undue influence over other jurors, such as lawyers. See ibid.

[137] See ibid. [138] Ibid.

[139] Ibid. (citing American Bar Association Project on Minimum Standards for Criminal Justice, Standards Relating to Trial by Jury § 5.4 (1968)).

[140] See ibid., at 174.

facts.[141] 'Much to Asch's surprise, the sixth person (and real subject) conformed with the incorrect majority 37 percent of the time.'[142] There could be two reasons for this result. First, the subject could have publicly voted with the majority because he felt pressure to conform, even though he privately continued to disagree. And, secondly, the subject could have re-evaluated the evidence, truly changed his mind, and voted in accordance with his conscience. The first is a danger to the ideals of the jury system because it could mean that criminals are being convicted by nonunanimous juries.[143] Even in the United States, which has had over 200 years of experience with the jury system, and which is not known as a culture that values 'harmony', there is a danger that jurors are not expressing their true opinions in an effort to avoid confrontation.

Nor are jury deliberations in the United States free from hierarchical influences. Many trial attorneys believe that most juries consist of 'one or two strong personalities with the rest more or less being followers'.[144] The empirical literature on small group discussions supports this assertion: '[p]articipation by the individuals is very uneven, and a few people dominate'.[145] Many scholars conclude, therefore, that the ideals are seldom ever realized because of these differences.[146]

Could Japanese society support the three ideals of the Anglo-American jury system? First, to what degree does the hierarchical nature of Japanese culture allow the Japanese juror to maintain his independence and equality and to make an informed and rational decision? Because of the lack of empirical evidence, this question is difficult to answer.

American jurors often lose their independence and acquiesce to the views of the majority even though they privately feel otherwise. Because of the greater importance of hierarchy in Japanese society, this could be

[141] See ibid.

[142] Ibid. 'Only when this person had an ally were subjects able to resist the pressure to conform.' Ibid. (citing Solomon Asch, Social Psychology (1952)).

[143] A vivid example of this is the result of a jury trial of a narcotics case in Miami in 1981. In this case, four defendants were on trial for allegedly having purchased drugs from undercover agents. During deliberations, the jurors reported they were deadlocked, and the judge instructed them to try further to reach agreement. Three hours later, they returned with verdicts. The judge then polled them in open court about whether they agreed in conscience with their decisions. The very first juror said 'no'. After being sent back to the jury room twice, the jurors returned with the same verdicts. It turned out that some jurors had been pressuring others to agree with them so the jury would reach a unanimous verdict and allow certain jurors to go on vacation. See ibid., at 176.

[144] Ibid., at 177.

[145] Ibid. (citing F. Stephan & E. Mishler, *The Distribution of Participation in Small Groups: An Exponential Approximation*, 17 Am. Soc. Rev. 598 (1952)).

[146] See ibid., at 180.

a greater problem in the Japanese jury. For example, in the United States, those that 'acquiesce' to the opinions of others do so not because American culture dictates that they do so, but because they are shy, have little interest in spending more time in the jury room, have weak personalities, or for other reasons. In Japan, a juror could acquiesce for these very same reasons. However, on top of these noncultural reasons, Japanese culture dictates that one should not contradict one's superiors. Therefore, a Japanese juror might adopt a superior's opinion because this would be the acceptable behavior in Japanese culture. Hence, a greater degree of frustration would exist with the ideals of independence and equality among jurors.

In contrast, Japanese 'group consciousness' and the desire of Japanese to maintain 'harmony' may have less of an effect on the Japanese jury than one would assume. Although it is clear that Japanese culture tends to be more group-oriented than individualistic cultures such as in the United States, the jury may not fit the definition of a 'group' as this word is used in the literature discussing Japanese culture. A jury composed of twelve randomly selected individuals, although a group temporarily, is by no means an institution or even a relationship that binds people together. A Japanese would most likely not identify himself as being part of the group that is the jury because he knows that once the case is over, the jury will break up and no longer exist. Therefore, although much literature exists describing the behavior of Japanese when interacting with members of a 'group', it is important to keep in mind that because the jury does not seem to qualify as a typical group, Japanese members of the jury may behave more individualistically. 'Group consciousness' may not be a threat at all to the effective functioning of the all-layperson jury system in Japan.

The desire to maintain harmony, unlike Japanese group consciousness, is a cultural attribute that could strongly influence jury deliberations. A heated issue at present is whether the desire to maintain harmony in Japan extends past the boundaries of one's immediate group to Japanese society in general.[147] If we assume that the cultural trait of maintaining harmony would continue to exist in the jury room, this could undermine the ideals of independence and equality, openness to

[147] Many scholars claim that the latter is true, and it is for this reason that the rate of litigation in Japan is so low. However, John Haley, in his piece *The Myth of the Reluctant Litigant*, 4 J. Japanese Stud. 359 (1978), claims that it is not a desire to maintain harmony that keeps Japanese from suing, but various logistical factors such as economics and access to courts and lawyers.

be influenced by information, and persuasion only by the substance of arguments. In an effort to maintain harmony, jurors might be willing to give up their personal beliefs and be persuaded for reasons other than substantive reasons. However, the desire to maintain harmony may be thrust aside by Japanese jurors, especially if the judge instructs them to do so, and an open debate could occur where each juror votes his independent mind. Without empirical evidence, it is difficult to say just what part this aspect of Japanese culture would play inside the four walls of the jury room.

B. Japanese Society

Culture is not the only consideration when discussing whether a jury system should be introduced into a society. One must also look at societal factors such as level of education, race, citizen participation, and other factors to determine whether a jury system could function effectively. J. H. Jearey argues that three conditions are necessary for a jury system to function effectively.[148] First, the society in which it operates must be for the most part racially, culturally, linguistically, and religiously homogeneous.[149] Secondly, the members of the society must be sufficiently educated to understand their responsibilities as jurors and understand that they must set aside private prejudices when fulfilling these responsibilities.[150] Thirdly, the members of the society must generally agree with the laws which, as jurors, they are required to enforce.[151]

The reasoning behind Jearey's list of conditions is clear. First, the more socially homogeneous a society, the less chance there will be that jurors from that society will base their decisions on racial, religious, or ethnic bias.[152] Secondly, the more educationally advanced a society becomes,

[148] See J. H. Jearey, *Trial by Jury and Trial with the Aid of Assessors in the Superior Courts of British African Territories: I*, 4 J. Afr. L. 133, 143 (1960). Jearey uses these conditions to assess the reason why the jury system plays such a small part in the African territories under discussion.

[149] See ibid., at 136, 138.

[150] See ibid., at 141.

[151] See ibid., at 135–6.

[152] One of the biggest problems with the jury system in the United States is the well-documented racism of juries. See Nathaniel R. Jones, *Race and American Juries—The Long View*, 30 Creighton L. Rev. 271, 273 (1997) ('increasingly, jury watchers are concluding that . . . race plays a far more significant role in jury verdicts than many people involved in the justice system prefer to acknowledge'); Nancy J. King, *Postconviction Review of Jury Discrimination: Measuring the Effects of Juror Race on Jury Decisions*, 92 Mich. L. Rev. 63, 66 (1993) (arguing that the influence of jury race discrimination on jury decisions is real and can be measured by judges in certain circumstances).

the more jurors will be able to understand their roles and put aside personal views on an issue not based on the facts and law. Furthermore, better educated juries will be able to comprehend more complex evidence used at trial directly, rather than through the statements of a zealous attorney or expert.[153] Finally, if jurors do not agree fundamentally with the laws on which they are supposed to base their decision, jury verdicts may be primarily based on factors other than the law, frustrating the concept of rule of law.

Because all three of these conditions are present in Japanese society, it seems that from a societal perspective, Japan is ripe for the reintroduction of the jury system. First, Japan is overall one of the most socially homogeneous societies in the world. Unlike in the United States, where citizenship is determined by place of birth, in Japan, citizenship is determined by the nationality of one's parents.[154] As a result, except in a few specific instances,[155] almost all Japanese citizens have the same ethnic and historical background. Also, although most Japanese claim to practice Shinto, Buddhism, or both,[156] few are serious about religion. Religion neither unifies nor divides the Japanese people—it simply exists neutrally. Finally, Japan has as little linguistic diversity as can be found in countries in Europe or in different regions of the United States. Japanese is spoken throughout Japan, with variations in dialect in the North and the South. Japan is also one of the most educationally advanced countries in the world. With a literacy rate of close to 99 percent and a rate of advancement to universities and junior colleges of over 37 percent,[157] the pool of jurors in Japan would allow for well-

[153] See Comment, *supra* note 130, at 125 (stating that one reason mitigating against adopting the jury system in South Africa is that jurors are not considered knowledgeable enough to decide complex cases).

[154] See Onuma Yasuaki, *Interplay Between Human Rights Activities and Legal Standards of Human Rights: A Case Study on the Korean Minority in Japan*, 25 CORNELL INT'L L.J. 515, 515 n. 3 (1992).

[155] These include the case of later generations of North and South Koreans whose parents were brought to Japan against their will during the Japanese occupation of Korea and who were naturalized. See Comment, *Local Public Employment Discrimination Against Korean Permanent Residents in Japan: A U.S. Perspective*, 7 PAC. RIM L. & POL. J. 197, 201–2 (1998).

[156] The total number of adherents to 'religion' in Japan in 1993 was 219,723,000. This figure exceeds the total population of Japan because most people belong to both Shintoism and Buddhism. See STATISTICS BUREAU, GOVERNMENT OF JAPAN, 1998 JAPAN STATISTICAL YEARBOOK 743, tbl. 21–17 (1998) (noting statistics on religious bodies, clergymen, and adherents).

[157] See Japan Information Network, *Rate of Advancement to Universities* (visited June 30, 1999) <http://jin.jcic.or.jp/stat/stats/16EDU72.html> (citing Minister of Education,

educated juries. And because over 90 percent of Japanese view themselves as members of the middle class, criminal defendants would, most of the time, truly be receiving a trial by their peers. Finally, because Japan follows the rule of law and the Japanese Constitution puts the power in the hands of the people, Japanese are in basic agreement with the laws they are required to enforce. If this were not so, these laws could be changed by democratic means.

A fourth factor that Jearey does not mention that could affect the success of a jury system is the degree to which a society has allowed or is willing to allow citizen participation in the system. In countries that have had no experience at all with citizen participation in the legal system, a switch to either an all-layperson jury system or a mixed court system could be difficult. On the other hand, societies that have a history of citizen participation in the legal system may be more welcoming of either type of jury system. Traditionally, Japan did not offer laypersons an opportunity to participate in the criminal adjudication process. However, laypersons did have the opportunity to participate in civil conciliation proceedings (*chotei*) during the Tokugawa period,[158] and they were able to participate on juries during the years 1928 to 1943.[159] During the Allied Occupation, prosecution review commissions (*kensatsu shinsakai*) were created to allow public participation of Japanese citizens to control abuses of prosecutorial discretion.[160] There are also various other areas where layperson participation in Japan exists. For example, 'laypersons may participate in quasi-judicial affairs as civil liberties commissioners (*jinken yogo iin*), local administrative counselors (*gyosei sodan iin*), welfare commissioners (*min'ei iin*), conciliation commissioners, expert commissioners, judicial commissioners, probation officers, and family court counselors'.[161]

Science, & Culture, The Research and Statistics Planning Division, School Basic Survey (Dec. 21, 1998) (university advancement rates); U.S. Dep't of State, Bureau of East Asian & Pacific Affairs, Background Notes: Japan, March 1999 (visited June 30, 1999) <http://www.state.gov/www/background_notes/japan_0399_bgn. html> (literacy rate); see also 5 Historical Statistics of Japan 260 (Japan Statistical Ass'n, 1987) (giving comparable statistics from 1985).

[158] See Mark D. West, *Prosecutorial Review Commissions: Japan's Answer to the Problem of Prosecutorial Discretion*, 92 Colum. L. Rev. 684, 695 (1992) (citing 1 Dan Fenno Henderson, Conciliation and Japanese Law: Tokugawa and Modern (1965)).

[159] See *supra* text accompanying notes 64–72.

[160] Prosecution review commissions are lay advisory bodies that review a public prosecutor's exercise of discretion not to prosecute. They are composed of 11 members who are chosen at random from voting lists. See West, *supra* note 158, at 694–8.

[161] Ibid., at 695 (citing Lawrence Ward Beer, Freedom of Expression in Japan 140 (1984)).

Furthermore, certain scholars have noted a change in 'law consciousness' of the Japanese from the 1950s to today.[162] This change is simply that more Japanese are willing today to bring their disputes to court than in the 1950s, signaling a more active role for citizens in the system.[163] The formation of popular movements, the use of prosecution review commissions in certain highly publicized cases, and the increase in academic writings and programs concerning forms of citizen participation evidence the citizen participation that is currently occurring.[164]

Japan's recent history with layperson participation in the judicial system will make it easier for the country to readopt a jury system for two reasons. First, the basic idea of layperson participation in the judicial system is already accepted in Japanese society, and calling citizens to serve on a jury would not be a foreign idea. Secondly, because Japan had a jury from 1928 to 1943, many of the facilities for jury trial still exist in the old courtrooms. Japan need not go further than these courtrooms for an example on which to base the design of new courtrooms.

C. Japanese Legal System

There is no technical legal barrier preventing Japan from readopting the jury system. The Jury Act was never repealed; rather, it was suspended until World War II was over.[165] The Japanese Diet could either repeal the Act to Suspend the Jury Act or enact a new law altogether establishing jury trial for criminal cases.

From a practitioner's perspective, the reintroduction of the jury system would change life drastically. One significant change would be that of timing. Under the present system, a long trial is not conducted in one continuous sitting.[166] Rather, the case is tried in short sessions,

[162] See, *e.g.*, Hideo Tanaka, *The Role of Law in Japanese Society: Comparisons with the West*, 19 U.B.C. L. Rev. 375, 384 (1985).

[163] See ibid. Professor Tanaka points to large pollution cases in the 1970s as an example. See ibid.

[164] See West, *supra* note 158, at 715.

[165] The Act to Suspend the Jury Act states that '[t]he jury system will be reinforced when the war is over'. Baishinho no Teishi ni Kansuru Horitsu (An Act to Suspend the Jury Act), Law No. 88 of 1943.

[166] See Foote, *supra* note 9, at 84 (describing this phenomenon in the criminal context); Glenn Theodore Melchinger, *For the Collective Benefit: Why Japan's New Strict Product Liability Law Is 'Strictly Business'*, 19 U. Haw. L. Rev. 879, 940 n. 11 (1997) (stating that civil trials in Japan are composed of monthly meetings rather than one continuous trial).

usually for a few hours each month.[167] The introduction of juries would require cases to be tried in one continuous time period, certainly changing the method of preparation of the attorneys.[168]

Another significant change would be that a trial by dossier would be replaced by bouts of live witness testimony.[169] The predictability of the old system would be gone. Japanese attorneys would have to learn the art of trying a case in front of laypersons rather than experienced career judges. The focus will be shifted from the papers to the live witnesses testifying.[170]

Adoption of a jury system would also certainly affect the appellate system in Japan. Presently, a defendant may appeal both factual and legal findings to the first level of appeal (*koso* appeal).[171] The Jury Act of 1923 abolished the *koso* appeal for jury trials on points of fact.[172] Any law re-adopting the jury system would probably do the same, or risk undermining the factual determinations of the jury. As Professor Lempert states, this '[c]ould fundamentally alter the power relationship between trial and appellate courts, and the rules of first level review might be similar to the rules that confine the Japanese Supreme Court to questions of law when it reviews intermediate court decisions'.[173] For defense attorneys, the primary effect would be to curtail opportunities for appeal or post-conviction review on factual grounds. However, presumably the better factfinding by juries would make up for this.

It is also likely that, through the adoption of a jury system in Japan, the near 100 percent conviction rate would decline.[174] Prosecutors may also push for the adoption of a U.S.-like plea bargaining system,[175] which could be used to save the courts time by preventing many cases from reaching the jury.[176]

Also, from a purely practical perspective, although some Japanese courtrooms continue to have jury boxes and jury rooms, the great majority do not. Certainly the cost and effort of adding such necessities for

[167] See Foote, *supra* note 9, at 84.

[168] See Lempert, *supra* note 4, at 67.

[169] See Foote, *supra* note 9, at 84.

[170] See ibid.

[171] See ibid., at 85.

[172] See Baishinho (Jury Act), Law. No. 50 of 1923, art. 101.

[173] Lempert, *supra* note 4, at 68.

[174] See ibid., at 67. As discussed *supra* in the text accompanying notes 30–3, laypersons may be able to avoid biases of experienced career judges concerning the presumption of innocence and correctness of prosecutors.

[175] Presently, the Japanese criminal justice system does not allow for plea bargaining. See Desombre, *supra* note 29, at 123–4. Prosecutors have discretion whether to prosecute based on the evidence gathered. See ibid.

[176] See Lempert, *supra* note 4, at 67.

jury trials, in addition to juror wages and travel, are factors to be considered in how smoothly a jury system could be adopted in Japan.[177]

Thus, although there is no legal obstacle preventing Japan from bringing back the jury in criminal trials, reintroduction of the jury system would take time and effort on the part of both the Japanese government and attorneys. At least one commentator has stated that the need for such efforts, in addition to skepticism about the jury system, may be enough to prevent adoption of the jury system in Japan in the near future.[178]

VI. Conclusion

Japanese jurists and scholars are presently studying various forms of the jury system around the world to determine which would be most suitable if Japan were to decide to readopt such a system for criminal trials. The probable success of a jury system in Japanese culture and society would depend entirely on the details of the system adopted. Obviously, it is necessary to avoid the many pitfalls of the original jury system used in Japan from 1928 to 1943, such as nonbinding verdicts and prohibition of objections to the jury instructions. Factors such as these served to delegitimize the jury system at that time and greatly contributed to its failure.

Assuming that a legitimate and binding system were adopted, the all-layperson Anglo-American jury system, as opposed to the German mixed court system, seems most suited for Japanese culture.[179] Japanese cultural characteristics such as the hierarchical nature of Japanese society, the high level of trust for authority figures in Japanese society, Japanese group consciousness, and the desire to maintain harmony would make it difficult for a mixed court system to function effectively.

[177] See Marshall S. Huebner, *Who Decides? Restructuring Criminal Justice for a Democratic South Africa*, 102 YALE L.J. 961, 975 (1993) (discussing administrative costs such as construction of jury boxes and deliberation rooms, and juror stipends and travel, in the context of whether South Africa should adopt the jury system).

[178] See Foote, *supra* note 9, at 85:

> '[I]n view of all the other elements of the criminal justice system that would be affected by reintroduction of the jury system, not to mention widespread skepticism of the jury among judges and prosecutors (as well as some segments of the defense bar), it seems unlikely that any jury system will be adopted in Japan in the near future.'

[179] It is important to note that the cultural characteristics come into play mostly in the deliberation phase of a jury trial, and it is from this perspective that I have formed these conclusions.

If the mixed court system were adopted in Japan, there is a fear that the laypersons would always defer to the opinions of the judges, even if not rationally persuaded, thus defeating their purpose. Certainly, the same cultural factors come into play in an all-layperson jury as well. However, there is a large difference between disagreeing with a professional judge and disagreeing with a fellow citizen. In the latter case, a deference to authority may still exist (such as if the other layperson is much older), but it would be less pronounced. Therefore, an all-layperson jury would be more successful than a mixed court in Japan.

From a cultural perspective, therefore, a jury system could be successful in Japan. None of the cultural attributes serves as a complete bar to the functioning of a jury system. Just as in the United States, the system will not function completely in line with its ideals, but it would still be able to function effectively. Likewise, Japan is ripe for the re-introduction of the jury system from a societal perspective. Japanese society is, for the most part, well educated, homogeneous, and middle class. These factors would facilitate the functioning and goals of a jury system in Japan. From a legal perspective, there is no barrier *per se* preventing Japan from reintroducing the jury system. However, it may be difficult to convince judges and prosecutors to change the *status quo*. Therefore, although it is presently unclear whether the Japanese will reintroduce a jury system in criminal cases, Japanese culture and society, as well as the Japanese legal system, would be conducive to a jury system, preferably one based on the Anglo-American model.

11 The Civil Jury in America

Stephan Landsman*

I. An Introduction—Texas Style

Americans have relied on juries of ordinary citizens to resolve their civil disputes since the beginning of the colonial period.[1] Juries were available in virtually all civil, as well as criminal, cases in Virginia no later than 1624.[2] They were specifically provided for in the 1641 Massachusetts Body of Liberties.[3] Indeed, in seventeenth and eighteenth century Massachusetts, juries were the primary instrument of governance.[4] Those who ratified both the state and national constitutions viewed juries as a critical component of the justice system. And juries have endured. Today, men and women from all walks of life are still called upon to resolve the most significant civil disputes confronting American society.

This was the case in 1985 when Pennzoil and Texaco, two of America's petrochemical giants, clashed over the acquisition of Getty Oil, the corporate creation of billionaire J. Paul Getty.[5] At Getty's death, the assets of his company had been divided between a family trust containing approximately 40 percent of outstanding shares, the Getty Museum, holding about 11 percent of the company's stock, and the public. The trust was governed by Getty's son Gordon, the museum was directed by Harold Williams, and the oil company was managed by CEO Sidney Peterson. In 1984, a simmering dispute between Gordon Getty and Sidney Peterson came to a head. The two fought each other for control of Getty Oil. A key prize in their contest was the swing block of shares controlled by the museum's Williams. Players representing all the interests in this high-stakes game engaged in a series of nasty tricks and betrayals that degenerated into a no-holds-barred struggle for dominance. The fight eventually spilled over into the public arena where

* Robert A. Clifford Professor of Tort Law and Social Policy, DePaul University.

[1] For an extended discussion of the early history of the American civil jury, see Stephan Landsman, *The Civil Jury in America: Scenes from an Unappreciated History*, 44 Hastings L.J. 579 (1993).

[2] See ibid., at 592. [3] See ibid.

[4] See generally William E. Nelson, Americanization of the Common Law: The Impact of Legal Change on Massachusetts Society, 1760–1830 (1975).

[5] Unless otherwise noted, my description of the *Pennzoil* litigation is based upon Thomas Petzinger, Jr., Oil and Honor: The Texaco–Pennzoil Wars (1987).

others interested in acquiring Getty Oil might compete. In Wall Street parlance, Getty Oil had been 'put in play' and might be seized by the highest bidder.

Pennzoil, hoping to obtain control of Getty's huge oil reserves, made an offer of $100 per share for the company. This bid was rejected as too low by Getty's board but led to further bargaining and an offer of $110 per share. This too was rejected. Certain 'sweeteners' were then added by Pennzoil resulting in a final offer of approximately $112.50 per share. This proposal was embedded within a highly complex legal package that was accepted 'in principle' by the negotiating parties. The deal was to be consummated through the drafting of a series of contractual documents. For a variety of reasons, the drafting dragged on for several days. During this delay, Texaco, which had been watching developments, came forward with an offer that eventually totaled $125 per share. The Getty stockholders abandoned their agreement with Pennzoil and accepted Texaco's proposal.

Pennzoil, believing it had been deprived of the fruits of a binding agreement, decided to sue. After preliminary legal skirmishing, Pennzoil and Texaco squared off in Texas state court on the question of whether Texaco had improperly interfered with a completed Pennzoil deal. The case, as required by law, was to be heard by a jury of twelve ordinary Texans. Their job was to decide if Texaco ought to be required to pay compensatory and punitive damages that might rise as high as $15 billion or more.

The case was assigned to Judge Anthony Farris. As the trial date approached, Texaco discovered that Pennzoil's lead attorney, the flamboyant Texan Joseph Jamail, had contributed $10,000 to Judge Farris's re-election campaign, which was the largest single contribution received by the judge. Texaco's lawyers asked Judge Farris to recuse himself from the case but the judge refused. His decision was affirmed by a Texas appellate court.

The first step in the trial process was jury selection. Before jurors were chosen, the lawyers were given an opportunity to question potential panel members about their possible biases. This questioning process, or *voir dire* as it is usually called, was effectively used by Jamail to lay out Pennzoil's key trial theme: that a deal, sealed with a handshake, had been consummated. In response, Texaco's chief lawyer, Richard Miller, asked potential jurors whether they could accept the limits imposed by law on corporate acquisitions and reject as incomplete the complex series of negotiations carried on by Pennzoil and Getty. After questioning that took five days, the contending parties were each allowed to remove by peremptory challenge as many as eight potential jurors they suspected of being either biased or unsympathetic. Pennzoil would later claim that Texaco had tried to exclude African-Americans, although four were empanelled, and Texaco would accuse Pennzoil of trying to remove Jews, although at least one sat on the panel as originally constituted.

The simple handshake theme so effectively exploited by Jamail during *voir dire* was diluted in Pennzoil's eight-week presentation to the jury. Pennzoil's case featured long and repetitive questioning, mind-numbing videotapes of pretrial witness examinations, and a mass of complex expert testimony including a claim for $7.5 billion in damages. Texaco did no better with its case. Before it could conclude, however, Judge Farris became mortally ill and was replaced by Judge Solomon Casseb. In the end, the trial took a total of seventeen weeks, involved thirty-five witnesses, and produced a transcript of more than 23,000 pages.

At the conclusion of the evidence, the jury was given five questions (or 'special issues' in Texas parlance) to answer, including whether there had been a Pennzoil–Getty contract, whether Texaco had interfered with that contract, what damages might be assessed if interference were found, and what punitive damages might be awarded. On its initial vote on the first jury question, the jury was divided seven to five in favor of Pennzoil. It reached a nine to three majority quickly but appeared stuck there. The majority needed just one more vote, because Texas law allows a nonunanimous verdict of ten to two.[6] After a weekend off, one juror switched sides and agreement was quickly reached on all five questions (the two dissenting jurors eventually joined their ten colleagues). The jury awarded Pennzoil $7.5 billion in compensatory damages and $3 billion in punitive damages.

This $10.5 billion judgment threatened Texaco's very existence. Under Texas law, defendants are required to post a bond in the total amount of the award against them before being allowed to appeal. In Texaco's case, this turned out to be a financial impossibility, because no one could or would write such a bond. Texaco turned to the federal courts for relief from the state court judgment. The question of federal intervention went all the way to the United States Supreme Court, which denied that Texaco had any federal claim.[7] Faced with a crushing judgment, Texaco chose to declare bankruptcy. In the ensuing legal

[6] See TEX. R. CIV. P. 292.

[7] See Pennzoil Co. v. Texaco, Inc., 481 U.S. 1, 2 (1987).

scramble, Pennzoil and Texaco came to a reluctant agreement in which Pennzoil accepted a payment of $3 billion to settle the case. A jury of twelve ordinary Texans had brought one of the country's largest and most powerful corporations to its knees.

The *Pennzoil* case raises a host of questions about the function of the modern jury. This chapter will explore a number of them, including why juries have been given so important a place in the judicial process, and how the jury ought to be constituted to carry out its work. The chapter also examines the process used to select a jury, instructions used to structure decision-making, and the nature as well as the form of jury verdicts. Despite many challenges to the jury system, careful assessment suggests that the jury is still an effective and necessary part of the judicial system.

II. Why Do American Civil Juries Have So Much Power?

Looking at the *Pennzoil* case, one might be moved to ask (as were many critics at the time): why does the United States allow twelve ordinary citizens to make such momentous decisions? The answer to this question involves a complex blend of historical and theoretical factors. Chief among the theoretical considerations is that the United States relies on a robustly adversarial form of justice. This means that Americans trust neutral and passive bodies to render decisions on the basis of the sharp clash of proofs presented by adversaries in a highly structured forensic setting.[8]

The jury is the most neutral and passive decision-maker available. It is not called upon to rule on any pretrial disputes, nor is it involved in the administration of the lawsuit. At trial, it hears only evidence that has been screened for objectionable and prejudicial material. Juries are made up of people who come together to hear one case; they are, therefore, unlikely to be tainted by the sorts of predispositions judges may develop over the course of their careers either about certain sorts of claims or certain lawyers or litigants. Because the jury comprises a group, no single juror's prejudices can destroy its ability to reach a fair decision. Moreover, its members may be questioned before trial in *voir dire*, which facilitates the removal of potentially biased individuals. All this is to be contrasted with the position of trial judges, like Judge Farris, who

[8] For a more complete description of America's adversarial system, see Stephan Landsman, Readings on Adversarial Justice: The American Approach to Adjudication 1–39 (1988).

have to labor unceasingly to manage the litigation before them, who inescapably bring their legal and political experiences into the courtroom with them, and who cannot be questioned regarding their opinions or sympathies.

The United States's allegiance to the civil jury is the product both of its early colonial history and the constitutional debates at the conclusion of the Revolutionary War.[9] The jury trial came to the New World with the English colonists and was, from the earliest times, the established means of resolving legal disputes. In the Revolutionary era, its value in American eyes was dramatically enhanced because juries regularly thwarted British objectives and provided a bulwark against royal tyranny. All the former colonies enthusiastically embraced the jury. 'The right to trial by jury was probably the only one universally secured by the first American state constitutions.'[10]

When the initial draft of the United States Constitution failed to make a specific provision for trial by jury in civil cases,[11] a cry of protest went up across the new nation. The Federalists, who had been primarily responsible for drafting the proposed constitution, were forced to defend their choice to omit the civil jury trial right. In pieces like Hamilton's essay number 83 in the *Federalist*, they argued that, although valuable, the jury might not be essential, especially in civil cases.[12] These and similar arguments were challenged by the Antifederalists, who treated failure to insist on jury trials as sufficient reason to reject the proposed constitution. The Antifederalists believed that juries were essential in both criminal *and* civil litigation to offset judicial power and overzealous legislatures. They drew support for their argument from Blackstone:

> The impartial administration of justice, which secures both our persons and our properties, is the great end of civil society. But if that be entirely entrusted to the magistracy, a select body of men, and those generally selected by the prince or such as enjoy the highest offices in the state, their decisions, in spite of their

[9] For a discussion of the colonial period and developments with respect to the jury trial during the era of the drafting of the Constitution, see Landsman, *supra* note 1.

[10] LEONARD W. LEVY, LEGACY OF SUPPRESSION: FREEDOM OF SPEECH AND PRESS IN EARLY AMERICAN HISTORY 281 (1960).

[11] The right to jury trial was provided for in criminal cases. See U.S. CONST. art. III, § 2, cl. 3 ('The Trial of all Crimes, except in Cases of Impeachment, shall be by Jury; and such Trial shall be held in the State where the said Crimes shall have been committed. . . .'); cf. ibid., amend. VI ('In all criminal prosecutions, the accused shall enjoy the right to a speedy and public trial, by an impartial jury of the State and district wherein the crime shall have been committed. . . .').

[12] See THE FEDERALIST No. 83 (Alexander Hamilton).

own natural integrity, will have frequently an involuntary bias toward those of their own rank and dignity; it is not to be expected from human nature that the few should always be attentive to the interests and good of the many.[13]

In the end, a compromise was reached: The jury trial right in civil cases did not appear in the body of the Constitution but was incorporated into that document as part of the first ten amendments. The Seventh Amendment declares:

In Suits at common law, where the value in controversy shall exceed twenty dollars, the right of trial by jury shall be preserved, and no fact tried by a jury, shall be otherwise re-examined in any Court of the United States, than according to the rules of the common law.[14]

Although much criticism has been leveled at the civil jury since 1791, it is inextricably woven into the fabric of the American justice system. It is the counterweight to a powerful professional judiciary and the occasional, antidemocratic tendencies of the various branches of government.

III. The Use of Juries in Civil Litigation Today

The jury remains a significant part of the United States's civil justice system. The National Center for State Courts estimates that there are approximately 150,000 state jury trials per year.[15] In the federal courts, there are about 10,000 jury trials a year, of which about half are civil.[16] Civil jury trials in state courts account for about 1 percent of all civil case dispositions.[17] In the federal system, this figure was about 2 percent for 1990.[18] Hundreds of thousands of Americans serve on juries in any given twelve-month period. In the federal system alone, more than 400,000 citizens were involved in *voir dire* in 1990 and more than 100,000 were chosen to serve as jurors.[19]

Although incomplete, there are data available that help us refine our picture of the civil jury at work. In one of the primary areas of civil litigation—torts—jury verdicts are returned in about 2.7 percent of all state court cases.[20] Juries do most of their tort work in simple cases involv-

[13] Ehrlich's Blackstone 682 (J. W. Ehrlich ed., Nourse Publishing Co. 1959).

[14] U.S. Const. amend. VII.

[15] See Jeffrey Abramson, We the Jury: The Jury System and the Ideal of Democracy 251 (1994).

[16] See ibid. [17] See ibid., at 252. [18] See ibid. [19] See ibid.

[20] The data in this para. are drawn largely from Brian J. Ostrom *et al.*, *A Step Above Anecdote: A Profile of the Civil Jury in the 1990s*, 79 Judicature 233, 234–40 (1996).

ing auto accidents and premises liability claims. Often these two categories account for 50 percent of the total civil jury caseload. Plaintiff win rates in tort cases vary widely, but in the aggregate plaintiffs win about half the time. This figure drops to 40 percent in products liability actions and to 30 percent in medical malpractice cases. Plaintiff win rates are virtually identical against individual and corporate defendants but awards against corporations are, on average, substantially larger. The median jury award in state courts is about $52,000, of which about half is consumed in fees and costs. Approximately 8 percent of jury awards exceed one million dollars. Punitive damage awards, as in *Pennzoil*, are infrequent and are most likely to be made in contract-related cases. The median punitive award in tort cases is quite modest ($38,000), but the mean is much higher ($590,000) because of the existence of a number of very large awards. The vast majority of tort plaintiffs are individuals rather than corporations. A typical state court trial usually takes about two years from case filing to jury trial.

IV. The Question of Jury Size

The Texas jury in the *Pennzoil* case had twelve jurors and four alternates. One of the alternates eventually took the place of a juror who was excused—thus ensuring that twelve jurors were present for deliberations.

From the late thirteenth century on, the Anglo-American legal system recognized that the jury should have twelve members, and, in the fifteenth century, a twelve-member jury definitively became the law of England, unless the parties consented otherwise.[21] In 1898, the United States Supreme Court held, in *Thompson* v. *Utah*, that a 'jury' in the constitutional sense of that term must be 'composed of not less than twelve persons'.[22] The legal implication of this decision was that all jury trials conducted under the mandate of either the Sixth (criminal) or Seventh (civil) Amendment to the United States Constitution (at a minimum all those trials conducted in federal court) had to utilize twelve-person juries. This requirement did not necessarily extend to all state court civil jury trials—a question turning on a difficult question of constitutional interpretation regarding the 'incorporation' of various aspects of the Bill of Rights into state proceedings.

[21] See Richard S. Arnold, *Trial by Jury: The Constitutional Right to a Jury of Twelve in Civil Trials*, 22 Hofstra L. Rev. 1, 8 (1993).

[22] 170 U.S. 343, 350 (1898).

Over the past three decades, the requirement of twelve jurors has come under sustained attack. In 1970, the Supreme Court, in *Williams* v. *Florida*, upheld a Florida statute mandating six-person juries in all state court criminal prosecutions except those involving the possible imposition of the death penalty.[23] In the *Williams* decision, the Supreme Court referred to reliance on twelve jurors as an 'historical accident'[24] and, in an act of analytical oversimplification, declared the only essential purpose of the criminal jury to be the prevention of oppression by government.[25] Based on the assumption that the jury was necessary only to serve this one purpose, the Court could discern no difference between the effectiveness of six- and twelve-person juries and, therefore, upheld the use of a six-person panel.[26] Three years later, the Court extended the six-person rule to federal civil trials in *Colgrove* v. *Battin*.[27] This decision was particularly noteworthy because the requirements of the Seventh Amendment specifically applied to the federal civil trial under consideration in that case. The court thus declared that whatever the term 'jury' had once meant, it was no longer to be defined as a body of twelve. This redefinition opened the way to significant downsizing.

The Court in *Colgrove*, in passing, noted that its analysis was supported by 'convincing empirical evidence'.[28] Later examination would disclose that this evidence was hardly empirical and far from convincing.[29] In fact, research would strongly suggest that smaller juries are no more efficient than larger ones[30] (efficiency was an important selling point for the Supreme Court majority in *Colgrove*), that the use of smaller juries is likely to lead to more wildly fluctuating verdicts,[31] that smaller panel size reduces the opportunity for minority jurors to serve,[32] and that smaller juries place added pressure on minority jurors who do serve to surrender to the majority point of view.[33]

[23] 399 U.S. 78 (1970). [24] Ibid., at 89. [25] See ibid., at 100.

[26] See ibid. [27] 413 U.S. 149 (1973). [28] Ibid., at 159 n. 15.

[29] See Hans Zeisel & Shari Seidman Diamond, *'Convincing Empirical Evidence' on the Six Member Jury*, 41 U. Chi. L. Rev. 281 (1974).

[30] See William R. Pabst, Jr., *Statistical Studies of the Costs of Six-Man Versus Twelve-Man Juries*, 14 Wm. & Mary L. Rev. 326, 327 (1972); Hans Zeisel, . . . *And Then There Were None: The Diminution of the Federal Jury*, 38 U. Chi. L. Rev. 710, 710–12 (1971).

[31] See Michael J. Saks, *The Smaller the Jury, the Greater the Unpredictability*, 79 Judicature 263, 264 (1996).

[32] See Michael J. Saks, *Ignorance of Science Is No Excuse*, Trial, Nov.–Dec. 1974, at 18, 19; Zeisel, *supra* note 30, at 716.

[33] See *Development in the Law—The Civil Jury*, 110 Harv. L. Rev. 1408, 1485–6 & n.165 (1997).

As evidence mounted regarding the inferiority of six-person panels, the court was confronted with a Georgia effort to reduce the size of its criminal juries to five. In *Ballew* v. *Georgia*, the Supreme Court rejected five-member juries as constitutionally inadequate in criminal cases.[34] Justice Blackmun's explanation for the court's decision suggested that a line had to be drawn somewhere.[35]

The research Blackmun relied on, however, suggests that the line should have been drawn at twelve, not between five and six. Nevertheless, in 1996, the Judicial Conference of the United States rejected the recommendation of its own Standing Committee on Rules of Practice and Procedure that the federal courts return to twelve-person juries in all civil cases.[36]

V. Selecting a Jury in a Civil Case—*Voir Dire*, Peremptory Challenges, and Jury Consultant Advice

In the *Pennzoil* case, the opposing lawyers spent five days questioning potential jurors about their sympathies. After this *voir dire*, each side used its eight peremptory strikes to remove those individuals who were perceived to be biased or unsympathetic. These two processes, *voir dire* and peremptory strikes, are at the heart of the civil juror selection system; however, each has become controversial over the last quarter-century.

Lawyer-conducted *voir dire* is the traditional American method of screening the members of the panel called for jury service.[37] In some states, *voir dire* has been left so completely in lawyers' hands that the judge does not even preside at the sessions in which opposing lawyers question potential jurors. Over the course of the past two decades, however, the feeling has grown among judges and rules drafters alike that lawyers have been abusing *voir dire* to indoctrinate the jury and to cultivate friendly relationships with individual jurors. Moreover, critics of the traditional approach have suggested that lawyer-directed questioning is inordinately time consuming and likely to veer into inappropriate areas touching on jurors' private lives and specific views about evidence they have not yet heard.

In reaction to the feeling that lawyers have abused *voir dire*, various courts have imposed substantial restrictions on lawyer participation in

[34] 435 U.S. 223 (1978). [35] See ibid., at 239.

[36] See *Development in the Law—The Civil Jury*, *supra* note 33, at 1478 & nn.106–8.

[37] For a general review of *voir dire*, see Barbara Allen Babcock, Voir Dire: *Preserving 'Its Wonderful Power,'* 27 Stan. L. Rev. 545 (1975).

the questioning process. In the federal courts, the civil rules today authorize judges to conduct the entire *voir dire* themselves.[38] Federal judges have exercised their rule-granted authority and in about 70 percent of cases conduct all *voir dire* alone.[39] This approach has yielded remarkably mechanical questioning that seldom vigorously pursues the issue of bias. Moreover, research suggests that judges are not as effective at eliciting juror self-disclosure as are lawyers.[40] Despite these drawbacks, *voir dire* has, more and more, become the judge's province.

Two techniques have been developed in recent years that promise to reinvigorate *voir dire* while restraining lawyer excesses. The first of these is to allow lawyer supplementation of the judge's questioning, thereby making it possible to secure both the benefit of judicial restraint and lawyer probing. Such an approach is authorized by the rules of procedure and is becoming more popular.[41] The second technique is to supplement oral *voir dire* with a written questionnaire answered by each potential juror. Questionnaires have been used in a number of high-profile civil trials, including the massive litigation regarding the safety of the pregnancy drug Bendectin, where a forty-six question form was distributed to potential jurors before oral *voir dire* began.[42]

Once *voir dire* has been concluded, each side is allowed to exercise its peremptory strikes. These strikes have, traditionally, been exercised without explanation or justification. As in a number of other areas, the Supreme Court has challenged tradition, in this instance by requiring that at least certain peremptory strikes be scrutinized and, in some circumstances, justified by counsel. The case requiring such scrutiny was the 1986 decision in *Batson* v. *Kentucky*.[43] In that criminal case, the Court held that it was improper for lawyers to use peremptory strikes to remove African-American juror candidates simply because of their race. The Court mandated a three-step process beginning with the complaining party making a 'prima facie [showing] of purposeful discrimination' based on race.[44] Once the complainant has made such a showing, the burden shifts to the party who exercised the peremptory strikes to articulate a 'neutral explanation' for his or her selections.[45] Then it is up to

[38] See Fed. R. Civ. P. 47(a).

[39] See Jury Trial Innovations 54 (G. Thomas Munsterman *et al.* (eds.), 1997).

[40] See Susan E. Jones, *Judge- Versus Attorney-Conducted Voir Dire: An Empirical Investigation of Juror Candor*, 11 Law & Hum. Behav. 131 (1987).

[41] See Jury Trial Innovations, *supra* note 39, § III–1 (lawyer-conducted *voir dire*).

[42] See *In re* Richardson-Merrell, Inc. 'Bendectin' Prod. Liab. Litig., 624 F. Supp 1212, 1258 (S. D. Ohio 1985).

[43] 476 U.S. 79 (1986).

[44] Ibid., at 93–4.

[45] Ibid., at 97–8.

the trial court to decide whether unlawful discrimination has been proven. Subsequent cases have expanded and contracted *Batson* by turns. The Supreme Court has extended *Batson* protection to juror candidates in civil actions[46] and to peremptory challenges that discriminate on the basis of gender.[47] The Court has, however, given trial courts virtually unfettered discretion in deciding *Batson* claims,[48] thereby declining to fix any firm or predictable guidelines. It remains to be seen whether *Batson* and its progeny will rein in discrimination in the use of peremptory challenges. In the *Pennzoil* case, each side accused the other of *Batson* violations, but the accusations were rejected.

The task of selecting jurors has become increasingly difficult as America's population has grown, the diversity of the jury pool has increased, and lawyers with a national practice find themselves more frequently trying lawsuits in communities they do not know. In these circumstances, at least when the stakes are high, lawyers will be attracted by any technique that offers the prospect of making more effective juror selections possible.

Since the early 1970s, one method said to 'improve' jury selection has become increasingly popular.[49] This is the so-called 'scientific selection' of jurors, which relies on the input of social scientists, or those claiming social science expertise ('jury consultants'), to help lawyers exercise their peremptory strikes. In the 1971 case of the Harrisburg Seven, a group of anti-Vietnam War protestors, Dr Jay Schulman and a number of confederates sought to use social science methods to help the defense select a more sympathetic jury in the generally hostile community of Harrisburg, Pennsylvania. To do this, the scientists conducted an opinion poll in the Harrisburg area, analyzed it in a search for correlations between favorable juror attitudes and demographic traits, and used a variety of in-court observational techniques to help counsel make their jury selections. When the ensuing trial ended in a jury deadlocked ten to two for acquittal, a new science (or, more accurately, business) was born.

The new business is premised on the notion that statistical assessment of community attitudes can significantly improve the identification of

[46] See Edmonson v. Leesville Concrete Co., 500 U.S. 614, 616 (1991) (prohibiting private litigants in a civil case from using peremptory challenges to exclude jurors based on race).

[47] See J.E.B. v. Alabama *ex rel.* T.B., 511 U.S. 127, 129 (1994).

[48] See, *e.g.*, Purkett v. Elem, 514 U.S. 765, 769 (1995) (*per curiam*).

[49] On scientific jury selection, see generally Valerie P. Hans & Neil Vidmar, Judging the Jury 79–94 (1986).

favorable jurors. If true, jury trials might be reduced to contests to see whose social scientists are better at profiling favorable jurors. Fortunately for the jury system, such a scenario is unsupported by careful research. First, the overwhelming majority of decisions are dictated by the weight of the evidence rather than any trait of the jurors.[50] It is almost always the way the witnesses and proof sound that makes or breaks a case. Secondly, the most significant benefit to be derived from the use of jury consultants is not related to peremptories at all but to the pretrial rehearsal and critique such consultants provide for lawyers.[51] Thirdly, careful assessment of the link between demographic traits (age, sex, race, educational background, employment, etc.) and juror decisions suggests that, even under optimum conditions, jury selection will not be improved by more than 10 percent over traditional methods.[52]

Despite all this, great concern has been expressed about scientific jury selection, and, at least in one sense, that concern is justified. Such methods clearly rely on demographic stereotypes,[53] the very thing that has been condemned in some contexts by *Batson* and its progeny. Moreover, effective or not, such techniques give the impression that favorable juries can be bought,[54] as was suggested in the aftermath of the William Kennedy Smith rape trial. It remains to be seen whether any restrictions should be imposed on the use of jury consultants.

VI. Trying Civil Cases

Pennzoil's lawsuit against Texaco resulted in a seventeen-week trial with thirty-five witnesses and a great deal of highly technical expert testimony.[55] It was, by virtually any measure, a complex case. Many critics of the civil jury have suggested that one of the jobs it cannot satisfactorily perform is the resolution of such complicated matters. It may be all well and good for the jury to resolve simple disputes, so the argument goes, but it is a serious mistake to let a group of laymen decide the fate of giant corporations or ponder weeks of esoteric expert testimony. In *Pennzoil*, there was a chorus of complaints of exactly this sort when the

[50] See SAUL M. KASSIN & LAWRENCE S. WRIGHTSMAN, THE AMERICAN JURY ON TRIAL: PSYCHOLOGICAL PERSPECTIVES 61 (1988).

[51] See Ross P. Laguzza, *Voodoo Jurynomics*, L.A. DAILY J., Apr. 9, 1997, at 6.

[52] See Reid Hastie, *Is Attorney-Conducted Voir Dire an Effective Procedure for the Selection of Impartial Juries?*, 40 AM. U. L. REV. 703, 719–20 (1991).

[53] See ABRAMSON, *supra* note 15, at 146–7.

[54] See ibid., at 149.

[55] With respect to details of the *Pennzoil* litigation, see generally PETZINGER, *supra* note 5.

jury's $10.5 billion award was announced. What few of the critics noted was the fact that Texaco offered no evidence on damages and did not in any way help the jury assess the punitive question. Whatever one thinks of the *Pennzoil* decision, the case typifies the new breed of information-intensive, expert-populated, lengthy cases that critics suggest juries should never be allowed to decide.

Under the Seventh Amendment, most civil actions involving monetary claims filed in federal courts must be tried by a jury if either party so requests. However, at least one federal court of appeals has indicated that if a case is too complex, it is unfair, and a violation of the Fifth Amendment right to due process, to insist that a jury hear the matter.[56] This complexity exception to the right to jury trial in civil cases has not been reviewed by the Supreme Court, but at least one other federal circuit court has denied the existence of such an exception.[57]

The most significant problem with a complexity exception is that over the long run it is likely to swallow the jury trial right. Almost every substantial lawsuit will have something difficult or complicated in it. To bar the jury from such cases is to invite their ouster from all meaningful civil litigation. Moreover, a complexity exception fails to take into account the difficulties a lone judge may have in dealing with a complex case. There is little basis for assuming that the judge will be any more effective than a properly informed group of jurors. Professor Richard Lempert, a lawyer and sociologist, has made another telling point about complexity:

> A close look at a number of cases, including several in which jury verdicts appear mistaken, does not show juries that are befuddled by complexity. Even when juries do not fully understand technical issues, they can usually make enough sense of what is going on to deliberate rationally, and they usually reach defensible decisions. To the extent that juries make identifiable mistakes, their mistakes seem most often attributable not to conditions uniquely associated with complexity, but to the mistakes of judges and lawyers, to such systematic deficiencies of the trial process as battles of experts and the prevalence of hard-to-understand jury instructions, and to the kinds of human error that affect simple trials as well. The anecdotal evidence should also remind us that it is difficult to predict which complex cases will trouble juries and which they will handle well.[58]

In light of the Supreme Court's avoidance of the issue, it does not appear that entire trials are likely at the present time to be treated as too

[56] See *In re* Japanese Elec. Prod. Antitrust Litig., 631 F.2d 1069, 1086 (3d Cir. 1980).
[57] See *In re* United States Fin. Sec. Litig., 609 F.2d 411, 432 (9th Cir. 1979).
[58] Richard Lempert, *Civil Juries and Complex Cases: Taking Stock After Twelve Years*, in VERDICT: ASSESSING THE CIVIL JURY SYSTEM 181, 234 (Robert E. Litan ed., 1993).

complex for jury adjudication; yet there is some indication that specific issues raised in certain cases may be kept from juries because of their complex nature. On the strength of such an assessment, the Supreme Court in *Markman* v. *Westview Instruments, Inc.*[59] unanimously concluded that in patent infringement cases the judge retains responsibility for construing the patent's language, despite a finding that the jury trial right is applicable.[60] This decision was based, in part, on a functional assessment that concluded 'judges . . . are better suited to find the acquired meaning of patent terms'.[61] Although the jury were left to decide the question of infringement, the Supreme Court's focus on judicial competence and juror limitations may signal future receptivity to the narrowing of jury responsibility in areas other than the language of patents.

Comparable attitudes may explain judicial reliance in difficult or complex cases on a procedure generally referred to as bifurcation (meaning a cutting into two pieces). Pursuant to this approach, exposure to certain issues in a case may be delayed until the jury has decided a number of preliminary questions. This sequenced approach to trial has been popular in cases concerning such questions as exposure to toxic chemicals, involvement in a mass disaster, and injury from a potentially dangerous product. It has also frequently been considered in cases containing claims for punitive damages. In all these situations, bifurcation serves to screen the jury from arguably prejudicial information about the extent of a claimant's injury or the scope of a defendant's wrongdoing until preliminary questions like responsibility for manufacture or conformity to industry-wide standards have been answered.

It has been argued on bifurcation's behalf that it simplifies the jurors' task by placing one issue before them at a time and eliminating exposure to potentially biasing or confusing information until absolutely necessary to the resolution of that issue. Research suggests that while bifurcation is helpful in some situations, it is no panacea. It has been found to increase significantly the percentage of defendant victories.[62] Paradoxically, it has also been found to increase the likelihood of large punitive awards.[63]

[59] 517 U.S. 370 (1996). [60] See ibid., at 391. [61] Ibid., at 388.

[62] See Hans Zeisel & Thomas Callahan, *Split Trials and Time Saving: A Statistical Analysis*, 76 Harv. L. Rev. 1606, 1612 (1963).

[63] See Stephan Landsman *et al.*, *Be Careful What You Wish for: The Paradoxical Effects of Bifurcating Claims for Punitive Damages*, [1998] Wis. L. Rev. 297, 329–30 (finding large punitive damages in cases where a jury reaches the punitive issue after having decided against the defendant on the preliminary question of liability).

Juries are expected to decide the case presented to them on the strength of the evidence adduced by the contending parties. The introduction of evidence is regulated by a series of rules circumscribing the use of certain sorts of proof. The most important evidence restrictions require that only relevant materials be presented in court and that prejudicial materials be excluded.[64] The judge must serve as gatekeeper by deciding what is relevant and what is prejudicial. In the course of making those decisions, the judge is, of course, exposed to the challenged proofs. Preliminary psychological investigation suggests that the judge may, unwittingly, be biased by what she or he hears.[65] One of the values of the jury is that it will not, generally, be exposed to prejudicial material and, therefore, will be more likely to decide cases without the biases with which judges must contend. A famous study by legal scholars Harry Kalven, Jr., and Hans Zeisel concluded that judicial exposure to inadmissible prejudicial materials concerning criminal defendants' prior records clearly affected judges' judgments about guilt and innocence and led them to decide more cases against defendants than untainted juries did.[66]

Many of the rules of evidence operate on psychological assumptions about how jurors will react to various sorts and forms of proof. It is assumed by the rules that things like criminal records are powerfully biasing, both in criminal and civil litigation[67]—leading juries to decide against those who have been previously convicted.[68] This assumption has been borne out in a variety of experiments.[69] Another assumption made by the rules is that hearsay (the in-court use of material from a person not available for cross-examination) will be overvalued by jurors. For this reason, among others, hearsay is usually barred from being introduced. However, experimental testing suggests that this assumption may not be warranted and that jurors instinctively tend to discount hearsay materials.[70] Be that as it may, American courts tend to shield jurors from this form of proof.

[64] See FED. R. EVID. 401, 403 & advisory committee note.

[65] See Stephan Landsman & Richard F. Rakos, *A Preliminary Inquiry into the Effect of Potentially Biasing Information on Judges and Jurors in Civil Litigation*, 12 BEHAV. SCI. & L. 113, 125 (1994).

[66] See HARRY KALVEN JR. & HANS ZEISEL, THE AMERICAN JURY 121–33 (1966).

[67] See FED. R. EVID. 609 (allowing court to admit evidence of a conviction only if it determines that its probative value outweighs its prejudicial effect).

[68] See ibid., advisory committee note.

[69] See, *e.g.*, Roselle L. Wissler & Michael J. Saks, *On the Inefficiency of Limiting Instructions: When Jurors Use Prior Conviction Evidence to Decide on Guilt*, 9 LAW & HUM. BEHAV. 37 (1985).

[70] See Richard Rakos & Stephan Landsman, *Researching the Hearsay Rule: Emerging Findings, General Issues, and Future Directions*, 76 MINN. L. REV. 655 (1992).

For much of the last century, it was felt that members of the jury panel should remain absolutely passive during the trial of a case.[71] Pursuant to this view, it was believed that jurors should be allowed neither to take notes nor to ask questions. Furthermore, they were strictly prohibited from discussing the case before the evidentiary presentation was concluded. These precepts consigned jurors to almost total inactivity, increasing the risks of inattention and disengagement.

Recently, there has been a substantial shift in thinking about juror passivity. A number of judges and scholars have attacked the idea and have suggested that jurors should be encouraged to participate more actively in the trial process. To this end, many courts have embraced juror note-taking.[72] In addition, some courts have adopted a somewhat more controversial step by allowing jurors to present judges with written questions that the judges may screen and ask if appropriate.[73] This is more controversial because of the risks that jurors may come to see themselves as advocates or seek answers to improper or prejudicial questions.[74] Both these techniques have been adopted in an effort to engage jurors more fully in the trial of the case they are to decide.[75] Perhaps the most radical proposal along these lines is to allow jurors to discuss the lawsuit while it is in the process of being tried. The risks here—premature decision, loss of neutrality, and heightened inter-juror conflict—are serious; nevertheless, some courts have begun experiments to determine the usefulness of such discussions.[76] It would appear that America is moving toward a new jury concept, one based on the active engagement of jurors in the cases they hear.

It should be noted, however, that there are countervailing trends in the law regulating juror conduct. Some recent legislation has attempted to blindfold jurors by depriving them of a number of critical pieces of information as they hear and decide cases. The Illinois legislature, for example, has sought to hide from jurors the fact that a plaintiff in a tort case will be barred from all recovery if he or she is found more than 50 percent responsible for the accident in question as well as the fact that there are legal ceilings on noneconomic and punitive damages.[77]

[71] For a careful examination of the issues of note-taking and question-asking, see Larry Heuer & Steven Penrod, *Juror Note Taking and Question Asking During Trials*, 18 Law & Hum. Behav. 121 (1994).

[72] See Jury Trial Innovations, *supra* note 39, § V–6 (juror note-taking).

[73] See ibid., § V–7 (juror questions to witnesses).

[74] See ibid.

[75] See ibid., at 142, 145.

[76] See ibid., § V–5 (juror discussions of evidence during the trial).

[77] See 735 Ill. Comp. Stat. 5/2–1107.1 (West 1992).

Additionally, the United States Court of Appeals for the Fifth Circuit has held that juries should not be informed of the rule that damages awards in civil antitrust cases under the Clayton Act will be trebled.[78] These and similar blindfolding exercises seek to keep the consequences of their decisions from jurors, apparently on the assumption that doing so will help to control or steer those decisions. Such an assumption conceptualizes jurors as passive sponges, who will 'soak up' only what they are permitted and then 'squeeze' out a decision. Such an image is deeply flawed and often yields skewed and unsatisfactory results distorted by juror speculation about embargoed information concerning legal consequences. Dr Shari Diamond and Professor Jonathan Casper have studied blindfolding and concluded: '[w]hen jurors are taken seriously and efforts are made to deal with their concerns and expectations, that is, when they are treated as active co-participants rather than passive sponges, they appear to be willing and able to respond more appropriately to the dictates of legal rules'.[79]

VII. Instructions to the Jury at the End of the Case

Once all the evidence has been presented, it is the judge's job to inform the jury of the law to be used in deciding the case. Depending on the practice of the locality, the judge may do this either before or after the lawyers have been given an opportunity to make their closing arguments; traditionally, instructions come last.[80] In the federal courts, since at least 1895 and probably a good bit earlier, it has been insisted that it is the jury's duty in a criminal case 'to take the law from the court, and apply that law to the facts as they find them to be from the evidence'.[81] This view is clearly at odds with the proposition that the jury may reject or 'nullify' the law. The question of nullification is explored in another chapter.[82]

In most cases, the judge's legal instructions are drawn from previously drafted models.[83] Quite often, these models are produced by officially

[78] See Clayton Act § 4, 15 U.S.C. § 15 (1994); Pollock & Riley, Inc. v. Pearl Brewing Co., 498 F.2d 1240, 1242 (5th Cir. 1974); see also Shari Seidman Diamond & Jonathan D. Caspor, *Blindfolding the Jury to Verdict Consequences: Damages, Experts, and the Civil Jury*, 26 L. & Soc'y Rev. 513, 517–18 (1992).

[79] Diamond & Caspor, *supra* note 78, at 558.

[80] See Jury Trial Innovations, *supra* note 39, at 161.

[81] Sparf v. United States, 156 U.S. 51, 102 (1895).

[82] See Nancy Jean King, *The American Criminal Jury*, this vol.

[83] On the question of jury instructions, see Hans & Vidmar, *supra* note 49, at 120–7.

constituted groups of lawyers, judges, and legal scholars whose primary goal is to reflect as accurately and fully as possible the current state of the law. What these so-called pattern instructions have generally lacked is concision and plain English. They tend to be long, repetitive, and filled with legal jargon. It has generally been thought more important that instructions be complete than comprehensible.

Unfortunately, but not surprisingly, such attitudes have produced instructions that are difficult for jurors to understand. In an archival study of 400 cases from the State of Washington, it was discovered that about one quarter of all juries halted their deliberations to request judicial clarification of one or more instructions.[84] It should be noted that in virtually all these cases the courts refused to elaborate on the original instructions provided.[85] Experimental work regarding the comprehensibility of instructions has found that jurors frequently fail to understand what instructions are saying.[86]

In light of such findings, a number of lawyers and scholars have asked what steps might be taken to improve juror understanding of instructions. Several quite simple steps that have been proposed have focused on the timing of the delivery of instructions and the format of their presentation.[87] As things now stand, jurors are usually given instructions only once—after all the evidence has been heard and the lawyers have made their closing arguments. This arrangement keeps jurors in the dark about the law throughout the case and allows them only a single chance to learn about its requirements. If relevant instructions were given at the start of the case or before final arguments, jurors would be afforded extra opportunities to consider the law's import and apply it to the facts. Moreover, lawyers would have a clearer picture of the law being presented to the jury and could more effectively tailor their proof and remarks to the legal principles laid down. On the question of format, it was traditionally believed that the proper way to instruct a jury was by means of a single oral recitation of the law. Jurors were not given a copy of the instructions but were expected to reconstruct the law from memory. Recent practice has moved away from this approach by providing jurors

[84] See Laurence J. Severance & Elizabeth F. Loftus, *Improving the Ability of Jurors to Comprehend and Apply Criminal Jury Instructions*, 17 L. & Soc'y Rev. 153, 172 (1982).

[85] See ibid.

[86] See Amiram Elwork *et al.*, Making Jury Instructions Understandable 12 (1982); Robert P. Charrow & Veda R. Charrow, *Making Legal Language Understandable: A Psycholinguistic Study of Jury Instructions*, 79 Colum. L. Rev. 1306, 1358 (1979).

[87] On the question of the improvement of jury instructions, see Jury Trial Innovations, *supra* note 39, §§ VI–1 to VI–11.

with a written copy of instructions. The supplying of written copies (or, in some cases, tape recordings) facilitates jury review during deliberations, enhances the accuracy of recollection of legal requirements, and focuses jurors on the precise legal questions to be resolved.

Beyond these simple steps, a number of reformers have set about the task of rewriting a vast array of legal instructions in plain English. It has been the hope of the drafters that the rewritten instructions will more effectively communicate the law's goals and requirements. Judges have not been particularly receptive to rewritten instructions.[88] As one group of commentators has put it: '[i]t is as if the courts prefer not to communicate clearly to their juries'.[89]

While, at first blush, this may seem an absurd attitude, there are several considerations that may help us understand it. First, the present pattern instructions have been carefully vetted and accepted by appellate courts. If they are used, there is little danger of appellate reversal. The same may not be true of plain English replacements. Until such time as the substitutes are officially endorsed, they remain a legally risky choice. Secondly, and perhaps more importantly, the present instructions often represent a compromise about difficult legal questions, granting each contending interest some part of its objective. This fine balance of interests is likely to be undone by plain English instructions. Indeed, research suggests that changing the wording of instructions often has a profound impact on the percentages of plaintiff and defendant victories.[90] If outcomes are likely to be affected, then redrafting is a far from neutral exercise and poses serious social and political questions.

VIII. Verdict Forms and Special Verdicts

Along with its instructions, a court may specify what sort, or form, of verdict a jury must reach in order to resolve a civil case. There are, essentially, three forms of verdict possible: a general verdict, a general verdict with interrogatories, and a special verdict. The most frequently used form is the general verdict, which leaves all questions about the legal and factual merits in the jurors' hands. It asks the jury only to declare which side has prevailed and fix damages, if appropriate. This form cedes the

[88] See Kassin & Wrightsman, *supra* note 50, at 152. [89] Ibid.

[90] See generally Michael J. Saks, *Judicial Nullification*, 68 Ind. L.J. 1281 (1993); Walter W. Steele, Jr. & Elizabeth G. Thornburg, *Jury Instructions: A Persistent Failure to Communicate*, 67 N.C. L. Rev. 77 (1988).

jury maximum authority. Jurors do not have to explain or justify their decision in any way.

General verdicts with interrogatories take a significant step away from jury control toward judicial management and oversight. The jury is still asked to deliver a verdict but is also required to answer a series of supplemental questions. These questions focus on the factual underpinnings of the verdict and require the jurors to specify a number of their factual conclusions. The jury's responses allow the court to scrutinize the soundness of the panel's reasoning. If the interrogatory answers are consistent with the verdict rendered, then the judgment is fully validated.[91] If the verdict is inconsistent with the interrogatories but the interrogatories are internally consistent, the court may enter a verdict on the interrogatories, ask the jury to deliberate further, or order a new trial. When the interrogatories are internally inconsistent, the jury may be asked to deliberate further or a new trial may be required. The point of the exercise is to make sure that the jurors have understood the case and rationally integrated facts and law. The general verdict with interrogatories is viewed as particularly useful in complex cases.

The special verdict is a device which shifts even more responsibility to the court. When used, it requires that jurors answer a series of special questions about the facts of a case. The court then uses these answers to determine the legal outcome. The special verdict removes the jury's ultimate decision-making power. This restrictive device, obviously, raises serious questions about respect for the civil jury as an adjudicatory body.

IX. Jury Decisions—Unanimous or Not?

By the fourteenth century, if not before, it was agreed that jury verdicts should be unanimous—that all jurors should agree on a decision or the case should be retried. This proposition was specifically embraced by the United States Supreme Court in 1897 in *American Publishing Co.* v. *Fisher.*[92] *American Publishing* stood until 1972, when, in reviewing a pair of state criminal decisions, the Supreme Court held that less than unanimous verdicts are constitutionally permissible.[93] In *Apodaca* v. *Oregon,*[94] the Court upheld an eleven-to-one verdict in an assault with a deadly weapon case,[95] while in *Johnson* v. *Louisiana,*[96] a nine-to-three conviction

[91] See Fed. R. Civ. P. 49(b). [92] 166 U.S. 464 (1897).

[93] See Apodaca v. Oregon, 406 U.S. 404 (1972); Johnson v. Louisiana, 406 U.S. 356 (1972).

[94] 406 U.S. 404 (1972). [95] See ibid., at 406. [96] 406 U.S. 356 (1972).

regarding a robbery charge was accepted.[97] As had been the case in its jury size decisions, the Supreme Court attributed the most narrowly circumscribed functions to the jury—claiming that the criminal jury does little more than serve as a counterbalance to the exercise of official power by the government. As the Supreme Court saw it, the size of the jury majority has little to do with containing government overreaching. The court also argued that unanimity is another historical accident that can be disposed of in the name of efficiency, the efficiency here being the avoidance of hung juries, at least down to the nine-to-three level.

Today, more than thirty states permit nonunanimous verdicts in civil cases.[98] Interestingly, only two, Oregon and Louisiana, allow such decisions in felony prosecutions. Due to an anomaly regarding interpretation of the Seventh Amendment, federal courts are still required to seek unanimous verdicts in civil cases.

One of the first questions that comes to mind about the nonunanimity rule is whether there is any limit whatsoever on how small the majority must be to satisfy constitutional constraints. In criminal matters, the Supreme Court has provided at least a partial answer. In *Burch* v. *Louisiana*,[99] the Court held that conviction by a vote of five to one is unacceptable because it yields fewer than six votes for conviction, thereby, arguably, offending the six-person jury rule articulated in *Ballew* v. *Georgia*.[100] Still unanswered are questions about the validity of votes like eight to four and seven to five. These numerical questions point up the absence of any principled rationale for the Supreme Court's preference, since it appears to rely on neither historical tradition nor authoritative empirical assessment.

In fact, the empirical data on nonunanimous juries suggest that such juries do not function as well as their unanimous counterparts. Reid Hastie and his colleagues, in a book-length study published by the Harvard University Press, detailed a series of alarming findings about nonunanimous juries.[101] First, they discovered that majority rule juries virtually always cease serious deliberations once they have reached the required majority for decision.[102] Moreover, the smaller the size of the required majority, the faster the deliberations.[103] For example, juries that

97 See ibid., at 358–9.

98 See Michael H. Glasser, Comment, *Letting the Supermajority Rule: Nonunanimous Jury Verdicts in Criminal Trials*, 24 Fla. St. U. L. Rev. 659, 671 (1997).

99 441 U.S. 130 (1979).

100 See ibid., at 138.

101 See Reid Hastie *et al.*, Inside the Jury (1983).

102 See ibid., at 95.

103 See ibid., at 60, 76.

needed only to reach an eight to four verdict in a particular mock case deliberated seventy-five minutes on average, while their unanimous-jury counterparts needed 138 minutes, and ten-to-two juries needed 103 minutes.[104] Perhaps most troubling, majority rule juries felt significantly less certain about the correctness of their decisions and the winning majority tended to 'adopt a more forceful, bullying, persuasive style' of deliberating.[105]

What is lost under a nonunanimous rule, suggests Jeffrey Abramson, is respect for genuine and robust deliberations as well as a commitment to strive for real consensus.[106] The loss of all this undermines the deliberative ideal, thereby challenging the central purpose of the jury—to have the entire community meaningfully contribute to the search for justice in our courts. Under a majority rule regime, minority viewpoints and contributions may be marginalized or even disregarded altogether.

X. Postverdict Review

A jury's decision is subject to review both at the trial court level and on appeal. After a verdict has been returned, the losing party may ask the trial judge for any one of a number of different forms of relief. The process of trial court review has its roots in eighteenth century common law procedure and was well established by the time the United States Constitution was adopted, thereby bringing such review into conformity with the Seventh Amendment's requirement that facts tried by a jury not be 'otherwise re-examined [except] according to the rules of the common law'.[107]

The primary sort of relief available for a fatally flawed jury decision is a new trial of the case before a new jury.[108] This may be ordered if the trial judge feels she or he has committed a serious error with respect to such matters as jury instructions or the application of the rules of evidence. Alternatively, a judge may grant a new trial if jurors may be shown to have seriously misbehaved, for example, by considering evidence not presented at trial. Finally, the trial court may grant a new trial if the verdict is against 'the clear weight of the evidence'.[109] This last

[104] See Reid Hastie *et al.*, Inside the Jury (1983), at 60. [105] Ibid., at 112.

[106] See Abramson, *supra* note 15, at 183. [107] U.S. Const. amend. VII.

[108] See Fleming James, Jr. *et al.*, Civil Procedure 382 (4th ed. 1992). Much of the following discussion is based upon this text.

[109] Ibid., at 393 (quoting Aetna Cas. & Sur. Co. v. Yeatts, 122 F.2d. 350, 352–3 (4th Cir. 1941)).

ground is generally said to be available only when the original decision is manifestly unjust. A new trial may not be ordered simply because a judge disagrees with the jury's assessment of the credibility of a witness or the weight of the evidence; instead, it must be dictated by the overwhelming weight of all the proof taken together.

The reviewing judge may use several alternative procedures rather than requiring a new trial. She or he may grant judgment to the losing party (called a judgment notwithstanding the verdict) if such a result is the only one rationally possible. Alternatively, the judge may insist that a new trial be held unless the plaintiff accepts a reduction in the damages award (*remittitur*) or, in rare cases, the defendant agrees to an increase in the award (*additur*).

Despite this impressive array of possible responses to jury error, trial courts are expected to respect jury decisions. The case law regarding review stresses the latitude a jury has in assessing the believability of the witnesses and persuasiveness of the proof. Inquiring into the mental processes of jurors after the rendering of a verdict is prohibited.[110] The rules regarding appellate court reversal are even more circumscribed. When an appellate court reviews a jury's decision about the facts of a case, it is limited to asking whether 'the jury "might reasonably" have found as it did'.[111] If there is some basis for the jury's choice, it must be upheld.

XI. Conclusion

The American civil jury is vested with enormous power and responsibility. Its authority touches virtually all sorts of civil disputes. Despite substantial modification of a number of jury mechanisms over the past several decades, the jury still occupies the exalted place originally envisioned for it in the Seventh Amendment. When the likes of Texaco and Pennzoil prepare for legal combat, it is likely they will be required to make their case before a group of ordinary citizens called away from their normal tasks to decide the most momentous questions of the day.

[110] See FED. R. EVID. 606(b).

[111] JAMES *ET AL.*, *supra* note 108, at 669.

12 'Guardian of Civil Rights . . . Medieval Relic': The Civil Jury in Canada

W. A. Bogart*

I. Introduction

The civil jury in Canada dangles on a shoestring despite the fact that the available evidence indicates that it enjoys broad public support.[1] It exists in some jurisdictions in little more than name only, while in a few jurisdictions it has been abolished outright. However, in Ontario, the largest province, civil juries appear to be used more than in other provinces. In fact, there was strong reaction when the Ontario Law Reform Commission ('OLRC') suggested in a recent Study Paper[2] that civil juries be drastically curtailed. As a result, the OLRC reversed itself and actually recommended expanding the use of lay decision-makers.[3] Nevertheless, juries in civil matters still exist only at the periphery, playing nowhere near the central role in administering justice that their counterparts do in the United States.[4] This chapter offers some explanations of why Canadian civil juries exist only at the margins by examining the availability of civil juries, empirical evidence regarding their use and cost in Ontario (the only province for which such information exists on a systematic basis), and academic and policy debates concerning their role.

* Professor of Law, University of Windsor, Ontario, Canada. My thanks go to Vishva Ramlall for painstaking research assistance, and to Linda Bertoldi and Justice Thomas Granger, Regional Senior Justice, Ontario Court of Justice, for very helpful comments.

1 See *infra* section III.C.

2 Ontario Law Reform Comm'n, Consultation Paper on the Use of Jury Trials in Civil Cases (1994) (hereinafter OLRC, Study Paper).

3 See Ontario Law Reform Comm'n, Report on the Use of Jury Trials in Civil Cases (1996) (hereinafter OLRC, Report).

4 In contrast, the jury plays a vital role in the administration of criminal justice in Canada. The right to a jury in a criminal trial (where the maximum punishment is five years or more) is constitutionally protected in the Charter of Rights and Freedoms (an entrenched bill of rights) enacted 15 years ago. See Can. Const. (Constitution Act, 1982) pt. I (Canadian Charter of Rights and Freedoms), § 11(f).

II. The Availability of Civil Juries in Canada

A. A Brief History of Civil Juries

Canada had imported the institution of civil juries from England before confederation in 1867. Initially, at least in Ontario, juries were mandatory in civil trials. Their obligatory use was seen as a safeguard against the domination of the courts by the merchant classes and served as a bulwark against threats to fundamental freedoms.[5]

Unfortunately, civil juries in Ontario suffered from abuses that limited their effectiveness. Sheriffs had absolute control in composing juror rolls, which led to frequent allegations of corruption and 'packing' to favour the interests of those in the Sheriff's office.[6] After decades of such charges, Ontario adopted a comprehensive statutory reform of the jury system in 1850.[7] However, in 1868, the presumption that civil trials were to be tried by a jury was reversed by passage of the Law Reform Act of 1868:[8] subject to a few exceptions, civil actions were to be tried by a judge unless one of the parties requested trial by jury.[9]

After the implementation of much-needed reform, criticisms of civil juries, once well-founded, were transformed into attacks on the institution itself. Opponents of the civil jury argued that trial by jury was too costly and time consuming, and they questioned the ability of lay people to grapple successfully with complicated legal and factual issues.[10] As a result, the use of civil juries was drastically curtailed. Thus was established a tone of judgment from which the Canadian civil jury has never fully recovered: '[i]ts reputed age-old role as guardian of civil rights and liberties was forgotten; suddenly it was a medieval relic, costly and inefficient, which continued to clog the machinery of justice only through the inertia of public will'.[11]

B. Conditions for Civil Trial by Jury

Despite its tumultuous history, the civil jury is still available in Canada. However, its availability varies among the Canadian jurisdictions. Even

[5] See OLRC, Report, *supra* note 3, at 5–6.

[6] See Paul Romney, *From Constitutionalism to Legalism: Trial by Jury, Responsible Government, and the Rule of Law in the Canadian Political Culture*, 7 L. & Hist. Rev. 121, 130 (1989).

[7] See OLRC, Report, *supra* note 3, at 5–6.

[8] Law Reform Act of 1868, ch. 6, § 18(1), 1868–69 S.O. 18, 25 (Ont.).

[9] See ibid.

[10] See OLRC, Report, *supra* note 3, at 26–9.

[11] Ibid., at 6 (quoting Romney, *supra* note 6, at 138).

those provinces that most widely encourage the use of juries still impose substantial conditions on their employment.

At one end of the spectrum are Quebec[12] and the Federal Court of Canada,[13] both of which unqualifiedly prohibit civil juries. Occupying the middle ground are provinces such as Alberta[14] and Saskatchewan,[15] where civil juries are available for certain types of claims. Generally, juries are available in cases in which the amount in controversy exceeds $10,000. In Alberta, for example, such claims are limited to those in tort and those for the recovery of property valued in excess of $10,000.[16] In addition, in Saskatchewan, a jury may be ordered where '(a) the ends of justice will be best served if findings of fact are made by representatives of the community; or (b) the outcome of the litigation is likely to affect a significant number of persons who are not party to the proceedings'.[17] Finally, at the other end of the spectrum are provinces like British Columbia[18] and Ontario.[19] Although jury trials are available there for certain kinds of actions, the list of excluded actions is significant and includes claims for equitable relief and claims against the crown and municipalities.[20]

C. *Judicial Attitudes Toward the Civil Jury*

As seen above, the role of the civil jury, at minimum, is subject to significant limitations in all Canadian jurisdictions. This tenuous hold is partially attributable to hostile judicial attitudes. Except for the limited instances where juries are mandatory, judges retain discretion to conduct a trial without a jury. In addition, judges retain power to intervene in juries' verdicts. Examining cases where these powers have been invoked provides insight into the courts' understanding of the decision-making capacity of lay jurors and reveals that Canadian judges are at best ambivalent toward civil juries.

[12] See Jurors Act, ch. 9, § 56, 1976 S.Q. 59, 68 (Que.).

[13] See Federal Courts Act, R.S.C., ch. F-7, § 49 (1985) (Can.).

[14] See Jury Act, ch. J-2.1, § 16, 1982 S.A. 37, 44 (Alta.); Alberta Rules of Court 234, 235.

[15] See Jury Act, ch. J-4.1, §§ 14–22, 1980–81 S.S. 53, 57–9 (Sask.); Queen's Bench Rules of Sask. 196.

[16] See *supra* note 14.

[17] Jury Act, ch. J-4.1, § 17(1), 1980–81 S.S. 55, 58 (Sask.).

[18] See Jury Act, R.S.B.C., ch. 210, §§ 13–21 (1979) (B.C.); Supreme Court Act, ch. 40, § 15, 1989 S.B.C. 327, 330 (B.C.); Supreme Court Rules 39(24)–(30) (B.C.).

[19] See Courts of Justice Act, R.S.O., ch. C.43, § 108 (1990) (Ont.); Rules of Civil Procedure 47 (Ont.).

[20] See *supra* notes 18, 19.

Canadian judges and justices have long saluted the importance of the civil jury, characterizing trial by civil jury as a 'substantive right' not to be taken away except for 'cogent reasons'.[21] Nevertheless, courts retain the ability to strike civil juries.[22] In all provinces, a party may move to have a jury notice struck out,[23] and the judge may rule on the motion as an exercise of his or her discretion. The most frequently cited ground for eliminating the jury in a civil case is the undue complexity of the factual issues to be decided.[24] Less frequently, the judge eliminates the jury because of the potential for prejudice to a party arising from the determination of issues by laypersons.[25] Furthermore, judges have developed specific guidelines, almost all of which militate against juries and favour striking their use in certain circumstances.[26] Although most of these strictures have been removed or significantly loosened in the last two decades, courts in some provinces are inclined to make findings of complexity that result in juries being eliminated relatively easily.

Traditionally, courts restricted the use of juries in civil cases to guard against a jury becoming overwhelmed by 'complexity' in cases involving complicated issues of law, medical malpractice actions, and in cases where the jury might discover that the defendant had insurance that would apply toward any adverse judgment. Recently, however, these categorical bars on the use of civil juries have been eliminated.

The first categorical bar previously recognized by Canadian courts occurred when the case involved complex legal issues. Although questions of law are left to judges, courts, particularly those in Ontario, have held that the presence of complicated issues of law in a case swamped the issues of fact, thus rendering the action inappropriate for determi-

[21] *King* v. *Colonial Homes Ltd.* [1956] S.C.R. 528, 533 (Can.); *Such* v. *Dominion Stores Ltd.* [1961] O.R. 190, 193 (Ont. C.A.).

[22] See, *e.g.*, Jury Act, ch. J-2.1, § 16(2), 1982 S.A. 37, 44 (Alta.).

[23] See, *e.g.*, Rules of Civil Procedure 47.02 (Ont.).

[24] This is underscored by legislation in some provinces. See, *e.g.*, Supreme Court Rules 39(27) (B.C.) (permitting the Court to strike out a civil jury where the issues require prolonged examination, scientific investigation, or are of 'an intricate or complex character').

[25] See generally Garry D. Watson & Craig Perkins, Holmested and Watson: Ontario Civil Procedure, vol. 3, 47 §§ 12–14, at 47–24 to 47–27 (Oct. 1997).

[26] In contrast, courts are disinclined to strictly review the means by which juries are selected. See *Hrup* v. *Cipollone* (1994) 19 O.R.3d 715, 723 (Ont. C.A.) (holding that failure to follow statutory stipulations for peremptory challenges is not a miscarriage of justice); *Thomas-Robinson* v. *Song* (1997) 34 O.R.3d 62 (Ont. Gen. Div.) (holding that the right to challenge potential jurors for cause, whether for racial bias or otherwise, does not exist in civil cases).

nation by a jury.[27] However, appellate courts in Ontario recently have reasoned that because only judges decide legal questions, the complexity of the legal issues in an action are irrelevant to the appropriateness of trial by jury.[28]

Another categorical bar to the use of the civil jury occurred in medical malpractice cases. Courts were reluctant to allow the use of juries in these cases because of the perception that the factual issues were too complex and that the risk of prejudice against doctors was too great.[29] By the 1970s, reservations expressed by Ontario courts about the use of juries to determine issues of negligence in medical malpractice cases led to their prohibition.[30] This prohibition was not based on any evidence suggesting that juries favoured plaintiffs in such cases or that juries are incapable of understanding factual issues in medical cases.[31] But in the 1980s, Ontario courts dropped the strict rule against civil juries in such cases, although they retained the power to eliminate juries in specific cases deemed too complex or involving the potential for prejudice.[32]

A final categorical bar recognized by Canadian courts occurred when the jury 'might reasonably infer' that the defendant was insured against a finding of liability. In such cases, the Supreme Court held that the panel must be released.[33] The Court reasoned that jurors would be more likely to find liability if they knew that an insurer would pay any judgment against the defendant.[34] Although such reasoning may have been sound decades ago, compulsory automobile insurance and the prevalence of liability coverage in other areas calls into question an automatic assumption of prejudice so severe as to require the removal of the case

27 See *MacDougall* v. *Midland Doherty Ltd.* [1984] 48 O.R.2d 603, 606 (Ont. H.C.J.); *Fulton* v. *Town of Fort Erie* (1982) 40 O.R.2d 235, 237 (Ont. H.C.J.); *Damien* v. *O'Mulvenny* (1981) 34 O.R.2d 448, 451 (Ont. H.C.J.).

28 See *Cosford* v. *Cornwall* [1992] 9 O.R.3d 37, 48 (Ont. C.A.); *Murray* v. *Collegiate Sports Ltd.* (1989) 40 C.P.C.2d 1, 3 (Ont. C.A.).

29 See *Law* v. *Woolford* [1976] 2 C.P.C. 197 (Ont. H.C.J.); *Kingbury* v. *Washington* [1925] 4 D.L.R. 632 (Man. C.A.). While the position in other provinces varied, only Alberta seemed to approach Ontario's hostility toward the use of juries in medical malpractice litigation. For a discussion of the various positions, see W. A. Bogart, *The Use of Civil Juries in Medical Malpractice Cases*, in Studies in Civil Procedure 1, 5–9 (Eric Gertner ed., 1979).

30 See *Law* [1976] 2 C.P.C. at 197.

31 See Bogart, *supra* note 29, at 9–14.

32 See *Strojny* v. *Chan* (1988) 26 C.P.C.2d 38 (Ont. H.C.J.); *Anderson* v. *Wilgress* (1985) 6 C.P.C.2d 172 (Ont. H.C.J.); *Zeller* v. *Toronto Gen. Hosp.* (1984) 45 C.P.C. 221 (Ont. H.C.J.); *Soldwisch* v. *Toronto W. Hosp.* (1983) 43 O.R.2d 449 (Ont. H.C.J.); *Archibald* v. *Dixon* (1981) 24 C.P.C. 235 (Ont. H.C.J); *Lalonde* v. *Sudbury Gen. Hosp. of the Immaculate Heart of Mary* (1980) 19 C.P.C. 147 (Ont. Dist. Ct.).

33 See *Bowhey* v. *Theakston* [1951] S.C.R. 679, 683 (Can.).

34 See ibid.

from the jury. Indeed, in the face of silence concerning such matters, juries might well assume that the defendant is insured.[35] As a result, many lower courts have found ways around automatically releasing juries just because they had acquired information from which they 'might reasonably infer' that insurance coverage played a role in the case.[36] In 1997, the Supreme Court put its imprimatur upon such efforts and abolished the rule.[37] Judges may now exercise discretion in determining whether to release a jury which has come to know that the defendant carries insurance that would cover any judgment against him or her.[38] Although such discretion is entirely defensible given the modern reality of ubiquitous insurance coverage, the prohibition against the mention of insurance continues to prevail in the United States.[39]

Though these strictures against the use of juries have been eliminated or drastically modified, the authority to strike out a jury on the grounds of the complexity of the issues or potential prejudice to one of the parties continues. Courts employ this discretion to strike juries in many debatable circumstances.[40] Nevertheless, courts of some provinces are more inclined to exercise this discretion to strike a jury demand than others. Alberta, where civil jury trials are rare, stands out. A search of cases decided in Alberta in the 1990s reveals four judgments in which the application for a jury was denied on the ground of complexity, which is a significant number given the otherwise few cases in which there is a jury.[41]

Furthermore, courts retain the authority to interfere with the judgment of a jury once it has reached its verdict.[42] Yet, in contrast to the

[35] The Supreme Court's rule was widely criticized. See, *e.g.*, John Sopinka, The Trial of an Action 31–2 (1981).

[36] See *Cameron* v. *Excelsior Life Ins. Co.* (1978) 27 N.S.R.2d 218 (N.S.S.C.T.D.); *Morin* v. *Rochon* (1983) 42 O.R.2d 301 (Ont. H.C.J.); *Alden* v. *Hutcheon* [1960] Q.L.R. 539 (Que. Q.B.).

[37] See *Hamstra* v. *British Columbia Rugby Union* [1997] 1 S.C.R. 1092, 1106 (Can.).

[38] See ibid.

[39] See McCormick on Evidence, vol. 1, § 201 (John W. Strong *et al.* eds., 4th ed. 1992), cited in *Hamstra* [1997] 1 S.C.R. at 1103.

[40] See *Babyn* v. *Patel* [1997] A.J. No. 261 (Alta. Q.B.) (striking jury because of difficult issues of causation and the likelihood of conflicting expert testimony); *Taguchi* v. *Stuparyk* [1993] A.J. No. 843 (Alta. Q.B.) (striking jury because the trial would involve lengthy examination of documents and actuarial reports as well as much conflicting expert testimony).

[41] See *Babyn* [1997] A.J. No. 261; *Sharma* v. *Smook* [1996] A.J. No. 22 (Alta. Q.B.); *Baker* v. *Suzuki Motor Co.* [1993] A.J. No. 240 (Alta. Q.B.); *Meyer* v. *Royal Bank of Canada* [1993] A.J. No. 705 (Alta. Q.B.); *Taguchi* [1993] A.J. No. 843. But see *Wilton* v. *Royal Bank* [1991] A.J. No. 770 (Alta. Q.B.).

[42] See *Malloch* v. *Moenke* [1996] B.C.J. No. 399 (B.C.C.A.); *Hill* v. *Church of Scientology* [1992] 7 O.R.3d 489, 498 (Ont. Gen. Div.); *Loffredi* v. *Simonetti* (1988) 29 C.P.C.2d 10, 15 (Ont. Dist. Ct.).

penchant of some courts to dispense with lay decision-makers, judges express substantial deference to juries once they have completed their task. Appellate courts consistently have held that it is only in limited circumstances—when there is no evidence to support the findings or the verdict cannot in law be a foundation for judgment—that the trial judge can disregard a jury's verdict.[43]

Moreover, the Ontario Court of Appeal seems disinclined to respond to even a legislative invitation to substitute its views for that of a civil jury. A recently enacted law empowers appellate courts to substitute their own assessment of damages on appeal in both jury and bench trials.[44] Nevertheless, the Ontario Court of Appeal has decided that, where the jury has awarded damages, the court will not interfere with the award unless there has been a 'wholly erroneous estimate of the damages'.[45]

D. Academic Attitudes Toward the Civil Jury

Another factor possibly explaining the (non)use of the civil jury is academic influence. Academic legal education in Canada, particularly in Ontario, is of comparatively recent origin. Until the 1950s, lawyers were largely educated as apprentices. One of the main architects of academic legal education was Cecil Wright, a tort scholar. Wright was adamantly opposed to civil juries, viewing them as ill-equipped to respond to the many theoretical and policy arguments essential to the development of tort law and policy.[46] Wright had tremendous influence and may have inculcated in several generations of lawyers a deep skepticism about the role, if any, that civil juries should play in the administration of civil justice.[47]

Another academic perspective, developed in the 1970s, came to view civil litigation as an ill-suited mechanism for providing compensation and effecting deterrence in most areas of torts.[48] Scholars in this school of

43 See cases cited *supra* note 42.

44 See Courts of Justice Act, R.S.O., ch. C.43, § 119 (1990) (Ont.) ('On an appeal from an award for damages for personal injury, the court may, if it considers it just, substitute its own assessment of the damages').

45 *Koukounakis* v. *Stainrod* (1995) 23 O.R.3d 299, 305 (Ont. C.A.).

46 See Edson L. Haines, *The Future of the Civil Jury*, in Studies in Canadian Tort Law 10, 10–11 (Allen M. Linden ed., 1968) (recounting Wright's hostility toward the civil jury).

47 See OLRC, Report, *supra* note 3; 2 Ontario, Royal Commission Inquiry into Civil Rights: Report Number One 859–60 (1968).

48 For a critical yet sympathetic evaluation (based on empirical studies) of this position, see Don Dewees *et al.*, Exploring the Domain of Accident Law: Taking the Facts Seriously (1996).

thought instead looked to the administrative state to provide redress, at least in the area of personal injuries.[49] For example, they advocated expanded versions of worker compensation programs, no-fault regimes for automobile accidents, and compensation for damages suffered as a result of medical treatment.[50] They were also largely unenthusiastic about civil juries, seeing them as inextricably linked to a system of tort adjudication that should, by and large, be abolished.[51] Some judges may agree with the view that juries are part of an outmoded system of compensation for personal injuries. In any event, judges might emphasize the burden on the judiciary in preparing what are contended to be long and intricate charges to civil juries.[52]

Whatever the merits of the stance taken by either Wright and his acolytes, on the one hand, or those advocating administrative regimes, on the other, these positions were highly influential in law and particularly legal policy-making. The civil jury for a very long time, especially in Ontario, thus had very few advocates among those in a position to recast the civil justice system.

III. Some Empirical Evidence: The Use and Cost of Civil Juries in Ontario

It is one thing to detail how the courts—or anyone else—believe civil juries should be employed. It is quite another to determine empirically the frequency with which they are used, in what category of cases, and at what cost. Research on the use of juries in most provinces is essentially educated guesswork. In some provinces, such as Manitoba, there were no civil jury trials for extensive periods of time.[53] In British Columbia, the frequency of use of the civil jury has been estimated at between 3 and 10 percent.[54] The OLRC tried to discover such facts, with regard to Ontario, in its recent report on the civil jury.[55] Due to the state of the

[49] See Don Dewees *et al.* (1996). [50] See ibid.

[51] See OLRC, Report, *supra* note 3. The Commission relied heavily on the advice of academics in coming to its recommendations in these studies. In addition, the leading casebook on civil procedure, Garry D. Watson *et al.*, Civil Litigation: Cases and Materials (4th ed. 1991), contains only a few scant references to civil juries. See, *e.g.*, ibid., at 280. Indeed, it is not an exaggeration to say that academics have ignored the civil jury, largely hoping it would go away.

[52] Letter from Justice B. T. Granger, Regional Senior Justice, Ontario Court of Justice (Feb. 23, 1998) (on file with author).

[53] See OLRC, Report, *supra* note 3, at 16–17. [54] See ibid.

[55] See ibid.

records used as the basis of this study, caution is required when examining its findings.[56] On the other hand, the OLRC report provides the only current, systematic attempt at assembling facts regarding the use of juries in any province.

A. The Use of Civil Jury Trials in Ontario

Although the use of civil juries in Ontario had been declining in recent decades, over the last several years their employment has increased by about 7 percent.[57] Specifically, civil jury trials have generally increased from 15 percent in 1988–89 to 22 percent in 1994–95.[58] Further breakdown of these figures indicates that approximately three-quarters of all civil jury trials involve claims arising from motor vehicle accidents.[59]

B. Expense of Civil Jury Trials in Ontario

There is a widely held perception that jury trials take longer and cost more than bench trials.[60] The accuracy of this view depends on whether the trial is concluded and how one determines the cost. The OLRC found that this perception is correct for those actions in which the trial is concluded.[61] It determined that the median length of trials determined by jury verdict exceeds by three-quarters of a day the median length of bench trials.[62] However, when cases that go to trial but settle before their

[56] The OLRC study indicates that justice system statistics in Canada, generally, and in Ontario, in particular, are not what they should be. See also RODERICK A. MACDONALD, STUDY PAPER ON CIVIL JUSTICE 20–3 (1995); W. A. Bogart *et al.*, *Current Utilization Patterns and Unmet Legal Needs*, in REPORT OF THE ONTARIO LEGAL AID REVIEW, A BLUEPRINT FOR PUBLICLY FUNDED LEGAL SERVICES, vol. 2, 316 (1997).

The researchers candidly acknowledge that they experienced significant difficulties, including establishing precisely how many jury trials actually took place in the last several years as opposed to actions in which a jury trial was scheduled but, for whatever reason, was not heard. See OLRC, REPORT, *supra* note 3, at 43–5.

[57] See ibid., at 8.

[58] See ibid., at 8–9. Statistics are last available for 1994–95.

[59] See ibid., at 9. This despite the fact that motor vehicle litigation in Ontario has declined in the last few years because of a move away from tort-based litigation to an administratively based 'no-fault' regime with exceptions for severe and permanent injuries. See INSURANCE BUREAU OF CANADA, FACTS OF THE GENERAL INSURANCE INDUSTRY IN CANADA 8–9 (1997); ALLAN O'DONNELL, AUTOMOBILE INSURANCE IN ONTARIO 229–50 (1991).

[60] See OLRC, REPORT, *supra* note 3, at 26–7.

[61] See ibid., at 54–5.

[62] See ibid.

conclusion are included, the average length of jury trials is less than that of bench trials.[63] This reflects the impact that juries have in promoting settlement: More jury cases settle prior to trial, and the jury cases that reach trial settle earlier than bench-trial cases that settle.[64]

With respect to the cost of a civil jury, the OLRC concluded that the jury is not as expensive as is widely thought.[65] There are several reasons why the jury might, in fact, be less costly. For example, the OLRC concluded that the administrative costs it identified and totaled were not substantial.[66] In addition, civil actions set to be tried by juries result in less courtroom time overall because of the higher rate of settlement and an apparently lower rate of appeal.[67]

C. *Experience of Jurors*

The OLRC found that citizens of Ontario generally approve of the use of the civil jury.[68] Perhaps of even greater importance, the study reports findings that actual jury service increases approval. The OLRC studied the experience of jurors by surveying former jurors and those who were part of civil jury panels but who did not actually serve.[69] Of those who had a favourable impression of the jury before serving, 40.2 percent had a more favourable impression after serving on a jury, while only 20.2 percent had a less favourable impression.[70] This finding apparently is consistent with an American study that found that 63 percent of jurors reported having a more favourable attitude to jury duty after serving.[71]

Respondents to the survey were also asked whether they thought the jury should be available for most civil trials, and whether they would seek a civil jury for an action in which they were a party. Most, 64.5 percent, were in favour of the continued availability of the jury for most civil actions.[72] For an action in which they were a party, 61.6 percent stated that they would prefer a judge and jury, 30 percent stated that they would select a judge alone, and 8.4 percent stated that their decision would depend on the particular case.[73]

63 See OLRC, Report, *supra* note 3, at 55.
64 See ibid., at 54–6.
65 See ibid., at 55.
66 See ibid., at 56.
67 See ibid., at 55–6.
68 See ibid., at 69.
69 See ibid., at 63–73.
70 See ibid., at 69.
71 See ibid., at 70 n. 52 (citing Shari Seidman Diamond, *What Jurors Think: Expectations and Reactions of Citizens Who Serve as Jurors*, in Verdict: Assessing the Civil Jury System 282 (Robert E. Litan ed., 1993)).
72 See ibid., at 71.
73 See ibid.

IV. Arguments About Civil Juries

The OLRC report on civil juries conveniently summarizes the perceived strengths and weaknesses of this institution.[74]

A. Arguments Favouring the Civil Jury

1. *Safeguard Against the Abuse of Power.* One reason identified by the OLRC as justifying the civil jury is that the jury is viewed as the bulwark against misuse of official power.[75] This notion finds its most robust expression in the institution of criminal juries. It also could be applied in civil matters in areas concerning misdirected activities of government. The difficulty, however, is that the use of juries often is forbidden in such matters. For example, in Ontario, lay decision-makers are statutorily precluded in actions against all levels of government: federal, provincial, and municipal.[76] Notably, the OLRC has recommended the removal of statutory proscriptions against the use of juries when governments are sued.[77]

Some proponents of the jury system have argued that juries are also a safeguard against abuse of power by protecting litigants from judicial bias.[78] The OLRC, however, found no evidence that litigants systematically believe that judges are biased.[79] On the other hand, the OLRC did find that some lawyers occasionally choose juries in order to avoid particular judges who they believe would not afford their client a good hearing.[80]

2. *Due Process, Community Standards, Law Reform.* Another reason identified by the OLRC as justification for the civil jury is that juries uphold the administration of justice by permitting the law to treat each case as unique while reflecting contemporary community standards.[81] This argument is particularly relevant in defamation and false arrest and imprisonment actions, because of the need to apply contemporary community standards in such cases. Others contend that this argument supports the use of juries in a wide range of cases because lay decision-makers are a strong protection against assembly-line justice.[82]

3. *The Jury as Catalyst.* A third reason justifying the use of the civil jury is that juries promote settlement and thereby save cost and time in

[74] See ibid., at 19–30. [75] See ibid., at 19. [76] See ibid., at 20.
[77] See ibid., at 82–3. [78] See ibid., at 20. [79] See ibid.
[80] See ibid. [81] See ibid. [82] See ibid., at 23.

the administration of justice.[83] As discussed earlier, the OLRC has found evidence supporting this conclusion.[84] However, doubters of lay decision-makers argue that these economies stem merely from the jury's unpredictability—litigants settle out of fear of the gyrations that take place in the jury room.[85]

4. *Competence.* A fourth reason cited by the OLRC as justification for juries is that group decision-making by juries is as good as or superior to solo decision-making by judges.[86] Psychological studies support this contention, particularly regarding credibility findings and damage assessments.[87] In addition, studies based on archival investigations and interviews with judges suggest that there is as much as an 80 percent overlap between what juries decide and what judges would have decided in the same cases.[88] Such studies, and the difficulty of establishing the 'correct' outcome in a disputed case, suggest that, at the least, it is difficult to disprove arguments that juries are as competent as judges at determining factual issues.

5. *Confidence in Fair Treatment.* Another reason cited by the OLRC as justification for juries is that a decision from representatives of the community is more likely to be accepted by the public than a decision from a judge alone.[89] For example, a survey of former jurors found that many prefer the decisionmaking of juries to that of judges.[90]

6. *Participation.* A sixth reason cited by the OLRC as justifying the civil jury is that jury duty provides citizens with an opportunity to participate in the administration of justice.[91] Such activity underscores a commitment to the fundamentals of society. Nevertheless, skeptics point out that only a small percentage of individuals actually serve on a jury.[92] Moreover, since juries are most often used in cases involving motor vehicle accidents, the beneficial effects of jury service are questionable. On the other hand, the very day-to-day nature of such cases may allow citizens to relate more easily to the justice system.

7. *Burden of Proof.* Finally, proponents of the civil jury insist that the public burden of persuasion is on those who would abolish it.[93] They cite two reasons for this contention. First, civil juries claim the protec-

[83] See OLRC, REPORT, *supra* note 3. [84] See *supra* section III.B.
[85] See OLRC, REPORT, *supra* note 3, at 23. [86] See ibid., at 23–4.
[87] See ibid., at 23 (citing CHARLES W. JOINER, CIVIL JUSTICE AND THE JURY (1962)).
[88] See ibid., at 24 (citing HARRY KALVEN JR. & HANS ZEISEL, THE AMERICAN JURY 58 (1966), and Harry Kalven Jr., *The Dignity of the Civil Jury*, 50 VA. L. REV. 1055, 1065–6 (1964)).
[89] See ibid. [90] See ibid., at 63–75. [91] See ibid., at 25–6.
[92] See ibid., at 25. [93] See ibid., at 26.

tion of a long history and tradition.[94] Secondly, contemporary values regarding society contain strong elements of both skepticism toward government and a claim of direct citizen participation.[95]

B. Arguments Against the Civil Jury

1. *Cost-benefit.* One reason cited by the OLRC for abolishing the civil jury is that any benefits that civil jury trials bestow are outweighed by their costs.[96] Jury trials are contended to be more lengthy and more expensive than bench trials. However, as discussed earlier,[97] the existing evidence throws this argument into question. Jury trials do not appear to be more time consuming, especially taking into account those actions which are settled during trial. Moreover, as also discussed earlier,[98] studies undertaken by the OLRC do not support the conclusion that jury trials cost more, or at least substantially more, than bench trials.[99]

2. *The Jury as Tactic.* Another reason suggested for abolishing the civil jury is that juries allow parties to gain an unfair tactical advantage.[100] Juries are sought by those with weak cases because they feel the unpredictability of jury outcomes will promote settlement or will allow some emotional appeal to succeed.[101] Institutional defendants, particularly insurance companies, select jury trials because juries in Canada award lower damages than do judges.[102]

Proponents of juries reply that, at a general level, there appears to be congruence between juries and judges;[103] juries are not any more unpredictable than judges in reality. Additionally, the mere fact that a rule gives one side a tactical advantage is not, in itself, a reason to abandon the rule—after all, the adversary system is premised on tactics. Finally, while there is evidence that juries do award lower damages than judges, there is no evidence to suggest that juries are awarding damages outside an acceptable range, whether established by experts at trial or otherwise.[104]

3. *Competence.* A final argument cited by the OLRC for abolishing the civil jury is that juries are not competent decision-makers.[105] In support of this contention, the OLRC points to the alleged unpredictability of juries and their inability to understand the evidence.[106] However, assumptions about the uncertainty of jury verdicts and the jury's failure

[94] See ibid. [95] See ibid. [96] See ibid., at 26–7.
[97] See *supra* section III.B. [98] See OLRC, REPORT, *supra* note 3, at 26–7.
[99] See ibid., at 27. [100] See ibid., at 27–9. [101] See ibid., at 27–8.
[102] See ibid., at 28. [103] See ibid. [104] See ibid.
[105] See ibid., at 29. [106] See ibid.

to understand the evidence are questionable for the reasons just discussed.[107] Furthermore, judges retain the authority to strike out a jury altogether in cases with complex factual issues.

V. Conclusion: Assessing the Arguments

The OLRC began its canvassing of the arguments relating to juries with some important observations. At base is its suggestion that promoters and skeptics of the civil jury are prompted by values that are hard to test empirically and difficult to reconcile in terms of basic views regarding the administration of justice.[108] For example, the OLRC correctly observed that there is no agreement about the criteria that should be used to measure the performance or contribution of judges or juries.[109]

Nevertheless, in assessing the arguments, we can begin with what we do know about the civil jury:

(1) The civil jury is rarely used in some provinces, while in others its use appears to range from 3 to 10 percent of civil trials. In Ontario, where the most systematic study has been done, juries are used in about 20 percent of civil cases.[110]

(2) Juries are employed primarily in tort cases, the vast majority of which are motor vehicle accident cases.[111] In such cases, juries are often sought by institutional litigants such as insurance companies.[112]

(3) Civil jury trials that go to completion do take somewhat longer than bench trials. However, because of the effect that the presence of a jury has on settlement rates, jury trials take less time overall.[113] Moreover, there is no clear evidence that civil jury trials cost substantially more.[114]

(4) Juries tend to award damages that are lower than those of judges, but jury verdicts remain within appropriate ranges.[115]

(5) The use of civil juries is circumscribed. First, the statutory proscriptions against their use vary among the provinces, but include prohibitions for suits against governments, for domestic

[107] See OLRC, REPORT, *supra* note 3. [108] See ibid., at 30.
[109] See ibid. [110] See *supra* text accompanying notes 53–9.
[111] See *supra* text accompanying note 59.
[112] See *supra* text accompanying note 102.
[113] See *supra* text accompanying notes 60–4.
[114] See *supra* text accompanying notes 60–7.
[115] See *supra* text accompanying note 102.

> issues, and for claims for equitable relief.[116] Secondly, judges retain discretion to strike out juries, most prominently on the ground of factual complexity.[117] In some provinces, this power has recently been limited by the courts, while in others the general authority to strike out a jury continues to be employed quite readily by judges.

Civil juries are not widely used in Canada. However, there is no clear evidence that their use imposes any burden on the justice system or that their verdicts are aberrant. At the same time, the use of lay decision-makers is limited in significant ways, with the result that juries are mostly used in litigation arising out of motor vehicle accidents and are frequently sought by institutional parties. Yet, if those boundaries were removed, or at least loosened, the use of juries could very well increase.

Nowhere are the contradictions regarding the civil jury more clearly apparent than in Ontario. Civil juries appear to be used most frequently in that province, despite the stringent qualifications on their use and the systematic opposition to their existence by official reports.[118] The Ontario Law Reform Commission has been especially prominent in its opposition. In numerous reports over several decades, it has consistently opposed the use of the civil jury.[119] As indicated earlier, in its most recent assessment of the role of lay decision-makers, it suggested again that civil juries be abolished.[120] However, this suggestion created such a strong reaction that the OLRC changed its position and actually recommended expansion of the role of civil juries.[121] Similarly, in the 1980s, the Ontario legislature, prompted by the OLRC, enacted legislation clearly authorizing appellate courts to modify jury awards in some circumstances.[122] Yet the response by the Court of Appeal has been to indicate that it will overturn jury verdicts only in extreme instances.[123]

A 'guardian of civil rights'? A 'medieval relic'? The civil jury in

[116] See *supra* text accompanying notes 12–20.

[117] See *supra* text accompanying notes 27–32.

[118] See ONTARIO, vol. 2, *supra* note 47, at 859–60.

[119] See, *e.g.*, ONTARIO LAW REFORM COMM'N, REPORT ON CLASS ACTIONS 461 (1982); ONTARIO LAW REFORM COMM'N, REPORT ON PRODUCTS LIABILITY 102–4 (1979); ONTARIO LAW REFORM COMM'N, REPORT ON THE ADMINISTRATION OF ONTARIO COURTS—PART I, at 329–50 (1973). But see MANITOBA LAW REFORM COMM'N, REPORT OF THE ADMINISTRATION OF JUSTICE IN MANITOBA PART II—A REVIEW OF THE JURY SYSTEM 48–50 (1975).

[120] See OLRC, STUDY PAPER, *supra* note 2.

[121] See OLRC, REPORT, *supra* note 3.

[122] See Courts of Justice Act, R.S.O., ch. C.43, § 119 (1990) (Ont.).

[123] See *Koukounakis* v. *Stainrod* (1995) 23 O.R.3d 299, 305 (Ont. C.A.).

Canada is a bit of vota. What is more, it is an institution that has simply fallen into disuse. In this regard, civil juries stand in marked contrast to the critical—and constitutionally entrenched[124]—role that juries play in the administration of criminal justice. Furthermore, there are no compelling policy reasons, or justifications based on costs, that can establish the case for consigning the jury to such a small role in the administration of civil justice.

Perhaps it is appropriate to end on a note of irony regarding the ill-fitting civil jury. The OLRC, the institution that worked for so long to bring about the end of the civil jury, was abolished in 1996[125]—a victim of governmental austerity and the politics of law. The civil jury, at least, continues to survive.

[124] See CAN. CONST. (Constitution Act, 1982) pt. I (Canadian Charter of Rights and Freedoms), § 11(f).

[125] The OLRC has never formally been abolished by having its statutory authorization repealed. Rather, it has been ended by the government refusing to fund it. See ONTARIO LAW REFORM COMM'N (revised May 1998) <http://www.attorneygeneral.jus.gov.on.ca/olrc/olrchome.htm>.

13 The Jury Elsewhere in the World

Neil Vidmar*

I. Introduction

The English jury was not confined to the countries that are covered in the other chapters in this book. Along with many other aspects of its culture and its laws, the jury system was transported to colonies in Africa, Asia, and the Caribbean as England built an empire. In other instances the English jury was spread by an indirect route. Admiration for the English jury accompanied the French Revolution, and Napoleon included a form of the jury in the Napoleonic Code of 1808. Through Napoleonic conquests or other routes, jury systems were introduced into other parts of Europe, including Belgium, parts of Germany, Switzerland, Austria, Hungary, Sardinia, Greece, Russia, Norway, Spain, and Portugal. Through influences of Spain and Portugal juries were introduced into some of the countries of Central and South America, including Ecuador, Uruguay, Paraguay, and Bolivia.[1] Although the jury did not take permanent root in some of these countries and in others it was radically transformed, a very substantial number of jury systems remain viable today.

A book entitled *World Jury Systems* must, therefore, acknowledge these other jury systems, and this final chapter attempts to do so. It is a sketchy and incomplete chapter. Writings on many of these systems are sparse, or at least inaccessible in the scholarly literature, particularly up-to-date writings. However, following my inquiry about the jury, in June 1999 the Legal and Constitutional Affairs Division of the Commonwealth Secretariat in London graciously sent a survey to all members of that organization asking whether they had a jury system and, if so, about its basic characteristics.[2] Most of the countries,

* Russell M. Robinson II Professor of Law and Professor of Psychology, Duke University.

[1] Alex Brown, The Juryman's Handbook (1951).

[2] Mr Richard C. Nzerem of the Legal and Constitutional Affairs Division of the Commonwealth Secretariat sent a questionnaire to all members and associated states of the Commonwealth on June 14, 1999. It requested information about the existence and operation of criminal and civil juries. Margaret A. Bruce compiled the data and forwarded them to Duke. The responses took a number of forms, from brief replies to more detailed

dependencies, and associated states responded, and the Commonwealth Survey is a major source for this chapter. A second source of information came from The International Conference on Lay Participation in the Criminal Trial in the 21st Century held in Siricusa, Sicily on May 26–29, 1999. That conference produced a number of papers on jury systems that will be produced in a book edited by Professor Stephen Thaman under a title similar to that of the conference. Scholars will also want to consult Thaman's book, but I have drawn on some of the papers to briefly sketch juries in countries outside the common law system.

Finally, I conducted library research that turned up additional sources, particularly ones dealing with the history of diffusion of the jury. I did not conduct primary research on these discoveries and cannot vouch for their accuracy, but in most cases I found more than a single source stating the same information.

Consistent with the focus of this book, I have limited the survey to jury systems that vest decision-making on guilt or negligence solely in the hands of the lay person members and excluded systems that have mixed tribunals of judges and lay persons. There are, of course, degrees of judge control over the jury, and sometimes it is so substantial that the line between the conception of the independent jury derived from England and mixed tribunals is not very distinct. As was the case for Chapter 1, it is helpful to have a brief historical overview to put the contemporary material into perspective.

II. The English Jury Exported to Other Colonies: A Historical Sketch

Wherever English colonists settled, they tended to import the jury system as a means of ensuring their own rights. It usually co-existed with the indigenous laws of the original inhabitants.[3] Native peoples were frequently tried by a judge assisted by lay assessors.[4]

descriptions, sometimes with appended copies of relevant statutes. In reporting these data (hereinafter, 'Commonwealth Survey') in this chapter I have usually used the phrasing of the original correspondence rather than risk an interpretation that might be erroneous. Copies of the responses are held on file at Duke Law School.

[3] T. O. Elias, British Colonial Law: A Comparative Study of the Interaction Between English and Local Laws in British Dependencies (1962).

[4] Ibid.; J. H. Jearey, *Trial by Jury and Trial with the Aid of Assessors in the Superior Courts of British African Territories: I*, 4 J. Afr. L. 133, 134 (1960).

Consider first the continent of Africa. Sierra Leone was England's oldest African colony.[5] It was settled by freed slaves from England in 1787. Along with other aspects of English law, the grand and petit jury systems were adopted in ordinances passed in 1799 and 1801. Sierra Leone also provided for civil jury trials. However, by the early 1800s there was considerable dissatisfaction with the jury system. The grand jury system apparently hampered attempts to stop the internal slave trade. Fair trials with petit juries were viewed as difficult to obtain because jurors were affected by community pressures and jealousies and rivalries between different tribes. The civil jury was abolished in 1866. The criminal jury survived, but in 1864 the Juries Amendment Ordinance required only a two-thirds majority for conviction, except capital trials still required unanimity. In 1895 defendants in non-capital cases were allowed to elect to be tried by a judge sitting with three assessors whose function was purely advisory. In 1932 the law providing trial by judge and lay assessors was amended to provide that if the three assessors were unanimous on the facts the judge was bound by their decision. Further changes provided for jury trial in cases in which a non-native was tried for a capital offense and where a native was charged with the murder of a non-native. By the mid-1950s the right to jury trial remained, but the racial problems associated with it had resulted in a substantial reduction in its popularity. Compared to other African colonies, however, race had never been an issue in the qualification to serve as a juror. Sierra Leone has been in political turmoil for most of the last part of the twentieth century and it is unlikely that the jury has survived.

The colony of Gambia also adopted jury trial in 1845.[6] However, from the beginning it was recognized that the system would have to be modified from that of England. The Gold Coast (Ghana) took a slightly different route. Lack of eligible jurors and racial factors led to provisions enabling the Attorney General to order trial by judge with lay assessors and allow nonunanimous jury verdicts in non-capital cases. Natives could serve on the jury if they were fluent in English, and in 1953 women were made eligible for jury service. When Ghana became an independent nation in 1957 the right to jury trial was maintained, but it was not expanded.

[5] Jearey, *supra* note 3 is the source for this paragraph. [6] Ibid.

In Nigeria the right to jury trial was provided for capital cases in the area of Lagos in 1865.[7] Initially, the jury was composed of seven persons, but in 1866 the size was increased to twelve. The law on the jury system was complicated by changes in its status as a colony. However, in 1945 capital trials and a number of other offences were made eligible. For capital trials the size of the jury was fixed at twelve, but for other offences it was fixed at eight. The law further provided for racial quotas: if the accused was a non-native the court was allowed to direct that not more than half of the jury should be non-natives. By the early 1970s, after Nigeria had become an independent nation, jury trial was reserved mostly for capital cases and appears to have been in use only in the Lagos area. One interesting aspect of jury trial involved changes in the unanimity rule that predated change in the unanimity rule in England in 1967. The jury was encouraged to deliberate to reach a unanimous verdict, but if, after two hours, it could not reach a consensus, the judge could accept the majority verdict of ten of the twelve jurors on that offence. In Lagos jurors were selected without regard to race or nationality, but it appears that the three peremptory challenges or unlimited challenges for cause might be used to excuse a juror who was a member of a tribal group that was traditionally hostile to the tribe to which the accused belonged. Since the 1980s Nigeria has been ruled by military governments; it is unlikely that the jury system has survived.

On the eastern side of Africa the jury system was utilized in Zanzibar (now Tanzania) until it was abolished in 1949.[8] Kenya provided trial by jury only for whites and the system was abolished upon independence in 1963.[9] Southern Rhodesia, now Zimbabwe, also had a jury system, but it was abolished in 1973.[10] In each of these countries jury service was *de jure* or *de facto* reserved for whites.[11] Jury trials of Africans accused of indictable crimes existed until 1927, but after that trial was by judge and lay assessors. African hostility to the Rhodesian jury system

[7] Emmet V. Mittlebeeler, *Race and Jury in Nigeria*, 18 How. L.J. 88, 90 (1973); and Jearey, *supra* note 3 at 144 (stating the date to be 1844). Both of these sources form the basis of this paragraph.

[8] J. H. Jearey, *Trial by Jury and Trial with the Aid of Assessors in the Superior Courts of British African Territories: II*, 5 J. Afr. L. 36 (1965).

[9] Ramesh Deosaran, Trial by Jury: Social and Psychological Dynamics 18 (1985); See also Elias, *supra* note 2 at 262.

[10] Justice Georges, *Is the Jury Trial an Essential Cornerstone of Justice?*, in Proceedings and Papers of the 7th Commonwealth Law Conference 30 (Hong Kong, September 1983).

[11] See Jearey, *supra* note 3 at 40–5; Georges, *supra* note 10, at 31.

developed out of perceived injustices favoring whites, and it was not re-established upon independence.

The jury was also introduced into South Africa, beginning with the Cape in 1828.[12] Shortly afterwards it was adopted in Natal and the Orange Free State.[13] The typical jury consisted of nine white males; a majority of at least seven was required for a verdict of guilty. Jury trial was reserved for the most serious crimes, but an accused could opt instead for trial by judge and lay assessors. Jury trials declined steadily until, in 1968, they constituted less than half of one percent of trials in the superior courts.[14] Jury trial was abolished altogether in 1969.[15] When one scholar suggested reviving jury trials for the new South Africa, he was strongly rebuffed by the legal and scholarly community.[16] The reasons involve a history of all-white juries rendering unjust verdicts against non-white defendants and the problems of devising a jury system for a complex multi-racial society.[17]

South West Africa, now the Republic of Namibia, also had a jury system for a period.[18] English law, including accusatorial procedure, replaced Dutch-influenced law in the beginning of the nineteenth century, and a jury system was introduced in the 1880s. However, in the course of the twentieth century South African criminal law replaced the older English law. Jury trial was abolished in 1969. In the territories of Basutoland, Bechuanaland, Swaziland, Northern Rhodesia, and the Gambia Protectorate, trial was by judge, usually accompanied by lay assessors when indigenous peoples were involved.[19]

Trial by jury was introduced into other British colonies. The laws of the East India Company in 1670 provided for trial by jury by twelve Englishmen, except if any party to a dispute was not English, half of

[12] J. A. Chubb, *Some Notes on the Commonwealth and Empire Law Conference, 1955, and an Address on the Jury System*, 73 S. AFR. L.J. 191, 197 (1956); Martin Seligson, Lay Participation in South Africa: From Apartheid to Majority Rule, Paper presented at the International Conference on Lay Participation in the Criminal Trial in the 21st Century, Siricusa, Sicily, Italy, May 26–29, 1999.

[13] Emmet V. Mittlebeeler, *Race and Jury in South Africa*, 14 How. L.J. 90, 93 (1968).

[14] Marshall S. Huebner, *Who Decides? Restructuring Criminal Justice for a Democratic South Africa*, 102 YALE L.J. 961 (1993).

[15] P. R. Spiller, *The Jury System in Early Natal*, 8 J. LEGAL HIST. 129 (1987); Huebner, *supra* note 14.

[16] Huebner, *supra* note 14. [17] Ibid.

[18] The Commonwealth Survey, *supra* note 1: Letter from the Namibia Ministry of Justice dated 9 July 1999 to the Legal and Constitutional Affairs Office of the Commonwealth Secretariat.

[19] J. H. Jearey, *Trial by Jury and Trial with the Aid of Assessors in the Superior Courts of British African Territories: III*, 5 J. AFR. L. 82 (1961).

the jury would be non-English.[20] In 1923 the law was changed to require that at least half of the members of the jury should be of the color or nationality of the accused, but by 1949 racial quotas on juries had been abolished.[21] After India became an independent nation jury trials were retained for offences tried in the High Courts,[22] but today jury trial no longer exists.[23] Singapore also had jury trial, but it was abolished in 1969.[24] Malaysia used trial by jury until around 1900.[25] Following independence in 1957 it was reintroduced for most capital offences in 1958.[26] Malaysia suspended its constitution in 1971 and jury trial was formally abolished in 1995.[27]

The last official survey of the British Commonwealth,[28] reported in 1942, indicated that there were thirty-eight 'colonies, dependencies, protectorates and other territories under the jurisdiction of the Crown in which the jury in full form or limited form had been introduced: Aden, Bahamas, Barbados, Bermuda, British Guiana, British Honduras, Brunei, Cayman Islands, Ceylon, Dominica, the Falklands, Federated Malay States, Fiji, Gambia, Gibraltar, Gold Coast, Grenada, Hong Kong, Jamaica, Johore, Kelantan, Kenya, Leeward Islands, Malta, Mauritius, Nigeria, North Borneo, Nyasaland, St Helena, St Lucia, St Vincent, Sierra Leone, Straits Settlements, Tonga, Trinidad, Turks and Caicos Island, and Zanzibar.

In many of these places the jury was reserved only for Europeans, or the Europeans had the right to request that half or a majority of the jury be composed of Europeans.[29] In some instances jury trial was available only for charges involving the death penalty as a possible punishment. Jury size ranged from the traditional twelve members to as few as seven members, although twelve members were usually required when the potential penalty was death. In all instances the juries were composed exclusively of males. In Aden, Barbados, Brunei, the Federated Malay States, the Gold Coast, Johore, Kelantan, Kenya, Malta, Nigeria,

[20] Charles Fawcett, The First Century of British Justice in India 15 (1934); A. C. Banerjee, English Law in India (1984).

[21] Deosaran, *supra* note 9, at 19. [22] Ibid.

[23] Commonwealth Survey, *supra* note 1; G. L. Sanghi, *Trial and Court Procedures in India*, in Trial and Court Procedures Worldwide 21, 31 (Charles Platto ed. 1991).

[24] Commonwealth Survey, *supra* note 1; Jaya Prakash, *Trial and Court Procedures in Singapore*, in Trial and Court Procedures Worldwide 66, 71 (Charles Platto, ed. 1991); Ramesh Deosaran, *supra* note 9.

[25] Deosaran, *supra* note 9 at 19. [26] Ibid.

[27] Commonwealth Survey, *supra* note 1.

[28] The survey is reported in Alex Brown, The Juryman's Handbook (1951).

[29] Ibid.

North Borneo, Nyasaland, and Zanzibar Europeans who were on trial had juries composed of special lists of English-speaking persons, or they had the right to have a majority of their race on the jury. In Zanzibar jury trial was available only for Europeans.

Many of these territories are now independent nations under new names and ruling regimes and the jury has been abolished or fallen into disuse. There are a number of explanations for discontinuation of the jury in these countries. When colonies or territories became independent, indigenous law or some other form of law replaced English law. In some instances there was an explicit rejection of the jury because of experience with it as a vestige of oppressive colonial rule.[30] Another explanation is that the jury system was seen as not adaptable to multiracial societies.[31] In other instances political turmoil and military governments have meant the suspension of many rights associated with civilian rule. Nevertheless, as documented in the next section, juries continue to survive in some of these former colonies.

Peter Duff and his colleagues[32] undertook a study of the Hong Kong jury at the beginning of the 1990s that reflects interesting light on one colonial jury system that may provide insights into jury systems that are now extinct.

Jury trials in Hong Kong are reserved only for major crimes tried in the High Court. The jury is composed of seven members and the agreement of five is necessary for a verdict. Although the population of Hong Kong is composed overwhelmingly of uni-lingual Cantonese speakers, and the majority of the accused are Cantonese, the trial is conducted in English and a working knowledge of English is a requirement for eligibility to serve. Most judges and barristers do not speak Cantonese. The majority of evidence in trials is in Cantonese, which is then translated into English. Jurors who speak Cantonese have an advantage over the judges and barristers because they hear the testimony of witnesses

[30] See, *e.g.* J. Georges, Is the jury trial an essential cornerstone of justice? Proceedings and Papers of the 7th Commonwealth Law Conference, Hong Kong, September 18–23, 1983.

[31] Allott summarized the basic problem in an article for the Fifth Commonwealth Magistrates Conference in 1979: 'The unwillingness to introduce jury trials in countries of mixed races, cultures, and levels of development has been provoked by doubt whether a jury would give persons of a different background a fair trial, and would be overready to acquit persons of the same background.' See also Elias, *supra*, note 2 for a discussion of specific problems in African and Asian colonies and Deosaran, *supra* note 9 for a discussion of similar problems in Caribbean and South American countries.

[32] Peter Duff, Mark Findlay, Carla Howarth and Chan Tsang-Fai, Juries: A Hong Kong Perspective (1992).

directly while the judge and lawyers are dependent on translators. On the other hand, judicial instructions are given in English, and the deliberations are carried out in English. Duff *et al.* reported that one juror informant complained that two Cantonese jurors on one jury could not conduct a simple conversation in English.

Duff *et al.* argued that the jury symbolizes the supremacy of English culture through its English qualification rules. Moreover, research showed that the majority of members of the Chinese community did not know what the jury is or anything about its role in the criminal justice system. However, in the unique anxiety anticipating reversion of the Hong Kong territory to China in 1997 the Chinese community strongly supported English law, including the jury system. As Hong Kong passes the millennium mark, the Basic Law, built upon English law, and its incorporation of trial by jury have, at least for the immediate future, survived the transfer of Hong Kong back to China.[33] Nevertheless, some of the problems of fairness, performance, and legitimacy associated with a colonially imposed jury system are clear.

III. The 'English' Jury on the Continents of Europe and South America: A Historical Sketch

Basic legal concepts of evidence and proof, procedural justice, and fairness developed hand in hand with the rise of the English jury,[34] and these ideas were intimately tied to the jury in legal writings and discourse.[35]

[33] Yash Ghai, Hong Kong's New Constitutional Order (1999).

[34] Stephan Landsman, *The Rise of the Contentious Spirit: Adversary Procedure in Eighteenth Century England*, 75 CORNELL LAW REVIEW 497 (1990); Stephan Landsman, *From Gilbert to Bentham: The Reconceptualization of Evidence Theory*, 36 WAYNE LAW REVIEW 1149 (1990).

[35] Although I footnote some statements, this section is derived from a number of sources. They overlap a great deal and I have checked them for consistency of dates and substantive material wherever possible. The sources are as follows: ALEX BROWN, THE JURYMAN'S HANDBOOK (1951); Gerhard Casper & Hans Zeisel, *Lay Judges in the German Criminal Courts*, (1972) 1 JOURNAL OF LEGAL STUDIES 135; RAMESH DEOSARAN, TRIAL BY JURY: SOCIAL AND PSYCHOLOGICAL DYNAMICS (1985); WILLIAM FORSYTH, TRIAL BY JURY (1875/1994); François Gorphe, *Reform of the Jury System in European Countries*, 27 JOURNAL OF THE AMERICAN INSTITUTE OF CRIMINAL LAW AND CRIMINOLOGY 17 (1937); Eberhard Knittel & Dietmar Seiler, *The Merits of Trial By Jury* (1972) 30 CAMBRIDGE LAW JOURNAL 316; Hermann Manheim, *Trial by Jury in Modern Continental Criminal Law* (1937) 53 LAW QUARTERLY REVIEW 99; ANTONIO SCHIOPPA, THE TRIAL JURY IN ENGLAND, FRANCE, GERMANY: 1700–1900 (1987); William Seagle, *Jury*, in Edwin Seligman (ed.), ENCYCLOPEDIA OF THE SOCIAL SCIENCES, Vol. 7 (circa 1930); William Seagle, *Jury*, in Edwin Seligman (ed.), ENCYCLOPEDIA OF THE SOCIAL SCIENCES, Vol. 8 (circa 1937); Fredrick Whitridge, *Trial by Jury*, CYCLOPEDIA OF POLITICAL SCIENCE, Vol. II, (ed., John Lalor) (1886).

French philosophers such as Voltaire, Montesquieu, and Diderot had great admiration for English procedure.[36] It is also claimed that the writings of Thomas Paine, so important for the American Revolution, and the assertion of the right to jury trial in the U.S. Declaration of Independence were influential.[37] Between 1789 and 1790 reformers of France's legal system had much enthusiasm for English modes of procedure, but it appears that they had little direct and practical knowledge of the way it worked in practice. Understanding of the jury was largely through reading of Blackstone and De Lolme, already outdated by evolutionary developments in England. As a consequence, the jury system was interpreted through the lens of existing French legal procedure. Following the French Revolution, reforms of the legal system were debated by the Assembly between 1789 and 1790 and in 1791 resulted in the adoption of a criminal jury system, though the civil jury was rejected. The jury became a mockery during the Reign of Terror, but it re-emerged during the reign of Napoleon.

The Napoleonic Criminal Code of 1808 contained provisions for the French form of the criminal jury. The French form merged some aspects of the English oral evidence requirement with French traditions of inquisitorial investigation and procedure relying on written documents. The sharp distinction between the functions of the judge and the functions of the lay jurors was also blurred, and the selection of jurors was left in the hands of government functionaries. Verdicts were rendered by a majority. The French jury subsequently went through a number of changes, most of which gave more power to the judge. Finally, in 1942, under the Vichy government, the jury system was replaced with a German-style procedure involving a system of judges and lay assessors. The contemporary French 'jury' actually is a mixed tribunal of lay persons and judges.[38]

However, through French conquests that resulted in adoption of the Napoleonic Code or more indirectly through the influence of English procedural ideas modified by French interpretations, juries were

[36] BROWN, *supra* note 28 at 118; SCHIOPPA, *supra* note 35.

[37] BROWN, *supra* note 38 at 118–19.

[38] Michel Bonnieu, The Presumption of Innocence and the French Cour d'Assises: Is France Ready for Adversary Procedure? Paper presented at the International Conference on Lay Participation in the Criminal Trial in the 21st Century, Siricusa, Sicily, Italy, May 26–29, 1999. For a detailed account of the French system in action see Bron McKillop, *Anatomy of a French Murder Case*, 45 AMERICAN JOURNAL OF COMPARATIVE LAW 527 (1997).

introduced into other European countries.[39] Napoleon had installed the French version of the jury into Rhenish provinces, which maintained the jury after downfall of the Napoleonic regime, but it was not until 1848 that juries were adopted in Prussia, Bavaria, Würtemberg, and Hesse-Darmstadt. Their adoption was under the influence of German liberal thinkers who associated the jury with other democratic ideas. The juries were modified to fit the German legal culture and were used only for the most serious crimes. However, they were often held in contrast to the older Schoffengericht consisting of two lay persons and a professional judge. The jury system declined and was permanently abolished in 1924 during the Weimar Republic.

Austria had limited forms of jury trial as early as 1850, but it was adopted more formally for press trials in 1869 and for general criminal procedure in 1874.[40] In form the Austrian jury followed the French model. Belgium introduced trial by jury in 1830 when it separated from Holland and adopted many of the principles of the Napoleonic Code.[41] Portugal adopted a jury in 1830 and expanded the system in 1837.[42] The Portuguese jury consisted of six members and a verdict of acquittal or conviction required a two-thirds majority, but the trial judge could annul it if he believed it improper. Portugal abolished jury trial in 1927 during the government of dictator Gomes da Costa.[43] A number of Cantons in Switzerland introduced jury trials around 1844. Greece had a form of the jury in 1834, and trial by jury was guaranteed in its constitution of 1844. For almost 150 years ten or twelve lay magistrates were exclusively competent to decide felony cases, including murder, but the jury was abolished under the dictatorship of the Greek Colonels in 1967. A form of 'jury' was restored in 1974, but it consists of a mixed court of laypersons and judges.[44] Hungary introduced a concept of the jury closer to the English jury in 1861. Russia adopted the jury system in 1864 and the first jury trial was held in 1866. Spain experimented with juries earlier, but juries were not

[39] Brown, *supra* note 38 at 119; Schioppa, *supra* note 38 at 10; Casper and Zeisel, *supra* note 35 at 136.

[40] Brown, *supra* note 28 at 121.

[41] Philip Traest, Country Study: Belgium, Paper presented at the International Conference on Lay Participation in the Criminal Trial in the 21st Century, Siricusa, Sicily, Italy, May 26–29, 1999.

[42] Forsyth, *supra* note 35 at 312.

[43] Knittel and Seiler, *supra* note 35 at 324.

[44] J. G. Tsiganou, *Juries or Judges? Decision-making Process in the Greek Felony Courts*, in J. F. Nijboer and J. M. Reijnjes, eds. Proceedings of the First World Conference on New Trends in Criminal Investigation and Evidence (1997).

firmly established there until 1888.[45] Japan introduced trial by jury in 1929 but abandoned it in 1943, as discussed in Chapter 10 in this volume. Holland abolished jury trial in 1813 immediately after it became an independent state.[46] Luxembourg followed in 1814. In 1848 the Kingdom of Sardinia introduced trial by jury. Subsequently, the Italian Kingdom developed a jury system in 1860, but abolished it in 1931 after the Fascist Party formed the government. Rumania adopted a French code, including provisions for jury trial, in 1864.

Legal scholarship in the English language is sorely lacking, but it appears forms of the jury may have existed in other countries that were often under the influence of Russia. Bulgaria began a jury system in 1895 but it sat with a judge. Serbia adopted trial by jury in 1892 and reintroduced it in 1918 but abolished it in its 1929 Code of Criminal Procedure.[47] The criminal codes of Poland and Czechoslovakia after 1918 also required jury trial.[48]

Undoubtedly through the influence of Spain and Portugal adopting forms of the jury, a number of countries in South America also made provisions for trial by jury, although in many instances primarily for charges involving the press. Uruguay introduced the jury in 1830. In Chile a law of 1872 mandated the trial of press offences by a jury of seven. Ecuador provided for jury trial in 1890, and the Venezuelan Code of 1898 allowed the various provinces to introduce it if they desired. Argentina made provision for jury trial in its 1853 Constitution.[49] In Brazil the jury system was adopted in 1822.[50] In 1832 Brazil had two jury councils, one for deciding guilt and one for sentence, but after 1841 only the former was maintained.

Scandinavian countries developed forms of the jury that, some assert, were independent of English law. Other scholarship disputes this

[45] See Thaman's Ch. on Spain and Russia for more details; see also Michael Burros, *The Spanish Jury: 1888–1923*, 14 Case Western Journal of International Law 177 (1982).

[46] Manheim, *supra* note 35.

[47] François Gorphe, *Reform of the Jury System in European Countries: England*, 27 Journal of the American Institute of Criminal Law and Criminology 17 (1937).

[48] Brown, *supra* note 28; Gorphe, *supra* note 35.

[49] Edmundo S. Hendler, Social Integration and Lay Participation: The Situation in Argentina, Paper presented at the International Conference on Lay Participation in the Criminal Trial in the 21st Century, Siricusa, Sicily, May 26–29, 1999.

[50] Luiz Flavio Gomez and Ana Paula Zomer, The Brazilian Jury System, Paper presented at the International Conference on Lay Participation in the Criminal Trial in the 21st Century, Siricusa, Sicily, Italy, May 26–29, 1999.

interpretation. It has been argued, for example, that the Swedish jury system for press cases of 1815 was influenced by the English trial jury.[51] Similarly, Norway used the English jury as model for its jury system in the Criminal Procedure Act of 1887.[52] On the other hand there appears to be evidence that Scandinavian use of lay persons in tribunals predated the juries that they developed in the nineteenth century. Arguments regarding which cultures invented the jury and whether they were independent inventions cannot be resolved to everyone's satisfaction.

IV. Jury Systems at the Beginning of the Twenty-first Century

A number of jury systems influenced by English law have survived the test of time and political change and appear to be heading into the twenty-first century as integral parts of the justice process. Presentation of these systems is organized around geographical areas.

A. British Isles

The *Isle of Man*[53] has a jury system for criminal cases triable on indictment. It is used on a regular basis. A jury of twelve persons is required for charges of treason or murder. Seven persons are used for other cases, except that if a judge determines that the crime has special gravity, a jury of twelve may be ordered. A unanimous verdict must be rendered in all instances. Any person registered to vote or who has been resident in the Islands for five years is eligible to serve unless he or she is ineligible under certain exemptions. The Isle of Man also has a civil jury. It is composed of six persons, and a unanimous verdict is required.

Jersey[54] likewise maintains a criminal jury system. Any person committed for trial in the Royal Court has the right to elect trial by jury. Jury trials take place, on average, once or twice a month. The jury is composed of twelve members. Unanimity is encouraged, but a majority of ten is sufficient for conviction.

[51] Torbjorn Vallinder, *The Swedish Jury System in Press Cases: An Offspring of Trial by Jury*, 8 Journal of Legal History 190 (1987).

[52] Asbjorn Strandbakken, Country Study: Kingdom of Norway, Paper presented at the International Conference on Lay Participation in the Criminal Trial in the 21st Century, Siricusa, Sicily, 26–29 May 1999.

[53] Commonwealth Survey, *supra* note 1.

[54] Commonwealth Survey, *supra* note 1.

Guernsey[55] does not have a traditional jury system. Instead, it utilizes twelve Jurats who are elected by an electoral college which comprises the Guernsey members of the Island's legislature and other elected officials, of which there may be in total as many as 104 members. Jurats are the arbitrators of fact. There must be a minimum of seven Jurats sitting for the full court to be properly constituted. A verdict on a simple majority is permitted. Jurats are also arbiters of fact in civil matters and there must be at least two Jurats in addition to the presiding judge.

B. *Africa*

Ghana, formerly The Gold Coast, retains a criminal jury system.[56] It is used for serious offences tried on indictment in the High Court. There is a provision for an alternative trial with a judge aided by assessors for non-murder trials, but it has not been used for over two decades. The jury is composed of seven persons. They must be residents of Ghana, be between 25 and 60 years of age, and be able to speak the English language. The jury panel is selected by the Chief Registrar of the High Court, who sends requests to heads of departments who then submit names of potential jurors. The petit jury is chosen from the panel by random selection. In cases of offences not punishable by death, a majority decision of five to two is allowed, but in cases carrying a death sentence a unanimous decision is required. If one juror has to be discharged for any reason, the jury is discharged and a new one empanelled. The court is bound by the verdict of the jury. Civil juries are not used in Ghana.

Malawi, formerly Nyasaland, maintains a jury system for charges of homicide and very serious cases, such as armed robbery, that are tried in the High Court.[57] The majority of criminal cases are tried by magistrates sitting without a jury. Every person between the ages of 21 and 65 is qualified to serve on the jury, but legal officials, politicians, law enforcement officers, ministers, and medical practitioners are exempt from duty. A jury is composed of twelve persons. The jury must return a unanimous verdict or a majority verdict consisting of not fewer than eight members. Judges can sit with assessors only when the case involves customary law. Malawi also maintains a civil jury system, but in practice the judge sits without a jury.

[55] Commonwealth Survey, *supra* note 1.
[56] Commonwealth Survey, *supra* note 1.
[57] Commonwealth Survey, *supra* note 1.

Uganda's district of Karamajoa attempted to establish a jury system in 1964.[58] Chapter 35 of the Administration of Justice (Karamoja) Act of the Laws of Uganda provided a complete blueprint for a jury system, including development of the panel, the offences that would be triable by jury, composition of the jury (eligible women could asked to have their names included in the pool), its size (seven) and decision rule (unanimity in death penalty cases, majority of five otherwise), the duties of the judge and even the travel allowances for jurors. However, the legislation was never implemented. Instead, cases in the High Court are tried by a judge and two assessors.

St Helena Island, a British dependency off the western coast of Africa, utilizes a jury system for either way or indictable offences.[59] Eight persons are required to constitute a jury, and a unanimous verdict is required. Over the past twenty years there have been only seven jury trials.

Botswana, *Cameroon*, *Tanzania*, and *Zimbabwe* reported that they do not have jury systems.[60]

Liberia was founded by freed American slaves and was never part of the British Empire, but its constitution, modelled after the United States Constitution, also provided for trial by jury.[61] Article I, Declaration of Rights, of the Constitution (as amended in 1955) provided for presentment by a grand jury and provided that 'every person criminally charged shall have a right . . . to have a speedy and impartial trial by a jury of the vicinity'. However, since the 1980s Liberia has been ruled by military governments or government that subordinated the judiciary to the executive branch. The jury system appears to be inoperative.

C. *Mediterranean Sea*

Gibraltar has a Crown Court system, and any offence that has a penalty greater than six months must be tried to a jury.[62] The jury is normally composed of nine persons, but if the potential penalty is life imprisonment the jury must have twelve members. Jurors must be between the ages of 18 and 65. Men have no choice regarding jury service, but

[58] Commonwealth Survey, *supra* note 1. The specific provisions are contained in the Administration of Justice (Karamoja) Act (Chapter 35) of the Laws of Uganda.

[59] Commonwealth Survey, *supra* note 1.

[60] Commonwealth Survey, *supra* note 1.

[61] Lawrence Marinelli, The New Liberia (1964); J. Gus Liebnow, Liberia: The Quest for Democracy (1987).

[62] Commonwealth Survey, *supra* note 1.

women may volunteer for duty. The jurors are told that the verdict must be unanimous, but in the nine-person juries a majority of seven is sufficient for a conviction.

Malta did not respond to the Commonwealth survey. However, an article written in 1964 indicated that a jury system was in existence at that time.[63] Maltese law was a mix of Napoleonic code and English law. The jury was originally introduced in 1829 in a limited form and contained provision for a special jury of three Maltese and three British members. The form existing in 1964 was confined to criminal charges. Ordinarily the trial was conducted by a single judge, but in cases punishable by death or by imprisonment exceeding twelve years it was composed of three judges. All trials by indictment involved a jury. The jury was composed of nine members. There were two jury lists, depending on the defendant. One list consisted of Maltese-speaking persons and another was composed of English-speaking persons. Property ownership was not a condition for jury eligibility, but there was an income level qualification. The jury foreman was one of the nine members, but he was chosen separately and was required to have had experience serving on a previous jury. The prosecution and the accused each had three peremptory challenges. A two-thirds majority of the jurors was necessary for conviction. However, in capital cases in which the verdict was not unanimous, the court was authorized to substitute a sentence of between twelve years and life at hard labour instead of death, and in practice it always did so.

Cyprus does not have a jury system.[64] Summary criminal jurisdiction is exercised by a single judge. More serious charges are tried by the Assize Court, a three-member court composed of a President of the District Court, a Senior District Judge, and a District Judge.

D. Asia and the South Pacific

The *Democratic Socialist Republic of Sri Lanka*, formerly Ceylon, maintains a jury system for the following offences: murder, culpable homicide, attempted murder, rape, certain offences associated with its Offensive Weapons Act, and abatement and conspiracy associated with that Act.[65] The jury is composed of seven persons. The law permits a verdict if five

[63] J. J. Cremona, Comment, *Jury System in Malta*, 13 AM. J. COMP. L. 570 (1964).
[64] Commonwealth Survey, *supra* note 1.
[65] Commonwealth Survey, *supra* note 1.

of the seven members agree. Every person residing in Sri Lanka over the age of 21 who has obtained a pass on the General Certificate of Education or an equivalent examination in six subjects including the Sinhala or Tamil language and has an income of not less than 300 rupees per month is qualified to serve. Additionally, anyone who is a graduate of a recognized university or holds an equivalent professional qualification is eligible to serve as a special juror. Sri Lanka does not have a jury for civil disputes.

The nature of the *Hong Kong* jury was described earlier in this chapter. It remains a part of the English law that has been kept in place under the agreements worked out between China, Hong Kong, and Great Britain.[66]

The *Kingdom of Tonga*, a former British protectorate consisting of 169 islands in the southwestern Pacific and a population of just over 100,000 also retains a jury system under Clause 99 of the Tongan constitution.[67] Indictable offences where the available penalty is two years or more and a fine of TOP $500 or more are eligible for jury trial. Juries are used for no more than approximately 10 percent of cases heard. Civil juries are available for cases under Supreme Court jurisdiction but are hardly ever used. Seven jurors are needed to constitute a jury. In criminal matters the verdict must be unanimous, but in civil matters a majority of five of the seven members is sufficient for a verdict.

The *Cook Islands*,[68] a protectorate of New Zealand, have twelve-person juries as part of prescribed criminal procedure for all major crimes. The defendant may elect for trial by judge and jury for other offences if the punishment exceeds six months in prison. The 1968 Juries Act provided for a valid verdict of eight jurors after three hours of deliberation. It is noteworthy that recent amendments to the Judicature Act significantly reduced the right to trial by jury.

In the *Marshall Islands*,[69] formerly under United States trust, any person accused of a criminal act punishable by three or more years in prison has the right to trial by a jury of four persons. The state and the defendant are allowed two peremptory challenges. Jurors must be able to read, write, or speak Marshallese or English.

[66] See text accompanying note 33. [67] Commonwealth Survey, *supra* note 1.

[68] Isaacus Adzoxornu, *The Cook Islands*, in Michael Ntumy, ed., South Pacific Islands Legal Systems (1993).

[69] Jean Zorn, *The Republic of the Marshall Islands*, in Michael Ntumy, ed., South Pacific Islands Legal Systems (1993).

American Samoa's[70] judicial system conforms closely with the U.S. legal system. Provisions in the U.S. Constitution requiring a jury trial have been held to be applicable in Samoa.

Guam[71] also uses the U.S. legal system, specifically the Federal Rules of Criminal Procedure and Federal Rules of Civil Procedure. Thus both civil trials and criminal trials are conducted with juries.

The *Commonwealth of the Northern Marina Islands*[72] provides for jury trial of six persons in civil cases. In criminal cases a person accused of committing a felony punishable by more than five years imprisonment has a right to trial by a jury of six persons.

Brunei,[73] *India*, *Kiribati*, *Malaysia*,[74] *Tuvalu*,[75] *Singapore*, *The Solomon Islands*, and *Fiji*[76] reported in the Commonwealth Survey that they do not have jury systems today.

E. The Carribean

The Eastern Carribean territories, comprised of the *British Virgin Islands*, *Montserrat*, *Tortola*, *The Commonwealth of Dominica*, *Anguilla*, *Antigua* and *Barbuda*, *St. Lucia*, *St. Vincent*, *the Grenadines* and *Grenada* all share a common Court of Appeal and Chief Justice.[77] However, they differ in some characteristics. All make distinctions between indictable and non-indictable

[70] Mary McCormick, *American Samoa*, in MICHAEL NTUMY, ed., SOUTH PACIFIC ISLANDS LEGAL SYSTEMS (1993).

[71] Mary McCormick, *Guam*, in MICHAEL NTUMY, ed., SOUTH PACIFIC ISLANDS LEGAL SYSTEMS (1993).

[72] Bruce Ottley, *The Commonwealth of the Northern Marina Islands*, in MICHAEL NTUMY, ed., SOUTH PACIFIC ISLANDS LEGAL SYSTEMS (1993).

[73] Commonwealth Survey, *supra* note 1. Until 1988 Brunei utilized two assessors for trials in its High Court. Since 1988 capital trials have been tried by two judges; other trials are tried by a single judge.

[74] Commonwealth Survey, *supra* note 1. Amendments to the 1995 Malaysian Criminal Procedure Code abolished jury trials and trials with the aid of assessors.

[75] Commonwealth Survey, *supra* note 1. Tuvalu allows two or three assessors. The accused may challenge the appointment of the assessors. However, the judge may overrule the assessors, and a trial held without assessors does not invalidate a conviction.

[76] Commonwealth Survey, *supra* note 1. Fiji tries crimes in its Supreme Court with a judge and assessors. The assessor list, with certain exemptions, is compiled of all males and females with a competent knowledge of English. Three assessors are used, except there are four for murder trials. A majority verdict is acceptable but the judge has the power to overrule the assessors.

[77] This information was obtained from a joint reply to the Commonwealth Survey by the members of the Eastern Carribean Territories. However, some of the individual territories submitted separate replies and the information that follows is a composite of all replies.

offenses (tried by judges or magistrates acting alone) and offenses triable either way. In Anguilla, Tortola, the Commonwealth of Dominica, Montserrat, and Antigua and Barbuda the jury is comprised of nine persons regardless of the offence with which the person is charged. In St. Lucia, St. Vincent, and the Grenadines and Grenada the jury usually consists of nine persons except that for trials involving potential capital punishment (murder and treason) the jury is comprised of twelve persons. In Grenada the Jury Act provides for the empanelling of not more than six alternate jurors, but the current practice is that two alternates are chosen for murder cases. In Antigua a statute also makes provision for eight of nine jurors to continue if one member becomes ill or is discharged for some other reason. In St. Lucia the judge, in his or her discretion and with the consent of the accused and the prosecutor, may proceed to render a valid verdict with six jurors in trials involving nine person juries and ten for capital offenses.

In all of the Eastern Carribean Islands a unanimous verdict is required for capital offences. For other offences in Antigua and Barbuda, Anguilla, the Commonwealth of Dominica, the British Virgin Islands, and Montserrat the jury must be unanimous if the verdict is rendered within two hours, but after two hours a majority of seven is accepted. In Grenada and St. Vincent and the Grenadines murder trials a verdict for a lesser included offence by ten jurors can be accepted after two hours of deliberation. For other trials a majority verdict from seven members can be accepted after two hours. In St. Lucia valid verdicts may be returned in non-capital cases by eight jurors after the first hour of deliberation and a majority of seven after two hours. However, the Criminal Code also provides that if majority of seven cannot agree, and are not likely to agree, after three hours the jury may be discharged by the judge.

Qualifications to serve on the jury also vary somewhat between the territories.[78] In St. Lucia citizens or residents between 18 and 65 years of age may serve if they can read and write the English language. In addition owners or lessees of property of an annual value of not less than $120 or an annual salary of $240 may also serve. Antigua and Barbuda qualifies everyone between 18 and 65 who has property of at least $5,000 in value or has a salary exceeding $5,000 or income from any source exceeding $2,000. In Grenada jurors must be between 21

[78] The are disqualifications, such as conviction of a serious offense, and exemptions for certain categories of persons, such as those involved in law enforcement, government, teaching, health care, and telegraphic services but these will not be detailed here.

and 65 years of age, be able to read and write English, and have property in the value of $2,000 or income equal to or exceeding $200 per year. Notwithstanding these criteria of eligibility in the High Court of Grenada women may be excluded from the jury in any particular case if the judge thinks it is proper or desirable to do so. In Anguilla anyone between the ages of 21 and 60 years who is a qualified voter is eligible to serve. In Montserrat jurors are between 21 and 65 years and must own land in the amount of at least $2,000, rents in the annual amount of at least $400, a salary of at least $2,000 *per annum*, or other income in the amount of at least $1,500 *per annum*. In St. Vincent and the Grenadines jurors are between the ages of 18 and 60, must read and write the English language and possess a property leasehold of $40 annually, occupy a house of annual rent of at least $240 or have a net annual income of $480. The British Virgin Islands and Anguilla also make provisions for special juries, as opposed to common juries, with qualifications for special jurors involving higher income or property values than for common jurors. For instance in the Virgin Islands to be eligible as a special juror a person must have lands or tenements in the value of at least $4,800, or own land in excess of 100 acres, or hold an office with an annual income of not less than $960 or be in receipt of income from any source of at least $720.

Anguilla also maintains a civil jury system on the books, but it has not been used during the past twenty years. In Montserrat Part V of the Jury Ordinance also provides for a party to request a special jury in civil cases. An array of special jurors cannot be empanelled unless the party requesting the jury deposits money determined sufficient by the Registrar of the court to pay the fees of the jurors included in the array. The civil jury is rarely used. St. Vincent and the Grenadines maintain a civil jury system, but civil juries are rarely used. The Virgin Islands also maintains a civil jury.

Bermuda has a criminal jury for serious crimes.[79] It can also be used for less serious crimes that allow the defendant to choose between a jury and a magistrate. The jury panel is drawn from the voters' list. The jury has twelve members. A unanimous verdict is required only when a verdict is returned in less than one hour. Thereafter, nine of twelve jurors may return a competent verdict. Civil juries are maintained for libel,

[79] Commonwealth Survey, *supra* note 1. In addition, see Ian Kawaley, *The Fair Cross-Section Principle: Trial by Special Jury and the Right to Criminal Jury Trial under the Bermuda Constitution*, 38 Int'l & Comp. L.Q. 522 (1989) and Deosaran, *supra* note 39, at 28.

slander, malicious prosecution, false imprisonment, seduction, or where a charge of fraud is in issue. Civil juries consist of eight persons, and six may return a verdict.

Cayman Islands juries sit on trials of indictment in the Grand Court. They also sit on some categories of lesser crimes (Category 2) if the prosecution and defence cannot agree on a summary jury trial.[80] Drug cases and minor crimes are heard by a magistrate. In the Grand Court the defendant can elect to be tried by judge alone. Twelve jurors are needed for murder and ten need to agree for a verdict. Juries for other cases are composed of seven members and five need to agree for a verdict. There are also provisions for civil juries at the request of the parties and with the consent of the court, but civil juries are rare. The civil jury is composed of seven persons and a majority of five can return a verdict.

In the *Turks and Caicos Islands* juries are mandatory for the most serious crimes, and they are also used for categories of crimes deemed triable either way.[81] Unless exempted every person between the ages of 21 and 65 who is registered as an elector is eligible for jury service. For treason and capital offences the jury is composed of twelve members, but otherwise it is composed of seven members. In capital cases a majority of eleven of twelve is allowed after a minimum of four hours of deliberation. In all other cases a majority vote of five of seven constitutes a competent verdict after three hours of deliberation. The Civil Procedure Ordinance also provides for civil juries. Either party to the lawsuit may demand a jury. However, an exception can be made if a judge determines that the matter requires prolonged examination of documents, if any scientific or local investigation cannot be conveniently tried by a jury, or if the matters fall under the Court of Chancery. The jury size is seven, and a majority of five can return a verdict. The party requesting the civil jury is responsible for paying the juror fees.

In *The Bahamas* the jury is used for all indictable offences tried in the Supreme Court.[82] Twelve persons are required for the jury. Jurors are chosen from the voter Register. Unanimous verdicts are required only when the death penalty is to be imposed upon conviction. Otherwise a two-thirds majority is required for conviction or acquittal.

Barbados maintains a general jury system.[83] It is used for all serious crimes and for crimes triable either way in which the accused person has

[80] Commonwealth Survey, *supra* note 1.
[81] Commonwealth Survey, *supra* note 1.
[82] Commonwealth Survey, *supra* note 1.
[83] Commonwealth Survey, *supra* note 1.

opted for trial by judge and jury. For murder and treason the jury consists of twelve members. The verdict must be unanimous. For a verdict of manslaughter a majority of nine can return a valid verdict. For other crimes the jury is composed of nine members and a majority of seven is required for a verdict. The Jurors Act also provides for civil juries of seven members. To be eligible to serve on a jury a person must be between 18 and 65 years old, a resident citizen, and be able to read and write in English. An additional requirement is that the person must be in possession of land worth not less than $960 or an occupier of land having a value of $1,400, or have an annual income of $1,400.

In *Saint Christopher and Nevis* the Jury Act provides for a jury of twelve for capital offences and a nine-member jury for other offences.[84] Any verdict returned in under two hours of deliberation must be unanimous. After two hours ten of the twelve jurors are sufficient to return a verdict in a capital murder case and seven of nine are sufficient for a verdict in other cases. With certain statutory exemptions the jury pool is derived from voter registration lists. There is a provision for a civil jury, but it is not maintained nor operated. The relevant act states that the party requesting the civil jury must deposit a sum of money sufficient to pay for the fees given to the jurors. All indictable offences are tried by jury. It was estimated that there are between 75 and 90 jury trials per year.[85]

Jamaica[86] maintains a jury system for indictable offences. Twelve jurors are required for murder and treason. Seven-person juries are used for other indictable offences. A unanimous verdict is required for murder and treason, but a majority of nine is sufficient for a verdict of manslaughter after a lapse of one hour after the jury retires to deliberate. With respect to other offences, a majority of five of seven is sufficient for a verdict after an hour of deliberation. Section 2 of the Jury Act states the qualifications for jury service: a resident of Jamaica, between the ages of 16 and 65 years, and named on the current list of electors for elections to the House of Representatives, able to speak and write in the English language. Non-Commonwealth citizens are not eligible to serve, nor are persons awaiting trial for an indictable offence or persons convicted of an offence for which they have been imprisoned for more than six months. Jamaica also has a civil jury system that can

[84] Commonwealth Survey, *supra* note 1.

[85] Commonwealth Survey, *supra* note 1. Information about jury size, decision rule, and jury composition was not provided.

[86] Commonwealth Survey, *supra* note 1. See also DEOSARAN, *supra* note 39; and *Legal System of Jamaica* 40 ST. LOUIS UNIVERSITY LAW JOURNAL 1381 (1996).

be convened at a litigant's request. The jury is composed of seven persons, but the Jury Act is silent regarding unanimous versus majority verdicts. The civil jury is rarely used but recently one was summoned for a case involving a claim of libel.

Trinidad requires twelve jurors for murder or treason trials and the verdict has to be unanimous in those cases for conviction or acquittal.[87] A verdict of manslaughter to a charge of murder, however, can be returned after three hours of deliberation if nine of the twelve jurors agree, but the trial judge has the discretion to discharge the jury if there is no verdict after three hours. A jury composed of nine persons is required for other cases and a judge can accept a verdict of seven of the nine after three hours of deliberation. The 1975 Jury (Amendment) Act provided that the Chief Election Officer draw up the jury list; the officer is also given access to income tax returns and names and addresses of employed persons from the National Insurance Board to ascertain eligibility of jurors. Jurors are required to be able to speak and write the English language. The Act also provides that each accused person and the prosecution have the right peremptorily to challenge up to three jurors, but any additional challenges must be supported by 'good cause', and the power to allow or disallow the challenge resides in the judge.

Puerto Rico is a self-governing island commonwealth in the West Indies that is associated with the United States. Spanish is the mother tongue of more than 90 percent of the population, and the majority of inhabitants are monolingual.[88] Puerto Rico's jury system and procedures in both criminal and civil cases mirror U.S. law with the exception that all matters in the Commonwealth courts are officially carried out in Spanish.[89] However, a U.S. federal court has jurisdiction over both criminal and civil matters associated with U.S. law, and all matters tried in the federal court are carried out in English.

F. South and Central America

Guyana, formerly British Guyana, on the north eastern coast of South America requires a jury for all indictable criminal offences.[90] Trials take

[87] Deosaran, *supra* note 39; Ramesh Deosaran, ***The Jury System in a Post-Colonial, Multiracial Society: Problems of Bias***, 21 British Journal of Criminology 305 (1981).

[88] Jose Alvarez-Gonzalez, *Law, Language and Statehood: The Role of English in the Great State of Puerto Rico*, 17 Law and Inequality 359 (1999).

[89] People v. Superior Court, 92 P.R.R. 580 (1965); Jackson v. Garcia 665 F. 2d 395 (1981).

[90] Commonwealth Survey, *supra* note 1.

place at four assizes every year. A jury is composed of twelve persons. Every citizen between the ages of 18 and 60 who can read and write English is eligible, but judges, members of the legislature, mayors, members of the military and constabulary forces, public officers, ministers, lawyers, and medical personnel are exempt. For capital offences the jury must be unanimous. In other cases verdicts returned before two hours of deliberation have elapsed must be unanimous. After two hours a verdict can be turned in with a majority vote of ten of the twelve members. There is no provision for civil juries.[91]

Belize, formerly British Honduras, in Central America also has a jury system.[92] In its Supreme Court criminal cases are tried by judge and jury. In capital cases the jury size is twelve but in other cases the jury is composed of nine persons. Civil cases are seldom tried by juries.

Panama, also in Central America, utilizes juries in its Superior Courts.[93] These courts try crimes such as homicide, abortion, crimes against the security of means of transportation or communication, and crimes against public health when they involve the death of a person. The accused may waive the right to jury trial and be tried by judge alone. The jury is composed of non-lawyer citizens and an alternate juror. The final verdict is determined by majority vote. The judge decides the punishment.

Nicaragua had provisions for trial by jury in its 1912 Constitution and its use continued even during the Sandinista government.[94] Its 1995 Constitution retains the right to trial by jury in an expanded form. Nicaragua's mode of criminal procedure remains basically inquisitorial so that the jury, composed of four lay persons and a judge are prepared

[91] Deosaran, *supra* note 39, discussed political and racial problems with the jury in Guyana in his 1985 study. These included a 1978 amendment transferring to the presiding magistrate the decision to choose between trial by judge and jury or by magistrate alone in indictable offenses, a decision that was very controversial among members of the Guyanese Bar. Part of the rationale for the change was the fact that delays in the criminal justice system had become onerous, but there were other factors as well. Deosaran discussed racial and political conflicts between Guyanese of African and East Indian descent. His discussion of racial and political problems in Guyana and other nations in the Caribbean is an important source of information about the effects in small populations in which there are sometimes community pressures to render verdicts based on friendships or social ties, lack of competent veniremen, and hostilities between different racial groups. See also Deosaran, *supra* note 87, for similar discussion on Trinidad.

[92] *Legal System of Belize*, 40 St. Louis University Law Journal 1333 (1996).

[93] *Legal System of Panama*, 40 St. Louis University Law Journal 1387 (1996).

[94] Sergio J. Cuarezma Teran, The Nicaraguan Jury System, Paper presented at the International Conference on Lay Participation in the Criminal Trial in the 21st Century, Siricusa, Sicily, May 26–29, 1999.

by files and other written documents before the oral part of the trial begins. The jury's decision is guilty or not guilty.

Brazil also has a jury system for criminal cases that was guaranteed in its 1937 Constitution.[95] In fact the jury system has been in continuous operation since 1822. The right to jury trial extends to all cases involving homicide, infanticide, abortion, and aiding suicide. The jury is composed of seven persons who have been selected from a list of twenty-one jurors drawn from a general list of certified jurors. The jurors listen to the evidence in a trial in which a single judge presides. They may ask for clarification of facts before judgment, but they do not deliberate. Their votes are made by secret ballot and a majority of four is need for a verdict of guilt. Their decision can be overturned by the Court of Appeal if it is manifestly contrary to the evidence, and the case can be ordered to be retried by a second jury.

Venezuela has made provisions for a jury system for serious cases, but it has yet to be implemented.[96]

G. *Contemporary Juries in Europe*

Austria retains a jury system for serious crimes in its Landesgerichte, or regional courts.[97] Juries must be used for crimes involving a potential sentence of more than ten years and may be used for those involving a sentence of five years. Juries are also required for all political crimes, such as high treason or collecting weapons for combat. Three judges preside over each trial, but the eight jurors are solely responsible for deciding the issue of guilt. If the defendant is found guilty, the jurors decide the punishment collectively with the three trial judges.

Belgium still retains a jury system.[98] In theory all criminal cases before

[95] Luiz Flavio Gomes and Ana Paula Zomer, The Brazilian Jury System, Paper presented at the International Conference on Lay Participation in the Criminal Trial in the 21st Century, Siricusa, Sicily, May 26–29, 1999.

[96] Rafael Quintero-Moreno, Il Nuovo Sistema Processale Penale in Venezuela. La Guria E Il Tribunale Misto [Venezuela's New System of Jury and Mixed Courts], Paper presented at the International Conference on Lay Participation in the Criminal Trial in the 21st Century, Siricusa, Sicily, 26–29 May, 1999.

[97] Herbert Hausmaninger, The Austrian Legal System (1998) at 114; Willibald Posch, Einführung in das Österreichische Recht (1985) at 234.

[98] Philip Traest, Country Study: Belgium, Paper presented at the International Conference on Lay Participation in the Criminal Trial in the 21st Century, Siricusa, Sicily, Italy, 26–29 May, 1999; Philip Traest, *Juries, Evidence and the Role of Lay Participation in the Belgian Criminal Process*, in J. F. Nijboer and J. M. Reijnjes, eds., Proceedings of the First World Congress on New Trends in Criminal Investigation and Evidence (1997).

the assize courts can be tried by jury, but in practice their use is limited to murder and other crimes for which the penalty is more than twenty years in prison. Even some of these crimes, such as rape of a minor or some forms of taking of hostages, can be tried instead by a court of professional judges. The Belgian jury consists of twelve members, but up to twelve alternate jurors can be sworn in the event that original jurors become ill or have to be replaced for other reasons. The jurors are chosen randomly from the jury pool, but both the prosecutor and the accused have the right to challenge six members of the jury and some of the alternate jurors. After hearing the evidence and being instructed by the judge the jury deliberates in a separate room and are not allowed to leave until a verdict is reached. The verdict of the jury is a special verdict involving questions about the elements charged in the crime and, upon discretion of the president of the court, questions about aggravating and mitigating circumstances relating to the crime. The jury's vote is by secret ballot. A majority of eight to four is sufficient for conviction. If a jury's decision is only seven to five in favour of guilt regarding a question about a main fact in the case, the three judges who preside at the trial have to express their opinion about the question of guilt. If they do not join the majority on the jury, the result is an acquittal. There are other complications to the Belgian jury system that are beyond the scope of this synopsis.

Denmark has a jury system that in its modern form began in 1919.[99] There are only about 100 jury trials per year. Most criminal cases in Denmark are decided by a single judge or by a mixed court using lay assessors. Juries are used in one of Denmark's two High Courts when the prosecution demands a prison sentence of at least four years, when the prosecution demands placement of an accused in a mental institution, and in cases involving political offences. Juries are composed of twelve persons sitting with a panel of three professional judges. The jury decides the question of guilt and a majority of eight is required to render a verdict adverse to the defendant. No reasons are given for the verdict. The jury may also be asked to decide other questions, including elements relating to intention, aggravation, mitigation, or insanity. During deliberations the chairman of the court may be called into the room to answer questions. If the verdict is guilty the jury sits with the three judges to decide punishment. However, in the punishment phase each juror has

[99] Peter Garde, Country Study: Kingdom of Denmark, Paper presented at the International Conference on Lay Participation in the Criminal Trial in the 21st Century, Siricusa, Sicily, Italy, May 26–29, 1999.

one vote but each of the three judges has four votes, thus providing parity between judges and jurors in a total of twenty-four votes.

Norway's criminal procedure is based on an adversary system.[100] Courts of first instance involve mixed tribunals of judges and lay persons. Juries are used only in the Court of Appeal, which can deal with the question of guilt. The cases involve crimes punishable with more than six years' imprisonment. The pool of lay persons from which the jury is composed are nominations of residents who have high moral character and knowledge of the Norwegian language, but in practice nominees are also members of political parties. They serve terms of four years. In attempting to ensure gender parity separate lists of males and females are kept. Seven men and seven women are chosen from the list. The jury is composed of ten persons from this list. The parties are allowed to exclude the four jurors that are not needed for the trial. Although professional judges conduct the hearing, the jury rules on the issue of guilt with a simple verdict of guilty or not guilty. A majority of seven of ten is required for a verdict of guilty. No reasons for the verdict are required, and disclosure of the number of guilty votes is forbidden. Other questions may be put to the jury that assist the judges in evaluating the verdict. It is possible for the judges to conclude that, despite a verdict of acquittal, the evidence indicates guilt; they may then order a new trial using a mixed tribunal. Following guilty verdicts the jury foreperson and three jury members are chosen to sit with the three judges to determine sentence, thus providing a layperson majority for deciding punishment.

Switzerland[101] still has provisions for trial by jury, composed of twelve persons, involving parts of its federal penal law. The Canton of Geneva provides for trial by jury of either six or twelve persons, depending on the gravity of the offence charged. However, jury trial has disappeared in other Swiss cantons and its use in federal trials and in Geneva is rare.

V. Concluding Comment

In contrast to the other chapters in this book, this final chapter must be treated as an incomplete work. I am confident that I have not covered

[100] Asbjørn Strandbakken, Country Study: Kingdom of Norway, Paper presented at the International Conference on Lay Participation in the Criminal Trial in the 21st Century, Siricusa, Sicily, Italy, May 26–29, 1999.

[101] Bernhard Strauli, La Participation de Magistrats Laïques a l'Administration de la Justice Pénale en Suisse. Paper presented at the International Conference on Lay Participation in the Criminal Trial in the 21st Century, Siricusa, Sicily, Italy, May 26–29, 1999.

every country and territory that has a jury,[102] but time has run out as the publication deadline nears. Even for those countries that are described, the sketch provides little information about the laws, the procedures, and the political and legal context on which the jury operates. Nevertheless, the chapter does provide ample documentation that the English invention of a jury composed of lay members of the community who have sole responsibility for deciding factual matters relating to guilt or innocence remains a viable institution in many parts of the world, even if the civil jury has all but disappeared.

The jury remains an intriguing institution that grew out of ideas associated with democracy and legal justice. Its development in nineteenth-century democratic movements and its wane with authoritarian governments reflects upon its democratic character. The historical sketch indicates, however, that it was also an institution frequently associated with colonial injustice, and it was and remains an institution that is difficult to implement in racially divided societies. It can also be an expensive institution to maintain. Its absence in many modern countries with strong democratic cultures indicates that it is not essential for democracy to flourish. Yet, its retention in some form in many countries, its reintroduction in Spain and Russia, and interest in its revival in Japan suggest that it has merits that legal systems that rely on professionals alone and those that utilize mixed tribunals may be lacking. Perhaps these merits are not sufficient to overcome its liabilities for some cultures, but in any event it remains a cornerstone of justice in many parts of the world. By placing what I have uncovered in this final chapter, my hope is that even with its shortcomings, the information will provide a broader perspective on the jury and spur additional interest among scholars to complete the picture, a picture that will include, I hope, analysis of its role in theories of democratic participation.

[102] These include countries that had not responded to the Commonwealth Survey by the time that the final proof of this volume was prepared.

Index

Index compiled by Frank Pert